"From June 24, 1981, five teenagers and a younger boy from a small village in Bosnia-Herzegovina called Bijakovici near Medjugorje first began seeing apparitions on a local hill of someone they called 'Gospa'—Croatian for 'Our Lady.' It is this phenomenon that Foley, author of the scholarly *Marian Apparitions, the Bible, and the Modern World*, seeks to investigate. He has conducted a painstaking and thorough investigation of every aspect of the case and, in an area fraught with strong, even aggressive, opinions his tone is moderate and charitable throughout."
　—JACK CARRIGAN, *Catholic Herald*

"Donal Foley takes the reader on a journey of discovery through the formidable information maze that surrounds Medjugorje. His tenacity in not losing the narrow path to the truth about the Balkan prodigy among many false trails and dead alleys would make Hercule Poirot jealous. Foley unearths little known Croatian sources and calls upon Catholic scholars to shed light on the enigma of Medjugorje. He delivers what he promises and takes his readers to the heart of the matter. *Understanding Medjugorje* is excellent!"
　—JOHN HAUF, Editor Emeritus, *SOUL* magazine

PRAISE FOR EARLIER EDITIONS OF THE BOOK:

"It has long seemed to me that a team of experts fluent in Croatian would be needed to untangle the complex phenomenon of Medjugorje. I am now convinced that Donal Foley has done a great deal of that necessary work by sorting out and assembling the studies already carried out by experts and then weighing and evaluating them."
—MSGR ARTHUR B. CALKINS

"Donal Foley is well qualified to inform readers about the events at Medjugorje in a balanced way, and from a Catholic point of view. He gives an excellent introduction to the Medjugorje phenomenon and explains many aspects that are not generally known. He is meticulous regarding the historical foundations of his work, but also provides an exemplary theological evaluation. Whoever wants to deepen their understanding of Medjugorje will find this book a rich source of information."
—PROF. DR MANFRED HAUKE

"*Medjugorje Revisited* is a thorough presentation, in their historical context, of the alleged apparitions in the former Yugoslavia. Applying traditional Catholic criteria for assessing visions, the author lays out the various problems that arise from the testimony of the alleged visionaries. He amply shows why successive local bishops have refused to declare the claimed apparitions worthy of belief. *Medjugorje Revisited* deserves to be widely studied."
—FR THOMAS CREAN, OP

"Donal Foley's comprehensive and convincing study of Medjugorje, *Medjugorje Revisited*, is a superb analysis of the alleged apparitions of Our Lady. It exposes what amounts to a pathological religious phenomenon that has duped millions of people seeking spiritual consolation in especially troubled times, when God seemed dead and the Church torn by dissent and disobedience. May this book's discerning judgment find definitive reinforcement in the long-awaited Vatican decision on Medjugorje!"
—JAMES LIKOUDIS

"Donal Foley has done lovers of accuracy a favor, and provided believers in Christ and children of the Blessed Virgin Mary a signal service with this book. Stick with the Church's approved apparitions and accept no dodgy substitutes!"
—MARK P. SHEA

FROM REVIEWS OF *UNDERSTANDING MEDJUGORJE*

"Foley's book on Medjugorje defends the rational basis of faith, sound common sense, and the traditional wisdom of the Church in his argument that Medjugorje has created 'a misguided quest for "signs and wonders,"' and developed into 'a vast, if captivating religious illusion.' Examining the entire phenomenon of the apparitions, from their inception in 1981 to the present, Foley mounts compelling evidence that questions the authenticity of the visions of the seers. The most cogent aspect of his argument contrasts the approved miracles at Fatima and Lourdes with the alleged appearances of the Holy Mother at Medjugorje. In short, this book views the events at Medjugorje from a comprehensive, historical, objective point of view that avoids the religious enthusiasm and charismatic emotionalism of its advocates. This is an arresting book that poses an impressive intellectual and religious challenge to those who have never honestly questioned the authentic nature of the events at Medjugorje."
—**DR MITCHELL KALPAKGIAN**, *The Wanderer*

"It is a good time to have a cool look at the claims and the truth about Medjugorje. This is done admirably in this book by Donal Foley—an expert on the appearances of Our Blessed Lady and, even more important, one with great devotion to her. It is well written, examines all the available evidence and is, above all, clear. This is a scholarly book but is easy to read even when it guides the reader through the Hampton Court Maze of Balkans history and Church feuds. If you only read one book on Medjugorje, then make it this one."
—**ERIC HESTER**, *Catholic Times*

"In one of the few books available today offering a critical look at Medjugorje, Donal Foley performs an excellent service in unraveling the many threads that comprise the genesis and history of the phenomenon. He discusses the significant role of the charismatic movement and tourism industry in propagating the visions, and shows how Medjugorje compares unfavorably to approved apparitions, especially Fatima. He presents an excellent overview of the complex historical backdrop preceding the apparitions to the six visionaries. The book is extremely well written, employing a clear, captivating, and engaging style. It contains neither rancor nor bitter accusations, but rather presents an unrelenting examination of the vast set of problems that encompass Medjugorje. This is required reading for anyone who wants to understand the profound difference between Medjugorje and Church-approved apparitions of the Blessed Virgin Mary."
—**FRANK REGA**, author of *St Francis of Assisi and the Conversion of the Muslims*

BY THE SAME AUTHOR:

Comprendere Medjugorje. Visioni celesti o inganno religioso?
(Eupress FTL-Edizioni Cantagalli s.r.l., Lugano/Siena, 2017)

Medjugorje verstehen: Himmlische Visionen oder fromme Illusion?
(Dominus-Verlag, Augsburg, 2011)

Marian Apparitions, the Bible, and the Modern World (Gracewing, Leominster, 2002)

Italian translation:

Il libro delle Apparizioni Mariane (Gribaudi, Milan, 2004)

Understanding Medjugorje: Heavenly Visions or Religious Illusion?
(Theotokos Books, Nottingham, 2006)

Christian Living: The Spirituality of the Foyers of Charity
(Theotokos Books, Nottingham, 2006)

More details at: www.theotokos.org.uk

MEDJUGORJE COMPLETE

Medjugorje COMPLETE

The Definitive Account of the Visions and Visionaries

DONAL ANTHONY FOLEY

Angelico Press

First published in the USA
by Angelico Press 2021
Copyright © Donal Anthony Foley 2021

All rights reserved:
No part of this book may be reproduced or transmitted,
in any form or by any means, without permission

For information, address:
Angelico Press, Ltd.
169 Monitor St.
Brooklyn, NY 11222
www.angelicopress.com

ppr 978-1-62138-746-6
cloth 978-1-62138-747-3

Book and cover design
by Michael Schrauzer

The Catholic Edition of the Revised Standard Version of the Bible, copyright 1965, 1966 by the Division of Christian Education of the National Council of the Churches of Christ in the United States of America. Used by permission. All rights reserved.

Disclaimer: the opinions expressed in this book are the responsibility of the author, and should not be taken as representing the views of any particular group or organization. The information in this book—which was mostly obtained from sources in the public domain—is, to the best of the author's knowledge, accurate and true. If any unintended errors are found, please notify the publisher so these can be rectified in future editions.

Web addresses in endnotes, etc. accessed between
27th July and 3rd August 2020.

*...for even Satan disguises himself
as an angel of light.*
2 Cor 11:14

"*Oftentimes, to win us to our harm
the instruments of darkness tell us truths;
Win us with honest trifles, to betray us
In deepest consequence.*"
Macbeth, Act 1, Scene 3

CONTENTS

FOREWORD by Prof. Dr Manfred Hauke xvii
PREFACE by Dr William A. Thomas xix
ACKNOWLEDGMENTS xxi
INTRODUCTION. xxiii

1 MEDJUGORJE: THE HISTORICAL BACKGROUND 1
 The Franciscans, the Bogomils and Islam—1; Rome and the Church in Bosnia-Herzegovina—2; The Franciscan Problem—3; The End of Communism—3

2 MEDJUGORJE AND THE CHARISMATIC MOVEMENT . . 5
 The Charismatic Movement and the Franciscans—5; Charismatic Problems—6; Medjugorje and the Visionaries—8; Unlikely Marian Seers—9; The Corrupting Influence of Communism—10; Charismatic "Prophecies" about Medjugorje—12; The Charismatic Movement and the Church—13; Medjugorje and Montanism—15; Medjugorje and Montanism Compared—18

3 THE MEDJUGORJE TAPES AND THE VISIONARIES . . . 23
 Questions about the Visionaries—23; The Medjugorje Tapes—24; The Importance of the Tapes—26; Reasons for Differences—27; The Tape Transcripts Are Reliable—29; First Day—Wednesday, 24 June 1981—30; The Blessed Virgin or Something Diabolical?—32; The Smoking Visionaries—33; The "Gospa" and the Light—35; More Questionable Evidence—36; Second Day—Thursday, 25 June 1981—37

4 TRUE AND FALSE VISIONS OF LIGHT 39
 Third day—Friday, 26 June 1981—39; Fourth day—Saturday, 27 June 1981—40; Fifth and Sixth Days of the Visions—41; Fr Zovko is Skeptical . . . and Concerned—42; The Move from Podbrdo to the Church—43; The Light and the Mist—45; The Angel of Portugal—46; Some Examples of Suspect Visions—47

5 THE VISIONS CONTINUE 51
   Did the Visionaries Really See Something?—51; Bishop Zanic's Difficult Situation—51; Criticism of the Local Bishops—53; Pressure on the Visionaries—54; Ivanka and the "Unbelieving Judases"—55; Fr Zovko Takes Control—56; Mirjana and "Two or Three More Days"—57; Vicka and Fr Vlasic—58

6 THREE MORE DAYS OF VISIONS 61
   Fr Zovko Interviews Five of the Visionaries—61; Mica and the Visionaries—61; Three More Days of Visions—63; Fr Rupcic's Criticism of Fr Sivric—66; Three Days or Three Times?—66; Some Untenable Arguments—67; Personal Criticism of Fr Sivric—68; Fr Rupcic and the Medjugorje Tapes—70; The Visionaries as Reliable Witnesses?—72; The Silent "Gospa"—74; Fr Zovko Commits Himself to the Visions—75; The Last Vision—76; Medjugorje and Lourdes—78; The Visionaries and Lourdes—80

7 MEDJUGORJE: GOD OR THE DEVIL?. 83
   Medjugorje: A Diabolical Origin?—83; Garabandal and Medjugorje—84; There is No Message—86; The Pattern of the Approved Apparitions—87; Our Lady's Words at Fatima—88; The Vision is Reluctant to Go to Church—90; A Visionary Pattern Established—90; The "Sign" Promised—91; The Garabandal "Great Miracle"—93; Garabandal Not as Popular as Medjugorje—94; Fr Zovko is Arrested and Imprisoned—94

8 PROBLEMS WITH THE MEDJUGORJE MESSAGES 97
   Some Unbelievable Messages—97; The Medjugorje Culture and Folklore—98; Questionable Content of the Messages—99; Theologically Suspect Messages—100; Further Suspect Messages—101; Themes of the Messages—103; The Duration of the Approved Apparitions—104; The Medjugorje Visions and False Prophets—105; Why So Many Messages?—106; Problems with the Franciscans—107; "The Pope can say what he wants..."—108; The Apostolic Signatura Decision—110; Problems with Fr Vlasic and Fr Barbaric—111; Dangerous Manipulation and More Problems—112; Ivan's Threatening Letter—113

9 MEDJUGORJE: MESSAGES AND SECRETS 115
   The Origin of the Messages—115; The Nature of the Medjugorje

Messages—115; No Turning Back—116; Archbishop Franic Intervenes—117; More Negative Evidence—118; Summarizing the Situation—119

10 FATIMA AND ITS EFFECTS 121
The Fatima Apparitions—May to August 1917—121; The Vision of Hell—122; The September and October Apparitions, 1917—123; Later Apparitions to Sr Lucia—124; Sr Lucia and the Consecration of Russia—125; The Portuguese Bishops Consecrate Their Country—126; Sr Lucia and the Consecration of 1942—126; Portugal before and after Fatima—128; A Country Transformed—128; Further Consecrations—130

11 THE MEDJUGORJE PROPAGANDA OFFENSIVE 133
A Rush of Books on Medjugorje—133; Criticism of the Medjugorje Critics—134; Incorrect Methodology—137; Denis Nolan and Medjugorje—138; Fr Laurentin's Pro-Medjugorje Arguments—140; The Prolonging of the Visions—142; The Visionaries Compared with the Saints—142; The Verbose and Repetitive Nature of the Messages—144; Medjugorje and the Post-Conciliar Period—145

12 MEDJUGORJE AND THE THEOLOGIANS 149
Theologians Pronounce on Medjugorje—149; Criticism of Bishop Zanic—151; Fr Michael O'Carroll on Medjugorje—152; A False Analogy—153; Bishop Zanic a Communist Collaborator?—154

13 MEDICAL AND SCIENTIFIC INVESTIGATIONS 157
Medical & Psychological Examinations of the Visionaries—157; Dr Henri Joyeux's Medical Experiments—158; Dr Margnelli's Other State of Consciousness—160; The EEG Results of the Visionaries—162; The Visionaries' Ecstatic Experiences Analyzed—163; Inaudible Voices—166; Multiple Conversations—167; Further Experimentation in 1985, 1986 and 1988—168; The 1987 Medjugorje Commission—170; Further Tests in Italy in 1998—171; More Research on Mirjana, Vicka and Ivanka—173; The Uncooperative Visionaries—174; Tests during the Nineties—175

14 MEDJUGORJE AS CULT RELIGION 179
Ivan and the Rosary—179; Strange Lights and Signs—179; Miracles

of the Sun?—180; A Dangerous Desire for the Miraculous—181; Diabolical Power and Influence—183; Solar Miracles and Golden Rosaries—183; Natural Explanations for the "Miraculous"—184; The Results of Sun-Gazing—186; The Dangers of Medjugorje Sun-Gazing—187; Miraculous Cures at Medjugorje?—188

15 THE CHURCH AND MEDJUGORJE 191
The Holy See and Medjugorje—191; Vatican Concerns about Medjugorje—193; A New Commission of Inquiry—195; Pope John Paul II and Medjugorje—195; Fr Sivric's Book on Medjugorje—196

16 MEDJUGORJE CREDIBILITY PROBLEMS 199
The Credibility of Vicka—199; Vicka and Hell—200; More Problems with Vicka—201; Some Alternative Explanations—202; St Bernadette's Genuine Ecstasies—203; Ivan and the "Sign"—204; Ivan's Apologists Regarding the "Sign"—206; Marija's Messages and Her Retraction—207; Problems with Mirjana—208; Vicka's Physical and Psychological State—209; Problems with the Religious Vows—211

17 MEDJUGORJE, THE ZADAR DECLARATION
   AND THE WAR 213
The War in Yugoslavia—213; Medjugorje and the Yugoslav Bishops' Conference—213; The Zadar Declaration as Pro-Medjugorje?—214; Yugoslavia Disintegrates—216; The War Comes to Medjugorje—217; Violence in Medjugorje—219; The War around Medjugorje—219; Religious Aspects of the War—222

18 CLARIFYING THE CASE OF MEDJUGORJE 225
The Poem of the Man-God and the Visionaries—225; Bishop Peric, the Pope and Medjugorje—226; Circulating Accounts of Alleged Visions—227; St Louis de Montfort on False Devotion to Our Lady—228; Apocryphal Writings and the Bible—229; Some Guidelines for Discernment—231; The Position of the Church on Visions—233; The Role of the Local Bishop—235; *Normae Congregationis* and Discernment—236; The Competent Authorities—238; Bishop Peric on Medjugorje—240; Franciscan Disobedience Continues—241; The Letter to Bishop Aubry—243; *Romanis Pontificibus* Implemented—244

19 THE GOOD AND BAD FRUITS OF MEDJUGORJE. . . . 247
Good Fruits in the Early Years—247; The Good Fruits Analyzed—248; Some Genuine Good Fruits?—250; Movements and Communities—251; Emotional Enthusiasm—252; Medjugorje and Franciscan University of Steubenville—253; "Imprinting" Medjugorje—255; The Impact of Medjugorje—256; Dangerous Desire for the Miraculous—259; Christ's Teaching on Good Fruits—260; False Prophets—262; Modern False Visions and Visionaries—263

20 MEDJUGORJE: PROBLEMS AND DANGERS 267
Focusing on Negative Elements—267; The Lifestyle of the Medjugorje Visionaries—269; Medjugorje—Why so Popular?—270; Medjugorje from a Spiritual Perspective—272; Medjugorje and the Crisis in the Church—273; A Diabolical Atmosphere—275; Some Diabolical Incidents—276; The Real Power behind Medjugorje?—278

21 MEDJUGORJE DEVELOPMENTS 281
A Medjugorje Conference—281; Bishop Peric's Indictment—282; The French Bishops and Medjugorje—282; Role of Local Bishop Crucial—283; Warnings from Prominent Churchmen—285; Visions and Secrets: An Ongoing Situation—286; Some Recent Medjugorje Books Considered—287; Denis Nolan on Medjugorje (Again)—289; Miravalle and Weible on Medjugorje—292; Fr Mulligan on Medjugorje—295; Damage Limitation—297

22 THE VATICAN AND MEDJUGORJE 299
Pope Benedict and Bishop Peric—299; The CDF and False Visionaries—299; Pope Benedict and Fatima—300; Bishop Peric Preaches at Medjugorje—301; Cardinal Bertone on Medjugorje—301; More Medjugorje Controversy—303; Fr Tomislav Vlasic is Investigated—304; The Devil's Battle Plan—306; Fr Laurentin Backpedals on Medjugorje—307; Fr Tomislav Vlasic is Laicized—308; Bishop Peric on Medjugorje Irregularities—309; Congregation for the Doctrine of the Faith Position—310; The Importance of Episcopal Collegiality—312; The International Commission on Medjugorje—314; Cardinal Ruini and the Commission—315; The Papal Nuncio on Medjugorje—317

23 MEDJUGORJE AND THE CULT MENTALITY 321
Caritas of Birmingham a Medjugorje Cult?—321; Caritas a Major Medjugorje Organization—323; Caritas and the Church—324; The Danger of a Breakaway Church—325

24 THE IMPORTANCE OF FATIMA 327
Pope John Paul II and the Consecration of 1984—327; The Collapse of Communism—329; Further Fatima Developments—329; The Conversion of Russia—330; Fatima and Medjugorje Contrasted—331; Some Questions for Medjugorje Supporters—332; More Recent Fatima Developments—333; Pope Benedict in Fatima—335; Medjugorje a Continuation of Fatima?—336; The Five First Saturdays Devotion—337

25 MEDJUGORJE DEVELOPMENTS FROM 2011 341
The Work of the Commission—341; Medjugorje Developments in 2012—343; Medjugorje Developments in 2013—344; Publication of *Medjugorje: The First Days*—345; Pope Francis and Medjugorje —347; Medjugorje Developments in 2014—349; Medjugorje Developments in 2015—350

26 THE RUINI COMMISSION REPORT 353
More on Pope Francis and Medjugorje—353; Pope Francis's Statements on Medjugorje—355; Medjugorje Developments in 2016—356; Mirjana's Book, *My Heart Will Triumph*—357; Cardinal Müller Interview and Pope Francis's Medjugorje Remarks—359; Medjugorje Developments in 2017—359; Pope Francis and "Tourism in Medjugorje"—361; Pope Francis and the Ruini Commission—362; Ruini Commission Report Details Leaked—363; The Implications of the Ruini Commission Report—364; Numerous Medjugorje Anomalies—365

27 THE VATICAN AND MEDJUGORJE 369
Further Medjugorje Developments in 2017—369; Archbishop Hoser on Medjugorje—369; Mirjana and Demonic Activity?—370; Cardinal Parolin and Archbishop Hoser on Medjugorje—371; Archbishop Hoser as Special Envoy to Medjugorje—372; Fr Manfred Hauke on Medjugorje—372; Expansion Plans for Medjugorje—373; Pope Francis and Chiara Amirante of New Horizons—374; Medjugorje Mladifest Youth Festival—375

28 THE CONTENTS OF THE RUINI COMMISSION
     REPORT ARE REVEALED. 377
     Leaked Copies of Ruini Report Published—377; Report Highlights
     Problems with Visionaries—377; Ruini Report Published as Two
     Separate eBooks—379; General Analysis of the Ruini Report—380;
     Report Posits "Two Phases" to the Visions—381; The Influence
     of Fatima and Kibeho on the Report—382; The Report on the
     First Seven Visions—384; The Vision as "Queen of Peace" and
     Her Messages—385; Queen of Peace or Blessed Virgin Mary?—387

29 THE MEDJUGORJE MESSAGES AS SUSPECT 389
     The Content of the Medjugorje Messages—389; There Is No
     Message—390; Fr Zovko and Ivanka . . . and Fr Vlasic—392; Fr
     Zovko's Frustration at Visionaries' Responses—394; Visions in a
     Police Van and at the Church—395; No Coherent Messages Given
     to the Visionaries—395; The Report and Demonic Influences—397;
     Holy Water Not Infallible Regarding the Demonic—398

30 MORE PROBLEMS HIGHLIGHTED BY THE REPORT . 401
     The Commission Report vs the Zadar Declaration—401;
     Problematic Elements—402; Money and Lies—404; Three More
     Days . . . and Subjectivism—405; Pastoral Recommendations—406;
     The Visionaries as an Embarrassment—408; More Bad Fruits—409;
     Dr Sumanovic-Glamuzina's Testimony—410; The Doctor Changes
     Her Mind—412; From Skepticism to Belief—413; Votes of the
     Commission—415; Verdict on the Report—416

31 SOME CONCLUSIONS 419
     The Church in Crisis—420; Pope John Paul II's Position—420;
     The Truth of Fatima: The Problems with Medjugorje—421;
     Triumph of the Immaculate Heart of Mary—422; Fatima Is the
     Answer—425; Problems and Dangers—427; Forty Years of Visions
     or Religious Fraud?—428; The Future of Medjugorje?—429

ENDNOTES 431
BIBLIOGRAPHY 475
RECOMMENDED RESOURCES 481
INDEX 483

FOREWORD

MANY PEOPLE WILL CELEBRATE THE FORTIETH anniversary in June 2021 of the extraordinary events which started at Medjugorje, believing them to be authentic Marian apparitions. But the last official declaration of the Church, from the Yugoslav bishops in 1991, does not support this enthusiasm and indicates that no supernatural origin can be affirmed for the alleged visions ("non constat de supernaturalitate").

In March 2010, a Vatican commission under Cardinal Camillo Ruini began to study the phenomenon of Medjugorje; the report of these studies was transmitted to the Congregation for the Doctrine of the Faith for further evaluation. The final report of the Commission was "leaked" in 2020; it suggests a recognition of the first seven presumed apparitions, but mentions many problems concerning subsequent developments at Medjugorje.

It does not seem, however, that the phenomenon can be limited to the first seven apparitions. To understand what happened initially at Medjugorje it is necessary to closely examine the transcripts of the tapes of the interviews with the visionaries that took place during the first week or so of the alleged visions, which is precisely what Donal Foley has done in the present work.

The overall situation is that the Holy See has permitted official pilgrimages to Medjugorje, but has also underlined the fact that this pastoral procedure does not entail any recognition of the supernatural character of the presumed apparitions. Given this situation, it is an urgent necessity to offer all interested readers a balanced treatment of the Medjugorje phenomenon, one based on an intensive study of the sources. At the same time it requires a Catholic sense of faith that is ready to accept genuine supernatural manifestations of Mary, the Mother of God, in history, without succumbing to credulity.

Donal Foley is very well equipped for this task of informing readers about the events at Medjugorje in a balanced way, and from a Catholic point of view. His university formation includes Humanities and Theology. He has written a work on Marian apparitions—*Marian Apparitions, the Bible, and the Modern World*—which takes seriously the prophetical significance of the authentic manifestations of the Virgin Mary, and which carefully explains them for contemporary readers. This standard work of reference appeared in 2002 and was translated into Italian soon after, in 2004.

In 2006, Foley published the first version of the present work, which looked at how we should understand Medjugorje, and posed the question: Are we confronted with heavenly visions or a religious illusion? That work received a very positive response. In 2011, it appeared in an updated and revised form; it was translated also into German. The second edition offered some innovative points of view; for instance, the comparison of Medjugorje with Montanism in the ancient Church, a movement that presented itself as "charismatic" and "prophetic," and that was accepted initially even by many ecclesiastical dignitaries, but which was ultimately rejected by the Church. A subsequent update was made for the Italian translation that was published in 2017. Now the author proposes a new edition with a further supplement to include recent events.

This important work avoids any polemics, but also studies the problematic aspects of Medjugorje, not shrinking from the critical question: Are there elements which suggest even a diabolic influence? And, in fact, a close analysis of the first ten days of the presumed apparitions does indeed point to this conclusion. Along with the human factor there seems to be a preternatural influence "from below."

In sum, Foley gives an excellent introduction to the Medjugorje phenomenon. He explains many of its aspects that are generally unknown. The author is very careful regarding the historical foundations of his work, but also provides an exemplary theological evaluation. Whoever wants to deepen their understanding of Medjugorje will find this book a rich source of information on which to assess it. The study is written in a very fluent way and is accessible to a wide readership. At the same time, it offers the necessary specialist information required for an accurate theological understanding and evaluation of Medjugorje.

Prof. Dr. Manfred Hauke,
Theological Faculty of Lugano (Switzerland)

PREFACE

MEDJUGORJE IS SOMEWHAT OF A JIGSAW PUZZLE that has been in existence now for the past 40 years. Few people have been able to grasp what is really happening there—rather they have allowed themselves to be carried off on a self-satisfying emotional wave which is both charismatic and euphoric.

There are so many stories or apparitions and messages that have emanated from there that it's hard to keep up—at the last count there were over 70,000 alleged apparitions contained in the over 500 volumes on the subject held by the Congregation for the Doctrine of the Faith.

Donal Anthony Foley has followed the events at Medjugorje closely and has amassed a great deal of the documentation publicly available in his updated work, *Medjugorje Complete: The Definitive Account of the Visions and Visionaries*. In this, Foley again lays out the available evidence so that the reader may see that all is not what is seems.

He begins by giving an account of the relationship between the Franciscan Friars and the Church. This has involved disobedience on a grand scale and has had its own tragic fruits, which have led to the suspensions of several priests and the dismissal from the priestly life and excommunication of another, namely Fr Tomislav Vlasic, OFM.

Basing much of his work on the taped testimonies of the alleged visionaries, Foley exposes the lies and contradictions of the seers that have to this day continued. Their actions have become the catalysts for many other alleged seers around the world, a world in chaos, a world where now, it seems, almost everyone claims to have visions, messages and miracles.

Foley then contrasts the authentic Marian Apparitions of Fatima, Lourdes and others with Medjugorje, in order to highlight the differences between the sublime and profound messages of the approved apparitions, such as Fatima, and the theologically suspect so-called messages of Medjugorje.

Foley includes all the major Medjugorje players in this book, highlighting their roles in the "Medjugorje Phenomena," alongside a detailed analysis of what has taken place there. This is what makes *Medjugorje Complete* a must-read for any serious Marian devotee who genuinely wants to discover what is really happening there.

He indicates that there is almost a parallel church being born in Medjugorje which is favorable to the charismatics and to those who seek to put emotion before devotion on a wave of Medjugorje emotionalism.

Despite the persistent propaganda about Medjugorje and the insistence by some about its being authentic, Donal Foley correctly indicates that all of the canonical Commissions arising from the relevant theological investigations came to the conclusion that there was nothing of a supernatural nature taking place there. That position was also upheld by the Zadar Commission in 1991.

There is an expectation by those in favor of Medjugorje that all of these decisions by the local bishops and experts will be overturned in favor of these alleged apparitions and messages, given the findings of yet another Commission under Cardinal Ruini, the former Vicar of the Diocese of Rome.

But in reality, this cannot happen, and as the reader begins to comprehend the realities that Foley lays bare, it is clear that the Church cannot overturn the conclusions of previous Commissions just to appease certain people. Moral principles do not depend on a majority vote.

In reading this book, the reader may feel that the Catholic Church at the highest level has failed to accept the findings of the previous Commissions because it has allowed itself to be swayed by the millions who visit there every year looking for signs and wonders.

Those who wish to develop an authentic Marian devotion would do well to buy and study this book and thereafter to focus on the approved and authentic Marian Sanctuaries such as Fatima and Lourdes.

Dr. William A. Thomas,
professor of Mariology, 25 March 2021

ACKNOWLEDGMENTS

I WOULD LIKE TO THANK THE FOLLOWING FOR their help in the preparation, production and promotion of this book: particular thanks to Fr Manfred Hauke for agreeing to write the foreword and for his general help and encouragement; and also to Dr William A. Thomas for his forthright preface. Thanks also to Marco Corvaglia for his extensive help and for permission to summarize and reference material from his excellent "The Medjugorje Illusion" website, and for his valuable assistance in reading through the typescript. Likewise, thanks to Kevin Symonds for his advice and comments.

I would also like to thank those who have helped with previous editions, including Patrick Coffin, Richard Chonak, Diane M. Korzeniewski OCDS, Fr Peter Joseph, Prof. Arpad Szakolczai, Louis Bélanger, Fr Thomas Crean OP, James Likoudis, Mark Waterinckx, Frank Rega, Laurette Elsberry, Mary Shepley, Martin Blake, Dr Pravin Thevathasan and Nick Lowry.

Details of various websites and blogs associated with some of the people mentioned above, which have information about Medjugorje and associated matters, can be seen in the section entitled "Medjugorje/Fatima Resources" at the end of this book.

INTRODUCTION

THE ORIGINAL VERSION OF THIS BOOK, *Understanding Medjugorje*, was published in 2006, and five years later, in 2011—thirty years after Medjugorje began—a revised version, *Medjugorje Revisited*, was issued. That same year, a German translation was published, and this was followed by an Italian translation which came out in 2017.

There have been a number of important developments over the last fifteen years regarding Medjugorje. Arguably, the most prominent development was the formation of the International Commission of Inquiry on Medjugorje in March 2010 by Pope Benedict XVI. Headed by Cardinal Camillo Ruini, the work of the Commission went for about four years, concluding in 2014. Its report, however, only became available when it was leaked in 2020. These new developments justify a further revised and updated edition to coincide with the fortieth anniversary of the beginning of the events at Medjugorje in June 1981.

The basic facts about Medjugorje can be related quite quickly. Beginning on 24 June of that year, six young people from a small village in Bosnia-Herzegovina, five of them in their mid-teens and one aged ten, began to claim that they were seeing the Blessed Virgin Mary on a nearby hillside. Four were girls, and two boys. News of this spread very rapidly—initially in the village itself and then throughout still-Communist Yugoslavia.

Great crowds of pilgrims congregated as the days went on and the visionaries claimed that they were still seeing Our Lady, or the *Gospa*, as she is known in Croatian. Some of the local Franciscan priests supported these claims, and even the bishop, Msgr Pavao Zanic, was open initially to this possibility, although over a period of time, he began to have serious doubts.

Meanwhile, increasing numbers of pilgrims from further afield came to visit during the 1980s, as Medjugorje became better known in the Catholic Church. The civil war in Yugoslavia in the early 90s only temporarily affected its popularity, and for forty years now, some of the visionaries have been claiming to receive daily visitations from the Blessed Mother.

Large numbers of pilgrims still journey to Medjugorje, even though Msgr Zanic's successor, Bishop Ratko Peric, declared himself opposed to the visions, and despite the fact that in 1991 the Bishops' Conference of ex-Yugoslavia came to the conclusion that it could not be affirmed that "supernatural apparitions and revelations" had taken place there. In addition, the majority of the claims of the visionaries have received no official support from the Vatican, although the Ruini Report is supportive of the authenticity of seven of the earliest alleged visions. That, very briefly, is an outline of what has taken place regarding Medjugorje, but there are other aspects related to these events which this work also focuses on.

One of these is the historical background to Medjugorje, including the local Franciscan dispute with official Church authority—and the accompanying disobedience—which affected Bosnia-Herzegovina, and which was an important factor as regards the growth of Medjugorje. This disobedience has been exemplified in the actions of the three priests most closely associated with the visions and the visionaries: Fr Tomislav Vlasic, Fr Jozo Zovko and Fr Slavko Barbaric.

Another major contributory factor was the conjunction between the Charismatic Movement and the visions. Without this factor of a Charismatic network already in place around the world—and supportive of the visions and the visionaries—it is doubtful if Medjugorje would have had anything like the impact it has had on the Church. Similarly, support from clerical figures, and in particular Fr René Laurentin, was crucial in giving Medjugorje an apparent air of orthodoxy.

A crucial point is that most of the early books about Medjugorje were based on quite late interviews with the visionaries, while the primary source material—tapes made during the first week or so of the visions—is still to a large extent unknown by most Medjugorje pilgrims. On examination, transcripts of these tapes reveal some illuminating facts about Medjugorje, and this book is thus, amongst other things, concerned with assessing the importance of that evidence.

In particular, the tape transcripts show that the manner in which the Medjugorje "Gospa" appeared to the visionaries is at variance with what happened previously during those apparitions of the real Blessed Virgin which have been approved by the Church.

What the transcripts also reveal is that there is a very high probability that what the visionaries saw during the first week or so of visions was not the Blessed Mother, but actually a diabolical counterfeit. Likewise, the number of claimed visions is far in excess of what has been the norm for approved apparitions over the centuries.

Introduction

Saverio Gaeta, a proponent of the alleged visions, in his *Medjugorje: 1. La vera storia*, criticizes information regarding the above point about the diabolic in the Italian translation of *Medjugorje Revisited*. He seems to make the allegation that the position adopted in this book regarding possible diabolical influence on the events at Medjugorje is largely due to the influence of the work of Mart Bax, a retired Dutch anthropologist, rather than, as is actually the case, the transcripts of the tapes made of the visionaries in June and early July 1981.

But it should also be said that serious problems relating to Bax's work have become apparent in recent years, including those highlighted in a report from VU University Amsterdam, and also in a critique of Bax's book entitled "Fabrications on Medjugorje: on Mart Bax' Research," by Robert Jolic. For this reason, almost the entirety of the information based on Bax's work in the previous editions of this book has been removed.[1] This does not affect the essential arguments found in this present work.

This book also explores many other aspects of Medjugorje, including the medical and scientific tests done on the visionaries. These are examined in detail, and their many deficiencies and lack of rigor demonstrated, as also is the fact that, apart from the tests done under the auspices of the Yugoslav Bishops' Conference, none of them have any validity in the eyes of the Church. And the same can be said for the claims of miraculous cures at Medjugorje, many of which have involved diseases such as multiple sclerosis, which can go into spontaneous remission.

The text examines, too, how Medjugorje has led to divisions amongst the faithful, and even between members of the hierarchy, and also looks at the affluent lifestyle of the visionaries and how this contrasts with the way genuine seers of the past lived and behaved.

Similarly, the shocking violence which took place around Medjugorje during the civil war in the 90s is examined, especially regarding the concentration camps in the vicinity. In fact, as will be seen, the perverted nationalism which some Hercegovina Franciscans indulged in was one of the contributory factors in bringing about this violence.

In sum, most pilgrims to Medjugorje have been unaware of many of the less savory aspects of what has taken place there. Medjugorje is still very popular, but it is worrying to note that many of its devotees are either unaware of or unwilling to face up to the serious problems associated with believing in the claims of the visionaries. And likewise, there is a lack of appreciation that Medjugorje contrasts very unfavorably with Fatima, and can actually be seen as one of the most serious obstacles to the widespread implementation of the Fatima message in the Church.

It is to be hoped, then, that sensible Medjugorje supporters will look at all this evidence with an open mind and realize that there are indeed issues regarding acceptance of Medjugorje which do need to be faced up to.

In sum, the purpose of this book is to bring the hidden side of Medjugorje into focus, so that people can make an honest assessment of it based on facts rather than fallacies or fantasies.

I
Medjugorje:
The Historical Background

THE FRANCISCANS, THE BOGOMILS AND ISLAM

It is important to become familiar with the historical background if we are to understand the root of the religious problems connected with Medjugorje. These go back as far as the fourteenth century, and even further, when Franciscan missionaries were given the task of bringing Bogomil heretics in the Bosnia-Herzegovina area back to the Church. The Bogomils were a dualistic neo-Manichaean sect who originated in tenth-century Bulgaria before spreading to Asia Minor and the Balkans. Their beliefs were related to those of the Albigensians of southern France, but in particular, they seem to have regarded both Christ *and* Satan as sons of God the Father. For them, Satan was the creator of the world, and thus we see here a type of equivalence between Christ and the devil in the Bogomil mind. Nor is this all ancient history, given that one commentator felt obliged to speak of the local Croatians as still having certain traits typical of the Bogomils.[1]

This interesting remark is borne out by history. The Papacy attempted to deal with this movement by sending out missionaries, originally Dominicans, in 1240, and then Franciscans a century later, in 1340. But it was only in the mid-fifteenth century that the campaign to uproot the heresy began to really bear fruit, and those local Church leaders who refused to recant were forced to emigrate. But despite this, a legacy of Bogomil influence was left in which the local Church was not closely linked to the Papacy, and this was to sow the seeds of future problems.[2]

When the Franciscans arrived in the area, they soon made local recruits, but disaster struck in the fifteenth century when the area was conquered by the Ottoman Turks. Only the Franciscans remained to minister to the people after the secular clergy fled, and four hundred years of persecution began.

ROME AND THE CHURCH IN BOSNIA-HERZEGOVINA

In 1878, Bosnia and Herzegovina were liberated from the Turkish yoke and came under Hapsburg rule. Three years later, Pope Leo XIII issued a bull establishing the authority of the secular clergy, and a new hierarchy was set up, with the Franciscans of Bosnia and Herzegovina losing their privileged position. This is the modern origin of the disputes between the Franciscans and the secular clergy which have dominated Church life in Bosnia-Herzegovina in recent years—the so-called "Herzegovina problem."

Regrettably, the Franciscans did not cooperate with the new hierarchy, and their example was followed by many of the ordinary faithful. Thus, the Catholic Church in Bosnia-Herzegovina was not able to mature properly, and the area remained in many respects a missionary territory.[3]

When the Hapsburg Empire fell in 1918, the Kingdom of the Serbs, Croats and Slovenes was founded, and following a coup in 1929, the Serb king enforced policies favoring his kinsmen, using Chetnik militants, while the kingdom was renamed Yugoslavia—the "land of the South Slavs."

The administration of the new state was virtually monopolized by ethnic Serbs, especially in the judiciary and the military, and the combination of Serb nationalism and the Orthodox Church resulted in a policy of institutionalized discrimination against the Catholic Church in Yugoslavia.

The more recent history of Bosnia-Herzegovina is equally relevant if we are to understand the background to the religious phenomenon of Medjugorje. This particularly applies to the atrocities that happened in the area during the Second World War, in 1941, when a fascist state was created by Croatian Ustasha forces in alliance with the Nazi occupiers of the country.

In Medjugorje itself, the Ustasha gathered together about six hundred Serbs from western Herzegovina and brutally murdered them at a place near the hamlet of Surmanci, not far from the village, mostly by throwing them off precipices into a mass grave. Survivors were finished off with hand grenades, or in some cases buried alive. This was almost exactly forty years before the alleged visions at Medjugorje began in June 1981.[4]

THE FRANCISCAN PROBLEM

Returning to the religious situation, we can note that in 1923 the Vatican had facilitated an agreement between the local bishop and the Franciscans regarding the sharing of parishes. However, at the request of one of his successors, Bishop Petar Cule, the Ordinary of Mostar-Duvno, the Holy See agreed to annul this agreement. Thereafter, the Franciscans were supposed to hand their parishes over to the jurisdiction of the bishop; but they refused to do so, claiming that the annulment had been reached without their agreement. As more diocesan clergy were ordained from the 1950s onwards, the Franciscans came under increasing pressure to relinquish control over the parishes they had looked after, but they were still unwilling to do this.

By 1975, the situation had become so serious that the Holy See issued a special decree—*Romanis Pontificibus*—demanding their obedience on this matter; but the Franciscans continued their resistance, and in consequence were penalized with various disciplinary measures. Hence, at the time of the Medjugorje visions, they were, in the main, in a state of active disobedience to both the local bishop and Rome, and clearly this was not a happy portent for the future.[5]

But in fairness to the Franciscans, it should be said that they had maintained the Faith in Bosnia-Herzegovina during four hundred years of Muslim persecution, when it was cut off from the mainstream Catholic world, and so it is understandable that a spirit of self-reliance should have developed amongst them. The tragedy was that self-reliance turned into stubbornness, and stubbornness into open disobedience.

By September 1980, less than a year before the alleged visions began, Bishop Pavao Zanic, having taken over from Bishop Cule, decided to create a new parish in Mostar, one which would be composed of three-quarters of the parishes being run by the Franciscans. This led to recriminations on the part of some Franciscans, and this defiance was not limited to the clergy: it seems that many of the local faithful, too, from 1975 onwards, were unwilling to accept secular priests in their parishes.[6]

THE END OF COMMUNISM

Another vital factor in this complex situation was the effect that Pope John Paul II's policies were having in Eastern Europe, particularly after his visit to Poland in 1979. Following the death of Tito in 1980, Croatian nationalism began to reawaken; after the Second World War, Tito had governed the various fractious Yugoslav states with an iron hand, but now a new era had arrived, and no one was quite sure what would happen, particularly with the advent of the Solidarity movement in Poland. When it became known in June 1981 that teenagers in Medjugorje were claiming to have seen the Blessed Mother, the final critical element was added to an already volatile mixture, one that would see, within a decade, the eruption of a bloody civil war, as Yugoslavia tore itself apart.

For the pope, however, the problem which would emerge as support for Medjugorje grew was that, on the one hand, he wanted to encourage a grassroots Marian movement in Croatia along the lines of traditional Marian devotion in Poland, as a way of hastening the end of Communism—but, on the other hand, he also wanted the dispute with the Franciscans to end. It was a very difficult situation, and one which could have been made much worse by hasty action.[7]

Undoubtedly, the vast majority of pilgrims to Medjugorje have known little or nothing about the complicated history of the region, as outlined above. We are not dealing with a normal Catholic culture here, but one with a strange and checkered history, comprised of heretical sects, pagan religion, seemingly endless violence and a long-running dispute between official Church authority and local Franciscans.

2
Medjugorje and the Charismatic Movement

THE CHARISMATIC MOVEMENT AND THE FRANCISCANS

Apart from the history of the region, it is important to understand the spiritual atmosphere in parts of Bosnia-Herzegovina in the years leading up to the visions. It seems that the Charismatic Renewal had become popular, due in particular to the efforts of two Franciscan priests, Jozo Zovko and Tomislav Vlasic. But the prayer meetings organized by them were far from traditional, and often involved people wandering about with their eyes *closed*, or alternatively having them open in order to look other participants in the eyes, before confessing their sins (non-sacramentally) to each other. Some meetings could also include speaking in tongues.

The whole idea was to break down barriers, and the group dynamics of these meetings were very effective, indeed too effective, in doing just that. These techniques were developed from the sensitivity-training programs promoted by W. R. Coulson and Carl Rogers. Indeed, the process of milling around a room in a disordered way was actually known as the "milling around" exercise, while another technique was known as "boundary breakers." These techniques have since become notorious for their ability to manipulate people, in what can be a type of "brainwashing," particularly when used in "encounter" groups.[1]

However, it should be noted that it is not being suggested here that such encounter groups have been, or are, common amongst Charismatics—they obviously represent an aberration which is outside the mainstream of Charismatic activities. Nevertheless, it is clear that they did have quite a strong influence on certain individuals in the early days.

The above-mentioned Fr Jozo Zovko was the parish priest at St James's Church in Medjugorje in June 1981, when the visions began, and according to Marijan Pehar, another local Franciscan, had previously held similar prayer group/encounter meetings. Regarding the testimony from Pehar in the E. Michael Jones book *The Medjugorje Deception*, Saverio Gaeta says that according to Fr Svetozar Kraljevic,

Pehar "went to live in the U. S. and left the priesthood around 1979. I don't believe that the two have ever met."

This rather vague testimony has to be set against that of Jones, who, according to his text, actually interviewed Pehar, who quite categorically stated that he was discussing events which took place in 1975. And Jones also says that a year later Pehar "was living in a sort of co-ed monastery in Zagreb with a number of nuns and Franciscan priests, including Father Tomislav Vlasic."

Mary Craig, a Medjugorje author, describes Fr Zovko as "an enthusiast for the charismatic movement, [who] was disappointed by Medjugorje's lukewarm response to the changes he was trying to bring about in its prayer-life, and was inclined to dismiss the village's spiritual state as 'stunted and anaemic.'"[2]

Fr René Laurentin, the well-known mariologist and Medjugorje author, had this to say in 1998 about these Charismatic activities: "If Fr Jozo has charisms, they have blossomed from natural gifts. That might explain why, when he lays hands on people, so many fall in the total physical, psychic and spiritual relaxation we call 'Resting in the Spirit.'"

However, despite this clear example of Charismatic activity, Fr Laurentin denied that Fr Zovko was "involved in the Charismatic Renewal," which would appear to be rather a strange statement to make. Regarding Fr Vlasic, he said that he is "very much involved with the Charismatic Renewal," but that he "purposely avoided all interference of charismatic activities in order to dedicate himself to the spiritual awakening of the parish."[3]

CHARISMATIC PROBLEMS

There was apparently something of a crisis in the Charismatic Movement in the late 1970s and early 1980s, prompted by the general tendency of "enthusiastic" movements like that of the Charismatics to run out of steam. This "crisis of faith" was revealed at the time in a number of articles in Charismatic publications such as *New Covenant* magazine. Attendance at the Notre Dame Charismatic Renewal conferences from 1979 to 1981 had dropped appreciably, and the movement seemed to be entering a period of decline. Something was needed to give it new impetus, and that something would come from a quite unexpected quarter, that is, interest in Medjugorje amongst Charismatics, an interest that would have huge repercussions for the Church in the West.

Meanwhile, two priests, Frs George Kosicki and Gerald Farrell, had written a book entitled *The Spirit and the Bride Say "Come!"*, which was published in early 1981. In this work, they argued that the Charismatic movement within Catholicism was becoming too ecumenical, and was losing its Catholic identity. Having read Fr Gobbi's *Our Lady Speaks to Her Beloved Priests*, they concluded that what was needed was an injection of his type of Marian apocalypticism, a message they saw as "a prophetic word to the Church in our time." They envisioned a Charismatic mass-movement, which would fulfill the message of Fatima:

> We believe that the promise of our Lady concerning the final triumph of her Immaculate Heart, the conversion of Russia and the ensuing world peace is soon to be fulfilled.... Those who are spiritually attuned to the needs of our time agree that only a sovereign act of God can meet our present needs, an outpouring of the Spirit such as occurred at Guadalupe.

As for prayer, they seem to have been thinking in terms of a mixture of the rosary and speaking in tongues.[4] It is interesting to note that at this stage, in the very early 80s, even Charismatics such as the authors of the above book thought in terms of Fatima as the natural place for Catholics to turn to when thinking of prophetic Marian teachings.

This is not to suggest, though, that a conscious process of manipulation was taking place regarding the Charismatic Renewal assuming a more Marian aspect: clearly it was, and is, far too diverse a movement for a few individuals to have brought this about. Rather, it is probably more accurate to see this process as part of a more general return to Marian devotion, in the aftermath of the upheavals which took place after the Second Vatican Council (1962–65).

Be that as it may, it would be through the Charismatic Renewal that a great deal of the publicity about Medjugorje would be generated worldwide—one only has to look at the writings of Charismatic authors such as Fr Robert Faricy to appreciate this.[5] And even as vocal a supporter of Medjugorje as Denis Nolan was obliged to admit later that "some have tried to 'create' Medjugorje in their own image. Perhaps this charge could be made in regard to some involved in the Charismatic Renewal."

Nolan also said that "It is unfortunate but true that perhaps the worst enemies of Medjugorje are sometimes proponents of the apparition themselves." He then went on to list Charismatic elements, and those who have disparaged Fatima and Lourdes at the expense of Medjugorje, as examples of this. In fact, he actually uses the words, "Other excesses abound."[6]

The fact is that the Franciscans most involved in promoting Medjugorje were undoubtedly heavily influenced by the Charismatic Renewal, and this symbiotic relationship between Medjugorje and the Charismatics would only grow stronger in succeeding years.

However, once again, this is not meant as a general criticism of the Charismatic Movement, as such, given that under the right conditions, it is quite possible that the Holy Spirit will grant extraordinary graces and charisms, such as healing gifts, to particular individuals. However, while acknowledging this, the *Catechism of the Catholic Church* also cautions that authentic discernment is critical, and in particular tells us that: "No charism is exempt from being referred and submitted to the Church's shepherds" (799–801).

MEDJUGORJE AND THE VISIONARIES

At the time the visions began, in June 1981, Medjugorje was a village with a population of about three thousand, situated in Bosnia-Herzegovina, in what was then Yugoslavia, about twenty-five miles from the Adriatic coast. However, most of the visionaries were born in nearby Bijakovici, situated nearer Podbrdo, the hill where the first visions took place, which is a short distance away from Medjugorje itself. Two bigger mountains, Crnica and Krizevac, form a backdrop, and the latter was known as Sipovac until 1933, when a massive stone cross was built on its summit. Krizevac has become a focus for pilgrims to Medjugorje, while Podbrdo is a foothill of the mountain Crnica. The population of western Herzegovina was mainly composed of Catholic Croats at this time, with some Muslims and fewer Orthodox Serbs.[7]

The visionaries were Vicka Ivankovic, aged nearly seventeen (born 3 September 1964); Mirjana Dragicevic (born 18 March 1965), Marija Pavlovic (born 1 April 1965) and Ivan Dragicevic (born 25 May 1965), all aged sixteen; Ivanka Ivankovic aged fifteen (born 21 June 1966) and Jakov Colo (born 6 March 1971), aged ten.[8]

Thus, there were four girls and two boys, Ivan and Jakov, and although some others were present at the beginning, these six have become the focus of the worldwide attention that Medjugorje has generated.[9] An important point to note is that, apart from Jakov, we are not dealing with *children* here, but rather with *young adults,* young people who had been exposed to many of the corrupting influences of the modern world, including television. This contrasts strongly with the young seers of approved Marian apparitions of the past, whose average age was about eleven and who were brought up in the generally much better moral atmosphere then prevailing.

UNLIKELY MARIAN SEERS

The fact is that the seers of approved apparitions have almost invariably been very innocent in the sense of being uncorrupted by the world. Most of them have been children or very simple adults. Only the children at Beauraing and Banneux had been exposed to modern communications in the form of the cinema — and clearly, 1930s cinema cannot be compared in terms of its corrupting influence with late twentieth-century television. At Medjugorje, the young people, despite Communism, had all been exposed to modern Western culture — including a disco — with all its power to degrade and undermine Christian values.

Compare this factor with the situation of most of the recognized seers who lived in previous centuries, often in rural areas far from cities, and most of whom were quite young children. It is true that Juan Diego of Guadalupe in Mexico, in 1531, was an adult, but he had only been baptized a few years previously and was spiritually childlike, while Catherine Labouré, who saw Our Lady at Rue du Bac in Paris, in 1830, was a reserved young nun in her twenties. At La Salette, which is also situated in France, in 1846, Mélanie was fourteen and Maximin eleven, while at Lourdes, likewise in France, in 1858, Bernadette was fourteen. The latter three in particular came from extremely poor backgrounds, both materially and culturally.

At Pontmain in northern France, in 1871, the four main seers were aged between ten and twelve, while at Knock in Ireland, in 1871, those present were mainly adults, although adults with a very simple faith. Fatima, in 1917, is outstanding in this respect since Lucia as the eldest was only ten, with Francisco and Jacinta aged only eight and seven respectively at the outset. At Beauraing, the eldest of the five children was about fifteen, and at Banneux, Mariette Beco was eleven. Both of these apparitions took place in Belgium in the early 1930s.

In the majority of these cases, then, we are dealing with *very* unsophisticated seers, some of whom had not even reached puberty, and thus their testimony has been intrinsically more believable than that of many more modern visionaries, including those at Medjugorje. The latter, as young people living in the 80s, would not have escaped the serious contamination which is present in the modern world. All of this tells us that the Medjugorje visionaries were far from ideal candidates as prospective Marian seers. It would seem that they were mostly too old and too worldly, and came from a mixed culture which was influenced by both Communism and television. They also had to contend with the effect of living in a distorted Catholic culture in which the disputes between the Franciscans and the secular clergy were a significant disturbing factor, one that was bound to have an effect on the young people.

THE CORRUPTING INFLUENCE OF COMMUNISM

The point about the corrupting influence of Communism needs to be further explained. It is very difficult for Westerners to really understand what life was like under Communism. We are so used to the freedom of thinking, saying and doing more or less what we like that trying to grasp what it was like to live under a system which was essentially a vast prison camp is practically impossible. Under Communism, people learned to practice self-censorship in order to survive, in the face of a party apparatus, a vast system of repression, which was omnipresent in the old Soviet Union.

In more or less closed societies, such as Yugoslavia under Communism, the air of unreality was compounded by the difficulty of getting reliable news about the outside world, apart from what could be learned via the state-controlled media. Speaking of this system, and its effects on the individual, Agnes Horvath and Arpad Szakolczai say that it "had a severe, often devastating impact on everybody, by destroying values, social connections, [and] forms of behaviour." This was because Communism, "tried to influence and supervise all decisions, all movements, all initiatives; it dreaded anything that was new, spontaneous, uncontrolled."

They also speak of the "most lasting and dangerous" impact of Communism as being its effects on the "depth" of personality of those living in such societies, because of the way it forced people to make unsatisfactory life decisions, and then "made them identify themselves with the results of their own decisions." Thus, there was a huge pressure to conform, to go along with the system, to think with the system, and at the same time a constant feeling of being under "their" control, of being observed, in a way that allowed no real freedom and little chance of escape.[10]

That this abnormal, indeed absurd, system should have finally collapsed was inevitable, but while it existed it was able to do enormous psychological and emotional damage to many of those imprisoned within it. The whole economic system under Communism was topsy-turvy. It was simply not set up for, or capable of meeting, the needs of ordinary individuals, and thus there were widespread shortages and inefficiencies, along with interminable queuing for basic needs. This constant struggle for economic survival was another debilitating influence of Communism. When we add to this the system of surveillance which was firmly in place, and which included a network of informers and collaborators, we have a situation where individuals could never know who they could trust—or what was in government files about them.[11]

But perhaps the most insidious effect of a "pressure-cooker" system like Communism was the way its mentality also affected those opposed to it. That is, such was the power of the Communist system, of its propaganda, that it affected not only the external behavior of those living under it, but also their thinking, indeed their very selves. People could begin to lose their moral bearings as the corrosive effects of years of Communist misrule would gradually wear them down, and their own "collaboration" with the system would be a further negative influence.

This type of thing could also affect the way that ordinary believers would interact with their priests and bishops. It was not unknown for the latter to be "co-opted" by the regime—that is, to collaborate with it in some respects—and so people lost their sense of trust even towards Church officials. This was obviously very corrosive of basic Christian charity, and undoubtedly created a great deal of mistrust and suspicion—which no doubt suited the Communists very well. And given the situation in Bosnia-Herzegovina, with its long running Franciscan-Secular dispute, this was bound to create special difficulties.

Putting all this together, we have, under Communism, an intrinsically corrupt and corrupting system, and it is also in the light of this that the experiences of the Medjugorje visionaries have to be assessed and understood.

CHARISMATIC "PROPHECIES" ABOUT MEDJUGORJE

Shortly before the visions began, an important Charismatic conference was held in Rome, in May 1981. We are told that:

> Fr Tomislav Vlasic... had gone to Rome for an international meeting of leaders of the Charismatic Renewal. During the conference, he asked some of the leaders to pray with him for the healing of the Church in Yugoslavia. One of those praying, Sr Briege McKenna, had a mental picture of Fr Vlasic seated and surrounded by a great crowd; from the seat flowed streams of water. Another, Emile Tardiff [sic] OP, said in prophecy: "Do not fear, I am sending you my mother." A few weeks later Our Lady began appearing in Medjugorje.[12]

Fr Ivo Sivric, in his important book *The Hidden Side of Medjugorje*, tells us that "according to Marija Pavlovic, in front of certain visionaries that...[Fr Vlasic] knew, one month in advance,...[he] mentioned that the Gospa would begin appearing in Yugoslavia. He did not, however, specify the place." This probably took place at a meeting he had with the visionaries in Medjugorje on 29 June 1981, during the first week of the visions. At this time, he was the chaplain at Capljina, a town to the south of Medjugorje.[13] It is worth noting that in no other approved apparitions do we find anyone coming forward in advance of them, to say when they are going to begin.

What is even more revealing, though, is that, according to Wayne Weible, the Protestant convert and Medjugorje advocate, Briege McKenna's "vision" actually contained further details, and that she had seen Fr Vlasic "in *a twin-towered church* sitting in a chair and surrounded by a great crowd." As Weible notes, this is an important point because the only church with twin towers which Fr Vlasic knew of was St James's parish church at Medjugorje.[14]

There was a continuing Charismatic interest at Medjugorje, too, even after the visions had begun. This is apparent from the fact that an important Charismatic service was held there from 23–25 August 1983. It seems that all the visionaries, as well as some priests and nuns connected with the parish, received the "baptism of the Spirit." The organizers of this meeting were Dr Philippe Madre of the Charismatic "Lion of Judah" community (later renamed the "Beatitudes" community); Fr Tardif, the priest mentioned previously who had spoken in "prophetic" terms to Fr Vlasic in Rome; and Fr Pierre Rancourt. Fr Tardif apparently "taught the faithful to prophesy, [and] to speak in tongues." Because of government opposition, however, the three visitors were arrested by the police, interrogated, searched and finally given the choice of prison or leaving the country immediately. Not surprisingly, they chose the latter.[15]

Fr René Laurentin, the French mariologist, claims that the influence of the Charismatic Renewal was not at work in the early days of Medjugorje, but his arguments do not seem credible in the light of the above evidence. It is certainly worth noting that he refers to "certain fears" that were expressed, "especially at Rome in September, 1983," about mixing Charismatic elements with the activities of the visionaries. He raises the question as to whether such a combination might "produce excesses," but reassures his readers as follows: "No doubt precautions must be taken against such a thing happening if the apparitions go on for a long time, but it is more likely that they will soon cease."[16]

Elsewhere, he tells us he believed this because at that point, the duration of the visions had been constantly diminishing from about twenty minutes in 1983, to about a minute in early 1984, while his other reason was that nearly all the alleged secrets had been revealed. This belief has clearly turned out to be quite mistaken — and indeed how empty that reassurance now seems so many years later.

THE CHARISMATIC MOVEMENT AND THE CHURCH

The modern Charismatic Movement, in the sense of *glossolalia*, or speaking in tongues, began in the American Midwest in the 1870s, and it received further impetus in the early twentieth century at Topeka, Kansas, and later at Los Angeles. This led to a massive growth in Pentecostal churches throughout the United States, so that now they number their adherents in the millions. There were also revivals in European countries, which were characterized by episodes of "weeping, moaning and shaking."[17]

The Charismatic Movement bases itself on the descriptions found in passages from St Paul's Epistles, such as 1 Corinthians 12:8–10. Those who are said to have received this "baptism of the Spirit" are said to show signs such as speaking in tongues, interpreting the *glossolalia* of others, demonstrating healing and prophetic powers and displaying the ability to discern spirits.

The Charismatic Movement, as it has become established within the Catholic Church, however, is essentially a post-Vatican II phenomenon. Pope John XXIII had called for a spiritual renewal within the Church, and one of the results of this was the formation of a group of students and staff at Duquesne University in Pittsburgh, in the 1960s, to explore new forms of spirituality. Some individual priests and lay people had taken part in Pentecostal "Full Gospel Fellowship" meetings as early as 1962, but it was in 1966–67 that Catholic participation really blossomed at Duquesne. Those involved began to pray in the Charismatic manner, experiencing glossolalia, and thus began the movement within Catholicism, which later spread with great rapidity to other centers, such as the University of Notre Dame in South Bend, Indiana. It was also taken up at Ann Arbor, Michigan, ultimately becoming a worldwide movement of Charismatic groups and communities.[18]

The worrying thing about the origin of this movement within the Catholic Church, then, is that it was not a spontaneous and entirely "Catholic" experience, but rather was derived at least in part from Protestant Pentecostalism.[19] It also seems that the "healing ministry" within the Charismatic movement, with all its claims for the "miraculous," was also strongly influenced by Protestant sources, remotely, in the nineteenth century, by groups such as the Christian Science movement of Mary Baker Eddy and more recently by Episcopalian and Presbyterian "healers."[20]

The movement was characterized by days of renewal and yearly conferences, such as those held at Notre Dame, and it attracted influential sponsors such as Cardinal Suenens of Belgium, who was given responsibility for the Charismatic Renewal within the Church by Pope Paul VI. It is certainly the case that the Charismatic Movement has had a very large impact on the Church, and many clergy and religious have testified that it has "saved their vocation." However, one sympathetic observer, Morton Kelsey, had this general comment to make about glossolalia: "Tongue speaking is a powerful invasion of the unconscious. It can be dangerous for the weak ego and should never be forced on anyone."[21]

Similarly, regarding the particular messages "given" to individuals via this approach, Kelsey notes that a number of religious leaders have come to regard such practices as divisive. He also points out that it can lead to a certain spiritual pride, as some Charismatics begin to feel that they are better than "ordinary" Christians. In particular, he makes the following rather illuminating remark: "Some persons who speak in tongues suddenly find themselves getting God by the tail and receiving messages that 'God told me this about you...' or 'God wants you to do this...' and these are usually the very people who receive messages for everyone but themselves."

Kelsey also notes the adverse psychological effect glossolalia may have for some people, since it can be "a liberating experience, freeing the unconscious to flood out into the individual." Such a "liberation" may clearly be extremely dangerous for certain unbalanced individuals,[22] and so the problems involved in some Charismatic practices are clear.

Fr Laurentin wrote a book on the Charismatic Movement entitled *Catholic Pentecostalism*, which was published in 1977, in which he tells us that he "became interested in Catholic Pentecostalism as early as 1967, the very year of its birth." The very fact that such a title could be used—with its emphasis on the word *Pentecostalism*—clearly indicates the actual origins of this movement within Catholicism. He goes on to say that he spoke with Fr Edward O'Connor, one of the "founders of the movement," who assured him that the future of the Church was bound up with this movement, a feeling Fr Laurentin apparently eventually came to share. Certainly, he took more than a passing interest in the work of the Charismatics, since he informs us that during the 1970s he attended a number of their conferences, gathering information about the movement.[23] It is probably worth noting that Fr O'Connor later wrote a largely uncritical work entitled *Marian Apparitions Today: Why So Many?*

Reading Fr Laurentin's book, published only four years before Medjugorje began, it is clear that by then he was completely committed to the Charismatic Renewal, and thus he cannot really be said to have approached the visions and the visionaries in a detached and objective manner: the work even has a chapter entitled "Mary, Model of the Charismatic." Rather, he was predisposed to see the actions of the Holy Spirit behind all their activities, and this bias has clearly colored his later writings on the subject. He admits as much himself, in speaking of the "harmony... established between the apparitions and the charismatic renewal."[24]

MEDJUGORJE AND MONTANISM

That there are important lessons from Church history concerning previous charismatic movements is clear from what happened during the Montanist crisis, which began in the mid-second century,

15

when Montanus initiated a movement with apocalyptic undertones. He claimed that the Holy Spirit was about to be poured out on the Church, and also that the heavenly Jerusalem had descended on the small village of Pepuza in Phrygia, in what is now western Turkey, a place described by St Cyril of Jerusalem as "a most insignificant hamlet."

It is interesting to note that this is the same area that had been the center of worship of Cybele, the Mother Goddess, whose ecstatic rites were administered by the Galli, "priests" given to self-castration. They also seem to have practiced other forms of self-mutilation with weapons, somewhat akin to the activities of the prophets of Baal as encountered by Elijah in the Old Testament. It certainly does not seem that the supporters of Montanus denied that he had been a "priest" of some form of idolatrous cult—a charge made by St Jerome specifically regarding the cult of Cybele—and was a recent convert; it was acknowledged, too, that he was a "considerable organizer."

Montanus was closely associated with two female prophetesses—Priscilla, or Prisca, and Maximilla—who were referred to as "madwomen" by orthodox writers. It is said that when carried away by "inspiration," Montanus would fall into a trance and start to speak wildly, possibly in tongues, while "prophesying." Indeed, Montanists described their movement as "The New Prophecy," and it became quite widespread, reaching Rome, North Africa and beyond.

Supporters of these innovators wrote down their declarations, regarding them as "sacred" writings, and it is clear that these were taken seriously in many quarters. Eusebius, the Church historian, tells us that there was a famous debate in Rome between Gaius and Proclus on whether these should be regarded as "scriptural." According to Eusebius, Montanism was characterized by the false prophet speaking in a trance, which induced irresponsibility and freedom from restraint, a condition which originated in a deliberate suppression of conscious thought, and which ended in an uncontrollable delirium. The general view of the early Church was that genuine prophecy did not involve this kind of "alienation of the senses." As Msgr Ronald Knox points out, Montanism was "a new type of prophecy altogether... not some casual variation on the prophetic *charisma* which still persisted, at that date, in Christendom proper."[25]

This is evident from the type of language used by Montanus and his followers, since, amongst other things, he said: "I am the Father, the Word, and the Paraclete," while Maximilla said: "I am the Word, and spirit, and power." They saw three separate dispensations corresponding to the Trinitarian persons, and identified their own movement with the coming of the Paraclete, the Holy Spirit. It seems that Maximilla regarded herself as the "last of the prophets," and thus there was certainly an apocalyptic strain in Montanist thinking.

Most of what has been recorded about the Montanists has come from their opponents; we are told that they had a "fondness for taking up collections," while "insinuations about dyed hair, pencilled eyebrows, and gaming tables" were also made. They were apparently well organized, and "itinerant preachers of the new prophecy were supported from ... central funds." Amongst the later developments noted by Epiphanius, a fourth-century bishop, we hear of followers of the sect sleeping in the temple at Pepuza in the hope that they might have a vision of Christ, and also of processions of virgins who would enter the church "in order to speak to the people, and deliver prophetic utterances calling to repentance."[26]

There was a definite feminine aspect to Montanism, with women prominent amongst the leaders of the sect, and there were clashes with the orthodox Church regarding prophecy, authority, the interpretation of Christian writings and just how significant Montanism was in terms of salvation history.

A later prophetess of Montanism, Quintilla, managed to generate her own band of followers, the "Quintillanists." She had claimed that Christ had come to her while she was asleep, in the form of a woman dressed in a bright robe, and that he was responsible for "putting wisdom into her." It has been claimed that this "vision" was not heretical because it points to the idea of "wisdom" having female characteristics, but it is hard to see how this sort of thing can really be equated with orthodox Catholic thinking.

This feminist streak in Montanism went beyond prophetesses, since later on there were "female Montanist presbyters [priests] and bishops" — both Epiphanius and St Augustine drew attention to this fact.[27]

As regards their "hierarchy," according to St Jerome, the Montanists gave first place to the "patriarchs of Pepuza," putting the so-called "koinonoi" in second place, followed by the bishops. The exact meaning of this term *koinonoi* is not known, but it may possibly point to a group functioning as "financial officers/collectors," based on Philippians 4:15, where it expresses the notion of "giving and receiving," or more literally partnership or fellowship. Whatever the exact organization of their "church," like many another sect, Montanism gradually became more heretical as time went on.[28]

MEDJUGORJE AND MONTANISM COMPARED

With respect to Medjugorje, there are certainly similarities to the way Montanism developed. We can see this in the Franciscan involvement at Medjugorje, which has led to the creation of a "parallel" church, one which was in a state of rebellion against the Vatican and the local hierarchy. And this is also evident regarding the *koinonoi*—assuming they were some sort of financial officers—in the focus on money in connection with Medjugorje. Likewise, Medjugorje has had more than its share of "itinerant preachers."

Fr René Laurentin, in his enthusiasm for all things charismatic, goes so far as to question the veracity of St Jerome on the above points, and implies that the *koinonoi* were "a kind of synod associated with the patriarch." Similarly, he questioned whether St Epiphanius was right on exactly what Montanus did or did not say. But given that these writers were over 1500 years closer to the events in question, it seems more than likely that they were better informed than Fr Laurentin. The basic problem for him is that many of the characteristics of Montanism seem to parallel the activities of the modern Charismatics, particularly as expressed at Medjugorje. Thus he is forced into the difficult position of trying to find positive things to say about Montanus and his followers.

Saverio Gaeta seems to be confused regarding these points made about Fr Laurentin's positive position on aspects of Montanism. Gaeta makes much of the fact that Fr Laurentin's book, *Catholic Pentecostalism*, was published in 1977—that is, four years before Medjugorje began—and as such claims that it does not make sense to criticize the French priest as a defender of Medjugorje in relation to Montanism. But the point is that his support for aspects of Montanism had nothing to do with Medjugorje but was made because he wanted to defend the Charismatic movement as a whole from charges that it did in fact have similarities to Montanism.[29]

Another point of resemblance between Montanism and Medjugorje can be seen in the similar spirit of rigorism that both movements have exhibited. Prisca and Maximilla both insisted on celibacy, to the extent that they apparently abandoned their husbands so as to devote themselves to preaching the new doctrines. We are also told that Montanus, on the basis of his new revelations, apparently had a very severe attitude towards the remarriage of widows. Similarly, Montanists fasted several times a year in order to differentiate themselves from ordinary Catholics, and in times of persecution they would deliberately court trouble.

As Msgr Knox observes, "To justify itself, the new prophecy must find something to forbid which the Church tolerates." The excessive focus on fasting, to the extent that some people were too weak to carry out their normal duties, as happened in the early days following the Medjugorje visions, is one example of this type of thing as regards Medjugorje itself. Another is the idea that believers were supposed to spend excessive amounts of time praying, following the lead of Ivan, who claimed that he needed over two hours to say the rosary.

This similarity between Montanism and "Medjugorism" even comes down to matters such as the predictions made by Maximilla before her death, that is, that a period of persecutions and wars would follow, whereas actually 13 years of peace and calm ensued. Conversely, the "Gospa" of Medjugorje proclaimed, in the mid-1980s, that she had come to bring peace to Yugoslavia and the world, a prediction made before the region experienced the worst fighting in Europe since the Second World War.[30]

It is even more pertinent to compare the attitude of the higher echelons of the Church in both cases. Montanism was clearly perceived as a very serious threat. The local bishops tried to expose Maximilla as a false prophetess but were forcibly prevented from doing so by her supporters, and so the Asian bishops met together in council to condemn the growing movement, as its influence began to be felt further afield.[31] Compare this with the treatment that has been meted out to the successive bishops of Mostar by the supporters of the visionaries, and the way that Medjugorje is now being dealt with at a very high level within the Church.[32]

In speaking of Montanism, Msgr Knox stated that: "The sect would have made but a small ripple on the surface of Christendom, if the wayward genius of Tertullian had not lent energy to its propaganda." Likewise, it is distressing to report that Medjugorje would probably have had much less of an impact on the Church if it had not been for the vocal support of important clerical figures such as Fr Laurentin.[33]

According to Tertullian, the pope of the day, Victor, was poised to recognize the prophecies of the Montanists but a certain Praxeas made allegations about the prophets and their activities, and pointed to previous papal teaching, considerations which caused Victor to draw back. Msgr Knox says that all this is possible, but "it reads very much like one of those Vatican rumours which in all ages have been so plentiful, and so untrustworthy. It depends on no other authority." Tertullian's witness is somewhat suspect since he eventually became a Montanist.[34]

It is certainly very instructive to compare this incident with the attitude expressed by some supporters of Medjugorje, who have been at great pains to demonstrate papal and other ecclesiastical support for the "shrine" and the "messages."

Another negative characteristic of Montanism was its longevity: in the year 250, the city of Thyatira, in the heart of Phrygia, was completely devoid of Catholic Christians—the Montanists were in charge—while "Constantine's laws were not enforced against Montanism in Phrygia itself, where it still had many adherents as late as the middle of the fifth century." There may even have been cases of Montanism surviving until the time of St John Damascene in the eighth century.[35] Thus, it was a long time before Montanism died out—perhaps an indication that support for Medjugorje will not disappear quickly, regardless of what the Church finally says.

The difference nowadays, as regards the propagation of Medjugorism, is that its rate of expansion has been very much more rapid due to modern methods of travel and communications.

As indicated, Montanism's greatest prize was the theologian Tertullian, a defection described by Msgr Knox "as if Newman had joined the Salvation Army." But the movement never succeeded in forming particularly deep roots, apart from in its native Phrygia. It was regarded by orthodox writers as being due to diabolical possession, but it is equally the case that hysteria or even deliberate fraud may have been responsible for some aspects of Montanism.[36]

Clearly, the history of Montanism shows how a "charismatic" movement can have a negative influence on the Church, and as Msgr Ronald Knox's famous book, *Enthusiasm, A Chapter in the History of Religion*, shows, there have been outbursts of this sort of behavior throughout Church history. Medjugorje is another such outburst, and the longevity and influence of Montanism are a clear warning from history that the threat presented by Medjugorje has to be taken seriously by the Church.

* * *

IT SHOULD BE REITERATED THAT THIS CHAPTER HAS not been meant as a general criticism of the Charismatic Movement, since clearly, given the right conditions, good leadership and proper discernment, such activities may well have a part to play in the life of the Church. But regrettably, it is precisely in the area of discernment, and particularly the discernment of Medjugorje as an overall phenomenon, that the modern Charismatic Movement has been found wanting. It is impossible to get around the fact that right from the beginning there has been an intimate link between the Charismatic Movement and the growth of Medjugorje. This link goes so far as to include the initial Charismatic "prophecies" about the visions themselves, as well as the subsequent publicity campaign conducted preeminently by Fr Laurentin. More than anyone else, he was responsible for the worldwide fame of Medjugorje.

3
The Medjugorje Tapes and the Visionaries

QUESTIONS ABOUT THE VISIONARIES

If we look at the visionaries as individuals, and likewise at their general backgrounds, we can better understand the *milieu* in which the visions arose. It certainly seems fair to describe their family life as less than ideal: for example, Vicka Ivankovic's father was an overseas worker, while her mother may have suffered from depression; in addition, Ivanka Ivankovic's mother had just died, and according to Fr Sivric, another, Mirjana Dragicevic, may well have had emotional problems.[1]

This general point is backed up in an interview, which took place on 27 February 1983, between Marinko Ivankovic, a "father figure" to the visionaries, and Fr Svetozar Kraljevic, the author of *The Apparitions of Our Lady at Medjugorje*. Marinko, the next-door neighbor of both Marija and Vicka in Bijakovici, was asked by the priest why he had involved himself with them, given that he was nearly forty, and a grown man with a family of his own. He responded to this by saying,

> The children have sometimes found themselves in difficult circumstances, especially Ivanka. She was the first in the group who saw the light and the Madonna. Her mother was dead and her father was in Germany. Practically, too, Jakov does not have a father; he lives in Bosnia but rarely visits here. Then Mirjana's family lives in Sarajevo. *In one way or another, the children did not have parental advice or the protection of parents.*[2]

Mary Craig described them as follows: "They were very different in temperament, social background and mental capacity — their intelligence ranging from slightly above to way below average."[3]

These are indications that the visionaries were to a greater or lesser extent emotionally vulnerable in some way, and therefore susceptible to the risk of things going wrong in any encounter with the preternatural, to say nothing of the diabolical.

As noted above, it is also the case that the visionaries were apparently not part of Fr Zovko's Charismatic prayer group, that is, they were not particularly "religious," and thus to some extent were outsiders.[4] Contrast the above deficiencies with the beautiful picture of family life which emerges from Sr Lucia's second volume of her autobiography, *Fatima in Lucia's Own Words II*.[5] This gives us the background to the apparitions, and shows how the three seers of Fatima, Francisco, Jacinta and Lucia, were very privileged in that they were brought up in a wonderful Catholic atmosphere, both in terms of their home life and the surrounding culture. Although they were relatively poor in economic terms, they were very rich in the blessings of the Faith, and in particular they did not come from families which were to some extent or other troubled.[6]

THE MEDJUGORJE TAPES

Many of the standard accounts of Medjugorje are based on interviews made by Frs Tomislav Vlasic and Svetozar Kraljevic about a year and a half after the original visions began in June 1981, or on the interviews with Vicka conducted by Fr Janko Bubalo. These were published later on, in 1987, as part of *A Thousand Encounters with the Blessed Virgin Mary in Medjugorje* — the title being a reference to Vicka's alleged claims of daily visions since 1981.

Obviously, eighteen months or more is a long time during which to retain detailed memories of the crowded first days of the alleged visits of the Blessed Virgin, and so it is legitimate to raise questions as to just how reliable those interviews really were. This is especially so since some of the information in these later interviews cannot be reconciled with what is on the transcripts of the interviews with the visionaries which were taped at Medjugorje by Fr Zovko and Fr Cuvalo, the parochial vicar, from 27–30 June 1981. This is not the case with, for example, the Fatima seers, since Sr Lucia's recollections have proved to be very trustworthy, to say nothing of the fact that Fatima has been fully accepted by the Church, and that Jacinta and Francisco have been canonized, while Sr Lucia is on the road to beatification.

The great value of these tapes lies in their spontaneity, in the fact that they are true-to-life dialogues between the two priests and the visionaries, in which all the essential details about what happened during the first week or so become apparent. They are a "warts and all" depiction of what really took place, and as such they are innately superior to the better-known but much later Medjugorje accounts. It is true that sections of the tapes are indistinct, but overall there is certainly enough clear information on them to justify regarding the tapes as primary source material on Medjugorje; in any case, the quality of the tapes is understandable given the circumstances under which they were made. Clearly, these contemporary interviews are far more likely to give an accurate record of what actually took place during those crucial first days than any interviews conducted later on; but they have either been ignored or mostly downplayed by the principal Medjugorje chroniclers.

This is rather ironic, since, as Medjugorje insider Daria Klanac relates, many pro-Medjugorje authors have used the same materials, particularly Fr Laurentin, Fr Janko Bubalo, Fr Svetozar Kraljevic and Fr Ljudevit Rupcic.[7]

These tapes correspond in timing with the earliest records of some of the major approved Marian apparitions, such as those at La Salette. In this case Mélanie, one of two seers, after being interviewed by the local mayor the day after seeing Our Lady, had her story taken down in writing by her employer, Baptiste Pra. He had called in two neighbors as witnesses, and while she dictated, he wrote down her words and the others checked her account and jointly signed it. Thus the most important basic text of the apparition was written only a day after the event.

Similarly, at Lourdes, Bernadette had to undergo bouts of questioning and her replies were taken down, so again we have a very full record of what happened, with the first major interview, at the hands of the local Police commissioner, Dominique Jacomet, in the presence of two other witnesses, taking place only a week after the first vision on 14 February 1858.[8]

At Fatima, too, the children were interrogated by Dr Manuel Formigão, a seminary professor, after both the September and October 1917 apparitions, with their replies being noted in detail. Likewise at Beauraing, the five children involved were questioned separately after the later apparitions, with their replies being taken down by a lawyer, Adrien Laurent. And at Banneux too, the local priest, Fr Louis Jamin, was careful to ensure that the seer, Mariette Beco, gave him a report of what happened after each apparition.[9]

So Fr Cuvalo's initiative in starting to record his conversations with the Medjugorje visionaries was extremely valuable and has given us the best record we have of what happened right at the beginning. In fact, in some respects, they are superior to a purely written record, because in listening to recorded speech, one can quite often catch nuances of meaning through manner of expression and tone of voice.

This is what Fr Augustin Poulain, the noted spiritual writer, said on this point: "Is there an absolutely authentic text? Have ... certain expressions been corrected as inexact or obscure, or have ... certain other passages been actually suppressed?" He then goes on to say that this is inadmissible from the critical viewpoint, since it means we are "depriving ourselves of very important data." Furthermore, he says: "Instead of curtailment, have there, on the contrary been additions to the revelation.... This would be a real falsification."[10]

Clearly, the tape transcripts represent the closest we are going to get to an "absolutely authentic text," and regarding his other points, concerning suppressions of, and additions to, the alleged revelation, the evidence concerning the Medjugorje messages on these points is examined further on in this book.

THE IMPORTANCE OF THE TAPES

Mary Craig details a conversation between Fr Zovko and his housekeeper immediately on his return to Medjugorje, during the first week of the visions, in which he asked her if Fr Cuvalo had spoken to the visionaries. She responded: "Yes, and he's recorded the conversations." Craig then tells us that Fr Zovko found the cassette and listened to it, and that he "began tape-recording all his conversations with the children." Further on, she even mentions the 30 June interview between Fr Zovko and the visionaries, saying "the tape of this interview still exists."

Similarly, Fr Michael O'Carroll, another pro-Medjugorje author, in speaking of the fifth day of the visions, Sunday 28 June, mentions that after Mass that morning "the children went through a wearying interrogation by the parish priest, Fr Jozo."[11]

Likewise, as we will see, Fr Janko Bubalo was certainly aware of these tapes, and challenged Vicka about elements from them during his interviews with her. But apart from Daria Klanac, and more latterly Fr James Mulligan, pro-Medjugorje writers do not give us any extended details of them, and thus in their accounts we are asked to rely largely on recollections which were recorded much later.

Regarding these original tape-recorded interviews, then, although the methodology used by the priests was far from perfect, they do give essential source material about the visions. It was believed that the

Communist authorities had confiscated these tapes when Fr Zovko was arrested, but Fr Sivric relates that his friend, Grgo Kozina, had managed to copy them beforehand, and was then able to pass on duplicates to him. From the evidence provided by sources such as Fr Bubalo, it is clear that other copies of these tapes must also have been in circulation.

Fr Sivric then painstakingly transcribed their contents and published them in full in the lengthy appendices to his book on Medjugorje.[12] Daria Klanac, a Canadian citizen of Croatian origin and a Medjugorje supporter—who by 2001 had organized more than sixty pilgrimages to the town, involving thousands of pilgrims—has also published transcripts of the tapes in her book *Aux Sources de Medjugorje*. She tells us that she likewise obtained her tapes from Grgo Kozina.[13]

And as we will see, Fr James Mulligan has also published a textual version of the tapes. This will be dealt with further on, but for the moment, we will just concern ourselves with the Sivric and Klanac versions of the transcripts. When these are compared—one by a pro-Medjugorje writer, and the other by a critic—they are found to be substantially the same.[14] However, it is rather curious that Klanac completely omits the first three tapes recorded by Fr Cuvalo, before the return of Fr Zovko. In any event, of the remaining tape transcripts, as regards the essential points, they are substantially in agreement.

Such variations as there are mainly involve differences in word order, which are understandable given that the transcriptions in Fr Sivric's *French* edition of his book were translated from the original language into English, and then into French, whereas Daria Klanac did her translation directly into French. Also, naturally enough, in the process of translation, since words can have more than one meaning, a particular word in the original language can be translated in more than one way—and this clearly also affects phrases and indeed whole sentences.

REASONS FOR DIFFERENCES

The remaining differences between the transcriptions can be categorized in a number of ways. These include short sections which Fr Sivric was presumably unable to satisfactorily translate, perhaps because of the poorer quality of the tapes he had to work with, or because he was older and thus his hearing was less acute than that of Daria Klanac—always bearing in mind, of course, that at times the material on the tapes was very confused, with interruptions or voices being mixed up indiscriminately. This also led Fr Sivric to occasionally mistake one speaker for another. But equally, Klanac acknowledges the difficulties involved in transcribing the tapes, and admits that some words and phrases escaped her.[15] Another category of differences involves sections of the tapes which Klanac includes, but which are missing in Fr Sivric's text—although, in one instance, involving the tape made of the interview between Fr Zovko and Ivan on the evening of 28 June, Fr Sivric has more material than Klanac.[16]

The essential point to note is that the "missing" material is not crucial to the arguments presented in this book. This mainly comes from two of the interviews with Jakov, the youngest of the visionaries. In the interview carried out on the morning of 27 June 1981, Klanac has approximately 40% more material than Fr Sivric,[17] while in the interview on 28 June, there is a more serious discrepancy, since Klanac's has approximately 80% more material.[18]

In her transcripts, Klanac includes material in which Jakov elaborated on his experiences, including information about the purported words of the "Gospa." These included the Vision remarking in a number of places that the visionaries were her "angels"; that everyone, including the Franciscans, should believe as though they could see the Vision too; and that "she" had come because there were a lot of believers there. Interestingly, according to Jakov, the Vision did explicitly claim to be the Blessed Virgin Mary, but apart from this, there is nothing to compare with what was said by the real Blessed Virgin at Lourdes and Fatima. During these interviews Jakov also indicated how the visionaries had prayed on the hillside and had asked for a sign, and he also gave the reaction of his mother.

Regarding the material on the tape of the interview with Mirjana on the morning of 28 June, Klanac has just under 50% more material, but again it is essentially a question of her describing her experiences in more detail, under questioning from Fr Zovko.[19] There are also a few other instances of this type amongst the other transcripts.

It is not clear why this material was missing on Fr Sivric's tapes, but it may well be that during the process of copying it was not thought worth preserving, or perhaps practical considerations such as fitting the interviews onto tapes of differing lengths were involved. Or the person doing the copying, Grgo Kozina, may have mistakenly failed to copy some of the interviews in their entirety. Certainly, it does not seem that any sinister motive can be imputed for these particular differences because the material involved is really quite innocuous.

The last category of differences would appear to be easier to explain, as it involves statements which might well have proved embarrassing if not dangerous for those involved, had they been widely circulated during the early 80s, when Communism was still in place. An example of this is found in the interview with Mirjana of 27 June, in which Fr Zovko asked her if she had been persecuted at school in Sarajevo because she went to church, to which she replied in the affirmative.[20]

There are further examples in the transcript of the last tape, which involved five of the visionaries. One section, which mentions the Communist militia, is missing in Fr Sivric's version, while another, which mentioned that one of the young women present with the visionaries that day, Ljubica Vasilj-Gluvic, worked for the local Communist "executive committee," is also missing. There is also a missing section which speaks of the mother of Vicka—arguably the "principal" visionary—as being depressed, and which also gives personal details about her family. There is mention, too, of cassettes with Croatian hymns which were decorated with forbidden nationalist symbols. A section which refers to the chief of the militia, a certain Zdravko, has also been removed, as have two further references to the executive committee, including the name of a certain Marinko Sego, who is described as its president.[21]

It is important to realize, however, that the majority of the tapes, as transcribed by the two authors, are virtually the same, once allowance is made for differences in word order, and the points noted above. This also includes other minor considerations, such as short unintelligible sections which Fr Sivric conscientiously noted. The material on seven of the twelve tapes dealt with by Daria Klanac is virtually the same as that found in Fr Sivric's transcripts, and overall, if we exclude the three tapes indicated above, those involving Jakov and Mirjana, then approximately 92% of the material is common to both authors. If we include those tapes, then approximately 85% of the material is substantially the same.

THE TAPE TRANSCRIPTS ARE RELIABLE

Clearly, these tapes are of primary importance in understanding Medjugorje, and that is why a study of their contents forms one of the central aspects of this book. The reality is that they are a severe embarrassment to the official position held by supporters of Medjugorje. The most important sections of the tapes are fully dealt with in the chapters which follow, and it is undoubtedly providential that they survived. No one of any credibility has challenged the fact of their existence and importance, but there have been attempts to question the validity of Fr Sivric's transcriptions by Fr Ljudevit Rupcic, a zealous Medjugorje supporter. He argued that because the transcriptions in Fr Sivric's *French* edition of his book have been translated from the original language into English, and then into French that this somehow calls into question their content. But this is clearly not the case since all that matters is whether or not these translations have been accurate.[22]

Louis Bélanger, the Canadian researcher who collaborated with Fr Sivric in the production of *The Hidden Side of Medjugorje*, points out that the original tapes were stored at St James's parish church in Medjugorje, with copies being held in the Mostar diocesan chancery archives, and, as we have seen, Grgo Kozina also made duplicates. Bélanger also tells us that:

> It was important to me that the taped documents...[Fr Sivric] had be carefully translated, tapes that were apparently identical to those given to me by the Bishop of Mostar. At my request, Father Sivric began to make a Croatian transcript and then dictated an English translation...in July, 1986 we exchanged tapes and verified that our sources were complementary.

In 1987, Bélanger asked Bishop Zanic to confirm that the 38 transcripts of the tapes, and their French translations, which he and Fr Sivric had produced, were accurate; Bishop Zanic, who understood French, did this.[23] This is what he had to say about Fr Sivric's book: "I can say that the work is solid, professional and excellent in every regard. The cassettes were reproduced faithfully, as well as the documents."[24]

FIRST DAY—WEDNESDAY, 24 JUNE 1981

Fr Laurentin claims that Fr Jozo Zovko only arrived at St James's parish in Medjugorje shortly before the first vision, but this is incorrect. In fact, Fr Zovko had been appointed pastor nine months before, in October 1980, but he was not present when the visions began, and only learned of them on 27 June, when he returned from a retreat he had been giving at a convent in northern Croatia.

Just before the first vision, Medjugorje was struck by a particularly violent thunderstorm, which raged during the early hours of the morning of Wednesday, 24 June. The post office was struck by lightning, caught fire, and was half burnt down. The lightning strike put the phones out of order and thus Fr Zovko was not fully aware of what was going on in Medjugorje; on his return he was confronted by a huge crowd outside his church.

To put all this in the context of the ongoing situation in Eastern Europe and further afield, the assassination attempt on Pope John Paul II had taken place only the previous month, on 13 May 1981, and there was rising tension between the Solidarity movement in Poland and the Communist leadership. Thus, the visions began at a critical moment.[25]

The first vision allegedly took place later that afternoon, as Ivanka Ivankovic and Mirjana Dragicevic were walking along the road near Bijakovici. Ivanka claimed that she could see the "Gospa," although Mirjana was apparently uncertain.

Later on, having left a message for Vicka Ivankovic, the pair climbed up to Podbrdo — to collect the sheep, according to Ivan Dragicevic's testimony — and saw a vision. Ivan was close to them, having been picking apples nearby with another Ivan, Ivan Ivankovic, a twenty-year-old local man who later dissociated himself from the visionaries because he disapproved of their behavior.[26]

In his taped interview with Fr Cuvalo, which took place on the afternoon of 27 June, Ivan Dragicevic says that he heard somebody saying: "The light is appearing up there." Then Vicka and Ivanka called to him inviting him to go up, since they said that something "like the Gospa" had appeared to them. He then said that they went up and had a similar experience. Fr Cuvalo asked Ivan what he saw once he had reached the girls and looked up, to which he replied: "I saw the light." However, he was not very articulate, and could hardly find the words to describe what he had seen, but it appears that he saw a vision of a "feminine" figure bathed in light, wearing a veil, and a crown which "shone like silver," hovering on a cloud above the stony ground.[27]

THE BLESSED VIRGIN OR SOMETHING DIABOLICAL?

One of the strangest aspects of Ivan Dragicevic's testimony on this occasion is that he tells us that the hands of the Vision were "trembling." This is clearly out of character with regard to the Blessed Virgin, who is by nature calm and serene. So this raises the question as to whether it might indicate a diabolical involvement. This point is emphasized by Msgr Farges, author of the celebrated study entitled *Mystical Phenomena:*

> The signs of diabolical intervention are well known. The devil's deeds always carry with them at least some ridiculous, unseemly, or coarse details; or even something opposed to faith and morals. If his vices were too obvious his influence would soon be unmasked; they are therefore always disguised under more or less inoffensive appearances, even under deceitful traits of virtue and sanctity. He transforms himself at will into an angel of light. God occasionally allows him to assume the most majestic forms, such as those of our Lord, the Blessed Virgin, or the saints. Nevertheless — for God could not otherwise permit it — the disguise, no matter how bold, is never complete, and he always betrays himself in some particular which cannot escape an attentive and prudent observer. Furthermore, the work of the devil becomes very soon unmasked by evil results, for an evil tree cannot bring forth good fruit.[28]

Fr Manfred Hauke, the theologian and mariologist, also comments on this point, saying: "The form of the apparition must correspond to the work of God, which is always perfect. Any physical or moral defects in appearance, attitude, or movements of the Mother of God are to be excluded."[29]

According to Vicka's first *Diary*, as translated by Fr Sivric, which he tells us was actually written for her by one of her sisters, Ana, she returned to the apparition site at around 6:30 p.m., with Mirjana and Ivanka, and it was the latter who then first saw the "Gospa," at which point the others also saw her. In fact, Vicka was responsible for three "diaries," which were three notebooks covering the time from the start of the visions until 25 March 1982, but not in a continuous manner. She wrote the third herself, with her sisters being responsible for writing the others, based on information supplied by Vicka.

Vicka claims that the Vision was holding a baby-like object, while waving at them to come closer, but that she got frightened and ran back to the village. The visionaries told everyone that they had seen the *Gospa*, and some apparently responded that since that day was the feast of St John the Baptist, perhaps they could expect something miraculous. During the vision, Mirjana had apparently asked for a sign so that everyone would believe them, and, according to Vicka, the hour hand on a wristwatch turned right around, which she took as a sign. However, Bishop Zanic later took this particular watch to a watchmaker who confirmed that it was broken, and because of this, the dial could rotate and thus, at the least touch, modify the position of the numbers. Vicka reports that: "We kept touching her and kissing her, and she kept laughing."[30]

THE SMOKING VISIONARIES

It seems that Fr Cuvalo had suspicions that Podbrdo was a place which some young people visited to smoke—this certainly seems to be the drift of some of the questions he put to Vicka, Ivanka and Marija during the first interview he tape-recorded. Regarding the people who were with them during the first vision, he asked if they had smoked.[31] They denied this, but it would be a strange question to put unless he had suspicions on the matter. Certainly, according to René Laurentin and René Lejeune, the girls *had* been smoking—they describe Mirjana's embarrassment at Ivanka saying she was seeing the "Gospa," because "they had been out smoking secretly."[32]

Fr Laurentin later made the position even clearer when he wrote: "The first two visionaries, Ivanka and Mirjana, held back for some time the fact that they were not only going to listen to some tapes that day, but were actually planning to go and smoke some of the tobacco which they threaded all day long with their families." He then says that "personal details" like this should remain private,[33] but this is ridiculous: the beginning of the visions is such a crucial moment that we are entitled to know as much about it as possible.

The evidence indicates, then, that the two visionaries did indeed smoke once they arrived at Podbrdo. In other words, just prior to their supposed meeting with the Blessed Virgin, the Mother of God, the Queen of Heaven, the two visionaries had been smoking. This certainly puts the initial stages of the Medjugorje event in a new light and makes it very difficult to accept that this was a genuine supernatural visitation.

Wayne Weible gives us even more of these "personal details," telling us that on the first evening, "Ivanka and Mirjana, having finished evening chores, had slipped off to a secluded spot to listen to rock music while smoking cigarettes pilfered from their fathers."

Sadly then, not only had the visionaries been smoking and listening to music, but they had also stolen the very cigarettes that they smoked. It would be interesting to know exactly what music they had been listening to, given the way that some types of rock music clearly have evil, not to say diabolical, connotations. Weible argues that: "To millions who would later journey to Medjugorje on pilgrimage, this venial act of experimentation would serve as an example that God chooses ordinary people for extraordinary missions."[34]

Or alternatively, and more accurately, one could argue that these further details make it even more unlikely that the visionaries did actually see the Blessed Virgin. And there is a curious parallel here to what took place at Garabandal in Spain, in the 1960s. There, the four young visionaries involved had been stealing apples immediately prior to the first vision they saw, allegedly of an angel, on 18 June 1961.[35] Like Medjugorje, Garabandal has never received any official Church approval.

When Mirjana was interviewed by Fr Zovko on 28 June, she described what had happened at the local hospital at Citluk, where she had been offered a cigarette by one of the doctors and had refused, saying: "I don't smoke." He had responded by saying: "You don't smoke this kind?" — undoubtedly a reference to the possibility in his mind that she may have been smoking drugs — to which she even more emphatically responded: "No cigarettes at all!"[36] Clearly, on this occasion she had not told the truth, which certainly calls her general credibility into question.

In fact, according to Mary Craig, rumors that at least some of the girls were smoking drugs were circulating in the village within the first few days; she reports that Fr Cuvalo said to Fr Zovko on his return: "One of the girls, Mirjana Dragicevic, comes from a grammar school in Sarajevo and they're saying she brought drugs with her, maybe in cigarettes. She's started giving drugs to the children, and now they're claiming to see visions." Following intervention by the increasingly concerned authorities, on the afternoon of Saturday, 27 June, the visionaries had been taken to a nearby town, Citluk, for medical tests. Fr Cuvalo, though, expressed his displeasure that no blood or urine tests for drugs had been taken: "Look, we've heard that the girl from Sarajevo brought in drugs. And another thing, they say that one of the children is an epileptic and a hysteric."

However, on 27 June 1981, Mirjana said to Fr Zovko, in connection with her alleged drug use, that she would like to "see a doctor so that he can establish that I don't use drugs." But since she didn't tell the truth about her smoking, it is difficult to know how to assess this statement.[37]

All of this indicates that the accounts of the first day's visions were unclear. Moreover, as we will see, these accounts are totally unlike those found in cases of authentic apparitions of Mary.

THE "GOSPA" AND THE LIGHT

As regards the actual appearance of the "Gospa," the tapes give us the basic details. The visionaries described her as being aged between nineteen and twenty, with a white veil and gray dress. Her veil covered her black hair, her eyes were blue, and her head was crowned with stars. She was said to float above the ground. Of particular note is the fact that the visionaries saw her gradually emerge from a "light"—the importance of this point will become apparent as we proceed—and that the Vision was prone to appear and disappear.[38] This mention of a "gray" dress being worn by the Vision is something of a problem, since gray isn't a color normally associated with the Blessed Virgin.

Jakov's remarks certainly seem to indicate that he really did see something. This is apparent in his taped interview with Fr Zovko, which took place on the afternoon of 27 June. In response to the priest's question as to the appearance of the "Gospa," when she manifested herself, he said: "It lighted up three times when I saw her. Three times, it lighted up and all of a sudden, the Gospa appeared up there."[39] So once again, the theme of "light" is present, but the indications that the visionaries were able to touch and kiss the Vision, and that she was laughing, seem rather strange, and indicate that the Vision was not the Blessed Virgin. The last point in particular, that the Vision was laughing, is quite disturbing, and completely out of character with the deportment of Our Lady during her approved apparitions—she has been known to smile on occasion, but there is obviously a big difference between this and outright laughter.

MORE QUESTIONABLE EVIDENCE

Mirjana's testimony, available to us in an interview taped by Fr Zovko on the afternoon of 27 June, substantially supports what was said by the other visionaries. Her response to the Vision, however, did not follow the traditional pattern. She describes how she became excited at seeing the "Gospa," saying how the experience was "delightful" for her, and that she wasn't afraid.[40]

Msgr Farges, however, has this to say on the difference between divine and diabolical visions:

> The divine vision produces at first a feeling of fear and astonishment in the soul that is conscious of its unworthiness, but it ends by bringing peacefulness and heavenly joy. The diabolical vision, on the contrary, begins by bringing joy, a sense of safety and sweetness, and ends in anxiety, sadness, fear, and disgust. The first develops the virtues, especially humility, in the soul of the seer, who will seek to hide such great favours in silence and secrecy. The second, on the contrary, develops feelings of vanity, vainglory, and a wish to parade the visions. *The public effects should also be noticed. Divine visions never produce scandal, disorder, or trouble in the Church, while the others inevitably engender these evils.*[41]

In particular, the last sentence of this quotation is one that should be seriously pondered given that it is precisely such effects which have accompanied the growth of the whole Medjugorje phenomenon.

Regarding Mirjana's experiences, it is clear, in the light of the above points from Msgr Farges, that what she was describing does not seem to bear the characteristics of the divine. Ideally, Fr Zovko should have asked her about how she had felt later on, but he neglected to do this, and so all that can be said with certainty is that her initial reaction followed the negative pattern outlined above by Msgr Farges.

Regarding his second point, on the way the vision ends, that is, with feelings of "anxiety, sadness, fear, and disgust," the following testimony from Marija, as taped on 27 June, is very interesting. She told Fr Cuvalo that on returning home on the second evening, she had to repeatedly explain to her parents what had happened. They then prepared supper for her and placed it before her on the table, but she reacted as follows: "I was scared, I wasn't able to eat, my hands were completely white; when I saw her for the first time my hands were cold like ice."[42]

In the interview with three of the visionaries taped by Fr Cuvalo on 27 June 1981, it emerges that the visionaries saw the "Gospa" holding something on the first evening. Ivanka testified that, "We saw something like a baby... then she covered it up..." They were apparently not close enough during this first vision to see any more, and it does not seem as though the Vision said anything on this occasion, although she did nod her head when Vicka asked if she was going to come the next day.[43]

It is hard to imagine why the Vision would have wanted to cover up the Baby Jesus, if it really was the Blessed Virgin, so this is not a good sign.

SECOND DAY — THURSDAY, 25 JUNE 1981

Ivan Dragicevic was absent on this occasion, having decided to spend the evening picking tobacco. According to the interview taped by Fr Cuvalo on the morning of 27 June, Vicka said that other people could see something on the hill, and she tells us that a woman told them to go up since they were being invited. It is apparent, too, that the visionaries were receiving directions from onlookers, and that when they reached Podbrdo, they "spotted her," and that "the light" was all around them.[44]

The mention of other people seeing "something" is very interesting, and certainly goes a long way towards explaining why the visionaries' stories were taken seriously by some villagers right from the beginning—although it seems that by the end of the first week the general mood had grown less supportive. Certainly, Vicka's testimony here seems convincing, since, given that she was speaking only a few days after the event, it would have been very easy for Fr Cuvalo to have checked up on this point regarding other witnesses. It is hard to believe that he would not have already spoken to local people, and thus have instantly contradicted Vicka if he had thought she was not telling the truth. Ivanka also made similar claims of other people seeing "the light" on Podbrdo, including her sister, and some other women.

We also have this testimony from Marinko Ivankovic, who claimed that about three weeks into the visions, one evening at about 11 p.m., he was on Podbrdo with a group of people, including the visionaries. He looked up and could see a very bright light coming towards them. Marinko was the local man, who, as has been noted above, initially acted as the unofficial "protector" of the visionaries.

Generally speaking, then, the information on their contact with the "Gospa" given in the taped interviews by the visionaries certainly does have the ring of truth about it. They speak of coming very close to her, and even touching her, although Vicka makes the quite extraordinary comment that "when you touch her ... the fingers bounce off as if they were of steel." Once again, though, the "Gospa" said nothing on this, the second day.[45]

* * *

IN ASSESSING THESE VISIONS OF THE FIRST COUPLE of days, then, what surely strikes the impartial observer is firstly, the absence of factors that are normally observed in apparitions which have been subsequently accepted by the Church, and secondly the presence of other factors which raise serious doubts as to their authenticity. Whether it is the fact that the Vision's hands were trembling, or that at one point the Vision was laughing—while in general she said nothing—all of this is very strange. None of this accords with the serene, calm presence of the Blessed Virgin, speaking words of reassurance to those who have been favored with her presence that one finds in her recent recognized apparitions. But conversely, it does seem that some people did see strange lights, and so we do not seem to be dealing with hallucinations. It appeared that something was happening up there on Podbrdo, but the exact nature of that "something" still had to be determined. However, the initial signs were hardly encouraging.

4
True and False Visions of Light

THIRD DAY—FRIDAY, 26 JUNE 1981

The information from Fr Cuvalo's first taped interview of 27 June has Marija testifying that she saw the "Gospa" on the third evening, but the impression we get from her words is that the Vision only gradually appeared: "At first, I saw a little cloud below, then her [*the Gospa*], her body and head."[1] Ivanka then testified that they asked her why she had come there, to which the reply was given: "Because there were a lot of faithful, that we must be together."

Ivanka also asked about her recently deceased mother, and was told that she was with the "Gospa," and that she should obey her grandmother. Mirjana asked about her grandfather, and was apparently reassured in a similar manner. They also asked if she was going to come again, to which the reply came: "Tomorrow at the same place," although no reply was made to their request for a sign.

Vicka tells us that she took along blessed salt and water, as a way of testing the Vision to see if it really was the "Gospa," on the assumption that the devil would be driven away by such sacramentals. After invoking the Trinity, she sprinkled the Vision while saying, "If you are the Gospa, remain with us. If you are not, get lost." There is some confusion in the ordering of events on the tape, but according to Jakov's interview with Fr Zovko, on the afternoon of 27 June, the sprinkling of the "Gospa" coincided with the moment when, according to Ivanka, she herself, Marija, and Mirjana, lost consciousness, at least to a degree.[2]

According to Fr Bubalo's interview with Vicka of December 1983, this "holy water" consisted of blessed salt and ordinary water, and had been made up by her mother, who merely mixed the two together.[3] This certainly calls into question whether this really was holy water, although the blessed salt on its own should have provoked some sort of reaction.

Ivan Dragicevic was also present on this occasion, and says in his interview with Fr Cuvalo that he, too, once again saw and heard the "Gospa," substantially confirming what the girls had told the priest in their interview with him. He was quite insistent that he was not lying when pressed by Fr Cuvalo. He said that on this occasion, he didn't see the "Gospa" straight away, rather Vicka saw her first; he didn't hear her say anything. When asked how his family had reacted to this news of visions, he remarked that they had said that they believed that the visions were true because so many other people had seen something.[4]

FOURTH DAY — SATURDAY, 27 JUNE 1981

Fr Cuvalo interviewed Marija on the evening of 28 June in the rectory at St James's Parish Church. He began by saying that the previous evening he had been with the crowd which had gathered and had seen her looking upwards and heard her exclaim: "There she is!" She confirmed this, and then he asked her exactly what she had seen. She responded, "The light." From the conversation which follows, it is unclear whether Marija actually said, "there *she* is," or "there *it* is," but from her later responses it seems that she just saw a light initially, rather than a figure, since further on she says that the first things that she saw were the "light and the stars." Fr Cuvalo then asked her what kind of light she saw, and where it was situated, on the ground or in the sky. Marija said that it was in the sky, and that she saw "the Gospa, her body," and that she wanted to see how close to the ground she would lower herself.[5]

Fr Cuvalo then established exactly where the other visionaries were positioned in relation to Marija, and got her to confirm that she had indeed seen the light first before seeing any figure. It is noteworthy that she did not see a rosary on the hand of the "Gospa," and that in particular the Vision made no attempt to initiate a conversation.[6] According to Marija, the Vision disappeared and reappeared, ascending and descending, while Vicka "loudly asked her questions."[7]

Mirjana's taped interview with Fr Zovko gives us more information about exactly how the "Gospa" disappeared. She told him that: "She goes slowly. She is disappearing slowly. She is climbing up there and then, the sky lights up.... She goes straight and disappears, little by little. There is more and more mist.... Mist appears all around her and she goes towards the sky."[8]

At this stage, on the fourth day, Fr Zovko was clearly concerned that the "Gospa" was not saying anything of particular importance to the visionaries, and he insistently questioned Mirjana about this, and about what they were all expected to do.[9]

FIFTH AND SIXTH DAYS OF THE VISIONS

By the fifth day, June 28, it appears that the initial light phenomena, which were certainly seen by some of those on the hillside, were no longer present.[10] But Mirjana was still speaking about the "light" that the visionaries could see as the "Gospa" appeared to them, since in an interview on that same evening she testified that: "I first spotted the light. Then I poked the others: 'Do you see the light?' They responded that they did. Then I saw how she is gradually descending and it is becoming clearer and clearer as she descends lower and the little stars all around her. It is so beautiful." A little further on Mirjana clarified this point: "As soon as I spot her, it becomes clearer and clearer. When she descends down, then it becomes completely clear that I see her."[11]

Mirjana, at least according to the taped interviews we have, was the first one to mention that the visionaries asked the "Gospa," on the fifth evening, to appear in the church, "so that everybody can see her." It may well be, though, that they were prompted to ask this question by someone else. Certainly, a little later in this interview, Fr Zovko made his concerns plain, asking why there was no message, and why the "Gospa" wasn't appearing in the church. Apparently, Mirjana had absolutely nothing to say to either of these questions.[12]

Apart from Fr Sivric's transcriptions, and those of Daria Klanac, both of whom obtained their copies of the tapes from Grgo Kozina, the latter also tape-recorded the visionaries while they were on Podbrdo on 28 June. Fr Janko Bubalo had a copy of this tape and played it for Vicka during one of his interviews with her:

> Fr Janko: "If you aren't too tired, would you listen to a live tape taken at one of the apparitions? To help you recall how it was."
>
> Vicka: "Why, of course. Where did you get it?"
>
> Fr Janko: "That is not important at this point, but, let's listen. The tape isn't the best. You know how it was to record in the midst of all the thorns, but, nevertheless ... listen ... "
>
> "The wind is blowing ... the thornbushes sway ... there they are, the six of them ... They stand ... They pray the Hail Mary ... " [Commentary by Grgo Kozina — the following sentences record what Vicka said, and include her repetitions of the "Gospa's" words in italics].

"My Lady, what do you wish of us?"
"My Lady, what do you wish of our priests?"
"She said they should be firm of faith."
"Lady, why don't you appear in the church, so that all can see you?"
"Blessed are they who do not see, but believe."
"My Lady, will you come to us again?"
"I will, at the same place."
"Lady, do you prefer that we sing or that we pray?"
"She said both."
"My Lady, what do you wish of the people gathered here?"
"She did not respond."
"The Virgin appears again, and the visionaries in one voice: 'Here she is!'..." [Commentary by Grgo Kozina]
"My Lady, what do you wish of the people here?" [Vicka, three times]
"She said that she gave the response, that the people here who do not see her should believe just as we six who see her do." [Vicka]
"My Lady, will you leave us some sign here on earth so that we can convince the people that we are not... lying, that we are not using you?" [Vicka, but no apparent response]
"The Virgin disappears... Will she come again? Little room for passage... the road is full... cars lined up to Beljina's store... All full..." [Commentary by Grgo Kozina][13]

Thus the contents of this tape give us a verbal snapshot of what actually happened on Podbrdo during that vision, and provide valuable additional information to supplement the transcripts from Fr Sivric and Daria Klanac.[14]

FR ZOVKO IS SKEPTICAL... AND CONCERNED

Fr Zovko's interview with Ivanka, made that same evening, also brought out the point that there was no definite message emerging from the visions, and his unease at this: "Why did she appear to you when there is no message?... That looks like clowning to me. She came in vain and she doesn't have anything to say." In his interview with Ivan, too, it is clear that Fr Zovko was concerned about this lack of a message, pressing him on this point. By this stage, Fr Zovko was getting worried about the size of the crowds gathering on the hillside, and also by the lack of any sign to show that the visionaries were telling the truth.[15]

Fr Sivric describes the atmosphere at the time as being explosive, since with each day the crowds thronging Podbrdo were growing ever larger. This ultimately led to the Communist authorities blocking all access roads.[16]

After raising the possibility with Mirjana that she could be seeing Satan, an idea which she rejected, Fr Zovko went on to ask her what else she saw in her vision apart from the "Gospa." She responded:

> When I look at her, the images come to me from the birth of Jesus when the angel approached her while saying to her: "Hail Mary," that she was going to conceive the Lord and become his mother. All that turns and comes into my head. Then, I saw it, how she was poor ... I see all that in front of my eyes as in a film ... I look at her and all that appears in my head.

This mention of images turning over in her head certainly sounds much more like an hallucination than a genuine divine apparition. And surely, the fact that Fr Zovko could ask Mirjana during this interview if she wasn't afraid that Satan could pretend and say he was the Blessed Virgin Mary is a clear indication of the way his thoughts were running at this stage of the visions.[17]

THE MOVE FROM PODBRDO TO THE CHURCH

By the time Fr Zovko came to interview Ivanka, that same evening, 28 June, it is apparent that he wanted to try and arrange for the visions to take place in the parish church from that point onwards. He queried if they had asked the "Gospa" about that—but she could not remember.[18]

The only comment to be made about this idea is that in none of the authentic apparitions of the Blessed Virgin has there been any suggestion that their location is in any way subject to human considerations or desires.

In fact, one of the most curious aspects of the whole Medjugorje affair is that during this crucial early period, the "Gospa" didn't ask for a chapel to be built at Podbrdo, although in her major approved apparitions, she has usually done that. Certainly, this was the case at Guadalupe, and also at Lourdes, while Rue du Bac was itself a church, so there was no need for this there. She didn't ask for a chapel at La Salette, but that was probably because the apparition site was located at the top of a mountain. Despite this, because of the enthusiasm of the local people, a church was eventually built at the site. At Fatima, too, she requested a chapel, and the same was true of Banneux and Beauraing in Belgium.

But at Medjugorje—which, as we will see, according to Mirjana, is to be the "last apparition on earth," and thus presumably at least as important, if not more important than Fatima—there was no request for a chapel to be built at Podbrdo.

And in fact, Vicka specifically asked the "Gospa" what she wanted to happen, "right here in this place"—that is, at Podbrdo—but she had to confess, during her interview on 30 June that the Vision "didn't know what to say," to which Fr Zovko responded: "What kind of Gospa is it who doesn't know? Then she is smaller than a child."[19]

On Monday, 29 June, the feast of St Peter and St Paul, Fr Zovko wrote out a declaration on the visions which was read out after Mass. In this, as reported by Mary Craig, he stated that he had talked to the youths and recorded the conversations, but, having "listened again to the cassettes, I must insist that there is no public revelation here. If anything is being revealed, it is of a private nature, for the children's benefit alone. Whether this will change I do not know. So far, Our Lady has said nothing that is meant for anyone else."

So, on the sixth day of the visions, Fr Zovko was openly acknowledging that there was no substantial public message being given to the visionaries.

That same evening, according to Mary Craig, the people of Bijakovici were summoned to an emergency meeting of the local Socialist Alliance, and were given explicit instructions by the local Communist leaders that the gatherings on Podbrdo were to be obstructed by all necessary means, and were also informed that, "If you must do these things, do them in church."

The same message was given to Fr Zovko the next day, when both he and Fr Cuvalo were summoned by the Communist authorities to a further meeting at the regional center of Citluk, and informed that it was necessary that the crowds be moved into the church where the situation could be controlled. This helps to explain why Fr Zovko became so insistent on the tapes that the visionaries should move into the church and away from Podbrdo.[20]

THE LIGHT AND THE MIST

Fr René Laurentin comments on the "light" associated with the "Gospa," and its influence on the visionaries, as follows: "The Gospa... attracted them by her sweet tonic and therapeutic light. Just like at Lourdes, this light preceded her. She came in this light, which illuminated like an interior sun."[21]

However, there are important differences between the "light" surrounding the "Gospa," and the light which preceded the Blessed Virgin at Lourdes. One of the early chroniclers of the apparitions there was J. B. Estrade, and he recorded Bernadette's recollections on this point as follows. She told him that there "came out of the interior of the grotto a golden-colored cloud, and soon after a Lady, young and beautiful, exceedingly beautiful... came and placed herself at the entrance of the opening above the rose bush."[22]

In this instance, we get the impression that rather than the Vision coalescing from the light which preceded her, as appears to have happened at Medjugorje, for Bernadette the apparition of the Lady was *distinct* from the golden-colored cloud, and was not a part of it. This is an extremely important point, as is clear from these further examples.

At Rue du Bac, Catherine Labouré initially heard a sound like the rustling of a silk dress, before seeing the Blessed Virgin descend the altar steps of the convent chapel and seat herself on the director's chair. Catherine then threw herself at Mary's feet, put her hands on her lap and looked up into her eyes, later describing that moment as the sweetest of her life.[23] Here, once again, there is no suggestion of the apparition of Mary gradually appearing, rather she was fully formed from the first moment that Catherine was aware of her presence, to the extent that she heard the noise of her dress, and could even physically touch her.

The same is true of the apparition seen by the children at La Salette. Mélanie was the first to see a dazzling globe of light at the top of the mountain, and called to Maximin. Both children shaded their eyes from the glare of the globe as it grew bigger and began to open, revealing a seated woman with her head in her hands. She then stood up and spoke to them: "Come, my children. Do not be afraid. I am here to tell you great news."[24] Thus, although the children saw the Blessed Virgin emerge from the globe of light, she was not part of that light, but quite distinct from it.

The situation was similar at Fatima, where we read that while the three little children were at the Cova da Iria with their flocks, on 13 May 1917, suddenly there was a bright flash of something like lightning. They looked up, thinking a thunderstorm was coming; but to their surprise the sky was clear and there was no wind. They had just agreed to go home in case it was a storm when there was another flash, and they looked up to their right to see, in Lucia's words, "a lady, clothed in white, brighter than the sun, radiating a light more clear and intense than a crystal cup filled with sparkling water, lit by burning sunlight."[25]

Here, too, it is clear that the children saw the apparition immediately and distinctly, and so we can see that there is a definite pattern to the way that Mary has been seen by the seers of her recognized apparitions. Although an aura of light usually accompanied her, it was distinct from her person. There was no question of her gradually appearing out of this light in an indistinct way, as at Medjugorje, but rather the apparition was fully formed and recognizable right from the beginning.

THE ANGEL OF PORTUGAL

Incidentally, this is also the case with the apparition of the Angel of Portugal seen by the Fatima shepherds on three occasions in 1916. In her *Second Memoir*, Lucia tells us that previously, in 1915, along with some other young companions, she had seen a mysterious being which she described as follows: "We saw a figure poised in the air above the trees; it looked like a statue made of snow, rendered almost transparent by the rays of the sun." The indications are, then, that because of its brilliance she couldn't discern its features.

Then, in the spring of the following year, while she was looking after the sheep with Francisco and Jacinta, following their lunch and the rosary, they began to play a game; but they were interrupted by a strong wind which shook the trees. She continues:

> Then we saw coming towards us, above the olive trees, the figure I have already spoken about. Jacinta and Francisco had never seen it before, nor had I ever mentioned it to them. As it drew closer, we were able to distinguish its features. It was a young man, about fourteen or fifteen years old, whiter than snow, transparent as crystal when the sun shines through it, and of great beauty.[26]

Here, too, it isn't the case that the figure gradually emerged out of a light; rather it was as if made of light and the very intensity of this light made it difficult to distinguish its features.

Msgr Farges has some very interesting observations about the process of a false vision gradually appearing. He is speaking particularly about hallucinations, but from what he says, it is clear that in certain cases such phenomena may be diabolically induced. He describes the way certain visions only become "gradually visible, with increasing clearness," beginning as a "vague light."

As an example, he speaks of crystal-gazing as related to fortune-telling: "The visionary who gazes into the mysterious crystal begins by seeing nothing at all, then he sees there vague clouds, then in these clouds personages are traced; finally these become clearly defined, move, and often they speak."[27] While this analysis can be applied to subjects who are hallucinating, it is also a classic description of the activities of fortune tellers, some of whose powers, historically, can undoubtedly be related to diabolical activities.

SOME EXAMPLES OF SUSPECT VISIONS

Certainly, this idea of Mary gradually appearing out of a cloud or mist, or being obscured in some way, or as associated with unusual types of light, is present in false or suspect visions. For example, this is what happened during some of the false visions which followed Lourdes. The first great chronicler of the apparitions, Fr Cros, interviewed some of these false visionaries as adults in 1878, including one Laurent Lacaze, who said that he remembered going "to the Grotto with other children: [and] that I saw a *kind of shadow*, but I have no idea whether *it* had any outline, or whether it was a man or a woman." Another, Jean-Pierre Pomiès, went into more detail:

> I used to go often to the Grotto, attracted by all the stories of what was going on there. During these visits I twice had a vision, the first time I saw a *dazzling light* in the hollow of the rock, and in the middle of it, *a rather thick shadow*. The light was neither red nor white, and stood about three feet high. I could not distinguish any face. This lasted about a quarter of an hour.[28]

The theme of "light" was certainly present during the first alleged apparition to Ida Peerdeman, the visionary from Amsterdam, Holland, associated with the "Lady of All Nations," who claimed that she saw Mary on 25 March 1945. She described her experience as follows: "I suddenly saw a light and said to myself: 'Where is this light coming from? What a curious light?' The wall then disappeared before my eyes. There was instead one sea of light in an empty space, and out of it I suddenly saw a figure moving forward, a female figure."[29]

The idea of the apparition Peerdeman saw appearing out of a very bright light is a recurring theme in her later experiences. An instance of this is the beginning of the twenty-seventh vision about which she says: "A bright, a dazzling light preceded the Lady." The twenty-eighth vision is even more explicit in this respect: "There was a bright light. From the centre of the light the Voice was heard. 'Here I am once more.' And I saw the Lady standing in the light." Similarly, the same pattern is found in the twenty-ninth vision (28 March 1951), which begins: "A brilliant light. From the depths of the light a voice makes itself heard: 'Here I am once more: the Lady of All Peoples.' And suddenly I see her there in front of me."

All of this is suspicious, and this view is definitely confirmed by the following further examples, which provide evidence of a gradual appearance of the Vision, with the first from the thirty-first vision (15 April 1951): "A great light. And the Lady, *slowly, very slowly*, emerges from this light and comes forward," while the thirty-second vision (29 April 1951) has, "The light; and the Lady, *little by little*, emerges from the light."[30]

Another example comes from the experiences of Mary Ann Van Hoof, the visionary associated with Necedah, Wisconsin, in the United States, who described how the Blessed Virgin emerged from a "blue mist" in her backyard on 28 May 1950. On another occasion, she described how she went out into the yard about midday, to the "Sacred Spot," where she "did not see Our Lady, only a sort of haze." She did however feel her "Heavenly Presence."[31]

A more recent example comes from Falmouth, Kentucky, where a woman called Sandy claimed visions and locutions during the 1990s which have not been approved. She described one of these events as follows: "I heard a sound. I've heard this before. It's like a musical, heralding-type sound from off in space. Then I looked up, and I saw a brightness...and she [Mary] started to appear through this brightness."[32]

True and False Visions of Light

* * *

THIS IDEA OF VISIONS OF MARY GRADUALLY APPEARING out of cloud or mist, or an unusual type of light, or in an indistinct form, then, certainly raises suspicions as to authenticity. We do not find this type of detail in the approved Marian apparitions, but it is one of the main characteristics of false or suspect visions. Thus, the fact that this is precisely how the "Gospa" appeared to the visionaries at Medjugorje is not a good sign, and points to the extremely doubtful origin of these visions.

5
The Visions Continue

DID THE VISIONARIES REALLY SEE SOMETHING?

The transcripts of the tapes certainly give a very strong impression that the visionaries did actually see something during those first crucial days on Podbrdo, and that on this point they were telling the truth. For example, in response to the question from Fr Zovko, on how she felt about the fact that people didn't believe her, Ivanka was adamant that she had seen the "Gospa," whether or not other people believed her, and also that a sign would be left.

It is hard to imagine that only five days into the visions she would be making such a vehement statement unless she really was seeing something.

This was certainly also the feeling expressed by Bishop Zanic in his 6 August 1981, press release, wherein he said of events at that stage: *"Everything indicates that the children are not lying.* However, the most difficult question remains: Did the children have subjective, supernatural experiences?"

The first part of the above statement has been extensively quoted by supporters of the visions — who have tended to ignore the qualification which followed — but it has to be borne in mind that this was just his first impression, gained only a matter of weeks into the visions, when the excitement over the whole affair was still very palpable. The bishop was certainly open to the possibility that the visions were authentic at this stage, and only gradually came to view them as false. It seems, too, that Bishop Zanic was being advised by the Holy See "to proceed slowly and not to make a hasty official judgement," and if we also remember the critical political situation, both within the country and with regard to Communism in Eastern Europe generally, we can see that he was under pressure from all sides.[1]

BISHOP ZANIC'S DIFFICULT SITUATION

Fr Robert Faricy, who went to visit Bishop Zanic in the autumn of 1983, acknowledged that the situation had been vastly complicated by the "strong opposition of the Communist government." This opposition meant that Bishop Zanic was being "closely supervised," and, according to Fr Faricy, if the Bishop had approved the visions at that time, the government would certainly have taken "severe repressive action" against him, and also presumably against the local Church. That these were no idle threats is clear from the fact that in the autumn of 1981, following Fr Zovko's imprisonment, two other Franciscans were given jail sentences of eight and five-and-a-half years respectively for publishing articles favorable to Medjugorje.

At this time, Bishop Zanic assured Fr Faricy that he had appointed an "investigating commission" to look into the visions, but the vicar general also pointed out that there was no hurry. Fr Faricy accepted this, saying that "given the opposition of the government and other local governing authorities and the police," he understood the need for great caution.

However, it should be noted that Fr Sivric, perhaps with the benefit of hindsight, while acknowledging the great pressure Bishop Zanic was under, expressed criticism of him for not adopting a more conciliatory tone towards supporters of the alleged visions, and also for not organizing a commission of inquiry much sooner.[2]

Fr Faricy once again visited Msgr Zanic, in May 1986, but this time he was more critical of his role, despite having earlier acknowledged the constraints hampering the bishop. Fr Faricy mentions the document issued in February 1978 by the Congregation for the Doctrine of the Faith, under its then head, Cardinal Seper, which gave guidance to bishops on how they should deal with reports of alleged apparitions. In 1986 this document was still secret, that is, it was not to be publicly disclosed, but since then it has become available. Given that the instructions in the document were general guidelines, it seems fair to say that Bishop Zanic probably did as much as he could in the circumstances to carry them out.[3]

It is certainly the case that on 11 January 1982, Bishop Zanic did institute a commission of inquiry comprising four members, and that he studied the events at Medjugorje carefully, while also keeping the Vatican informed of developments. This led to the submission, on 2 June 1982, of a report to the Congregation for the Doctrine of the Faith. The commission of inquiry was enlarged in 1984 to fifteen persons, made up of clerics from different dioceses and faculties of theology in the country, as well as some doctors. On 30 October 1984, Bishop Zanic published his *Position* document, and in April 1986, he sent his definitive negative conclusions on Medjugorje to

Cardinal Ratzinger, who later became Pope Benedict XVI.[4] By the mid-80s, then, Bishop Zanic's stance on the visions was quite clear: he had definitely decided that they were not genuine.

CRITICISM OF THE LOCAL BISHOPS

Bishop Zanic was later criticized by Fr Ljudevit Rupcic, a Croatian Franciscan, on the grounds that he had not sufficiently involved himself personally in events at Medjugorje. He argued that: "Nothing can substitute for 'on the spot' verification and personal insight. But the bishop has deliberately kept some distance from the facts."[5]

Actually, during the major approved apparitions of the 19th and early-20th centuries, avoiding personal contact with alleged sites of visions has been precisely the policy of those bishops charged with investigating such incidents. They have almost invariably adopted such a policy because it was the only way to avoid being unduly influenced in their decisions.

Fr Laurentin thinks that the relevant part of the 1978 CDF document on apparition discernment, which states that "the competent ecclesiastical Authority has the serious obligation to inform itself without delay and to carry out a diligent investigation," implies that the bishop involved should not stand back, "as many did," but "should quickly discern the facts."[6] This is true as far as it goes, but it certainly does not indicate that any bishop has to personally investigate such reports. It is sufficient, surely, that he oversees the investigation; in fact, the word bishop comes from the Greek word *episkopos*, which literally means "overseer."

Fr Rupcic, in collaboration with Fr Viktor Nuic, also criticized Ratko Peric, who visited Medjugorje in the first half of August 1981, while he was still resident in Rome, over a decade before his appointment as Bishop Zanic's successor. They describe how Bishop Peric interviewed some young girls who had been present at a number of late night visions on the hillside, during which he was told that "an unnamed visionary said in a raised voice: 'Turn off your batteries [torches], Our Lady will not appear if you do not turn off all the lights!'" Something similar happened the next night, as someone cried out: "Put out your cigarettes! If you do not put out your cigarettes, Our Lady will not appear."

Bishop Peric's response to this was to say to his companion, "We could leave now. There is nothing authentic here! Our Lady is not as sensitive as we that she would be bothered by — a cigarette!"

Although his companion was more open to the possibility that something genuine was going on, surely Bishop Peric was right to come to this conclusion.[7] And obviously, this situation, of bystanders smoking at the site of an alleged vision, is quite different from the case of Ivanka and Mirjana smoking before the first vision, when they actually claimed to have seen the Blessed Virgin.

As we will see further on, this idea that the visionaries or their supporters could somehow "stage manage" particular visions is completely unsustainable. If Our Lady really is appearing somewhere, then such an appearance is *not* dependent on the moment-by-moment behavior of particular individuals in the crowd, nor on essentially trivial points such as whether or not people had turned off their torches. We can be quite certain that when she appeared on 13 October 1917 at Fatima, in the presence of an estimated crowd of 70,000 people, a good number of these were openly skeptical and scoffing of the whole idea, and no doubt acting in a far from reverential way — and yet this did not prevent her from appearing.

PRESSURE ON THE VISIONARIES

Returning now to the taped interviews, concerning the one conducted with Ivanka on 30 June 1981, it emerges that Fr Zovko was worried at the way things were turning out regarding the visions. He asked her what they were planning, and what the people should be told. To this Ivanka responded that they would discourage the people from coming to Podbrdo.

It was apparent, too, that Ivanka and the other visionaries were also under pressure, including pressure from their friend Marinko, since further on in the tape she tells us that he had told them to say that there would be no more visions. Up to this point Marinko had been providing questions for the visionaries to put to the Vision. Farther on, Ivanka said that she was going to ask the "Gospa" if they were allowed to tell the people that the visions would soon be ending.

But at times, the contradictory nature of what the visionaries were saying is clear from the further questions that, prompted by Marinko, they asked the "Gospa." The first of these, put by Ivanka, concerned their ability to endure their new situation, to which the "Gospa" apparently replied: "You will be able to, my dear angels!" The second, of far greater importance, concerned "how long she was going to remain with us." Ivanka told Fr Zovko that she had replied: "As long as you want, as long as you wish!"[8]

Once again, it is totally inconsistent with authentic manifestations of the supernatural that Our Lady's appearances should in any way depend on human desires or wishes.

So, on the one hand, the visionaries were apparently looking to find a way out of their predicament as public figures, while on the other hand, the claim was being made that the "Gospa" was prepared to appear to them almost indefinitely. It may well be that by this, the seventh day, 30 June, Ivanka, and perhaps some of the other visionaries, were beginning to lose the ability to discern the reality of what they maintained was happening. This is perhaps not surprising when one considers all the pressures they were facing from their families, the local community, the Franciscans and the Communist authorities.

IVANKA AND THE "UNBELIEVING JUDASES"

Then, as the tape continued, there is the incident concerning the lady doctor present during the vision, who asked if she could touch the unseen "Gospa." Ivanka recounted how the Vision had apparently responded: "There are always unbelieving Judases. Let her come near!" Fr Zovko immediately seized on this remark: "But Judas was not without faith," to which Ivanka responded: "Without faith! But he was a traitor!" Vicka also used the word "Judases" in recounting this incident to Fr Janko Bubalo. Fr Zovko was puzzled by this phrase, as he couldn't understand why the "Gospa" had mentioned Judas since he believed he had faith like the other apostles.[9]

On this evidence, we are obliged to ask why in his reputedly authoritative *Chronological Corpus of the Messages,* Fr Laurentin should have changed the "Gospa's" response to: *"There have always been doubting Thomases. Let her come."*[10] Why should he have been willing, in this instance, to change the wording of a message in order to present it in a better light? Whatever the explanation might be, it seems beyond doubt that the Blessed Virgin could never have used such an expression. And the word "Judases" is also found on the tape-recording made by Grgo Kozina at Podbrdo, which further corroborates Fr Sivric's transcription.[11]

FR ZOVKO TAKES CONTROL

At this point, it seems that Fr Zovko came to a decision to try to put a stop to the visions, or at least bring them under control, endeavoring to get the visionaries to say that the "Gospa" had said that she wouldn't be coming any more, and thus the people should stay at home. He also put the accusation that Marinko not only wrote the questions put to the "Gospa" but also her answers, an accusation which Ivanka strongly denied.[12]

Fr Zovko then asked why the "Gospa" didn't appear in the church, before asking Ivanka to explain what was really happening. Her reply was revealing, in the sense that it seems to indicate that she sincerely believed she was seeing *something:* "I believe in it, I see her. What can I do? If people would see her and I wouldn't, I wouldn't believe it either."

It hardly needs to be pointed out that asking the Blessed Mother to do what we want, in the manner here being suggested by Fr Zovko, is quite unthinkable.[13] Farther on, Fr Zovko asked about the sign the "Gospa" would leave, to which Ivanka replied hesitantly that people were "talking about water," presumably in the hope that some sort of miraculous spring would appear. The most natural interpretation for this is that a connection with Lourdes was being made, and this is a point which will be discussed in more detail further on.

Fr Zovko's suspicions are equally evident in the following statement: "Can't you see that satan [sic] is present there and not the Gospa?" He said this because of the amount of cursing that was still going on amongst the local people, before coming back insistently to his point that the visions would have to stop: "Listen, Ivica [*Ivanka*], are you going to obey me? Go and tell the people!"[14]

After once again discussing Marinko's role in formulating the questions put to the "Gospa," Fr Zovko then began to insist to Ivanka that he should be the one to compose what they would say to the people. But she was not happy with that and said that she wanted to ask the "Gospa." In response, he strongly insisted that the people should come to the church and pray there, and she agreed to this, but only if that was what the "Gospa" wanted. He pressed on, however, despite her objections, and told her she should come into the church and pray the rosary before the congregation.[15]

MIRJANA AND "TWO OR THREE MORE DAYS"

Fr Zovko also taped his interview with Mirjana that same morning, 30 June, and she told him that some other Franciscans had said that the visionaries should now come down to the church to have their visions, rather than go to Podbrdo. She also said: "Today, I want also to ask her how many days she is going to remain with us. Let her tell us exactly how many days she can remain with us, because this evening, it is already the seventh evening!"

Fr Zovko expressed his exasperation at the whole business, and asked her how she would "get out of this?" She responded: "What can I do, if I see her and they don't see her?" He then came back to the important point of how much longer the visions were to last: "What do you think about it? How many more days will you be seeing her?" Mirjana replied: "Something tells me, two or three more days."[16]

Mirjana also told him that when "Vida [*Vicka*] sleeps, she keeps saying in her sleep: 'Leave a sign!'" This information came from her cousin who slept in the same room, and is a further indication of the probability that Vicka really was seeing something.

As in his interview with Ivanka, Fr Zovko was preoccupied with the question of how the affair was going to be resolved: "Oh, what are we going to do with the people? That's my difficulty. Give me a solution!" Mirjana told him that she needed to ask the "Gospa," but he expressed his concern that they were not seeing the *Gospa* — that the behavior of the onlookers, and particularly the cursing, just did not fit in with that. He went on to point to the severe punishments meted out by God to those in the Bible, or the early Church, who propagated "wrong messages," saying that he was "terribly afraid."

It seems that at this point Fr Zovko may have come to the conclusion that the visionaries were hallucinating or seeing something non-supernatural, since he then said: "If those messages are only in your mind, not for the people: that's the problem. Listen, you can have [visions], but she isn't giving any message to the people. You shouldn't have spread it around."[17]

As in the case of Ivanka, he tried to persuade Mirjana to move the visions from Podbrdo to the parish church: "You invite people this evening to come to church, agreed?" She was still noncommittal, though, and so he tried to convince her to ask the "Gospa" to appear in the church, but she remained unsure. She pointed out that people began to go up to Podbrdo from the early afternoon, so how could she convince them to go to the church? But Fr Zovko continued to press his point, agreeing with her that the Communist militia were less likely to harass the visionaries if they were inside the church, rather than on the hillside. Eventually she agreed to do what he asked and go to the hillside at 6 p.m. and tell the people to go to the church; but then she brought up the question of what Marinko might think of all this, and so this particular dialogue ended on an uncertain note.[18]

VICKA AND FR VLASIC

Fr Zovko similarly taped an interview with Vicka on the same morning, 30 June, and she told him that they were going to ask the "Gospa" some questions — including a request for a sign — in addition to asking how many more days she would be appearing to them. He then went on to point out to her that the "Gospa" had not answered any of the questions on the previous evening, saying, "All right, it means that you didn't see her [*the Gospa*], my Vicka."

He also asked her what she was going to tell the people that evening, to which she responded: "I am going to tell the people not to come at all." As with the other visionaries, he then tried to persuade her to invite the people inside the church, but she, too, was uncertain. Fr Zovko then put a straight question: "When are the apparitions going to end?" Vicka responded by saying that she thought they would end after the "Gospa" gave a sign.

There was also an interesting exchange concerning Fr Tomislav Vlasic. Fr Zovko commented on how popular the visionaries had become and Vicka responded by telling him that a Franciscan from Capljina had asked her to go there. It emerged that this Franciscan was Fr Vlasic,[19] and this certainly seems to indicate that he was expressing a keen interest in the visions and the visionaries during the first week, and that he had already visited Medjugorje. According to his own testimony, as recorded in Fr Kraljevic's book, Fr Vlasic met five of the visionaries at the house of Marinko Ivankovic, on "St Peter's Day" — presumably a reference to 29 June, the solemnity of Saints Peter and Paul.[20]

This was quite possibly the occasion on which, as already indicated above, Fr Vlasic told the visionaries that he had already predicted, one month in advance, that the "Gospa" would begin appearing in Yugoslavia — this would certainly explain why he was so anxious to meet them once news of the visions reached him.[21]

The Visions Continue

* * *

THUS, THE EVIDENCE FROM THE TAPES CONTINUES TO present a strange paradox: it seems evident that the visionaries really were seeing something, but at the same time it is pushing the boundaries of credibility too far to believe that what they were seeing really was the Blessed Virgin.

6
Three More Days of Visions

FR ZOVKO INTERVIEWS FIVE OF THE VISIONARIES

One of the most important interviews took place at about 6:30 p.m. on the evening of 30 June, after their vision that day. This involved Fr Zovko and five of the six visionaries, as well as two other young women, Mica Ivankovic and Ljubica Vasilj-Gluvic, who were called into the interview about half way through. Ivan Dragicevic was not present during the evening vision, nor had he been with the others in the afternoon.

Mica was a social worker, and at the time a practicing Catholic, while Ljubica worked for the Bosnia-Herzegovina Executive Council in Sarajevo and was a member of the Communist party. There is nothing necessarily suspicious about that, though, since many people felt it necessary to be party members in order to safeguard their jobs. As Fr Sivric points out, "Later, all sorts of disparaging stories were circulated in many places about these two fine people," but he argues these were without foundation.

The young women had driven them, via a roundabout route stopping at various points, to a place called Cerno, near Medjugorje, where their visions took place that day. The idea has grown up that the visionaries were in some way "abducted" by the women, as part of a Communist plot to discredit them. But the visionaries knew them and agreed to go; in fact, Mica was a near neighbor of some of them.

As Fr Sivric points out, Mica said that the authorities in Citluk "were not considering removing the visionaries from Medjugorje that day, nor that they, Mica and Ljubica, had been sent by any official to carry out that task." If anything, the taped evidence shows that Mica came in for some criticism when she defended the children at a meeting connected with her work.

MICA AND THE VISIONARIES

However, it does seem possible that Mica decided to "unofficially" persuade the visionaries to go somewhere different from Podbrdo that day, by telling them that otherwise they would have to undergo some sort of "inspection." This is a reference to the police — the

Milicija — interviewing them. This is what Mirjana said about this at the interview, before the two young women were called in by Fr Zovko: "We were just eating and Mica said that some sort of inspection would take place, so it would be better if we would move ... to see if ... the Gospa was going to appear in another place." A little further on, Vicka corroborates what Mirjana said.

And later in the interview, Mica stated that, while in Vicka's house, she told Vicka and Mirjana that she had heard from Zlata, Vicka's mother, that they, the visionaries, had decided not to go to Podbrdo that day. At this, Mica asked them what they were going to do then, to which Mirjana responded: "We are going to lock ourselves up in my room!" Mica pointed out the impracticality of this, given the mood of the people coming to Medjugorje, who would expect to see them that evening on Podbrdo. According to Fr Sivric, she then continued, saying: "Then they [the visionaries] told me: 'It just occurred to us. Do you think it would be possible for us to go someplace else?' I said: 'There's no problem. Let's go!' Then they notified Marija and Jakov.'" However, according to Daria Klanac, it was Mica's idea, which the visionaries then accepted.[1]

Either way, the visionaries went of their own free will, so there was no question of force being used, or their being "abducted."

And regarding the "inspection" and what that might involve, Mirjana was certainly worried that they would be taken away by the authorities: "We thought they would take us to the mental asylum or to the hospital, either today or tomorrow. The people certainly think so." Mica then confirmed to Fr Zovko that during a meeting she attended as part of her work, she was told that the visionaries would be taken to the hospital. She also said that later on she had been told to talk to both the visionaries and their parents, but she denied that anyone had suggested that she take the visionaries to another place.[2]

According to Mica's account, when they were about to set off for the afternoon, there were quite a lot of people about, and also a police car, which was apparently outside one of the visionaries' houses, but they managed to depart without any serious problems. She did confess that she was worried that people might think she had taken away the visionaries, but actually it seems that her motives were a mixture of trying to help them avoid the inspection and also wanting to "see the reality of how the children would behave at the other place." She had been at Podbrdo on previous evenings but had been too far away from the visionaries to see what was going on.³ So it would seem that her motives were a combination of protectiveness and curiosity.

In any event, the result was that the visionaries didn't go to Podbrdo that evening, but from other indications on the transcript, it is clear that a crowd did gather on the hillside in their absence. Vicka said she was worried that the crowd would be angry that they hadn't appeared on Podbrdo, while Mirjana believed that "the people think that they took us somewhere, that the militia [*Milicija*] took us somewhere. We should calm down the people. The people might become violent."⁴

Vicka also speaks of a "Commission," and three automobiles, the mayor and the Milicija, but it doesn't seem as though the visionaries actually spoke to any of the police officials. Fr Sivric understood the Commission to be a group of county officials from Citluk. Then Vicka said to Fr Zovko: "They [the Commission] told us if we intend to go to church: 'You shouldn't lead the people by the nose to make them follow you,' but rather that we should be alone." Fr Zovko asked when they had said that, but Vicka didn't respond to this question directly, but just carried on, saying: "The Commission told us and everybody says the same thing: 'The people are leaving their work, and nobody is working anymore, they simply come to the hillside.'"⁵

Precisely when they were told this is uncertain, and likewise exactly how the Commission, the "inspection" and the Milicija all fit into this general picture is unclear from the transcript. But we need to bear in mind that the situation at this time was very fluid, indeed somewhat chaotic, as the authorities struggled to cope with what was happening. Pressure was building up on everyone involved: the visionaries, Fr Zovko and his assistant priests, and the Communist authorities, who were increasingly anxious over the crowds that were thronging Podbrdo. And certainly one of the themes of this transcript is Fr Zovko's concern and insistence that the visionaries should move into the church from that point on for their visions of the "Gospa," and thus bring the people down from the hillside.

THREE MORE DAYS OF VISIONS

Fr Zovko also asked Mirjana if she had said anything to the "Gospa." She replied that she had asked her "how many [more] days she is going to stay with us," the response being, "Three [more] days." Mirjana continued, "which means until Friday."

Fr Zovko made no particular comment about this response from the "Gospa," and Mirjana continued: "Then we asked her if she would be angry if we don't go to the hillside [Podbrdo] anymore but rather into the church. She was rather indecisive when we asked her this question. It looked as if she didn't like it. But finally, she said she wouldn't be angry."[6]

At this point, it must be emphasized that it is ridiculous to imagine that the Blessed Virgin could possibly have acted in such a hesitant and uncertain manner.

One of the other visionaries then said that the Vision would appear at the same time as usual, before Mirjana related that the "Gospa" had asked about Ivan, saying: "Where is the other boy?" This is rather strange, since when asked by Fr Bubalo if the "Gospa" knew their names, Vicka responded: "Ah! Does she know our names! Why she called us by our names the very first day."

This event certainly does not fit in with the principle that Mary is the universal spiritual mother, who has a personal care and concern for each and every human being, which includes knowing their names and using them, rather than impersonal terms such as "the other boy." Fr Zovko returned to this point later on, pointing out that if they were really seeing the *Gospa* she ought to have known Ivan's location and what his name was.[7]

Meanwhile, he realized that the visions would now be taking place in the church, in the evening, and that the "Gospa" had agreed to this. But as Mirjana once more pointed out, this would only be until Friday, "which means Wednesday, Thursday, Friday."

A heated debate then followed in which they discussed the best way of informing the people of these new developments, and it is clear that although some of the visionaries were still unhappy about the proposed move from the hillside to the church, they were prepared to accept this.[8]

Fr Zovko also questioned Mica Ivankovic and Ljubica Vasilj-Gluvic about how things had developed that afternoon; both testified that they had watched the visionaries while they were having their visions, hearing the questions put to the "Gospa," and noting their responses. To the question of how many more times the "Gospa" would be appearing, Mica Ivankovic said that she heard them say together: "Three times," repeating the response of the Vision.

This point was taken up further on in the tape when Mica, and

Three More Days of Visions

one of the visionaries, again related that "three more times" were specifically mentioned by the "Gospa," and that everything would end on Friday.[9]

Thus, we have independent confirmation that at this stage, 30 June 1981, there were only supposed to be a further three visions.

Indeed, Fr Bubalo brought this up in his interviews with Vicka, when, after saying that he had been playing back the cassettes made during the first week, he challenged her on this point. Her response was rather uncertain: "I really don't know that. I don't recall." She then went on to explain things as follows: "Someone said that just so that they would leave us in peace. Fra Jozo really wore us out. Here, there. Ask this, then that. And, then again. Your mind stands still!"[10]

It is clear from the further explanations she gave on this point that she was seeking to put this clear discrepancy in a positive light. But the taped evidence does not support such an explanation, and Vicka's account here is very unsatisfactory. And what about her explanation as to how the idea had arisen that there would be only three more visions — "Someone said that just so that they would leave us in peace." In other words, "someone" allegedly lied in order to avoid being questioned. What does that tell us about the slipshod attitude of the visionaries to the truth? The reality, though, is that "someone" didn't just say that; rather it was quite clearly said by Mirjana in the presence of Vicka. And as we will see, Vicka is quoted by Randall Sullivan, a pro-Medjugorje writer, as saying, following the vision on the last of the "three more days," 3 July: "This evening the Madonna gave messages for us, and not for the world... *She appeared for the last time this evening.*"

It is significant, too, that while Mica was relating the afternoon's other events, which included a confrontation with the police, Jakov, the youngest of the visionaries, burst into the conversation and claimed that one of them had pulled out a gun and threatened to kill them. But he was quickly rebuked for making this up.[11] This type of thing is perhaps attributable to Jakov watching violent TV shows or films, and is another indication that his "cultural formation," and presumably that of the other visionaries, was quite different from that of the authentic Marian seers of the past.

To sum up, by the end of the first week, the clear expectation amongst the visionaries was that the visions were only supposed to go on for another three days.

FR RUPCIC'S CRITICISM OF FR SIVRIC

Frs Ljudevit Rupcic and Viktor Nuic, however, take issue with Fr Sivric's approach. They claim that because, on the morning of 30 June 1981, Fr Zovko questioned the three visionaries Ivanka, Mirjana and Vicka separately, and asked them different questions about how much longer the visions would go on for, and received different answers, then it is inadmissible to only choose Mirjana's reply. This, as the reader will recall, was: "Something tells me, two or three more days." Ivanka had reported the "Gospa" as saying: "As long as you want, as long as you wish!" while Vicka thought that a sign would be left before the visions ended.

However, it has to be borne in mind that Fr Zovko was not conducting a methodical series of interviews with the visionaries, in which exactly the same set of questions was put to each of them. Moreover, they would naturally have focused on what concerned them and what they could remember, as well as the general tenor of the questions. Their testimony on other points is not in exact agreement, so why should we expect that to be the case in this instance?[12]

Frs Rupcic and Nuic then go on to discuss the recording of the meeting between Fr Zovko and five of the visionaries on the evening of 30 June, immediately after their experience at Cerno, which has just been dealt with above. On that occasion, as we have seen, Mirjana said that she had asked the "Gospa" "how many days she is going to remain with us. Exactly how many days she will remain with us. She said: 'Three days'... that means until Friday."

Likewise, we have also seen how Mica Ivankovic, one of the young women who had driven the visionaries to Cerno, stated that in response to the question of how many more times was the "Gospa" going to appear to them, she heard them say together: "Three times."

THREE DAYS OR THREE TIMES?

Regarding these statements, though, Frs Rupcic and Nuic advance the rather strained argument that because Mirjana used the word "days," and Mica the different word "times," to describe the remaining visits of the "Gospa," then somehow this invalidates the fact that all the evidence does indeed indicate that there were only supposed to be a further three visitations. They accuse Fr Sivric of "manipulation," but surely no sensible person will read any great significance into the fact that these different words were used—and all Fr Sivric was actually doing was accurately transcribing the words on the tapes. Given that the visions had been taking place daily, then whether it is said they were going to go on for another three days or another three times, surely it is unreasonable hairsplitting—and a sign of some desperation—to argue that there is any real problem here.[13]

However, despite the above argumentation, Frs Rupcic and Nuic acknowledge that there is a discrepancy between Ivanka stating that the "Gospa" would remain with the visionaries as long as they wished and Mirjana stating that she would only be remaining with them for three days.[14] They attempt to explain this by attributing this difference to the pressure which the visionaries were under from the Communist authorities, but this does seem to be a case of grasping at straws. Rather it seems that the Vision uttered these contradictory statements, which once again indicates that we are not dealing with a genuinely supernatural event—the real Blessed Virgin would not speak in such a confusing way.

SOME UNTENABLE ARGUMENTS

Frs Rupcic and Nuic then go on to advance an even more precarious argument, namely, that the "three days" should not be understood chronologically but *theologically*. They put forward the idea that the "third day" in biblical use signifies a moment of salvation, as in Christ's resurrection from the dead taking place on the third day, saying: "If the expression 'three days' is taken this way in the Biblical revelation, then why cannot it be taken in the same way in Mirjana's prophetical statement?" Daria Klanac also takes a similar line, arguing that the three days can be seen in symbolic terms.[15]

All three accept, then, that Mirjana really did say that the visions would only be taking place for another three days, but it should be clear that there is nothing "prophetical" or "theological" about what Mirjana said; rather she precisely delineated the end of the three days by saying "until Friday."

Fr Laurentin, in commenting in a footnote in his own volume *Medjugorje Testament*, on Bishop Peric's book *Prijestolje Mudrosti (The Seat of Wisdom)*, attempts to argue that the three days can be understood in a different way:

> I've noted here the contradictions or lies with which the visionaries were trapped. Vicka would have said on June 30, 1981 that the apparitions would end in 3 days. During these

troubled times, under the threat of the police, she meant the end of apparitions on the hill, an error of perspective, as can occur, even in the Bible.[16]

Daria Klanac also apparently puts forward the view that the three days could be understood in this way.[17]

But in both cases, a plain reading of the text does not allow such an interpretation. The question asked was not, "how many more days was the 'Gospa' going to stay with them on the hillside before moving to the church," but, quite simply, "how many more days was she going to stay with them," to which the reply was "until Friday."

Sadly, these types of arguments only illustrate the lengths to which some Medjugorje proponents will go to in an attempt to justify the unjustifiable. They also indicate that there is an ambiguity in Klanac's thinking on this question of three days. She seems to be saying that they may be symbolic—but also that they are real as regards moving from Podbrdo to the church. It is difficult to see how both of these interpretations can be valid, and it is strange that Daria Klanac cannot see this, since her own transcription of the interview on 30 June makes this clear:

> Fr Zovko: "Well! This interests me. Three more times. So, when do these visions finish?"
> Mica: "They said: 'Immediately.' Later, they said: 'It finishes on Friday.'"
> Fr Zovko: "But where is it going to finish on Friday?"
> Jakov: "In the church."
> Mirjana: "If Gospa doesn't tell us, perhaps for the last day, she wishes that it may be on the hill!"[18]

PERSONAL CRITICISM OF FR SIVRIC

It is also necessary to assess Fr Rupcic's personal criticisms of Fr Sivric. Fr Rupcic claimed that because some of Fr Sivric's relatives in Medjugorje were opposed to the visions, then this affected his own objectivity;[19] but this is a rather insecure argument. As we have seen, Fr Sivric was away from Medjugorje from the early 1940s, and had in fact emigrated to the United States, where he taught for many years. Thus his links to his relatives were remote, to say the least, and far from his criticisms of Medjugorje being to his advantage, they were a cause of hostility from some of his fellow Franciscans—including Fr Rupcic. And in describing his sources in the village, he said that:

> A good number of Medjugorje's citizens have shown spontaneity and openness to my work by communicating to me everything which might be pertinent to the visions. From the beginning, some among them have been against the authenticity of the apparitions, seeing them as a "shady" affair, and unworthy of the Madonna. From others came testimony of contradictions and even of actual lies. These informants are even afraid to speak openly for fear of literally being banished from the village.

That was the atmosphere in which he had to operate, and indeed he tells us that in his book he felt obliged to conceal the identities of those who assisted him, surely a sign of the hostility he faced from many in Medjugorje.[20]

Fr Sivric openly acknowledged that Mica Ivankovic was his second cousin, but she was also related to Ivanka, who said of her, "She is our cousin."[21] In a small place like Medjugorje a lot of people are related to a lot of other people, and so we shouldn't read anything sinister into the fact that Fr Sivric had relatives locally. The argument could be turned on its head to say that the Medjugorje visionaries also had relatives in the area, and so this was to their advantage.

Denis Nolan claims that Fr Sivric's nephew was a Communist party official who was sent to Medjugorje to "put an end to the whole matter."[22] But he doesn't give the name of this individual, or any evidence to back up this allegation, and in any case what matters is what is on the tapes; and given that we can have confidence that they were accurately transcribed by Fr Sivric, then arguments about his relatives are ultimately beside the point.

On the other hand, if we examine Fr Rupcic's own attitude to Medjugorje, it is clear that he was not a disinterested and neutral observer. His writings reveal a fanaticism towards Medjugorje which will not accept even the possibility that the visions are not genuine. He made it his business to champion Medjugorje at a very early stage and was, according to Fr Michael O'Carroll, the first to "write substantially on Medjugorje." Indeed, Fr O'Carroll was content to include criticism of Bishop Zanic, from the pen of Fr Rupcic, comprising over thirty pages, in his own book on Medjugorje.[23]

Fr Rupcic was also the author of an intemperate book entitled *The Truth about Medjugorje*, which again was highly critical of Bishop Zanic. He followed this up with further books attacking those who questioned Medjugorje, including Fr Sivric. We also need to bear in mind that Fr Rupcic was a Franciscan and thus associated with the Herzegovina Franciscans who have been in dispute with both the local bishops and Rome for many years.

Who then is more likely to be biased? Fr Sivric, who opposed Medjugorje at some personal cost, or Fr Rupcic, who demonstrated an obsessive attachment to the visions and the visionaries, to the extent that he was prepared to defend Medjugorje with far-fetched arguments, such as those discussed above?

FR RUPCIC AND THE MEDJUGORJE TAPES

Fr Rupcic claims that the tapes are incomplete and unreliable, but as is clear from the appendices to his book, Fr Sivric was very careful to indicate when sections of the tape were incomprehensible, or where there was an interruption in recording.

These are the claims made by Fr Rupcic:

> It is important to note here that not all, including the most relevant facts and situations associated with the events at Medjugorje are recorded on tape. Beyond that, the author selects the tape recordings in harmony with the goal he has set for himself. Aside from that, the tape recordings used by Sivric are not the original tapes. The original tapes were entirely clear and complete. The police confiscated those tapes at the time they arrested the pastor, Fr. Jozo Zovko. The Bishop sought to retrieve the tapes so as to make use of them for his Investigative Commission, but was unable to get them. The tapes made use of by Sivric are copies of copies made by individuals for their private use. When the tapes are being copied, often individual parts of the conversations were deleted; thus, the spliced conversations are spread over a period of days and dates. Evidence of this is seen in the transcription of the tapes used by the author in his book. Sivric often notes that the tape has been cut, and notes that the tape recordings are undecipherable in at least 148 instances.[24]

But if we analyze these claims, it is clear that there is no real substance to them. Firstly, if the original tapes were confiscated by the police, how could Fr Rupcic have actually known what was on them in order to compare them with the copies? How does he know that what is on the copies does not give us the substantial truth about what was on the original tapes? Obviously, he couldn't know any of this and so his criticisms of Fr Sivric here are of little weight. There may well be other important information on the "missing" portions — if there are any significant missing portions — but that is not really relevant, since what *is* on the tapes gives us quite enough information to understand what went on during the interviews. And if there is any missing material that might eventually come to light, then the chances are that it would be even more damaging to the position of the visionaries than what the extant tapes have already revealed.

As we have seen, Fr Rupcic also stated that when the tapes were being copied "often individual parts of the conversations were deleted; thus, the spliced conversations are spread over a period of days and dates." Even if this was the case — and again, since the original tapes were not available, how could he have any certain knowledge of this — even then, we still have within the transcripts sections of text which are long enough to be confident that we are getting a good idea of not only what was said, but also the context in which it was said. We are not dealing with very short snatches of conversation which could possibly be misunderstood in that way, but mostly lengthy dialogues without any significant disruptions.

And as we will see shortly, Fr Rupcic's fellow Franciscan, Fr Bubalo, said this when challenging Vicka about some of her recollections: "Lately I replayed some of the cassettes including that conversation with Fra Jozo." He pointedly *didn't* say: "Lately I replayed some of the cassettes and they are so disjointed and unclear as to be useless," or anything of the sort. It's obvious from the context that he considered the quality of the tapes quite satisfactory. So if the tapes were good enough for Fr Bubalo, then they ought to have been good enough for Fr Rupcic, and any other critics.

And in addition to this, an audio file of one of the cassettes is available on the internet, that is, the interview between Fr Zovko and Jakov on the morning of 27 June 1981.[25] The quality of this file is surprisingly good, and on the assumption that the other tapes are of similar quality, we can have even more confidence that the transcripts of the tapes by Fr Sivric and Daria Klanac are reliable.

Overall, what really matters is this: does the material we have give us enough information about the first days of the visions to come to a balanced judgment about what happened? And the answer to that is positive, because a perusal of the tape transcripts in Fr Sivric's book—which comprise nearly half the text at 176 pages—shows that there is more than enough material available to justify that position.

Fr Rupcic also says, "Such tapes, 'documents' for the author, are seventh-hand witness, at best, which, by established principles, cannot be recognized as having the strength of proof."[26] To describe the tape transcripts as "seventh-hand witness" is just bizarre—surely anyone can see that they are the primary evidence we have for what took place during the first days at Medjugorje.

Fr Rupcic also quotes Fr Zovko as saying, after having read Fr Sivric's transcripts: "This is not my composition."[27] So he is saying that Fr Sivric made up the transcripts. But what about Daria Klanac—did she also make up her version of the tapes? And the person effectively accusing them of this, Fr Zovko, has been episcopally disciplined three times, and in 1985 was forbidden by Bishop Zanic to celebrate Mass or to preach at Medjugorje. Who therefore is more likely to be telling the truth?

THE VISIONARIES AS RELIABLE WITNESSES?

Fr Rupcic makes a further criticism of Fr Sivric, regarding those parts of the tapes which are unclear: "Since all the participants in these taped conversations are still living, it boggles the mind that the author does not attempt to fill in or clarify those missing parts. The participants to the conversations were all available to him at the time of his sojourn in Medjugorje."[28]

Surely, though, it would be asking too much to expect the visionaries to remember later exactly what they had said while they were being recorded. What guarantee do we have that their recollections after such a period of time would do anything to clarify what was on the tapes? And that is assuming that those recollections are reliable, whereas there is evidence that some of their later accounts contradict what is on the tapes, as in the case of the discrepancy between the reason given by the visionaries for going with the two social workers on 30 June, and the later accounts of this incident that were circulated.

This is what Vicka said to Fr Bubalo about this outing: "Two girls came for us about two in the afternoon. And, they offered to take us about a bit in their car. Not suspecting anything, we got ready and left." However, on the 30 June tape, when asked by Fr Zovko if someone else had told them to try "another hill," Vicka explicitly says, "we chose the place and the rest and we didn't need anyone to tell us what to do," while Jakov adds: "We marked the place."

Fr Bubalo challenged Vicka about this discrepancy saying: "It's uncomfortable for me, but I must. Lately I replayed some of the cassettes including that conversation with Fra Jozo. And, I came across one of your assertions that does not agree with what you just told me ... you told me here, and you always maintained it, that the girls tricked you into that outing."[29]

Vicka attempted to explain all this away, but the fact is that her later account does not tally with what is on the tapes.

This is what Denis Nolan says about this incident: "As the hour of the apparition drew near, the social workers refused to take the visionaries back to the village. The visionaries forced them to stop the running car by threatening to jump out and then witnessed the apparition on the roadside."[30]

It is unclear where this story actually came from, but perhaps it arose out of a desire to emulate the way the children of Fatima really were kidnapped by the Mayor of Ourem on 13 August 1917. Whatever its origins, it clearly bears about as much relationship to reality as Jakov's claim that one of the policemen had pulled out a gun and threatened to kill them. In fact, this story clearly puts Vicka in the same category as Jakov — a young fantasist who cannot be relied on.

Another example of this type of thing concerns the "anniversary" of the visions. This is commemorated on the 25th of each month, although the first vision actually took place on 24 June 1981. But the 25th has become important for Medjugorje supporters, as the day when the monthly message from Marija Pavlovic is communicated to the world. Fr Bubalo also asked Vicka about this point and was told that, in 1982, "the Virgin herself decided it." He pursued the matter, asking why she had said this, and was told that the "Gospa" had said to the visionaries: "Why, my angels, isn't it clear to you that we really met that day for the first time."

But the only problem with this response is that it contradicts the facts as revealed on one of the other tapes transcribed by Fr Sivric, since all the visionaries were *not* present on the second day — Ivan Dragicevic was missing. This is clear from his interview with Fr Cuvalo on the afternoon of 27 June 1981. In this, after describing the events of the first day, Ivan says: "The first evening I was with them, the second I wasn't." And further on, he was asked: "Did you go [to the hill] the next day," to which he responded: "No, I didn't." And finally, towards the end of the interview when Fr Cuvalo again asked him what happened on the second day, and if he had gone to Podbrdo, Ivan responded: "The second evening I didn't go. I worked in the field, I was picking tobacco leaves."[31]

So the explanation given for the change of day by the Vision, that they "really met that day for the first time," isn't tenable, and once again Vicka's recollection of events is faulty.

Fr Rupcic also says: "The true sources still today are the living people, the partakers of those events: in the first place, the Seers, their families, and the Pastors and Assistants. The author, nonetheless, relies on a few taped conversations involving some of the direct witnesses."[32]

This betrays a fundamental misunderstanding of what constitutes reliable evidence as opposed to the unreliable variety. It must be apparent that tape-recordings of the events done within a matter of days, even allowing for certain sections which are unclear, are a far superior source of evidence than recollections gathered months or even years later.

THE SILENT "GOSPA"

The conversation of the "Gospa" — or rather the lack of it in the early days — is an extremely important point to note. There was apparently no message for mankind during these days, a point which disturbed Fr Zovko. In speaking to Mirjana on the evening of 28 June, he got a negative response to the question: "And she does not say anything?" He then continued: "She never says anything first if you do not ask her a question." To this Mirjana replied: "Nothing. First of all, we ask her something." This prompted Fr Zovko to say: "So there is no message. Good, Mirjana!"[33]

Similarly, in his interview with Ivanka on 30 June, Fr Zovko was still worried about the lack of any message from the "Gospa," and particularly about the lack of any specific prayer for the visionaries. He questioned Ivanka on this point, but her reply was negative. He responded by saying that in previous apparitions, such as Fatima, there had been a message to pray the rosary. Ivanka's retort was extremely revealing: "Nothing like that! She answers all that we ask her but nothing else." One can sense the frustration in Fr Zovko's answer: "But how is it that she doesn't say anything new to you, but always answers the same thing?" Ivanka responded weakly: "What do I know?"[34]

This failure to take the initiative on the part of the "Gospa" is, of course, completely out of line with authentic Marian apparitions, where the Blessed Virgin has always known exactly what she was doing. Later on, in the messages produced over the last quarter century and more, the "Gospa" would find her voice, and produce a veritable torrent of words — but much of this, as will be seen, is completely out of character with what we know of the utterances of the Blessed Virgin during her approved apparitions.

During his long interview of 30 June, Fr Zovko also remarked on the "Gospa's" request that the visionaries "reconcile the people," questioning them as to whether this referred to everyone or just to local parishioners. They responded that it referred to the neighbors. On this point, Fr Sivric observed that there was a definite need for reconciliation in the locality.[35]

FR ZOVKO COMMITS HIMSELF TO THE VISIONS

Fr Zovko's general impressions of the first days of the visions, and of the visionaries, as reported by Mary Craig, are worth noting. He complained that their answers were "terribly vague," and that he found them "ignorant and shallow," to the extent that he was "terribly afraid" that the whole thing was "just a joke with them." His concluding thoughts were particularly disturbing:

> How can these children possibly have seen the Blessed Virgin? It was unthinkable that anyone could have seen her and not be radically changed by the experience. There was tension among them too. They argued a lot and disagreed among themselves about what had happened. Vicka and Mirjana seemed to be jostling for position as leader.[36]

But as time went on, it became clear that the parish priest had radically changed his position. Fr Svetozar Kraljevic spoke to Fr Zovko on 11 August 1983, and during this interview the latter related "the first sign from God which led him to believe in the apparitions." He was apparently speaking of the events which took place on 1 July 1981, when the authorities were looking for the visionaries while he was in the church. He claimed that despite the fact that the building was empty he heard a "voice" saying: "Come out and protect the children."[37]

Thus, two years after the visions began, Fr Zovko was claiming his own locution, although he had been highly critical of the visionaries up to 30 June 1981. Was this the reason why he changed his mind about the visions?

According to E. Michael Jones, Thursday, 2 July 1981, the day when the visionaries alleged that the Virgin had appeared to them in the afternoon, in the parish church, with Fr Zovko and a large crowd present, was the "the crucial turning point in the history of the so-called apparitions." The priest had preached a revivalist sermon which whipped up the emotions of those present to fever pitch. It was really from this point on, when the visions were henceforth said to take place in the church, that the community as a whole took them on board and accepted them as real in their own minds, and in the sight of the world.[38]

From this point, Fr Zovko became one of the prime movers behind the visions, and it was his premature acceptance of them as genuine, at least as far as informing his parishioners was concerned, which was a crucial catalyst in the formation of the whole Medjugorje edifice. We will perhaps never know the ultimate reason why, instead of adopting an attitude of "wait and see," he suddenly changed his mind about the visions and rushed to judgment. It was certainly a strange about-turn—perhaps his account of hearing something in the church was genuine? But whatever the reason it was a decision which would have far-reaching consequences.

THE LAST VISION

Regrettably, there is no tape of the events which took place on Friday, 3 July, the day on which the visionaries had said they would experience their final encounter with the "Gospa." But Fr Sivric was able to interview one of the witnesses present at the rectory at St James's church, Fr Tadija Pavlovic, who, as a neighboring parish priest, was in Medjugorje helping with confessions. He heard the visionaries state quite clearly that this was indeed the last vision. Additional witnesses at this meeting included local priests Frs Umberto Loncar and Stojan Zrno, as well as Mijo Gabric, a reporter for the paper *Glas Koncila*, and Ivo Magzan. On the next day, Saturday, 4 July, however, Fr Pavlovic was surprised to hear from his own parishioners that the "Gospa" had apparently once again appeared, and the same thing was reported to him the following day, Sunday, 5 July.

Three More Days of Visions

Fr Sivric notes that after this he refused to return to Medjugorje to say Mass or to hear confessions. Fr Pavlovic was also somewhat scandalized when, on returning to Medjugorje on 25 July, to visit his mother, he was present at the feast day Mass at St James's church, and was struck by the lack of devotion displayed towards the Eucharist by the visionaries, and the way they talked, and walked around the church.[39]

According to Frs Rupcic and Nuic, Fr Zovko "categorically denies that after the apparition the visionaries stated that Our Lady told them that this was the final apparition." They go on to say that Fr Umberto Loncar recorded in his diary that the visionaries "did not say anything about the vision but immediately left the church." However, we then learn that Jakov and Vicka spoke to those gathered outside, via loudspeakers, and that although Jakov did not say anything about a last vision, amongst other things Vicka stated: "Tonight she appeared for the last time..."

The rather incredible response of Frs Rupcic and Nuic to this is to say, "Vicka said that and not Our Lady. At least Vicka does not say that Our Lady told them this!"[40]

The fact is that Fr Rupcic, in a separate earlier account, contradicted himself when, in one of his polemics against Bishop Zanic, he said: "Nor was he right in saying that there were some priests present during the *last apparition* on 3 July because Fr Jozo was actually the only one present at that apparition."[41]

Note here that Fr Rupcic actually gives the game away by inadvertently admitting that this was the "last apparition." Given this, and the discrepancy on the number of priests present, there are certainly legitimate question marks about the accuracy of Fr Rupcic's recollections.

Even though the visions did not end on 3 July, it is clear that the expectation that they would not go on indefinitely was present during the early years. As an example of this, we have the testimony of Fr John Bertolucci, who was interviewed by Fr Vlasic. Although no date is given, this interview must have taken place sometime between 1981 and 1983. After expressing some reservations about exactly what was taking place in spiritual terms while the visionaries were experiencing their visions, he went on to say: "The children themselves... say the apparitions will end."

Fr Laurentin made the same point when writing in January 1984. He commented on the fact that one of the visionaries — Mirjana — was no longer seeing any visions, and that this was "a harbinger of their impending end."[42]

MEDJUGORJE AND LOURDES

The fact that the visionaries testified that the visions were due to end within "three more days" — in other words, less than two weeks after they had begun on 24 June 1981 — has proved a grave embarrassment to some promoters of Medjugorje. They have downplayed this fact and tried to explain it away in the face of the tens of thousands of further visions subsequently alleged to have taken place. An example of this is found in the interview between Fr Zovko and Fr Svetozar Kraljevic, which took place on 11 August 1983. In this interview, Fr Zovko claimed that he had given the visionaries a book on Lourdes and that from the number of apparitions which Bernadette experienced — nineteen — they too thought that they should expect a further three visions, since they claimed to have experienced sixteen visions up to that point.

It does seem, from the taped conversation of 27 June 1981, that Mirjana, at least, had read a book on Lourdes, possibly even before the first vision. Fr Zovko asked her if she was reading any book at the present time, and she responded: "I have read. It is about Lourdes. The day after, when they were telling me... what happened to that little girl."

Clearly this is a reference to St Bernadette, and Fr Zovko then asked: "When was that [the reading of the book], this year?" to which Mirjana responded: "Right after I came down here. They talked about it." This response could be interpreted as indicating that Mirjana had read the book before 24 June 1981; but according to Daria Klanac's transcript, Mirjana claimed to have read the book only after the first vision.

In any event, the above idea, that there would only be a total of nineteen visions, as an explanation for the "three more days" assertion, is completely unacceptable in the overall context of what was said both on this day and on 30 June. There was simply no mention of the figure nineteen; rather, as we will see, the visionaries were only aware of the *eighteen* main apparitions at Lourdes.

Apart from that, at least one other visionary, Jakov, was also aware of the basic story of Lourdes, as is clear from the tape of the interview he had with Fr Zovko, also on 27 June.[43]

Three More Days of Visions

The first taped interview, with only three of the visionaries, Ivanka, Vicka and Marija, was undertaken by Fr Zrinko Cuvalo, the parochial vicar at Medjugorje, on the morning of 27 June. In this interview, four days into the course of the visions, Fr Cuvalo asked them why they had returned to Podbrdo after the initial vision on 24 June, the feast of the birth of St John the Baptist. To this, Ivanka explained how they had been repeatedly told how the Blessed Virgin had appeared at Lourdes eighteen times.[44]

This is an interesting admission and indicates that already the visionaries were under some external pressure to carry on going to Podbrdo. It also indicates that the story of Lourdes was well known in the village, to the extent that at least some villagers were aware that there were eighteen main apparitions at the grotto — which is certainly not something the average Catholic would know. But we should note, too, that there is a discrepancy between the eighteen apparitions mentioned by Ivanka and the figure nineteen used by Fr Zovko to explain the problem of the "three more days." The last apparition to Bernadette took place sometime later, on 16 July, and is not considered to be part of the main sequence of Lourdes apparitions.

The point, however, as regards Fr Zovko's assertion, is that, if anything, the visionaries ought to have said, "*two* more days," given that they were aware of the number eighteen, rather than nineteen. So the whole idea that the "three more days" was somehow tied in with the young people's knowledge of Lourdes is untenable and breaks down completely under investigation.[45]

Fr Laurentin's explanation for all this is extremely feeble: "On that day [30 June] Mirjana thought that she understood that the Gospa would return for three more days, until Friday. But it was only her interpretation."[46] It is not clear exactly what he based this statement on, but it simply cannot be reconciled with the tape transcripts.

And in fact, we can go further than this, and say that Fr Laurentin is actually guilty of omitting important material in his *Chronological Corpus*, particularly on this point of the "three more days," as Louis Bélanger makes clear. He shows how when Fr Laurentin's accounts of the 29th and 30th June 1981 are compared with the tape transcripts made by Fr Sivric and Daria Klanac, it is quite clear that Fr Laurentin left out a good deal of material which was damaging to Medjugorje.[47]

THE VISIONARIES AND LOURDES

Apart from all this, there are points of contact between the accounts of the visionaries and the apparitions at Lourdes which certainly indicate that they were aware of what had happened there. Fr Sivric took the view that what happened at Medjugorje might well have been, to some extent, a "copying" of what took place at Lourdes. For example, as already indicated, he draws attention to the fact that on the third day, Vicka took along some blessed salt and water and sprinkled the "Gospa" with it. We find Bernadette also sprinkling holy water on the apparition she saw. The particular significance of this is that, as we have seen, on this occasion Vicka said: "If you are the Gospa, remain with us. If you are not, get lost," while Bernadette asked her beautiful lady "to stay if she came from God, to go away if not."[48]

Similarly, when Ivanka was speaking with Fr Zovko about a "sign," she said that while the best sign of all would be that the "Gospa" should appear to everyone, failing that, "she would cause 'water' to spring up," which equates with the appearance of the miraculous spring at Lourdes.[49]

Fr Sivric also considers the possibility that Medjugorje could have been a "pious initiative" on the part of the visionaries, but one which quickly went beyond their control. On this analysis, as he says, the "events at Lourdes would have served as catalysts for their own visions."[50]

But while the visionaries' knowledge of Lourdes undoubtedly did contribute to their perception of what took place on Podbrdo, it's hard to see how the visions could have been a purely "pious initiative." The evidence from the tapes does surely indicate that they saw "something," and that it wasn't just a case of an elaborate make-believe which got out of hand.

The evidence suggests, then, that the visionaries were aware of what had taken place at Lourdes, and this surely illustrates an important point which has not been sufficiently grasped. Because accounts of the recognized apparitions of Mary have been freely available now for decades, it is quite possible for individuals to be influenced by these accounts. This is not to say that the visionaries consciously set out to fabricate the entire manifestation right from the beginning — the evidence from the tapes strongly indicates that they did see something during the first week. Rather, once they came down to the church from Podbrdo, there was enormous pressure on them to maintain the stance that they really were seeing the Blessed Virgin.

* * *

THE TRAGEDY OF THIS WHOLE AFFAIR IS THAT THE visionaries have been as much the victims of what has taken place at Medjugorje as its originators. As we have seen, there were a number of factors at work in and around Podbrdo which led them to believe they were seeing visions of the Blessed Mother, and thus, it would be too simplistic to say that Medjugorje was fabricated according to a predetermined plan. Rather, it arose haphazardly, and there were a number of ingredients which contributed to it, among which accounts of the events at Lourdes were one factor. But in the end, its initial success can probably be attributed mainly to Fr Zovko, who after expressing clear disbelief during the early days of the visions, was led to change his mind and become a fervent supporter of Medjugorje.

7
Medjugorje: God or the Devil?

MEDJUGORJE: A DIABOLICAL ORIGIN?

In the light of the evidence cited above, it is legitimate then to ask whether or not the original visions, of the first week or so, were not in fact diabolical in origin, as Fr Zovko himself suggested on more than one occasion. If we look at the whole phenomenon from the perspective of the devil, then some very interesting points emerge. He has a great deal of experience in this area. He knows all about human weakness, foolishness and sinfulness — and how to exploit these to the maximum. And we always need to bear in mind St Paul's warning that Satan can disguise himself as an "angel of light" (2 Cor 11:14).

Regarding the storm which struck Medjugorje overnight, just before the visions began, which was mentioned previously, some older inhabitants of the village said that they could remember nothing like it in half a century. Repeated streaks of lightning flashed across the sky to the sound of deafening thunder, and as fires were started by lightning strikes, a hall, which had been turned into a disco, was burned down, and the post office badly damaged. One terrified inhabitant compared it to the "Day of Judgement."[1]

We have to ask why this significantly destructive storm happened just as the visions were beginning — could this have been a sign of a diabolical involvement at Medjugorje?

Be that as it may, another point to note is that in 1977, four years before the Medjugorje visions began, Bishop Zanic's predecessor, Bishop Cule, set up a Marian shrine dedicated to Our Lady as "Queen of Peace." This was done at Hrasno, which is situated about 25 miles away from Medjugorje, in the neighboring diocese of Trebinje e Mrkanin, a diocese which is administered by the bishops of Mostar-Duvno. Bishop Cule, by this act, specifically wanted the Blessed Virgin to heal the divisions within the area which were essentially caused by the disobedience of the Franciscans.[2] Why, then, would Our Lady want to begin to appear so close to this genuine shrine and create a rival to it in Medjugorje? It doesn't make sense, except as, again, a sign of the diabolical. Who else but the devil would want to initiate such a thing?

In any event, if it is the case that the devil — or some sort of diabolic vision — was in fact appearing during the first week at Medjugorje, it can be said that his main concern, initially, would be to avoid frightening the visionaries away by acting in a precipitate way. Therefore, he would, of necessity, adopt a non-threatening attitude towards them. The devil does not know the future with precision — the fact of human free will and the power of God's grace make that too difficult — and therefore each case like this has to be treated on its own merits.

So, following the above scenario, on the first day, the Vision said nothing, but just allowed the visionaries to get used to their new experience. Similarly, the Vision did not say anything on the second day, but did allow the visionaries to touch its form. Fr Cuvalo questioned them on this point, asking if the Vision said anything as they were doing this. Marija replied: "Nothing at all, she kept looking... She told us, she laughed, what else..."[3]

Thus, if the Vision was in fact diabolical, that would explain why Satan first of all ingratiated himself with them, by allowing them to touch the visionary form he had assumed, and also by laughing, thus putting them more at ease.

GARABANDAL AND MEDJUGORJE

This parallels what happened at Garabandal, a Spanish village, where in the early 1960s four young girls claimed to have had visions of the Blessed Virgin, visions which have not been accepted as authentic by the Church. On Sunday, 2 July 1961, they alleged that she had appeared to them as Our Lady of Mount Carmel, and that they spoke to her for a long time. One of them, Conchita, later recorded in her diary that they told her mundane details about the village haymaking, and that "Mary's" response was to laugh at the things they told her.[4]

It is hard to believe that the real Blessed Virgin would have engaged in such trivial chit-chat with the girls. But as a diabolical method of drawing the children more closely into visions which were not supernatural, as also seems to have happened during the first week at Medjugorje, it makes perfect sense. We only have to recall the way the Serpent beguiled Eve to realize that this is exactly the way we should expect the devil to behave in such situations.

On 3 August 1961, the Garabandal visionaries made the first of their "ecstatic walks," which involved their walking either forward or backwards, without apparently looking where they were going. These walks were often conducted at tremendous speed, to the astonishment of onlookers who could barely keep up.[5] There are interesting parallels here to some of the accounts of the Medjugorje visionaries during the first week, including those recorded on the tapes transcribed by Fr Sivric. For example, Marija spoke of following people down the hill, and moving to another location after one of the visions, and of feeling "as if somebody got hold of me and kept dragging me.... Something kept attracting me."

In Fr Sivric's translation of her first *Diary,* Vicka makes a similar claim, speaking of how on the second day, 25 June 1981, she ran up the hill with the other visionaries who were present, because the "Gospa" was calling them: "We felt as if some force were drawing us up there." Speaking of this occasion, Mirjana related that they had quickly climbed up the hill, "but...did not become tired," despite the fact that it was a long way up.[6] Vicka also had this to say about that day's events:

> The Madonna called to us to go up on the hill, and we went. When you look up there from the bottom of the hill, it looks close, but it is not. We ran quickly up the hill. It was not like walking on the ground. Nor did we look for the path. We simply ran toward her. In five minutes we were on the hill—as if something had pulled us through the air. I was afraid. I also was barefoot, but no thorns had scratched me. When we were about two meters away from the Madonna, we felt as if we were thrown to our knees. Jakov was thrown kneeling into a thorny bush, and I thought he would be injured. But he came out of it without a scratch.

The interesting thing is that these experiences were not just the subjective feelings of the visionaries, but were also witnessed by onlookers, as Fr Kraljevic indicates: "Those who watched the children run up the hill testify to the truthfulness of Vicka's words. They were amazed by the speed with which the children ran, and were not able to follow them to the top of the hill."[7]

We do not find anything like this "ecstatic" running in the approved apparitions of the Blessed Virgin, whereas it is disturbing to note this clear parallel with the activities of the Garabandal visionaries.

THERE IS NO MESSAGE

As we have seen, on the third day, Ivanka asked the Vision why she had come there and was told: "Because there were a lot of faithful, that we must be together." She asked, too, about her recently deceased mother and was told that she was with the "Gospa." Mirjana, too, was reassured about her grandfather. The visionaries then asked if she was going to come again, and they were told: "Tomorrow at the same place"—but their request for a sign was ignored.[8]

Here, too, we can see how this "small talk" was conducive to this process of ingratiation with the visionaries, while the "message" itself—"that we must be together"—is completely trite and unnecessary.

And as Louis Bélanger points out, too, the fact that Ivanka's mother had died, alone, quite recently, at the early age of thirty-nine, is an important factor which has to be taken into account when assessing what really happened. Naturally she would still have been grieving for her mother, and so could be expected to interpret her experiences that day in the light of her bereavement.[9] She may have had a desire to see her mother, and as we will see further on, the desire to see something "supernatural" is dangerous because it gives the devil an opportunity to satisfy such a desire. So Ivanka's fragile emotional state at the time of the first apparition, so soon after her mother's death, and her possible *desire* for some sort of contact with her mother, may help us to better understand her frame of mind at the time.

In the light of what has taken place during genuine apparitions, it is astonishing to note that up to this point, the Vision had made no serious attempt to initiate any conversation, or pass on any message of substance, and in this regard, it was exactly the same on the fourth day. Rather, the Vision allowed the visionaries to take the initiative and become used to its presence. Indeed, as already indicated, by this stage, Fr Zovko was becoming somewhat exasperated at the lack of any clear message from the Vision, and he pressed Mirjana on this point.[10]

His perplexity continued following the events of the fifth day, when he was not able to get a straight answer on this point of a lack of a specific message, neither from Mirjana, nor Ivanka, nor Ivan. Finally, as already noted, on the sixth day, Fr Zovko publicly acknowledged that no official message was being given and that, "Our Lady has said nothing that is meant for anyone else."[11]

This virtual non-communication to the visionaries from the "Gospa," during the crucial first week or so of visions, contrasts very strongly with the way that the approved apparitions of the Blessed Virgin have developed. In most such cases, a week has been quite sufficient for her to say everything she wanted to say, but at Medjugorje during this period the "Gospa" did not pass on anything of significance.

This does not mean, though, that everything about Medjugorje is necessarily diabolically inspired. As we have seen, Medjugorje almost certainly arose in part because of the weakness of fallen human nature, especially on the part of the visionaries and their immediate associates. These elements facilitate the work of the devil, but as this work is invisible, it is therefore difficult to identify. Satan achieves his objectives by a kind of counterfeit "grace" in the heart and mind, by which people are drawn into believing in false visions almost without being aware of what is happening. For, clearly, the vast majority of those who have been to Medjugorje have gone there in good faith.

THE PATTERN OF THE APPROVED APPARITIONS

Whether it is the Blessed Virgin speaking to Juan Diego at Guadalupe, in 1531, when she imparted a series of messages to him, or Rue du Bac, where Mary spoke in detail about the mission she was giving Catherine Labouré, or Fatima, where the message contained a specific request to the pope, the pattern of the approved apparitions of the past has been consistent: the Blessed Virgin has something definite and of vital supernatural importance to say regarding mankind's salvation, and she wastes no time in conveying her message.

This is also true of her apparitions at Lourdes, La Salette, Beauraing and Banneux. She always leads the conversation and is the one who initiates important elements. This does not mean, however, that she unthinkingly brushes aside unimportant questions; rather, as a true mother, she shows that she understands the mentality of her children, and where their questions can be answered, she does so. But her intention is very definitely to convey a specific spiritual message in a relatively short space of time. In most cases, she did this with very few words, and this aspect seems to coincide with her reticence in the Gospels, where likewise, she said very little. In addition, her words are concerned with her mission as the spiritual mother of mankind, and not with generalities or matters not related to salvation: she says nothing unseemly or contrary to the Faith.[12]

Indeed, it is fair to say that if *all* the reported words of Mary during her major apparitions, in the period of over four hundred years between Guadalupe and Banneux, were put together, they would not amount to much more than a document of ten or eleven sheets. How many people realize how little she actually said during her recognized apparitions? At Knock and Pontmain, she said absolutely nothing—although a few words did appear on a banner at her feet during the latter apparition—and, for example, the following words at Banneux were so few, that they could easily be written on the back of a postcard:

> "This stream is reserved for me. Good evening."
> "Push your hands into the water."
> "I am the Virgin of the poor."
> "This spring is reserved for all the nations—to relieve the sick."
> "I shall pray for you. Au Revoir."
> "I come to relieve suffering."
> "Believe in me, I will believe in you. Pray much. Au Revoir."
> "My dear child, pray much. Au Revoir."
> "I am the Mother of the Savior, Mother of God. Pray much. Adieu."[13]

OUR LADY'S WORDS AT FATIMA

The same principle can also be illustrated by looking at the following dialogue with Lucia which took place during the first apparition at Fatima, and which began with Mary smiling and reassuring the children:

> "Do not be afraid, I will do you no harm."
> "Where are you from?"
> "I am from heaven."
> "What do want of me?"
> "I have come to ask you to come here for six months in succession on the 13th day, at this same hour. Later on, I will tell who I am and what I want. Afterwards, I will return here yet a seventh time."
> "Shall I go to heaven too?"
> "Yes, you will."
> "And Jacinta?"
> "She will go also."
> "And Francisco?"
> "He will go there too, but he must say many rosaries."

Lucia then asked about two young women who had died recently, and was told that one was in heaven, and that the other would be in purgatory "until the end of the world."

"Are you willing to offer yourselves to God and bear all the sufferings He wills to send you, as an act of reparation for the conversion of sinners?"

"Yes, we are willing."

"Then you are going to have much to suffer, but the grace of God will be your comfort."

Lucia recounted that at that moment the Lady opened her hands:

> communicating to us a light so intense that, as it streamed from her hands, its rays penetrated our hearts and the innermost depths of our souls, making us see ourselves in God, Who was that light, more clearly than we see ourselves in the best of mirrors. Then, moved by an interior impulse that was also communicated to us, we fell on our knees, repeating in our hearts: "O most Holy Trinity, I adore You! My God, my God, I love You in the most Blessed Sacrament!"

After a few moments, before she disappeared, the Lady left them with a request: "Pray the Rosary every day, in order to obtain peace for the world and the end of the war."[14]

We can see here that Our Lady initially reassured the children that she is indeed from heaven, and that they will go there too, before answering the questions which naturally come to Lucia's mind. Then she moves straight on to the important spiritual substance of her message, namely, asking them to offer themselves to God, to accept suffering in reparation for sin and to pray the rosary. The contrast with the lack of any substantial spiritual message from God on the part of the Medjugorje Vision during the first few days could hardly be greater.

To sum up what we have been considering so far, the primary evidence provided by the taped interviews recorded at the time of the visions clearly demonstrates that the first week's visions at Medjugorje present us with major difficulties. They bear no resemblance to the way the approved Marian apparitions developed during a similar, or an even shorter period, sometimes amounting to as little as a single apparition, as in the case of La Salette.

THE VISION IS RELUCTANT TO GO TO CHURCH

What really seems to clinch the argument that the Vision was not the Blessed Virgin is the following very important admission, which, as we have already noted, was made by Mirjana during Fr Zovko's interview with the visionaries on 30 June: "We asked her if she would be annoyed to see us going to the church rather than to the hill. However, she seemed indecisive when we asked this question, as if she did not like it. Nevertheless she said that she wouldn't be annoyed."[15]

The whole idea that the Blessed Virgin defers to purely subjective human whims, as to where she is to appear, is absolutely out of the question, and by itself, raises very serious doubts as to the nature of the Medjugorje Vision. However, if, for the sake of argument, we assume that it was Mary, how can one then explain that she was "indecisive" and at first looked "as if she did not like it" when the visionaries asked if they could go to the church in future, rather than return to the hillside? To think that Mary could not have been pleased that they wanted to go into the church, where her divine Son is really present in the tabernacle, is frankly quite unbelievable. However, if the Vision was not in fact Mary, but in some sense diabolical, then its reluctance to appear before the Blessed Sacrament in the church becomes understandable.

Regarding this question of a diabolical deception, on Tuesday, 30 June, while Fr Zovko was interviewing some of the visionaries individually, two other Franciscans, Frs Pervan and Dugandzic, arrived at his office. Fr Zovko refused to allow them to participate in the interviews, but when he emerged later on, he found Fr Pervan proclaiming that the children were possessed by the devil. He suggested exorcism but Fr Zovko, in the words of Mary Craig, "dismissed [this] as too alarming for all concerned and unlikely to bring them any nearer to the truth."[16] It is certainly significant that Fr Pervan should have thought of diabolical possession as an explanation for the visionaries' activities, and this indicates that at this stage he felt there was something unwholesome about the whole business.

A VISIONARY PATTERN ESTABLISHED

Once the visionaries had moved from Podbrdo to the church, a pattern was established, which remained practically unchanged until 1985. Every evening, after saying the rosary in the church, they would assemble in a room opposite the sacristy, which became known as "the chapel of the apparitions." This had a crucifix on the wall above a movable altar, and a statue of Our Lady of Lourdes to one side. This mention of the statue is an interesting point in itself, since it adds to the evidence that the apparitions at Lourdes formed an accepted part of parish life. During their visions, they would stare at a precise spot on the south wall of this room, having fallen to their knees as a group.

Within a month, this pattern, according to Vicka's first *Diary*, involved the "Gospa" appearing to the visionaries at half past six, greeting them with the words, "Praised be Jesus," and then engaging them in conversation. The themes at this stage apparently centered on the need for conversion and penance, and it seems that her customary saying as she departed was: "Go in God's peace!" Exactly a month after the visions began, on 24 July 1981, Vicka was still describing the arrival of the Vision in similar terms to those used right at the beginning, that is of a light slowly descending.[17]

THE "SIGN" PROMISED

From the second day onwards, 25 June 1981, the visionaries were very concerned that the "Gospa" should provide a "sign" in order to indicate that they were telling the truth, and thus satisfy the understandable expectations of the crowd.[18] It certainly seems that the visionaries thought that this sign would appear "very soon," and the common opinion amongst both them and the Franciscans at this time was that this sign would be given during 1981. According to Fr Sivric, Fr Zovko had announced in a sermon that a sign would be given roughly about the time of the feast of the Assumption — that is, around 15 August 1981.[19]

Fr Laurentin reports that Vicka recorded in her first *Diary*, for the entry dated 27 August 1981, that when she asked the Vision about the sign, the response was: "Very soon, I promise you." This theme was repeated on 29 August, when in response to a question on the sign by Ivanka, they were told: "Again, a little patience," with similar answers coming on 30 August and 3 September.

When interviewed by Fr Bubalo about the sign, Vicka confirmed that, according to the "Gospa," the sign would be at Podbrdo, that it would appear instantaneously and not gradually, and that everyone would be able to see it. In addition, Vicka said that it would be permanent and indestructible, and that she knew exactly what it would look like, and when it would appear.[20] The problem with this is that if a permanent, but obviously miraculous, sign is to be left at Podbrdo, then this would tend to do away with the need for faith—unlike the case with relics such as the Shroud of Turin, or the Mexican Guadalupe *Tilma* with Our Lady's miraculous image on it.

Frs Rupcic and Nuic dispute that the "Gospa" explicitly promised the visionaries a "sign," but there is no question that according to the testimony of the latter they certainly expected something to happen. As we have seen, when questioned concerning a sign by Fr Zovko, Ivanka had replied: "She certainly is going to leave it," while Vicka maintained that she thought the visions would end after the "Gospa" had given a sign. This point is even clearer in Vicka's first *Diary*, as translated by Fr Sivric, where in the entry for 27 August 1981, she tells us that in response to their further questions about a sign, the "Gospa" responded: "It is going to be soon since I have promised you."

Once again, Frs Rupcic and Nuic attempt a "theological" explanation, this time for the use of the word "soon," arguing that because in the Bible "thousands of years can mean one day," therefore "Vicka's statement should not be any more suspicious than the statements by Biblical prophets."[21] The danger with this type of approach, of course, is that it can be used to twist the plain meaning of a word into whatever we want it to mean.

However, it might be further argued by Medjugorje supporters that this use of the word "soon" by the Vision parallels the way that Our Lady at Fatima told Lucia that unlike Jacinta and Francisco, who would *soon* go to heaven, she would have to stay on earth, "some time longer," whereas in fact, Lucia lived on into her nineties. But clearly, it would have been heartbreaking for her to have been told this as a young child, and we can see in the words "some time longer" Mary's motherly concern to spare her unnecessary anguish. And indeed, in saying that she would take Jacinta and Francisco to heaven "soon" she was saying nothing other than the truth, since both of them died shortly after—here "soon" was used very literally.[22] The other point to make is that when Our Lady spoke of the miracle that was to come at Fatima, she did not use a vague word like "soon," but specified the very month—October—and indeed the very day—the thirteenth.

THE GARABANDAL "GREAT MIRACLE"

In any event, something similar to what was claimed for Medjugorje, a future "great miracle," was also prophesied at Garabandal, and this was supposed to occur in such a manner that it would be seen by all in the vicinity of Garabandal on a particular day, with an advance notice of eight days. According to Sanchez-Ventura y Pascual's book *The Apparitions of Garabandal*, originally published in English in 1966, it was also foretold:

> The Pope and Padre Pio will see it from wherever they happen to be; that the sick who are present will be cured, that sinners will be converted, that the miracle will last some fifteen minutes; that the Bishop will raise his prohibition beforehand, so that priests may be there; and that a permanent sign will be left as a proof of the miracle...

According to one of the visionaries, the miracle was to be "as great and spectacular as the world needs," and she also claimed to know its date.[23]

Needless to say, there has been no great miracle at Garabandal, and the chances of there being one in the future would appear to be remote. Padre Pio died in 1968, and this talk of a sign seems to have been nothing less than a device to keep up some sort of interest in Garabandal, by attempting to force the Church not to come to any definite decision about the alleged visions until they had been "proved" by this expected miracle. There have been attempts to circumvent the inconvenient fact of Padre Pio's death by claiming that he had a private vision of the miracle beforehand, but this goes against the plain sense of the above "prophecy."[24]

Indeed, the only genuine Marian "great sign" of recent times has been the one to which Our Lady referred in July 1917, when as part of the Fatima secret she foretold the strange illuminations in the night sky which would be seen in many parts of the world, and which took place in 1938. "When you see a night illumined by an unknown light, know that this is the *great sign* given you by God that he is about to punish the world for its crimes, by means of war, famine, and persecutions of the Church and of the Holy Father." Of course, the miracle of the sun itself at Fatima was also an extremely important sign, given so that all might believe.

GARABANDAL NOT AS POPULAR AS MEDJUGORJE

Garabandal was very popular at the time, and still has a sizable following to this day, but it never managed to attract anything like the support garnered by Medjugorje. There are probably a number of reasons for this, including the fact that despite the problems emerging at the time of the Second Vatican Council, the Church was still in an essentially healthy condition at that time. But a case can certainly be made that Garabandal, and other claimed apparitions, including those to Ida Peerdeman at Amsterdam in the 1940s and 1950s, prepared the minds of many Catholics for the possibility of a lengthy series of visions. In addition, such alleged visions, which often involved opposition to the wishes of the local bishop, also prepared the way for the sort of confrontation with the episcopacy which has developed at Medjugorje.

But what was missing at Garabandal was a worldwide support network of the sort provided by the Charismatic Movement, and also very crucially, a group of religious and priests, the Franciscans of Bosnia-Herzegovina, prepared to back Medjugorje. In addition, the early 80s were one of the low points of the Church's fortunes in recent years. Pope John Paul II had only been in power for a brief period, and it would be some time before his policies and personality would begin to have an impact on the Church. All of these factors combined to provide a suitable atmosphere in which Medjugorje could flourish.

With the passage of time, though, it must be obvious to any unbiased observer that Garabandal and Medjugorje have much more in common with each other than either of them has with any of the approved Marian apparitions, and that sensible Catholics ought to be supporting the latter instead.

FR ZOVKO IS ARRESTED AND IMPRISONED

On 11 July 1981, Fr Zovko preached a fiery sermon, taking as his subject the Israelites wandering in the wilderness for forty years. The authorities regarded this sermon as having veiled political and nationalistic implications in connection with the years of Communist rule in Yugoslavia. *Novosti* (*The News*), a daily newspaper, accused him of wanting to revive the Ustasha nationalist movement, "in the very place of the crime." Fr Laurentin links this to the killing of some local Marxists and the atrocities carried out by Tito's partisans, but fails to mention the brutal massacre of the Serbs at Surmanci, which is surely the crime to which the paper was referring.[25]

Meanwhile, Bishop Zanic had visited Medjugorje on 25 July, and it seems that at this very early stage he was open to the possibility that the visionaries might be telling the truth. He was also aware of the hostility of the government, and, on 6 August, he issued a press release in defense of the priests and the visionaries, who were being attacked in Communist newspapers. Indeed subsequently, on 12 August, Podbrdo was put off-limits by the civil authorities.

We can gauge the impact the Medjugorje phenomenon was having locally by noting that on the Feast of the Assumption Fr Zovko was able to announce to a huge crowd of 25,000 that a sign would be given by the "Gospa" on 17 August 1981. Meanwhile, another indication of how feverish things had become during the early days came from the variously timed announcements by Marinko that a large church would suddenly appear on Podbrdo, or that a local hill would simply disappear. These statements were reported to Fr Sivric by his various informants in the village.

There was a sign on 17 August, but it wasn't quite the one Fr Zovko had expected; rather it was the arrival of the police to arrest him because of his earlier "political" sermon, which led to a summary trial for the priest. His place was taken by Fr Tomislav Vlasic who was to remain the pivotal influence over the visionaries, as their spiritual director, until September 1984, being later followed in this role by Fr Slavko Barbaric. In 1988, Fr Vlasic would begin a mixed religious community in Italy, one involving young people, including the visionary Marija Pavlovic and a German woman named Agnes Heupel who had supposedly been cured of a partial paralysis at Medjugorje.[26]

Fr Zovko was put on trial in Mostar on 21 October 1981 and convicted the following day, receiving a prison sentence which would only see his release in February 1983.[27] This crackdown by the authorities illustrates another of the factors which helped to fuel support for Medjugorje in the early days, namely, the opposition of the Communists, which led many people to conclude that the claimed visions must be genuine. They had suffered for so long under a Communist regime which was maintained by lies that it almost seemed natural to believe the opposite of what they said, regardless of whether or not it might be true.[28]

8

Problems with the Medjugorje Messages

SOME UNBELIEVABLE MESSAGES

At this stage, early in the life of Medjugorje, some of the visionaries were prone to making rather extreme statements. For example, Fr Sivric reports that in late August or early September 1981, Vicka announced, in front of a certain Jure Ivankovic and a priest, that "Germany and the United States will be destroyed... that the Pope will be exiled in Turkey, [and] ... that Bisce, the plain south of Mostar, will be covered in knee-deep blood." Fr Sivric notes that this supposed prophecy did not originate with Vicka, because as a child he could remember similar prophecies being repeated. This illustrates the effect of the popular culture on her, and her difficulty in differentiating between fantasy and reality. But the fact that she should have said such a thing at all is clearly disturbing.

Similarly, Fr Sivric tells us that on 4 September 1981, Vicka wrote in her first *Diary* about the infamous "bloody handkerchief" incident, which concerned a meeting between a "driver" and a man covered in blood — Christ, according to the visionary — who ordered that a handkerchief soaked in blood should be thrown in a river. This driver then met Mary who asked for the handkerchief, although he was apparently reluctant to hand it over. Then the Blessed Virgin reportedly said, "If you had not given it to me, that would have been the end of the world." Vicka stated categorically that: "The Gospa said that was the truth."

However, by the time Vicka was speaking with Fr Bubalo, in 1983, she was putting forward a different version of this story, saying: "I'm surprised that people continue to associate me with that hankie, when it really isn't my affair." She goes on to attempt to distance herself from this bizarre account, but it is all very unconvincing. She does not deny, however, that the "Gospa" *had* corroborated the story, when she said that she later asked her about it.

But as Marco Corvaglia, an Italian Medjugorje researcher, points out, this story is actually a re-working of an ancient legend that has been in circulation in Europe for centuries. For example, the Italian writer Giovanni Sercambi wrote a very similar story not about a handkerchief, but rather about some loaves, in his fifteenth century *Croniche* ("Chronicles"). Again, this is evidence of the effect of the popular culture on Vicka rather than of anything supernatural.

Rather surprisingly, Fr Laurentin did not include this incident in his *Chronological Corpus of the Messages*,[1] and attempted to justify himself regarding it as follows: "I will not go back on this story which has been badly attested. I had suggested to Father Bubalo to eliminate this confusing and insignificant event from his book."[2]

THE MEDJUGORJE CULTURE AND FOLKLORE

It is important to put the visions and the visionaries in the context of the local culture of which they are part. Fr Sivric speaks of a very specific culture and folklore in the area, one which is quite credulous in believing tales of miraculous events, and thus very open to the possibility of visions. Further on he speaks of a "tendency to dramatize" in the culture. It is worth noting, too, that the local villages had their own "prophets" and "prophetesses," whose predictions were remembered and passed on orally within the community. During the summer of 1986, Fr Sivric heard of a local prophetess who had apparently often said: "Woe to the people of Medjugorje when they have bad priests!" Thus, when the accounts of the visions began to circulate, they found a ready local audience happy to absorb them and then pass them on to others. This attitude also influenced individuals who claimed that they too were seeing visions.[3]

The question of alleged cures at Medjugorje will be dealt with in a subsequent chapter, but there is also apparently a cultural factor to take into account in assessing these claims. Paolo Apolito, an Italian researcher, makes the following comment on this point, arguing that the visions at Medjugorje became mixed up with elements of local medicinal folklore: "At Medjugorje... an entire pre-existing tradition of popular medicine connected to poultices of plants and flowers mixed with earth was revived and found new efficacy through the phenomena of the apparitions." He then cites instances where pilgrims seem to have relied as much for relief from illness on infusions of soil and grass found on Podbrdo, as on prayers to the *Gospa*.[4]

QUESTIONABLE CONTENT OF THE MESSAGES

It can certainly be argued that the content of the Medjugorje messages leaves a lot to be desired. Some Medjugorje supporters have claimed that they have a cohesiveness and spirituality which could only have come from heaven, but it is a mystery how anyone who has looked at them in any detail can seriously maintain that argument. The fact is that there is nothing inherently unlikely about the proposition that the majority of the messages do not have a supernatural origin. Regarding their intrinsic nature, it is certainly true to say that they have a quality of "sameness" about them, which of itself is highly suspect, to say nothing of the questionable theology some of them contain.

On this point, Fr Augustin Poulain says: "The revelation can also be mistrusted, if, although good from the spiritual point of view, it is a *truism*, occurring in all ascetic writings. God would not employ such great means for such a small result."[5]

There is an element of flattery in the following message, from 1 March 1984, the idea that the parish had been "specially chosen," an approach which is completely foreign to the genuine messages of Our Lady:

> Dear children! *I have chosen this parish in a special way and I wish to lead it.* I am keeping it in love and I want everyone to be mine. Thank you for your response this evening. I wish that you will always be in greater numbers with me and my Son. Every Thursday I will speak a special message for you.

This idea is repeated in the following message, from 15 November 1984:

> Dear children! *You are a chosen people and God has given you great graces.* You are not aware of the importance of every message I am giving you. Now I only wish to say: Pray, pray, pray! I do not know what else to tell you because I love you and wish that in prayer you come to know my love and the love of God. Thank you for your response to my call.[6]

The idea that the Blessed Virgin would continually thank people for responding to her call is, of course, completely untenable. It suggests that people are conferring a favor on her, and as such, it is without precedent in any of the major approved apparitions.

The following message, from 21 February 1985, seems to disclose a rather petulant "Gospa," who will go away and sulk in the corner if her demands are not met:

Dear children! From day to day I have been appealing to you for renewal and prayer in the parish. But you are not responding. Today I am appealing to you for the last time. This is the season of Lent, and you, as a parish in Lent, should be moved to love by my appeal. *If you are not, I do not wish to give you any more messages.* Thank you for your response to my call.7

THEOLOGICALLY SUSPECT MESSAGES

Bishop Peric had occasion to highlight a number of Medjugorje "messages" which are problematical. For example, he mentions this one, dated 16 September 1981, which is found in the *Chronicle* of the Medjugorje visions which was edited by Fr Tomislav Vlasic between 11 September 1981 and 31 August 1984. He reported that the Vision "told them also that they do not have to pray for themselves, because she has rewarded them in a better way. Let them pray for others." As Bishop Peric points out, "No private apparition on earth substitutes for the necessity of prayer to God."

In a *Chronicle* entry dated 21 July 1982, following an alleged vision, Fr Vlasic asked the visionaries questions about purgatory and hell. Regarding hell, amongst other things, they responded: "God permits his children to suffer in Hell because they have committed grave sins that he cannot pardon." This answer is suspect because it is not a question of God not being able to pardon grave sins, but rather the willingness or otherwise of the person to seek forgiveness. As Bishop Peric noted, "The Faith teaches that there is no sin that God cannot pardon if man repents."

The visionaries also said: "In Hell everyone suffers in the same way." This response, too, is suspect, because it is unlikely that this is the case. In the book of Revelation we read that everyone will be judged according to what they have done, so presumably too, they will be punished according to the seriousness of their sins (Rev 20:12–13). And so some people will suffer more in hell than others.

Another suspect message from the *Chronicle* is dated 6 May 1982: "This evening the young people posed a theological question and received an answer. They asked: 'Are the people in Heaven present only with the soul, or with the soul and the body?' They are present with the soul and the body: that was their answer."

This answer doesn't make sense, since apart from Jesus and Mary, the saved are present in heaven only as rational souls, without their bodies, which they will only receive again at the resurrection of the body.8

Problems with the Medjugorje Messages

On 1 October 1981, a particularly contentious response was recorded to the question: "Are all the faiths good? Are all the faiths identical?" The response was: "Before God all the faiths are identical. God governs them like a king in his kingdom..."

But as Bishop Peric points out, if all religions are equal then why are we obliged to believe in Christ? Fr Laurentin attempted to justify this statement by going into the ethnic and religious differences in Yugoslavia, and quoted Vicka as saying: "The Blessed Virgin told me that 'All religions are equal before God.'" Vicka then went on to say, "That is to say, that all men are equal before God..."

Obviously, though, this is not an adequate explanation — how can there be an equivalence between religions and individuals on this point? Fr Laurentin rather lamely speaks of "ambiguities" in a number of places in his extended commentary on this troubling answer.[9]

Vicka's third *Diary* also has a questionable entry, dated 28 February 1982, in which the Vision praised Fr Vlasic for his work in guiding the visionaries. In this, Vicka says: "I and Jakov were there. The Gospa came at 6, 3 minutes, she looked kindly at us. Then the Gospa spoke about Tomislav, first she looked at him, and then said: 'you can thank Tomislav very much because he is guiding you so well.'"[10]

Clearly, to anyone who is familiar with the recognized apparitions of Our Lady, the idea that she would praise anyone in this way is untenable. And this is particularly the case here since, as we will see, Fr Vlasic was laicized in 2009, because of, in the words of the Franciscan minister general Fr José Rodriguez Carballo, "conduct harmful to ecclesial communion both in the spheres of doctrine and discipline."

FURTHER SUSPECT MESSAGES

Some other messages are also theologically suspect, or at least ambiguous. For example, the message dated 24 July 1982 is as follows: "The body, drawn from the earth, decomposes after death. *It never comes back to life again.* Man receives a transfigured body."[11]

While it is true to say that our bodies will be transfigured at the resurrection, it is clearly not true that they will never come back to life again, since this would imply that the same bodies that we have on earth are not part of the resurrection of the body. That this is not the case is clear from Scripture (cf. Rom 8:11; Phil 3:21), and was also proclaimed at the Fourth Lateran Council as follows: "They will arise with their bodies which they have now."[12]

Similarly, this message, dated 31 August 1982, calls into question Mary's mediatory role: "*I do not dispose all graces.* I receive from God what I obtain through prayer. God has placed His complete trust in me."[13]

This first sentence is clearly contrary to Church teaching regarding Our Lady, that she is indeed the Mediatrix of all graces.[14] In contrast, this is what St Louis de Montfort, the great Marian saint, had to say on this point: "God has entrusted Mary with the keeping, the administration and distribution of all His graces, so that all His graces and gifts pass through her hands."[15]

This part of the message is also at odds with the experience of St Catherine Labouré at Rue du Bac, during the apparition on 27 November 1830, when she saw Mary standing on a globe with rings on her fingers flashing with light rays, which she was explicitly told represented graces.

Surely, then, this "message," of itself, disqualifies Medjugorje from being seriously regarded as a supernatural event?

There is also an unhealthy preoccupation with the devil in many of the messages, a preoccupation which is absent in the approved Marian apparitions. Satan is mentioned in over sixty of the messages listed between 1984 and 2004.[16] This appears to be, though, more an indication of the dualistic tendency already noted in Croatian popular religion than evidence of truly supernaturality.

A particular point to note is that the Wisdom literature in the Bible has a number of passages which are critical of excessive talk, a quality which certainly seems to characterize the messages from the "Gospa." For example, Proverbs 17:27 tells us that: "He who restrains his words has knowledge," while Ecclesiastes 5:2 is even more explicit: "Be not rash with your mouth, nor let your heart be hasty to utter a word before God . . . therefore let your words be few." Mary's words in both the Gospels and in her approved apparitions have generally been few but to the point.

Sometimes, too, the encounters with the "Gospa" could descend to the level of farce. Mrs. Patricia Waters, an ex-promoter of Medjugorje, describes how she was present at one of these in the early 80s, during which Jakov asked the "Gospa" about a football match, and how his favorite team had done. This caused the other visionaries to burst out laughing. Wayne Weible confirms that this bizarre incident did in fact take place.[17]

Fr Jordan Aumann, OP, in his *Spiritual Theology*, makes the following general comment on the above points: "Revelations concerning merely curious or useless matters should be rejected as not divine. The same is to be said of those that are detailed, lengthy, and filled with a superfluity of proofs and reasons. Divine revelations are generally brief, clear, and precise."[18]

THEMES OF THE MESSAGES

It is possible to discern, from a very early stage, a predominance of Franciscan themes in the messages. For example, the emphasis on Franciscan prayer formulas, such as the seven Our Fathers, Hail Marys and Glorias, an old Franciscan devotion, is evident, as is the stress on fasting on bread and water.[19] An important part of the worldwide message being propagated in the name of Medjugorje has been one of "prayer, conversion, and fasting." Undoubtedly, this focus on such traditional Catholic practices was a great help, in the early days, in convincing many that Medjugorje might well be genuine. But as we have seen, these elements were conspicuous by their absence from the messages of the first week or so — in fact, the message of the first week was that there was no message!

And specifically regarding fasting, Fr Laurentin is quite clear that this did not come about as a result of a request of the "Gospa." He tells us that it "began as an initiative of the parish priest: there was not as yet a message from the Virgin. How did he get this idea? Perhaps it was inspiration but above all he was basing himself on an ancient tradition of Bosnia-Hercegovina."

Apparently, following his experience on 2 July, when Fr Zovko claimed he had heard a voice telling him to "protect the children" and had subsequently preached to his parishioners, he had challenged them thus: "Are you ready to pray and fast (for three days)?" Their response had been strongly affirmative.

And even before this, on 28 June, during his interview with Mirjana, while complaining that the "Gospa" wasn't giving them any sort of coherent message about prayer or what to do, he also commented that, "She doesn't tell you to fast," with the implication that is what she ought to have done if she really was the *Gospa*. This then is another indication of how fasting was one of the prevailing religious practices in the locality, and definitely not an initiative of the "Gospa."[20]

THE DURATION OF THE APPROVED APPARITIONS

There is also the problem of the sheer volume of messages, as well as the length of time the visions have apparently been continuing. Most recognized apparitions have begun and ended in a relatively short time. As we have seen, all the words of the approved modern apparitions come to no more than about a dozen pages of text at most. Why after being so sparing of words in the past, to the point of taciturnity, why should Mary suddenly become so expansive and talkative? It just doesn't make sense.

At Guadalupe, Mary appeared only four times to Juan Diego, while at Rue du Bac, Catherine Labouré was privileged with only three major apparitions. At La Salette, Mary appeared only once to the two children, while at Lourdes she appeared less than twenty times to Bernadette. Both Pontmain and Knock involved only a single apparition, while at Fatima, Mary appeared on six occasions. The number of apparitions at Beauraing was something over thirty, and at Banneux, eight.

Thus, the average number of apparitions for the major approved visitations of the Blessed Virgin was only just over eight, and their longest duration, in the case of Fatima, was less than six months. Although it is true that Mary appeared to Sr Lucia on a number of occasions in later years, it is clear that these events were of a different order and thus were not a part of the original series of apparitions, although they were organically linked to them and represent important developments of the message of Fatima.

Thus, the norm for the major approved apparitions is one which has, for each particular place, a number for apparitions usually in single figures, and a duration of weeks, or possibly months, but not years.

Some Medjugorje supporters, though, have claimed that the Marian apparitions at Notre-Dame du Laus, in southeastern France, to seventeen-year-old Benoîte Rencurel, between 1664 to 1718, show that the long duration of the Medjugorje visions is not exceptional. This series of apparitions was finally recognized in May 2008, by Bishop Jean-Michel di Falco Leandri, bishop of the diocese of Gap and Embrun, after three years of research by a team of historians, psychologists and theologians. Benoîte saw daily apparitions of the Blessed Virgin for four months, but from that point on only had intermittent apparitions until 1718. So there is a clear difference between this and Medjugorje, where some of the visionaries have claimed daily visions now for forty years.[21]

And this point is only further emphasized by the approval, on 8 December 2010, by Bishop David Ricken, of the apparitions of Our Lady to Adele Brise in Champion, Wisconsin, in 1859, the first such apparitions to gain approval by decree in the United States. The Blessed Virgin appeared to 28-year-old Adele, a Belgian immigrant, only three times, and the shrine of Our Lady of Good Help was thereby eventually established. As is usual with approved apparitions, Mary passed on only brief messages to Adele, focusing on her role as "the Queen of Heaven who prays for the conversion of sinners," while asking her to do the same.[22]

THE MEDJUGORJE VISIONS AND FALSE PROPHETS

But it is claimed that the Blessed Virgin has been appearing daily to at least some of the visionaries for forty years now — that is, tens of thousands of times. What this means in practice, if these events are genuine, is that for some reason Mary has abandoned the approach she has previously taken, of appearing only a relatively small number of times and over a brief period, and instead has been appearing virtually "on demand." As detailed above, the average number of appearances for genuine Marian apparitions has been in single figures — but if Medjugorje is authentic, then suddenly this average has been boosted by a factor of a thousand! And there still seems to be no end in sight to all this activity.

Does this seem probable? Would God change, in such a dramatic fashion, a method of approaching humanity which has been in place for hundreds of years? Is it not rather evidence, as was the case with the large numbers of false prophets who contended with the genuine prophets sent by God in the Old Testament, that these messages are not supernatural?

This is evident, for example, from the fact that Elijah had to face the false prophets of Baal in his struggle against the paganism encouraged by the wicked king of Israel, Ahab, and his wife Jezebel. It is significant that there were four hundred prophets of Baal ranged against the solitary Elijah (1 Kings 18). Likewise, the prophet Micaiah had to face a further four hundred false prophets who foretold victory for Ahab and Jehoshaphat, the king of Judah, if they attacked Ramoth in Gilead. But Micaiah said that it had been revealed to him that a deceptive spirit had been put into the mouths of the false prophets, in order that Ahab should be led to his death, as subsequently happened (1 Kings 22:5–38).

Later on, the prophet Jeremiah complained about the false prophets he had to face (Jer 14:13–15), and similar condemnations are found in Ezekiel against both male and female false prophets (Ezek 13:2–16). Thus, there is nothing new about false prophecies or false messages being propagated. In addition, as the prophet Isaiah indicated (59:1), God's hand is not shortened, that is, he does not have to struggle or shout to get his message across: he is omnipotent. This point is emphatically made in another passage from Isaiah:

> For as the rain and the snow come down from heaven, and return not thither but water the earth, making it bring forth and sprout, giving seed to the sower and bread to the eater, so shall my word be that goes out from my mouth; it shall not return to me empty, but it shall accomplish that which I purpose, and prosper in the thing for which I sent it. (Isa 55:10–11)

God's "word," in the form of the approved Marian apparitions, has been extraordinarily fruitful, and with a minimum of words and appearances. Mary appears once, and for a few hours, at Pontmain and Knock—and probably for no more than half an hour at La Salette—and three great pilgrimage sites spring up: she allegedly appears thousands of times at Medjugorje, and the result for the last forty years has been a story of confusion, disobedience and disorder in the Church.

WHY SO MANY MESSAGES?

Why are there all these messages, then, if they don't tell us anything new? The simplest reason would appear to be that if these alleged visions do not come from God, then unless there was this element of repetition they would quickly have been forgotten.

Vicka spoke about this point in one of her conversations with Fr Bubalo. He asked her why she thought the "Gospa" was appearing to the visionaries for so long a time, and she responded by saying that the Virgin had said that "this was her last appearance on earth," and that she couldn't "accomplish what she wants so fast either." Fr Bubalo then asked her to clarify what she meant by that, to which Vicka replied: "Why, think about it: how would all this seem if the Virgin had appeared only ten or twenty times, and then disappeared. Why, in the hustle and bustle it would have been forgotten by now. Who would believe that she was here?"[23]

Indeed, we have to question whether people would still be going to Medjugorje if the visions had stopped very quickly. As we have seen — according to clear taped testimony — this is what was supposed to have happened; but instead people continue to go there in large numbers, primarily because it is alleged that Mary continues to appear to some of the visionaries every day. Without these daily visions, the whole phenomenon would no doubt have dried up and been long forgotten by now — but instead it is promoted as vigorously as ever, regardless of the problems this is causing for recognized shrines which promote approved messages.

Apart from all that, there is also the rather puzzling aspect of what the messages *haven't* been saying. Given the situation of the Church and the world, and the fact that these alleged messages have been promulgated now for forty years, one would have expected them to be somewhat more relevant than is actually the case. A search of a concordance of Medjugorje messages from 1984 to 2009 reveals that words such as abortion, contraception, pornography and homosexuality are missing. The same is true of adultery, divorce and fornication. Likewise, drugs, murder, lying, lust, and impurity don't get a mention, nor stealing, theft, idolatry, wrath, despair or greed. One exception is "pride" but that refers to the sin of Satan, and not to a human sin.[24]

Conversely, what we do find are references to things like "consumerism," "carelessness" and "curiosity," in the midst of hundreds of commonplace messages. Surely, the great crime of legalized abortion alone would merit repeated references if these messages really did come from the Blessed Virgin. This situation is all the more strange given that the visionaries have hinted at various "chastisements" which will happen unless mankind repents of its sins. This is clear from the letter sent to Rome in 1983 by Fr Vlasic, in which he summarized Mirjana's claims regarding her "secrets," saying: "The ninth and tenth secrets are serious. They concern chastisements for the sins of the world."[25]

PROBLEMS WITH THE FRANCISCANS

Turning now to the Holy See's reaction to Medjugorje: at the beginning this was one of extreme caution and indeed suspicion, as is evident from the following remarks of Cardinal Seper, the then head of the Congregation for the Doctrine of the Faith, which were made in 1981. He was asked to comment about Medjugorje, and, given that he was a Croat and was fully aware of the religious situation in the country, his remarks are doubly significant:

> When the Franciscans obey the decrees of the Holy See then I shall consider this phenomenon, not before. For me, the sign of obedience is the sign of a genuine Catholic faith. Its absence in Medjugorje on the part of the Franciscans, its sponsors and advocates, renders the whole enterprise suspect.[26]

Indeed, as Joachim Bouflet points out, obedience is one of the main criteria for the proper discernment of private revelations — that is, obedience to the legitimate pastors of the Church, and particularly to the local bishop of the diocese where the alleged revelations have taken place. This obedience is linked to humility, and without these two central virtues there can be no question of an authentic private revelation. Padre, now Saint, Pio is a good example of a model religious who submitted without murmur to the disciplinary measures taken against him, even when it could be said that he was treated unjustly.[27]

Obedience was also the central point in the dispute between Bishop Zanic and Frs Ivica Vego and Ivan Prusina. The sections following on this topic are a summary of the relevant material on Marco Corvaglia's "The Medjugorje Illusion" website. This dispute arose because the two Franciscans, who were chaplains in Mostar, refused to accept the bishop's decision that the existing Franciscan parish there should be reduced in size, with the remainder being entrusted to the secular clergy. Frs Vego and Prusina were opposed to this, even though such an action was valid in the light of the papal decree *Romanis Pontificibus*. Accepting this decision was not optional for the Franciscans, since under Canon Law, they were obliged, in line with their vow of obedience, to accept what the bishop wanted, regardless of whether or not they felt they had been badly treated. This incident happened in 1980, the year before the alleged visions began.[28]

"THE POPE CAN SAY WHAT HE WANTS..."

To understand exactly how the two Franciscans became bound up with Medjugorje, we need to examine some of the alleged messages of the "Gospa" relating to them. Fr Vego went to Medjugorje in December 1981, met the visionaries and through them consulted the "Gospa" about his position, and that of Fr Prusina. The result was that messages began to appear defending the rebellious Franciscans, encouraging them in their opposition to the bishop. These messages are found in Vicka's *Rokovnik* (Notebook). In this, for the entry dated 19 December 1981, she writes that she asked the "Gospa" about the Herzegovina "problem" and that the "Gospa" had said that the more guilty party was Bishop Zanic. Regarding Fr Vego, in particular, "she" said that he was not guilty, and should remain in Mostar.[29]

Another message was given on 3 January 1982, and according to Vicka, the "Gospa" said that "Ivica is not guilty. Have him keep the faith even if the Franciscans expel him.... He is not guilty. The bishop does not see to it enough that there is order. It is his fault. But he will not always be bishop. I will show justice in the Kingdom."[30]

Then, less than two weeks later, on 14 January 1982, Vicka, Marija and Jakov went to see the bishop, who was by now aware, through a member of the Franciscan Provincial Council, that Frs Vego and Prusina had said that they would not leave Mostar, citing the above supportive messages. Bishop Zanic asked Vicka whether the "Gospa" had said anything about Frs Vego and Prusina, and she, in union with the other two said, "She did not, we don't know them." Bishop Zanic taped this interview, and repeated this question several times, always getting the same answer. Further messages of support from the "Gospa" to the two Franciscans were issued on 15 and 26 April 1982.[31]

In 1983, Bishop Zanic learned through Fr Radogost Grafenauer, a Slovenian Jesuit who had met the visionaries, about the existence of Vicka's literary output, and the messages from the "Gospa" concerning himself. Fr Grafenauer had copied the relevant passages and let Bishop Zanic see them, and also taped an interview he had with Vicka. A copy of this was also given to Bishop Zanic, and we can look at some of the dialogue:

> Fr Grafenauer: "You told the bishop that he is to blame and that those two [Frs Vego and Prusina] are innocent and that they can perform their priestly duties?"
> Vicka: "Yes I did."
> Fr Grafenauer: "Can they hear confessions? Did Our Lady mention this?"
> Vicka: "Yes."
> Fr Grafenauer: "If Our Lady said this and the Pope says that they cannot..."
> Vicka: "The Pope can say what he wants, I'm telling it as it is."[32]

THE APOSTOLIC SIGNATURA DECISION

Because of their stance, the two Franciscans were repeatedly admonished by the General Curia of the Franciscan Friars Minor in Rome, and were then suspended *a divinis*, before being reduced to the lay state by the Vatican Congregation for Religious. Finally they were dismissed from the Order by the Franciscan General Curia in Rome. But Bishop Zanic reported that they continued to act as priests in the area of the newly founded parish, while also promoting Medjugorje.[33]

The two Franciscans appealed to the Vatican Congregation for Religious on 18 February 1985, but their appeal was unsuccessful. Meanwhile, Fr Vego, having fathered a child by a nun from Mostar, abandoned the religious life, thus leaving Fr Prusina to pursue the matter further.[34]

But on 27 March 1993, the Apostolic Signatura, which, after the pope, is the highest judicial authority in the Catholic Church, recognized that there had been errors made regarding the dismissal from the Order of the two Franciscans, and their reduction to the lay state. This was because the accused had not had a proper opportunity to defend themselves, and also because of procedural errors by what was, at the time, the Congregation for Religious (and is now the Congregation for the Institutes of Consecrated Life). Thus the judgments against them were overturned.

Regarding the role of Bishop Zanic, though, in his action against Fr Prusina in requesting his reduction to the lay state, as presented on 7 January 1983, it should be noted that the Apostolic Signatura did not question the validity of his request, but only the procedural methods of the Congregation for Religious with regard to the decree of dismissal from the Franciscan Order. Where Bishop Zanic is mentioned, his judgment in this case is seen as falling within his sphere of competence.[35]

This case has become something of a *cause célèbre* for Medjugorje supporters, who seem to believe that it shows that Bishop Zanic erred; and indeed there is a good deal of misinformation about this on the internet. In reality, though, Bishop Zanic was not at fault, and, in October 1997, Don Ante Luburic, the chancellor of the Mostar diocese, issued a communiqué in which he accused Fr Laurentin of spreading "disinformation" over this case, while denying his claim that the two Franciscans had been "rehabilitated." He indicated that this was not the case "as regards the abuses they committed," while noting that there had been an "error by omission" by the Congregation for the Institutes of Consecrated Life. He also said that the "interdict" issued against Fr Prusina by Bishop Zanic retained "all its validity, and he has no jurisdiction whatever nor canonical mission in the diocese of Mostar-Duvno," while also pointing out that Fr Vego had "left the Order and the priesthood in 1988."[36]

PROBLEMS WITH FR VLASIC AND FR BARBARIC

During the summer of 1984, Fr Tomislav Vlasic was responsible for a campaign to celebrate the birthday of the Blessed Virgin on 5 August, instead of 8 September, the day on which the Church keeps this festival. The cause of this claim was an alleged interior locution given to Jelena Vasilj, a twelve-year-old girl from Medjugorje. Fr Vlasic tried to persuade Bishop Zanic to comply with this idea, but the bishop declined. And of course, it is hard to see how he could have been expected to change the date of a liturgical feast observed by the universal Church. However, this did not stop news of this new celebration being widely circulated, and as a result, many people came to Medjugorje on 5 August, when the Church actually celebrates the feast of Our Lady of the Snows.

This is a good example of the mischief that can be caused by individuals who try to persuade people that their own ideas are of more importance than the Church's position. It is also further evidence of the Franciscan influence on the visionaries, since the above idea, that 5 August is the birthday of the Blessed Virgin, is apparently a Franciscan tradition.[37]

According to Mrs. Patricia Waters, in April 1984 she was present in the sacristy with about fifty other people waiting for the visionaries to enter, when Fr Slavko Barbaric came in and said: "Unless some of you go out of this room, the apparition will not take place." This was the point at which she began to have suspicions about the whole Medjugorje edifice. How could Fr Barbaric possibly decide on the conditions for Our Lady to appear? Her own explanation for the demeanor of the visionaries at these times was that she thought that they might well have been hypnotized in some way.[38]

In August 1984, in a letter to Bishop Zanic, the Franciscan Provincialate proposed that Fr Barbaric should move to Medjugorje as parish priest, and this request was approved by the bishop. But less than five months later, on 3 January 1985, Bishop Zanic wrote to the

Provincialate asking that Fr Barbaric be transferred from Medjugorje to another position. This was because he was promoting the visions in opposition to the bishop's wishes, despite having been warned about this orally and in writing on numerous occasions.

However, a month later, on 3 February 1985, there was an alleged vision, and Fr Barbaric wrote in the *Chronicle of the Apparitions* that:

> The vision came suddenly. Shorter this evening than in some days, just 2 minutes. Marija, Ivan, and Jakov were present. The message was for friar Slavko, as promised in the vision yesterday. It was given by Ivan. It went as follows: "I would like that Slavko remain here, and attend to all the details and the notes so that at the end of my visit we will have a synoptic image of everything. I am praying especially for Slavko at this time and for all those who work in the parish."[39]

So the bishop requested that Fr Barbaric be removed from Medjugorje because of his persistent disobedience, but the Vision, supposedly the Blessed Virgin, wanted him to stay. The idea that Our Lady is going to explicitly oppose the wishes of the local bishop is clearly fantastic, and indeed another sign of the falsity of these claims.

In addition, as the official newsletter of the Archdiocese of the Metropolis of Sarajevo, *Vrhbosna*, noted early in the year 2000:

> Following a number of official letters between the Episcopal Curia, the Franciscan Provincial and Fra Slavko Barbaric concerning the friar being sent away from Medjugorje, where he had for years been carrying out pastoral work illegally, without the approval of the diocesan curia, the diocesan Ordinary proclaims that Fra Slavko Barbaric is deprived of confessional jurisdiction (the faculties of hearing confessions) in the territories of all dioceses of Hercegovina.[40]

DANGEROUS MANIPULATION AND MORE PROBLEMS

There is also evidence of a tendency on the part of some of the Franciscans to induce other young people to have visions. Louis Bélanger wrote to Fr Laurentin about an incident, in January 1985, when Fr Slavko Barbaric showed him a video in which Fr Ivica Vego was with some youngsters from a village near Medjugorje. He was apparently encouraging them to "see" the "Gospa," insistently asking them if they could see her and giving them writing materials to note any messages they might receive. Bélanger comments that: "It was in the purest tradition of the occult. We know that those who induce automatic writing in young people can cause them more or less permanent damage in their identity formation."

It does not seem that either Fr Barbaric, a psychotherapist, or Fr Vego were concerned about this danger.[41]

This incident is reminiscent of an experiment conducted by the writer Carlos Staehlin, as reported by Fr Karl Rahner, on six youths aged between fifteen and eighteen. They were told to imagine that a battle between medieval warriors was going on above a tree; two apparently saw or heard nothing, two saw the battle and the last two both saw and heard it, with their reports apparently agreeing.[42] Staehlin's experiment was clearly hazardous. He deliberately encouraged the youths to fantasize in what could have been a psychologically dangerous manner, to say nothing of inviting a possible diabolical intervention. Comparisons with experiments with "Ouija" boards, and all the hazards involved in such matters, come to mind.

IVAN'S THREATENING LETTER

Prior to this, as Fr Sivric reports, Bishop Zanic had received what can only be described as a threatening letter from Ivan Dragicevic, dated 21 June 1983. In this, he claimed he had received a message from the "Gospa," in which she demanded the bishop's "immediate conversion on [sic] the happenings in the Medjugorje parish before it is too late," and warned him not to "cause nor incite dissension among the clergy," nor emphasize the "negative side" of the visions. This was to be a "last warning" that he should "convert and change," otherwise the "verdict" of the "Gospa" and her Son would "reach him."

Does it need to be pointed out that it is completely beyond the bounds of credibility to believe that the Blessed Virgin Mary could possibly have given such a message? Although it was established that this letter was written in Ivan Dragicevic's hand, it does not seem at all likely that he actually composed it.[43]

Medjugorje supporters ask why Bishop Zanic changed his mind about the visions, having initially been supportive, with the implication that he had an ulterior motive; but surely no bishop could take Medjugorje seriously after a message like that. What other reason would be required for any sensible person to reject it?

* * *

TO CONCLUDE, THE EVIDENCE EXAMINED IN THIS chapter has brought to light many of the serious problems associated with Medjugorje, including both the content and duration of the messages as they began to develop after the initial visions of the first week, when effectively no messages of any substance were given by the "Gospa." It has also become quite clear that both the visionaries and the Franciscans who have been most involved with them have emerged with serious question marks as to their credibility. But for the most part these negative points have not been disclosed as part of the publicity surrounding Medjugorje. Instead, it has been presented as perfectly acceptable in a religious sense, and this is the impression that most of the pilgrims to Medjugorje have received.

9
Medjugorje: Messages and Secrets

THE ORIGIN OF THE MESSAGES

As we have seen, by mid-1982 Bishop Zanic was quite clear that the visions and the messages associated with them were not genuine, and this was the conclusion he steadfastly maintained from this point onwards, a position maintained by his successor, Bishop Peric. If these later messages are not genuine — and the evidence suggests that this is the case — then we have to ask how they arose.

Fr Rudo Franken tells us that in March 1985, Bishop Zanic wrote to Fr Tomislav Pervan, who at that time was the parish priest at Medjugorje, setting out a list of demands which included preventing the visionaries from appearing in public, and stopping any of the visions taking place in the parish church, or in any building adjacent to it. These demands were partly met in that the visions no longer took place in the "apparition chapel," which was near the sacristy, but moved instead to the presbytery. This took place at the suggestion of Archbishop Franic of Split. But as Fr Franken further points out, what sort of figure does this turn the Blessed Virgin into, that she is unable to decide herself where to appear?[1] How can this possibly be consistent with how Our Lady has appeared in her approved apparitions? Does this not further indicate that Medjugorje cannot be of supernatural origin?

THE NATURE OF THE MEDJUGORJE MESSAGES

Despite the fact that the messages emanating from Medjugorje have been coming out now for forty years, and that this is, in reality, one of the major factors arguing *against* their authenticity, paradoxically, it is precisely this factor which has so greatly impressed many Medjugorje supporters. The argument is put forward that surely "these children" could not possibly have maintained this performance if the whole thing were not genuine. This ignores the fact that in the first place we are mostly not dealing with children, but rather young adults, who now, forty years later, have fully grown up.

Thus, so far, all the evidence we have considered strongly suggests that Medjugorje is not authentically supernatural, but rather that the whole situation was thrust on the visionaries, because within a matter of days thousands of people were thronging the hillside, as the movement quickly gathered momentum. Within the first week or so, they had to make a crucial decision. It is clear from the "three more days" statements on the tape-recordings that they expected the visions to end shortly. But by then an expectation had built up, and it seems as though all the major participants were largely swept along by events, in the face of the rapidly growing crowds and a hostile government.

NO TURNING BACK

It may be that after the visionaries had come down to the church and nothing happened, with a large expectant crowd before them they then felt obliged — or were pressurized — into pretending that once again they had seen something. Or alternatively, those involved may have very quickly realized that unless they continued to act as though they were having visions, the whole thing would just fizzle out — or, more seriously, that some of the villagers would turn against them. The expectations of the local populace had been raised, and they would not take kindly to being fooled. In the volatile and brutal culture of that area, any reaction against them would have no doubt been violent.

Thus, as we have seen, the evidence presented so far strongly suggests that after the first week or so, there was pressure on the visionaries to carry on claiming that the Blessed Virgin really was continuing to appear to them. Once they had given in to this situation, and continued to issue messages, there could be no turning back without great danger. And, of course, with time, and with the growing number of pilgrims, to admit that the whole thing was not genuine would become increasingly difficult, particularly when the community as a whole had effectively committed themselves to the visions.

As the years went by, and the hotels, pizza parlors, restaurants and piety stalls established themselves in Medjugorje, the local population progressively acquired as much of a vested interest in the continuation of the visions as did the visionaries themselves. The visions had brought unprecedented prosperity to the area, and the truth is that if the visionaries or the Franciscans had admitted that the whole phenomenon was not genuine, as Michael Davies points out, they would probably have been lynched.[2]

Wayne Weible describes the situation five years after the visions began, in June 1986:

> Away from Saint James Church, new buildings dotted the landscape. Commercialism grew at a rampant pace, and taxis roamed like a swarm of bees over decrepit bridges and dirt roads that were never intended to support such traffic. The roads were filled with pilgrims, and many villagers were busy adding extensions of rooms to their dwellings to house more pilgrims. For many villagers, the changes were uncomfortable annoyances, offset only by the good fruits of the apparitions.[3]

But no doubt other villagers were quite content with this new influx of wealth into their community.

The overall situation may be even more complicated in that the visionaries and their immediate supporters may have somehow managed to convince themselves that, although the later visions and messages were not genuine, the whole enterprise was justified because of the "good fruits" which were coming from it.

ARCHBISHOP FRANIC INTERVENES

The archbishop of Split, Frane Franic, visited Medjugorje early on, and after seeing the visionaries during an ecstasy, and interviewing them, became convinced "as a private Christian... of their authenticity." It seems that he was swayed, too, by the enormous crowds at Medjugorje, and certainly, despite the fact that he had no direct jurisdiction in the Mostar-Duvno diocese, he apparently implied such authority in his public remarks.

In addition, it seems that, during a December 1984 visit to Medjugorje, he went so far as to consult the "Gospa" about some of his own affairs through the visionary Marija Pavlovic. As Fr Sivric comments, "It is both irritating and deplorable to watch him treat the Virgin Mary like a fortune teller."[4] Thus, it is clear that Archbishop Franic was an early, enthusiastic and uncritical supporter of Medjugorje, and it seems that he played a role amongst fellow ecclesiastics not unlike that played by Fr Laurentin with regard to other theologians. Before his visit to Medjugorje in December 1984, he had been to Rome, and had "discussed the whole matter with John Paul II." He also tells us that "many are calling me from Italy and France and different journalists come to see me."[5]

MORE NEGATIVE EVIDENCE

Bishop Zanic issued a declaration on Medjugorje on 25 July 1987, in which, after detailing his own work and that of the various commissions, he made this heartfelt plea:

> It was said that Our Lady started to appear at Podbrdo on Mount Crnica. When the police stopped people going there, she appeared in people's homes, on fences, in fields, in vineyards and tobacco fields. She appeared in the church, on the altar, in the sacristy, in the choir loft, on the roof, in the bell tower, on the roads, on the road to Cerno, in a car, on a bus, in schools, at several places in Mostar and Sarajevo, in monasteries in Zagreb, in Varazdin, in Switzerland, in Italy, then again at Podbrdo, in Krizevac, in the parish, on the presbytery and so on. This does not list even half the number of locations where apparitions were alleged to have taken place, so that a sober man who venerates Our Lady must ask: "My Lady, what are they making of you?"[6]

Meanwhile, Mirjana Dragicevic had made it known, on 25 December 1982, that she would no longer be receiving daily visions, and that from now on would only see the "Gospa" once a year, on her birthday. She also claimed to have received the last secret of the ten which had been allegedly given to her by Mary. As we will see, Mirjana also said that there would be no more visions of Jesus or Mary on earth. There were also claims of secrets being received on a miraculous sheet of paper made of an indescribable material. Later, another account emerged in which the secret was now in a special code, which would only be revealed when the paper was given to a particular priest, Fr Petar Ljubicic, who would have the grace to understand it. In December 1982, it was stated that the first of the secrets would soon be revealed.[7]

After his release from prison in February 1983, Fr Zovko was sent to a different parish, leaving Fr Vlasic in charge of the visionaries. In December of that same year, the latter wrote to the pope outlining events in his parish. This letter claimed that the visions at Medjugorje were the "last apparitions of the Blessed Virgin on earth," and that this was "why they are lasting so long and occurring so frequently." The visionaries also reiterated their claims that they had received numerous secrets, and spoke of the "visible" sign that would be left at Medjugorje.[8]

SUMMARIZING THE SITUATION

At this stage, it is probably good to summarize some of the main points discussed previously regarding the visions, so that the reader has clearly in mind the grave difficulties associated with accepting Medjugorje as genuine.

Firstly, there are the problems regarding the difficult family background of a number of the visionaries. We also have the inconsistent phenomena surrounding the appearances of the "Gospa," such as the light which preceded her, and the way the Vision emerged from this light. This contrasts markedly with the way Our Lady appeared in her recognized apparitions at Lourdes, Rue du Bac and Fatima, and points strongly to a non-divine source. Then, there are the unthinkable things said or done by the Vision — that, for example, the visionaries saw it holding something like a baby which was then covered up, or that the Vision's hands were trembling, or that they were allowed to touch and kiss the Vision, which was laughing — or equally, the contents of Ivan's letter with their threat that Bishop Zanic should "convert and change" or face the consequences. All of these things, amongst others, raise very serious doubts about the supernatural authenticity of the alleged visions.

Similarly, the fact that the "Gospa" never spoke until one of the visionaries asked questions, and that there was no message of any substance during the first week, such that Fr Zovko was forced to ask why she had appeared at all if this was the case, and then remark that the whole thing looked like clowning to him: all of this is completely out of line with what has happened during the authentic apparitions of Mary. In addition, we have the concerns raised by Fr Zovko that the visionaries might well be seeing Satan, because of the amount of cursing that was still going on in the locality, even as the Vision was supposedly appearing.

There is also the problem of the "Gospa" being asked to do what the visionaries or Fr Zovko wanted, specifically, to appear in the parish church. Or the idea that Mary would continue appearing to the visionaries for as long as they wanted. Since when have authentic visions of the Blessed Virgin ever been "arranged" like this? Then we have Fr Zovko's negative conclusion at the end of the first week, that the "Gospa's" message was only meant for the visionaries, followed by his swift about-turn to support them, possibly on the strength of the idea that he had heard a locution of his own.

There must also be serious reservations about the conduct of those most involved in spreading the messages of Medjugorje, as for example in the way that Fr Laurentin altered the message about the "unbelieving Judases." In fact, just how reliable are any of the messages, given the ample evidence suggesting that they do not have a heavenly origin? And of course, the admission that there were only supposed to be "three more days" of visions — that on Friday, 3 July 1981, the last appearance of the "Gospa" should have taken place — is absolutely fatal to the idea that any of the subsequent messages are genuine.

* * *

IN THIS CHAPTER, THEN, APART FROM THE ABOVE GENeral considerations, we have seen how the evidence suggests that Medjugorje, after the first week, developed as a "pious deception," which could be justified because of the good fruits that the pilgrims were experiencing. But as we have also seen, since then Medjugorje has grown enormously, and taken on a life of its own, to the great detriment of genuine Marian shrines.

10
Fatima and its Effects

THE FATIMA APPARITIONS — MAY TO AUGUST 1917

Having looked in detail, then, at the events of the first week at Medjugorje and their aftermath, we are in a better position to contrast this with the basic details of what happened at Fatima. This should be regarded as the most important Marian apparition, primarily because of its unique approval by and association with the papacy from its inception, culminating in the exceptional developments in the pontificate of Pope St John Paul II, as will be discussed in a later chapter.

Fatima occurred just as the Russian Revolution was unfolding during World War I. As the war dragged on, by 1916, Russia was in a state of crisis, and this gave the Communist revolutionaries under Lenin their chance: just as the Blessed Virgin was appearing in Fatima, between May and October 1917, they were gradually positioning themselves to take power, which they did in November 1917. During the war, Pope Benedict XV made repeated but forlorn pleas for peace, and finally, in May 1917, he made a direct appeal to Mary to intercede for peace in the world. The response was her first appearance at Fatima just over a week later.[1]

Portugal was suffering greatly during this period under an anticlerical republican regime, which freely persecuted the Church. At this time Fatima was just a small village, situated about seventy miles north of Lisbon; the three children to whom the Blessed Virgin appeared were Lucia dos Santos, aged ten, and her cousins Francisco and Jacinta Marto, brother and sister, aged eight and seven respectively.

As already noted, in the spring of 1916, the three children had their first joint encounter with a being who would later identify himself as the "Angel of Portugal." This angel appeared to them twice more with a message emphasizing the necessity of prayer and reparation. These visits prepared the children for their meetings with Mary from May to October of the following year.[2]

The first of these took place on 13 May 1917, when the three children saw the Blessed Virgin at the Cova da Iria near Fatima. She smiled and told them not to be afraid, before saying that she was from heaven. Lucia then asked her what she wanted: "I have come to ask you to come here for six months in succession on the thirteenth day of the month at this same hour. Then I will tell you who I am and what I want. And I shall return here yet a seventh time." The Blessed Virgin finished with a request: "Say the Rosary every day, to bring peace to the world and the end of the war." With that, she began to rise into the air, moving towards the east until she disappeared.

At the next apparition on June 13, the Blessed Virgin again asked Lucia to pray the rosary every day. In reply, Lucia asked her to take them to heaven, but was told that although Jacinta and Francisco would shortly go to heaven, Lucia's task was to promote devotion to her Immaculate Heart throughout the world.[3]

THE VISION OF HELL

On 13 July, Mary again asked Lucia to continue to pray the rosary every day in order to obtain peace for the world and the end of the war. Lucia asked her who she was and for a miracle so everyone would believe: "Continue to come here every month. In October, I will tell you who I am and what I want, and I will perform a miracle for all to see and believe." After this, Mary opened her hands and rays of light from them seemed to penetrate the earth so that the children saw a terrifying vision of hell; this was the first part of the "secret" of Fatima, and was not revealed until much later. She then related the second part of the secret as follows:

> You have seen hell where the souls of poor sinners go. To save them, God wishes to establish in the world devotion to my Immaculate Heart. If what I say to you is done, many souls will be saved and there will be peace. The war is going to end; but if people do not cease offending God, a worse one will break out during the pontificate of Pius XI. When you see a night illumined by an unknown light, know that this is the great sign given you by God that he is about to punish the world for its crimes, by means of war, famine, and persecutions of the Church and of the Holy Father.
>
> To prevent this, I shall come to ask for the consecration of Russia to my Immaculate Heart, and the Communion of Reparation on the First Saturdays. If my requests are heeded, Russia will be converted, and there will be peace; if not, she will spread her errors throughout the world, causing wars and persecutions of the Church. The good will be martyred, the Holy Father will have much to suffer, various nations will be

annihilated. In the end, my Immaculate Heart will triumph.
The Holy Father will consecrate Russia to me and she will be
converted, and a period of peace will be granted to the world.

The first two parts of the secret only became publicly known in 1942, and the third part was only divulged in June 2000.

The children were kidnapped on the morning of 13 August by the mayor of Vila Nova de Ourem and interrogated about the secret; but despite his threats and promises of money, they refused to divulge it. In the afternoon, they were moved to the local prison and threatened with death but determined that they would die rather than reveal the secret. The mayor admitted defeat and they were released. On August 19, Lucia, Francisco and Jacinta were together at a place called Valinhos, near Fatima, where they again saw the Blessed Virgin, who spoke to Lucia: "Go again to the Cova da Iria on the 13th and continue to say the Rosary every day." Mary also repeated her promise to perform a miracle so all would believe, and again asked for prayer and sacrifice for sinners.[4]

THE SEPTEMBER AND OCTOBER APPARITIONS, 1917

On 13 September, the Blessed Virgin once more spoke to Lucia, asking her to continue to pray the rosary in order to obtain the end of the war, again promising a miracle in October so that all would believe. This proclamation of a public miracle naturally caused the most intense speculation throughout Portugal.

On October 13, Mary appeared before them for the last time, as Lucia asked what she wanted: "I want to tell you that a chapel is to be built here in my honor. I am the Lady of the Rosary. Continue always to pray the Rosary every day. The war is going to end, and the soldiers will soon return to their homes." She reported too that Mary grew very sad and said: "Do not offend the Lord our God any more, because He is already so much offended."

Then rising into the air and opening her hands towards the sun, growing more brilliant as she did, she disappeared, to be replaced by various visions of the Holy Family seen only by the children. At the same time, the crowd of 70,000 saw a true miracle. The black clouds parted, and the sun became visible as a dull gray disc that could be looked at directly quite easily. It then began to gyrate and send out different colored rays of light, before appearing to descend towards the ground, such that many of those present thought it was the end of the world. Other people witnessed the solar miracle from a distance, thus ruling out the possibility of any type of collective hallucination.[5]

Francisco and Jacinta were amongst the victims of the influenza epidemic which swept Europe in the autumn of 1918, just as the war was finishing. Francisco received his first Communion, and on the next day, 4 April 1919, he died. Jacinta had to endure much suffering as various attempts were made to treat a painful chest abscess which developed following pneumonia. She finally died on 20 February of the following year, 1920.[6]

LATER APPARITIONS TO SR LUCIA

Lucia was sent away to school, later becoming a religious sister. On 10 December 1925, while at the convent in Pontevedra, Spain, she saw a further apparition, this time of the Blessed Virgin with the Child Jesus. Mary told Sr Lucia to announce that she promised all the graces necessary for salvation to those who, on the first Saturday of five consecutive months, confessed, received Holy Communion, recited five decades of the rosary, and meditated on the rosary for fifteen minutes, all with the intention of making reparation to her Immaculate Heart.

On 13 June 1929, Sr Lucia, while at prayer in the convent chapel at Tuy, to which she had transferred, saw another apparition, this time a representation of the Holy Trinity. She also heard the Blessed Virgin speak to her, asking that the pope, in union with all the bishops of the world, make the consecration of Russia to her Immaculate Heart which she had spoken of during the July 1917 apparition:

> The moment has come in which God asks the Holy Father, in union with all the Bishops in the world, to make the consecration of Russia to my Immaculate Heart, promising to save it by this means. There are so many souls whom the Justice of God condemns for sins committed against me, that I have come to ask reparation: sacrifice yourself for this intention and pray.[7]

The Church, meanwhile, had maintained silence about the apparitions during the years from 1917, and it wasn't until May 1922 that Bishop Correia da Silva issued a pastoral letter on the subject, indicating that he would set up a commission of inquiry. In 1930, he issued another pastoral letter on the apparitions, which, after recounting the events at Fatima, contained the following brief but very important statement:

Fatima and its Effects

In virtue of considerations made known, and others which for reasons of brevity we omit; humbly invoking the Divine Spirit and placing ourselves under the protection of the most Holy Virgin, and after hearing the opinions of our Rev. Advisors in this diocese, we hereby: 1. Declare worthy of belief, the visions of the shepherd children in the Cova da Iria, parish of Fatima, in this diocese, from the 13th May to 13th October, 1917. 2. Permit officially the cult of Our Lady of Fatima.[8]

SR LUCIA AND THE CONSECRATION OF RUSSIA

In September 1935, the remains of Jacinta were removed to Fatima, and, on opening the coffin, her face was found to be incorrupt. This led the bishop to ask Sr Lucia to write what she knew of Jacinta, and this is how she came to compose her *First Memoir*, under obedience, which recounted the basic facts about Fatima, and which was ready by Christmas 1935.

In passing, it might be remarked how this contrasts strongly with the actions of the Medjugorje visionaries and their supporters, who, purely on their own initiative, have propagated accounts of their visions and publicized themselves worldwide, without any reference to the local Ordinary.

Following the outbreak of the Spanish Civil War, apparently a fulfillment of the prophecy about Russia spreading its errors, Sr Lucia's confessor, Fr Gonzalves, wrote to her asking what should be done. She replied in May 1936, and again pointed out that it was necessary that the Holy Father make the consecration of Russia, before describing how she had asked Jesus in prayer why he would not convert Russia without it. She received the following answer as an interior locution: "Because I want My whole Church to acknowledge that consecration as a triumph of the Immaculate Heart of Mary, so that it may extend its cult later on, and put the devotion to this Immaculate Heart beside the devotion to My Sacred Heart."

To this, Sr Lucia replied: "But my God, the Holy Father probably won't believe me, unless You Yourself move him with a special inspiration." She then heard the following answer: "The Holy Father. Pray very much for the Holy Father. He will do it, but it will be very late. Nevertheless the Immaculate Heart of Mary will save Russia. It has been entrusted to her." After consulting a colleague, Fr Gonzalves wrote to Bishop Correia da Silva urging him to contact Rome on the matter of the consecration of Russia, and this the bishop did early in 1937.[9]

THE PORTUGUESE BISHOPS CONSECRATE THEIR COUNTRY

In 1931, the Portuguese bishops had collectively consecrated Portugal to Mary's Immaculate Heart, and in 1936, at the site of the apparitions, with the prospect of the country being afflicted with Communism because of the conflict raging in neighboring Spain, they made a vow to organize a national pilgrimage to Fatima if Portugal was delivered from this fate. Their country was indeed preserved from Communism, and as a result they were able to return in May 1938 to fulfill their vow and renew the previous consecration, being joined by half a million ordinary Portuguese. Following a spiritual retreat, under Fr Pinto, the spiritual director of Alexandrina da Costa, a Portuguese mystic beatified in 2004, the Portuguese bishops also petitioned the pope, asking that he consecrate the whole world to the Immaculate Heart of Mary, so that it could be saved from disaster, just as Portugal had been delivered from the threat of Communism.

On 25 January 1938, a strange light filled the skies of northern as well as, most unusually, southern Europe. It was described as a particularly brilliant display of the *aurora borealis*, but Sr Lucia realized that it was the "unknown light" foretold by the Blessed Virgin during the July apparition. Sr Lucia apparently informed the bishop of the importance of this sign and again referred to it in her third memoir.[10]

SR LUCIA AND THE CONSECRATION OF 1942

In December 1940, Sr Lucia, under obedience, also wrote to the new pope, Pius XII, telling him that part of the secret that concerned the consecration of Russia and the Communions of reparation. In this she asked the pope to extend the First Saturdays devotion to the whole world, and revealed that Jesus had made it known to her that he would shorten the "days of tribulation" that mankind was then undergoing. But this was on condition that Pius XII "consecrate the world to the Immaculate Heart of Mary, with a special mention for Russia, and order that all the Bishops of the world do the same...."

The time was not ripe, then, for the particular consecration of Russia, but God was prepared to accept a general consecration of the world, with mention of Russia, as a means of shortening the war. In this letter to the pope, Sr Lucia also made the following statement, which included a reference to the consecration of Portugal to Mary's Immaculate Heart made in 1931, and renewed in 1938, as the situation in Europe worsened:

> Most Holy Father, if in the union of my soul with God I have not been deceived, our Lord promises a special protection to our country in this war, due to the consecration of the nation by the Portuguese Prelates to the Immaculate Heart of Mary; as proof of the graces that would have been granted to other nations, had they also consecrated themselves to Her.

The fact that Portugal was able to keep out of the Second World War, in contrast to its involvement in World War I, was undoubtedly a sign for the pope and the bishops of the world of the power of this consecration, and probably contributed to Pius XII's decision to go ahead with the consecration of the world in 1942. In 1940, it looked as though Hitler's forces would soon overrun the whole of Europe, including Portugal, and so this was no empty promise on Sr Lucia's part. The danger of Spain entering the war, and the pressure Portugal was under from the Allies to be allowed to use its territories, meant that all through 1941 the threat of the country being forced into the war was certainly real.

On 31 October 1942, Pope Pius XII spoke to the Portuguese people in a radio message. In this, he alluded to the way that his predecessor, Pius XI, had acknowledged the miraculous intervention of the Blessed Virgin in Portugal, and how this had led to the transformation of the country. He invited them to trust in Mary's maternal protection and pray for an end to the war, before continuing with the formula of consecration of the globe, including Russia, although this was not mentioned specifically by name. Thus, in this act Pope Pius XII consecrated the whole world to Mary's Immaculate Heart, whilst also going on to recall the consecration of the world to the Sacred Heart of Jesus, made by Pope Leo XIII in 1899.

This was not the complete consecration asked for by the Blessed Virgin at Fatima, but it was sufficient for God to intervene and shorten the war. This is apparent from a letter written by Sr Lucia to Fr Gonzalves in May 1943, in which she stated that the true penance that God demanded was for everyone to fulfill their religious and civil duties, before going on to say: "He promises that the War will soon end, on account of the action that His Holiness deigned to perform. But since it was incomplete the conversion of Russia has been put off to later."

It certainly seems that Winston Churchill, the British wartime leader, thought that the turning point in the war came a few days after the date of the consecration, a reference to the Second Battle of El Alamein, in North Africa, between 23 October and 4 November 1942, which saw the defeat of Rommel's forces.[11]

PORTUGAL BEFORE AND AFTER FATIMA

A common claim made by Medjugorje supporters is that it represents the continuation or fulfillment of Fatima. But if we compare the events which have taken place in and around Medjugorje since 1981 with what happened in Fatima and Portugal from 1917 onwards, then the contrast between the two is quite stark. To do this it is necessary to retrace our steps somewhat.

During the nineteenth century, a rising tide of anti-clericalism in Portugal culminated in the assassination of the king and his son on 1 February 1908, and the proclamation of a republic on 5 October 1910. This revolution led to a period of vicious persecution of the Church, resulting in the law of the separation of the Church and state, which was voted in on 20 April 1911. When Pope St Pius X denounced this law's enactments most of the bishops were exiled and many priests were imprisoned, including the future bishop of Leiria-Fatima, Bishop Correia da Silva. The author of this law, Afonso Costa, openly boasted that "thanks to this law of separation, in two generations Catholicism will be completely eliminated from Portugal." Such was the ferocity of the campaign against the Church, and the power of the anti-clerical movement, that there appeared to be nothing to stop the Church's enemies from achieving their objective.

So what happened after 1917 to cause the bishops of Portugal to make the following declaration, on the occasion of the silver jubilee of the apparitions in May 1942: "If someone had shut his eyes twenty-five years ago and were to open them again today, he would no longer recognize Portugal, so profound and vast is the transformation brought about by the factor of the modest and invisible apparition of the Holy Virgin at Fatima"? On the same occasion, the Patriarch of Lisbon, Cardinal Cerejeira, said there was only one word to describe what had happened in the past twenty-five years: "miracle."

A COUNTRY TRANSFORMED

This astounding transformation, peacefully and from within, was brought about by two principal factors. The immediate cause was the tireless response of the poor and simple people of Portugal, who came on pilgrimage to Fatima in their tens of thousands from all over the country, praying the rosary, singing hymns and doing penance. They rejoiced that Our Lady had come down to them from heaven, in the midst of their sufferings, with her message of consolation and salvation.

October 1922 saw the publication of the first edition of the Fatima shrine's journal for pilgrims, *Voz da Fatima*, in order to make known her message and the marvels of grace and conversion that were taking place. It began with three thousand copies. In just three years, this figure had risen to fifty thousand, and by 1937, it had a circulation of 380,000. As well as the pilgrimages, there were also miraculous cures. These were collected in a book by the first historian of Fatima, Canon Formigão, who cited some twenty-four cases between 1917 and 1922. *Voz da Fatima* described more than eight hundred cures which took place in the twenty years from 1922 to 1942.

The substantial numbers of people coming on pilgrimage — 300,000 by May 1931 — and the remarkable conversions taking place, in turn won over those priests who had been indifferent or even hostile, and resulted in an explosion of vocations. When Bishop da Silva was appointed to the diocese of Leiria in 1920, the seminary was closed; by 1933, it had seventy-five seminarians. In the diocese of Portalegre, there were eighteen seminarians in 1917; by 1933, the number had risen to 201, and there was a similar steady and marked upsurge in the numbers of priests, which continued to rise until the 1960s.

The second factor in the miraculous transformation of the country was the willingness of the Portuguese bishops to accept Our Lady's message, and in particular, as has been previously noted, their action in consecrating Portugal to the Immaculate Heart of Mary in 1931. This saved the country from the Communist revolution that was engulfing Spain. Later, in 1938, this consecration was solemnly renewed in thanksgiving for Portugal's preservation from that tragic conflict.

By the time of the silver jubilee of the apparitions in 1942, it was apparent that during the preceding eleven years, Portugal had been miraculously preserved in peace and freedom from the fearful persecution suffered by the Church during that period in Spain. And it had also been preserved from entanglement in the Second World War. The transformation was so extraordinary that Cardinal Cerejeira was able to tell a French journalist in 1942, "Today you would hardly be able to find a handful of enemies of religion throughout the entire country."[12]

To sum up, this was all brought about by the great fidelity of the people in responding to Our Lady's requests, particularly the daily recitation of the rosary, done, as her message of 13 May 1917 had said, "in order to obtain peace for the world and the end of the war." This was in conjunction with the bishops signifying their formal acceptance of the Blessed Virgin's message by consecrating the country to her Immaculate Heart, in 1931, in 1938 and in 1940. In short, one can say that the apparitions of the Blessed Virgin at Fatima, and her message of prayer, penance, reparation and the rosary, brought about nothing less than the resurrection of the Church in Portugal.

FURTHER CONSECRATIONS

Nor was Portugal the only country to benefit from a Marian consecration. The intervention of Mary to obtain the deliverance of Poland from Communism in recent years can be traced back to the consecration of the country to the Immaculate Heart of Mary made on 8 September 1946. This was done at the Marian shrine at Jasna Gora in the presence of 700,000 Poles, using the same form of words that Pius XII had used in his consecration of the world to Mary's Immaculate Heart in 1942. Poland was thus the first country to follow the example of Portugal in making this consecration.

In 1952, as a further sign of the importance he attached to Fatima, Pope Pius XII had specifically consecrated Russia to Mary's Immaculate Heart, on 7 July, the feast of Saints Cyril and Methodius. This, however, was not done in union with all the bishops of the world, and so it did not qualify as the full collegial consecration asked for by Mary.

Pope Paul VI recalled the 1942 consecration of Pius XII, and also referred with approval to Fatima, during the Second Vatican Council, but he chose not to make the collegial consecration asked for by the Blessed Virgin, even though he was in the presence of the world's bishops. He did, however, declare Mary "Mother of the Church" at the close of the third session of the Council, on 21 November 1964. In 1967, he went to Fatima, on 13 May, the Golden anniversary of the first apparition, and presented Sr Lucia to the assembled crowds, thus giving further papal approval to Fatima. At this stage, no reigning Pope had even been to Lourdes, let alone the shrine of any other modern Marian apparition, so this was a very significant move.[13]

* * *

Fatima and its Effects

JUST ABOUT EVERYTHING, THEN, IN THE ABOVE ACCOUNT indicates that there are very sharp, indeed irreconcilable, differences between what happened and Fatima and the events at Medjugorje. The children of Fatima were innocent, the apparitions they experienced were few in number, the message itself was coherent and has proved to be of vital importance for the Church, while the whole series of events was confirmed by the miracle of the sun. Medjugorje, though, by contrast, has shown itself to be deficient in all these areas. Similarly, as we will see, there is no comparison between what happened in Portugal after Fatima and what has taken place in the Balkans following Medjugorje. Regarding the former, the apparitions at Fatima led to a profound change in Portugal, while ten years after the first visions at Medjugorje, Yugoslavia became embroiled in a vicious civil war.

All of the above points, then, indicate the powerful influence that Fatima has had, not only on Portugal but also on world history. In subsequent chapters this influence will be contrasted with Medjugorje and its aftermath, in a way that will make it clear that it is completely fanciful to regard Medjugorje as any sort of continuation of Fatima.

11

The Medjugorje Propaganda Offensive

A RUSH OF BOOKS ON MEDJUGORJE

By 1984, Medjugorje was starting to become known in the wider Catholic world, principally because of the appearance of publications promoting it, some of which were authored by well-known theologians. Among these, as noted previously, Fr René Laurentin was certainly the most prominent, and it is hard to overstate his role in the worldwide promotion of Medjugorje. It is not an exaggeration to say that without his backing, it could not have attained such a prominent role in the Church. He tells us that he was the first to make Medjugorje known in France, in an article in *Figaro*, as early as 23 February 1982. He was also responsible for translating and supplementing a book on the alleged visions by Fr Ljudevit Rupcic, which was eventually published in English, in 1984, under the title, *Is the Virgin Mary Appearing at Medjugorje?* This was described by E. Michael Jones as "the book that launched the entire Medjugorje phenomenon," and an indication of its popularity can be seen on the cover of the 1988 edition (the sixth printing), which was emblazoned with the slogan, "90,000 sold in the U. S. A.!"[1]

To grasp Fr Laurentin's crucial role in the promotion of Medjugorje, it is necessary to realize the high reputation he had previously gained as a mariologist. He had written a number of very influential Marian books, and in particular was regarded as an expert on Lourdes, having authored the standard six-volume work on the subject. He had also produced studies of the apparitions at Rue du Bac and Pontmain, and in addition had worked as a *peritus* or expert at Vatican II.[2] Thus, when he threw his weight behind Medjugorje such support was bound to be of great significance.

But the crucial point is that there is a big difference between the type of historical-theological investigations into past apparitions which he had previously undertaken, and a "hands-on" study of an ongoing phenomenon as complex as Medjugorje. The undoubted skills which he possessed in investigating the former were not the only ones that were required in order to discern and correctly explain a continuing series of alleged visions. With regard to Medjugorje, it would regrettably appear, as we will see further on, that Fr Laurentin found himself drawn into the whole phenomenon and became too personally involved in it, and thereby lost that very necessary sense of detachment which is essential if one is to arrive at a properly informed judgment which is both impartial and objective.

Another very early and influential book was *The Apparitions of Our Lady at Medjugorje*, by Fr Svetozar Kraljevic. This was published by the Franciscan Herald Press, also in 1984. It consists of an outline of the visions, along with various testimonies and interviews. A similarly important promoter has been Fr Robert Faricy, SJ, an emeritus professor of spirituality formerly at the Gregorian University in Rome, who coauthored, with Sr Lucy Rooney, *Mary Queen of Peace: Is the Mother of God Appearing in Medjugorje?* This, too, was published in 1984, by Alba House. The book by leading mariologist Fr Michael O'Carroll, CSSp, *Medjugorje: Facts, Documents, Theology*, was published in 1986, as was Mark Miravalle's *The Message of Medjugorje: The Marian Message to the Modern World*, while Mary Craig's *Spark from Heaven: The Mystery of the Madonna of Medjugorje*, was published in 1988. Like the other works mentioned above, this last volume presented Medjugorje in a largely favorable light.

Thus, even before the end of the 80s, a whole series of publications promoting Medjugorje were in wide circulation amongst Catholics in the West, and were having a marked effect. At this time, the only substantial titles to appear in English criticizing the Medjugorje phenomenon were E. Michael Jones's *Medjugorje: the Untold Story* (Fidelity Press, South Bend, 1988), and Fr Sivric's *The Hidden Side of Medjugorje* (Psilog, Québec, 1989). But their impact was limited in the face of the flood of books and media publicity in favor of Medjugorje.

CRITICISM OF THE MEDJUGORJE CRITICS

One critic of E. Michael Jones's work, Daniel Klimek, argues that his book "has been largely discredited... by a former supporter of Jones," that is Fr Robert Fox. But the fact that Fr Fox withdrew his support for Jones' first book on Medjugorje does not necessarily mean that the facts in the book are wrong. In order to determine that, we would need to have precise details of exactly what points Fr Fox was making, but these are not indicated by Klimek, who just gives some general reasons given by Fr Fox, including "the integrity of methodology and [his] journalistic responsibility." Those are serious charges but Fr Fox did not substantiate them (or at least Klimek provides no evidence of this), and so it's difficult to assess their weight.

In any case, just because one person, Fr Fox, withdrew his support for the book, that doesn't "discredit" it — there have to be precise reasons, supported by clear evidence, for making such a charge. In fact, the allegations that Jones made against Fr Vlasic, of sexual misconduct amongst other things, which is what Fr Fox was presumably referring to, have, it would seem, been substantiated, as we will see, in the Congregation for the Doctrine of the Faith declaration issued against Fr Vlasic in 2008; but exactly what these sexual matters are has not been revealed. The canonical status of Fr Vlasic was made public because his actions had led to him being reported to the CDF in connection with Medjugorje, for, amongst other things, charges "contra sextum," that is, in connection with the Sixth Commandment, and thus relating to sexual matters.

The specific sexual allegations dealt with by Jones are not discussed in this book, and so in this instance there has not been any reliance on him as a source. In any case, critics of Jones have not demonstrated that any of the material facts which he provides, and which have been quoted in this book, are incorrect.[3]

Fr Sivric's book came in for criticism from Randall Sullivan, the author of a later pro-Medjugorje book published in 2004, *The Miracle Detective*. In this, Sullivan stated that: "The volume was an astonishingly shoddy compendium of rumor, gossip, and outright falsehoods that concluded the apparitions had been produced by a combination of imagination and fabrication, and clearly were 'a copy of Lourdes.'"

As we have seen, though, Fr Sivric's book provides the primary evidence for what actually happened during the early days of the visions, and it would appear that Sullivan was relying on the views of his Medjugorje contacts. He provides no evidence of the "outright falsehoods" he mentions, or any hard evidence to back up his assertions. And this is despite the fact that he was obviously aware of the existence of the tapes and thus should have realized their significance. It is not clear if he used material from the tape transcripts, or from later interviews with the visionaries, in giving his own version of what happened, since, although he does mention some of the points found in Fr Sivric's book, the wording he uses is different and there are also discrepancies over dating; in addition, he gives no references to his sources.

What is clear, though, is that Sullivan definitely states that the visions were supposed to end on 3 July, and he even quotes Vicka as saying on that occasion: "This evening the Madonna gave messages for us, and not for the world... *She appeared for the last time this evening.*" However, despite this, bizarrely, he accepts the visionaries' later accounts of further visions.[4]

As for Randall Sullivan's knowledge of the subject, the problem is that he was not a Catholic, and indeed displays a degree of ignorance about the Catholic Faith and basic Catholic terminology. For example, he talks of priests who "take" rather than "hear" confessions, and also doesn't seem to realize that friars and monks are quite different. As he himself admits, "most of what I knew of the Catholic Church... had been learned through my liaisons with women who were fallen from the faith." Clearly, this is not likely to be the most reliable source of catechesis, and so Sullivan's expertise is questionable. Even if we grant that he learned a good deal about the Church during his investigations, the fact remains that he received much of his further "catechesis" within the environment of "Medjugorjean" emotionalism, rather than in a more sober setting.

Apart from that, it is clear that once the Medjugorje "apparatus" realized that he was a reporter from *Rolling Stone* magazine, he was welcomed with open arms, and given very privileged access to the visionaries and their Franciscan associates, to the extent of even being able to stay with Mirjana. This is his description of his first encounter with her:

> The moment I met Mirjana, I knew she was neither a liar nor a lunatic, at least not of any sort I knew about. The young woman's eyes were the blue of alpine lakes, luminous with clarity, unnerving in their repose. Her gaze was penetrating but did not probe. She struck me as quite sure of herself yet entirely unassuming.

This quote surely demonstrates that Randall Sullivan simply wasn't a suitable person to investigate alleged visions. His approach is based on feelings. He intuitively feels that Mirjana is genuine, therefore she must be genuine. *I feel therefore I am.* So much for a rigorous process of discernment.

Sullivan also had no difficulty in meeting most of the other visionaries, including Vicka. And just over a week after his arrival, he was introduced to Fr Slavko Barbaric, at the time the spiritual director of the visionaries. What becomes clear, as the text unfolds, is that Fr Barbaric and the visionaries entirely succeeded in persuading Sullivan that Medjugorje was genuine. The Franciscan priest even arranged for him to meet with a famous recipient of an alleged Medjugorje "miraculous healing," and from then on he was even more firmly in the Medjugorje camp.

In sum, Randall Sullivan goes into great detail about the visions, but everything is portrayed in an almost exclusively uncritical light.[5] This is not to say one cannot find some useful information in the book, but overall his conclusions need to be treated with great caution.

Summing up the situation regarding the effect of all the favorable books, Paolo Apolito did not hesitate to state that:

> With Medjugorje, we are dealing with one of the most powerful publicity campaigns ever conducted around a religious phenomenon, as was noted from the very beginning, and from the interior of the ecclesiastic world, when *La Civiltà Cattolica* remarked, diplomatically, on the "impression" that there might be "a publicity campaign, very well organized on a grass-roots basis."

He goes on to speak of a "veritable flood of books, articles, video-cassettes, film clips, radio and television programs...[which] poured first into the European countries that are traditionally most open to these phenomena, such as Italy, France, Germany, Spain, and Ireland, and then on to the rest of the world." He particularly points to Italy, and the Medjugorje periodical *Eco di Maria*, which in 2005 had a print run of 800,000 copies and was published in 15 different languages.[6]

INCORRECT METHODOLOGY

The main point to note about the above publications favorable to Medjugorje is that they all base themselves on testimonies from the visionaries recorded some time after the visions, rather than the transcripts of their talks with the parish clergy during the first week, as detailed in the books by Fr Sivric and Daria Klanac. For instance, the interviews conducted by Fr Kraljevic date from early 1983, that is, some eighteen months or more after the original visions. As we have seen previously, the tape transcripts are far more likely to be accurate than anything documented so much later. But that is just the problem: the whole Medjugorje movement has been largely built on these later testimonies, which do not reveal the whole truth about what happened in the critical first week.

In addition, the general level of compilation of the messages produced at Medjugorje has been less than perfect, as even Fr Laurentin acknowledges: "There are a great number of words, and they have not been kept methodically. The first register of the parish, where the events had been written, has been confiscated [by the authorities]. Many of the words have been repeated without anyone making an attempt to write them down."[7]

Mark Miravalle's *The Message of Medjugorje* is, in his own words, a "theological analysis of the content of the messages" given at Medjugorje, but he claims to make "no explicit judgment as to the supernatural character of the apparitions." Rather he is trying to determine if the essential content of the Medjugorje messages is in harmony with the Gospels and the writings of the Apostolic Fathers, as well as the documents of Vatican II and post-conciliar statements, and with what has taken place at approved apparitions.[8]

The problem with this approach is that it is putting the cart before the horse — before we can investigate the content of the messages in the above way, we should first determine if the messages themselves are credible. And looking at the sources used by Miravalle, this is not the case with his book; indeed, anyone with some theological knowledge can make up messages which conform to the above criteria. He relies almost exclusively on *Is the Virgin Mary Appearing at Medjugorje?* as co-authored by Fr Laurentin and Fr Rupcic, and Fr Kraljevic's *The Apparitions of Our Lady at Medjugorje*. But as we have seen, the information in these books is based on quite late interviews and not the tape transcripts. The same is true of Miravalle's attempts to see Medjugorje as a continuation of Lourdes and Fatima — unless we have accurate messages to begin with, it is impossible to do this.

DENIS NOLAN AND MEDJUGORJE

Denis Nolan's book *Medjugorje: A Time for Truth and a Time for Action* was published in 1993, at a time when the early practices associated with Medjugorje, the prayer, the fasting and so on, had certainly struck a chord with many Catholics. But already, the basic flaws in the approach taken by Medjugorje enthusiasts like Nolan were becoming apparent. This becomes obvious if we look at the structure of the book. After an introductory chapter, and some testimony from Pope John Paul II and Mother Teresa, the rest of the long first section of the book is taken up with testimonies from various cardinals, bishops and theologians in support of Medjugorje. This takes us up to page 105.

There are then further sections dealing with secular sources and Medjugorje; attempts to defend the authenticity of the visions; responses to criticism of Medjugorje from various Catholic authors; and finally, sections detailing some of the messages, and then further responses to criticisms in a lengthy series of appendices.[9] So all in all, Nolan had to adopt quite a defensive stance, a sign that not everybody was as enthusiastic about Medjugorje as he would have liked.

As regards the long initial sections, from the religious and secular sources in favor of Medjugorje, it must be emphasized that no matter how many churchmen have expressed their approval of it, or how eminent they are, that *of itself* adds nothing to the argument. This even applies to the pope. Their statements are just their private opinions and have no official standing. This obviously applies even more in the case of the views of secular publications and media outlets on Medjugorje. Piling up testimony after testimony of this sort is meaningless as regards *discerning* the authenticity of an alleged vision. It looks impressive and no doubt is influential for some people, but that is only because they don't understand the spiritual principles involved.

The opening quote to the section attempting to defend the authenticity of the visions is very revealing as far as Denis Nolan's attitude to Medjugorje is concerned:

> Let's face it. Prima facie, the Medjugorje apparitions appear to be "for real" beyond a shadow of a doubt. As the television cameras peered into the apparition room and zoomed in on the visionaries conversing with the Gospa, we knew in the pit of our stomachs that something extraordinary was taking place here.[10]

That sums up the attitude of convinced Medjugorje supporters such as Nolan: his espousal of the visions was not based on any objective discernment of the facts, but was quite literally a "gut-reaction." Nolan's views on the subject are colored by this highly emotive response, and so he sees everything about Medjugorje in a positive light. Thus legitimate critical points against Medjugorje are dismissed as "deceit-driven doubt and malicious attack."[11] The idea that anyone can have serious, objective criticisms of the phenomenon is dismissed as impossible and absurd.

The points which Denis Nolan puts forward in support of Medjugorje are dealt with elsewhere in this book, so there is no need for a detailed analysis of his position at this point, except to say that events have overtaken him and that many arguments which seemed supportive of the visions in the early days have subsequently been shown to be flawed.[12]

FR LAURENTIN'S PRO-MEDJUGORJE ARGUMENTS

Regarding Fr Laurentin and his participation in Medjugorje, this is what Fr Michael O'Carroll has to say about him in his book: because of "his unique qualification and of his entire involvement, *he is part of the event.*" Further on he says: "He became more and more deeply involved, *entangled is a better word,* in the subsequent development. He was, before long, entirely convinced of the authenticity and felt it his duty to answer criticism, to defend the visionaries."[13]

Here we come to the heart of Fr Laurentin's difficulty with regard to Medjugorje, namely that he allowed himself to become *entangled* in it. That is, instead of maintaining a proper attitude of reserve, as is fitting for a theologian investigating alleged mystical phenomena — and as the Church herself always does, when officially investigating such phenomena — he allowed himself to become too closely involved with proceedings, and ended up uncritically accepting Medjugorje.

If we look at some of Fr Laurentin's arguments in favor of Medjugorje in detail, we can see that they are essentially subjective. One of his major points is that although Beauraing and Banneux in Belgium, in the 1930s, are regarded as the last Marian apparitions to be accepted by the Church, many of the more than two hundred visions which are alleged to have taken place since then were, in his view, actually authentic. He questions whether we should consider that they are all illusory, before continuing: "Is it not rather that they took place in a cultural and ecclesial environment in which they could never have been recognized?" He also maintains that: "Real discernment such as that made by Bishop Laurence at Lourdes, in a manner exemplary for his day, does not seem possible any longer."[14]

He makes similar points in a later work:

Will the Church recognize the apparitions at Medjugorje? The presuppositions which are predominant today in theology (like exegesies [sic] and universal culture) are contrary to all recognition of apparitions. If none of those which occurred in the past 50 years received official recognition, Medjugorje has very little chance of escaping the common rule.[15]

It is difficult to see how these statements can be justified, since they imply that the various Episcopal commissions which investigated those alleged visions, and either refused to accept them or pronounced negatively, were in error. If we believe that the Holy Spirit is guiding the Church — and that includes the bishops who have to deal with visions and visionaries — then, assuming that they have carried out their job properly, and invoked the assistance of the Holy Spirit, Catholics loyal to the Church should give proper weight to their decisions.

The real reason, it would seem, that Fr Laurentin is apparently so keen to accept many of the visions alleged to have taken place since the 1930s is that they support his own position on Medjugorje, rather than that they have any intrinsic merit of their own. What he describes as a "hypercritical mentality" is actually just the normal functioning of the Church's hierarchy in this area, which always acts with great caution and prudence because of the ever-present danger of false visionaries disrupting the unity and peace of the Church.

This is evident from the work of researchers such as Bernard Billet who details 210 alleged visions which took place between 1928 and 1971. Although in most of these cases no decision was taken by the relevant ecclesiastical authority, as regards nearly thirty of these alleged visions a negative decision was returned. According to another researcher, Yves Chiron, the period between 1971 and 1981, when Medjugorje began, tells a similar story, except that of nearly thirty alleged visions nine were subject to a negative decision.[16]

This is a much higher percentage than was the case with the earlier period. In other words, the trend, if anything, prior to Medjugorje, was towards a greater likelihood of condemnation on the part of local bishops when dealing with such phenomena. More recent research, carried out by Paolo Apolito, claims that in the United States, between 1945 and 1979, a period of nearly 35 years, there were only 21 reports of visions, while in the 20 years following 1980, there have been more than 150 such reports.[17]

THE PROLONGING OF THE VISIONS

Another major argument advanced by Fr Laurentin involves his attempts to justify the very large number of visions. For example, he says: "The prolonging of the apparitions to an apparently excessive degree is justified by the spiritual formation that the young people and those of the town are receiving to an ever-greater degree. This is a major aspect of Medjugorje."[18]

At first glance, this seems plausible enough, but on examination, it proves to be a rather insubstantial argument. If the Medjugorje visionaries needed such an extensive "spiritual formation," extending, at the time, to three years of daily visions, how do we explain the fact that the illiterate Bernadette of Lourdes was privileged with fewer than twenty apparitions; or that the children of Fatima only saw Our Lady half a dozen times at the Cova da Iria and Valinhos? Note that this supposed paucity of apparitions was not a barrier to the sanctification of Bernadette, nor of Jacinta and Francisco.

Indeed, to argue that daily apparitions are necessary to "spiritual formation" suggests that at Medjugorje there was a real deficiency in the power of the Vision, who needed to prolong the apparitions over a period of years in order to bring about what the Blessed Virgin was easily able to achieve at Lourdes and Fatima in a matter of months. In short, how could extending such a "spiritual formation," to include daily visions for forty years now, possibly be justified?

THE VISIONARIES COMPARED WITH THE SAINTS

It has been argued that these daily visions for the Medjugorje visionaries follow the type of pattern that we find in the lives of some of the saints, and that this is thus an argument in their favor. It is certainly true that we can read of such events in the lives of modern saints and holy people such as Gemma Galgani, Padre Pio and Alexandrina da Costa, who were quite often privileged with apparitions or visions of Jesus or Mary. But there was usually a price to pay for this privilege, and that price was suffering—often extreme suffering. As we will see, this is in marked contrast to the affluent lifestyles of a number of the Medjugorje visionaries, with their large houses, expensive cars and frequent foreign trips.

Another characteristic of the holy persons mentioned above, and of many others like them, apart from the fact that they suffered, was their extreme humility, which made them shrink from any self-advertisement or self-promotion. Again, as we will see, this contrasts very sharply with the Medjugorje visionaries who have been very much a part of the whole process of promoting Medjugorje worldwide. In particular, we find that the saints were very reluctant to reveal that they had been recipients of divine favors such as visions or apparitions, a point that is confirmed by Fr Augustin Poulain. Although he wasn't focusing on alleged visionaries in the modern sense, but on what might be described as revelations to holy persons and saints, still, his approach can, by extension, also be applied to them. He says:

> Among those virtues that a revelation should bring in its train, one that should shine forth most brilliantly, and regarding which it is of paramount importance to be informed, is humility. It is the one most opposed to our nature and of which Satan has the greatest horror.... Pride, on the contrary, is the mark of diabolic illusion or imposture. It shows itself by... *an independent spirit with regard to Superiors and directors*... by the refusal to submit to the necessary examination and by anger. It is a sign of pride, and therefore of illusion, *to have a craving to divulge the graces we believe ourselves to have received*. Humility leads to their concealment, except in the somewhat rare cases of real utility.

He also says that in the case of a genuine revelation, we ought to expect real spiritual progress for the visionary concerned. He speaks of "a great advance in sanctification" as a positive sign, but conversely, "If the seer of the vision has remained at an ordinary level of virtue, his visions must be regarded with suspicion."

He also makes the point that any evil tendencies amongst visionaries "may not show themselves at the outset," before going on to say: "What the Devil cannot do is incline the soul towards solid virtues in a real and durable manner. But he can, by a ruse, feign to encourage them for a time... Provided the end is evil, the road leading up to it matters little to him."[19]

The problem, then, for acceptance of the claims of the Medjugorje visionaries is that their activities fall between two stools, so to speak. On the one hand, it is clear that they are definitely not in the same category as saintly individuals such as those indicated above, who were privileged with visions or apparitions, while on the other hand, their lives and experiences do not follow the pattern of the seers of genuine Marian apparitions, such as the children of Fatima. They lack the sanctity of the former and the innocence and youth of the latter.

Writing in 1986, regarding the possibility that the Congregation for the Doctrine of the Faith might form a new international commission to judge the visions, Fr Faricy noted that: "It seems to be quite unlikely that Cardinal Ratzinger will appoint a new commission before the apparitions have ceased to occur daily."[20]

That was over thirty years ago, and the visions are still said to be continuing up to this moment in one form or another. However, there have been visions which have been condemned as false by the local Ordinary even while they were allegedly going on, including those at Palmar de Troya in Spain in 1968, and at Bayside in the United States in 1970. The Holy See, too, has found it necessary to intervene in the past, as in the case of the false visions at Heroldsbach in Germany, in July 1951, even though these were said to have continued until October 1952.[21] So it would appear that there is no intrinsic reason why the visions at Medjugorje could not be condemned by the Church, even while they are alleged to be continuing. And equally, it would seem that there is no chance of them being approved while they are ongoing, in case there should be some future scandal — that is, a scandal even more egregious than some of the things that have already happened concerning Medjugorje.

THE VERBOSE AND REPETITIVE NATURE OF THE MESSAGES

Fr Laurentin also says that the verbose nature of the messages is justified because they were being given out in a country which at that time was under Communist rule: "Speech that is more frequent and more prolonged may be quite opportune for the church of silence." In reality, however, when an apparition is truly of divine origin, regardless of whether it takes place in a free or a totalitarian society, God only needs a few words and a short interval of time to get his message across.[22]

Fr Laurentin also says, in connection with the Old Testament era, during which, as he acknowledges, there were periods when there was little or no prophecy in Israel: "Perhaps the seriousness of the period in which we live and the inertia of the world despite the voices from heaven explain this large number of apparitions at Medjugorje."[23] These points, though, in themselves do not justify the excessive number of visions claimed to be taking place at Medjugorje, and rather imply that God is losing his touch and has to adopt the modern "advertising" mentality which insists on incessantly repeating a message.

Fr Laurentin further says: "We are in a repetitive world. There is television every day. What is not repeated is submerged. This renders the prolonged repetition of the message quite useful."[24] This is a purely materialistic, utilitarian argument, which fails to refer to the alleged divine truth of their origin, and only gives further cause for suspicion as to the ultimate cause of the visions.

With regard to the devil, Fr Laurentin maintains: "Satan seems to be excluded because these apparitions lead to Christ, to prayer, conversion, confession, and the Eucharist. If Satan were to work that way against himself we would have to say that he has had a conversion!"[25]

However, as demonstrated by Fr William Most, the devil is quite willing to encourage a certain growth in religious practices within the context of a series of false visions:

> The dangers of diabolical interference ... are very grave. Many cases are on record in which the devil appeared in the guise of Our Lord, and even gave true prophecies and urged people on to virtue. The devil is willing to tolerate some real good, so long as he has hope of accomplishing greater evil out of the affair in the long run. To distinguish a vision of divine origin from one that is diabolic is extremely difficult. Even skilled theologians may err in this matter. A large number of cases of alleged visions are probably diabolic.[26]

MEDJUGORJE AND THE POST-CONCILIAR PERIOD

Another of Fr Laurentin's arguments is expressed as follows:

> The Apparitions at Medjugorje do not give the impression of a step backward. Though they have points in common and are in harmony with the apparitions of the last century, they do not share the cultural peculiarities of these latter. They fit in with the pastoral life of the post-conciliar Church. The Virgin encourages openness and ecumenism.[27]

The reality is that the Medjugorje visions have essentially little or nothing in common with the approved Marian apparitions of either the nineteenth or twentieth centuries — apart from a surface similarity in terms of requests to say the rosary and so on — nor does

Fr Laurentin explain exactly what he means by "cultural peculiarities." On any sort of close analysis, in terms of the age of the seers, the number of apparitions, their duration and their reception by the Church, it is unquestionably the case that Medjugorje and the approved Marian apparitions are poles apart.

The dividing line between "ecumenism" and indifferentism in the reported remarks of the "Gospa" seems distinctly thin, as when Fr Vlasic interviewed Mirjana in 1983, and she said: "The Madonna always stresses that there is but one God, and that people have enforced unnatural separation. One cannot truly believe, be a true Christian, if he does not respect other religions as well."

To this, Fr Vlasic responded: "What, then, is the role of Jesus Christ, if the Moslem religion is a good religion?" Mirjana's rather lame response was: "We did not discuss that. She merely explained, and deplored, the lack of religious unity..."[28] Indifferentism is the principle that all religions, or the various Christian denominations, are more or less equally good and true, or that it does not matter which one you follow.

Fr Laurentin also speaks of how a "Muslim dervish from Blade (near Mostar), experienced in the mystical ways of Sufism, reacted very positively when he assisted at the apparitions..." That an exponent of a questionable form of mysticism should react in this way, however, is surely a warning sign regarding the visionaries and their experiences, rather than anything positive in their favor.

Similarly, the fact that Pentecostals such as David DuPlessis have visited Medjugorje and given it their support is not, as Fr Laurentin seems to believe, a positive factor, but rather a serious concern for any normal Catholic, given the subjective nature of Pentecostalism and its emphasis on the emotional. Indeed, Fr Laurentin, speaking of the praise lavished upon Medjugorje by DuPlessis, made the following rather astonishing statement: "This is a good indication that the apparitions of Medjugorje are without any of the historical particularities of Catholicism and thus have a better quality ecumenical dimension."[29] It is unclear exactly what Fr Laurentin meant by this, but the implication seems to be that the Medjugorje visions are so lacking in the supernatural norms of approved apparitions, that they can even appeal to a Pentecostalist.

* * *

The Medjugorje Propaganda Offensive

SUMMING UP, THEN, WE CAN SAY THAT THIS CHAPTER has indicated that one of the main reasons for the success of Medjugorje has been the massive publicity campaign waged on its behalf, principally by authors such as Fr Laurentin, whose books on the subject have sold in the tens of thousands worldwide. Similarly, a number of other prominent writers have endorsed Medjugorje whereas there have been relatively few critical works, none of which has succeeded in reaching a mass audience. As we have seen, the really vital testimony is contained in the tape transcripts of the interviews with the visionaries made during the first week or so—but with very few exceptions this evidence has not been reproduced in the popular works on Medjugorje, and to this day it remains largely unknown.

We have looked, too, at Fr Laurentin's pro-Medjugorje arguments, which, amongst other things, imply that a number of the Episcopal judgments on alleged visions made during the twentieth century have been faulty. Similarly, his arguments in favor of a large number of repetitive visions surely lack any sort of credibility in the light of what happened at places like Lourdes and Fatima. The reality is that the Medjugorje messages have more in common with the methods of modern advertising than with anything likely to have come from heaven. It is also clear that Fr Laurentin became personally "entangled" in Medjugorje, and thus he seemingly lost the ability to discern the visions in an impartial and objective manner.

12
Medjugorje and the Theologians

THEOLOGIANS PRONOUNCE ON MEDJUGORJE

Fr Laurentin lays great emphasis on the number of influential writers who have shown support for Medjugorje, in the belief that discernment is necessarily related to the number and reputation of those quoted. He cites the opinion of Fr Robert Faricy, in a 1983 article, to the effect that: "Medjugorje should be a place not only of national but international pilgrimage." Even before that, as early as December 1981, only six months after the visions had begun, Fr Faricy had both visited Medjugorje and spoken with Archbishop Franic. Fr Faricy also tells us that on his first visit he met Fr Vlasic, and that they were already acquainted through the Charismatic Movement.

These are surely indications of connections between Medjugorje and some important Charismatics at a remarkably early stage. It is also noteworthy that following his own visit to Medjugorje that same month, Archbishop Franic wrote a positive article in which he expressed the hope that "international experts like...[Fr] Faricy will be part of the Committee responsible for verifying the authenticity of the events of Medjugorje."

A more weighty witness is Fr Hans Urs von Balthasar, who spoke about Medjugorje in Rome in the early 80s. Undoubtedly, Fr Laurentin's public support of Medjugorje was a factor in persuading the celebrated Swiss theologian to take such a stance. And as Fr Michael O'Carroll put it, "The intervention of this giant among contemporary theologians caused much surprise." In December 1984, von Balthasar wrote a very critical letter to Bishop Zanic in response to the latter's warnings about Medjugorje, which had been widely circulated. The contents of this letter include these lines in which he accused the bishop of denigrating "people who are renowned and innocent, deserving your respect and protection," while he also spoke of his bringing out "accusations which have been refuted a hundred times over."

As the reader will realize from the evidence presented in preceding chapters, it seems apparent from this letter that von Balthasar was not really aware of what had actually happened during the first week at Medjugorje. Rather, he seems to have been unduly influenced by the views of Medjugorje supporters. He expressed himself equally vigorously in an interview given in November 1985, in which he said: "Medjugorje's theology rings true. I am convinced of its truth. And everything about Medjugorje is authentic in a Catholic sense. What is happening there is so evident, so convincing."

Sadly, this quote would seem to indicate that even as influential a figure as von Balthasar was not immune from the spirit of subjectivism which has made genuine discernment regarding Medjugorje so difficult.[1] Indeed, there is no indication that he made any detailed study of Medjugorje, rather than relying on the testimony of writers like Fr Laurentin.

In addition, von Balthasar's views in this area are open to question, given his long association with the alleged mystic Adrienne von Speyr. He claimed that her works could not be dismissed as "private revelations" or a "peripheral outgrowth of theology." Rather he saw her ideas as a form of "ecclesial mysticism" that contributed to a "deepening" of theology. Regarding the problems with accepting her experiences as genuine, Anne Barbeau Gardiner points to an investigation of one of her books, which indicates that "her revelations appear to conflict with Catholic teaching on key points." So von Balthasar may have been unduly influenced by his relationship with von Speyr, and thus looked too favorably upon claims of alleged mystical experiences, including Medjugorje.[2] Overall, this is perhaps as good an example as any of the modern excessive reliance on the "cult of the expert" as a means of discernment.

The Swiss theologian was also the recipient of a letter from Fr Vlasic, in 1983, which stated: "The children have decided to enter the religious life, but they are waiting for the right moment which only they know."[3] This certainly looks like a Medjugorje "prophecy" which hasn't come true, and in fact none of the visionaries has become a priest or religious, though this was the type of information about Medjugorje which figures like von Balthasar were receiving in the early days. Indeed, it appears that sometime after this, Fr von Balthasar withdrew his belief in the genuineness of the ongoing claims for apparitions at Medjugorje. Regrettably, he was less public in his retraction than in his original criticisms. He apparently told a group on retreat under him, around 1987, that he did believe in Medjugorje at one time but no longer. In any event, the result was no positive public statement on Medjugorje from him after this.[4]

Finally, however, after detailing all the points he considered favorable to Medjugorje, Fr Laurentin was obliged to acknowledge the major stumbling-block faced by its supporters, a stumbling-block which remained after the appointment of his successor, Bishop Peric: "The most serious objection...[is] the opposition of the Bishop to these apparitions."[5] This opposition was forthcoming and led to an unpleasant propaganda offensive against Bishop Zanic, which is dealt with below.

CRITICISM OF BISHOP ZANIC

This campaign of criticism and opposition towards Bishop Zanic developed quite early on, and was certainly well in place by the time Fr Laurentin made the following remarks with regard to the expanded Episcopal commission of 1984: "Those who were chosen for the Commission were among the most critically-minded of the available experts and they were, for the most part, opposed to the authenticity of the apparitions."[6]

However, as Fr Sivric notes, Bishop Zanic's Commission was certainly "open and independent" given that its members came from a wide variety of dioceses, provinces and theological faculties. He also notes that these individuals, who were mostly professors of theology, were actually recommended by outside authorities, and so it would be wrong to suggest they were handpicked by Bishop Zanic.[7]

Criticism of the bishop is also apparent in an interview with Fr Svetozar Kraljevic done as part of a CBC Fifth Estate program in September 1985. In the video of this interview, the reporter says to Fr Kraljevic: "The Bishop of Mostar is... unequivocal. He says the Virgin Mary is not appearing in Medjugorje." On hearing this, we can see Fr Kraljevic pause before shrugging his shoulders and making a gesture with his hands as if to indicate that the bishop's position is unimportant, before saying: "That is the opinion of a person who has a right to say so but if you talk to the..."

At this point the interviewer interjects sharply to say: "This is not just a person, this is the bishop you're speaking about," to which Fr Kraljevic responds: "His judgments, what I would like to say, are not professional and his judgments come from his inner disbelief that the children don't see the Blessed Virgin Mary."[8]

This revealing interview shows the attitude of disdain displayed towards Bishop Zanic which was present at the time amongst a number of the Herzegovina Franciscans, and which has also regrettably been displayed by many Medjugorje supporters since then.

Fr Laurentin also described the bishop in the following words, while at the same time managing to ingratiate himself with the Yugoslav government: "While the Bishop became adversary number one, the government recognized the peaceful order and the loyalty of this purely religious phenomenon, which was appreciated by official tourism."[9]

Fr Laurentin was openly critical of the bishop's negative stance on Medjugorje, holding his judgment to be "an error," because "except for new arguments...even the successors of the apostles are not exempt from any risks of human weakness." As we have seen, though, "new arguments"—in the form of the transcripts of the Medjugorje tapes—have become available, and indeed the tapes were themselves available at the time, as the evidence from Fr Bubalo's interviews with Vicka makes clear. In addition, it is rash to go against the judgment of the local Ordinary in such instances, providing he has acted properly, as was the case with Bishop Zanic.

Fr Laurentin went on to say: "Obedience to established authority...does not necessarily extinguish an *interior conviction,* nor the responsibility to prepare discreetly a historical revision." In other words, Fr Laurentin regarded his own subjective *feelings* about Medjugorje as superior to the judgments of the bishop. He also compared Bishop Zanic's actions to those of Msgr Cauchon, the bishop who was responsible for constituting the tribunal which condemned Joan of Arc to death by burning at the stake![10]

FR MICHAEL O'CARROLL ON MEDJUGORJE

Another example of this type of criticism came from Fr Michael O'Carroll, who made the following statement about the role of Bishop Zanic:

> There is no question of withdrawing the problem of authenticity of an apparition of Our Lady from the competence of a bishop. It is the bishop who really has the problem: How is he, in a case like Medjugorje, to assess the importance of worldwide opinion? It is clear...that the Bishop of Mostar has chosen to ignore this factor in his judgement of the reported visions.

Does "worldwide opinion" entitle Catholics to ignore the fact that it is for the local Ordinary to come to decisions about alleged visions in his diocese in the first instance? One might ask why, if Fr O'Carroll recognized the competent authority's power to decide in this case, he was unwilling to accept his decision?

Fr O'Carroll then goes on to mention the large Catholic response to Medjugorje, plus "enlightened disinterested theological opinion," and the various scientific studies carried out on the visionaries, before concluding thus: "In view of these facts now known through the Bishop's own mode of procedure, what value, if any, would attach to any judgement he chooses to publish?"[11]

So he accepts the bishop has the competence to pronounce on authenticity, but questions whether his judgment would have any value. We seem to be in a situation where theologians and intellectuals think they have some form of superior knowledge, which exempts them from Episcopal judgments in these matters.[12]

Leaving aside just how enlightened and disinterested the theological opinion mentioned by Fr O'Carroll actually was, as well as just how much we can expect scientific experiments to tell us about spiritual manifestations, Fr O'Carroll's main bone of contention is that Bishop Zanic was not prepared to take note of "worldwide opinion" in coming to a decision about Medjugorje. But looking at the activities of those Episcopal commissions previously set up to investigate reports of Marian apparitions, which were almost invariably made up of locally available theologians, there does not seem to be any solid reason why the bishop should have taken outside opinions into account. This is quite apart from practical matters such as the need to understand the local language in order to assess Medjugorje at first hand.

Regarding this idea, even Fr Laurentin could see the difficulties of supporting the views of figures such as Archbishop Franic on this point: "I did not support that opinion because the experts and native bishops have the advantage of speaking the language of the country, and are better situated for the understanding and the knowledge of the facts."

A FALSE ANALOGY

Fr O'Carroll also attempts to draw an historical analogy between Cardinal Newman's essay *On Consulting the Faithful in Matters of Doctrine* — which appeared in 1859, and which explained that during the Arian crisis of the fourth century it was the laity rather than the

bishops who saved the Church—and the more recent activity of
the laity in supporting Medjugorje. He then comments on the fact
that Pope Pius XII consulted the bishops of the world before pro-
mulgating the dogma of the Assumption in 1950, telling them that
they should take account of lay devotion in this area: "Here too was
recognition of the role of the laity in the area of doctrine." He then
puts the question: "Has this truth... relevance to the happenings at
Medjugorje over the last five years?"[13]

What Fr O'Carroll seems to be saying is that the Arian crisis can
be seen as a model for the way Medjugorje has developed, that is,
just as erring bishops in the fourth century were countered by an
orthodox laity, so the "erring" Bishop Zanic was being confounded
by the crowds of pilgrims manifesting their "orthodoxy" by coming
to Medjugorje. Regrettably, this is a false analogy, since it was Bishop
Zanic who acted in an orthodox manner, in the way he responded
to events, as detailed above. It is rather the theologians and pilgrims
who have flocked to Medjugorje, despite all the problems associated
with it, who have been misled by the complicated series of events
described above, and who, in consequence, are in error. Furthermore,
the Arians denied a dogma of the Church. No one who disbelieves
in an apparition—proven or doubtful—can ever be called a heretic
just for that reason, since private revelations, even when approved,
are not a part of the deposit of faith.

BISHOP ZANIC A COMMUNIST COLLABORATOR?

Fr Ljudevit Rupcic accused Bishop Zanic of changing his mind
about Medjugorje under Communist pressure, basing himself on the
testimony of Fr Zovko,[14] and this was a charge that was repeated
in the film entitled *Gospa*, a Hollywood production, which starred
Martin Sheen in the role of Fr Zovko and Morgan Fairchild as a Franciscan nun. In the film, Bishop Zanic was portrayed as a Communist
collaborator. Thus, it was a slur on his good name, and the Vicar
General of Mostar diocese issued an official rebuttal on 17 June 1995.
His statement categorically denied this charge as follows:

> The Chancery office of the diocese of Mostar fervently con-
> demns as untrue all the scenes and words regarding the eccle-
> siastical behaviour of Msgr. Pavao Zanic, the former diocesan
> bishop (under the name of Petar Subic in the film) with
> respect to the events of Medjugorje.... Not even a shadow

of cowardliness or easing-off of the Bishop before the communist authorities was ever in question, let alone any type of collaboration with them.... Instead, the bishop always behaved in a courageous and dignified way.[15]

So it's a question of either believing the Chancery office of the diocese of Mostar, which denies that Bishop Zanic was a Communist collaborator, or Fr Rupcic, the fanatical Franciscan Medjugorje supporter, and Fr Zovko, the thrice-disciplined Franciscan priest. In fact, in 1985, Fr Rupcic, along with Frs Zovko and Fr Vlasic, was forbidden by Bishop Zanic to celebrate Mass or to preach at Medjugorje.[16]

* * *

TO CONCLUDE, A MAJOR PART OF THE PRO-MEDJUGORJE campaign has involved an over-reliance on the opinions of well-known theologians, but in reality it turns out that these have either not been in full possession of the facts, or alternatively, not particularly objective—rather, as regards some of the latter, a pre-existing Charismatic mindset has colored their views. Even apparently objective scientific analysis of the visionaries turns out to be not as decisive as has been claimed, since diabolical activity or a lack of truthfulness cannot be detected using scientific methods, as will be seen in the next chapter.

The other part of the campaign in favor of Medjugorje has involved attacks on the person of Bishop Zanic, which largely succeeded in undermining his credibility in the minds of many Catholics. Would the supporters of a genuine apparition of Mary have resorted to such methods? This was certainly not the case with previous approved apparitions. Does not this intensive propaganda onslaught rather reveal an absence of certainty that the visions are divinely inspired, and a determination by some Medjugorje supporters to force their subjective views on the whole Catholic world, without respecting the authority of the Church to decide such matters?

13
Medical and Scientific Investigations

MEDICAL & PSYCHOLOGICAL EXAMINATIONS
OF THE VISIONARIES

We learn from the tape transcripts that on 27 June 1981, three days after the visions began, the visionaries were taken for a police interrogation and medical inspection at Citluk. They were examined by a psychiatrist, but this procedure was apparently inconclusive, and the evidence on the tape suggests that at least some of the visionaries were far from cooperative. Two days later, on 29 June, they were again taken for a medical examination, firstly to Citluk, and then to Mostar. Here they saw a Dr Dzudza, a female psychiatrist, who, according to Ivanka, apparently threatened them with incarceration in a psychiatric ward if they continued to go to Podbrdo; but she could find no definite grounds for detaining them. They were also examined by various doctors including Dr Ludvik Stopar, who is described as a "psychiatrist and parapsychologist." Parapsychology is the study of claimed psychic phenomena such as near-death and out-of-the-body experiences. His conclusion was that they were not suffering from mental illness, and this seems to have been the position of those doctors who did examine them in the early years. Given the evidence presented previously, though, particularly that pointing to a diabolical origin for the visions, and also the likelihood of later visions and messages being fabricated, this is perhaps only to be expected.

And in any case, as Fr Laurent Volken says, in his *Visions, Revelations, and the Church,* an important work on the subject, it is crucial to realize that "the examination of the psychological make-up alone can never be the basis of a judgment in favor of the divine origin of a revelation. Only by a supernatural process can we in the long run judge supernatural facts."

The initial commission set up by Bishop Zanic also did some basic work in this area, with a priest member, Fr Nicolas Bulat, applying an old-fashioned test to Vicka during one of her visions. He pricked her in the shoulder with a needle, drawing blood, but there is some dispute as to exactly how much of a reaction there was to this on her part.[1] In fact, this first commission did not apparently carry out any detailed medical examination of the visionaries, because over time they had gradually come to the conclusion that their ecstasies were not genuine—thus they did not see such examinations as a necessity.

DR HENRI JOYEUX'S MEDICAL EXPERIMENTS

Dr Henri Joyeux, a French cancer expert, assembled a team of specialists to examine the visionaries on three occasions in 1984, from 9–10 June, 6–7 October, and 28–29 December. After numerous tests, they came to the conclusion that they were not suffering from individual or collective hallucinations or hysteria. They also concluded that the visionaries were not subject to neurosis, phobias, depression, nor to catalepsy, a condition characterized by lack of response to external stimuli and by muscular rigidity. Similarly, they denied that the visionaries' ecstasies were "pathological" in nature.

However, it is unclear how they could have come to such definite conclusions, since of the five members of the team, only one, Dr Jean Cadhilhac, a neurophysiologist—that is, someone concerned with diagnosing problems with the functioning of the nervous system—could be said to have qualifications directly pertinent to some of those conclusions; the other members of the team were qualified in ophthalmology (eyes), otorhinolaryngology (ear, nose and throat) and cardiology (heart). The type of conclusions they came to would seem to require specialists more in the realms of psychiatry and psychology.[2]

Apart from that, there are also questions concerning the objectivity of Dr Joyeux, since, as Marco Corvaglia points out, he had links to the Charismatic Renewal and was close to Dr René Lejeune, a leader of the movement in France. And as we have seen, Dr Lejeune was the co-author, with Fr Laurentin, of the *Chronological Corpus of the Messages*; in addition, Dr Joyeux also wrote the preface to one of Lejeune's books.[3]

This is not to question his basic competence, but just to point out his connections with the Charismatic Renewal which may have colored his attitude to the visionaries and their claims. Certainly, he and his team can be criticized for a lack of rigor in their dealings with them.

In connection with the medical and psychological status of the visionaries, Bishop Zanic wrote to Fr Laurentin in January 1985, pointing out: "It is not hallucinations that I wish to stress. That was the interpretation of one of my doctors. I now believe that it was something worse—simulation." In response, Fr Laurentin claimed, "Our tests... ruled out the possibility of simulation," but there is no clear indication in the text he co-authored with Dr Henri Joyeux, *Scientific and Medical Studies on the Apparitions of Medjugorje*, that tests for simulation, that is, lie detector tests, were carried out by the French medical/scientific team assembled under Dr Joyeux. In any event, as we will see, there is no guarantee that such tests are accurate.

Indeed, the French doctor was conscious of the possibility that the visionaries could have been lying, as this statement from his evaluation makes clear: "Perhaps we are dealing with collective deceit? Would not a lie detector eventually unmask such deceit? In facing up to these... questions our team was conscious of a number of handicaps which are important to define." He then goes on to pinpoint the linguistic and logistical difficulties they faced in carrying out their tests—the team had to rely on translators, and faced difficulties in transporting their scientific equipment back and forth from France to Yugoslavia.[4]

Fr Laurentin makes much of the fact that the visionaries, during their alleged ecstasies, did not feel pinching, touching or other stimulation. But the tests carried out—on brain activity, the heart, eyes, hearing, and larynx function—were clearly not capable of eliminating the possibility that the visionaries were able to enter into self-induced trances. Just because the tests apparently ruled out factors like hallucination or mental illness, this does not rule out the possibility of deception.

Fr Laurentin points to the encephalogram done by Dr Joyeux's team on Ivan, on 10 June 1984, and claims that this rules out epilepsy and "pathological" hallucination. However, the crucial fact, surely, is that it does *not* exclude the possibility that Ivan was not necessarily telling the truth, that he was not actually in any sort of genuine "ecstasy."[5]

It is interesting to note that another test had been planned, to verify the claim of the visionaries that they could "touch" the Vision. This would have involved photographing them from the side and noting the position of their hands. But on the same day, 10 June, Jakov claimed that he had forgotten to ask the "Gospa" about this, and later, in October, Ivanka and Marija said that the Vision would not agree to it.[6]

A test done on Marija and Ivanka, on 7 October 1984, illustrates the essential weakness in the approach adopted by the investigators. During an alleged vision on this day, Dr Jacques Philippot placed what is described as a "screen" in front of their eyes, and we are told that neither of them "noticed the screen that was placed between them and the apparition and it did not interfere with the perception of the apparition."[7] Photographs of these incidents in the book show that this screen was actually a small piece of card, which would not have interfered with their peripheral vision.

The important point to notice, however, is that the researchers, instead of adopting a critical attitude to the claims of the visionaries, assume that they really are seeing something supernatural. Thus, they did not take a truly scientific approach to their task. A much more rigorous and questioning attitude was required. How did they know that the visionaries were actually seeing anything? The only evidence they had was what they were being told by the visionaries themselves.

DR MARGNELLI'S OTHER STATE OF CONSCIOUSNESS

An Italian doctor, Dr Marco Margnelli, in an interview given in 1988, following his investigations, stated that the visionaries "pass into another state of consciousness — a condition that one can also reach through meditation techniques, such as auto-training, though not as profoundly." He went on to say that he didn't believe that they were lying because "otherwise they would react to tests of a sensory and painful kind."[8]

It is not clear how the latter points rule out the possibility of lying, since it is quite possible to envisage a person in such a trance becoming largely impervious to pain — and as we will see, the tests in these areas were inadequate in some important respects. But it is interesting that he can describe the ecstasies of the visionaries in terms of a condition akin to a self-induced state of alternative consciousness, with the difference between them being their depth or intensity. Certainly if one can enter a self-induced trance, then presumably with practice this process could be refined to produce a much deeper state of mental and bodily abstraction. This factor may well explain why during their ecstasies some of the visionaries were allegedly impervious to loud sounds or very bright lights.

But even here, there is room for doubt regarding the test on Ivan's hearing done by Dr Francois Rouquerol. He reacted to a sound of 70 decibels before entering his "ecstasy," but apparently didn't react to one of 90 decibels — equivalent to the sound of heavy traffic — *during* his ecstasy, telling the investigators that he heard nothing. The problem with this test, though, is that there was no objective and independent way that the doctor could verify this; he relied entirely on Ivan's testimony. And even though this test was only done on Ivan, a few pages further on in the Laurentin/Joyeux book we are told that "the visionaries do not hear [a] noise level of 90 decibels." Thus the unscientific result of Ivan's test was improperly applied to *all* the visionaries, giving a false picture of the situation. This procedure, again, shows a lack of scientific rigor on the part of the investigators, and a tendency to give far too much credence to the visionaries' claims about seeing the Blessed Virgin.[9]

And regarding the claim that the visionaries could have very bright lights shone in their eyes, without their pupils reducing in size, as is normally the case, such assertions are questionable. Dr Maria Magatti claimed that during a test, which she herself admitted was "inadequate, and too quick," she shone a 1000-watt cine-projector light onto the eyes of the visionaries during their ecstasies "without causing any modification in the diameter of the pupils" — normally, this type of thing will cause the pupil to contract. But this finding was contradicted by the results of later tests. Dr Jacques Philippot, an ophthalmologist, carried out tests on the visionaries on 6–7 October 1984, and discovered that: "The pupil continues to react to light during the ecstasy." And this was also the case during later tests carried out by Dr Frigerio and his associates, and Dr Mario Cigada.[10]

All of this is quite apart, of course, from the possibility of a diabolical involvement in these "ecstasies," which could equally account for their claimed qualities.

Returning to Dr Margnelli's claims, he thus argues that people can pass into another state of consciousness via meditation techniques, but qualifies this by saying that in his opinion they cannot do this to the extent found regarding the Medjugorje visionaries' ecstasies. Surely, though, it's legitimate to ask whether Dr Margnelli was justified in being so certain that this couldn't happen. He is described as a neurophysiologist, that is, a specialist in the functioning of the nervous system. He is usually dealing, presumably, with people with various abnormal conditions, and so trying to analyze exactly what is behind the Medjugorje visions is something really beyond his experience. Whether the visions are supernatural, or merely preternatural or diabolical, or even just fabricated, then this is certainly the case.

Thus, his conclusion that the "other state of consciousness" assumed by the visionaries could not be due to meditation techniques is not justified. Had he examined anyone else who had been claiming visions for what was at the time a period of seven years? That was certainly a long enough time for the visionaries to have practiced techniques enabling them to enter into deeper trance-like states. How many other people in a similar state had he studied, and of those how was he able to determine which ecstasies were genuine and which false? The reality is that scientific methods, on their own, cannot tell us the exact nature of such alleged visions, which can only ultimately be judged through a process of spiritual discernment.

Dr Margnelli also stated that he had *not* done an electroencephalogram on the visionaries as this had already been done by the French investigators; he relied rather on "several other checks and investigations."[11]

THE EEG RESULTS OF THE VISIONARIES

Electroencephalography (EEG) records electrical activity in the brain using electrodes placed on the scalp; it is used in neurology mainly to diagnose epilepsy. If we turn to some of the EEG work carried out by the French team we can see the results they obtained. Regarding Ivan, during a test which lasted about thirty minutes, covering the time before, during, and after his vision, he did not sleep or dream, but remained in a state of "alpha rhythm" brain activity, which is described as a "rhythm of wakefulness and receptivity, *the rhythm of a contemplative in calm prayer.*" The test was regarded as eliminating the possibility of pathological hallucination.

Regarding the tests done on Marija and Ivanka, there was apparently no sign of any "cerebral anomaly" or "pathological symptoms." Fr Laurentin tells us:

> The graphs recorded before, during and after the apparition *show only minimal differences*. Before the apparition, especially in Marija's case, we find the presence of the beta rhythm, the rhythm of attention and reflection, and also the alpha rhythm, indicating the state of wakefulness. *The latter predominates progressively from the beginning of the ecstasy.*[12]

It's hard to see how, from these results, it can be claimed that there is any proof that the visionaries tested were in a "deep ecstasy." Ivan's brain rhythm is described as being like that of someone calmly praying, while in the case of Marija and Ivanka the graphs show only minimal differences in their brain activity before, during, and after the test, with a state similar to wakefulness developing as Marija's vision, in particular, went on.

The Italian neurophysiologist, Dr Francesco D'Alpa, is critical of both of these tests. In the case of Ivan this is because of the "short duration of ecstasy, about 62 seconds, a time quite insufficient to assess any possible changes relative to the basic graph."

Regarding Marija, he says:

> As regards the EEG obtained on Marija...the new datum would be the observation that alpha rhythm "predominates progressively from the beginning of the ecstasy." One may legitimately ask what is the reliability of this information, which comes from a subjective assessment on an encephalogram of very poor quality.

He goes on to say, "The 'ecstasy' of Marija lasted only 102 ± 2 sec, a period during which it is very difficult to assess...the percentage amount of the various sequences of rhythms."

Overall, Dr D'Alpa points to deficiencies in the planning, implementation and evaluation of these tests, and sees them as characterized by "methodological deficiencies" and "arbitrariness of evaluation," criticisms which he also applied to many other aspects of the group's work. He concluded that a report such as the one produced by Dr Joyeux could never be accepted by a serious medical journal.[13]

THE VISIONARIES' ECSTATIC EXPERIENCES ANALYZED

Fr Laurentin describes one of the visions videoed by the scientific team as follows:

> To prepare themselves for the apparition the visionaries, standing, recite several Our Fathers, Hail Marys and Glory Bes until "The Gospa" appears. During the early months they usually recited each prayer twice or three times before the apparition took place. Since the end of 1983, ecstasy begins before they have finished the first Our Father.[14]

The first thing to notice about this, from a critical perspective, is that by this time, the ecstasies of the visionaries were happening at a particular moment which they knew was coming, that is before they had finished the first *Our Father*. It is not as if these visions were happening completely unexpectedly. In fact, what is actually taking place here is that from the end of 1983, it was the visionaries themselves who were effectively determining when their visions began, rather than waiting for the "Gospa" to appear. This point on its own raises numerous problems and is a very strong indication that nothing supernatural was going on. Fr Laurentin continues:

> Suddenly their gaze, already fixed on the location of the apparition, becomes more intense. There are hardly any movements of the eyelids.... They kneel down very naturally, all at the same moment. The movement is not perfectly synchronised, a fact that might be attributed to their differing reaction times, or the difference in their reflexes. But we have never noticed a signal being given.[15]

Of course, there would be no need for an obvious signal to be given because the very act of kneeling down, which he admits was not done exactly simultaneously, coming as it did during the *Our Father*, could have acted as a cue in itself. In other words, one of the visionaries could have begun to kneel down and the others followed very quickly. We should remember that these were fit youngsters, who had been having these experiences since mid-1981.

Video evidence makes it clear that this act of kneeling down by the visionaries was not simultaneous on other occasions too. For example, footage from one video clearly shows Ivanka kneeling down more quickly than Vicka,[16] while another video again features Ivanka, but this time standing behind Jakov, so that she was outside his field of vision. Again, her kneeling down is noticeably quicker than his.[17]

A word or two about "reaction time" is appropriate here. A good deal of research has been carried out on this subject, and "the accepted figures for mean simple reaction times for college-age individuals have been about 190 ms (0.19 sec) for light stimuli and about 160 ms for sound stimuli." As might be expected, with practice, reaction time can be reduced, and being warned in advance also leads to a faster reaction time.[18]

This means that the reaction time of a fit young person to a visual stimulus can certainly be of the order of 2/10 of a second, and even quicker for sound stimuli. Since such short reaction times are possible, it is clear that claims of apparent simultaneity for the visionaries in response to alleged supernatural stimuli are very difficult, if not impossible, to verify.

Nor is it really possible to argue that if the visions were false, then we might expect a "ripple" effect, in which one visionary would quickly follow another in kneeling down, followed by another, followed by another, each within their own reaction times, a process which would naturally take longer than a single person's reaction time. This is because they were generally very close together, and could either hear the air movements from those around them, or through their peripheral vision see movements and react very quickly to them.

So it is not a question of falsity requiring a time-consuming "cascade" of movements, but rather of one visionary kneeling, and then the others very quickly following suit, with all this generally happening within the approximate duration of one person's reaction time. But having said that, as already pointed out, the video evidence indicates that at least on some occasions there was a noticeable time lag between the movements of particular visionaries.

Fr Laurentin then comments on what happened next: "Their lips can be seen moving but no voices are heard... Suddenly, all their voices become audible, and they say, in Croatian, 'who art in heaven'; 'hallowed be thy name' etc. The opening words, 'Our Father' are not pronounced."[19]

Once again, there is nothing necessarily supernatural about this, and whether a group begins to say a prayer with the first word, or, as in this case, with the third word, this does not of itself rule out a natural explanation. It would only be necessary for one of the visionaries to begin on the third word, and then, as in the case of their kneeling down, for the others to follow quickly.

What is certainly clear from these observations of the visionaries in "ecstasy" is that the scientific experiments designed to test these claims were far from rigorous. Pictures in the book, and video evidence, show the visionaries wired up to various pieces of apparatus, but there is no indication that they were blindfolded, or fitted with earplugs, so as to exclude visual or auditory cues from one to another. Similarly, if the experiments had been conducted with true scientific rigor, surely a far more accurate analysis would have been obtained if they had been placed in separate partitioned areas, so as to exclude cues from air disturbances caused by the person next to them kneeling down quickly.

INAUDIBLE VOICES

Ivanka's voice and larynx function were tested on 28 December 1984, by Dr Francois Rouquerol. This was to discover why the visionaries' voices became inaudible once ecstasy proper had begun. At this time, according to the evidence recorded by the instruments, there was no longer any larynx movement, only that of the lips—a process which is described as "articulation without phonation." The problem with this is that there is no way of determining whether these lip movements without sound actually corresponded with genuine language. Fr Laurentin acknowledges that they were unable to find anyone capable of lip reading in order to determine this point. And it is just as easy to argue that all that was happening was that the visionaries were moving their lips without making any sounds—something anybody can do.

This question could possibly have been decided on Friday, 8 March 1985, when Dr Luigi Frigerio, accompanied by two colleagues, attempted to test Vicka during a vision, by attaching a laryngophone to her larynx (voice box). This device can pick up very low-level sounds produced by a patient's larynx. But this vision only lasted 22 seconds, well below the usual length, and thus there was no time to properly check Vicka's larynx function during ecstasy. Her explanation for this was that the "Gospa" had looked at the apparatus and said: "It is not necessary."[20]

We can contrast this incident with one involving Ivan. He was videoed while in an alleged ecstasy during a Medjugorje celebration at Aylesford in Kent, England, in 1996. From the footage it seems as though Ivan's lips are moving without any words being audible, but when the sound is turned up, speech can clearly be heard coming from him. So on this occasion at least, there was no question of "articulation without phonation." What is particularly disturbing about this incident, though, is the expression on Ivan's face: it is totally bland and unenthusiastic, with a complete lack of evident joy or intimacy, let alone rapture.[21]

Dr Frigerio went on to claim that the experiences of the visionaries could only be preternatural or supernatural, and further stated that if they were preternatural then the visionaries would not be free, but, since they were apparently free, then they must be supernatural.[22] But this idea goes against the basic Catholic principle of the freedom of the human will, that is, that no outside spiritual agency can absolutely control how we act—except possibly in exceptional cases of diabolical possession—although they can influence or tempt us. So even if someone is experiencing a preternatural experience, they still retain their essential ability to act and make free choices.

MULTIPLE CONVERSATIONS

One of the strangest aspects of the whole Medjugorje story is the way that, according to Fr Laurentin, the "Virgin may give a message to one without the others hearing and *they can hold independent conversations simultaneously.*" Dr Joyeux made a similar observation, saying, "each one of them appeared *simultaneously and successively*, to receive information from and converse with a person whom we as doctors have never seen."[23]

In other words, it is claimed that the "Gospa" could speak with more than one visionary at the same time. This is certainly an interesting claim in the light of what has taken place during the approved Marian apparitions. We do not find this happening at Fatima, nor at Beauraing, which in terms of the number of seers and their ages is the approved apparition which most closely corresponds with Medjugorje—although not as regards duration, since the apparitions at Beauraing only lasted between November 1932 and January 1933, a matter of a few months. At La Salette, Our Lady did speak to the two children separately, but only in order to impart separate secrets to them, which the other child could not hear. Regarding Beauraing, at various times during the apparitions, she spoke to one or another of the children, but again when she gave the three youngest personal secrets during the last apparition, this was done to each of them separately and not concurrently.[24]

In the light of all this, it does not seem at all likely that the visionaries were actually speaking in this manner to a genuinely supernatural visitor.

Fr Laurentin explicitly states that the visionaries recited the Our Father *with* the "Gospa,"[25] and this fact of itself raises an acute problem. Would the sinless Blessed Virgin Mary repeatedly recite this prayer which includes the phrase, *and forgive us our trespasses [sins]?*—this would not appear to be theologically possible.[26]

Fr Laurentin also comments on the fact that Dr Ludvik Stopar hypnotized Marija, and that under hypnosis she gave the same account of her experiences as when in her normal condition, except that she also revealed the alleged secrets she had received.[27] This is taken as proof that the secrets are genuinely supernatural, but, of course, that is not necessarily the case. The secrets may not have been genuine supernatural revelations, yet the visionaries may well have not told of their contents to anyone outside their particular circle.

Dr Joyeux gave an interview to *Paris Match* in the summer of 1985, during which, speaking of the various experiments that had been carried out on the visionaries, he acknowledged quite plainly that, "None of them gave scientific proof that the Virgin is appearing to the visionaries and this is impossible to achieve." Even Fr Laurentin was forced to admit that "the object [sic] who appears to the young people ... will always remain outside scientific experimentation. We will always be limited to hypotheses in that regard."[28]

Interestingly, Louis Bélanger tells us that his own researches in Canada showed that it is quite possible — using volunteers in tests done under laboratory conditions — to duplicate the states of consciousness found during the above medical tests done on the visionaries, and thus that there is nothing necessarily supernatural about them. Specifically, Bélanger's team recorded the following data with one adolescent subject: non-blinking of the eyes; acceleration of the cardiac rhythm; and a pattern of continuous alpha brain waves with the eyes open — with all of these phenomena produced in a normal state of consciousness, as the subject was aware of his environment and able to respond to instructions.[29]

FURTHER EXPERIMENTATION IN 1985, 1986 AND 1988

In September 1985, Dr Luigi Frigerio led a group from the *Associazione Regina della Pace* ("Queen of Peace Society"), which carried out further tests on the visionaries. It should be noted that this society was specifically pro-Medjugorje, and that Dr Frigerio is something of a Medjugorje devotee, so its objectivity can certainly be called into question.

One of these tests was the algometric test, and this was done by Professor Maurizio Santini, who was in charge of examining the visionaries' sensitivity to pain. This test involved using an algometer with a metal plate that could be heated up and applied to the subject's skin. Three of the visionaries, Jakov, Ivan and Marija, were tested while in "ecstasy," with Professor Santini limiting the reaction times for the pain threshold, in order to prevent skin lesions. The device was attached to various parts of the visionaries' bodies, including the fingers, wrist and forehead, and it was claimed, to give one example, that when in "ecstasy," Ivan's reaction time when tested on the forehead increased by a factor of 700%, from 0.4 seconds while outside ecstasy, to 2.8 seconds during his ecstasy. In other words, it was being claimed that the visionaries' pain threshold greatly increased during ecstasy, and that this was a sign that these ecstasies were "supernatural." But it should be noted that 2.8 seconds is not very long, and the experiment had been specifically set up to avoid the danger of skin lesions, therefore the device could not have been excessively hot.

And also, as Marco Corvaglia points out, there is quite a subjective element to these tests since it would have been quite possible for the three visionaries, while not in "ecstasy," to react as soon as possible to the pain, and conversely, while in their alleged ecstasies, to resist the pain as long as possible, bearing in mind that we are not talking about extreme levels of pain here, or excessive time durations. And as he also notes, the difference in reaction times for Jakov was only 0.6 seconds, which is hardly exceptional, while with Marija, since she was recovering from a form of stroke at the time, and the resultant hypoesthesia — that is, a diminished sensitivity to touch, temperature and pain — her test results are clearly unreliable.[30]

The following year, on 14 January 1986, a self-appointed "French-Italian scientific theological commission," which consisted of "seventeen renowned natural scientists, doctors, psychiatrists and theologians," following tests on the visionaries, issued a twelve-point conclusion, which amongst other things made the following four assertions:

> 1. On the basis of the psychological tests, for all and each of the visionaries it is possible with certainty to exclude fraud and deception. 2. On the basis of the medical examinations, tests and clinical observations etc., for all and each of the visionaries it is possible to exclude pathological hallucinations. 3. On the basis of the results of previous researches for all and each of the visionaries it is possible to exclude a purely natural interpretation of these manifestations. 4. On the basis of information and observations that can be documented, for all and each of the visionaries it is possible to exclude that these manifestations are of the preternatural order, i.e., under demonic influence.[31]

We can agree that the scientists were competent regarding the second point, that is regarding "pathological hallucinations," but it is obvious that they exceeded their competence with regard to matters such as excluding fraud and deception, or the demonic. Such scientific investigations, of their very nature, cannot categorically exclude the latter, while deception is always a possibility which must be taken into account.

Apart from the fact that the Medjugorje visionaries were in some way "disconnected" from the real world during their trance-like condition, there was, according to Dr Philippe Loron in an interview published in 1989, a very close synchronization between the eye movements of the visionaries while they were "seeing" their alleged visions — to within 1/5 of a second when the ecstasy began, and when it finished.[32]

On the face of it, this seems like strong evidence to support the genuine nature of what the visionaries experienced, but we have to bear in mind what was said above about reaction time, which, for visual stimuli, is of the order of 0.19 seconds. This makes it clear that this figure of 1/5 of a second for eye movement (0.2 seconds) is only what we would expect given a normal reaction time.

THE 1987 MEDJUGORJE COMMISSION

In January 1987, the formation of a new commission to study Medjugorje was jointly announced by Cardinal Franjo Kuharic and Bishop Zanic. It was composed of theologians and medical specialists, who met twenty-three times in Zagreb, between April 1987 and September 1990. Following their work, the Yugoslav Episcopal Conference issued the Zadar declaration in April 1991. This stated that: "On the basis of investigation up till now, it cannot be established that one is dealing with supernatural apparitions and revelations."

This was thus, in essence, a judgment of *non constat de supernaturalitate*, that is, the supernaturality of the alleged visions had not been proved. Nineteen out of twenty bishops on the commission voted in favor of the declaration, with only one abstention.[33]

The Commission had established a medical sub-committee of six specialists to examine the psychological status of the visionaries; their work involved looking at the available medical documentation, and also examining the six visionaries in the light of *Normae Congregationis*. This is the 1978 document, issued by the Congregation for the Doctrine of the Faith, which is concerned with the discernment of claims of private revelations. We will be looking at this document in detail in a later chapter. The sub-committee included three neuropsychiatrists, a psychiatrist and a psychologist, and concluded that the visionaries were "psychically balanced," and that they didn't show signs of mental illness, or "psycho-pathological inclinations." They also concluded that there was no evidence of mass hysteria or psychosis or other phenomena of that kind.[34]

The results of the various medical examinations done prior to the publication of the negative decision of the earlier diocesan commission of inquiry in 1986 had not been considered valid by that body,[35] and despite the above medical sub-committee giving the visionaries what was effectively a clean bill of mental health, as we have seen, the Commission itself came to an, at best, "neutral" conclusion. So clearly, they did not consider any of the thousands of alleged visions claimed by 1991 as proven. And so, it comes down to a choice between either believing that the visionaries did really see the Blessed Virgin thousands of times between 1981 and 1991, that they were deceived by the devil, or that they were not telling the truth. These would appear to be the stark alternatives.

FURTHER TESTS IN ITALY IN 1998

Further medical tests were done on three of the visionaries, Marija, Ivan and Vicka, in Italy, from 22–23 April 1998, at the insistence of Fr Ivan Landeka, at that time the parish priest of Medjugorje, at a religious house in Capiago Intimiano, Como, Italy. The tests were conducted by a research team led by Dr Giorgio Gagliardi and Fr Andreas Resch, and their findings were published in book form in 2000. As Fr Laurentin tells us, though,

> Vicka was there only for some general tests because Our Lady had asked her on the 20th of April to accept being deprived of the daily apparitions until June 4th. Vicka, who could refuse Our Lady nothing, accepted. It was difficult for her, but even so she remained in perfect joy.[36]

In other words, Vicka did not subject herself to any particular tests to determine her condition during any of her alleged ecstatic states during this period.

Because of Vicka's stance, the research team was only able to study Ivan and Marija, and on 22 April, Dr Gagliardi suggested that they be kept separate, in different rooms, when they were next in ecstasy; but as the time of the expected vision at 6:30 pm approached, this idea was frustrated by Ivan's insistence on staying with Marija.

As Marco Corvaglia points out, this refusal has to be understood in the context of Ivan spending half the year in the United States, where he claims daily visions, and Marija experiencing her own alleged visions at her home in Monza, Italy. Thus there was no good reason for them refusing the perfectly reasonable request of Dr Gagliardi, and this gives rise to suspicions as to why there was this insistence on their being together. In the event, the "ecstasies" experienced by the visionaries were simultaneous, coming during the recitation of the Our Father.

However, the next day, Dr Gagliardi once more requested that the visionaries be tested separately, so that they could not see or hear each other, and also be without access to a timepiece. On this occasion the visionaries agreed, and the result was there was a time difference of almost five minutes between the onset of the ecstasies of Ivan and Marija, although they are supposed to be synchronized.[37]

Marija also underwent tests on the same day with the aim of verifying whether her physiological state was altered during an ecstasy, a fact which might indicate an altered state of consciousness. One particular test involved ophthalmologist Mario Cigada assessing Marija's photomotor reflex and her blink reflex. The first of these involved seeing whether her pupils contracted when a beam of light from a small torch was directed at them, and the second was an assessment of whether or not Marija blinked when the cornea of her eye was touched with a piece of cotton wool. In the video of this experiment, it can be clearly seen that during her alleged ecstasy, Marija not only maintained her normal rate of blinking, but also exhibited the photomotor and blink reflexes of someone not showing any signs of an altered state of consciousness.[38]

It is worth noting that Dr Giorgio Gagliardi has adopted an attitude of great caution regarding the interpretation of the phenomenon of Medjugorje. From 1985 to 2002 he served as deputy director of the Center for Study and Research on Psychophysiology of States of Consciousness in Milan, and thus he is one of the few people involved in research on the Medjugorje visionaries to actually have first-hand experience in the relevant disciplines.[39]

MORE RESEARCH ON MIRJANA, VICKA AND IVANKA

Further research was carried out from 23–24 July 1998 at Medjugorje, this time on Mirjana, Vicka and Ivanka; while what is described as "psychodiagnostic" research involving Jakov also took place, and on 11 December 1998, psycho-physiological research involving Marija was undertaken in Italy. This work involved a team of scientists, who carried out a wide variety of tests, and came to the conclusion that the "results of the investigation carried out demonstrate that the ecstatic phenomenology can be compared to the one from 1985 with somewhat less intensity."

They went on to say that they did not believe that the visions were states of "hypnotic trance," but there does not seem to have been any particular focus on the possibility of the visionaries entering self-induced trances.

The statement issued by the research team mentions the "Valsecchi truth and lie detection test," so this time they were definitely tested on this point. But there is no consensus that such tests are accurate or scientific. They are subjective and rely on changes in emotional responses; it is quite possible for someone who is telling the truth to be falsely accused of lying, and conversely for a determined liar to avoid detection. For the above reasons, evidence obtained from lie detector tests is generally inadmissible in American courts, and in those of a number of other countries.[40]

More recent tests were apparently done on Ivan and Marija, on 25 June 2005 (the "anniversary" day of Medjugorje), by Dr Philippe Loron. However, no report has ever been published on these tests, and the only documentation available about them consists of statements by Dr Loron to the Croatian newspaper *Slobodna Dalmacija*, dated 27 June 2005. These statements give no information about the members of the investigating team, nor an accurate description of which tests were carried out, nor provide any quantitative, and thus precise and verifiable results. Thus they are deficient from all points of view.[41]

Marco Corvaglia points out too that none of the findings of any of these medical teams has ever been published in a recognized, peer-reviewed scientific journal. Only by doing this, and being accepted as such, could any of these studies really be considered "scientific."

THE UNCOOPERATIVE VISIONARIES

At this point, it's worth summarizing some of the points made above, and including some additional information, to show how the visionaries were, at times, very uncooperative, and put the researchers to unnecessary trouble, or avoided the tests altogether by simply absenting themselves for various reasons. This is a summary of the relevant information in Marco Corvaglia's book.[42]

During Professor Joyeux's first visit to Medjugorje in 1984, on 9 June, three of the visionaries—Jakov, Ivanka and Marija—refused to subject themselves to the tests, even though the doctors had made the lengthy journey from France just for this purpose. But instead of being critical of this, Fr Laurentin merely commented that the "refusal was characterised by that solidarity so remarkable among the group." In response, the doctors pointed out that such a refusal made it appear that they were "afraid of the outcome." In reply, Jakov agreed to ask the "Gospa's" permission, which was duly given during that evening's vision.

Surely, though, the researchers should have realized at this point that they were being manipulated. They should have packed their bags and departed, rather than go along with the charade of accepting what one of the visionaries claimed he had heard. The whole point of such a scientific appraisal is that they were there to *critically* test the visionaries' claims, not to become part of an alleged response from the "Gospa." That was the fatal flaw in their approach: they effectively became part of the experimentation.

The next day some of the visionaries did consent to be tested, but that meant that only one day of actual testing was possible, and there were further problems during the October and December sessions, and indeed during some of the later series of tests as well.

Jakov was not present for the 6–7 October sessions because he said he was ill, and Vicka was also absent on 7 October, again because of alleged illness. Vicka was again absent for the tests on 28 December, and the next day, both Jakov and Ivanka failed to turn up for their scheduled tests.[43]

Moving on now to Dr Frigerio's tests in March 1985, as we have seen, Vicka managed to avoid one particular test by claiming that the "Gospa" had looked at the apparatus and said: "It is not necessary." Dr Frigerio returned to Medjugorje the following September, but again, Vicka claimed that according to the "Gospa" such testing was unnecessary.[44]

Dr Giorgio Valli, a neurologist from Milan, went to Medjugorje in January 1987 to conduct comparative studies on the visionaries during their alleged ecstasies. But they all refused apart from Marija. Fr Laurentin commented on this as follows: "Since it was necessary to have two seers for this synchronic study, Professor Valli, who had brought, at great expense, a considerable amount of material with him, renounced his project."

There were more problems a few months later: "Professor Joyeux, who came back with the team on April 4–5, met with similar difficulties. He waited a whole afternoon at Vicka's house... [hoping] to be able to observe and film during her apparition; but she had the apparition in a purely private way." This led Fr Laurentin to further comment: "We admire the patience, the spiritual comprehension and the grandeur of the soul, with which several doctors have accepted the 'no' of the seers."[45]

It might also be said that "credulity" or "naivety" are more suitable words to describe their attitude. But showing admirable perseverance, Dr Joyeux returned in January 1988, intending to conduct comparative studies in the laboratory, rather than use less reliable portable equipment. This would have involved the visionaries traveling to France. Jakov, however, refused to be involved, and although tickets for the others were bought, the day before departure, Vicka announced that the "Gospa" had asked for a pause in her visions, and that for some time she would not be appearing to her, while Marija claimed to have the flu. So, once again it was impossible to do a comparative study and everything had to be called off.[46]

Fr Laurentin summarized why it had become impossible to persuade the visionaries to undertake new tests, citing the unwillingness of some to be involved, the opposition of others, or their claiming to be too busy, or what he characterized as the "indifference of certain others." But even so, he strove to minimize all this, saying: "Of course, for the Virgin these scientific studies are minor things."[47]

TESTS DURING THE NINETIES

Two years later, in 1992, Fr Laurentin was forced to admit that while Dr Joyeux had "multiplied his attempts to gather at least 2 or 3 visionaries together (since we are talking about comparative studies)," all such attempts had failed.[48]

Four years after this, in 1996, the situation had still not improved, leading Fr Laurentin to comment that Professor Joyeux was still having to deal with indifference, disinterest and even opposition from the visionaries, who were apparently unconcerned about the tests. He continues:

> For them the situation is this: Our Lady said to them, when they asked her about the opportuneness of these tests: "It is not necessary".... But the Professor did not give up. He came back to Medjugorje on May 15, 1995. But it was a useless journey. According to Vicka, all depends on Our Lady: "She is the one who decides."[49]

The situation had scarcely improved by the time the 1998 tests were conducted: on 22 and 23 April of that year, both Marija and Ivan agreed to be tested, but the results obtained on Ivan were largely unusable because of his high state of tension when connected to the equipment. And Jakov refused to be tested.[50] Moreover Vicka, as we have seen, although she was present, could only be given general tests, since she claimed she was having no visions at that time because the "Gospa" had asked her for this sacrifice between 20 April and 4 June.

As Marco Corvaglia notes, the last "pause" in visions for Vicka had taken place over ten years previously, in January 1988, and that pause, too, had coincided with medical tests—in that case, those planned by Dr Joyeux.[51]

Three months later, Dr Gagliardi and Fr Resch went to Medjugorje, arriving on 23 July, confident, now that Vicka's "pause" was over, that they could conduct tests on Jakov and her; but as before, the journey turned out to be largely fruitless. Although Mirjana and Ivanka said that they were ready to take part in some tests, since they no longer had daily visions it was clearly impossible to study them while in ecstasy, while Jakov was again unwilling to be tested apart from a simple psychodiagnostic examination.

But with regard to Vicka they were in for a surprise: she now claimed that she was undertaking another "pause" in visions, set to last five days, and that this had begun on 20 July. Fr Resch complained that something like this happened every time they came, to which Vicka responded: "As for your visit, Brother Slavko asked me if I could stay home from July 20 to St James [Feast of St James, 25 July], but I did not know if you'd come."[52]

In other words, Vicka's "pause" began on the very day that Fr Barbaric had informed her that the scientific team's arrival was imminent.

This certainly seems like a very convenient "pause," giving rise to the suspicion that Vicka was avoiding having to submit herself to any detailed tests.

Fr Resch then attempted to make new arrangements for September, and Vicka agreed to go to Italy on 7 or 8 September, but according to Marco Corvaglia, there is no record of any tests having been carried out on those dates. He contacted Fr Resch about this, and was told that tests did not take place then and that instead he met Vicka in Medjugorje, but that no ecstasy took place during their meeting, and thus there was no opportunity to do any tests.[53]

The impression is given in some Medjugorje books that the visionaries willingly cooperated with all that was expected of them regarding the various tests, but as the above litany of evasion and excuses makes clear, this was far from the case. Apart from the very early tests, which focused on the mental health of the visionaries, and which involved most if not all of them, the various later tests are all, for one reason or another, unsatisfactory.

In particular, Mirjana, Ivanka and to a lesser extent Jakov, none of whom now claims daily visions, have undergone little or no scientific testing, while of the other three, Vicka has managed to avoid a good number of the tests, mainly by claiming that the "Gospa" had requested "pauses" in her visions. Rather conveniently, these pauses just happened to coincide with the times when the tests were being done.

In all this, the chief apologist for the uncooperative and obstructive attitude of the visionaries was Fr Laurentin, and in sum, the only rational conclusion that can be reached is that no credence should be given to the exaggerated claims made about these tests.

Thus we can say regarding all the various tests to which the Medjugorje visionaries have been subject that none of them categorically demonstrates that their experiences are supernatural—indeed, this is in any case impossible to verify scientifically—nor have they been able to determine whether or not the visionaries have been lying. The other crucial point to make regarding these tests is that since none of them—apart from those conducted by the above-mentioned medical sub-committee of the Yugoslav Episcopal Conference—was commissioned by the proper spiritual authority, strictly speaking they have no relevance regarding the accurate discernment of what has been happening at Medjugorje. Only the Church possesses the divine authority and competence as regards such discernment.

* * *

AS WE HAVE SEEN, THEN, THERE IS CLEAR EVIDENCE to suggest that the initial stages of the visions at Medjugorje were diabolically inspired, but as time went on there does seem to have been far less activity of that sort there. Thus, the later ecstasies at Medjugorje seem to have had more of a human element in them, and the conclusion that they are largely self-induced "trances" seems very likely.

That is of course assuming that the use of words like "ecstasy" or "trance" can be justified, when in fact the EEG tests seem to indicate nothing particularly out of the ordinary was happening during the claimed experiences of the visionaries. Conversely, if individuals claim to see visions, then, as in the case of those who desire signs and wonders, this in itself opens up the possibility, if not the certainty, of diabolical intervention. Thus, the later activities of the Medjugorje visionaries during their trances may well have also unwittingly been subject to diabolical influence.

14
Medjugorje as Cult Religion

IVAN AND THE ROSARY

E. Michael Jones describes his experience of an encounter with Ivan Dragicevic in Medjugorje in May 1988. The visionary was with a group of international pilgrims at midday, standing by the side of the road in Bijakovici, about a hundred yards from his house. He was speaking to them with the translation being done by two tour guides. Jones describes him as looking "a little hot and a little bored." In response to one question, as to whether or not he had seen the Blessed Mother lately, one of the guides said: "Every day he sees our Lady at twenty to seven... at the choir loft."

The conversation then turned to prayer and Ivan told the crowd that Our Lady wanted them to spend ten minutes saying the Our Father, and he further informed them that he personally needed "two to two-and-a-half hours" to say a full rosary. The pilgrims were suitably impressed by this, but as Jones remarks, it would have been hard to imagine someone like Sr Lucia of Fatima acting in a similar fashion, speaking about herself by the side of a road.[1] And in point of fact, it is obvious from her memoirs that the children of Fatima did everything they could to avoid broadcasting the details of their experiences to curiosity seekers.

STRANGE LIGHTS AND SIGNS

Alleged signs and wonders in the vicinity of Medjugorje have been widely publicized in books favorable to the visions; for example, there have been many reports of lights on the hill Crnica which were taken to be supernatural. But according to Fr Sivric's investigations, these were simply fires lit on the hillside, some by shepherds as a precaution against wolves, and others by young people playing practical jokes. He also came across an account of somebody burning gasoline on Podbrdo.

Another common sign taken to have a heavenly significance concerns the massive cross on Krizevac, which some witnesses claim to have seen bathed in light, or assuming the shape of a woman, or even the "Gospa." However, it turns out that such phenomena have been observable for many years, and are due to a combination of weather and atmospheric conditions. According to Fr Sivric, who made his own investigations, this effect is linked to rain and quite easy to verify. Similarly, Mark Waterinckx reports that on a number of occasions, while present in Medjugorje, he saw that when the sun was shining at about 10 o'clock in the morning, at a particular angle, the cross on Krizevac seemed to disappear.

All of this indicates that these perceptions were not supernatural but most probably optical phenomena or illusions, which witnesses nevertheless interpreted in a supernatural way.[2]

MIRACLES OF THE SUN?

However, there have been apparently trustworthy witnesses who have stated that they have seen strange phenomena associated with the sun at Medjugorje—but these can probably be seen as having a rational explanation, or alternatively, as being due to diabolical influence. For example, in September 1986, Mary Craig was with a BBC crew who were making a film about the visions. After interviewing a good number of individuals, they returned to the village one evening, waiting outside the church at about 6:15 p.m. for two of the visionaries to appear. She then tells us that a

> sudden flash of light and tremor of excitement in the crowd made me turn and look in the direction of the sun. Almost to my horror, I witnessed what so many have called the "dance of the sun": the sun moving back and forth as though on a yo-yo string, its central incandescent white disk surrounded by spinning circles of yellow, green and red light, for all the world like a Catherine-wheel firework.

She then heard a fellow onlooker say that he had just realized that he had been staring directly at the Mediterranean sun for fully ten minutes, and was not dazzled in the slightest. Craig was startled by this and realized that she too had been looking at the sun for the same period, as had her companion. When she questioned him, he agreed that he had also been able to look directly at the sun without ill effect. Interestingly, both of them felt that there must be a rational explanation for what they had seen, and she explicitly said that she "had no sense of the numinous, only of the passing strange."[3]

Assuming for the moment that this incident was genuinely beyond nature—although as we will see, a scientific explanation may also be

Medjugorje as Cult Religion

possible — we have to bear in mind that that does not necessarily mean it was supernatural. There is a genuine "middle ground," the preternatural, where Satan is able to intervene under the right conditions. Given the questionable atmosphere surrounding Medjugorje, and given particularly the great desire of many pilgrims to see something, it wouldn't have been difficult for the right conditions to arise, in order to enable the devil to produce a false miracle.

And apart from that, it's obvious that what pilgrims like Craig saw — and the same could be said for any of the other alleged solar miracles at Medjugorje — is that they are outclassed by the Fatima miracle of the sun from every conceivable angle, whether it is the fact that the Fatima miracle was *genuinely* predicted three months in advance, or that it was seen over a huge area, or that it resulted in thousands of conversions and a complete renovation of Portuguese society.

A DANGEROUS DESIRE FOR THE MIRACULOUS

A good example of a possible false miracle took place during the approved appearances of the Blessed Virgin to the five children at Beauraing in Belgium in the early 1930s. A much larger than usual crowd of about fifteen thousand persons assembled on the evening of 8 December 1932, the feast of the Immaculate Conception, for that particular day's expected apparition. The atmosphere was highly charged, primarily because of an expectation that a miracle would be performed. This was despite the fact that Our Lady had said nothing to the children to encourage this belief. Some of those present that evening, who had been standing on a nearby railway embankment, claimed they had seen "on the mountain far over toward the east a whitish light having a human form." Thus, a rumor spread through the town that others, apart from the five children, had also seen something.

When about ten of these persons were questioned the next day, they were in a frightened and emotionally upset state, and some said they had seen something like Our Lady of Lourdes, but others gave different accounts — some "saw a blue belt, others saw blue rays emanating from the head, others saw a ball of fire." It is difficult to decide the exact cause of these visions, and although some form of multiple hallucination is possible, it seems more likely that they are evidence of a demonic intervention.[4]

There is quite a difference between these events and what happened regarding the miracle of the sun at Fatima. On 13 October 1917, a miracle had been promised and a huge crowd of 70,000 had assembled there with the expectation of seeing something, but without knowing exactly what would happen. But at Beauraing, no promise of a miracle had been given in advance, and so we can probably explain the strange visions which were seen by certain members of the crowd as resulting from an intense expectation.

This desire to see something, as St John of the Cross notes, is extremely dangerous since the devil is well able to satisfy such desires. He tells us that,

> the devil rejoices greatly when a soul desires to receive revelations, and when he sees it inclined to them, for he has then a great occasion and opportunity to insinuate errors and to detract from the faith in so far as he can, for ... he renders the soul that desires them very gross, and at times even leads it into many temptations and unseemly ways.

Elsewhere he makes a similar point: "Those who now desire to question God or receive some vision or revelation are guilty not only of foolish behaviour but also of offending him by not fixing their eyes entirely on Christ and by living with the desire for some other novelty."[5]

St John of the Cross (1542–1591) was one of the greatest writers on mystical theology in the history of Catholicism, and was made a Doctor of the Church in 1926.

St Teresa of Avila, another Doctor of the Church and mystical writer, also spoke about the dangers for those who desire spiritual favors, saying: "Such a one is certain to be deceived, or at least is in great danger of delusion, *for a door is thus left open to the Devil.*" She also pointed out another danger: "When people strongly desire such a thing, the imagination makes them *fancy they see or hear it,* just as when one's mind is set on a subject all day, one dreams of it at night."[6]

Regarding this idea of an intense desire for "signs and wonders," which has certainly been present among pilgrims at Medjugorje, Denis Nolan says, "It would be foolish to conclude ... that apparitions and supernatural phenomena exist merely because this thirst exists."[7]

But on this point, Nolan is completely wrong, as the teaching of St John of the Cross makes clear — apparitions and other apparently supernatural phenomena *can* very definitely occur if a sufficient desire for them is present.

DIABOLICAL POWER AND INFLUENCE

We read in the book of Revelation about the Beast who will wage war against the Church towards the end of time. He is to be assisted by a second beast whose task will be to make all the inhabitants of the earth worship his master. To this end, he works "great signs, even making fire come down from heaven to earth in the sight of men; and by the signs which it is allowed to work in the presence of the beast, it deceives those who dwell on earth..." (Rev 13:13–14).

This illustrates the way that during the "end times" the devil will be able to intervene in order to deceive mankind. So there is nothing inherently unlikely in his being able to exercise such powers to a lesser extent in our own days. Then, there will be an almost universal reign of evil on earth, which will give Satan great scope to act—but who will deny that the level of evil in our own days has not reached immense proportions?

It is only necessary to point to the huge number of abortions worldwide, to the great prevalence of pornography in the media, to drug use, to widespread secularization, and to oppression and injustice around the globe to realize this. Thus, with respect to Medjugorje, some sort of diabolical influence cannot be ruled out as the most likely explanation for many of the alleged solar miracles in the vicinity.

We have already looked at a possible sign of diabolical influence in the vicinity of Medjugorje with regard to the great storm which struck the village on the eve of the first vision in 1981. And if that is the case with thunder and lightning, then there is no reason why such an influence might not also extend to general atmospheric conditions around Medjugorje, and thus to the illusion of solar "miracles," since the sun's light has to pass through the atmosphere to reach us.

SOLAR MIRACLES AND GOLDEN ROSARIES

There is also the case of the false visions at Necedah, Wisconsin, which, as we will see in a later chapter, strongly savor of the diabolic. Here, on 7 October 1950, up to 100,000 people gathered to witness a promised miracle of the sun. This is what one person, Eloise Vlasak, claimed she saw:

> I looked at the crowd and everyone had golden patches on them.... [The sun] seemed to be spinning clockwise so fast; it turned a pale gold, silver and then... green. When it turned

green it still showed a luminous disk. It was as if God held a giant spotlight and [was] changing it with color prism slides.

Most people, however, including newspaper reporters, didn't see anything unusual. But the fact that some people did see a "solar miracle" indicates that under the right conditions, diabolical influences are very possible, although in this case hallucination cannot be ruled out.[8]

Claims that metal rosary links have changed color at Medjugorje, often assuming a golden hue, have been widely reported. For many people this has become the standard Medjugorje "miracle," but it cannot be emphasized strongly enough that such phenomena can likewise also have a preternatural explanation, as a result of an intense desire to experience something "miraculous." At best, such a "miracle" can only be described as trivial and unworthy of God, and regrettably it has not been unknown for such things to have happened in association with false visionaries.

One example of this concerns the Necedah visionary, Mary Ann Van Hoof, who "blessed" religious items and rosaries, and similarly, there were reports of rosaries turning to gold at Necedah. When the journalist Marlene Maloney investigated Necedah in the late 80s, she was able to see one of these rosaries, confirming that the chain had indeed "changed to a gold color." But she goes on to say that this effect "certainly didn't suggest the work of God: the wooden beads had turned a dull, nauseating golden green." She took the rosary to a jeweler who explained that, on a natural level, this change could have taken place if the rosary had been dipped into a particular chemical and then warmed.[9]

NATURAL EXPLANATIONS FOR THE "MIRACULOUS"

It is probable, too, that some of the alleged miracles of the sun at Medjugorje can be explained in natural terms. Fr Sivric deals with the way it supposedly danced a little before sunset on 2 August 1981, pointing out that talk of the "Gospa's" visions was naturally on everybody's lips, and so there was a heightened expectation of signs and wonders in the air. Recalling that he was born and brought up in Medjugorje, he relates that as a child, during the warm summer months, he can remember seeing spectacular sunsets, which, due to particular atmospheric conditions, would give the impression of two or even three "suns" one on top of the other. It seems that most of these unusual signs took place during the early months of the visions, when excitement was at its height, in a psychologically charged atmosphere, and thus there was a predisposition to believe they were true.[10]

In addition, Paolo Apolito points to research carried out to investigate alleged solar prodigies which are supposed to have happened at Medjugorje and many other visionary sites. He particularly cites experiments by two researchers, Malanga and Pinotti, who, after studying films taken at Medjugorje and some Italian sites—films which consistently show the sun pulsating—were able to replicate the effects produced. These seemed to show the sun rotating or turning green, amongst other effects. Malanga and Pinotti thought that these effects might be due to videotaping solar light, and noted that they only occurred when the camera was set up with a particular lens aperture. At this setting:

> When too much light hits the electronic circuits of the video camera, it tends automatically to close the electronic shutter which in automatic mode remains closed, but in manual mode reopens, returning to the conditions set by the operator, which produces the phenomena cyclically.[11]

So it is perfectly possible to explain, in purely natural terms, through the particular settings on a video camera, these different motions of the sun and different colors emanating from it, which thousands of people have been led to believe were of truly miraculous origin. Moreover, in an interview given by Bishop Ratko Peric, and published in the diocesan newspaper *Crkva na Kamenu* (*The Church on the Rock*), he made the following interesting comment:

> Medjugorje was already "phenomenal" in the last century. Fr Petar Bakula, OFM, noted in a book he wrote in 1867 that people were even then claiming to see a very strong and pinkish light in and around Medjugorje. So the "phenomenon of light" did not start to fascinate people for the first time in 1981, but rather goes back to the last century.[12]

Even Fr Laurentin accepts that the majority of these miracles can be explained in a natural way:

> If one watches the sun near its setting (dazzling and not yet turned red), it ceases to dazzle at the end of a second [sic]. The center becomes dull in color, "like a Host," say those who are religiously struck by this sign, while the periphery stays luminate and radiant. Those phenomena do not require supernatural explanations at all.[13]

THE RESULTS OF SUN-GAZING

Marco Corvaglia describes the work of Professor Auguste Meessen, of the Department of Physics at the Catholic University of Louvain, Belgium, who produced a report entitled, "Apparitions and Miracles of the Sun." In this, he gives details of some experiments in which he looked at the sun in particular conditions, including the following instance:

> In November 2002, I looked directly into the sun, at about 4 p.m. The sun was relatively low above the horizon and its light intensity was attenuated, although the sky was clear. I was able to look right into the sun and was amazed to see that the sun was immediately converted into a grey disc, surrounded by a brilliant ring. The grey disc was practically uniform, while the surrounding ring was somewhat irregular and flamboyant, but did not extend beyond the solar disk. It coincided with its rim.

He goes on to hypothesize that the sun became gray because of a reduction in sensitivity of his eyes due to "bleaching of pigments in the colour-sensitive cones of the fovea," as well as secondary processes in the eye. He comments that this is an automatic adaptation and a purely natural process.

Professor Meessen also investigated the production of the different colors that the testimonies from some Medjugorje witnesses speak of:

> In a second experiment, realized at 3 p.m. in December 2002, I looked straight at the sun during a much longer time. After some minutes, I saw impressive colours, up to 2 or 3 times the diameter of the sun. They changed, but were mainly pink, deep blue, red and green. Further away, the sky became progressively more luminous. I stopped there, since I understood that these colours resulted from the fact that the red, green and blue sensitive pigments [of the eyes] are bleached and regenerated at different rates.

He concluded that the brain analyses these changes, but in the process of making sense of the information it is receiving, *illusions* are possible.

And as Marco Corvaglia notes, in a place like Medjugorje, where sun-gazing is a recognized pilgrimage activity, it is inevitable that when the necessary conditions are present, a number of pilgrims will see "something" when staring at the sun. These will then invite other pilgrims to do likewise, with the result that some will also see a "solar miracle," while others will see nothing.[14]

Overall, these experiments indicate that a natural explanation for many of the "solar miracles" reported at Medjugorje is quite possible, although further research into this area is required. But that this is the case is apparent from video evidence.

The documentary "The Visionaries from Medjugorje tried by Science," which is available in Medjugorje, has scenes relating to one of the alleged miracles of the sun that occurred at Medjugorje. They show people looking at the sun, while a "miracle" is supposedly happening, but the camera focuses on these individuals and not the sun itself. During these scenes people are obviously reacting to "something," with one woman clasping her hands together, close to tears, and a young boy actually weeping. But at the end of the scene we finally see that the sun, as recorded by the camera—and apart from the sort of "flaring" which happens when a video camera is turned towards the sun—looks absolutely normal. Many other instances of alleged solar miracles are given at YouTube, for example, but on examination they can be explained as effects due to the nature of the cameras or camcorders being used.[15]

THE DANGERS OF MEDJUGORJE SUN-GAZING

Staring at the sun at Medjugorje has also had its tragic side, concerning those people who have seriously damaged their eyes because of a desire to see something miraculous. E. Michael Jones recounts his own meeting with two sisters who were fellow pilgrims to Medjugorje, one of whom, on hearing that a friend of hers had seen the sun spin, decided the next day to stare at the noonday sun, until, as she related, "an arrow of pain" hit her eyes and "everything went orange." The result was permanent eye damage due to scarring of the retina.[16]

This dangerous side of Medjugorje sun-gazing is clearly indicated in the relevant scientific literature. For example, the *British Journal of Ophthalmology* published a paper in 1988 entitled, "Solar retinopathy following religious rituals," written by three doctors. The term "solar retinopathy" refers to damage caused to the retina of the eye by the sun. The paper detailed four cases of such damage due to pilgrims gazing at the sun during "religious rituals," three of which were directly related to Medjugorje. As the paper states: "All four patients suffered irreversible visual loss."

And these were not isolated incidents: similar cases are recounted in the *Journal of the Louisiana State Medical Society* and the *New England Journal of Medicine*.[17]

MIRACULOUS CURES AT MEDJUGORJE?

As regards talk of miraculous cures at Medjugorje, this, too, seems to have been greatly exaggerated. A dossier of over fifty alleged cures, compiled by Fr Ljudevit Rupcic, joint author with Fr Laurentin of the bestselling Medjugorje book mentioned earlier, was presented to Dr Mangiapan, the head of the medical bureau at Lourdes, but his conclusions were negative. In the April 1984 edition of the *Association Medicale Internationale de Lourdes*, he stated that the cases he had been presented with were described very briefly and without adequate supporting evidence.

Dr Mangiapan wrote to Bishop Zanic, saying "this whole file [on miracles] has practically no value... and, such as it is, it could not serve to mount any weighty argument for a place of apparitions."[18]

There is the case of the alleged cure of Venka Bilic-Brajcic, a woman suffering from cancer. After a mastectomy in 1980, and radiation treatment, scabs began to appear on one of her breasts. Her sister urged her to pray to the Gospa, and according to Frs Laurentin and Rupcic she began to feel better, returned to Medjugorje to give thanks, and also submitted medical documents in September 1982. However, sadly, she died, in June 1984. An even more famous supposed miracle involved Diana Basile from Milan, who was allegedly cured of multiple sclerosis, and attendant blindness in one eye, in May 1984. This event received a great deal of publicity, but when Bishop Zanic arranged for the medical records of the case to be sent to the medical bureau at Lourdes, Dr Mangiapan responded that, because multiple sclerosis can go into spontaneous remission, it was very difficult to verify whether a cure had really taken place.[19]

It is interesting to note that Fr Rupcic, writing during the 1980s, describes the case of Diana Basile as not only "the one that has been most thoroughly examined," but also as "the most important among the healings in Medjugorje."[20]

Randall Sullivan says that in investigating accounts of alleged cures at Medjugorje, he was forced to admit that he

> could not help but notice how many of them involved either MS [multiple sclerosis] or some other disease that attacked

the nervous system. Difficult to diagnose and impossible to cure, such illnesses also are remarkably resistant to scientific study, making it very difficult to prove that a healing has been miraculous.

He goes on, though, to say: "Many of the cases in the files at Medjugorje involved injuries and diseases more suitable to scientific certification. At least two of those who claimed miraculous healings were themselves medical doctors."[21]

The problem with this approach is that it is somewhat contradictory and vague—in both quotes Sullivan talks in terms of "many" cases but doesn't give us any idea of numbers so we can judge what percentage of alleged cures are more likely to be genuine. And this is quite apart from the fact that no matter how many such "cures" are brought forward, they have no standing in the eyes of the Church since they have not been verified by the legitimate spiritual authority.

So we are clearly a long way here from the astounding cures of organic diseases which have taken place at authentic Marian shrines such as Lourdes, and which *have* been verified by the Church.

The Australian investigative journalist, Terry Willesee, a Catholic, traveled to Medjugorje and was responsible for producing a video on the subject, in 1991, entitled *All I Need Is a Miracle*. Despite serious investigation he was not able to uncover any alleged miraculous events which could be substantiated as being of genuinely supernatural origin.[22]

* * *

TO CONCLUDE, ALL THE ABOVE EVIDENCE INDICATES that what has happened in Medjugorje, as regards claims for miraculous signs and wonders, is far from decisive, and indeed, while many of them can be explained in natural terms, again there is a real possibility that some of them may be due to diabolical activity. Regarding the claims for miraculous cures, it is clear, too, that none of them can be accepted from a rigorous medical viewpoint. Regrettably, all of this is further evidence of the defective nature of critically important aspects of Medjugorje which have rarely been exposed to proper public scrutiny.

15

The Church and Medjugorje

THE HOLY SEE AND MEDJUGORJE

During the 1980s, the apparently impressive reports about a religious revival emanating from Medjugorje had to be taken seriously. But it seems that, as time went on, the Holy See adopted a more realistic approach, taking account of the various negative elements which also become evident. No doubt, the Vatican also had to bear in mind the fact that, as the movement in favor of Medjugorje increased in popularity, attracting not just thousands but in due course millions of pilgrims from all over the world, there was an increasing possibility that a negative judgment might lead to the formation of an alternative, breakaway Medjugorje-based "Church."[1] This, of course, wouldn't necessarily have had to be very big to cause considerable confusion and problems.

Certainly, as in so many areas of Church life which were proving contentious in the post-Vatican II era, the Holy See was keen to take a non-confrontational approach in trying to sort out problems, as, for example, those caused by dissident theologians. The same approach also seems to have been adopted with regard to alleged visions.[2]

In *The Ratzinger Report*, published in 1985, the then Cardinal Ratzinger, who replaced Cardinal Seper as the Prefect of the Congregation for the Doctrine of the Faith in the early 1980s, was queried by the Italian journalist Vittorio Messori, who asked him if he thought some sort of "clarifying statement" on Medjugorje from the Congregation was needed. The question arose because of the large number of pilgrims who were by then going to Medjugorje, and was also prompted by the ongoing conflict between the Franciscans and the local bishop.

The first part of the Cardinal's response was as follows: "In this area, more than ever, patience is the fundamental principle of the policy of our Congregation." He then went on to say, "One of the signs of our times is that the announcements of 'Marian apparitions' are multiplying all over the world." Just prior to this, he had remarked that, "we certainly cannot prevent God from speaking to our time through simple persons and also through extraordinary signs that point to the insufficiency of the cultures stamped by rationalism and positivism that dominate us."[3]

From these words, it seems that Cardinal Ratzinger was at least open to the possibility that these reports of apparitions should be taken seriously, and moreover, according to Fr Michael O'Carroll, the cardinal was here specifically speaking about Medjugorje. Given the support Medjugorje was receiving from theologians such as Fr Hans Urs von Balthasar and Fr Laurentin, it would have been difficult for him to think otherwise at this stage, especially taking into account all the information circulating about Medjugorje at the time regarding its positive fruits. In respect of the conduct of pilgrims, conversions, fasting, and so on, much of this was apparently genuine in the early days.

In addition, in February 1985, Archbishop Franic had sent a report on Medjugorje to Cardinal Ratzinger, in which he gave his support to the Franciscans and particularly Fr Vlasic. He pointed to the great number of pilgrims and the other fruits, and characterized the letter circulated by Bishop Zanic as having "already caused scandal." In particular, he called for an "International Commission dependent on the Holy See itself, to evaluate the difficulties raised by His Excellency, the Bishop of Mostar." He made the same point further on, and said that action needed to be taken "before the Bishop succeeds in banning pilgrimages to Medjugorje definitively."

Meanwhile, Bishop Zanic had sent a letter of his own to the Secretariat of State at the Vatican, in January 1985, complaining about the books published by Fathers Laurentin and Rupcic, and likewise about the activities of Archbishop Franic, saying that his attitude in supporting "all this propaganda...has appeared most improper and troublesome." He described the latter's archiepiscopal Curia as a "kind of Medjugorje Centre," and stated that the archbishop had visited Medjugorje, preached there, and had given interviews in *Glas Koncila* to the Medjugorje Franciscans. He had also "visited the homes of the visionaries without any notification to the local bishop or Father Provincial, as if these did not exist." He finished by saying: "I beg the Holy See to be good enough to issue enlightened directives on the subject."[4]

To return to Cardinal Ratzinger, Messori asked what other criteria the Congregation was using to judge these events, to which the cardinal replied: "One of our criteria is to separate the aspect of the true or presumed 'supernaturality' of the apparition from that of its spiritual fruits." He then went on to speak of ancient pilgrimage sites which might not have much in the way of "scientific truth" about their traditions, but which were nevertheless spiritually fruitful at the time. He concluded by saying: "The problem is not so much that of modern hypercriticism (which ends up later, moreover, in a form of new credulity), but it is that of the evaluation of the vitality and of the orthodoxy of the religious life that is developing around these places."[5]

VATICAN CONCERNS ABOUT MEDJUGORJE

The great difficulty for the Church is that it cannot rush in and make a hasty judgment, and thus it has to be open to the possibility that any claimed vision may be genuine, at least initially, assuming that there are some good aspects present. And in the case of Medjugorje, the initial signs — prayer, fasting, conversions — did seem good, at least to the outside observer. It was only gradually that the negative aspects became apparent, and by then the whole Medjugorje movement had built up an appreciable momentum worldwide.[6]

Meanwhile, by the mid-1980s, the early hostility of the Yugoslav government was abating, as it adopted a different attitude towards Medjugorje. With pilgrim numbers increasing, it was realized that it was a potentially lucrative source of income, and thus from this time onwards, pilgrimages were encouraged. All this was taking place against the backdrop of the severe economic crisis which had developed following the death of Tito in 1980. The government was careful to ensure that accommodation costs were paid directly to it, but clearly there were many other ways that local people could make a profit even though this financial activity mainly took place in the local currency, the dinar, which had no value outside Yugoslavia.[7]

And as Marco Corvaglia points out, there is clear evidence of a softening of the government's attitude towards Medjugorje over time in the 1980s. Indeed, in 1983, a state publishing house, AG Matos, published a pro-Medjugorje work by Fr Ljudevit Rupcic, *Gospina ukazanja u Medjugorju* ("The apparitions of Our Lady at Medjugorje"). And from 1984, state travel agencies, such as Atlas in Dubrovnik, began providing pilgrim services, while articles in favor of the alleged apparitions were appearing in newspapers controlled by the Communist regime. There were even pro-Medjugorje television programs broadcast by Yugoslav state television, such as the documentary *Faith and Mysticism*, shown on 16 October 1985. Apparently, after this program pilgrim numbers to Medjugorje from within the country increased significantly.[8]

By the mid-1980s, Bishop Zanic was very concerned about the way the whole phenomenon of the visions was developing, and the wider effect they were having in Croatia. He wrote a prophetic letter to this effect to Fr Laurentin on 25 January 1985, arguing that a "fierce frenzy has taken hold of many faithful who were good until now; they have become excessive and peculiar penitents... One can look forward to a religious war here."[9] It seems, though, that the bishop was referring to a "war" between supporters and opponents of Medjugorje, rather than the violence which actually broke out in the region later on.

There was obviously some concern in the Vatican too, since, on 23 May 1985, a warning about Medjugorje was issued by Archbishop Alberto Bovone, Undersecretary of the Congregation for the Doctrine of the Faith, in the form of a letter sent to the bishops of Italy. This letter indicated that official pilgrimages to Medjugorje should not be organized, while also deploring the publicity campaign surrounding the alleged visions, and the confusion that was resulting. Here is the entire text of the letter sent to the secretary of the Italian Bishops' Conference, Msgr Egidio Caporello:

> Your Excellency, from many parts, especially from the competent Ordinary of Mostar (Yugoslavia), one can gather and lament the vast propaganda given to the "events" tied to the so-called apparitions in Medjugorje, for which pilgrimages and other initiatives have been organized that only contribute to the creation of confusion amongst the faithful and interfere with the work of the appointed Commission which is delicately examining the "events" under scrutiny. In order to avoid enhancing this mentioned propaganda and speculation going on in Italy, despite all that has been expressed and recommended by the Bishops' Conference of Yugoslavia, could this Presidency please suggest to the Italian Episcopate to publicly discourage the organizing of pilgrimages to the so-called centre of apparitions, as well as all other forms of publicity, especially written materials, which could be considered prejudicial to a sober assertion of the facts on the part of the Special Commission which has been canonically formed for this purpose. I take this opportunity to express the assurances of my highest regards....[10]

Clearly then, Cardinal Ratzinger's Congregation was concerned about the "vast propaganda" and "speculation" surrounding Medjugorje at this time.

A NEW COMMISSION OF INQUIRY

Then, during the following year, on 2 May 1986, the enlarged commission of inquiry presented its verdict to Bishop Zanic, criticizing the alleged visions, and the following month he sent this report to the Holy See. However, this was not made public, and instead, on 18 January 1987, the formation of yet a third commission was announced, but this time at the higher level of the Yugoslav Bishops' Conference. According to the joint statement on this commission issued by Cardinal Kuharic and Bishop Zanic, this step was taken because the events at Medjugorje were increasingly having a wider impact throughout the Church, and moreover, the formation of this third commission was a Vatican initiative. This is clear from the third paragraph of the joint statement, which, after pointing out that the CDF had been made aware of the most recent commission's work, said it had "urged that that work be continued at the level of the National Conference of Bishops."[11]

The immediate result was that the supporters of Medjugorje were able to claim that Bishop Zanic had been undermined and that the Holy See had removed the Medjugorje dossier from his jurisdiction, and this was the message that went out to the world, even though it was not actually the case. In reality, the situation was much more complicated, in that the transfer of the dossier released Bishop Zanic from having to make a difficult decision on his own, especially given the trying relationship he had with the Medjugorje Franciscans, while also allowing him to share the burden of responsibility with the Bishops' Conference.[12] As we will see, what happened here was actually in line with the provisions laid down in *Normae Congregationis*, the 1978 document on the discernment of claims of private revelations, which was issued by the Congregation for the Doctrine of the Faith.

POPE JOHN PAUL II AND MEDJUGORJE

As regards the role of Pope John Paul II in this whole question, Fr Laurentin claimed, in 1997, that he had given the pope a copy of his book on Medjugorje, and that this had influenced the pontiff. Given that Fr Laurentin had proved such a supporter of Medjugorje, he may well have given John Paul II an overly optimistic account of what was happening there. But having said that, the pope's sympathy towards movements involving young people was probably also a factor in the general mood of unwillingness to see Medjugorje condemned, in addition to the effect of the accounts then being circulated about its fruits. And as Fr Sivric points out, the fact that Medjugorje could well have been an indication of the presence of the Blessed Virgin in a Communist country, which would undoubtedly be a boost for Catholicism, was perhaps also a factor influencing the Vatican at this stage.[13]

Moreover, we also have a report published in 1987, following the *ad limina* visit of the Venetian bishops to Rome, during which they apparently asked the pope what he thought about Medjugorje, to which he gave a non-committal response, while encouraging any spiritual fruits obtained through Medjugorje.[14]

However, the following year, 1988, Archbishop (later Cardinal) Pio Laghi, the former Apostolic Pro-Nuncio to the United States, stated in a letter: "Although there have been made observations about Medjugorje attributed to the Holy Father or other officials of the Holy See, none of these have been acknowledged as authentic."[15] More recent evidence concerning John Paul II's private devotion for Medjugorje is given in a later chapter. But it should always be remembered that a pope's *private* opinion on this or any other matter has no binding authority for the faithful.

Much the same can be said for the support given to Medjugorje by individuals such as Mother Teresa and Fr Gabriele Amorth. While freely acknowledging Mother Teresa's outstanding holiness, this, of itself, did not make her an expert on Medjugorje. There is nothing to suggest that she had made any detailed examination of the facts and controversies surrounding it. Similarly, while acknowledging Fr Amorth's expertise as an exorcist, again, there is nothing to indicate that he had fully investigated Medjugorje. Indeed, it is clear from a 2002 interview he gave on the subject that he had been the leader of a Medjugorje prayer group since 1984,[16] and was thus an early and, it would appear, a largely uncritical devotee of the visions.

FR SIVRIC'S BOOK ON MEDJUGORJE

1988 also saw the publication of a book in French by Fr Ivo Sivric, which highlighted the problems that emerged when Medjugorje was examined seriously. In 1989 it was translated into English, under the title *The Hidden Side of Medjugorje,* and as we have seen, it detailed, amongst other things, the original interviews between Fr Zovko and the visionaries, which revealed a great deal of hitherto largely unknown material about how Medjugorje had really begun.

Fr Sivric was eminently qualified to write a book on Medjugorje, since it was his birthplace, and he was well acquainted with the local situation. In addition, he was a Franciscan, and so was fully aware of the nature of the problems involving some members of the Order and successive local bishops. After ordination in Yugoslavia, in 1941, he went to Rome for further studies, and then settled in the United States, teaching at Duquesne University and writing a number of books.

On hearing about the visions, he returned to his native country, and spent a total of about six months in Medjugorje at various times in 1983, 1984 and 1986. So he not only brought the right qualities to his studies, but had also benefited from his time abroad, which meant he had the ability to look at the situation from a broader perspective. Thus, for all these reasons, he was very well qualified to understand events in Medjugorje.

Fr Laurentin criticized this book in one of his periodic newsletters, but even so, he was obliged to admit that its "sources are fundamental.... The numerous translated Croatian documents are a service to specialists.... Thus, one can only congratulate him for having so carefully decoded and edited these probing interviews."[17]

* * *

WE HAVE SEEN IN THIS CHAPTER, THEN, THAT THE position adopted by the Church has gradually clarified over time. To begin with there was an attitude of openness to the possibility that Medjugorje might be genuine: the initial signs seemed good—what could be wrong with calls to prayer, fasting, and a return to the sacraments? But that attitude was gradually replaced with one of greater caution, as some of the doubtful elements regarding Medjugorje began to emerge.

By that time, though, the movement in its favor had grown to such proportions that Church authorities were faced with the dilemma of how to deal with the pastoral needs of the hundreds of thousands of pilgrims going there in good faith. Moreover, the political situation in Yugoslavia, and indeed Eastern Europe generally, was still causing concern. As a result, a definitive decision about Medjugorje has been consistently postponed, but surely such a delicate balancing act cannot be maintained indefinitely.

16
Medjugorje Credibility Problems

THE CREDIBILITY OF VICKA

Apart from the problems described above, the credibility of the visionaries has also come under increasingly close scrutiny as time has gone on. Regarding Vicka, the somewhat "difficult" side of her character comes across quite clearly in her talks with Fr Bubalo, as set down in his book, *A Thousand Encounters with the Blessed Virgin Mary in Medjugorje*. For instance, when he asked her about the nature of the holy water with which she sprinkled the "Gospa" on the third day, she responded thus: "Lord [!], why are you making like an Englishman? As though you don't know that in every christian home we have blessed salt, and also holy water."[1]

There are other examples of this type of thing found in the book, but suffice to say that she comes across as a difficult individual, one whose behavior is not consistent with what would be expected of a genuine Marian seer. Even Fr Vlasic could make a comment such as the following about Vicka: "this girl is choleric and has a brusque and sometimes aggressive style."

In another conversation, during which Fr Bubalo asked Vicka about her experience of heaven — which she alleged she had seen in a vision along with Jakov — he told her that somebody "once told me (and he was poking fun at it) that you said, telling of that Heaven, that Heaven has some kind of doors. What is your response now?" To this, Vicka replied: "Why the same as then! There where we stood with the Virgin there is some sort of tunnel, some sort of door, and next to them a man is standing. The Virgin said not everyone can enter. You need a *permit* there too. A narrow passage awaits everyone there."[2]

Whatever sort of reception people can expect at the gates of eternity, one thing is certain: permits will *not* be required to enter heaven! This episode, with its mention of "permits," is probably more due to Vicka's fertile imagination, and her experience of life under a Communist system, than any supernatural encounter.

Fr Bubalo then went on to discuss her alleged visions of purgatory and hell. She described purgatory as "some sort of dark chasm, some dark space between Heaven and Hell. It is filled with something like ashes and ... it looks awful!" Then she claimed to have been taken to hell by the "Gospa," describing it as a place of: "Fire ... devils ... awful people! All are horned, with tails ... all look like devils! They all struggle ... God deliver us, and that's all!"[3]

VICKA AND HELL

This text on hell raises a number of problems, particularly the point that *all* the inhabitants of hell are "horned" and "have tails." It is unlikely that any human beings in hell will assume the traditional form of demons, that is as horned and tailed, and this description probably owes more to pictures Vicka might have seen of hell, or books she had read on the subject, or sermons she had heard, than anything supernatural.

Also, the use of points of ellipsis [...] in the above quote could be due to one of two reasons: either that is the way Vicka spoke, in a disjointed way, or else there is material which has been deliberately omitted, possibly because of its foolish/embarrassing/heretical nature. Certainly, the use of ellipsis is not a feature of the book generally.

A more weighty objection is that it is clear from her account that these alleged visions were not momentary, as was the case of the vision of hell seen at Fatima by the three seers, but were quite extensive. Vicka claims that the "Gospa" took them, through the roof of Jakov's house, on this tour of heaven, purgatory and hell, and then dropped them back at his house again.

The children of Fatima only saw hell for an *instant*, but that instant was enough to completely change their lives. Jacinta in particular was very much affected by the vision of hell. As Sr Lucia recounts in her *Third Memoir*, it "made a very strong impression on her...[and] filled her with horror to such a degree, that every penance and mortification was as nothing in her eyes, if it could only prevent souls from going there."

Sr Lucia also tells us that Jacinta "often" sat on the ground or a rock and exclaimed: "Oh, Hell! Hell! How sorry I am for the souls who go to hell! And the people down there, burning alive, like wood in the fire!" Then "shuddering" she would kneel down and recite the prayer that Our Lady had taught them to say at the end of each decade of the rosary: "O my Jesus! Forgive us, save us from the fire of hell. Lead all souls to Heaven, especially those who are most in need."

Sr Lucia further reports that:

Jacinta remained on her knees like this for long periods of time, saying the same prayer over and over again. From time to time, like someone awaking from sleep, she called out to her brother or myself: "Francisco! Francisco! Are you praying with me? We must pray very much, to save souls from hell! So many go there! So many!"[4]

Clearly, too, Lucia and Francisco were also deeply affected by this vision, if not quite to the same extent as Jacinta. Contrast that, though, with the effects on Vicka and Jakov—they allegedly went on an extended excursion around the celestial and infernal regions, but is there any sign of their developing a spirituality even remotely like that of the Fatima seers? Where are the lives of intense mortification and penance that they ought to be leading if they really did see hell? The reality is that their lives are more like those of celebrities than saints, and this tells us all we really need to know about Vicka's alleged visions of the afterlife.

MORE PROBLEMS WITH VICKA

Further questions about Vicka can also be raised following an incident that took place on 14 January 1985. This event has to be understood in the context of Vicka's repeated claims that during their "ecstasies," the visionaries saw or heard nothing except the "Gospa." For example, during her interviews with Fr Bubalo, in 1983, she made the following statements: "We see the Virgin, but we don't see anything else or sense anything else," and: "As soon as we begin to pray, the wall disappears. All disappears," and also: "When the Virgin appears, I no longer see nor hear anything except her."[5] In theory then, Vicka shouldn't have responded to any outside stimulus.

What happened, though, was this: a pilgrim named Jean-Louis Martin, although initially enthusiastic about Medjugorje, gradually came to have doubts, and decided to put one of the visionaries to the test. Also present on this occasion were Fr Tomislav Pervan, who was the parish priest, Fr Slavko Barbaric, Fr Ivica Vego, and Louis Bélanger, who was there to film the visionaries in "ecstasy." While Vicka was in an apparent ecstasy in the apparition room at the church, Martin made as if to poke her in the eyes with his fingers, and she reacted as if she had been startled, moving her head *away* from him. Remember, according to her own testimony, she said: "We see the Virgin, *but we don't see anything else or sense anything else.*"

She left the room accompanied by Fr Vego, while Fr Barbaric confronted Jean-Louis Martin about the incident. Vicka returned after a while, with Fr Vego, and then offered the quite incredible explanation that she had moved her head away in order to prevent the baby Jesus from falling, as she was under the impression that the Blessed Virgin was about to drop him. This attempted explanation is clearly nonsensical on a purely physical level, because if the baby Jesus had really been about to slip, then Vicka ought to have moved *forward* to prevent this. This account was videoed too, because Louis Bélanger had inadvertently left his camera running; thus the whole incident was captured on film and has been widely circulated. No doubt this episode is the reason why the apparition room was closed to the public from 27 January 1985.[6]

SOME ALTERNATIVE EXPLANATIONS

Daria Klanac claims that on this occasion, Vicka was actually talking about a previous vision, but if we look at a transcript of what Vicka said to Fr Vego, this is not the case. Here are her words: "So, Ivica, I was on my knees here. I saw him (Jean-Louis) only when I entered.... I was on my knees here. And I was praying. Afterwards I saw nothing, neither him nor Pervan, nobody. I have not seen anything."

So at this point, Vicka was apparently claiming that once she had entered her "ecstasy" she saw only the "Gospa" and nothing else, and didn't see Jean-Louis Martin dart his fingers towards her head.

Vicka then went on to say: "Once, when the Madonna was narrating her life to me, when the Virgin showed me the Child Jesus in her arms, he bended so, while she was holding Jesus, I thought he would slip."

Here, Vicka is introducing the idea that in a *previous* vision she thought the baby Jesus would fall out of the Gospa's hands, before going on to say: "But I did not see anyone *here* [that is now, on this occasion]. Only, she has showed me the little baby. Yes, it is so, *I was only afraid that the child was slipping*. It was so, she kept her hand so. He was there, *as if I was going to take him*."[7]

So Vicka here clearly distinguishes between an alleged previous vision and what happened on this occasion, when she was "afraid that the child was slipping," and this was her explanation for why she moved. This is what Fr Laurentin says about this incident:

Medjugorje Credibility Problems

Ivica, a young Franciscan, was charged to ask Vicka about the fact. He had to provide an explanation (in German), requested by Bellanger [sic], a Canadian parapsychologist who has studied the apparitions. Harassed with questions, Vicka explained that during this apparition she had a moment of emotion, because the Virgin held the Infant Jesus in her arms and she was afraid that he was falling.

And this was the explanation which Vicka later gave to Fr Laurentin: "I have been questioned so much about this apparition that I have recounted this particular: The Infant Jesus seemed not to be safely held in the arms of his mother. I know that nothing can happen to Jesus in his glory. But I had the feeling that he was falling."[8]

The irony of this situation is that if Vicka had said nothing, Medjugorje apologists could probably have explained away her moving her head as evidence that perhaps her "ecstasy" wasn't as deep as expected, or that it was an unconscious reaction, or that, really, a lot more research into the precise nature of ecstasy is needed before we can fully understand it. But the fact that she felt obliged to say something is clear evidence that she was aware that all was not well, and that an explanation of some sort was required. Unfortunately for her, the explanation she gave, rather than clarifying the matter, only made it more obvious that her account was unbelievable.

ST BERNADETTE'S GENUINE ECSTASIES

And if we contrast this with an incident involving Bernadette Soubirous, which took place at Lourdes on 7 April 1858, the date of the seventeenth apparition, this becomes even more apparent. Bernadette saw the Blessed Virgin early that morning, and had already entered ecstasy, when Dr Dozous, a local medical man, and a skeptic, arrived. He was surprised to see that Bernadette, on her knees, had cupped her hands around the flame of a large candle before her, to protect it from the wind, holding on to it with her wrists. The flickering flame was touching the inside of her curved palms, and someone in the crowd shouted, "She's burning!" But Dr Dozous, anxious to determine whether Bernadette's claims were genuine or not, cried out: "Leave her alone." After the ecstasy, he examined her hands, and was astonished to discover not the slightest trace of any burns on them. As a result of this, the doctor became an instantaneous and enthusiastic convert.[9]

Most people realize that holding one's hand in a flame, even a candle flame, and even just for a moment, is very painful. But no one in a normal waking state could bear to have the flame of a large candle play on their fingers for even a few seconds without crying out and sustaining serious burns.

So Bernadette was in a genuine ecstasy, totally oblivious to the world, and that is the difference between a real ecstasy and a "Medjugorje ecstasy."

Contrast this incident, too, with the algometer test mentioned previously, which was designed to test the visionaries' sensitivity to pain. As we have seen, it was really quite inadequate, in that the amount of actual pain was not great, nor was the time duration of the test sufficient. But a real life "test" like Bernadette's is a very different matter — a candle flame can have a temperature of over 1,000°C — and just a few seconds in such a flame is absolutely agonizing. The maximum temperature the algometer could reach was just 50°C. In fact, any normal person, outside of a genuine ecstasy such as Bernadette's, would instantly withdraw their hand from a candle flame. When the Medjugorje visionaries submit to such a genuine test, and allow a candle flame to be played over their hands while they are in one of their alleged ecstasies, then skeptics will take their claims more seriously.

And there is another difference between genuine seers like St Bernadette and the Medjugorje visionaries: on one occasion, one of the visitors to her home — which was a one-room hovel at the old jail in Lourdes, the *Cachot* — tried to slip a gold coin into her hand; but she rejected it vigorously and exclaimed: "*It burns me.*" In fact she rejected all such offers of money,[10] which, as we will see, has apparently not been the case with the Medjugorje visionaries, who live in smart houses, drive expensive cars and, in general, live rather comfortable lives.

IVAN AND THE "SIGN"

In May 1982, Bishop Zanic sent two members of the investigative commission he had set up the previous January, to question the visionaries about the miraculous sign that had been promised. They were asked to describe this sign but refused, prompting suspicions that they had been tipped off. Mirjana was in Sarajevo at the time, and she too refused to comply, leading Bishop Zanic to suspect that somebody had contacted her by phone.

On this occasion Ivan Dragicevic was also absent, away at the Franciscan seminary in Visoko, but when questioned separately he readily agreed to write down details of the sign, which he did, and his text, plus a copy, were sealed in envelopes and held at the seminary archives and the bishop's office in Mostar respectively. When all the visionaries, including Ivan, came to Mostar later in the year, on 3 August, they were asked by the bishop to write down this "sign" on separate pieces of paper, but they refused, claiming they had a mandate not to do so from the "Gospa."

Bishop Zanic increased the size of his commission from five to fourteen members in 1984, and Ivan was interviewed about the "sign" by three members of this enlarged Episcopal commission in March 1985. Fr Puljic, one of the commission members, asked Ivan if he had written anything about the "sign," to which Ivan responded: "No." Fr Puljic then asked him what he had put in the envelope at Visoko, to which Ivan replied: "I put a blank sheet of paper in the envelope; then I sealed it; then the Gospa appeared to me and she smiled."

Such an answer is clearly disturbing, since it implies that the Blessed Virgin would make a special appearance just to condone this deception.

But in reality, when the contents of the envelope from the bishop's Chancery were examined, in the presence of all the commission members, it was found to contain not a blank sheet, but a signed statement from Ivan, dated 9 May 1982. This included information about the sign, apparently dictated by the "Gospa," that it would be "a huge shrine in Medjugorje in memory of my apparitions and this shrine shall be [dedicated] to my person." Moreover, according to the statement, this shrine "will appear in the sixth month." This presumably meant June 1982. As is well known, though, to this day nothing of the sort has occurred.[11]

Archbishop Franic, during his statement made at the Yugoslav Episcopal conference on 17 April 1985, made the following remarks: "The case of Ivan Dragicevic is held by certain members of the Commission to be proof positive that everything that happens in Medjugorje is pure fantasy. We must distinguish Ivan the seer from Ivan the human being." He then went on to say that Ivan the seminarian had a "reverential fear" of his superiors, and was afraid he would be expelled if he wrote nothing.[12]

IVAN'S APOLOGISTS REGARDING THE "SIGN"

Randall Sullivan puts forward his own version of this event, alleging that Ivan was "overwhelmed" by this encounter with the commission members, and when writing about the sign, after revealing the month, became aware within himself that he should not reveal the year.

Fr Laurentin, too, has his version of what happened, arguing that Ivan was "isolated ... misunderstood, [and] ill at ease with his studies" — he was expelled a month later — and having been "intimidated" by the commissioners, he "cracked." The French priest claims that what Ivan wrote was "so vague that in his mind he figured he had not 'written anything.'" Apparently, Ivan told him this in "all sincerity," and, according to Fr Laurentin, the result, once the envelope was opened, was that he "lost face, not only with the members of the commission but also with the parish priests and the other visionaries."

Then, we are told, after a "grueling" meeting on 7 March 1985, involving Fr Barbaric and the Commission members, the Franciscan "convened a meeting with the six visionaries in order to ascertain Ivan's veracity as a visionary." At this, the "other five confirmed his position as a visionary, all the while reprimanding him for his error. During the days to come, he would weep bitterly. But he did learn from his experience."[13]

This picturesque account is interesting for all sorts of reasons, but the idea of the other visionaries "confirming" Ivan as a visionary is surely completely surreal. If a seer is genuine, it is God or Our Lady who "confirm" them, not their peers, and on earth such confirmation, in the sense of approving the apparitions in question, or beatifying or canonizing the seers, is done by the Church. Surely this one incident, on its own, is enough to indicate the strange depths to which adhering to the "logic" of Medjugorje has led Fr Laurentin, and unfortunately, many others beside him.

In sum, readers will have to decide for themselves whether to accept Ivan's "explanation," or that of the official commission members. But apart from that, Ivan's description of the sign, as recorded by Sullivan, that it would be "a flame that burned continuously but without consuming," also raises problems. As with Vicka's description of the supposed "sign," Ivan's portrayal of it as something clearly miraculous, that is, something which will tend to obviate the need for faith, is difficult to accept.

MARIJA'S MESSAGES AND HER RETRACTION

Marija began giving out monthly messages from the "Gospa" on 25 January 1987. According to Wayne Weible, she would "write down the message and give it to Father Slavko Barbaric. It would then be checked thoroughly for adherence to Scripture and church doctrine, and in less than 24 hours, it would be transmitted to prayer groups and to others around the world."[14]

Had the Blessed Virgin Mary become so deficient in scriptural and doctrinal knowledge that her messages now needed to be vetted by Fr Barbaric? Is this not just more evidence that these statements are not supernatural?

But even as early as 1984, there was evidence of the visionaries being under the effective control of the Franciscans: the following comes from the *Chronicle of the Apparitions*, then being edited by Fr Vlasic, for the entry dated 12 April: "Today I spoke with all the seers. I brought to their attention again the necessity of not releasing statements to anyone without informing us."[15]

Marija was also closely involved in a rather strange project which was promoted by Fr Vlasic and Agnes Heupel. On 25 March 1988, Fr Vlasic issued an "appeal" from near Parma, Italy, in which he claimed that, since 1985, "Our Lord and Our Heavenly Mother" had been speaking to him in his heart, "in a special manner," giving him "special communiqués," which involved the setting up of a religious community.

As early as 7 October 1981, a little over three months after the visions began, Fr Vlasic had made the following request of the "Gospa": "Should we found here a community just like that of St Francis of Assisi?" Obviously, then, such an idea had been in his mind for a long time. Agnes Heupel also claimed to have received a message from Jesus in support of this community of young people of both sexes, and the idea received an apparent endorsement from Marija in April 1988, who said that she had seen a vision of the "Gospa" and that she was supportive of the idea.

In any event, when this proposal for a mixed community was put to the Vatican, permission was not forthcoming. Marija then issued the following statement in a letter dated 11 July 1988:[16]

> I feel morally bound to make the following statements before God, Our Lady, and the Church of Jesus Christ:... The message of the text *An Invitation to the Marian Year* and

the deposition which bears my signature is that I brought Our Lady's answer to Brother [sic] Tomislav Vlasic's question. That answer was supposedly: "This is God's plan." In other words, it follows from these texts that I transmitted to Brother Tomislav Vlasic, Our Lady's confirmation and express approval of this work.... I now declare that I never asked Our Lady for any confirmation whatsoever of this work by Brother Tomislav Vlasic and Agnes Heupel.... My first statement... does not correspond to the truth. Brother Tomislav Vlasic advised me, stressing the point again and again, that I, as a seer, ought to write a deposition which the world expected.[17]

Marija was due to marry her fiancée, Paolo Lunetti, in September 1993, and according to Wayne Weible, this "gave cause for concern among the Franciscans of Medjugorje. Would this marriage disrupt the flow of monthly messages, or the pattern of the apparitions, especially since Marija would be living in Monza, Italy?" Marija reassured them that she expected no change to her regime of daily visions, but concern remained because, "The other visionaries who had married had settled in the village. Marija would be the first one to be living away from the direct spiritual guidance of the Franciscans."[18]

PROBLEMS WITH MIRJANA

Regarding Mirjana, Fr Sivric comments about rumors as to her emotional stability. He cites an interview between her and Fr Tomislav Vlasic, which was taped on 10 January 1983, pointing out that although most of this interview can be found in the book by Fr Svetozar Kraljevic, regrettably, in this source, "certain passages have been omitted or have had their sense mitigated."

Since Fr Sivric had a copy of the complete Croatian text of the original interview, he was able to compare this with the translated text and detail important omissions. These include some of Mirjana's thoughts on purgatory, heaven, and hell. The section on purgatory has poor souls from that place of purification allegedly knocking on the window of a sixth-floor apartment in order to ask for prayers — Mirjana explicitly claims that the "Gospa" told her this. As regards hell, we are told that the "people begin feeling comfortable there."[19]

One remark that Fr Kraljevic did include from the interview was the claim that the visions at Medjugorje were "the last apparition on earth." When pressed on this point, Mirjana went on to say: "It is the last time that Jesus or Mary will appear on earth."[20]

Certainly, there is evidence of some problems regarding Mirjana's emotional state in the interview. At one point, Fr Vlasic asked her if she had been depressed after what had allegedly been her last meeting with the "Gospa." To this she replied: "Terribly sad. At school...everybody told me I'd gone mad. They laughed at me. I didn't want to talk to anybody.... I've just wanted to sit by myself, alone.... I start to cry, without knowing why."

In connection with this, it is perhaps worth noting that Fr Jordan Aumann lists "confusion, anxiety, and deep depression" as being amongst the recognized "signs of the diabolical spirit."[21] This is not to say that we have proof positive that Mirjana was suffering from a "deep depression" which was definitely linked to diabolical activity — or even a form of clinical depression — but her remarks are an indication of a possible problem in this area.

VICKA'S PHYSICAL AND PSYCHOLOGICAL STATE

In 1985, Vicka claimed to be receiving revelations about the life of the Blessed Virgin, and, more generally, about the future. She was also beset with headaches and blackouts — which went on for years — and which may indicate the sort of psychological strain she was under. It is certainly quite astonishing to read in an article by Fr Janko Bubalo, written in January 1986, that "Vicka lived a mysterious life of headaches and fainting which grew more and more difficult to bear and lasted longer and longer." These episodes were apparently impervious to medical treatment, even in Zagreb. Further on, Fr Bubalo tells us that her "fainting began to last longer and longer. Nearly every day it lasted fifteen hours or more," and she would only wake up for her encounter with the "Gospa."

All of this indicates that Vicka's physical and psychological state was far from normal during this period. Indeed, as Joachim Bouflet points out, Vicka had at this time all the characteristics of an hysteric, being subject to strange illnesses which appear suddenly and which defy diagnosis. According to Mary Craig, these characteristics were also noticed by a group of psychiatrists who came to examine the visionaries in January 1986. They saw Vicka one afternoon "when she was in what her family described as a 'coma,'" but which the psychiatrists described as an "hysterical stupor." In addition, one of the three psychiatrists "observed that she had a tendency to exaggerate for effect, always wanted to be the centre of attention, and was inclined to court popularity."

Louis Bélanger also mentions this visit, and points to the general conclusions reached by the group:

> The undersigned physicians ... recommend that the apparitions take place only in the presence of responsible priests, with the exclusion of any form of public presence. This is not only to render the spiritual atmosphere more adequate, but also to eliminate any reinforcement of a suggestive type.

Those signing the recommendations were Austrian professor Gottfried Roth, a neurologist and pastoral psychiatrist; Polish professor Wanda Poltawska, a pastoral psychiatrist and a close friend of Karol Wojtyła/Pope John Paul II; Italian psychiatrist Pietro R. Cavalleri; and Italian medical doctors Caterina Tribbia and Piergiorgio Spaggiari.

The group's recommendations have obviously not been followed, and as Bélanger also points out, a failure to do this has turned the appearances of the Medjugorje visionaries into the sort of thing that is more usually found on a Reality TV show.[22]

According to Craig, it was later claimed that Vicka had been suffering from a tumor on the brain, but that she was "cured on the date foretold her by the Lady — 25th of September 1988 — and is now in good health."[23] However, if she had been suffering from a brain tumor, how do we explain the fact that it had not been revealed by any of the previous medical examinations she had undergone?

This is what Fr Jordan Aumann has to say about the characteristics required if we are likely to be dealing with genuine divine revelations:

> The person who receives the revelation should be examined carefully, especially as to temperament and character. If the person is humble, well balanced, discreet, evidently advanced in virtue, and enjoys good mental and physical health, there is good reason to proceed further and to examine the revelation itself. But if the individual ... suffers nervous affliction, is subject to periods of great exhaustion or great depression, or is eager to divulge the revelation, there is cause for serious doubt.[24]

Regarding Vicka and Mirjana in particular then, as indicated above, there are definitely good grounds for believing that they have suffered some problems in the above areas. The question is, how can we reconcile this with the fact that the medical tests done on the visionaries as a group, in the early 1980s, seemed to indicate that they were psychologically healthy? This is not an easy question to answer, but perhaps we may be dealing here with the psychological effects of *guilt* at their being part of the deception maintained after Friday, 3 July 1981. As we have seen, this involved the claim that the "Gospa" was still appearing to the visionaries, even though we know, via the tape transcripts, and Vicka's explicit testimony, that that was supposed to be the date of the last vision.

And it is important to take the effects of guilt seriously, as philosopher Donald DeMarco notes:

> Throughout history, in both literate and nonliterate societies, the prevailing consensus has been that guilt is a natural human response to one's deliberate and voluntary complicity in moral wrongdoing, and that man persists in suffering both in body and in soul when his guilt remains unconfessed and unatoned.[25]

PROBLEMS WITH THE RELIGIOUS VOWS

Regrettably, the credibility of some of the Franciscans involved with Medjugorje has also been undermined by incidents in which it is alleged that the vow of chastity has been broken. While this would not constitute primary evidence against the visions — since given human frailty anyone can fall into sins of this kind — it would nevertheless indicate a further negative aspect which cannot be ignored. What *can* be said about these allegations, though, is that they would appear to relate, as we have seen, to one of the charges made against Fr Vlasic in 2008, namely that he acted "contra sextum," that is, against the Sixth Commandment, and thus concerning sexual matters.[26]

Similarly, serious sexual allegations were made against Fr Jozo Zovko, the parish priest in Medjugorje at the beginning of the visions, and as we have seen, one of the main Medjugorje promoters. These matters were brought to the attention of the Franciscan General, Herman Schalueck, and Fr Zovko was disciplined by Bishop Zanic in August 1989. He was also "disciplined a second time, in June 1994, this time under Bishop Peric, for pertinacious disobedience." Fr René Laurentin, in his *Dernières Nouvelles,* was forced to acknowledge that since the motives for the sanctions against Fr Zovko were not made public, they must have been serious.

And Fr Zovko was disciplined yet a third time, in 2004, being suspended from exercising any priestly act within the diocese of Mostar-Duvno by Bishop Peric, in the light of his "constant disobedience in this local Church" and his "lack of respect towards the decisions of the Diocesan Bishops." The decree indicating this was published in the Archdiocesan newsletter.

The testimony of Marija Pavlovic, from 21 October 1981, that, according to the "Gospa," Fr Zovko was "a saint" looks very suspect in the light of all this.[27]

It transpires, too, that in 1990, Fr Zovko was requested, by the Vatican Congregation for the Evangelization of Peoples, to move away from Medjugorje to a distant convent. But he only went as far as Siroki Brijeg, and still displayed evidence of disobedience by visiting Medjugorje. During the 1990s, he was involved in constructing, in the words of Bishop Peric, a religious house "of great proportions" in Siroki Brijeg without any ecclesiastical permission. In 1997, it was reported that up to 8 million Deutschmarks had been spent on this project, but it was unclear exactly where this money had come from.[28]

* * *

OVERALL THEN, WHAT ARE WE TO MAKE OF THE CREDibility of these visionaries and some of their main Franciscan associates? Whether it is Mirjana's reported emotional instability in the early days, Vicka's possible hysteria and her strange illnesses, Marija's humiliating retraction, or Ivan's "confusion" over the alleged sign, it seems clear from the evidence presented that they have almost nothing in common with genuine Marian seers, with the simplicity or holiness of St Bernadette or the children of Fatima. And likewise, regarding Frs Vlasic and Zovko, and the serious sexual allegations made against them, as well as the various disciplinary problems they have encountered, these things must surely make thoughtful supporters of Medjugorje uneasy.

All of the above illustrates the "hidden" side of Medjugorje, a side which most pilgrims know absolutely nothing about.

17
Medjugorje, the Zadar Declaration and the War

THE WAR IN YUGOSLAVIA

The Communist regimes in Eastern Europe began to unravel with great speed from 1989 onwards, a process which was definitively marked by the fall of the Berlin Wall in November of that year. By and large, this process was very peaceful, but the situation in Yugoslavia was different — and potentially explosive — given its rival groupings of Serbs, Croats, Slovenes and Muslims, in a country divided along religious and ethnic lines. Franjo Tudjman became leader of a new political party in Croatia, the HDZ, but his program did not include guarantees for ethnic minorities within Croatia, and particularly for the Serbs. In Serbia, meanwhile, Slobodan Milosevic had been promoting an increasingly xenophobic policy as he rose to power. As nationalist feelings continued to grow all over Yugoslavia, conflict became inevitable, particularly in Bosnia-Herzegovina, which was very ethnically diverse and had a large Muslim population.[1]

MEDJUGORJE AND THE YUGOSLAV BISHOPS' CONFERENCE

The findings of the Yugoslav Bishops' Conference on Medjugorje — the Zadar declaration — was officially published on 10 April 1991, and this clearly stated that, after nearly ten years of alleged visions, it could not be affirmed that "supernatural apparitions and revelations" had taken place. Equally, however, the bishops were concerned that pilgrims to Medjugorje, who, despite the dangerous situation in Yugoslavia, were still coming to the village, should have their spiritual needs cared for. The text of the declaration is as follows:

> On the basis of investigation up till now it cannot be established that one is dealing with supernatural apparitions and revelations. However, the numerous gatherings of the faithful from different parts of the world, who are coming to Medjugorje prompted both by motives of belief and certain other motives, require the attention and pastoral care in the first place of the bishop of the diocese and of the other bishops

with him so that in Medjugorje and everything related to it a healthy devotion toward the Blessed Virgin Mary would be promoted in conformity with the teaching of the Church. For that purpose the bishops shall issue separate appropriate liturgical-pastoral directives. Likewise by means of their Commission they shall further follow and investigate the total event in Medjugorje.[2]

The declaration illustrated the dilemma faced by Church authorities: they could not pronounce in favor of the alleged visions because, as was stated, they could not find anything supernatural about them, but equally they also had to respond to the spiritual needs of those who believed in the visions in good faith.

Previously, it had been reported that Pope John Paul II had met with one of the Yugoslav Bishops and assured him that a Vatican statement on Medjugorje would eventually be issued. According to John Thavis of the Catholic News Service, this meeting took place on 8 February 1991. Cardinal Ratzinger had made similar remarks to E. Michael Jones, who had put some questions to him during a visit to Dallas, Texas, on 7 February 1991: in agreeing with the stance of the Yugoslav Bishops, the cardinal indicated that the statement would be issued soon. Later in the year, though, the civil war had apparently complicated matters to the extent that this statement was postponed. When asked about his own opinion on Medjugorje, Cardinal Ratzinger responded: "I can have no other opinion than that of the [Yugoslavian] bishops."[3]

THE ZADAR DECLARATION AS PRO-MEDJUGORJE?

But some supporters of Medjugorje then attempted to explain how the Zadar declaration could be seen, from their perspective, in a positive light. A good example of this comes from Fr Robert Faricy, who wrote about the work of the Yugoslav Bishops' commission as follows, saying that it "released an inconclusive report in 1990 that... could not determine as yet whether the Medjugorje events were really from God in an extraordinary manner."[4]

This is a puzzling statement, and it is equally difficult to understand the following pronouncement from Archbishop Franc Perko of Belgrade, which was made in 1991:

> It is not true that the bishops' document... states there is nothing supernatural about Medjugorje. The prelates wrote:

> "*non constat de supernaturalitate*" ["the supernatural character is not established"]. They did not write: "*constat de non supernaturalitate*" ["the non-supernatural character is established"]. There is an enormous difference: the first cannot be interpreted definitively but is left open to new developments. This does not mean that I'm in favour of Medjugorje. I believe that we cannot make a definitive declaration but there are signs that perhaps there is, or has been, something supernatural about Medjugorje.[5]

That may have been the archbishop's own approach, and that of others on the commission, but is it really a logical position to take? On the face of it, it seems that the Bishops' statement indicates their acceptance of the traditional Latin phrase *non constat de supernaturalitate*, that is, that there was no direct evidence of supernaturality, and thus it was not an express denial of supernaturality, as would have been the case if they had used the phrase *constat de non-supernaturalitate*. But having said that, in the real world, can it seriously be suggested that although there had been roughly three thousand alleged visions by this time, none of which could enable the Bishops to state "that one is dealing with supernatural apparitions and revelations," nevertheless, the commission was genuinely holding out some hope that, perhaps after several thousand more visions, it would be able to come to a positive conclusion? Is that really a credible position to maintain?

In theory, the use of *non constat de supernaturalitate* could allow for further developments—but regarding Medjugorje is this at all likely? It *might* be possible if the commission had been dealing with a more normal claim of alleged apparitions, numbering in single figures, and one taking place over a short period, but surely not after ten years and thousands of alleged visions.

This becomes obvious if we use a more down-to-earth example to explore this situation. Supposing a person meets a new work colleague during a break and they get to know each other. Now, if after a week of such meetings, this person was to say that they could not affirm that anything that their new colleague had said during this time was true, then we could accept this as a reasonable situation. After all, a week is not a long time to get to know what another person is really like, and to be able to check up on what they have told us. But now, suppose that after working with this person for ten years, and talking with them every day, they were to turn around and say that they could not affirm that anything they had been told during this lengthy period was true, then unquestionably we would be in a completely different situation. In effect, they would be saying that they just could not trust the other person, and indeed were not even sure that anything they had been told was true. This type of example allows us to see the Zadar declaration in its proper perspective, and not through unrealistic, pro-Medjugorje, rose-tinted spectacles.

YUGOSLAVIA DISINTEGRATES

Meanwhile, the unstable political situation, one of the factors which had hampered a straightforward Vatican decision on Medjugorje since the mid-80s, was growing progressively worse as concerns about Communism were replaced by worries over a resurgent nationalism. This was increasingly reflected in violent incidents between the various ethnic groups, and acts of attendant ethnic cleansing, which were intensifying to the level of all-out war. From the Croat perspective, the Yugoslav army was acting exclusively at the behest of the Serbs, while for the latter an anti-Western siege mentality was developing.[6]

Around the same time that the statement of the Yugoslav Bishops' Conference was issued, the political situation in the country began to come to a climax. Franjo Tudjman and Slobodan Milosevic met in early 1991 and decided between them that they would partition Bosnia-Herzegovina, with the Croats to take the northwestern section, the Serbs the southeastern section, with a Muslim buffer zone in the middle. On 25 June 1991, almost exactly ten years after Medjugorje began, both Croatia and Slovenia declared independence. The result of these declarations was that the Yugoslav army, essentially a Serb-run military, invaded Slovenia, thus initiating full-scale hostilities.

The Yugoslav Bishops had been due to ratify their Medjugorje directives arising from the Zadar declaration in a plenary session on 27 June 1991, but were prevented from doing so by the war. The ultimate result was that the thorny question of Medjugorje then devolved onto the four bishops who made up the Bishops' Conference of Bosnia-Herzegovina. Thus, it can be said that the violent dismembering of Yugoslavia was one of the factors which saved Medjugorje,[7] although undoubtedly even quite restrictive directives would not have dampened the ardor of many enthusiasts for the visions.

The European Community recognized Croatia and Slovenia as independent nations on 6 January 1992, followed a week later by the Holy See, and in April both the EC and US recognized Bosnia-Herzegovina, in a move which intensified the fighting in that region. This had a direct effect on Medjugorje, to the extent that the parish church was closed for services, remaining locked for nearly three months from April to June. According to E. Michael Jones, the reaction of the visionaries and their Franciscan mentors was to send an increasingly desperate series of faxes to George Bush senior demanding intervention on the part of the US, while Yugoslav jets screamed overhead.[8]

THE WAR COMES TO MEDJUGORJE

It has been claimed that the "Gospa" at Medjugorje prophesied the war in Yugoslavia, but there are no unambiguous messages to this effect which can be cited to definitely prove this assertion. Randall Sullivan says that in 1982, a Franciscan friar asked Mirjana "if Croatia would ever be free," with the response being: "Yes, after a small war."[9]

The first thing to say about such a "prophecy" is that given the violent history of the Balkans, it wouldn't have been difficult to foresee that the end of Communism in Yugoslavia would almost certainly lead to bloodshed and war. And the downfall of Communism was on the horizon even before this alleged prophecy: workers in Poland had already gone on strike in 1980 and went on to form the Solidarity trade union in 1981. Many people in the Eastern bloc countries were anxious to be free of Communism, but feared the consequences of revolution, especially after what had happened in Hungary in 1956 and Czechoslovakia in 1968.

It was the bravery of the Polish people in standing up for their rights, following the historic visit of Pope John Paul II in 1979, which was the catalyst for the downfall of Communism. The situation in ex-Yugoslavia was somewhat different, but following Tito's death in May 1980, it became clear that it would be difficult to keep Yugoslavia together in the future, in the face of a resurgent nationalism. So overall, predicting the fall of Communism in Yugoslavia in 1982 would not necessarily have required any supernatural insight.

Apart from all that, anyone familiar with the message of Fatima could have logically predicted the fall of Communism without the need for any new apparition. So this could have been a purely "human" prophecy, or alternatively, a diabolical one: that is, assuming that the above dialogue did actually take place, which is by no means certain.

The second point is that describing the violence which actually took place in ex-Yugoslavia as a "small war" is an obscenity, especially given its horrific nature, the great sufferings of those involved and the large number of people killed, in what was the worst fighting in Europe since World War II.

Then regarding the "prophecy" itself, note how no precise date is given, nor is the "Franciscan friar" identified. And a search of the *Chronological Corpus of the Messages* for 1982 reveals no mention of "Croatia." The only reference to war is found in the following dialogue for 12 July 1982: Q. "Will there be a third world war?" A. "The third world war will not take place."

The "source" of this quote about a "small war" actually appears to be Fr Slavko Barbaric, who in his *Mother, Lead Us to Peace!*, published in 1994, said: "Recently I spoke with Mirjana and she told me that in 1982 a Franciscan priest asked her to ask the Gospa: 'Will Croatia ever be free?'... The answer was: 'Croatia as well as Bosnia will be free, but only after a small war.'"

In other words, he spoke to Mirjana, "recently," presumably in the early 1990s, and she then told him about this earlier prophecy, which only made it into print in 1994, well after the war started. These characteristics obviously make it very suspect.[10]

A common claim made by Medjugorje supporters is that the divine origin of the visions is indicated by the fact that the town itself was not seriously affected by the fighting, in contrast say to Mostar, which was devastated. This is to ignore the fact that wars, by their very nature, are chaotic, and that particular locations may well escape damage essentially because they are not of strategic importance.

If this argument is taken to its logical conclusion, then we would have to say that the famous Benedictine monastery at Monte Cassino in Italy, which was leveled during the Second World War, was somehow a place of infidelity, of God's *disfavor*. In fact, it was destroyed by warfare on two previous occasions, and also by an earthquake in the 14th century. Thus, whether or not a particular religious location is destroyed during a war is not necessarily relevant as regards authenticity, and this is just another example of a very weak argument being used to prop up Medjugorje.

In fact, though, Medjugorje and its surroundings *were* affected by the war, and this became apparent in the early 90s, since it seems that there was a factory there that was turning out hand grenades. In addition, radical rightwing Croat HOS forces based in the town, along with more regular HVO [Bosnian Croat army] forces, were attracting neo-Nazis from all quarters to fight alongside them—swastika pins were on sale alongside rosaries in the piety stalls of Medjugorje.[11]

VIOLENCE IN MEDJUGORJE

It was also claimed that at this time, due to longstanding clan vendettas, there were up to eighty killings in Medjugorje. But this figure has been disputed by writers such as Randall Sullivan, who claim that the violence was on a much smaller scale. Based on his own research, however, Sullivan admits that there was violence in Medjugorje, saying: "The Franciscans would acknowledge only that there had been 'a few' violent deaths in the parish during the war.'" But he adds, "That was almost certainly an understatement."

He also speaks of how, in August 1992, the monument to the hundreds of Serbs killed at Surmanci during World War II, not far from Bijakovici, was dynamited apart in a huge explosion, with its pieces being used to "fill in the pit where the bodies had been buried."[12]

Given all that, is it really possible to believe that Our Lady would have appeared in Medjugorje in 1981, knowing that within a decade the above types of activities would actually be taking place there?

THE WAR AROUND MEDJUGORJE

But if there are some question marks about the extent of the violence in Medjugorje itself, there can be no doubt about some other negative aspects of life in the town at this time, nor about the brutality and bloodshed that went on in some of the concentration camps in the locality.

Award-winning journalist Ed Vulliamy, in his *Seasons in Hell*, published in 1994, described how Medjugorje had become a "focus for other visitors, since it is now a seedy junction for black marketeering and dealing in arms and stolen cars." Vulliamy characterized Medjugorje and Siroki Brijeg as "party towns," with the latter having become a base for the then "imminent ethnic cleansing of the Mostar region," while the "HVO had put out a verbal warning that anyone found sheltering Muslims in the Holy City [Medjugorje] would have their homes blown up." He noted that, incredibly, pilgrims were still coming to Medjugorje, even as the HVO shelled Muslim Mostar only fifteen miles away.

Vulliamy also describes how, at the conclusion of peace talks in Medjugorje in May 1993, President Tudjman said that the appearance of the "Gospa" had "heralded 'the reawakening of the Croatian nation.'"[13]

Historian Michael Sells charges that, by 1992:

> Medjugorje-based Croat religious nationalists, some with openly neo-Ustashe affiliations, were cleansing non-Catholics from the region. Serbs and Muslims were expelled from all areas under Croat nationalist control and their shrines annihilated. Medjugorje was the staging center for some of the most brutal attacks, including an expedition to the Serb monastery complex at Zitomislic. In that expedition, HVO forces killed the priests and monks, expelled the Orthodox population, and then dynamited and burned the entire set of monuments dating from the 16th century.[14]

In doing this, they were only repeating the actions of their Ustasha predecessors, who in June 1941 attacked Zitomislic, torturing and killing the monks and throwing their bodies into a pit, before plundering and burning the buildings.

Sells also describes how, in April 1993, in "the southern Herzegovinian town of Capljina, Muslim civilians were raped and confined in concentration camps." Capljina is only a short distance away from Medjugorje. Later on, in August, the HVO attacked the nearby town of Pocitelj, destroying its Islamic landmarks, while "its Muslim population [were] driven off to detention camps."

Sells goes on to say that:

> In the same month, images of skeletal prisoners at the HVO concentration camp at Dretelj reminded the world of earlier images from the Serb nationalist camp at Omarska. The prisoners at Dretelj had been starved, forced to drink their own urine, and tortured sexually. As at Omarska, local criminals were invited in to kill Muslim captives.[15]

Ed Vulliamy describes in detail how the Muslim men of Capljina were rounded up in June 1993 and taken to the camps at Dretelj and Gabela, a town only thirteen miles away from Medjugorje. He was one of the first journalists to gain access to the concentration camp at Dretelj, and described the hideous conditions in which the prisoners had been kept and their horrific treatment at the hands of the HVO, which included routine beatings, general brutality and outright murder.[16]

Regarding the activities and attitudes of the Herzegovina Franciscans, Michael Sells indicates that Church leaders such as Cardinal Kuharic of Zagreb, Archbishop Puljic of Sarajevo and the superior of the Bosnian Franciscan Province, Fr Petar Andjelkovic, OFM, had "specifically and courageously condemned the crimes of Croat religious nationalists. In Herzegovina, however, the Catholic clergy played a different, more troubling role." He goes on to note that:

> When European mediators attempted to reconcile the Catholic and Muslim population of Mostar, they were opposed by elements within the local Catholic clergy such as Tomislav Pervan, the provincial superior of 250 Franciscan Friars in the Mostar region, who repeated the Tudjman propaganda that the Bosnian Muslims wanted an Islamic state.

Fr Pervan served as parish priest at Medjugorje in the 1980s and again more recently.

At the same time, we are told by historian Vjekoslav Perica that: "In the midst of the bloody war, the Herzegovina Franciscans, assisted by Croatia's defense minister, Gojko Susak, built in Croatia's capital, Zagreb, a new mammoth church and pastoral centre worth 12 million German marks." One wonders where the money for that came from and how the Franciscans could justify it in the light of their vows of poverty and the appalling sufferings going on amongst the people in the area, which should surely have had the first call on their funds.[17]

And in fact, Marco Corvaglia details how research carried out in 2014 showed that in the period from 1981 to 2013, a period of 32 years, the Franciscan-controlled parish church in Medjugorje had a total revenue of 290 million euros—which is over 300 million dollars at current exchange rates.

This huge revenue enabled the Franciscan Province of Herzegovina to become a shareholder in, and have some representation on, the management boards of two banks, Hrvatska banka and Dubrovacka banka. And beyond that, in 1997, the Province was among the founding members of another bank, the Hercegovacka banka.[18]

The Guardian newspaper reported that in 2001, police "backed by soldiers from the NATO-led Stabilisation Force (S-FOR) ... seized control of a bank in Mostar, Bosnia-Hercegovina, that is believed to be used by Bosnian Croat extremists pursuing the goal of an independent mini-state in Croat areas of Bosnia." This operation took place because of "'repeated concern over continued corruption,' a statement from chief international administrator Wolfgang Petritsch's office said."

The authorities also took over branches of the bank in other towns, including Medjugorje, and the report concludes by saying, "Records show the Hercegovacka Banka was founded in 1997 by several private companies and the Franciscan order, which controls the religious shrine in Medjugorje, a major source of income, both from pilgrims and from donations by Croats living abroad."[19]

RELIGIOUS ASPECTS OF THE WAR

Louis Bélanger points out how Fr Slavko Barbaric, some months before his death, in April 2000, visited some of the Croats accused of war crimes at the Hague International Criminal Court, men he described as "our prisoners." He had previously expressed the hope that the Court would "do justice and act worthily," but when their sentences, ranging from 8 to 45 years, were handed down, he lamented that the "Croatian people have been condemned in those good and noble men." It should be borne in mind that that these were not soldiers defending their "homeland," but men convicted of crimes against humanity. This incident perfectly captures and illustrates the twisted mentality of those Herzegovinian Franciscans, such as Fr Barbaric, who put nationalism before basic religious principles and the protection of innocent life, in an abject betrayal of the ideals of their founder, St Francis.[20]

Michael Sells also argues that the Medjugorje visions were "nationalized" by Croat politicians, giving as an example the way the independence of Croatia was announced on 25 June 1991, the supposed tenth anniversary of the visions, while noting that the "Franciscans at Medjugorje favored an association between the Virgin and the independent Croat state and were proud of it."

Vjekoslav Perica agrees with this position, recording that ten years later, on 24 June 2001, the twentieth anniversary of the beginning of the visions, 200,000 pilgrims gathered in Medjugorje, as Tomislav

Pervan told them that without the miracle at Medjugorje there would not have been the Croatian independent state existing today, and that it was the Madonna of Medjugorje who had put Croatia on the map of world nation-states.[21]

Perica also comments: "In the historical perspective of the twentieth century as a century of ideological wars, the Medjugorje 'miracle' fueled both Croat nationalism and [the] anticommunist struggle."

He likewise highlights the way the rise of Medjugorje caused resentment amongst Orthodox Serbs, since the visions were taking place only a few miles away from the mass grave at Surmanci — where, as we have seen, many Serbs were murdered during the Second World War — a site which was only one of a number of such graves in the vicinity.

Sells concludes by saying:

> If the Madonna of Medjugorje did insist on peace one wonders why those who heard her message gave such little thought to the Muslims confined to concentration camps at Gabela, Capljina, Dretelj, Ljubuski, and Rodoc, all within a few miles of Medjugorje. Did those busloads of pilgrims, filled with inner light and joy, hear the screams from the other side of the Medjugorje hills?

Perica is equally trenchant: "The Medjugorje apparitions of the 1980s were not a 'peace and prayer movement'... but a prelude to partition, war, and genocide in Bosnia-Herzegovina."[22]

In other words, far from being a beneficial influence on events during the breakup of Yugoslavia, the Medjugorje visions were actually a catalyst for the violence, with some of the Herzegovina Franciscans acting as macabre cheerleaders to these terrible events.

Looking, then, at all the above evidence for what went on in and around Medjugorje during this period, surely it is quite clear that the idea that it really was the Blessed Virgin who began to appear there ten years earlier is absurd. Could the Mother of God honestly have been expected to appear in such a place knowing what was going to be going on in the vicinity? Surely the black marketeering, the dealing in arms, the stolen cars, the rapes, the murders, the torture, the ethnic cleansing, the manipulation of religion for political ends — surely all of these things make such an idea impossible to believe.[23]

* * *

BY THE EARLY 90S, THEN, IT BEGAN TO LOOK AS IF Medjugorje was in a state of decline: Yugoslavia was rapidly fragmenting as the vicious civil war took its course, and the Yugoslav Bishops had clearly indicated that there was nothing supernatural about the visions. Somehow, though, once the war was over, the pilgrims returned *en masse*, and this is surely one of the most inexplicable aspects of the whole affair. Negative factors which would have been enough to destroy any normal enterprise many times over have been shrugged off by Medjugorje enthusiasts, with barely a ripple of concern being expressed. Further on in this book some reasons for this state of affairs will be discussed, including the idea that for some people, Medjugorje has developed a cult-like attraction which has put it beyond the realm of reason and common sense.

18
Clarifying the Case of Medjugorje

THE POEM OF THE MAN-GOD AND THE VISIONARIES

The Poem of the Man-God, the "life of Christ" by Maria Valtorta, was placed on the *Index of Forbidden Books* in 1959, but it still managed to impinge on Medjugorje in 1991. When the *Index* was abolished following Vatican II, previously banned works like the *Poem* were given a new lease on life, and this work was particularly popular with Medjugorje supporters. However, Cardinal Ratzinger had written to Cardinal Siri concerning the *Poem of the Man-God*, in January 1985, saying:

> After the dissolution of the Index, when some people thought the printing and distribution of the work was permitted, people were reminded again in *L'Osservatore Romano* (June 15, 1966) that, as was published in the *Acta Apostolicae Sedis* (1966), the Index retains its moral force despite its dissolution.

In March 1992, Marija Pavlovic appeared, with Fr Slavko Barbaric, on a call-in TV show from New Orleans entitled *Focus*. During the program, a caller asked what Our Lady had said about *The Poem of the Man-God*, and Marija responded in Italian, *si può leggere,* that is: "You can read it." Realizing belatedly that this was probably not a good answer, she turned to Fr Barbaric for help, and he attempted to rescue the situation by suggesting that viewers might like to consult their local bishop about Valtorta's work.[1]

It is clear that amongst the other visionaries, Vicka also had a similar approach to this work, which has been described, with good reason, as a "vulgar, blasphemous, and fraudulent 'revelation.'" In an interview, when asked about this, she said: "Marija asked the Virgin about that book, and the Virgin said that she should read that book, because it is like a poem between God and man."[2]

Surely this is another indication that Medjugorje is not supernatural, since it is impossible to believe that the Blessed Virgin could have suggested that dangerous nonsense such as the *Poem* was suitable as spiritual reading.

BISHOP PERIC, THE POPE AND MEDJUGORJE

In early May 1992, Bishop Zanic's episcopal palace in Mostar was shelled by artillery and destroyed. He was forced to flee and finally reached Rome, where he asked Pope John Paul II to be relieved of his duties, and that Ratko Peric be named as his successor.[3]

The pope had been due to visit Sarajevo in September 1994, but just before he arrived, the Serbs shelled a spot very close to where he had been scheduled to celebrate an outdoor Mass, and this part of the trip was canceled. According to E. Michael Jones, this happened after the visionary Marija Pavlovic had proclaimed a message from the "Gospa," on 24 August, to the effect that the pope *would* be arriving there as planned.[4]

Bishop Ratko Peric attended the Synod of Bishops in Rome in October 1994, and made a public plea for help in resolving the question of Medjugorje. He stated that many ecclesial problems were evident at Medjugorje, including unauthorized religious communities establishing themselves in the town, and religious buildings being erected without permission — such as the giant pavilion behind the local parish church of St James — as well as difficulties caused by the local Franciscans acting illicitly.

Jones reports that street protests against the bishop were organized in Mostar by supporters of the Franciscans, and the situation became so bad that on 2 April 1995:

> The Bishop was attacked by a mob in his chancery, and his pectoral cross was ripped from his person. He was then beaten up, forced into a waiting car, driven to an illicit chapel run by the Medjugorje Franciscans, and held hostage for 10 hours. It was only when the Mayor of Mostar showed up with UN troops that the Bishop was released.[5]

Fr Laurentin confirms that this incident did take place saying: "When Bishop Peric annexed the Franciscan parishes around Mostar, the Croatians wrongfully kidnapped him. No one was able to stop them, except for the Franciscans, I am told."[6]

What does this further incident reveal about the whole Medjugorje phenomenon?

The following statement from Pope John Paul II, as reported in the 18 September 1996 edition of *L'Osservatore Romano*, would appear to be a criticism of the spirituality which has developed out of alleged visions like Medjugorje, and represented an alternative aspect of his thinking on the subject: "Within the Church community, the multiplication of supposed 'apparitions' or 'visions' is sowing confusion and reveals a certain lack of a solid basis to the faith and Christian life among her members."7

CIRCULATING ACCOUNTS OF ALLEGED VISIONS

The 4 December 1996 English edition of *L'Osservatore Romano* carried a notification from the Congregation for the Doctrine of the Faith, principally on the questions raised by the case of Vassula Ryden; but it also contained a second section giving important general information relevant to the whole problem of alleged visions:

> 1) The interpretation given by some individuals to a Decision approved by Paul VI on 14 October 1966 and promulgated on 15 November of that year, in virtue of which writings and messages resulting from alleged revelations could be freely circulated in the Church, is absolutely groundless. This decision actually referred to the "Abolition of the Index of Forbidden Books" and determined that—after the relevant censures were lifted—the moral obligation still remained of not circulating or reading those writings which endanger faith and morals.
>
> 2) It should be recalled however that with regard to the circulation of texts of alleged private revelations, canon 823 §1 of the current Code remains in force: "the Pastors of the Church have the ... right to demand that writings to be published by the Christian faithful which touch upon faith or morals be submitted to their judgment."
>
> 3) Alleged supernatural revelations and writings concerning them are submitted in first instance to the judgment of the diocesan Bishop, and, in particular cases, to the judgment of the Episcopal Conference and the Congregation for the Doctrine of the Faith.

Regarding the belief amongst many Medjugorje supporters that "writings and messages resulting from alleged revelations" can be circulated freely in the Church, it is clear that this is incorrect. In reality, all such texts ought to be submitted to the "Pastors of the Church" for their judgment, which in this case means the local bishop, and if necessary an even higher authority. This has certainly not happened with many of the books supportive of Medjugorje, to say nothing of the periodic messages emanating from some of the visionaries.

Even as long ago as the 1950s, the Church had begun to warn ordinary Catholics about the dangers of a too credulous approach to accounts of visions. This is what Cardinal Ottaviani wrote on the subject, as reported in *L'Osservatore Romano* of 14 February 1951:

> Fifty years ago who would have believed that the Church today would have to put her children, and even her priests, on their guard against stories of visions, false miracles and of those so-called preternatural occurrences which from one country to another, from one continent to another, everywhere indeed, attract excited crowds.... We have for years been in the presence of a revival of a popular passion for the marvellous, even in matters of religion. Crowds of the faithful assemble in places where apparitions or miracles are supposed to have happened; but at the same time they desert their churches, the Sacraments, the hearing of sermons.... The Church certainly does not wish to hush up the wonders wrought by God. She only desires the faithful to distinguish clearly between what comes from God and what does not come from God and may come from our adversary who is also His. The Church is the enemy of false miracles.[8]

ST LOUIS DE MONTFORT ON FALSE DEVOTION TO OUR LADY

The following passage is from St Louis de Montfort's *True Devotion to the Blessed Virgin*. Although he lived before the era of the major modern approved apparitions, beginning with Rue du Bac in 1830, and is here dealing with the difference between false and authentic devotion to Mary, his words can also be applied to the problem of apparition discernment:

> It is all the more necessary to make the right choice of the true devotion to our Blessed Lady, for now more than ever there are false devotions to her which can easily be mistaken for true ones. The devil, like a counterfeiter and crafty, experienced deceiver, has already misled and ruined many Christians by means of fraudulent devotions to our Lady.... A counterfeiter usually makes coins only of gold and silver, rarely of other metals, because these latter would not be worth the trouble. Similarly, the devil leaves other devotions alone and counterfeits mostly those directed to

Jesus and Mary.... It is therefore very important, first, to recognise false devotions to our Blessed Lady so as to avoid them, and to recognise true devotion in order to practise it.[9]

If we substitute the word "apparition" or "vision" for "devotion" in the above passage, we can have a good idea of how important it is to differentiate between true and false apparitions, and also see how there must be many reports of false apparitions in circulation today.

The devil does not change his basic game plan, especially when it has worked so well in the past. In St Louis de Montfort's time, it was to encourage false devotion to Our Lady, by inspiring individuals to fall into the trap of embracing sham devotion through traits such as scrupulosity, presumption, inconstancy, hypocrisy and self-interest. And of course, those traits are still present today in Marian devotion, except now, with the flood of alleged visions, we have the added danger of a satanic influence through the devil playing on human pride, credulity and the desire for novelty, amongst other things, in order to promote false apparitions.

APOCRYPHAL WRITINGS AND THE BIBLE

And going back even further, we can see how this general principle of false ideas attempting to supplant what is true can also be applied to Public Revelation. Certainly, the New Testament writings were subject to imitation by false or apocryphal writings, and it was centuries before the New Testament canon, or agreed list of books, was established in the Church.

The four canonical Gospels, Matthew, Mark, Luke and John, suffered most from apocryphal mimicry, with this taking a number of forms, including Gospels containing heretical or invented material. Infancy Gospels such as the *Infancy Gospel of Thomas*, which has stories of Jesus as a child working miracles, were very popular, while the *Protoevangelium* of James gives details of Mary's early life and names her parents as Joachim and Anna. A partial listing of apocryphal Gospels indicates how popular this form of imitation was: there were Gospels of the Ebionites, of the Hebrews, of Peter, of Thomas, of Philip, of Bartholomew, of Matthias, of Barnabas, and even of Judas!

It is noteworthy how many of these spurious gospels there were, numerous enough to be a threat to the true "Good News." Similarly, there were quite a number of imitations of the canonical Acts of the Apostles, which in the main seem to have been composed by heretics, although some of them may have been revised by orthodox writers. Apocryphal editions of St Paul's epistles also exist, as do imitations of St John's Apocalypse.

The implications of all this are clear: of all the Gospels, epistles and apocalypses produced during the early Christian centuries, only a small proportion were authentic. The others were to a greater or lesser extent heretical, or pious forgeries. In some cases they may contain elements of truth, but the Church has not been able to accept them as canonical.

If we compare this with the situation regarding the approved Marian apparitions and their more modern alleged counterparts, we can see that there is a strong possibility that many of the latter are imitations and not genuine. And of course, given all the points made previously in this book, this argument applies particularly in the case of Medjugorje.

Thus we can draw some important conclusions from the history of the compilation of the biblical canon of books, and how this relates to judging the plethora of modern alleged Marian apparitions. Firstly it should be noted that biblical prophecy was not continuous, that is, prophets did not appear constantly throughout Israel's history, but only during specific periods. In particular from about 400 BC, when the book of Malachi was written, until the time of Christ, there were no authentic prophetic writings, although there were many spurious prophecies claiming to be genuine. God had given his message through the Law and the great prophetic figures and it was up to the people to accept and live up to it, in expectation of the Messiah.

Similarly, as difficult as it might be for some people to accept, there is no reason to expect that genuine Church-recognized Marian apparitions should have continued to take place with the same frequency as previously. Thus the proliferation of alleged apparitions from the mid-twentieth century onwards in particular may well be a counterpart to the situation which prevailed in Israel in the "intertestamental" period, the time between Malachi and Christ, and to that which prevailed in the early Christian centuries, when genuine New Testament writings were threatened by a host of imitations.

In fact it is possible to argue that God is actually "obliged," in a certain sense, to stop giving prophecies, writings or revelations once a certain point is reached, for fear of confusing people. Once a certain style of prophecy or writing is well known it is very easy to imitate it, as the extra-biblical writings indicate. Similarly, we reached the point long ago where the mechanism of the approved Marian apparitions could easily be copied.

The Church has been given a more than adequate "prophetic" message in Mary's approved apparitions, and particularly Fatima, and so it would seem presumptuous to expect anything more. And so while sites of alleged apparitions such as Medjugorje continue to attract large crowds, the sad fact is that ordinary Catholics are neglecting Fatima, despite its having attracted overwhelming approval from the Church.[10]

And it is likewise worth noting that St Louis de Montfort also went on to say that "among so many different forms of true devotion to our Blessed Lady we should choose the one most perfect and the most pleasing to her, the one that gives greater glory to God and is most sanctifying for us."

Without prejudice to the other approved apparitions, surely we can apply this idea in particular to the wholehearted promotion of Fatima in the Church, as the "most perfect and the most pleasing" form of devotion to her in our own times.

SOME GUIDELINES FOR DISCERNMENT

Fr Jordan Aumann, OP, in his *Spiritual Theology*, speaks of there being three different "types" of spirits which can affect us: that is, the divine spirit, the diabolical spirit and the human spirit. God always inclines us towards good, the devil always inclines us towards evil, while our own human spirits can be influenced either way.

While the devil, or a diabolical spirit, cannot, for example, produce any genuinely supernatural phenomena, such as raising the dead or predicting the future, evil spirits can produce corporeal or imaginative visions, or false ecstasies. They can also cure diseases due to diabolical influence, or cause individuals to hear sounds or voices.[11]

It is clear from the Bible that there have been instances when, by means of diabolical power, individuals have been able to mimic miracles. Thus, as we can read in Exodus, chapters 7 to 9, Pharaoh's magicians and sorcerers were able to imitate some of the miraculous deeds done by Moses and Aaron. But there was a limit to their power.

Fr Aumann also speaks of the following characteristics that can be taken as "general signs of the divine spirit." Amongst these he includes a tendency towards truthfulness, and also what he describes as "gravity," that is, the idea that "God is never the cause of things that are useless, futile, frivolous, or impertinent. When his spirit moves a soul it is always for something serious and beneficial."

As we have seen, it is highly questionable if truthfulness or gravity are words that could be justly used in describing many aspects of Medjugorje.

In the same way, Fr Aumann speaks about the quality of *docility,* namely the principle that:

> Souls that are moved by the spirit of God accept cheerfully the advice and counsel of their directors or others who have authority over them. This spirit of obedience, docility, and submission is one of the clearest signs that a particular inspiration or movement is from God. This is especially true in the case of the educated, who have a greater tendency to be attached to their own opinions.

He also has this to say about the quality of *humility* regarding those claiming divine favors: "The Holy Spirit always fills the soul with sentiments of humility and self-effacement. The loftier the communications from on high, the more profoundly the soul inclines to the abyss of its own nothingness. Mary said, 'I am the servant of the Lord. Let it be done to me as you say.'"

If we apply these criteria to both the visionaries and some of their associates, then clearly they cannot be said to have been acting with any great spirit of docility or humility.[12] Similarly, it is hard to believe that another quality he lists, that of *self-abnegation,* is a defining characteristic of the visionaries, given their strong tendency to court publicity.

Regarding "signs of the diabolical spirit," Fr Aumann gives the following points as being worthy of attention, and particularly, a *spirit of falsity,* since, because "the devil is the father of lies," he can cleverly conceal "his deceit by half-truths and pseudo-mystical phenomena."

He also speaks of *obstinacy* as being one of "the surest signs of a diabolical spirit," while "constant indiscretion and a restless spirit" are equally amongst his contra-indications.

Similarly, both a *spirit of pride and vanity,* and *false humility,* come in for censure. The former is apparently characteristic of those who are "very anxious to publicize their gifts of grace and mystical experiences," while the latter "is the disguise for their pride and self-love."[13]

The reader can make his or her own judgment as to how well the above description fits the activities of the Medjugorje visionaries.

THE POSITION OF THE CHURCH ON VISIONS

We can now review the position of the Church on the whole area of visions and apparitions. The various approved Marian apparitions, such as Guadalupe, Lourdes and Fatima, are classed as "private" revelations, in that the Public Revelation to and through the Church was completed during Apostolic times, and is now closed. All that the Church has done since then is to develop and clarify those public truths, and Catholics are bound to believe them as truths of the Faith. Private revelations, however, including the approved Marian apparitions, are given to an individual or group for their own good or that of others; Catholics are not obliged to believe in them, and they do not add to the sum total of Public Revelation,[14] as the *Catechism of the Catholic Church* (67) makes clear:

> Throughout the ages, there have been so-called "private" revelations, some of which have been recognized by the authority of the Church. They do not belong, however, to the deposit of faith. It is not their role to improve or complete Christ's definitive Revelation, but to help live more fully by it in a certain period of history. Guided by the Magisterium of the Church, the *sensus fidelium* knows how to discern and welcome in these revelations whatever constitutes an authentic call of Christ or his saints to the Church.

But as Fr Manfred Hauke notes: "The adjective 'private' does not imply a purely personal interest which does not involve the ecclesial community, but only distinguishes these messages from general revelation."[15]

There is always the danger of illusion or deception in visions or apparitions, and that is why the Church, in the person of the local bishop initially, has always been reluctant to accept them without a great deal of scrutiny. In approving particular private revelations, the Church is only proposing them for assent on the basis that they are worthy of an act of human faith, based on human testimony.

The classic view on this matter was expressed by Prospero Lambertini (the future Benedict XIV, d. 1758) as follows: "Although an assent of Catholic faith may not and can not be given to revelations thus approved, still, an assent of human faith, made according to the rules of prudence is due to them; for, according to these rules such revelations are probable and worthy of pious credence."[16]

It could be remarked in passing that Lambertini wrote in the period before the major modern Marian apparitions, and there has been some development in thinking since then. That is particularly so if we recognize the exceptional nature of the messages received and transmitted by the various more recent Marian seers, which seem to be a special case of private revelation, since they form a series which has been of great importance in strengthening the Church in modern times. They certainly differ from the various private revelations to individual saints, which have been concerned with, for example, the foundation of a religious order. That is, such revelations concern only part of the Church, whereas the major Marian apparitions have importance for the Church as a whole.

As Fr William Most states, "Some private revelations of our own times, such as those at Fatima, are directed to all Christians, not only to one individual; still they are technically called private, to distinguish them from that revelation which closed with the death of St. John."[17] Thus, we have to distinguish between those revelations made to individuals, for their own good, and those meant for the whole Church. Fatima, Lourdes and Guadalupe certainly fall into the latter category, and, given the miraculous events surrounding them, which are evidence of the divine, these seem to call for a greater commitment on the part of Catholics as a whole.[18]

Fr Hauke comments on this point:

> Since the distinction between "public" and "private" does not appear to be very useful in respect to apparitions that have an incisive message for the entire Church (such as Guadalupe, Lourdes, and Fatima), more recently a distinction has been proposed "between foundational revelation and particular revelations, which continue according to the diversity of times and places."[19]

The question also arises as to how certain we can be that an apparition really comes from God. In the Old Testament period, prophets such as Elijah appeared and claimed to speak in the name of God, proving this by miraculous signs accepted by the people. These signs were necessary because of the presence of false prophets, and so a process of discernment was needed. Likewise, Christ proved the divine nature of his person and mission by performing miracles.

This is the view of the French spiritual writer, Fr Poulain, on how much credibility we should give to revelations and visions generally, and, by extension, this also applies to Marian apparitions:

When a miracle is performed, and it is stated that it is worked with this intention [as a sign], or when circumstances show this to be the case, it is an undeniable proof of the divine nature of the revelation. A prophecy fulfilled will be the equivalent of a miracle, if it was couched in definite language and could not have been the result of chance or a conjecture of the Devil.[20]

The miraculous healings at Lourdes seem to fulfill these criteria, while at Fatima there was both a fulfilled prophecy and a miraculous sign in the foretelling and actual occurrence of the miracle of the sun. This indicates that these Marian apparitions really did come from God, and so we can be *morally certain* they are worthy of belief. In contrast, however, regarding Medjugorje, as we have seen, there is no clear-cut evidence of miraculous signs or genuine prophetic utterances.

THE ROLE OF THE LOCAL BISHOP

The decision as to the authenticity of an apparition rests in the first place with the local bishop, who is the "father in Christ" of his own diocese. If, after sufficient study, there is solid evidence to support the apparition, in terms of the facts surrounding it and the activities of the seer or seers, and likewise regarding such matters as miraculous healings, then the bishop is empowered to issue some form of edict declaring the authenticity of a particular apparition. While such a statement is not infallible, and no one is absolutely obliged to believe in that particular apparition, the position of the bishop as the spiritual ruler of the diocese does mean that his decision should be respected. The two extremes to be avoided are excessive credulity, which believes every report of an apparition, and excessive skepticism, which holds apparitions almost in contempt.

The attitude of the bishop, of course, also holds good with regard to alleged visions which show clear signs of being false, including Medjugorje. As we have seen, the position of the successive bishops of Mostar has been negative, and these have not been arbitrary decisions which can just be ignored, although unfortunately that seems to have been the attitude of many Medjugorje supporters.

Over time, the papacy may grant special privileges to particular shrines, and those are a sign of further approval by the Church as a whole.[21] One such liturgical sign is the granting of a feast day, as, for example, that of Our Lady of Lourdes on 11 February. In recent times, as already indicated, popes such as Paul VI and John Paul II have visited a number of Marian shrines, thus giving them the highest possible level of approval.

Fr Hauke emphasizes the importance of this point in connection with the holiness of the seer or seers:

> A Marian prophecy reaches the highest degree of credibility when the recognized sanctity of the seers and the liturgical celebration of events are united. For the liturgical aspect, the peak comes with a feast made obligatory at the universal level. Saint Catherine Labouré (Rue du Bac), Saint Bernadette (Lourdes), and Saint Juan Diego (Guadalupe) were canonized; two of the seers of Fatima have been beatified. There is an optional liturgical memorial for the entire Church in regard to Lourdes, Fatima, and Guadalupe, while the feast of Our Lady of Guadalupe was introduced for an entire continent (the Americas).[22]

In sum, then, the Church has consistently taken a very cautious attitude towards Marian apparitions, with only a very small minority of such reported events being accepted. Episcopal approval is the first step in such acceptance, but other factors such as general Church approval, expressed in the building of a basilica, for example, or a papal visit, would also seem to be important if an apparition is to be fully acknowledged.

NORMAE CONGREGATIONIS AND DISCERNMENT

In 1978, *Normae Congregationis*, a document on the discernment of claims of private revelations, was issued by the Congregation for the Doctrine of the Faith. This text was approved by Pope Paul VI and then made available to bishops and religious superiors worldwide. It was reproduced in an unofficial French translation in the book by Joachim Bouflet and Philippe Boutry, *Un signe dans le ciel: Les apparitions de la Vierge*.[23]

Although it is rather involved, it is necessary to look at this document in some detail in order to understand its implications for apparition discernment. *Normae Congregationis* begins with a preliminary note explaining how the document originated, and noting that because news of alleged apparitions spreads more quickly than formerly, and pilgrimages are easier to organize, ecclesiastical authority had felt it necessary to reconsider the subject. Because of scientific advances in this area, and the need for rigorous critical analysis, the text notes that it is more difficult to arrive at a speedy decision, one that is either *constat de supernaturalitate* ("the supernatural character is established") or *non constat de supernaturalitate* ("the supernatural character is not established").[24]

The text also discusses the option for the local bishop to permit or prohibit public veneration [*cultus*] and other forms of devotion by the faithful. It then goes on to say that to ensure that the devotion arising from any private revelation will be fully Catholic, and that the Church itself will be able to properly discern any claimed revelation, it is necessary to adopt a particular approach. This involves the event in question first being assessed according to positive and negative criteria, as subsequently set out, and then, while continuing to investigate the phenomenon "with great prudence," to allow certain public devotions. Subsequently, after some time, and in the light of any evident spiritual fruits, it is permissible, "if the case requires, to present a judgment on its validity and supernatural character."

It should thus be noted that *Normae Congregationis* envisages a three-stage process, and that it is not legitimate to jump straight to a consideration of the "fruits" of any alleged visions, without first establishing whether or not the claimed visions are worthy of belief. Regrettably this procedure has not been followed by many Medjugorje devotees and writers, who have acted as though the fruits were, in practice, the only things that mattered.

The text then discusses the positive and negative criteria for judgment of any alleged vision. The positive criteria include a "moral certitude," following a "serious investigation," that the claimed revelation is in fact genuine. Other factors include the personal qualities of the visionaries, with a focus on "mental equilibrium, honesty and rectitude of moral life, habitual sincerity and docility toward ecclesiastical authority."

The revelations themselves must be in conformity with "true theological and spiritual doctrine" and "exempt from error." Finally, the claimed revelation should have given rise to a "healthy devotion" and "abundant and constant spiritual fruits" with an emphasis on "the spirit of prayer, conversions, [and] the testimony of charity." Notice that the "spiritual fruits" are only considered as part of *one* of the positive criteria, in conjunction with "healthy devotion."

Rather surprisingly, there is no mention of miraculous healings or supernatural events, such as fulfilled prophecies, as positive criteria for authenticity. And the idea that the revelations should be in conformity with "true theological and spiritual doctrine" could possibly be understood in the sense that they ought to conform to the pattern of previous approved apparitions, although obviously this is not explicitly stated.

The negative criteria include obvious errors concerning the claimed revelation, as well as "doctrinal errors," allowing for the fact that the subject may unconsciously add things to a genuine revelation. Other negative criteria include an "evident seeking of money" in relation to the phenomenon, as well as "gravely immoral acts at the time of the event itself or in association with it, committed by the subject or by his close followers." Similarly, if the individuals are subject to "mental illnesses or psychopathic tendencies" or there is evidence of "psychosis or collective hysteria, or other things of this kind," then these too would be taken as negative criteria.

Regarding Medjugorje, there is certainly cause for concern on the particular point "evident seeking of money"; and likewise, regarding "gravely immoral acts," as we have seen, there are legitimate concerns regarding Frs Vlasic and Zovko, two close associates of the visionaries.

At this juncture, however, *Normae Congregationis* stresses the importance of seeing these positive or negative criteria as part of the whole investigation, and not as definitive one way or the other.

THE COMPETENT AUTHORITIES

The document then deals with those authorities able to judge the alleged event, beginning with the local Ordinary, who has a serious obligation to investigate it if a spontaneous devotion arises. The bishop can authorize various devotions if the above-mentioned positive criteria are present, but it must be made clear that this does not indicate approval by the Church. And if it is a question of the alleged phenomenon giving rise to serious abuses of devotion or false doctrines, or signs of a false mysticism, then the local bishop is obliged to intervene.

The local Ordinary can request that the regional or national Bishops' Conference intervene so that the event can be studied more fully, and these higher bodies can intervene if the phenomenon assumes regional or national importance. The Vatican can intervene at the request of the local bishop or of a qualified group of the faithful, or by means of its own universal authority.

Clarifying the Case of Medjugorje

The Congregation for the Doctrine of the Faith can also intervene in consultation with the Ordinary, after he has carried out his own investigation. In serious cases the Congregation can intervene on its own authority, particularly if the event affects a broad portion of the Church—but always in consultation with the bishop, and the Episcopal conference, where this is necessary.

It is clear that the way the question of Medjugorje has been dealt with, initially by the local bishop, and then by the Bishops' Conferences of first ex-Yugoslavia, and then Bosnia-Herzegovina, accords with the above provisions, and that the repetitive claim that Bishop Zanic was relieved of the Medjugorje "dossier" is incorrect. It would be more accurate to say that the CDF, in consultation with the successive bishops of Mostar, has been trying for many years now to find the best way to deal with Medjugorje. The relevant text from *Normae Congregationis* (IV, 1. b) makes this clear: "It is proper to the Sacred Congregation to intervene at its own initiative in more serious cases, especially if the matter affects a larger part of the Church; *the Ordinary is always to be consulted* and, if appropriate, also the Episcopal Conference."

The fact that this text speaks of the Ordinary being consulted indicates that any crude assertion that the local bishop, in this case Bishop Peric, has been deliberately snubbed or excluded is incorrect.

Part 2 of this final section of the document states: "The Sacred Congregation will be able either to evaluate the Ordinary's manner of acting and approve it, or, if possible and appropriate, to initiate a new examination of the matter, distinct from the study completed by the Ordinary, either on its own or through a special commission."

This can be read as though it implies "disapproval" as regards Bishop Peric's way of acting regarding Medjugorje, but the investigation had already passed beyond this point, to higher episcopal levels. And as we will see, the CDF announced the formation of a new Commission to study Medjugorje, in March 2010, in line with the provision in the quotation above.

It always needs to be borne in mind that *Normae Congregationis* was meant to be a set of guidelines and not a straitjacket, and that it was written before the advent of Medjugorje and its worldwide impact. Nothing comparable to Medjugorje in the realm of alleged visions had been seen in the Church in modern times before 1978, the year of its promulgation. Because of this, it would have been impossible to compose a document on apparition discernment prior to something like Medjugorje that could have taken account of every possible eventuality, and so it has to be interpreted in the light of experience, and of the facts on the ground, and not in an unreal or overly legalistic way.

BISHOP PERIC ON MEDJUGORJE

Bishop Peric was interviewed by the French writer Yves Chiron in the journal *Présent,* dated 25 January 1997, and was at pains to emphasize that the conclusions of the Zadar declaration of 1991 still held good—that it could not be affirmed that "supernatural apparitions and revelations" had taken place at Medjugorje. Similarly, he made it plain that there had been no recognition of any *cultus* there, in the sense outlined in *Normae Congregationis,* of allowing public veneration of the Medjugorje "Gospa," as a preliminary to recognition of the alleged visions themselves. He also pointed out, contrary to statements made by certain authors, that the inquiry into the visions had *not* been removed from his authority.

Bishop Peric commented on his parochial visits to Medjugorje as follows:

> There are many disorders there. There are Franciscan priests there with no canonical mission; religious communities have been established without the permission of the diocesan bishop, ecclesiastical buildings have been erected without ecclesiastical approval, parishes are encouraged to organize official pilgrimages, etc. Medjugorje, considered as a location of presumed apparitions, does not promote peace and unity but creates confusion and division, and not simply in its own diocese. I stated this in October 1994 at the Synod of Bishops and in the presence of the Holy Father, and I repeat it today with the same responsibility.

He further remarked that he did not see the need for any new commission of inquiry, and moreover, the Congregation for the Doctrine of the Faith had upheld his general position in letters to two French bishops, sent in July 1995 and March 1996. In these, after citing the 1991 Zadar declaration of the Yugoslav Bishops Conference, the text of the CDF letters had continued as follows: "Official pilgrimages to Medjugorje, representing it as a place of authentic Marian apparitions must not be organized either on a parish or diocesan level, because this would be a contradiction of what has been affirmed by the bishops of the ex-Yugoslavia in their previously cited declaration."[25]

Pope John Paul II was finally able to make his postponed visit to Sarajevo in April 1997, but during his homily, he made no mention of Medjugorje. Rather, he restricted his remarks to the Marian shrine at Hrasno, twenty-five miles away, which, as we have seen, was established in 1977—four years before Medjugorje—under the title "Queen of Peace"; on 9 May he sent a telegram to Bishop Peric in which he praised the shrine at Hrasno as a true center of Marian devotion.[26]

In October 1997, in response to a letter from Thierry Boutet of the French organization *Famille Chrétienne* ("Christian Family"), Bishop Peric stated that:

> On the basis of the serious study of the case by 30 [academics], on my episcopal experience of five years in the Diocese, on the scandalous disobedience that surrounds the phenomenon, on the lies that are at times put into the mouth of the "Madonna," on the unusual repetition of "messages" for over 16 years, on the strange way that the "spiritual directors" of the so-called "visionaries" accompany them throughout the world making propaganda of them, on the practice that the "Madonna" appears at the "fiat" (let her come!) of the "visionaries," my conviction and position is not only *non constat de supernaturalitate* [the supernaturality has not been proven] but also the other formula *constat de non supernaturalitate* [the non-supernaturality is proven] of the apparitions or revelations of Medjugorje.[27]

It should be noted that what Bishop Peric was doing here was changing his own stance from a somewhat neutral one to a negative position; but further on in the letter he acknowledges that he does not have the final say: "I am open to a study that the Holy See would undertake, as the supreme court of the Catholic Church, to speak the supreme and definitive judgment on the case, and that as soon as possible, for the good of souls and for the honor of the Church and of Our Lady."[28]

FRANCISCAN DISOBEDIENCE CONTINUES

On 22 June 1997, the Catholic Information Agency in Zagreb published an important document signed by Don Ante Luburic, the Chancellor of Mostar diocese, which detailed further instances of

Franciscan disobedience to Bishop Peric. He outlined some aspects of the history of the problem, before giving specific examples, including churches that had been built and blessed by the Franciscans without the knowledge of the bishop, and in contradiction of Canon Law. He also mentioned the fact that more than forty Franciscans did not have the necessary faculties for pastoral work in the diocese. In particular, he mentioned the case of those parishioners who, with the knowledge of the Franciscans, had bricked up the entrance of the church at Capljina, to prevent the bishop from sending secular priests to the parish. Similarly, he gave details of the numerous "religious" communities, including the charismatic Beatitudes community, that were operating at Medjugorje without the permission of Church authorities.[29]

Later in the year, on 24 October, Don Luburic issued a further communiqué, which has already been mentioned. A response to an article by Fr Laurentin, this communiqué accused the French priest of "disinformation" regarding some of his assertions on Medjugorje. These included statements about some Franciscans who had been disciplined, and an assertion that the Holy Father had asked Cardinal Kuharic, and even President Tudjman, to go to Medjugorje.

In particular, it described as "an invention" of Fr Laurentin the idea that Pope John Paul II, during his journey to Sarajevo, had "authorised a part of his retinue to leave him during the journey in order to go publicly on pilgrimage to Medjugorje: eleven persons, bishops and ambassadors, along with Vatican correspondents."

"In reality," continued Don Luburic:

> The Ambassador of Croatia to the Holy See, Mr Ive Livljanic, organised in his own capacity the journey of a group of ambassadors, bringing them from Rome to Medjugorje: these persons had nothing to do with authorisation by, nor with the retinue of, the Holy Father. Apart from this disinformation, one sees all sorts of things attributed to the Holy Father and to his "entourage," things which have no foundation in reality.[30]

Meanwhile, the situation had worsened at Capljina, Fr Vlasic's old parish, where, on 5 October 1997, a certain "Bishop" Srecko Franjo Novak conducted a Confirmation ceremony at the church; it turned out, however, that he had been expelled from the regular Catholic seminary, only to join the "Old Catholics" where he was, at most, a deacon. He apparently spoke in German, and one of the Franciscan priests acting illicitly at the parish translated for him. It does not seem that the Sacrament was validly conferred on this occasion, and it is certainly highly irregular for any bishop to attempt to confer Confirmation in another diocese without the permission of the local Ordinary, to say nothing of doing so in a church whose main entrance had been bricked up. Fr Laurentin confirms that this incident did indeed take place.[31] On 23 March 1998, the Congregation for Religious in Rome confirmed decrees dismissing two of the priests involved at Capljina, Frs Boniface Barbaric and Bozo Rados, from the Franciscan Order.[32]

THE LETTER TO BISHOP AUBRY

In May 1998, Archbishop Tarcisio Bertone, Secretary to the Congregation for the Doctrine of the Faith, responded to an enquiry from Bishop Gilbert Aubry of Saint-Denis de la Réunion, on the question of Medjugorje. This response has been taken by many adherents of Medjugorje as providing support for their position, but on examination it will be seen that this is questionable.

The first point to make is that this was a personal letter, addressed to one bishop, and not meant, initially, as a general response for the whole Church, although it was circulated more widely later on. In any case, in this letter Archbishop Bertone speaks of the "so-called apparitions of Medjugorje," thus indicating that the Holy See had not in any way approved the alleged visions. Furthermore, the archbishop says that it is impossible for him to answer all the questions put by Bishop Aubry on matters such as pilgrimages and the "pastoral care of the faithful who go there," because "the Holy See does not ordinarily take a position of its own regarding supposed supernatural phenomena as a court of first instance."

Archbishop Bertone then went on to speak about the "credibility" of the "apparitions" in question, stating that the Congregation accepts the Zadar declaration made by the Yugoslavian Bishops in April 1991, that is: "On the basis of investigation up till now, it cannot be established that one is dealing with supernatural apparitions and revelations."[33]

The archbishop indicated that Bishop Peric's statement to Thierry Boutet, as detailed above, that is, that the "non-supernaturality" of the visions or revelations of Medjugorje is "proven," was the "personal conviction" of Bishop Peric. But this does not mean that he was necessarily dismissing or contradicting the latter — he was merely stating a fact, while at the same time acknowledging that Bishop Peric, as the local Ordinary, was perfectly entitled to express such a conviction.

The reason Archbishop Bertone said this was that Bishop Peric was no longer in a position to make a definitive final judgment, since Medjugorje now had an influence and presence much wider than his diocese. And in fact the archbishop indicated that if the case were to be re-examined this would be under the aegis of the Episcopal Conference of Bosnia-Herzegovina, and it would be for this body "to make any new pronouncements that might be called for." But in saying this he wasn't stating that Bishop Peric shouldn't advance his personal opinion, nor act concerning Medjugorje within his own diocese.[34]

Finally, with regard to pilgrimages to Medjugorje, Archbishop Bertone reiterated the fact that "private" pilgrimages were allowed, provided that "they are not regarded as an authentication of events still taking place."[35]

ROMANIS PONTIFICIBUS IMPLEMENTED

Later in the year, in November 1998, there was a further development regarding the proper implementation of the special decree issued in 1975 by the Holy See, *Romanis Pontificibus,* which was mentioned previously. This demanded Franciscan obedience concerning the distribution of parishes between the Franciscans of the Herzegovina Province and the diocesan clergy of Mostar-Duvno diocese. The crux of this problem was not that it was a dispute between the bishops and the Franciscans, but rather between the Franciscans and the Vatican. Although most of the Franciscans involved did cooperate, a number (as we have seen above) resisted at Capljina to the point of usurping the parish, an action which ultimately led to their dismissal from the Order.

Then, on 20 February 1999, nearly twenty-four years after being issued, *Romanis Pontificibus* was definitively implemented by the then Vicar General of the Order of Friars Minor, Fr Stephan Ottenbreit, and Bishop Peric of Mostar-Duvno. The Holy See was represented by the then Papal Nuncio, Msgr Mario Cassari.

The important point to note here is that the usual task of an Order such as the Franciscans is to evangelize a new territory, and then, once this is done, to hand over control to the diocesan clergy. That is the way things normally work in the Church. So, the fact that the Holy See was prepared to allow the Herzegovina Province

Franciscans to keep half of their parishes—a situation which does not exist anywhere else in the world—was a significant concession.

Despite this, a number of Franciscans refused to sign the declaration of obedience this implementation required, and as a result, nine were dismissed from the Order, and a further twenty-three suffered other penalties, including the withdrawal of the faculty to hear confessions.[36] Furthermore, as part of the process of implementation, seven parishes were due to be handed over to the diocese, but this did not take place as planned because some parishioners physically resisted this move, a resistance which also involved "serious written and verbal threats, [the] occupation of churches and parochial houses and the removal of parish registers and stamps."[37]

* * *

SO, ONCE AGAIN, THE NEGATIVE ASPECTS OF MEDJUgorje become clear when the facts are examined. The widespread circulation of Medjugorje messages and books has led to many disorders. By rights, all of these writings ought to have been submitted to lawful Church authority. Bishop Peric's forthright interviews on the subject of Medjugorje, in which he details the problems which have arisen there, make his position very clear.

And this criticism could be extended almost indefinitely to ask why the "Gospa" didn't have anything negative to say about the activities of Frs Vlasic and Zovko, since the former, as we will see, would eventually be laicized and dismissed from the Franciscan Order, while the latter has been suspended three times. And the incidents involving these individuals are just the tip of the iceberg as far as problems with Medjugorje are concerned, and the lack of any response to these from the "Gospa."

19
The Good and Bad Fruits of Medjugorje

GOOD FRUITS IN THE EARLY YEARS

It would be wrong to claim that there have been no good fruits arising out of Medjugorje, at least as far as the early years were concerned. For example, Fr Sivric details the activities of a group of four Franciscans from a small friary seven or eight miles away, who, right from the beginning, came to Medjugorje practically daily to hear confessions, and had indeed heard tens of thousands of confessions as part of their ministry there. On the bigger feasts, when the crowds were even larger than usual, these priests were joined by other Franciscans from even further afield.[1]

But on a purely psychological level, if someone sees a long line of penitents at Medjugorje, that in itself may well prompt some soul searching even from somebody who might not have had any particular intention to go to confession. That is, such a sight might well act a catalyst in the process of their conversion. In the churches of the developed countries, though, such a sight is extremely rare, and thus frequent confession is something which needs more promotion in catechesis and homilies.

Undeniably, Medjugorje exerted a great attraction for people, and particularly young people, from a very early date. Sr Lucy Rooney tells us: "On the feast of the Exaltation of the Cross in 1983 (celebrated on a Sunday), over 100,000 came, over half of them young people. Transport being forbidden, they came mostly bare-footed, walking to the isolated village and climbing up the rocky mountain to the great cross on the ridge." She also tells us about the situation on 24 and 25 June 1984, the "third anniversary" of the beginning of the visions, when:

> So many pilgrims came from overseas that Masses were said each day in Italian, German, French and English, as well as Croatian. The majority of people were from Yugoslavia itself. They came on foot with no plans to stay anywhere, carrying what they would need for a night or two in the open.[2]

THE GOOD FRUITS ANALYZED

However, the fact that many people came to Medjugorje then, and continue to do so, does not of itself guarantee authenticity. The events at Necedah involving Mary Ann Van Hoof, who at the age of 40, in 1949, began to claim that she was seeing visions of the Virgin Mary, are a good indication of this. Nothing in anything she said was particularly credible, but she succeeded in deceiving large numbers of people.

The origin of her visions was almost certainly diabolical, given that her parents had been immigrants from Transylvania where they had dabbled in spiritualism — a career her mother continued in the United States, running a "spirit cabin" at Kenosha, Wisconsin. Mary Ann had acted as her assistant and was familiar with the activities of spirit mediums. It seems, too, that her mother was present during her daughter's later visions. When the La Crosse Diocese investigated the case, it transpired that neither Mary Ann, nor her husband, Fred Van Hoof, had been particularly zealous Catholics, and that they hadn't received the sacraments regularly until *after* the visions began. Almost unbelievably, too, for a supposed Marian visionary, it seems that she "detested Catholics and referred to them in derogatory terms, especially her husband's family whom she labeled, 'those damn Catholic farmers.'"

In any event, as news of her prophecies and revelations spread, pilgrims began to come in increasing numbers to the Van Hoof's Necedah farm, despite the strongly negative stance taken both by the local Ordinary, Bishop Treacy, and Cardinal Stritch. It is estimated that up to 100,000 people were present at the farm on 15 August 1950 for the feast of the Assumption.[3] This in itself is surely a clear indication that crowds coming to an alleged apparition site offer no guarantee of authenticity, and thus a warning that the number of pilgrims going to Medjugorje is no indication as to its real status.

Fr Michael O'Carroll was one visitor to Medjugorje, in 1986, who was obviously greatly impressed by what he saw: "The parish of Medjugorje is the first patent miracle of Our Lady, Queen of Peace. The parishioners are a case history. Their dissensions, at one time acute, have vanished. Their prayer is of a kind seen nowhere in the world." He also claimed: "The apparitions have sparked off a spiritual revolution in the parish of Medjugorje. Again, never has a whole community been so affected and transformed and brought to such a pitch of fervour."⁴ Fr Laurentin similarly lavished praise on Medjugorje, saying, "Because of false news having been published about it, we wish to stress that the parish of Medjugorje is the most normally operated in the world."⁵

These are the rather florid views of foreigners who had been drawn to Medjugorje from overseas, but Fr Sivric's investigations told a different story. The reader will recall that he was born and bred in Medjugorje, and was thus better equipped to assess the real situation. While conceding that in the early days there certainly was a change of attitude amongst many of the local people, according to his research it seems that over time they began to grow blasé, possibly because the threats issued in the name of the "Gospa" had progressively lost their impact. While acknowledging that there had been some improvements, he pointed to the persistence of "malicious and vindictive gossip." This was akin to Mark Waterinckx's experience in the 80s, when during his long stays in Medjugorje he frequently witnessed parishioners quarreling, despite stories of there being a new spirit in the village.⁶

In fact, Fr Faricy was forced to acknowledge that by 1986 the religious situation in Medjugorje had deteriorated, with fewer people attending the evening Mass and rosary.⁷ Regarding the activities of those pilgrims who came to Medjugorje in the early years, Mary Craig describes how one observer assessed the situation: "A lot of them weren't interested in praying. What they enjoyed doing most was looking at the sun and applauding the visionaries whenever they appeared."⁸

Wayne Weible was certainly disappointed with the way things had turned out at Medjugorje in comparison with the early days. He talks of how in the years that followed:

> [Its] pristine atmosphere began to show signs of pollution: Pilgrimages began to include curiosity seekers and those who came strictly as tourists. Travel agencies...[were] anxious to cash in on the growing popularity of the region.... The presence of the Virgin each evening became almost commonplace for many villagers.... Medjugorje had become a place of material opportunity for many. New entrepreneurs were coming to the village in droves. Their demeanor was that of rapacious wolves disguised as converted sheep, as they attempted to cash in quickly on the desires of those in search

of miracles. Cafés and souvenir stands sprang up almost overnight, along with hotels and barracks. There was constant construction as villagers continued to build additional rooms onto their homes to house pilgrims. Many villagers who had responded so fervently in the beginning months of the apparitions were now busy making money as they had never made it before. They were too busy to attend evening Mass, or to pray a family rosary, or to fast on Wednesdays and Fridays as requested by the Virgin.[9]

SOME GENUINE GOOD FRUITS?

Undoubtedly, though, there have been individuals and groups present in, or associated with, Medjugorje who have benefited from this. One example involves Moira Noonan, who, in her book *Ransomed from Darkness*, recounts her experiences as a New Age teacher—but one who eventually came back to the Catholic faith. This seems to have occurred to some extent through her contacts with Medjugorje. The negative side of all this, however, is that, in the words of Noonan, "an enormous false Mary movement" has grown up, principally through the writings of Sondra Ray, a well-known New Age practitioner, who has promoted the idea that the Blessed Virgin is a goddess who can be "channeled" in a spiritualistic fashion.

In any event, Noonan claims that while engaged in a spiritualistic "table rapping" session, she heard an "inner voice" from the "Queen of Peace" giving her an intuition that what she was doing was wrong. But she also tells us that she had started to wear a Miraculous Medal that had been left to her by her deceased grandmother. Other incidents seemed to be pointing her towards Marian devotion, including one where she was physically prevented from using her New Age crystals by an invisible force, and again heard an inner voice, this time telling her to pray the rosary. She was also led to go to confession, the first time she had received this sacrament in 25 years.

She now began to live a sincere Catholic life centered on Mass, prayer and spiritual reading, but breaking with her past was a long and difficult process. She finally managed to go to Medjugorje, where she went to confession to a priest with experience of the New Age movement. Her first confession to him lasted for 2½ hours, and in subsequent meetings with him she was gradually led to renounce all her past spiritualist activities, and was thus able to make a truly fresh start.[10]

The Good and Bad Fruits of Medjugorje

While applauding this outcome, the point clearly needs to be made that it was her participation in the sacrament of confession at Medjugorje which was the crucial part of her spiritual healing, rather than actually being present in the place itself. We also have to take into account the fact that she was wearing a Miraculous Medal. But having said that, it does seem possible that she did receive some extraordinary supernatural help to bring her back to the right road.

This has to be understood, though, in the context of her overall situation. It may well be that God had infallibly foreseen that it was only by means of her coming into contact with Catholics associated with Medjugorje that it would be possible for her to free herself from her New Age involvement. In other words, in an extreme situation like this, it might be necessary for God and the Blessed Virgin to have intervened miraculously in her life, given that she was so deeply involved in occult practices. However, this obviously does not imply a blanket endorsement of everything to do with Medjugorje.

MOVEMENTS AND COMMUNITIES

Another example is the international youth movement Youth 2000, whose origins have been linked with Medjugorje. But it emerges that the original impetus for the movement came to Ernest Williams while he was in Fatima in 1989, immediately following the World Youth Day at Santiago de Compostela—although the first Youth 2000 Festival of Prayer was actually launched in Medjugorje the following year. In any event, it is clear that later on, Youth 2000 was at pains to distance itself from Medjugorje. In the CTS booklet on the movement, in the question-and-answer section, the following statement appeared: "Ernest Williams, and many other young people who ran the first retreats in England, have visited Medjugorje. However, Youth 2000 has no official connection to Medjugorje and awaits the definitive ruling of the Church."

In fact, the spirituality of Youth 2000 has far more in common with the message of Fatima than that of Medjugorje, as a further quote from the CTS booklet indicates: "The charism of Youth 2000 is to draw young people through the Immaculate Heart of Mary to a deep and lasting union with the Eucharistic Heart of Jesus." At Fatima, Our Lady spoke of God's wish to "establish in the world devotion to my Immaculate Heart." As we will see, the Medjugorje messages make virtually no mention of this devotion.[11]

Various communities and organizations have established themselves in Medjugorje, including the charismatic Community of the Beatitudes, the New Horizons community, the Oasis of Peace community, the Cenacolo community, and the Mary's Meals movement. Sr Emmanuel Maillard, of the Beatitudes community, has published a number of pro-Medjugorje books, and has been described as "one of the most active figures in the promotion of Medjugorje worldwide." The Cenacolo community is involved in helping drug addicts to recover through adopting a Christian lifestyle, while the Mary's Meals movement has set up school feeding projects in the developing world. Generally speaking, these movements are clearly a force for the good, but regrettably there have been problems with some of them.

Regarding the Cenacolo community, Bishop Peric was obliged to write to Sr Elvira, the foundress, in December 2008, telling her that he had not given authorization for a chapel for her community in Medjugorje, nor permission for some of the visionaries to have their alleged visions there. The bishop also had to write to the Oasis of Peace community, in February 2009, pointing out that the community had not received permission to establish itself in Medjugorje, nor to have a perpetual adoration chapel. And as already indicated, previous to this, in May 1997, the Chancellor of the Mostar diocese, Dom Ante Luburic, had released a statement pointing out that at that time, many religious communities were "living and working within the parish of Medjugorje without the permission of the Church authorities." Amongst these he listed the Beatitudes community, Cenacolo and Oasis of Peace, before concluding: "Hence, Medjugorje has become a place of Religious disorder, disobedience and anti-ecclesiastical activity."[12]

So regarding these communities, quite serious disobedience was evident as long ago as the 1990s.

EMOTIONAL ENTHUSIASM

What, then, of those foreign pilgrims who have come to Medjugorje and claimed conversions and other spiritual benefits? The first point to note is that God does not deny his graces to those who go to a place of alleged visions in good faith to pray, attend Mass, join in the rosary and go to confession. The people who go to Medjugorje are clearly open to God's grace, otherwise they would not have gone in the first place. But having said that, we have to beware of transitory spiritual conversions which do not last, and also of emotional feelings of self-satisfaction which may lead individuals to believe that they are part of a spiritual elite, and thus better than the ordinary Catholic. The question then becomes: do those who have experienced a conversion at Medjugorje return home and show that their lives have been changed through becoming seriously involved in the day-to-day low-key work of building up the Church? Or are they more interested in trying to get other people involved in believing in alleged visions which have not been recognized?

Some of those caught up in the enthusiasm over Medjugorje were very influential:

> By chance, John Hill, a Boston millionaire and lapsed Catholic, heard an audio-cassette about Medjugorje, and instantly dedicated his entire fortune to promoting the messages. Setting up a Center for Peace in Boston, he dispatched a team to make an hour-long television film, began organizing monthly charter flights for pilgrims and arranging for the free distribution of booklets, video and audio cassettes, in a variety of languages, to people all over the world.[13]

What has certainly happened is that the large number of pilgrims returning from Medjugorje has precipitated an explosion in the number of major worldwide centers promoting the visions, as well as a vast number of smaller local groups often producing their own newsletters and literature. In addition, the fact that the visionaries have been very ready to travel, and can apparently experience "visions on demand," has greatly helped to promote Medjugorje. For all these reasons, and more, Medjugorje captured the imagination of many Catholics during the 1980s, when, for various reasons, people wanted something new, something exciting, something more than they were getting from their ordinary parish life.[14]

MEDJUGORJE AND FRANCISCAN UNIVERSITY OF STEUBENVILLE

To take one powerful example of this, we need only look at the relationship between the promotion of Medjugorje, the Charismatic Renewal and Franciscan University of Steubenville, in Ohio in the United States. The former chancellor of the university, Fr Michael Scanlan, was a long-time supporter of Medjugorje, and edited one of the earliest books in English on the subject, Fr Svetozar Kraljevic's

The Apparitions of Our Lady at Medjugorje, which was published by the Franciscan Herald Press as early as 1984.[15]

E. Michael Jones commented on this link:

> The University of Steubenville was a center for the specifically Kosickian brand of Charismatic Renewal—i.e., including devotion to Mary—and subsequently became a center for interest in Medjugorje. Video tapes on Medjugorje were shown in the university cafeteria, Sister Isabel Bettwy organized tours, and there is even a picture of the seer Marija Pavlovic wearing a University of Steubenville sweatshirt.[16]

In fact, the university's connection with Medjugorje goes back to the early 1980s, when it was reported in the student newspaper, *The Troubadour*, that a group from Steubenville, led by Fr Scanlan and Sr Bettwy, had visited there as pilgrims in 1983. There were further reports of Medjugorje-related events in subsequent years, such as the fact that in November 1986, Fr Tomislav Pervan, the then pastor of the Medjugorje parish, visited the university. It was also reported that Dr Mark Miravalle was commencing the first in a series of lectures on Medjugorje, while a story from March 1987 concerned a spring pilgrimage by seventy Steubenville students to the village, in what was still then Communist Yugoslavia. In February 1989, the paper ran a story about a student who had spent a semester in Medjugorje, while in September 1990, it reported that Fr Gobbi, the alleged locutionist, had appeared at the university. Medjugorje promoter Wayne Weible was another visitor in February 1992, and then in February 2000, it was reported that Fr Petar Ljubicic, who was described as the "spiritual director" of the visionaries, and was the priest to whom Mirjana will supposedly confide her secrets on a piece of paper similar to parchment, had spoken to students in the Christ the King chapel.[17]

So clearly, according to these *Troubadour* reports, there has been a long association between the university and Medjugorje, involving many aspects of student life. And given this, how could the students avoid coming to the conclusion that Medjugorje was worthy of belief? And this position has influenced a large number of young people over the years, many of whom have gone on to assume important positions at other universities and Catholic institutions, to say nothing of the diffusion of such a mentality throughout the Charismatic movement and the Church generally.

"IMPRINTING" MEDJUGORJE

One of the most intriguing aspects of Medjugorje is the intense devotion it seems to generate amongst its adherents, to the point that some devotees are unwilling to even consider the possibility—often following an emotional experience there—that it may not be genuine. An explanation for this intensity of devotion may come from the psychological process known as *imprinting*.

This idea was popularized by Konrad Lorenz, the Austrian ethologist, through his work on the behavior of birds. Lorenz showed how goslings hatched in an incubator would "imprint" on the first moving object they saw within a certain critical period after hatching, and regard that object as their "mother." Thus Lorenz was able to get the young goslings to imprint on him, and follow him around as if he was their mother. In the natural state, this is obviously very advantageous for the young birds, since they are then attached to their real parents and will follow them. This process also occurs with human babies, in the sense of them becoming attached to their parents, although obviously this is a much more complex process than with animals.

Regarding Medjugorje, and the principle of imprinting, we can perhaps see it in spiritual terms along the following lines. Catholicism, unlike Protestantism, has traditionally allotted a very important place to the veneration of the Blessed Virgin. There are many serious theological reasons for this, but psychologically and emotionally it's important to have a "spiritual" mother, just as a person's natural mother has an extremely vital role to play in their proper development. Indeed, it could be argued that without this maternal influence, whether on the physical or spiritual levels, the person will be severely disadvantaged. So devotion to Our Lady is clearly very important, which is why the Church has traditionally placed so much emphasis on it.

Now, if we consider what has taken place for many of the pilgrims to Medjugorje, it is the case that, given the confusion in the Church in recent years, many of them will have come from a very impoverished environment in their local parish with regard to devotion to Our Lady. In other words, they are "spiritual orphans," or "hatchlings" regarding her. They arrive in Medjugorje, and are suddenly immersed in a very powerful religious atmosphere, focused on practices such as the rosary, devotion to Our Lady, adoration of the Blessed Sacrament, the stations of the cross, prayer meetings, sacramental confession and so on.

They realize, perhaps for the first time in their lives, the vital importance of devotion to the Blessed Virgin, and develop an intense attachment to the "Gospa" and everything she stands for at Medjugorje. Of course, there is nothing wrong with this idea of a genuine devotion to Our Lady, and in fact it is a necessity for a truly Catholic spiritual life; but the problem is, like the young goslings who became "maternally" attached to Lorenz, the new Medjugorje devotees have not become attached to their *real* spiritual mother, but, according to all the evidence we have looked at so far, to a counterfeit, the Medjugorje "Gospa." God and Our Lady do not, of course, reject their devotion, even though it is misplaced, and this probably explains some of the conversions which have happened at Medjugorje, and equally, the intense, almost fanatical devotion which has developed around it over the last forty years.

This personal and intense devotion makes the problem of Medjugorje a very difficult one to solve, but it would appear that somehow the Church is going to have to develop a process whereby Medjugorje devotees are encouraged to "transfer" their allegiance to one of the other approved Marian apparitions, whether that be Guadalupe, Lourdes, Fatima, or another approved devotion. That will not be easy, but ultimately the alternative may well be their estrangement from the Church. Fortunately, in many cases, this transference of allegiance happens naturally, as the faith of these converts deepens.

But there is another situation in which the person is so affected by what they experience at Medjugorje, or in connection with it, that they are not in fact imprinted on Mary as such, but rather on "Medjugorje." Their loyalty is to "Medjugorje," and all that the word signifies for them—the visionaries, their spiritual experiences while there, the camaraderie with their fellow pilgrims, the atmosphere of the town, and so on. Then if someone questions Medjugorje, or criticizes it in any way, they take it personally. Thus for such individuals, "Medjugorje" has passed beyond devotion to Our Lady, and has assumed almost cult-like properties. They are so identified with it that their ego has become involved, and that is a much more difficult situation to deal with.

THE IMPACT OF MEDJUGORJE

Wayne Weible indicates the impact Medjugorje was having on the Church at this time:

The Good and Bad Fruits of Medjugorje

The month before the eight[h] anniversary celebration in Medjugorje, the first national conference in the United States on Medjugorje was held at the University of Notre Dame, in Indiana. More than 5,000 followers of the apparitions came to enjoy three days of retreat into holiness — very much akin to what takes place during pilgrimage at Medjugorje.... Within two years, similar conferences were springing up throughout the United States. Franciscan priests stationed at the parish in Medjugorje, and several of the visionaries themselves, were now coming to speak at these conferences, bringing their experiences to thousands who could not personally go to Medjugorje. Many skeptical and cautious priests and bishops who had journeyed there now urged the faithful to listen to and live the messages.[18]

Modern communications, initially via the telephone and fax machine, and later via the Internet, mean that the Medjugorje messages can now be instantly flashed around the world. This is something new, and has given many people a sense of belonging which, for them, was lacking in the institutional Church. They feel as though they are part of an extended Medjugorje family, and the monthly messages encourage this feeling.

This technological revolution, involving the internet particularly, but also television, video and the press, has meant that the visionaries and their supporters have been able to largely bypass Church authorities and the traditional forms of regulation and control which the latter have exercised. They have been able to take their message direct to potential pilgrims worldwide.[19]

Undoubtedly, though, one of the biggest reasons people have been drawn to Medjugorje, or to events involving the visionaries, has been the belief that the Blessed Virgin has been appearing on a daily basis, and that it may even be possible to receive a personal message from her, or see some sign. As we have seen above, though, St John of the Cross warns that the desire for revelations is very dangerous, and is almost guaranteed to lead to serious problems.

We can see this from the following section of an address by Fr Gianni Sgreva, given at the National Medjugorje Conference held at the University of Notre Dame in 1991. He told the audience how on the evening of 4 December 1985,

> I was taking off my priestly vestments in the sacristy of Medjugorje. Marija Pavlovic approached me and said, "Father Gianni, the Madonna spoke of you this evening." Immediately I answered, "What did she tell you?" "No, I won't tell you right away. You have to put yourself in prayer and recollection." I was left a little upset in the face of Marija's words. But I agreed to go with her together in prayer the following day. Then Marija gave me the message of the Madonna. Our Lady said: "Tell Gianni that I want to speak to him personally." I did not believe it. I told her, "If you see Our Lady again this evening, say to Our Lady that Fr. Gianni wants only facts and signs, and few words." But there was one thing that I liked right away. It came to my mind immediately that Our Lady said my name then.

Fr Sgreva goes on to say that "fruits and signs began right away," and that these prompted him to ask Marija to ask the "Gospa" if these signs were genuine. Not surprisingly, he was told that they were.[20] This was not the only occasion on which Marija delivered personal messages between the "Gospa" and a particular individual. As already noted, Archbishop Franic was also the recipient of one of these supposed messages. On 17 December 1984, he tells us:

> [I] asked Marija if I would be imposing too much if she were to ask Our Lady if there was a message for me. I expressly said I would be happy if she would give me some admonition for my conversion, if she would point her finger at my weaker points and tell me where I need to be careful and where I need to improve.[21]

The archbishop received the "message" that he should expect "greater sufferings" in the future.

The problem is that we don't find this type of thing—personal messages for individuals—in the accounts of the approved apparitions of Our Lady. She has certainly given instructions to individuals through the seers, that they should carry out a particular action to do with the establishment of a shrine, for instance, but this idea of the Blessed Virgin acting like the personal spiritual guru of particular individuals is just not present.

However, a similar type of thing did happen at Garabandal. We read of how:

> A totally skeptical priest... arrived wearing street clothes. He watched one of the children approach him. She offered him a crucifix to kiss several times. "If this is genuine," he thought to himself, "let the child come to." In an instant the visionary emerged from her ecstasy, smiled at the priest and turned to go home.

A further incident concerned another skeptic who:

> During one vision... thought to himself: "For me to believe this, the child will have to take my rosary from its case and hand it to me." The visionary immediately approached him, handed him his rosary and, to everyone's astonishment, said, "You didn't believe before, but now you do."[22]

Such incidents were by no means uncommon at Garabandal, and the mistake that such individuals made was to look for signs to indicate that the visionaries were genuine. The problem is that such an attitude is presumptuous and leaves the way open for diabolical involvement.

Thus, the attitude of those Medjugorje visionaries who have offered signs and messages to individuals, supposedly from the "Gospa," is totally at variance with what has happened during approved apparitions.

DANGEROUS DESIRE FOR THE MIRACULOUS

Generally speaking, we can say that this desire for the "miraculous" can partly be explained as the effect of a sort of spiritual lethargy which results in people not wishing to make the effort to pray as a means of discovering God's will, but rather to look for shortcuts and quick answers. However, believers should realize that it is contrary to faith to expect God or the Blessed Virgin to personally impart some sort of message to them. They are not there simply to do our bidding. The whole history of the Church makes this abundantly clear. Rather, we have to live by faith, and not by signs, wonders or messages. The very sobering words of Christ on this subject were that it was an "evil and adulterous generation [that] seeks for a sign" (Matt 16:4).

Medjugorje devotees should thus ask themselves this crucial question: do I believe in Medjugorje because my rosary has changed color, or because I have seen the sun spinning, or because alternatively, I have had a genuine spiritual experience which has had a lasting effect?

If the main focus has been on the former aspects, rather than the latter, then obviously that is inconsistent with the authentic way the Faith should be lived.

Ultimately, it seems that many Medjugorje supporters have come to believe the mistaken position that what counts is their personal opinion, rather than an objective discernment of the facts. And there is likewise the serious worldwide problem of all the alleged visionaries who have also been claiming to see the Blessed Virgin in the wake of Medjugorje, many of these being people who have been there.

Paolo Apolito lists the following individuals as being amongst those claiming to have started to receive their own revelations either following a visit to Medjugorje, or through some more general contact with it: Veronica Garcia; Br David, a Franciscan; Fr Jack Spaulding; Gianna Talone; Estela Ruiz; Lena Shipley; Alfredo Raimondo and Patricia Soto. And he also makes the very pertinent point that whereas prior to the modern era, with its explosion of visionary claims, individuals claiming such experiences would almost certainly have been shunned by the average Catholic, now they can expect to be treated as celebrities.[23]

CHRIST'S TEACHING ON GOOD FRUITS

On this question of the fruits arising from Medjugorje, reference is often made to the statement of Christ in the Gospels on the subject, with the implication that what has happened there is in line with his teaching:

> Beware of false prophets, who come to you in sheep's clothing but inwardly are ravenous wolves. You will know them by their fruits. Are grapes gathered from thorns, or figs from thistles? So, every sound tree bears good fruit, but the bad tree bears evil fruit. A sound tree cannot bear evil fruit, nor can a bad tree bear good fruit. Every tree that does not bear good fruit is cut down and thrown into the fire. Thus you will know them by their fruits. (Matt 7:15–20, 21–23 for further reading)

Yet a careful reading of the text makes it plain that Christ was *not* expressly talking about the spiritual fruits that might result from the actions of particular individuals, but rather was telling us to look carefully at the way those individuals themselves actually lived. The text is about false prophets, and Christ says we will know *them* by their fruits. This does not absolutely exclude the genuine good fruits which might proceed from the actions of individuals who themselves are not trustworthy, but it does seem that the emphasis being made here is on the activities of those individuals themselves, and not on any movements they might initiate.

Jesus gave us another solemn warning about "false prophets," which has been recorded in St Matthew's Gospel. Although this refers specifically to the "end times," it can also be applied throughout Church history, including in our own period: "For false Christs and false prophets will arise and show great signs and wonders, so as to lead astray, if possible, *even the elect*" (Matt 24:24).

Yes, even the "elect," which, as regards Marian apparitions, indicates those people with a genuine devotion to the Blessed Virgin; even they can be led astray by false prophets.

If we apply the "good fruits" criterion to Medjugorje as it should essentially be applied, that is, to the visionaries and their Franciscan associates, then as this book has clearly indicated it is obvious that they have been less than satisfactory. To take just a few examples, whether it is Vicka's "bloody handkerchief" story, or her activities as regards the laying on of hands, or the incident of the alleged dropping of the Baby Jesus by the Blessed Virgin, obviously the fruits in her case are suspect. Similarly, the threatening letter written by Ivan's hand to Bishop Zanic gives grave cause for concern, as does the emotional state of Mirjana, and the retraction of Marija's support for Fr Vlasic's idea of a community.

Regarding the Franciscans most involved with Medjugorje themselves, their long-running state of disobedience, both as regards the local bishop and the Holy See, is surely a very bad fruit. More recently, this disobedience has been expressed by other Franciscans through the erection of churches without permission, as well as irregular Confirmations. And as we will see shortly, the lifestyle of those principally involved in Medjugorje, as it has unfolded over the years, is a far cry from the poverty and simplicity one would expect of genuine seers or their associates.

This is what Fr Laurent Volken says on this point:

> Disobedience is a negative criterion of discernment and emphasized by theologians. And one of the reasons which bishops and other ecclesiastical authorities have given for condemning this or that apparition has been precisely the

disobedience of the visionaries or even of members of the Church who believed in the apparitions in question and disobeyed the instructions given upon the matter.²⁴

Thus, by the standards of Christ's teaching on good fruits it is hard to avoid the conclusion that both the visionaries and their Franciscan associates cannot be said to have lived up to its spirit or its letter.

FALSE PROPHETS

There seems to be a reluctance in some Catholic circles to believe that those involved in either receiving or promoting alleged visions or messages can possibly be acting from anything other than the highest motives. Sadly, such well-meaning but naïve support for Medjugorje has led many sincere people astray. It is an unfortunate fact that throughout Church history there have been false prophets and false visionaries at work. Where there is a group of religious enthusiasts, it is hardly surprising that out of self-interest people will be attracted to them purely for financial gain.

Is it really conceivable that these types of activities should have suddenly ceased following the Second Vatican Council? The answer is obviously no, and indeed all the evidence suggests that the situation has grown markedly worse since Vatican II, and this is only a reflection of the state of the secular world where the incidence of fraud of all types has exploded in recent years.

To use a concrete example, suppose a person has a $10 bill or a £10 note in their possession. How do they know that it is not counterfeit? Suppose it is believed that forgers have been working in the area, and that there is a possibility that an appreciable amount of forged currency is in circulation. The person has two basic options: they can either take the suspect note to the bank and have it checked, or they can just pass it on to the next person. They might argue that if that person accepts it then they will assume it is good, and if they don't, then they will regard it as a forgery. But that is faulty from a moral perspective. If someone has good reason to believe that a banknote is forged then it is their *duty* to have it checked.

If we apply this to the question of true and false visions, then it is obvious that checking the note with a bank is like finding out what the official spokesmen of the Church — the bishops in the first instance — have said about a particular vision. But just ignoring the status of the vision and relying on the alleged good fruits is like passing on the note the next time we shop—all that concerns us is whether or not the shop accepts it, and not whether it is forged or genuine. It might be said that a few forged notes in circulation are not going to do much harm, and that is true enough. But if the forgeries reach a certain percentage of the money in circulation then it will start to lose its value—the principle of bad money driving out the good comes into play. If the process goes on unchecked, ultimately the economy of the nation concerned will collapse, because its money will become totally worthless.

MODERN FALSE VISIONS AND VISIONARIES

Something like this has been happening with regard to visions. False or unapproved visions have been driving out the true. Yves Chiron lists seventy-one apparitions that are alleged to have arisen following Medjugorje, between 1981 and 1991. Of these, only Kibeho in Rwanda and San Nicolas in Argentina have gained any sort of support from the local bishop, while twelve were judged negatively, and no decision was taken about the others—which in effect means that they were not pronounced to be authentic.[25]

It should be noticed that this list is far from exhaustive, and in the intervening period there has been no slowdown in the number of alleged visions being reported. Yet, for many people, the very fact that all these reports are proliferating is a sign that the Blessed Virgin must indeed be appearing all over the world. What this means in practice is that many Catholics seem to have lost the ability or even the notion of seeking to discern between true and false visions.

Even Fr Laurentin, the foremost modern supporter of practically every conceivable allegedly "supernatural" event, has, in his *Apparitions of the Blessed Virgin Mary Today,* an appendix entitled: "Apparitions without credibility." These include Bayside in New York, where Veronica Leuken claimed to be receiving heavenly messages for many years, including the preposterous notion that Pope Paul VI had been replaced by an impostor whose features had been altered by plastic surgery. He also mentions an alleged female visionary at Belluno in Italy in the 1980s, and events involving a priest called Don Vincenzo and another female visionary, Maria Fioritti, who began to allege visions at Pescara following a visit to Medjugorje in 1987. Great signs were promised, and it was claimed that Pescara would be the conclusion of Medjugorje, and the "greatest apparitions in history." Fr

Laurentin describes this as "sensationalism" which "contradicts the messages of Medjugorje."

The French priest also deals with William Kamm, the German-born Australian visionary who styles himself as the "Little Pebble," and who claimed visions, including various unfulfilled prophecies and warnings, for many years. None of his claims has been given any credence by successive local bishops. Similarly, Fr Laurentin discusses the case of Marie-Paule Giguère, the founder of the Army of Mary in Quebec, Canada. This flourished during the 1970s, and even received local Episcopal approval for a while, but "serious errors," including the idea that the foundress was the "mystical reincarnation of Mary," became manifest after some time, and the organization was dissolved in 1987.[26] As we will see, followers of this woman were excommunicated in 2007, following a judgment handed down by the Congregation for the Doctrine of the Faith.

Nor are these the only alleged visions which by any standard must be regarded as false. There have been a great number of such incidents since Vatican II, particularly in the wake of Medjugorje, and thus the alleged events in Bosnia-Herzegovina have to be seen against this backdrop of large numbers of false or at best questionable visions.

Finally, we have to confront the startling fact that some of those involved in investigating Medjugorje have received death threats. Fr Sivric did not return to Medjugorje in later years because of such threats, while E. Michael Jones tells us that he "got a call from a man in England warning me that if I went back to Bosnia, the Franciscans were going to have me killed."[27] Would a genuine Marian apparition give rise to this sort of thing? These are some of the "fruits" of Medjugorje which we don't hear very much about.

* * *

WE CAN SAY, THEN, THAT ALTHOUGH THERE WAS EVIdence of good fruits arising from Medjugorje in the early days, particularly as reported by outsiders, those more familiar with the local culture, such as Fr Sivric, were more critical. In addition, while orthodox organizations such as Youth 2000 have distanced themselves from Medjugorje, the danger of excessive emotional enthusiasm for it has become clear, particularly in the mistaken belief that the Blessed Virgin has been appearing daily to the visionaries. Similarly, the problems engendered by an excessive desire for revelations, especially as expressed by writers such as St John of the Cross, have not been understood by Medjugorje supporters.

We have seen, too, that Christ's teaching on good fruits indicates quite clearly that the focus should be on the behavior of the individuals in question, and not on any movements they might initiate. Investigations along these lines have shown that the "fruits" exhibited by the Medjugorje visionaries and their Franciscan associates have left much to be desired. The strange reluctance of many Catholics to acknowledge that there is even a possible problem as regards false prophets has also been explored, as has the clear evidence that the vast majority of alleged visions reported in recent years are almost certainly false.

In sum, despite a number of positive points in its favor, the overall picture as regards good and bad fruits surely indicates that Medjugorje must be judged in a negative light.

20
Medjugorje: Problems and Dangers

FOCUSING ON NEGATIVE ELEMENTS

Apart from the considerations discussed in the last chapter, the attraction of going on pilgrimage to a shrine where Our Lady is allegedly appearing every day has proved irresistible for many. But one of the consequences of this development has been a general devaluation of Marian piety, and as a result all sorts of strange ideas have begun to circulate freely in the Church. For instance, there has been the focus on supposed "signs and wonders," on rosaries changing color, or the sun spinning, rather than on the real heavenly message of prayer and penance as found in the Gospels, and given at Fatima and other approved apparitions, such as Lourdes. Or in some cases, where these ideas have been taken up, they have been pushed to extremes, so that people fast excessively, or spend long hours in prayer, to the detriment of the duties of their state in life or their family commitments. The sound Catholic principle of observing a sensible balance has often been lost.

Denis Nolan effectively admits that there have been problems in this area, saying, "It may be true that some have gone to Medjugorje seeking some kind of supernatural titillation. There may be pilgrims who seek signs and wonders and who are disappointed if they do not end up with gold rosaries and a private apparition."[1]

Wayne Weible has this to say on this general point:

> Many pilgrims who had experienced a life-changing conversion through Medjugorje were now busy following after every claimed visionary and locutionist. They seemed driven by an insatiable thirst to know every possible detail about any supernatural event. The monthly messages given to Marija were now awaited more out of curiosity about what new things might be said, rather than out of a desire to learn from them and make them part of daily life.[2]

It has been argued[3] that this type of thing was also present at genuine apparition sites such as Fatima or Lourdes. But for the most part, there was a clear difference in the attitude displayed by people visiting those shrines formerly, and that displayed in recent times at Medjugorje, where "miracle seeking" has become something of a passion.

Yes, people did want cures at Lourdes, but usually, they did not display an unhealthy fascination with signs and wonders, or a desire to see rosaries changing color, or to spend time staring at the sun — with subsequent permanent eye damage for some — which we find associated with Medjugorje. The majority of people going to Lourdes were satisfied — and more than satisfied — with the miracles arising from the spring which Our Lady revealed to St Bernadette, or which took place during the Eucharistic processions. And regarding the miracle of the sun at Fatima, this was actually predicted three months in advance by Our Lady, so the people were not acting inappropriately in their expectation of a miracle.

But in neither case do we have the well-known phenomenon found at Medjugorje, and other alleged places of visions, of people deliberately seeking out signs and wonders, and traveling around from place to place to satisfy this desire.[4]

In addition, there has been too great a focus on apocalyptic elements, such as warnings, chastisements and signs, and particularly on the notion that the Second Coming of Christ is quite near. Apart from the fact that this type of message has been frequently advocated by false prophets, it is quite contrary to the genuine message of Fatima. It is true that the secret of Fatima does contain elements pointing to the future, but there is a complete lack of sensationalism. Rather, the emphasis is on what we can do to follow Our Lady's requests, so as to bring about the triumph of her Immaculate Heart, and not on a sort of fatalism which sees unavoidable impending disaster around every corner.

The fact is that the Blessed Virgin said nothing at Fatima about the Second Coming of her Son, but she did promise the world a period of peace provided that people complied with her requests. This period of peace may well be preceded by possibly great upheavals, but it would be wrong to describe the message of Fatima as apocalyptic or eschatological in the traditional sense of these words, that is, as related to the end of the world.

To return to Christ's teaching on false prophets, this also supplies the answer to those who might argue that it is unfair, or lacking in Christian charity, to bring up any negative points about the visionaries or the Franciscans. But unless people are informed about the nature of the activities of these individuals, how can they judge whether they are true or false prophets? If somebody begins to act as a visionary, or becomes closely associated with such a person, then they must expect to be submitted to a searching personal examination.

Unless we examine their fruits—that is, their actions and words—in some detail, it will be impossible to come to any balanced, objective conclusions about them. If the person is a genuine seer then any such investigation will only make this apparent, and they will grow in humility, as was the case with the little children of Fatima, or St Bernadette.

But if they are false prophets, if they exhibit pride or deceit, if the visitations, visions and messages which they say they are receiving in truth do not come from heaven, then for their own good ordinary believers need to be protected from unwittingly accepting communications which are not divine.

THE LIFESTYLE OF THE MEDJUGORJE VISIONARIES

Joachim Bouflet reproduces a non-exhaustive list of the various journeys which were undertaken by the Medjugorje visionaries between 1990 and 1998. They visited countries all over the world, but the emphasis was on the United States and Europe. He details twenty-six "apostolic" journeys undertaken by Vicka, twenty-three by Ivan, followed by Marija with seventeen, while Jakov, Mirjana and Ivanka made twelve between them.[5] Contrast this with the behavior of the seers of approved apparitions, such as St Catherine Labouré, St Bernadette, or Sr Lucia, who scarcely stepped outside her convent in Coimbra after 1948! Even if we consider the children at Beauraing and Banneux, who, like the Medjugorje visionaries, did not become professed religious, it is nevertheless the case that they certainly did not travel all over the world. Rather, they stayed out of the limelight, living quiet lives.

As regards the lifestyle of the Medjugorje visionaries, according to E. Michael Jones, in the late 1990s, Ivan Dragicevic was driving an expensive BMW car and living in a large mansion not far from the site of the alleged first vision, having married Loreen Murphy, "Miss Massachusetts," a former Beauty Queen. Mirjana Dragicevic was living in a similar dwelling right across the street.[6]

The following extract from a report in *The Sunday Times* (London), dated 29 December 2002, gave an update on the status of some of the visionaries:

Three of the six "seers," as they are known, have stayed in the town and their prosperity has risen to reflect the Madonna gold rush. Two of them, Jakov Colo, 31, and Mirjana Dragicevic-Soldo, 37, live in smart executive houses with immaculate gardens, double garages and security gates. On the other side of town the residence of Ivanka Ivankovic-Elez, 36, is even more sumptuous, with a brand new tennis court. All three refused to discuss their experiences and the huge wealth it has generated. Local Franciscan monks [sic] who gave credence to the visions preferred to say nothing, demanding that any questions be sent by fax.7

Amongst the visionaries, Mirjana has an interest in promoting Medjugorje pilgrimages, and has been associated with the *Medjugorje Web* site, which describes itself as the "first web site created in 1995 about Medjugorje," and claims to be "still the largest, most comprehensive, and [most] visited Medjugorje web site on the internet."

On its Medjugorje pilgrimage page, for the year 2019, it advertised pilgrimages, which, apart from daily Mass and other "spiritual activities," included, "6 nights staying with the visionary Mirjana Soldo," in an air-conditioned room with private bathroom. Included with this were breakfast and dinner, with wine being served at the latter.8

This does not sound like a particularly penitential pilgrimage, in line with the early Medjugorje "messages" about prayer and fasting, but sadly, this type of thing is now the norm at Catholic pilgrimage sites in general. They have lost sight of what the essence of a pilgrimage really is—that is, a chance, principally through prayer and penance, to break through the barriers of normal life and really experience the power of the supernatural.

The main point, though, about the above is the fact that for most of the pilgrimages to Medjugorje run by this company pilgrims stay with Mirjana, and presumably this is a lucrative source of income for her.

MEDJUGORJE—WHY SO POPULAR?

One of the enigmas about Medjugorje is why it has proved to be so incredibly popular with so many Catholics, despite all the negative points which have been detailed above. One answer, it seems, is that many people *want* to believe in Medjugorje, and simply assume Our Lady is appearing there daily, as it is claimed, without taking the trouble to investigate whether or not this is true. The reality is that people can quite easily be tempted to *believe what they want to believe*.

As Kevin Orlin Johnson says, for people in this enthusiastic frame of mind, with a predisposition to believe, there are only two possible verdicts on an alleged apparition, that is, either "yes," it is true, or alternatively it is probably true but "not yet proven." Thus, there is a failure to consider the very real possibility that the vision in question may well be false.

Johnson also comments on the mistaken perception that if enough people go to a particular site, then the Church will be obliged to reverse a negative judgment and call it positive. As he says, this is to mistake the Church's traditional approach for one where "reality can be determined by vote," and this attitude may well be due to "culpable negligence" regarding Church teaching on these matters.[9]

Such negligence may include an unwillingness to recognize that official ecclesiastical statements on a particular vision do have real meaning, and cannot be disregarded just because they don't fit in with our own point of view. Conversely, there is also a lack of understanding that no matter how many priests, bishops, or even cardinals believe in a particular alleged vision, that, of itself, does not make it true. Ordinarily, it is only the bishop of the particular diocese in question who has the authority to pronounce upon what is going on there.[10]

There is also the danger of people becoming addicted to the spiritual experiences generated by a visit to Medjugorje. This is particularly the case if the person who has been converted at Medjugorje was previously a lukewarm or non-practicing Catholic. If they experience signs and wonders such as their rosary turning to gold, they may find it very difficult to question the authenticity of the happenings at Medjugorje. One hears of people whose whole spiritual life revolves around the messages from various alleged visionaries, and who travel from one place to another to satisfy a craving for these phenomena.

However, one reason for this particular quest amongst many believers today is the undeniable fact that there is a spiritual vacuum in the Church, a vacuum which has arisen due to various factors. Many people get caught up in visions because they have a genuine thirst for the supernatural, and, not readily finding it in their local parish, are driven to look for it elsewhere, as in the area of alleged visions such as Medjugorje. This is a point which is dealt with in more detail below.

There are also many people today who have become bound up in a quest for religious novelties, and this is essentially the Catholic counterpart of what we see in society as a whole: that is, a restlessness and unease which can only be satisfied by new and exotic experiences. The timeless truths of Fatima are not exciting enough — some people need a ceaseless round of new messages or they are apparently not happy.

MEDJUGORJE FROM A SPIRITUAL PERSPECTIVE

Let us attempt to look at this situation from a spiritual perspective. We all have free will, so while it is possible it is not likely that there is going to be any dramatic supernatural intervention to prevent the visionaries from continuing their activities, nor will anything miraculous be done to prevent people going on pilgrimage to Medjugorje. In many cases, pilgrims going there may well be lapsed, or even living a sinful life. Given the condition of the Church, God may well foresee that, for a particular individual, as in the case of Moira Noonan, a visit to Medjugorje may be the only chance they will have to be converted.

The visions and messages are not approved, but the vast majority of pilgrims go there in all sincerity, and thus we can surmise that, in such genuine cases, God will grant the necessary graces of conversion. And this, of course, is to say nothing of the effects of the prayers and sufferings of their friends and relatives, who in some cases may have been interceding on their behalf for years.

However, in many cases, when such people are converted, after a time they realize the deficiencies of some aspects of Medjugorje spirituality, and move on to a properly regulated mainstream Catholic life, focusing more on prayer and the sacraments, and less on spiritual experiences. That is, they begin to live by faith, rather than by means of "signs and wonders."

We might compare this situation to that of a person who enters the unheated porch of a house on a bitterly cold day. Compared to the temperature outside, the porch feels warm, but if they remain in the porch for too long they soon feel the cold again, and have to move into the house itself. Medjugorje, taken as an overall phenomenon, can thus at best be regarded as a sort of porch or vestibule of the Church proper, a sort of halfway house; but it is not a place where one should remain, spiritually, for any length of time.

Another very powerful influence in favor of Medjugorje has been the Catholic media, which with very few exceptions has been reluctant to criticize Medjugorje in any way. It seems that many of those involved in the media have been afraid of losing readers if they publish anything even remotely critical. Similarly, editors have been reluctant to lose advertising revenue from those promoting pilgrimages to Medjugorje. This, of course, is to say nothing of those who have a vested interest in promoting Medjugorje, through publishing books, or organizing conferences and pilgrimages, activities which have naturally generated a great deal of money. To verify this, it is only necessary to look at the internet to see the large number of pro-Medjugorje websites, and those promoting pilgrimages and other events.

A further source of support — which at first sight might seem rather surprising — has been the secular media. For the most part, instead of the hostility which is usually shown towards all things Catholic, their approach to Medjugorje has been almost benevolent. Denis Nolan quotes excerpts from newspapers, magazines and journals ranging from the *Wall Street Journal* to the *Reader's Digest,* and television programs ranging from NBC's *Inside Edition* to the *Oprah Winfrey Show,* none of which has apparently had anything particularly critical to say about it.[11]

It could be argued that this in itself is rather suspicious: Christ told those of his "brethren" who did not believe in him that "the world cannot hate you, but it hates me because I testify of it that its works are evil." In other words, the Church, which is the body of Christ, can really only expect antagonism, even hatred, at the hands of the world — of which the secular media is the "conscience" — and yet Medjugorje has been treated with what amounts to kid gloves by the media.

MEDJUGORJE AND THE CRISIS IN THE CHURCH

In some respects, the desire to go to Medjugorje is understandable in the light of the serious problems that the Catholic Church in the West has been experiencing in recent years. Up until the Second Vatican Council, Marian devotion in the developed countries was strong and healthy. Organizations such as the Blue Army and the Legion of Mary thrived, and the rosary was a solidly rooted devotion. But following the Council, various liberal groups, with an agenda of their own, and acting in the alleged "spirit" of Vatican II, managed to foist their own ideas on ordinary Catholics in the United States and Europe. Distorting the true meaning of conciliar documents such as *Lumen Gentium,* they succeeded in virtually eliminating Marian devotions from many churches. As a result, many Catholics suddenly found themselves strangers in their own Church. This created a spiritual vacuum which various groups and individuals, including alleged visionaries, have been quick to fill.

The devotional and liturgical life of many parishes is still sadly inadequate, and thus numerous people are drawn to Medjugorje because they are looking for something with a more profound spirituality. However, as previous chapters of this work have demonstrated, the tragedy is that the Marian spirituality they will encounter at Medjugorje will not necessarily in the end prove to be a "healthy devotion toward the Blessed Virgin Mary... promoted in conformity with the teaching of the Church." This is because "it cannot be established that one is dealing with supernatural apparitions and revelations." As we have seen, both of these quotations come from the Yugoslav Bishops' Conference Zadar declaration of April 1991.[12]

Believing in visions which have not been approved by the Church — and which all the available evidence indicates are false — cannot be good for one's spiritual health in the long term. The counterpart to believing in Medjugorje is neglecting to profit from the genuine apparitions of Mary, and in particular Fatima. Unless one has moral certainty that a series of apparitions is genuine, one is on very dangerous ground in believing in them.

As indicated above, the picture which emerges if we analyze the good fruits that are claimed for Medjugorje is that these were certainly present to some extent in the early years. But as time has gone on, they have been noteworthy largely because of their absence. While there is much misunderstanding regarding exactly what Christ meant by the term "good fruits," a correct analysis of his teaching indicates that we are meant to look mainly at the activities of those claiming visions, or those closely supporting them, rather than at any general religious enthusiasm which might be generated. In this sense, the evidence which we have been considering in earlier chapters of this work demonstrates that the fruits at Medjugorje cannot be said to have been good.

Furthermore, it is clear that within the general Catholic community there is a widespread failure to realize that the fabrication of visions is a distinct possibility, or that the devil might well be involved in originating or sustaining them. This is what St John of the Cross says on this general point:

Among locutions and visions there are usually many that come from the devil. For he commonly deals with the soul in the same manner as God does, imparting communications so similar to God's that, disguised among the flock like the wolf in sheep's clothing, his meddling may be hardly discernible. Since he says many things that are true and reasonable and turn out as predicted, people can be easily misled, thinking that the revelation must be from God since what was predicted truly comes about.[13]

In the past, Catholics were warned about the wiles of Satan, and of the need to remain wary about apparently miraculous events, but in recent years, the Church's traditional caution in this area has been sadly neglected.

A DIABOLICAL ATMOSPHERE

Given, then, all of the evidence discussed previously, how is one to explain the origin of the Medjugorje visions? Regrettably, an impartial assessment of the facts clearly suggests the possibility, if not the probability, of a diabolical intervention. The Bible tells us that we should be sober and watchful, because our "adversary the devil prowls around like a roaring lion, seeking someone to devour" (1 Pet 5:8). Satan is perpetually on the lookout to ensnare the unsuspecting or unwary. Most of the time, he can do little damage to us, provided that we are in a state of grace and endeavor to resist his temptations. But if particular circumstances arise then problems may well begin.

As regards Medjugorje, these include the unstable family backgrounds and temperaments of some of the visionaries, which indicate that such persons would not be likely to receive communications from heaven. In addition, as already indicated, the fact that Ivanka's mother was recently deceased would have put her in a vulnerable emotional state, which might have predisposed her to see something. Moreover, we have noted, too, there is also the possible influence of the evil atmosphere resulting from the location of the visions, that is, a place associated with the wartime massacres at Surmanci near Medjugorje.

On this last point, Moira Noonan recounts a revealing incident. While still embroiled in New Age practices, she visited a spiritual "retreat center" in the northeast United States, which included a lake on the property. One hot summer's day while sitting on the lake shore she tells us that she "had the sensation that something was wrong. I felt that there was something very strange and forbidding about this lake." She attempted to shrug off this feeling by going for a swim out to a platform in the lake, but by the time she reached this, "the dark emotion I felt had completely overwhelmed me.... It was as if I had been literally swimming through spirits. It was just eerie and it was sickening. It felt like I was swimming through blood, it was just so thick. I couldn't stand it."

When she got back she discovered that the white settlers of the area had massacred the native people who lived there — killing men and women and children — and then thrown their bodies into the lake.[14] The parallel with the massacre at Surmanci is clear and disturbing.

Putting all this together, we can see that when Ivanka and Mirjana went up Podbrdo, to smoke and listen to rock music, the possibility of a diabolical intervention cannot be ruled out.

SOME DIABOLICAL INCIDENTS

That some of the visionaries were involved in occurrences which strongly suggest this is clear from the following examples. A strange incident involving Mirjana took place about a year after the initial visions, in mid-1982, and she recounted it to Fr Vlasic in January 1983. She tells us that as she was waiting in her room for her usual rendezvous with the "Gospa":

> I knelt down, and had not yet made the sign of the cross, when suddenly a bright light flashed and a devil appeared. It was as if something *told* me it was a devil. I looked at him and was very surprised, for I was expecting the Madonna to appear. He was horrible — he was like black all over.... He was terrifying, dreadful, and I did not know what he wanted. I realized I was growing weak, and then I fainted. When I revived, he was still standing there, laughing. It seemed that he gave me a strange kind of strength, so that I could almost accept him. He told me that I would be very beautiful, and very happy, and so on. However, I would have no need of the Madonna, he said, and no need for faith. "She has brought you nothing but suffering and difficulties," he said; but he would give me everything beautiful — whatever I want. Then something in me — I don't know what, if it was something conscious or something in my soul — told me: *No! No! No!* Then I began to shake and feel just awful. Then he disappeared, and the Madonna appeared, and when she

appeared my strength returned—as if she restored it to me. I felt normal again. Then the Madonna told me: "That was a trial, but it will not happen to you again."[15]

This was clearly a frightening incident, but the biggest problem with this particular vision is that, unlike genuine Marian apparitions, where there is a clear distinction between the divine and the diabolical, here they are intertwined. Thus, in an overall sense, this type of manifestation is far more characteristic of the diabolical.[16]

This is evident from an incident which happened to Francisco of Fatima. In her memoirs, Sr Lucia does not tell us exactly when this happened, but it is clear that it was quite separate from one of the Blessed Virgin's apparitions. She tells us how one day the three of them went to a rocky place called Pedreira, and while the girls played and looked after the sheep, Francisco withdrew to pray nearby. After a while, Lucia and Jacinta heard him shouting and crying out to Our Lady, and they ran to find him "trembling with fright... and so upset that he was unable to rise to his feet." They asked him what had happened, and in a very frightened voice he told them: "It was one of those huge beasts that we saw in hell. He was right here breathing out flames!"[17]

Marinko Ivankovic, speaking in February 1983, testifies to a strange event which took place "on the Feast of the Madonna of the Angels," 2 August 1981, in a field near Medjugorje, one evening after Mass. This was apparently a well-known meeting place for prayer. The visionaries were present, and claimed that the "Gospa" had appeared to them, and would allow all those who wished to do so, to touch her. The people duly came forward and "touched" the "Gospa," being told by the visionaries that they were touching her veil, her head, her hand, and so on. This apparently went on for ten or fifteen minutes, until Marija cried out to Marinko: "The Madonna is blackened all over!... there were sinners here who touched her, and as they touched her her robe got darker and darker, until it was black." Marija then told him that they should all go to confession as soon as possible.[18]

Fr Laurentin mentions this incident,[19] but surprisingly makes no comment. It hardly needs stating that the above scenario—the idea that the Blessed Virgin could somehow be contaminated by contact with human beings—is quite absurd. It is absolutely contrary to authentic communications with the Blessed Virgin, as experienced by true mystics and saints, such as St Catherine Labouré, who, as we have seen, was able to put her hands on Our Lady's lap.

THE REAL POWER BEHIND MEDJUGORJE?

As for the continuing "power" and influence of Medjugorje, one also has to ask if there isn't a diabolical element present here too. Specifically, has the effect of the long-running rebellion by the Franciscans of the Herzegovina Province given the devil the power to ensure that Medjugorje continues to thrive? This might seem like an improbable claim, but it's worth investigation.

The first thing to note is that, as discussed previously, the special decree issued in 1975 by the Holy See, *Romanis Pontificibus,* demanded Franciscan obedience concerning the distribution of parishes between the Franciscans of the Herzegovina Province and the diocesan clergy of Mostar-Duvno diocese. The crucial point about this is that it was a *Vatican* decree, and thus this dispute was essentially between the Papacy and the rebellious Franciscans.

So the Franciscans of the Herzegovina Province were in an active state of rebellion against the Vicars of Christ, even *before* the Medjugorje visions began. Just think of the power that must have given the devil to cause trouble. It was only in 1999, nearly twenty-four years after its promulgation, that *Romanis Pontificibus* was complied with, and even then a number of Franciscans refused to sign the declaration of obedience, resulting in nine being dismissed from the Order and a further twenty-three suffering other penalties.

Disobedience resulting from pride was, of course, the hallmark of the devil's primordial revolt against God. And the *non serviam* — "I will not serve" — of Satan has found a very powerful echo in the attitude of the Herzegovina Franciscans in their rebellion against official Church authority for so many years. And furthermore, this disobedience and pride has been compounded by the actions and attitudes of those Franciscans most involved with the Medjugorje visionaries, that is, Frs Vlasic, Zovko and Barbaric.

In addition to pride and disobedience, there is also the question of dishonesty. At the beginning it doesn't seem that there was outright dishonesty — the evidence from the tapes does suggest that the visionaries really saw something. So it is probable that the claims of the visionaries — that they saw what they believed was the "Gospa" — were genuine for most of what happened until about the tenth day. The argument which has been presented in this book, of course, is that this wasn't the real *Gospa*, the Blessed Virgin, but a diabolical imposture.

From that point on, though, things for the most part, it would seem, changed, and this passage from the *Catechism* holds good:

> Since it violates the virtue of truthfulness, a lie does real violence to another. It affects...[a person's] ability to know, which is a condition of every judgment and decision. It contains the seed of discord and all consequent evils. Lying is destructive of society; it undermines trust among men and tears apart the fabric of social relationships. (2486)

As we have seen, there is no question but that the visions were supposed to end on Friday, 3 July 1981, the end of the three-day period stipulated by both the visionaries and the two young women who were present during the vision on 30 June. But the visions didn't end on that day, and it is claimed that they have continued for the last forty years. Clearly, if that is the case, someone isn't telling the truth, and in a very big way.

It could be argued that if what the visionaries were seeing during this earlier period was actually diabolical in origin, then the evidence from the "three more days" dialogue suggest that they were being giving a chance to exit their role as visionaries. Maybe the devil had only been given a certain amount of time to tempt them, the ten-day period from 24 June to 3 July—but they didn't take that chance. Whatever the exact reason for the continuance of the visions, such a pretense involves an extremely grave violation of the truth, and this too plays into the hands of Satan, who, according to Christ, is "a liar and the father of lies" (John 8:44).

Thus, the whole Medjugorje edifice is built on pride, disobedience and, on the basis of the "three more days" dialogue, dishonesty; and this must, to some extent, account for the "spiritual power" which emanates from it. But the problem is that this power is not the grace which comes from God through Christ, but a sort of counterfeit "grace" which ultimately is a sign of the devil. Of course, there was, and is, "real" grace available at Medjugorje through sincere prayer and the sacraments, but it would be foolish to discount the presence of this diabolical "grace"—in the sense of deliberate serious sin putting a person under the power of the devil—as one of the "motors" for the Medjugorje phenomenon.

This last point, of course, doesn't apply to the visionaries during the period up to 3 July, but rather to the disobedience of the local

Franciscans. Even though the devil, unlike God, doesn't have the power to act directly on the human intellect and will, but only on the imagination and sensibility, he can still wield a powerful influence over individuals who freely commit sin. As Christ also noted, "everyone who commits sin is the slave of sin" (Jn 8:34). And ultimately, being a slave of sin means being a slave of the devil.

On that pleasant late June afternoon in 1981, when Ivanka and Mirjana went out to smoke on Podbrdo, the devil was waiting, prowling around "like a roaring lion, seeking someone to devour" (1 Pet 5:8), emboldened by the proximity of Surmanci, with its evil atmosphere, and no doubt strengthened by the long-running rebellion of the Herzegovina Franciscans. For whatever reason, it seems that the visionaries took the devil's bait, and the rest is history.

* * *

THIS CHAPTER, THEN, CLEARLY INDICATES THE FURther problems involved with believing in Medjugorje, including the "apocalyptic" character of some of the messages, which puts them into conflict with the genuine message of Fatima and other approved apparitions. Similarly, the necessity of being on guard against false prophets does not seem to have been fully realized by many Medjugorje devotees, nor the problems associated with aspects of the spirituality which has developed out of it. In particular, many have been largely oblivious to the potentially very dangerous results of having an excessive desire to see a vision. To a great extent, all of this has happened because of the crisis affecting the Church since the 1960s, which has resulted in many well-meaning Catholics becoming involved with Medjugorje—but tragically, they have not been aware of some of its darker aspects.

21
Medjugorje Developments

A MEDJUGORJE CONFERENCE

As time went on, the Medjugorje visionaries and their Franciscan associates continued to promote the claimed visions and messages, drawing crowds wherever they went. Laurette Elsberry attended a Medjugorje conference in Sacramento. She described how it was "so sad to see so many people being taken in by the tour operators, the religious goods peddlers and a vaudevillian cast of characters intent on making the Mother of God into someone who traipses all around the world following the 'visionaries' and hawking 'pilgrimages.'"

But what particularly appalled her was a joke told by one of the visionaries, Marija Pavlovic, who was there with her husband. This joke was taped and the following is an edited transcription:

> Jesus was in Paradise. The Apostles were a bit bored being in Paradise for such a long time...[and so] Jesus said, "Let's go for a tour on the earth."...So they went [to the Holy Land] and they decided to have a barbecue on the beach, on the lake, with fresh fish.... And since they were in Paradise where they had no more faith but they were completely sure about what they could do...they were all walking on the water. And so also Jesus went on the water but he started to go down—to sink. So he starts thinking to himself: "What's wrong with me? I'm Jesus. This is impossible. I'm sinking." And then Peter saw him, got close to him and said: "Rabbi, you forgot, your feet have holes."

Laurette Elsberry reports the reaction of the nearly two thousand attendees at the conference: "They broke out in loud, raucous laughs and applause." She then goes on to put the question as to how such people "could have laughed at such a blasphemous and sacrilegious joke, which ridiculed the Sacred Wounds of the Savior."[1]

Indeed, is it possible to imagine a genuine Marian seer acting in such a way?

BISHOP PERIC'S INDICTMENT

This is what Bishop Ratko Peric of Mostar had to say about Medjugorje, at a Confirmation homily, given in the village itself:

> [A] true believer can only remain amazed at the talk that here in Medjugorje, for almost twenty years now, day by day, Mary has been presumably "appearing" for five, ten or fifteen minutes to so-called "seers"; that she is presumably handing something over: in the form of so-called "messages," or "ten secrets," it's not sure if there are exactly ten, if each person has received the same number, or if there are six times more, meaning that each person received a different amount. Does this mean that this "apparition" up until this time has appeared 6,940 times (19 years multiplied by 365/6 days)? And that constantly, every day, she is speaking, and that only once in a month she leaves a "message," and thanks the so-called "seers" for responding to her call? And this has been going on for almost twenty years now, and could keep on going another ten, twenty or even more years? The official statements of the Church, starting from the local Bishop up to the Bishops' Conference has not in this case recognized a single "apparition" as authentic. The Church has clearly declared that it is impossible to affirm that these events involve supernatural apparitions.[2]

There could hardly be a more solid indictment of Medjugorje.

Meanwhile, the death of Fr Slavko Barbaric was reported in late November 2000. It appears that he died while climbing Mount Krizevac, and was actually in Medjugorje contrary to the wishes of Bishop Peric, who had withdrawn his faculties for hearing confessions the previous February. As might be expected, some of the Medjugorje visionaries claimed that the Blessed Virgin had appeared to them to inform them that Fr Barbaric was in heaven. It is worth noting that Bishop Peric personally came to conduct the funeral, despite all the problems the deceased had caused in the diocese.[3]

THE FRENCH BISHOPS AND MEDJUGORJE

In January 2001, during an assembly of the French Bishops, Msgr Henri Brincard, bishop of Puy-en-Velay, responded in writing to the following question put by a member of the conference: "Is there an authorised and official position of the Church concerning the events which motivate pilgrimages to Medjugorje?"

Msgr Brincard replied by outlining the official Church position on this subject, that it belongs to the local Ordinary of the diocese to investigate such events, as the 1978 Congregation for the Doctrine of the Faith instruction made clear, and that Bishop Zanic had acted correctly in carrying out his own investigations between 1982 and 1986. In other words, he had set up commissions as required, and had likewise provided general guidance for the faithful by indicating his own position.

Following advice from the Congregation, he had agreed that the Yugoslav Episcopal conference should study the dossier which had been compiled on Medjugorje, given that it was having an effect well beyond his own diocese.

Msgr Brincard then pointed out that "the Holy Father never intervenes directly in affairs of this kind," and that the Congregation had expressed its appreciation of "the work accomplished by the diocesan commission, under the responsibility of Bishop Zanic." When on 26 April 1986, he had delivered to Cardinal Ratzinger an outline of the expected negative judgment which the commission would reach, the cardinal asked Bishop Zanic to delay the publication of any definitive judgment.

On 2 May 1986, the commission voted against recognizing any supernatural character in the events at Medjugorje, and on 15 May 1986, Bishop Zanic informed the Congregation about the negative findings of the commission. Msgr Brincard was at pains to point out that it was "not correct to state that Bishop Zanic was relieved of the dossier," as some Medjugorje supporters had claimed. The Yugoslav Episcopal Conference of Yugoslavia then undertook its own study of the dossier on Medjugorje, by means of a new commission, and this ultimately resulted in the Zadar declaration of 10 April 1991.[4]

ROLE OF LOCAL BISHOP CRUCIAL

Summing up all these developments, Msgr Brincard stated quite clearly that:

> Up to this day, only the bishops of Mostar—Bishop Zanic, then Bishop Peric—and the Yugoslav Episcopal Conference (dissolved *de facto* by the partition of the country after the war) have expressed a judgement on the events of Medjugorje. The Congregation for the Doctrine of the Faith, on the other hand, has never issued an official judgement. It has only given directives of a pastoral order.

Msgr Brincard then went on to state that in previous cases dealing with apparitions: "Rome always remits... [finally] to the authority and the competence of the local Ordinary." To illustrate this he mentioned several approved apparitions including those at La Salette, Beauraing and Banneux, where the local Bishops were able to issue official pronouncements despite difficulties.[5]

On the vexed question of pilgrimages, Msgr Brincard was content to reiterate the advice, detailed above, which was given by Vatican officials, in particular Archbishops Bovone and Bertone, to the effect that official pilgrimages to Medjugorje should be discouraged. Regarding private pilgrimages, however, he makes the following pertinent point: "How, in fact, . . . [can one] organise a private pilgrimage without it being motivated by the conviction that the events of Medjugorje are of a supernatural origin?"

Regarding the question of the fruits which are supposed to have arisen from Medjugorje, Msgr Brincard pointed out that according to the 1978 CDF document, the alleged supernatural events themselves must first be evaluated before there can be any question of examining the fruits. And he emphasized this by saying: "When this order is not respected errors of judgment can arise." Moreover, he went on to make the following observations:

> If we examine the events of Medjugorje in the light of the fruits, what do we observe? It is first of all undeniable that at Medjugorje there are returns to God and "spiritual" healings. It is no less evident that the sacramental life there is regular and the prayer fervent. One could not deny these good fruits *in situ*. We should even rejoice in them. But can we say that they continue in our parishes? Difficult question, for we must note unfortunately that the susceptibility, even aggressiveness, of some partisans of Medjugorje towards those who do not share their enthusiasm is such that in some places it provokes serious tensions which attack the unity of the People of God.

Finally, he looked at the fruits in the lives of the visionaries, focusing particularly on the question of their obedience to the Bishop of Mostar. He was forced to conclude that many problems existed in this area. The importance of Msgr Brincard's response can hardly be overstated since it was made at the request of the permanent council of the French Episcopal Conference, in January 2001, and was published in their official bulletin.[6]

Medjugorje Developments

WARNINGS FROM PROMINENT CHURCHMEN

The divisive nature of the activities of some Bosnia-Herzegovina Franciscans was noted by Cardinal Vinko Puljic of Sarajevo, at the Synod of Bishops in Rome, in October 2001. He spoke of how:

> Certain members of the Order of Franciscan Friars Minor and those expelled try to impose their own points of view in the individual Dioceses, substituting the authentic charisms of their Institute with pseudo-charisms, a serious threat for the Church and for her organizational and doctrinal unity. Suffice it to recall the sad events last summer when the protagonists of the aforementioned Order and a self-declared bishop: an old-style Catholic deacon expelled from his community, or a systematic disobedience to the same religious persons who for years have been in the Diocese of Mostar-Duvno [sic].[7]

In July 2002, Cardinal Pell of Sydney refused to allow Vicka Ivankovic-Mijatovic, one of most prominent of the six alleged Medjugorje visionaries, now married, to speak in any Church building during a visit to his diocese.[8]

But in other dioceses this has not been the case, and the following is an example of the sort of "mania" which can develop around Medjugorje and its visionaries. In February 2011, Vicka came to Ireland to begin a "tour" of the country. Under the headline "Medjugorje visionary works her magic," it was reported in the *Irish Examiner* that she appeared at the Shelbourne Hall in Dublin before a crowd of 2,300 people who had gathered to see her have her scheduled vision of the "Gospa."

The reporter described the atmosphere as swinging between that of a "pious religious ceremony and [a] pop concert," and went on to say that the "mainly elderly crowd was not disappointed." Sad to say, Vicka was accompanied by nine priests on the stage. At the conclusion of her "performance" she was virtually mobbed by the crowd, and the same thing happened as she left the building after Mass. She also appeared on RTÉ's "Late, Late Show" and went on to visit Cork and Kerry.[9]

That so many people were prepared to turn out to see Vicka, to the extent that there was "standing room only" at the venue, is surely deeply worrying. How many of those people would be prepared to spend time in real prayer before the Blessed Sacrament? How many of them have done the Fatima Five First Saturdays devotion, or realize it is meant to be an ongoing devotion of reparation?

In late 2002, Fr Zovko was refused permission to celebrate Mass at the Immaculate Conception national shrine in Washington. Msgr Michael J. Bransfield, the rector, had written to Bishop Peric asking him to clarify the juridical status of the Franciscan. The bishop responded, in a letter dated 18 November, that Fr Zovko's disobedience had led to his faculties and canonical mission being revoked by Bishop Zanic on 23 August 1989, and that as his successor he had upheld this decision.[10]

As for Fr Vlasic, as we will see, after spending time at various communities and houses in Italy, Austria and Medjugorje, in July 2009 he was laicized and dismissed from the Franciscan Order.

VISIONS AND SECRETS: AN ONGOING SITUATION

According to one Medjugorje author, the situation as regards the visionaries and their secrets is as follows. Having ceased to receive daily visions in December 1982, Mirjana claimed visions on the second day of each month, with an annual one on her birthday—but the monthly visions, at least, are reported to have ceased early in 2020. In addition, she claimed to have received all ten secrets.

Ivanka supposedly stopped receiving daily visions in May 1985, though she too has an annual vision on 25 June, and has received the full complement of secrets. Jakov, likewise, has received all ten secrets, and ceased having daily visions in 1998. Marija, Vicka and Ivan all claim to continue to have daily visions, and similarly all claim they have received nine secrets.[11]

Regarding Ivanka's claim of an annual vision, it's worth noting that according to the pro-Medjugorje DVD "The Visionaries from Medjugorje tried by Science," her husband reported that she was very "uptight" for two or three days before her alleged annual vision, and that her children had also confirmed this, saying that their mother was "different."[12]

Why would this be the case? Why would she be "uptight" before seeing Our Lady? Speaking of her own experience of seeing the Blessed Virgin, St Bernadette said: "She is so beautiful that when you have seen her once, you would wish to die in order to see her again."[13] But Ivanka, far from looking forward to seeing the "Gospa" once more, is "uptight." Could this be an indication of *guilt*, that her claim to have an annual vision of the "Gospa" had become something of a burden?

Bishop Peric delivered an address at Maynooth College in Ireland, on 17 February 2004, in which he outlined the then situation regarding Medjugorje. He itemized the number of total claimed visions, which varied between about 770 for Ivanka, to over 8,000 for Vicka, Marija and Ivan, with a grand total for all the visionaries of over 33,000! As he notes, the Church has not accepted a single one of these visions as authentic.[14] This is what the bishop had to say about the various secrets confided to the visionaries, and the "sign":

> Those who have daily "visions" have received nine secrets, while those who have "apparitions" once a year, have ten secrets. It is not clear if nine or ten secrets have been given and are known to each of the "seers," or if each of the "seers" has his/her own number of secrets which differ from the rest. If we compare this to the authentic apparitions, then one can see that at Lourdes there were no secrets for the world, while at Fatima one secret was divided into three parts. Yet at Medjugorje till now there have been 9 or 10, or even 57 possible secrets, which have been divided by three "seers" who have received 10 and another three who have received 9. To this day not a single secret has been revealed. In the first years there was apocalyptic talk about a "great sign" to happen, yet to this day this "great sign" has not occurred, and the expectation of a sign has diminished.

SOME RECENT MEDJUGORJE BOOKS CONSIDERED

We can now consider some more recent books supportive of Medjugorje, one of which is *God-Sent: A History of the Accredited Apparitions of Mary*, by Roy Abraham Varghese. This is an unsatisfactory book, not least because of the inclusion of some alleged apparitions, and this is particularly the case with Medjugorje.

God-Sent is reminiscent of certain Protestant "histories" of Christianity, which pay lip-service to figures like St Augustine, and other Catholic pre-Reformation theologians, whereas their real interest is in figures such as Luther and Calvin, and some of their less well-known successors — of the great Catholic figures of the post-Reformation era, there is hardly a mention. With this approach Varghese is not alone, and a number of contemporary authors seem to have adopted a similarly mistaken approach of almost uncritically accepting every new claim of alleged visions and revelations, while virtually ignoring those which have been approved.

This was certainly the case with Fr Edward O'Connor's *Marian Apparitions Today: Why So Many?* This deals with a mixture of genuine approved apparitions and other suspect ones such as Garabandal, San Damiano and, of course, Medjugorje, as though they were all on the same footing. As we have seen, Garabandal has received no official Church approval, and indeed, San Damiano received a negative judgment from the local bishop in 1980,[15] sixteen years before the publication of Fr O'Connor's book.

The predominant theme of Varghese's book is that while apparitions like Lourdes and Fatima are all very well, we are now in the age of Medjugorje and Amsterdam, and similar alleged visions, and that these represent the continuation and fulfillment of the earlier apparitions. But, of course, it is possible to take a completely different view of this and see, for the most part, that the majority of these alleged visions are dubious when compared with the major approved apparitions.

And in fact, this has proved to be the case with one alleged visionary, Julia Kim of Naju in South Korea, whom Varghese described as "one of today's most famous visionaries: she has been privileged to witness or participate in a broad spectrum of supernatural phenomena ranging from bleeding statues and messages from the Virgin to the stigmata and Eucharistic miracles. She is a visionary, stigmatist and victim soul."[16]

Unfortunately, it also turns out that she is a fraud, who has now been excommunicated. She was subject to a critical declaration from her archbishop in 1998, two years before Varghese's book was published, and received further admonitions in 2005 and 2007, before she and her followers incurred *latae sententiae* excommunication in 2008.[17]

The uncritical tendency to "accredit" quite suspect apparitions becomes particularly marked when Varghese moves on to deal with Medjugorje, to the point that "messages" originating there are apparently placed in the same category as ones from approved apparitions, a process which can only lead to confusion. The author effectively states that Medjugorje is an authentic apparition of the Virgin, basing his conclusion on the fact that the visionaries display no apparent psychopathic tendencies, psychosis or hysteria.[18] However, he has failed to acknowledge that there is another possibility, that is, fraud, and in general his approach is rather presumptuous in the light of the many criticisms and concerns that have been voiced about Medjugorje.

The section of the book on Medjugorje has a number of questionable statements, including the following: "Other than Guadalupe, no other Marian apparition in history has been the direct cause of as many conversions as Medjugorje"; and, "There are over a thousand documented cures attributed to Medjugorje." Regarding conversions, there are no accurate figures, so such a statement is impossible to prove, and regarding the "documented" cures, documented by whom? Unless they are approved by the Church they have no validity.

Varghese also states: "In judging the authenticity of an apparition, what matters ultimately (in addition to the theological content of the visions) is the actual state of the visionary during the apparition."[19] This simply doesn't make sense — how can the validity of a vision possibly be assessed on such a narrow basis? What is to stop an alleged visionary faking a vision?

Varghese likewise states that: "Concerning the Medjugorje critics, it may be said that they are not developing arguments; they are painting a certain picture, creating a certain history of the events of Medjugorje."[20] Actually, the exact opposite is the truth — it is the propagandists for Medjugorje who have been guilty of "painting a certain picture" of Medjugorje, a picture heavily at odds with reality.

Mark Miravalle reiterated his support for the visions in his *Introduction to Medjugorje*, published in 2004, referring his readers to his 1986 work, *The Message of Medjugorje*, for a more comprehensive treatment. Again, Miravalle states that he wants to focus on the "message" of Medjugorje,[21] so this book, too, of which more than half is taken up with alleged messages, falls into the same trap of examining the messages without determining whether or not there are good grounds for believing that they are genuine. There was possibly some excuse for this type of attitude in the 1980s, but surely not in 2004, when anyone seriously interested in investigating Medjugorje ought to have been aware of the work of Fr Sivric and Daria Klanac, and their transcripts of the original interviews.

DENIS NOLAN ON MEDJUGORJE (AGAIN)

The fourth edition of Denis Nolan's *Medjugorje and the Church* was published in 2007, and is an attempt to argue that there is genuine Church support for Medjugorje. The blurb on the cover promises "shocking new revelations about the Catholic Church's true position on Medjugorje!"—but predictably, Nolan fails to deliver regarding these "revelations." He quotes Pope John Paul II as saying, "Medjugorje is the fulfillment and continuation of Fatima," but unfortunately his source for this is the rather suspect Bishop Hnilica.[22]

In any case, how could Medjugorje possibly be the "fulfillment" of Fatima, since the message of Fatima is self-contained, and needs no further "fulfillment"? Our Lady has given us, in the Fatima message, what has accurately been described as "a peace plan from heaven." There is nothing lacking in this message such that it needs to be supplemented or continued; the problem is that not enough Catholics have paid serious attention to it. And it will be fulfilled precisely when that happens, principally through the practice and promotion of the Five First Saturdays devotion. In sum, nothing in the Medjugorje "messages" adds anything meaningful to the message of Fatima.

Nolan's strategy in this book is quite simple—to attempt to pile up so many testimonies from various parties in favor of Medjugorje that the reader will apparently be forced to acknowledge that there must be something in it, otherwise, why would so many priests, bishops, cardinals and even, apparently, Pope John Paul II, have been supportive of it?

But in this he is making the fundamental error of equating the views of *members* of the Church with the actual position of the Church itself. No matter how many clerics have been to Medjugorje, no matter how many conversions or numbers of pilgrims have been claimed, these factors, of themselves, do not indicate any *official* Church support for Medjugorje. This is a point that cannot be stressed often enough, especially as so many Medjugorje supporters do not seem to appreciate its importance.

The majority of Nolan's book is, in fact, taken up with testimonies about Medjugorje, including those from various apostolates, and in particular he quotes Saint John Paul II as saying: "If I were not the Pope, I would be in Medjugorje already."[23] But that is just the point: he *was* the pope, and so realized that he couldn't go to Medjugorje in an official capacity, and that therefore his remarks were not authoritative, just an expression of his personal and private devotion. And this holds good for all the other figures quoted in the book, no matter how eminent they might be. Indeed, that so many of them have been to Medjugorje and are supportive of it is a sad indication of the present state of the Church, especially given the widespread lack of support for Fatima.

Nolan devotes an appendix to transcripts of letters received by Marek and Sophia Swarnicki, friends of John Paul II, who were clearly Medjugorje enthusiasts. He highlights the fact that the pope made the following statement about Medjugorje in one of his responses: "I thank Sophia for everything concerning Medjugorje. I, too, go there every day as a pilgrim in my prayers."[24] But it is easy to overstate the significance of this response: the pope had evidently received some Medjugorje literature from his old friends, so obviously politeness required that he express appreciation, and as a deeply spiritual man, he could hardly speak except in terms of prayer.

In the next letter the pope writes: "And now we every day return to Medjugorje in prayer."[25] But this too can be interpreted as a general remark about prayer tied in with his friends' appreciation of Medjugorje. The excerpts from the other letters are in a similar vein, and it is clear that the pope was essentially responding to the remarks made by his friends in a private manner, which could not possibly have any bearing on the official position of the Church on Medjugorje.

It's also worth noting that the letters were written in the early 90s, at the time when either the wars in ex-Yugoslavia were raging or the people of the area were suffering in their aftermath; the pope expressed his concern for the "poor little orphans and all the inhabitants of that land" in one letter, while in another, he writes of the "terrible events in the Balkans," which he says cannot be understood without Medjugorje.[26] That, of course, does not mean that the pope was accepting Medjugorje as supernatural, but rather just stating that it was one of the factors in the violent breakup of Yugoslavia.

Another appendix is devoted to "Critics of Medjugorje," and in this, Nolan condemns a previous version of this book, *Understanding Medjugorje*, as follows: "Foley's book...deploys a *Da Vinci Code* strategy in its polemics, creating a mosaic of half-truths and outright falsehoods which appear plausible to the ignorant or the innocent. There are no new facts, discoveries or insights in the book. It is a rerun of previous devious assaults."

It hard to see how anyone — except a person who is fanatically and uncritically committed to Medjugorje — could make such an overwrought statement, which bears no relationship to reality. The important thing to notice is that he does not actually detail any of the "half-truths or outright falsehoods" he mentions, but rather recommends his readers to his *Medjugorje: A Time for Truth and a Time for Action* for "detailed responses to these frequently reincarnated charges."[27]

The problem is that Nolan's earlier book was published as long ago as 1993, and much more has become known about the murkier side of Medjugorje since then. But apart from that, the major criticisms made in the previous editions of this book have not been adequately answered by Nolan or any of the other prominent Medjugorje writers — their general policy has been, and almost universally continues to be, to ignore the unpleasant facts about Medjugorje and continue to recycle the old propaganda.

MIRAVALLE AND WEIBLE ON MEDJUGORJE

Another book on the subject, *Are the Medjugorje Apparitions Authentic?* by Mark Miravalle and Wayne Weible, was published in 2008, and argues that criticisms of Medjugorje are unjustified.

Miravalle looks at the question of the inordinate length of time that the Medjugorje visionaries have been claiming visions, and argues that this is not a factor considered in *Normae Congregationis*. While this is true, it does not mean that it is irrelevant, since that document is clearly not exhaustive on the subject of claimed visions. He then goes on to argue that in Church history there have been even longer examples of "supernatural communications" to saintly figures, such as St Brigid, St Hildegard and St Pio of Pietrelcina.[28]

But as we have seen it is illegitimate to compare the "spirituality" of the Medjugorje visionaries with the genuine sanctity of the above canonized saints — there is just no comparison, not least because the mystical encounters granted to such saints are of a different order to those experienced by the seers of the genuine apparitions of the Blessed Virgin, let alone to what the Medjugorje visionaries have claimed to experience.

He also mentions Benoîte Rencurel of the Laus apparitions, but, as previously indicated, her daily apparitions of the Blessed Virgin only lasted for four months, and from that point on she only had intermittent apparitions, so what happened there is not relevant in this instance.

Miravalle states: "We must be careful not to use incidental criteria, such as the length of the series of the apparitions, as a fundamental reason to validate or invalidate a reported apparition."[29]

But is the fact that the general pattern of approved Marian apparitions involves a small number of appearances — in contrast to the tens of thousands claimed at Medjugorje—an "incidental" criterion? Surely common sense suggests that it is far from incidental, and actually it is an extremely useful aid in discerning the truth or falsity of an alleged series of visions.

On the question of whether or not the Medjugorje messages contain false ecumenical teaching, Miravalle states, as a general principle: "The messages of Medjugorje do not contain a single doctrinal teaching that runs contrary to authentic Catholic Magisterial teaching."[30] However, this is a difficult argument to sustain, since, as we have seen in chapter 8, some of the messages are ambiguous if not actually contrary to Catholic teaching.

Miravalle then quotes one particular ecumenical message as follows: "In God's eyes there are no divisions and there are no religions. You in the world have made the divisions." There are several points to note about this passage; firstly, there is that initial sentence: "In God's eyes there are no divisions *and there are no religions*." It is being stated that there are no religions in God's eyes—so does that mean the Catholic Faith, as founded by Christ, isn't a religion?

In addition, the reference given for this quote by Miravalle states that it comes from a "message of Medjugorje reported between 1981–1983." Surely though, something more precise than that is required in a book purporting to give "theological facts and first-hand accounts" on Medjugorje? And this is just the problem with some of these early Medjugorje messages—there is no way of really knowing how reliable many of them are.

Miravalle's next section looks at whether or not we are dealing with false visionaries at Medjugorje. He states that the "overwhelming consensus of public opinion for those who have had direct contact with these six visionaries is a profound respect for their manifest integrity, [and] straightforwardness," and that theologians "who have interviewed the visionaries have likewise concluded to the same obvious presence of moral integrity and personal authenticity."[31]

However, "public opinion" is a notoriously unreliable guide to the truth of any matter, given how easily it can be manipulated by the unscrupulous, through advertising, through propaganda and through the spreading of false reports and rumors. And as for the "manifest integrity" of the visionaries, as this book has amply demonstrated, that is a difficult, if not impossible, position to maintain. The same can be said for the ideas of the theologians Miravalle mentions, including Fr

René Laurentin, Fr Robert Faricy and Fr Michael O'Carroll, whose arguments in favor of Medjugorje and the visionaries have been discussed above and found wanting.

Miravalle then states: "Remarkable personal sacrifice rather than personal gain has been the foremost experience" of the visionaries.[32] In saying this he is ignoring the well-documented evidence concerning their lavish lifestyles, which has been discussed previously, including expensive cars and large houses with "immaculate gardens, double garages and security gates," and in one instance, a tennis court. In fact, "remarkable personal sacrifice" is probably the phrase least likely to be applied to the Medjugorje visionaries by anyone who is properly informed about them.

Regarding the medical tests carried out on the visionaries, he says:

> Two medical teams ... have scientifically examined the visionaries during the time of reported apparitions. Each has independently validated the legitimacy of their state of ecstasy as being in some form of true communication outside of their ordinary time-space experience. These scientific studies also ruled out any possibility of "collective hallucination" and, by deduction, any form of mere human deception of [sic] falsification.[33]

But as we have seen, these scientific tests have actually been seriously inadequate as regards determining the truth or falsity of the claims of the visionaries. This is so because some of the procedures used were flawed, and lacking in scientific rigor. The principal reason, though, is that no scientific tests can ever determine whether or not a supernatural event has taken place — science is incapable of that. As for ruling out human deception, again, as we have seen, the tests have provided no guarantee against that either.

In sum, the above arguments in favor of Medjugorje do not stand up.

The second half of the book, authored by Wayne Weible, looks at the alleged good fruits arising out of Medjugorje. It consists of a series of "feel good" stories of conversions and claimed miraculous cures, including his own conversion story. He tells us that this came from watching a video on Medjugorje:

> Within minutes of viewing the tape, I knew in my heart that Medjugorje was real.... As I watched, I suddenly "felt" that the Blessed Virgin Mary was speaking directly to my heart

and she was asking me to make the spreading of the Medjugorje apparitions my life's mission.³⁴

So after watching one video on Medjugorje, he proposes to completely change his lifestyle and become a fervent Medjugorjean missionary. Notice that this is the same type of reaction that Denis Nolan reported, one that is completely emotional and without any element of discernment. No doubt Weible is sincere in what he says, but clearly his account is entirely subjective. He also gives a number of accounts of allegedly miraculous healings, but offers no evidence that these have been investigated by any ecclesiastical body, as is the practice at Lourdes.

FR MULLIGAN ON MEDJUGORJE

Medjugorje: What's Happening? by Fr James Mulligan was also published in 2008, and, like Mark Miravalle, he claims: "All that has been reported from Medjugorje does not contain a single statement that in any way contradicts Catholic Magisterial teaching."³⁵ As we have seen, that is a questionable position.

Unlike most Medjugorje books, though, the author does include material which reveals some of the more disturbing historical aspects. For example, he includes information about the atrocities committed at Surmanci in 1941, that is, the mass murder of hundreds of Serbs at the hands of the fascist Croatian Ustasha forces, which happened, as he acknowledges, "within the parish of Medjugorje at the hamlet of Surmanci."³⁶

This is the first admission in the book, and it is followed by others, in what is arguably an attempt at "damage limitation." Previously, the most extravagant claims could be made about Medjugorje, but an increasing number of books have since been published highlighting the numerous problems involved with believing in it. The account of the first alleged vision, on 24 June 1981, has the following statement about the activities of the two initial visionaries, Ivanka and Mirjana, before they saw the "Gospa":

> According to some reports the girls were smoking cigarettes and listening to rock music on a radio/cassette player — perhaps for some not the most pious of preludes to what has become one of the most impressive claims of religious apparitions in Church history.

In other words, it is accepted that the girls were smoking and listening to rock music — in fact, as we have seen, it can't be denied now, since Medjugorje authors Fr René Laurentin and Wayne Weible have both admitted it. Fr Mulligan attempts to downplay the importance of this, but surely it does matter that the two visionaries were engaged in these not particularly devout activities immediately before claiming to have seen Our Lady. How could it not be important?

Fr Mulligan's accounts of the various visions of the first week or so then continue, but as with other Medjugorje commentators, there is a big problem: these accounts cannot be easily reconciled with the most crucial evidence of all, that is, the transcripts of the tapes made of the visionaries' experiences in June 1981. Before detailing what happened during the vision of Friday 26 June, he describes the various sources used in reconstructing the dialogue between the visionaries and the "Gospa" as including "interviews with the visionaries, records kept by the parish of St James, *various tape recordings* and statements by witnesses." He then goes on to say that these made it "possible to approximate the dialogue which took place at this and subsequent apparitions."[37]

The first point to note is that this is an admission that, almost certainly, the material from the original taped interviews has been used here. But the problem is that it has been mixed up with a number of other less satisfactory sources. The other point is to realize how vague it is to use words like "approximate," or to say, as he does in the next sentence, that "it *appears* the essential dialogue recorded was *something* of [sic] the following."

The interview between Fr Zovko and five of the six visionaries, on the evening of 30 June, has already been dealt with. This involved the two female social workers who had driven them to Cerno, near Medjugorje, where their vision that day took place. As we have seen, the idea has been propagated that the visionaries were "abducted" by these social workers, as part of a Communist plot, but we now know from the tape transcripts that they agreed to go.

However, Fr Mulligan's version of this event, following Denis Nolan, promotes the "abduction" story, and likewise has the visionaries threatening to jump out of the social worker's moving car if it didn't stop.[38] Such is the mythic power of Medjugorje.

DAMAGE LIMITATION

There is more attempted damage limitation further on, this time in connection with the fact that during this interview, as we have also seen, it became clear that the "Gospa" was only supposed to be appearing for another three days, a fact which is backed up in the transcripts by the witness of the two social workers, who heard the visionaries repeat the words "three times." So there is indisputable independent confirmation that at this stage, 30 June 1981, there were only supposed to be another three visions, and this is apparent even in the Klanac version.

Fr Mulligan, however, repeats the account in which Fr Zovko attempted to explain this discrepancy by invoking the number of apparitions at Lourdes, but as already indicated, this "explanation" is totally inadequate; and his alternative explanation, that the visionaries said this "in order to be left alone from [sic] the crowds" is equally unsatisfactory.[39]

Supporters of Fatima who have criticized Medjugorje are described as producing statements which appear "breathtaking in their vitriol," while those who have looked critically at the lives of the visionaries or the Franciscans — a procedure which is absolutely essential if the truth of their claims is to be assessed — are described as "obsessives." Presumably this means that those who swallow every claim made about Medjugorje, no matter how ridiculous it might be, are the sensible ones.[40]

There are clear signs that this work is a compilation taken from ultra-pro-Medjugorje sources: for example, the conflict around Medjugorje between 1991 and 1995 is described as the "Croatian Homeland War," which is hardly a neutral term. Letters to the Catholic Press and articles supportive of Medjugorje are also printed verbatim, as are interviews with various figures connected with the "shrine." But letters which were critical of Medjugorje, and which answered the points put forward by the pro-Medjugorje correspondents, are omitted.[41]

There is also an attempt to equate Medjugorje with approved Marian apparitions such as Guadalupe, Rue du Bac, La Salette, Lourdes, Fatima, Beauraing and Banneux, but as we have seen, these have little or nothing in common with Medjugorje.

The illustrations, many of them quite rare, are a clear sign of the privileged access which the author had to early Medjugorje sources — no one critical of Medjugorje would have been given such access.

There is a section entitled "Remarkable Priests," which devotes seven or eight pages to Frs Jozo Zovko and Fr Slavko Barbaric; but Fr Tomislav Vlasic, despite his early prominence on the Medjugorje scene, gets only the briefest mention, in passing at it were. This was probably because it was possible to see the way the wind was blowing regarding Fr Vlasic when the book was being written, and it was deemed prudent to only mention him very briefly.[42]

However, when an updated, hardback, version of *Medjugorje: What's Happening?* was published in 2010, the pictures of Fr Vlasic in the previous edition had mysteriously disappeared—he had been "airbrushed" out of the Medjugorje story. No doubt this was because by then Fr Vlasic had been dismissed from the Franciscan Order and laicized, and was thus something of an embarrassment. Moreover, his very name had been removed from an equivalent section of the revised edition.[43] He had become a "non-person" as far as Medjugorje promoters like Fr Mulligan were concerned.

Apart from that, what is the justification for describing Frs Zovko and Barbaric as "remarkable," when, as we have seen, they had to be disciplined for various offenses? They were certainly "remarkable," but not for the right reasons.

It's hard to see how one reviewer could describe the first edition of *Medjugorje: What's Happening?* as "balanced" and "well-grounded," or, on an even more bizarre note, state that it was "possibly the most comprehensive critique to date." How can a book which is so obviously slanted in favor of the usual material about Medjugorje possibly be described as a critique?

Many other critical points could be made about Fr Mulligan's book, but in sum, anyone looking for an objective investigation into Medjugorje will be disappointed by this flawed book, and the same must also be said of the other books discussed above.

22

The Vatican and Medjugorje

POPE BENEDICT AND BISHOP PERIC

In February 2006, Bishop Peric made his *ad limina* visitation to Pope Benedict XVI, and discussed the state of affairs in his diocese with the pontiff. He was able to note that there had been some progress as regards the Franciscan problem, although there were still a number of examples of disobedience. He also discussed Medjugorje with the pope, who intimated that for some time the Congregation for the Doctrine of the Faith had been skeptical as regards the claims of daily visions made by some of the visionaries. Bishop Peric confirmed that nothing had happened in the intervening period to affect the findings of the Bishops' conference of ex-Yugoslavia, the Zadar declaration, made in 1991. He then reiterated his own position as regards the non-supernaturality of the visions, before continuing:

> The numerous absurd messages, insincerities, falsehoods and disobedience associated with the events and "apparitions" of Medjugorje from the very outset, all disprove any claims of authenticity. Much pressure through appeals has been made to force the recognition of the authenticity of private revelations, yet not through convincing arguments based upon the truth, but through the self-praise of personal conversions and by statements such as one "feels good." How can this ever be taken as proof of the authenticity of apparitions?

At the conclusion of the meeting, Pope Benedict said the feeling at the Congregation had been that priests should be available to deal with the sacramental needs of pilgrims, but that this was to leave aside "the question of the authenticity of the apparitions."[1]

THE CDF AND FALSE VISIONARIES

However, previous to this, in July 2005, there was an important indication that the Congregation for the Doctrine of the Faith, under Cardinal William Levada, was going to take a firmer stance regarding alleged visionaries. It was announced that various prohibitions were being put in place against Fr Luigi Burresi, better known as Brother Gino, including his being forbidden to hear confessions, to give spiritual direction, to preach, to celebrate the sacraments in public or to grant any form of interview.

Until 1992, Fr Burresi was a member of the Oblates of the Virgin Mary, and had a reputation as a mystic and spiritual director, as well as allegedly being a stigmatic and a visionary. The decree from the CDF cites abuses in confession and spiritual direction as the reason for this action, but, according to Sandro Magister, in addition, Vatican sources confirmed that Fr Burresi had also been accused of sexual abuse by men who were part of his movement during the 1970s and 1980s. This was the first decree to be issued by the Congregation during Pope Benedict XVI's pontificate, who personally approved it on 27 May 2005.[2]

This action was followed, in September 2007, by the publication of a document from the Congregation concerning the excommunication, for schism and heresy, of members of the community of Our Lady of All Nations, better known as the "Army of Mary," a sect founded by one Marie-Paule Giguère in Canada, in 1971. Giguère claimed to be a reincarnation of the Blessed Virgin who had received visions and messages from God, to the effect that Mary was fully divine, and thus that Giguère herself was divine.[3]

POPE BENEDICT AND FATIMA

In May 2006, Pope Benedict XVI commemorated the 25th anniversary of the assassination attempt on Pope John Paul II, on 13 May 1981, remarking to the thousands of pilgrims gathered in St Peter's Square that the previous pope had felt he had miraculously escaped death due to the intervention of a "maternal hand." In the presence of the statue of Our Lady, which had been brought to Rome from Fatima for the occasion, Pope Benedict went on to link the message of Fatima with that of Lourdes, describing it as "an intense call to prayer and conversion." He also said that Fatima was a "truly prophetic" announcement, in the light of the destruction caused by wars, totalitarian regimes and persecutions against the Church during the twentieth century. He further noted that despite "reasons for apprehension about the future of humanity," what the Blessed Virgin promised at Fatima, that in the end, her Immaculate Heart would triumph, was very consoling. Cardinal Camillo Ruini later presided over Mass in St Peter's Basilica, at the end of which he read out a message from the pope in which the Holy Father expressed the hope that "the message of Fatima be increasingly accepted, understood and lived in every community."[4]

BISHOP PERIC PREACHES AT MEDJUGORJE

Not long after this, during a Confirmation Mass homily at St James's Church in Medjugorje, on 15 June 2006, Bishop Peric said that the Church "has not accepted, neither as supernatural nor as Marian, any of the apparitions" alleged by the Medjugorje visionaries. He then called on them, and "those persons behind the 'messages,' to demonstrate ecclesiastical obedience and to cease with these public manifestations and messages in this parish." He further stated: "In this fashion they shall show their necessary adherence to the Church, by neither placing private apparitions nor private sayings before the official position of the Church."

Bishop Peric said that his position, which echoed that of Bishop Zanic his predecessor, had papal support, and he thanked Popes Benedict and John Paul II, because they "have always respected the judgments of the bishops of Mostar-Duvno... regarding the so-called 'apparitions' and 'messages' of Medjugorje... [while he recognized] the Holy Father's right to give a final decision on these events."[5]

It's worth noting that the Bishops of Tuscany in Italy issued a press release following their *ad limina* visit to the pope from 16 to 20 April 2007. In this, they made it known that they had also had a meeting with the Secretary of the Congregation for the Doctrine of the Faith, Archbishop Angelo Amato, who, while speaking to them about Medjugorje, invited them to publicize the above-mentioned homily of Bishop Peric. The bishops particularly emphasized that they were asking their priests to "read it carefully and to draw the necessary consequences for the correct enlightenment of our faithful."[6]

CARDINAL BERTONE ON MEDJUGORJE

Meanwhile, in February 2005, Cardinal Tarcisio Bertone, the Vatican Secretary of State, had been interviewed on Radio Maria, an Italian radio station, and expressed skepticism about Medjugorje. The response from many of the listeners was quite aggressive, leading the cardinal to speak later of the "unseemly and offensive reactions of faithful and priests who describe themselves as 'Medjugorjean.'" The cardinal went on to deplore the "excesses of fanaticism, such as the events in various churches, in which they promise the possibility of being present at an apparition of the Madonna... at a scheduled time."[7]

Following this, early in 2007, the Italian edition of a book-length interview with Cardinal Bertone was published, and this was translated into English and published, in 2008, as *The Last Secret of Fatima*. In this book there is a short chapter dealing with Medjugorje, in which the cardinal makes the following statement about the alleged visions. It is significant because it points to the way a very senior Vatican official was then thinking about Medjugorje. When specifically asked whether Our Lady had appeared there or not, this was the response:

> The opinion of Tarcisio Bertone is that [Medjugorje] is a very big question mark. Medjugorje is to some extent an anomaly that doesn't completely square with other apparitions. It doesn't entirely follow the *traditio*, or tradition, of apparitions. Between 1981 and the present, Mary is supposed to have appeared tens of thousands of times. The volume of Our Lady's alleged messages does not reflect the usual pattern of Marian apparitions, which, like meteors from heaven, tend to have a clear beginning and a clear end. The counterargument, of course, is that the extraordinary times we're living in demand this kind of extraordinary response from Mary. When I say "the counterargument is," I'm speaking in a roundabout way in order to highlight a certain disagreement I have with this position, which is put forward by [those] who want the Church to go in a certain direction.[8]

What was perhaps equally significant was that the book contained a foreword from Pope Benedict XVI, in which he imparted his apostolic blessing on Cardinal Bertone, a sign surely that the pope was in agreement with the content of the book. And although Cardinal Bertone was not specifically referring to Medjugorje in the following quote, his remarks are relevant to the subject:

> The eclipse of the sacred has led to a do-it-yourself approach to the holy, a kind of supermarket of religious faiths. And, unfortunately, a lot of Catholics are in danger of completely losing their grip on the historical, physical aspect of religion. They'd rather gawk at a weeping Madonna than read a page of the Gospel.... This is Christianity à la carte — you order off the menu in the restaurant of religious experience. A lot of Christians are spiritually naïve, and this makes them vulnerable to the influence of superficial ideas and disinformation.[9]

MORE MEDJUGORJE CONTROVERSY

In June 2007, there was further controversy concerning Medjugorje when Fr Raniero Cantalamessa, the Capuchin preacher of the papal household, withdrew from a planned engagement to deliver a series of lectures at Medjugorje. This followed the decision of Bishop Peric to deny him permission to speak there. He was to have been the keynote speaker at the 12th International Seminar for Priests, from 3–5 July, an event at which Fr Jozo Zovko had also been billed to appear, even though Bishop Peric had revoked his priestly faculties in 2004. Fr Cantalamessa, who has been the papal preacher since 1980, is a high-profile figure at the Vatican, responsible for delivering weekly meditations during Advent and Lent to the pope, cardinals, bishops and other religious figures, so this was a significant prohibition.[10] And we should note that he acknowledged the authority of the local bishop, unlike many of those most involved in promoting Medjugorje.

In March 2008, Cardinal Vinko Puljic was interviewed by *Vecernji list*, a large circulation Croatian daily paper. It was put to him that a recently published interview with Cardinal Bertone had raised the question of a re-examination of the case of Medjugorje. He was then asked if the Bosnia-Herzegovina Bishops' Conference had discussed the matter, and whether Medjugorje would be officially examined. Cardinal Puljic responded by saying that the bishops had not discussed it, because "the phenomenon of Medjugorje does not come within our competence." He went on to say that when the "Holy See takes the decision and gives a task, we shall think about what to do."[11]

So by this time, it seemed that the decision had been made that an investigation of Medjugorje at Vatican level would be forthcoming, but there was still no definite announcement.

Meanwhile, in early June 2008, it was reported that Bishop Andrea Gemma, a retired exorcist, had said that it was his belief that the Medjugorje phenomenon was a "scandal" and a "diabolical deceit." He also stated that he believed that the Congregation for the Doctrine of the Faith would not ultimately rule in favor of the claims of the visionaries. *Petrus*, the online Italian Catholic journal, reported his remarks as follows: "You'll see that soon the Vatican will intervene with something explosive to unmask once and for all who is behind this deceit."

He further stated that it was:

a phenomenon which is absolutely diabolical, around which revolve many underground interests. Holy Mother Church, the only one able to pronounce, through the mouth of the Bishop of Mostar, has already said publicly, and officially, that the Madonna has never appeared at Medjugorje and that this whole sham is the work of the devil.

The bishop also contended:

> In Medjugorje everything happens in function of money: pilgrimages, lodging houses, sale of trinkets. So much so that abusing the good faith of those poor souls who go there thinking to encounter the Madonna, the false seers have organised themselves financially, have enriched themselves and live a rather comfortable life.... These don't seem to me to be disinterested persons. Thus, together with those who shore up this noisy deception, they patently have every interest in convincing people that they see and speak with the Virgin Mary.[12]

FR TOMISLAV VLASIC IS INVESTIGATED

It wasn't necessary to wait long for the "explosive" intervention from the Vatican which Bishop Gemma had predicted, which would "unmask once and for all who is behind this deceit." On 31 August 2008, Bishop Peric published—at the explicit request of the Congregation for the Doctrine of the Faith—a letter he had received from the secretary of the CDF, Archbishop Angelo Amato. This letter, dated 30 May 2008, informed the bishop of the Congregation's findings regarding Fr Tomislav Vlasic—the former spiritual director of the Medjugorje visionaries—and asked him to make public the canonical status of Fr Vlasic, whose actions had led to him being reported to the Congregation "for the diffusion of dubious doctrine, manipulation of consciences, suspect mysticism, disobedience toward legitimately issued orders" and charges "contra sextum," that is, in connection with the Sixth Commandment, and thus relating to sexual matters.

And just to make it clear that there was a definite Medjugorje link here—which some of its supporters denied—the letter also stated that it was: "Within the context of the phenomenon [of] Medjugorje, [that] this Dicastery is studying the case of Father Tomislav Vlasic OFM."

It seems that Fr Vlasic was disciplined after refusing to cooperate with the inquiry initiated by the Congregation, and had instead sought to justify himself by referring to his religious activities around Medjugorje. And it also emerged that a decree concerning Fr Vlasic had been jointly signed earlier in the year by Cardinal William Levada, prefect of the Congregation for the Doctrine of the Faith, and the Minister General of the Order of Friars Minor, Fr José Rodriguez Carballo.

This decree stipulated that Fr Vlasic should be confined to an Italian Franciscan friary and not allowed contact with the "Queen of Peace" community which he had founded without prior permission from his religious superior. It also banned him from public preaching and from hearing confessions, as well as requiring that he take a mandatory course of theological-spiritual formation and make a solemn profession of the Catholic faith. He was warned that he would be excommunicated if he violated any of the prohibitions, a point which surely indicates the extremely serious nature of the charges against him.

Bishop Peric finally noted:

> Father Vlasic is forewarned that, in the case of stubbornness, a juridical penal process will begin with the aim of still harsher sanctions, not excluding dismissal, having in mind the suspicion of heresy and schism, as well as scandalous acts *contra sextum* [against the Sixth Commandment] aggravated by mystical motivations.[13]

It's worth pointing out here that the fact that the Congregation asked Bishop Peric to publish this letter about Fr Vlasic, which specifically linked him with Medjugorje, negates the idea that he was no longer associated with the Medjugorje dossier.

Previous to this development, though, it was reported[14] that Fr Laurentin had responded to Bishop Gemma's remarks as follows:

> Usually, to be true, I don't like to speak about Medjugorje because I prefer to follow the line of silence chosen by the Church, but in this precise case I cannot be in agreement with Monsignor Gemma. The number of the apparitions of Our Lady is probably excessive, but I do not think that one can speak about a satanic deceit. On the other hand, we note in Medjugorje the most elevated number of conversions to the Catholic faith: what would Satan gain in bringing back so many souls to God? Look, in this kind of situation

prudence is an obligation, but I am convinced that Medjugorje is a fruit of the Good and not of the Evil.

Fr Laurentin's remark that he didn't "like to speak about Medjugorje" is surely unbelievable in the light of his involvement in promoting it for so many years. Indeed, for seventeen years, up until 1998, he published an annual report with constantly updated information about Medjugorje, his famous *Dernières Nouvelles* ("Latest News"), with the final edition running to 238 pages. This report only ceased publication at the express request of Bishop Peric. And this is to say nothing of Fr Laurentin's other publications on the subject.

But we should at least be grateful for his candor in admitting that the number of alleged visions is "probably excessive." Does that mean the "Gospa" doesn't know what she doing? Or perhaps the fault lies with the visionaries or the Franciscans? Whatever the explanation for this phrase, it certainly sounded as though Fr Laurentin was becoming more cautious about Medjugorje.

THE DEVIL'S BATTLE PLAN

And as to what Satan might gain by promoting false visions, apart from undermining Fatima and other genuine apparitions, what about the danger of Medjugorje devotees leaving the Church if it should be finally condemned? That would be a significant victory for the devil surely? The way some Medjugorje supporters talk, you would think the devil was a complete novice in spiritual matters, someone who would never dream of using a series of false visions to undermine the Church. The reality is Satan's intelligence far surpasses that of mankind, and it is only by a total reliance on God's grace that we can possibly hope to defeat his wiles and temptations.

In fact, it is precisely in the area of alleged revelations that he can do the most damage. Regarding Catholic dogmas, these are regarded by all loyal Catholics as non-negotiable, and thus it's hard for the devil to cause much mischief there. But regarding alleged visions, since a process of discernment is required by the Church, it is the ideal territory for him to cause trouble; it takes some time for the Church to come to a decision, so he has a period in which to engage in "guerrilla warfare" against it. And that is actually his whole battle plan. He knows he has lost the war against God — sentence has been passed against him and his rebellious followers and they will spend all eternity in hell. But he still has a chance to obstruct the Church in its own march towards eternity, to win some battles, whether regarding individual souls or movements such as the one which has grown up around Medjugorje.

And when we also consider Fatima, with its definite promise of the triumph of Mary's Immaculate Heart and a period of peace for the world, then we can see that this is a struggle with huge consequences. If the devil can subvert or delay the acceptance and implementation of the program outlined by Our Lady at Fatima, then that is a big victory for him. And what better way of doing that then by initiating and then encouraging a rival Marian apparition site at Medjugorje? Given the enormous official Church support Fatima has received, he cannot achieve this by a frontal assault, but has to do his work more subtly. And if he can get good Catholics hooked on false visions then that is a prize certainly worth working for.

This is what St Teresa of Avila said about the cold-blooded determination of the devil to do everything he can to bring humanity down to his level: "The devil's wiles are many; he would turn hell upside down a thousand times to make us think ourselves better than we are."[15] And if the devil is prepared to do that just to prevent a single believer advancing in genuine virtue, what malice will he not display in attempting to subvert Our Lady's role in the salvation of mankind? And since Fatima is one of the principal means by which that cause will be advanced in our times, then promoting a place like Medjugorje only makes sound satanic sense.

What does it really matter to Satan if there are some conversions, if people start to say the rosary and so on, if the Church as a whole continues to battle against the "culture of death," without properly employing the spiritual means we were given at Fatima, and particularly the Five First Saturdays devotion? And we should also remember that the Medjugorje "good fruits" have to be balanced against the chronic disobedience, the scandals and all the other "evil fruits" which have arisen from it.

FR LAURENTIN BACKPEDALS ON MEDJUGORJE

In October 2008, the Italian web site *Petrus* published a further interview with Fr Laurentin, which provided more evidence that the French priest was apparently backpedaling with regard to his previously fulsome support for Medjugorje—but perhaps this wasn't such an unexpected development after all, given the revelations about Fr Vlasic.

In response to a question from the interviewer, in which he described Fr Laurentin as a "supporter of the apparitions of Medjugorje," he asked him why the Vatican did not "appear to be convinced of the authenticity of the Medjugorje apparitions." His response was: "I am only an expert and I have no magisterium. And I never allow myself to give an opinion on the apparitions which I study. I only examine the facts, the reasons in favor and those against. I discern them, I explain them as clearly as possible, but I don't give any judgment."

This was news to the interviewer, who responded by saying: "Father Laurentin, what you are saying seems to be a step backward: you have written books upholding the thesis of the authenticity of the apparitions of Medjugorje...." But Fr Laurentin again insisted that he had not done this, a statement which is extremely difficult to reconcile with the large number of articles and books he has written supportive of Medjugorje.[16] This is clear, to give just one example, from his book published in 1984, *Is the Virgin Mary Appearing at Medjugorje?*, in which Fr Laurentin stated: "While reserving judgment to the Episcopal authority responsible in this matter, and simply in my capacity as an expert, well aware of my limits, *I would say that my analysis leads me to a positive evaluation of the apparitions.*"[17]

FR TOMISLAV VLASIC IS LAICIZED

There was a further development in the case of Fr Tomislav Vlasic in July 2009, when the news broke that he had been laicized by Pope Benedict XVI, who had "granted him the favor of reduction to the lay state (*amissio status clericalis*) and of dismissal from the Order." In addition, Pope Benedict had also "motu proprio" (that is, on his own initiative), granted him "the remission of the censure incurred as well as the favor of dispensation from religious vows and from all the responsibilities connected with sacred ordination, including celibacy."

All this became clear when a letter dated 10 March was made public on 24 July 2009. In this letter, the Franciscan Minister General Fr José Rodriguez Carballo informed Franciscan provincials in Bosnia-Herzegovina, Croatia and Italy that Fr Vlasic had himself requested laicization. In the letter, Fr Rodriguez said Fr Vlasic was "responsible for conduct harmful to ecclesial communion both in the spheres of doctrine and discipline."

The letter further stated that Pope Benedict had "under pain of excommunication" imposed conditions on "Mr. Tomislav Vlasic," including an "absolute prohibition from exercising any form of apostolate" and an "absolute prohibition from releasing declarations on religious matters, especially regarding 'the phenomenon of Medjugorje.'"[18]

Some Medjugorje supporters tried to claim that this was not as serious as it all seemed, and to distance the now ex-Fr Vlasic from the overall movement, but even if he had been laicized at his own request, this definitely looked like someone who had "jumped before he was pushed." And it is impossible to deny Fr Vlasic's crucial role in the early days at Medjugorje. Fr Bubalo has a picture in his book showing Fr Vlasic leading the visionaries in prayer at some point during this period, with the caption underneath telling us that: "From August 1981 until the end of 1984, he was the spiritual advisor of the seers." And this type of statement is found in a number of other early books on the apparitions by Medjugorje supporters. In addition, Fr Vlasic was responsible for the *Kronika ukazanja*, the *Chronicle of the Apparitions* during this period.[19]

And what are we to make of alleged statements from the "Gospa" in the early 1980s supportive of Fr Vlasic? Knowing that he would be a source of scandal is it likely that the Blessed Virgin would have said on 28 February 1982: "Thank Tomislav very much, *for he is guiding you very well*." Or what about this response on 3 June 1983, after Fr Vlasic had founded a prayer group, and the visionaries had asked: "What do you expect of Fr. Tomislav? Has he begun well?" to which they received the reply: "Yes, it is good. *Have him continue*."[20]

Surely the content of these alleged messages, given what has subsequently happened to Fr Vlasic, demonstrates beyond any doubt that they could not possibly have originated with the real Blessed Virgin?

BISHOP PERIC ON MEDJUGORJE IRREGULARITIES

In early June 2009, Bishop Peric spoke at a Confirmation Mass at Medjugorje, saying that while in Rome earlier in the year, he had talked to "top officials" at the Vatican Secretariat of State and the Congregation for the Doctrine of the Faith, and that they had confirmed that they were informing anyone who asked them that the Church has never recognized the alleged visions as authentic.

During his homily Bishop Peric likewise urged his listeners not to accept that the alleged visions reported in the parish were real, while after the Mass, he made a pastoral visitation of the parish, following which he sent letters to Fr Petar Vlasic, the current parish priest, and Fr Danko Perutina, one of the parochial vicars, both of whom are Franciscans.

In his letter to Fr Vlasic, which amongst other things concerned liturgical matters and the curtailing of the activities of the visionaries within the parish, the bishop reaffirmed that priests from abroad should not give conferences or retreats without his permission, and that "neither foreign nor domestic priests can promote alleged 'messages' or 'apparitions' which have not been proclaimed authentic in that church or on church property." He also said that the "parish of Medjugorje cannot be called a shrine, neither privately, nor publicly, not officially, because it is not recognized as such by any level of competent ecclesial authority."

Fr Vlasic was likewise asked to ensure that Fr Perutina did not give any more commentaries on the alleged monthly messages from Marija Pavlovic, which was the thrust of the bishop's letter to Fr Perutina himself. These documents were published on the Mostar-Duvno diocesan website on 26 September.[21]

Later in the year, in a Reuters interview dated 7 October 2009, Cardinal Vinko Puljic apparently said that he expected the Vatican to issue more explicit guidance to Catholics "soon" on the question of Medjugorje. The cardinal reportedly said: "We are now awaiting a new directive on this issue. I don't think we must wait for a long time, I think it will be this year, but that is not clear.... I am going to Rome in November and we must discuss this."[22]

CONGREGATION FOR THE DOCTRINE OF THE FAITH POSITION

Further controversy was aroused in mid-November 2009 by the news that Cardinal Christoph Schönborn intended to visit Medjugorje over the Christmas period. However, Fr Johannes Fürnkranz, a spokesman for the Archdiocese of Vienna, said that the trip was private and should not be taken as implying that the cardinal accepted the truth of the visions.

Perhaps the most interesting point to emerge from this development was the reaction of an official at the Congregation for the Doctrine of the Faith, who told a Catholic News Agency reporter that the Congregation remained supportive of the Bosnia-Herzegovina Bishops, and that specifically: "The local bishops have the ultimate authority on this matter, and their arguments against the alleged apparitions are doctrinally solid." When further questioned on whether Medjugorje be judged by its fruits of "conversions and vocations to the Church," the official responded: "It is not the duty of this Dicastery to make a pastoral assessment, but a doctrinal one. But regarding the argument, it can equally be argued that God can write straight with crooked lines, just as it has been proven in several previous occasions with patently false apparitions."[23]

This very revealing statement was a clear indication of the way the Congregation actually regarded Medjugorje at this time, and is a classic response to those who claim that because Medjugorje has given rise to vocations, then it must be genuine. Given the present crisis in the Church, many young people will have had their first real exposure to a more intense Catholic atmosphere through a pilgrimage to Medjugorje, and may then pursue a vocation to the priesthood or religious life. But that doesn't prove Medjugorje is genuine.

We have the sad example of the Legionaries of Christ. Consider how many vocations arose through the activities of the founder, Fr Marcial Maciel Degollado, who has now been exposed as a sexual deviant and fraud. Although Pope John Paul II gave him his support, Pope Benedict removed him from active ministry on becoming pontiff, and ordered that he lead a life of prayer and penitence. He even described Maciel as a "false prophet." How do we explain all of these vocations and conversions of heart if Maciel was a "false prophet"? The answer lies in St Paul's teaching in Romans 5:20: "Where sin increased, grace abounded all the more." The situation is no different with Medjugorje: conversions and vocations can take place because God's grace will always triumph, even in a place where the visions in question are not supernatural.[24]

Sadly, too, the fact that Pope John Paul II was deceived by Maciel indicates that his private judgment on Medjugorje cannot be regarded as sacrosanct.

On 20 November, Cardinal Vinko Puljic, while at the Vatican to attend the plenary session of a meeting of the Congregation for the Evangelization of Peoples, denied press reports which claimed that a commission concerned with the alleged visions at Medjugorje was being created by the Holy See. In an apparent reference to the 1991 Zadar declaration, he said: "The doctrinal issue of the Medjugorje phenomenon is resolved, but its pastoral significance must still be taken into account." He further stated: "For the moment, everything is under the jurisdiction of the local bishops.... Still, at any given moment, the Congregation for the Doctrine of the Faith could establish an International Commission in order to study the case of Medjugorje."[25]

In April 2007, Bishop Peric had noted that despite being forbidden from exercising his priestly ministry in the diocese, Fr Zovko had been invited to lead the Way of the Cross in Medjugorje, and to hear confessions. And in February 2009, Fr Zovko left Siroki Brijeg, and moved into a partially ruined convent on the uninhabited Croatian islet of Badija. He issued a statement which was faxed to his supporters, in which it was claimed that he had asked his superiors for permission to reside outside the province. But according to the 24 February 2009 edition of the Croatian magazine *Nacional*, he had actually been exiled from the Franciscan Province of Herzegovina after nearly 20 years of disobedience. Moreover, he was isolated and forbidden any contacts, either personally or by letter with the faithful, and was not to spread any further information about Medjugorje. According to another report, he was moved again, in November 2009, to Frohnleiten in Austria, by a decision of the Franciscan Provincial of Herzegovina.[26]

THE IMPORTANCE OF EPISCOPAL COLLEGIALITY

Cardinal Christoph Schönborn came in for criticism earlier in the year, in September, when he invited some of the Medjugorje visionaries for a public appearance at his cathedral in Vienna.[27] The essential problem with this type of thing, though, was that it was a radical departure from what used to happen in the Church. When priests, bishops and now even cardinals permit alleged visionaries to have "apparitions" in their churches or cathedrals, we are very much in uncharted waters.

Before Medjugorje, bishops didn't do this because it would have implied a clear lack of collegiality; that is, it would have been a violation of the principle that the world's bishops have a joint and collective responsibility for the governance and pastoral care of the Church. This obviously includes not encouraging movements in favor of suspect visions within their own diocese, nor within the diocese where the alleged visions are taking place.

But it seems that with the best of intentions, some bishops have allowed themselves to be swayed by the wave of enthusiasm over Medjugorje, to the extent that this has now caused divisions in the Church, with bishops holding differing views on the subject. This disharmony amongst the members of the hierarchy is unfortunately

The Vatican and Medjugorje

another of the bad "fruits" resulting from Medjugorje, and has also led to discord amongst the faithful who have become confused at this lack of concord amongst their spiritual leaders.

Acting in such a way is thus an affront to Episcopal collegiality, and it also gives credibility, or the appearance of Church approval, to the alleged visions, ahead of a definitive judgment from the Church. Regarding Medjugorje, the visionaries are not permitted to have visions on Church property in any diocese in Bosnia-Herzegovina or Croatia. Yet, there are frequent announcements that the "Gospa" will be appearing at a set time in parishes and cathedrals all over the world? How can such behavior be justified?[28]

In addition, as already indicated, we have Cardinal Bertone's complaint regarding Medjugorje, about the "excesses of fanaticism, such as the events in various churches, in which they promise the possibility of being present at an apparition of the Madonna... at a scheduled time." So here we had a highly placed cardinal expressing concern over such activities.

Meanwhile, another important figure, the Portuguese Cardinal José Saraiva Martins, had been interviewed by *Petrus*, and was asked if the alleged visions at Medjugorje should be considered true or false. He responded by saying: "The apparitions will not be considered authentic, as long as they have not been officially approved by the Church in the person of the Holy Father." He further stated that he didn't know

> if these apparitions were invented or if they have economic interests... in cases of this sort, the devil's paw may be here. But God is so great that he knows how to make even the evil one serve for the good of humanity: in this way, it is possible to explain the benefits which many people maintain they received at Medjugorje.

In response to a question about the assertion of the Medjugorje visionaries that it was a sequel to the Fatima apparitions, the cardinal was quite forthright:

> I don't believe that they are. I see too many differences. As I said before, the little shepherds of Fatima made themselves humble and chose silence; at Medjugorje, I don't know if that is going to happen.... No, I see nothing in common between Fatima and Medjugorje.[29]

THE INTERNATIONAL COMMISSION ON MEDJUGORJE

On 6 March 2010, it was reported in the Italian weekly magazine *Panorama* that Pope Benedict XVI had authorized an official inquiry, led by Cardinal Camillo Ruini, into the Medjugorje visions. The cardinal had collaborated with the pope on various projects previously, and was an ex-president of the Italian Bishops' Conference, as well as a former cardinal vicar of Rome. However, at this stage, there was no corroboration of this report from the Vatican.[30]

This came on 17 March, when a statement confirming the formation of a commission to investigate the "phenomenon" of Medjugorje was released by the Vatican. This read as follows:

> Under the auspices of the Congregation for the Doctrine of the Faith, under the presidency of Cardinal Camillo Ruini, an international commission of investigation on Medjugorje has been constituted. Said Commission, composed of cardinals, bishops and experts will work in a reserved manner, subjecting the results of their studies to the authority of the Dicastery.

Fr Federico Lombardi, the Vatican spokesman, confirmed the role of Cardinal Ruini as president, and indicated that the Commission would have approximately twenty members. Fr Lombardi explained that although Medjugorje began as a diocesan phenomenon, when it was seen to have passed beyond that level, it came under the aegis of the Bishops' Conference of the former Yugoslavia, which now no longer existed. The Bishops of Bosnia-Herzegovina had then ultimately asked the Congregation for the Doctrine of the Faith to take over the investigation because previous commissions had not come to a definitive conclusion on the supernaturality or otherwise of Medjugorje. Fr Lombardi said that he expected that the investigation would take "a good while" to be completed, and that the results would then be submitted to the CDF. Thus the Commission was to be an advisory body with the role of offering its findings to the Congregation, which would "make decisions on the case."[31]

Less than a week later, in the Italian newspaper *Il Giornale*, Vatican reporter Andrea Tornielli wrote that a new diocese could be created from territory currently within the dioceses of Dubrovnik, Mostar and Split — thus including Medjugorje — supposedly to "permit a better administration of the flow of pilgrims." This would have had the effect of making Medjugorje independent of Bishop Ratko Perić of Mostar-Duvno. Moreover, Tornielli claimed that the decision to create the new diocese was put off the previous September partly due to the opposition of Bishop Perić.

However, when Fr Lombardi was questioned about this, he said that he was unaware of this speculation and believed it was "baseless" that such a proposal would be included in the Commission's findings. Given that the three cities named by Tornielli — Dubrovnik, Mostar and Split — are within two different Bishops' Conferences and indeed two different countries, Croatia and Bosnia-Herzegovina, this proposal seems unlikely.

The Italian journalist also wrote that he understood that the Commission's deliberations would not be concerned with the "supernatural" aspects of Medjugorje, but rather focus on the Zadar declaration made by the Bishops of ex-Yugoslavia in April 1991.

Tornielli claimed that the Vatican has never pronounced a judgment on a case of apparitions that are still in progress,[32] but this is factually incorrect: as already indicated, the Holy See *has* condemned false visions in the past even while it was claimed they were still going on, as was the case regarding Heroldsbach in Germany in 1951.

CARDINAL RUINI AND THE COMMISSION

On 13 April 2010, a report came from the Vatican that the Commission to investigate Medjugorje had held its first meeting on 26 March. At the same time, the names of the members of the Commission were announced. These included Cardinal Camillo Ruini as president, as well as several cardinals and archbishops, many of whom served on Pontifical Councils or Vatican congregations. Specifically, these commission members were: Cardinal Jozef Tomko, Cardinal Vinko Puljic, Cardinal Josip Bozanic, Cardinal Julian Herranz and Archbishop Angelo Amato.

The commission also included various individuals, namely Msgr Tony Anatrella, a French psychoanalyst; Msgr Pierangelo Sequeri, an Italian theology professor; Fr David Maria Jaeger, OFM; Fr Zdzisław Józef Kijas, OFM Conv; and Fr Salvatore Perrella, OSM, a Mariology lecturer. Fr Achim Schütz, a theological anthropology professor, was included as secretary, with Msgr Krzysztof Nykiel, a CDF official, serving as an additional secretary. Other members were Fr Franjo Topic, a theology professor from Sarajevo; Fr Mijo Nikic, SJ, a professor of psychology and psychology of religion from Zagreb; Fr Mihaly Szentmartoni, SJ, a professor of spirituality; and Sr Veronica Nela Gaspar, a theology professor.[33]

The members of the committee were chosen with the expectation that they would be a body with the necessary authority and expertise. Cardinals Puljic and Bozanic, archbishops of Sarajevo in Bosnia-Herzegovina and Zagreb in Croatia, respectively, both formerly in Yugoslavia, had local knowledge and experience, while Cardinal Jozef Tomko was a retired prefect of the Congregation for the Evangelization of Peoples, and Cardinal Julian Herranz was the retired president of the Pontifical Council for Legislative Texts, and a priest of Opus Dei.

Archbishop Angelo Amato was responsible for signing the canonical sanctions against the then Fr Tomislav Vlasic when he was the secretary of the Congregation for the Doctrine of the Faith, and so was familiar with Medjugorje.

Of the other members of the Commission, three of them, Fr Franjo Topic, Fr Mijo Nikic, SJ, and Sr Veronica Nela Gaspar, were based in countries from the former Yugoslavia and thus were expected to have the necessary linguistic and theological skills, while the others were drawn from a variety of countries and had different areas of expertise.

The Commission had two Franciscan members, Fr David Jaeger and Fr Zdzislaw Jozef Kijas, a sign that a proper evaluation of Medjugorje was connected to the stance of the local Franciscans in relation to the Church in Bosnia-Herzegovina. In particular, Fr Jaeger, a canon lawyer, specialized in Church-State relations.

And since this was a new examination of the event, distinct from previous Episcopal commissions, and given the highly contentious nature of Medjugorje, presumably it was decided that Bishop Peric would not be a part of the special Commission. To have included him would only have invited charges from Medjugorje partisans that the Commission was "unbalanced" or "biased," although, as we have seen, *Normae Congregationis* clearly stipulates that the local Ordinary is always to be consulted regarding the investigation of alleged revelations.

In fact, the bishop contacted the Catholic News Service in February 2011, to say that he would "no longer comment about what is happening in Medjugorje out of respect for the Vatican commission." And it also needs to be pointed out that none of the local Franciscans were invited to join the Commission either.

An interesting point about Cardinal Ruini's role as the president of the Commission is that he had had previous experience of dealing with a Medjugorje-related incident. This concerned a small Marian statue from Medjugorje, which allegedly began to weep blood, beginning on 2 February 1995, in Civitavecchia, a city on the Italian coast about 70km to the northwest of Rome. A diocesan commission of inquiry, comprising eleven members, met to look into the case for the first time on 19 April of that year, and had completed its work by 22 November 1996.

Seven members of the commission expressed themselves in favor of the belief that the weepings from the statue were of a supernatural nature, with three opposed and one abstaining. But this position was rejected by the Vatican, most probably on the grounds that tests showed that the blood on the statue was male in origin, in addition to which all the male members of the family that owned the statue had refused to agree to a blood test.

In the year 2000, the Congregation for the Doctrine of the Faith, with the then Cardinal Joseph Ratzinger as its prefect, established a new commission under Cardinal Ruini, and this concluded that a more cautious verdict of *non constat de supernaturalitate* ("the supernaturality has not been proven") was more appropriate. News of this decision, however, was only made public on 17 February 2005, by Cardinal Bertone, the then secretary of the CDF, who explained that the diocesan commission had been set up hastily by the bishop.[34]

THE PAPAL NUNCIO ON MEDJUGORJE

Three days after the International Commission on Medjugorje was announced, Archbishop D'Errico, the Papal Nuncio to Bosnia-Herzegovina, was interviewed, and the question of Medjugorje was raised; the text of the resulting interview was placed on the website of the Bishops' Conference of Bosnia-Herzegovina. Archbishop D'Errico said that:

> From personal experience, every time I met the Holy Father he had great interest in the question of Medjugorje, a question to which he was directed...[since] he became prefect of the Congregation for the Doctrine of the Faith. It deals with a question for which he feels responsible as the supreme head of the Church to pronounce a clear message. The Holy Father personally knows it very well and he has told me

that several times—he is well acquainted with the whole phenomenon. He knows about the great good that is being done in this region by the priests, the Franciscan friars, and the laity. And on the other hand he asks himself how...[is there] such opposition to this phenomenon. For that reason he wanted to establish this commission which is on an especially high level to obtain a complete picture of it by persons who are highly qualified. So from different parts of the world he has invited cardinals, bishops, experts and expert witnesses to be part of this commission.[35]

Thus this interview revealed the personal interest that Pope Benedict took regarding the "question" of Medjugorje, and how he felt the need for a "clear message" to be pronounced by the Church—a further indication of an expectation that some definite decision would come out of the work of the Commission.

However, according to one of the Commission members, Fr Salvatore Perrella, speaking in January 2011, since the pope wanted a "decisive conclusion made," it was likely that the Commission's work would take quite some time. He further stated that the case of Medjugorje "is a serious thing," and that it was "very complex" but capable of resolution.

It was disquieting, though, to read that he also said that the extended length of the alleged visions at Medjugorje was not something that "generates suspicion" any longer. In saying this, he pointed to the recognition of "precedents" such as the apparitions of Our Lady of Laus, which spanned a period of 54 years and were recognized by the local bishop in 2008.

However, as indicated previously, the seer of Laus, Benoîte Rencurel, saw daily apparitions of the Blessed Virgin only for four months, and from then on only had intermittent apparitions until 1718. So this is a quite different situation to that at Medjugorje, where some of the visionaries have been alleging daily visions now for many decades.

In any event, to further emphasize the importance of the role of the local Ordinary, he also stated that at each step of the investigation, "the person in charge of everything is the bishop,"[36] which once again shows that the bishop of Mostar was not sidelined by the Commission, but that this new development was the culmination of a logical process.

The crucial point in all this, and the one which was surely of great significance for the Ruini Commission, was that up to that point, official Church pronouncements about Medjugorje had either been explicitly or implicitly negative — explicitly in the case of the local bishops, and, as has been argued previously, implicitly as regards the Zadar declaration. Other statements concerning, for example, pilgrimages, had essentially been of a pastoral nature, and designed to ensure that the genuine needs of pilgrims were taken care of. It seemed that some extraordinary supernatural facts about Medjugorje were going to have to suddenly emerge if the Commission was to overturn the previously established ecclesial positions.

23
Medjugorje and the Cult Mentality

CARITAS OF BIRMINGHAM A MEDJUGORJE CULT?

If the Church makes a final judgment on Medjugorje which is negative—definitely stating that it is not supernatural—it is to be hoped that most Catholics who support it will respect the Church's position. However, of the millions of supporters around the world, if only a tiny percentage of these reject such as decision, there is the real danger of a breakaway movement establishing itself. What if priests, or some of the local Medjugorje Franciscans, were to get involved with such a group? These are real dangers and this is the prize which the devil is no doubt doing his utmost to achieve.

And in fact, at least one group has adopted an openly "schismatic" attitude to Medjugorje, that is, Caritas of Birmingham, the well-known Medjugorje group in Alabama, although this stance has been repudiated by some of the more "official" Medjugorje organizations. The "Medjugorje WebSite" (www.medjugorje.ws) has a whole series of people and groups lining up to criticize Caritas, under the heading: "Keep extreme caution or totally avoid anything from this person, his organization and their websites." Underneath this is a sub-heading stating: "The people who live in Medjugorje, especially most of the visionaries, the guides and the priests, warn to stay away from Caritas of Birmingham. 'Cult' is a word that often comes up."

Fr Svetozar Kraljevic is then quoted, in a letter dated October 2000, as saying:

> Dear brothers and sisters, Here in Medjugorje, in the name of the priests who are working in the parish with pilgrims who are coming from all over the world, I express my deep concern for the organization called CARITAS from Birmingham, Alabama. It appears that the organization does not follow good practice of Church discipline as well as the discipline of its members in regard to their ways in which they are organized within. We are afraid that there might be elements of a lack of respect for family relationships, mutual respect, respect for the church authority, respect for the families where the members come from, respect for property

of family members who are there now and those who were there and left the community.

Beneath this, *EWTN* is listed as an organization disapproving of Caritas, and then there are whole series of links to documents accusing Caritas of being a cult-like operation, with testimonies from individuals, plus news stories detailing court cases involving it. There is even a letter from Denis Nolan, dated 25 November 2000, expressing concern about Caritas.[1]

One ex-member of Caritas is quoted as saying:

> Caritas of Birmingham, under the sole dictates of Terry Colafrancesco has developed a set of doctrines exclusively for itself. In many cases, these "doctrines" are in direct conflict with the teachings of the Roman Catholic Church. In light of this, Caritas can be seen as an isolated cult outside Catholicism.[2]

The site also features information from the International Cultic Studies Association (ICSA), formerly the American Family Foundation, which states:

> At the May 2001 American Family Foundation Conference in Newark, New Jersey, several ex-members of Caritas of Birmingham offered their stories to a distinguished panel of psychologists and cult exit counselors. It was the overwhelming opinion of the panel that the leader of Caritas of Birmingham, Terry Colafrancesco (self-styled "A Friend of Medjugorje"), fits the profile of a cult leader, much the same as David Koresh and Jim Jones were leaders of their groups. There are several factors that determine whether a group can be classified as a true cult.

In support of this assertion, the site then listed various qualities which qualify a group to be regarded as a cult, including unquestioning commitment to the leader, excessive control by the leader over many aspects of member's lives, and elitist claims that the group/leader have a special mission to save humanity. These points, and more, are then supported by various testimonies from ex-members of Caritas.[3]

So this apparently isn't a problem which developed recently, but has been going on for many years. We have to ask then, if Caritas has been plagued by these problems, why the "Gospa" didn't tell the visionary Marija Pavlovic-Lunetti — who was at least at one time a frequent visitor to Caritas — that it was a cult-like organization, or that she should have severed her connections with Colafrancesco?

Far from this being the case though, on the Caritas website there is an explicit claim that the organization owes its renewed impetus to her:

> We, as a people who make up Caritas, were directed, directly by a message from Our Lady given through Marija, the visionary, on May 31, 1995, to: "... get as many hearts as you can close to my heart and lead them to God, to a way of salvation..." This was a message given specifically for the Community of Caritas with only Marija and Caritas' founder, A Friend of Medjugorje, present. It was clear that Our Lady gave it specifically for him and the Caritas Community.

Colafrancesco goes on to apparently describe himself as one of the "instruments who have been designated as such by the Queen of Heaven Herself," and one of the Caritas websites, medjugorje.com, still features the latest messages from Marija.[4]

CARITAS A MAJOR MEDJUGORJE ORGANIZATION

Caritas of Birmingham is not a small-scale operation: it is run from the 35,000-square-foot "Tabernacle of Our Lady's Messages" building, which was purpose-built for spreading information about Medjugorje. It is on three floors, with the first floor being a printing facility, the second a shipping department and offices, and the third a retreat center, with chapels on each floor.[5]

According to Colafrancesco's own website, Caritas is "one of the largest non-profit organizations in the State of Alabama," while for a story in the *Birmingham News* dating from 2011, reporter Greg Garrison interviewed Colafrancesco, and reported:

> Caritas has just spent more than $8 million on expansion at its main building... The four-story [sic] Tabernacle of Our Lady's Messages contains a massive publishing operation that produces 500,000 booklets a week sent worldwide to promote the visions. "We're getting ready for a huge evangelization of the whole world," said Colafrancesco, who writes many of the booklets under his pen name, "A Friend of Medjugorje." Colafrancesco... pointed out a new $2.2 million binding machine churning out booklets. "We pay as we go," he said. "We don't borrow money." Despite the recession, annual donations to Caritas have tripled from a few years ago, to between $3 million and $4 million.[6]

Apart from this massive publishing operation, and its website, Medjugorje.com, Caritas also has a webcast, *Radio WAVE*, hosted by Colafrancesco, which focuses particularly on discussing the alleged messages given to Mirjana and Marija.[7] Caritas also runs pilgrimages to Medjugorje, through its "BVM Pilgrimages" arm. The site claims that: "BVM Pilgrimages is one of the longest running pilgrimage organizations for Medjugorje from the Americas and many other countries, having brought thousands of pilgrims to Medjugorje."[8]

Caritas also runs "Prayer Gatherings" attracting thousands of pilgrims; and in the past, as indicated, Medjugorje visionary Marija has been the star attraction at some of these gatherings, with claims that she had "apparitions" of the "Gospa" in the "apparition Field" and the "apparition Bedroom."[9]

According to the *Birmingham News* report, "Caritas is also a community of families with about 55 residents, who do daily prayers and chores on the farm and work in the printing operation." But echoing the concerns expressed on the Medjugorje WebSite, there are accusations that all is not well: "Some ex-residents of Caritas have left in anger and launched Internet attacks saying they were required to give up possessions and live in trailers while Colafrancesco lived extravagantly, exerted undue control over their lives and children and pressed them into unpaid labor."

Colafrancesco didn't specifically deny these claims, but did say this about these criticisms: "We don't respond to it, we don't want people who don't want to be here."[10]

CARITAS AND THE CHURCH

The local Ordinary, Bishop Robert Baker, did not allow priests to say Mass at Caritas, but apparently Colafrancesco, at that time, didn't "worry about church approval," and actually stated: "Our Lady does not have time to go through commissions for these messages and secrets. This is above that right now. It's for the whole world."[11]

But there is rather a big problem with that position. Here we have the head of an organization, stating he "doesn't worry about church approval" of Medjugorje. But where does that leave the visionary Marija? She is allegedly seeing the Blessed Virgin every day — but would the real Blessed Virgin appear on premises where the organizer has adopted such a position?

And these developments have even more significance, since they seem to indicate there was a division amongst the visionaries. If we look again at the sub-heading on the "Medjugorje WebSite" we can see a significant admission: "The people who live in Medjugorje, especially *most* of the visionaries, the guides and the priests, warn to stay away from Caritas of Birmingham. 'Cult' is a word that often comes up."[12]

Note that word "most" — they couldn't say "all," because clearly Marija was a Caritas supporter. Surely, though, this is a major embarrassment to the cause of Medjugorje? Ivan, Vicka and Marija were claiming daily visions — in other words they were saying that the same Blessed Virgin Mary is continually appearing to all three of them — but those same visionaries are divided over Caritas in a fundamental way. Why didn't the "Gospa" intervene to put them right on whether or not Caritas is an acceptable Medjugorje organization?

THE DANGER OF A BREAKAWAY CHURCH

Based on what Colafrancesco said about not worrying about Church approval for Medjugorje, and the size and scope of the Caritas organization, plus the support of Marija, it is clear that Caritas is unlikely to accept any negative decision about Medjugorje handed down by the Church. Thus it is very possible that some Caritas supporters could well end up estranged from the Church, and create their own parallel "Medjugorje Church."

This, in a nutshell, is the great tragedy of Medjugorje. If it had never been propagandized in the way it has, and Fatima had been properly promoted, then all those people with genuine Marian devotion would have gravitated towards Fatima, including individuals such as Terry Colafrancesco, whose energies could have been put to far better use, and within the Church. And it becomes even worse if we consider the tens of thousands, if not millions, of Medjugorje supporters who ought to have been behind Fatima, but instead have applied themselves to propagating the very dubious claims of the Medjugorje visionaries.

Fr Svetozar Kraljevic, who, in 2011, was running pilgrim-funded social projects in Medjugorje, was quoted as saying, "We are all a commission," in a Catholic News Service story. This was taken to be a reference to the "Magisterium" provided by "the local Franciscans, the townspeople and the pilgrims, who by their presence continue to study the claims about Mary's appearance in Medjugorje and to judge the authenticity of the messages the young people say she gives them."

No mention of the bishop of Mostar, the Bishops' conference of Bosnia-Hercegovina, the International Commission, the CDF or the pope here—apparently Fr Kraljevic, the local Franciscans, the townspeople and the pilgrims were a "commission unto themselves."

This attitude seemed to be backed up by one pilgrim who said, "Whether the Vatican says it's true or not really doesn't matter. What counts is what you believe inside, and I believe people need this." These sentiments probably represent those of a sizable number of Medjugorje supporters. But another local Franciscan, Fr Danko Perutina told a group of pilgrims that there had been numerous investigations into the Medjugorje visionaries' claims and that they must accept whatever the Vatican commission decides.[13]

So this could have indicated a possible split among the Medjugorje Franciscans themselves at the time, with some of the old guard, such as Fr Kraljevic, being unwilling to accept the possibility that Medjugorje might not be approved, while some of the younger Franciscans, such as Fr Perutina, were possibly adopting a more pragmatic approach.

24
The Importance of Fatima

POPE JOHN PAUL II AND THE CONSECRATION OF 1984

Pope John Paul II's formal association with Fatima stems from the attempt made on his life in Rome on 13 May 1981, the anniversary of the first apparition at Fatima, when he was shot in St Peter's square. Providentially, the bullet wounds were not fatal, and while in hospital recovering, the pope apparently reviewed all the documents on Fatima. He certainly felt that the Blessed Virgin's intercession had saved his life, and his reading convinced him that the consecration of Russia to Mary's Immaculate Heart was an absolute necessity if the world was to be saved from war and atheism.

Consequently, on 13 May 1982, exactly a year after the assassination attempt, Pope John Paul II went to Fatima, both to thank Our Lady for saving his life, and also to carry out a public act of consecration of the whole world, including Russia, to her Immaculate Heart. After this was accomplished, however, it became apparent that many of the world's bishops had not been informed in time. Thus, this consecration had not fulfilled the condition of collegiality asked for by Mary at Fatima, that is, that the pope, in union with the bishops of the world, should consecrate Russia to her Immaculate Heart. Sr Lucia, still living in the Carmelite convent at Coimbra, apparently later made this known to the Apostolic Nuncio in Portugal.

Interestingly, in this 1982 consecration, John Paul II specifically described Fatima as a place "chosen" by the Blessed Virgin, thus indicating official confirmation of its status and intimating that we are to understand it as the major "prophecy" of modern times, a prophecy whose urgent message cannot be ignored. During his homily, the pope made the following remarks:

> If the Church has accepted the message of Fatima, it is above all because that message contains a truth and a call whose basic content is the truth and call of the Gospel itself. "Repent, and believe in the Gospel" (Mk 1:15). These are the first words of the Messiah addressed to humanity. The message of Fatima is, in its basic nucleus, a call to conversion and repentance, as in the Gospel. This call was uttered at the

beginning of the twentieth century, and it was thus addressed particularly to this present century. The Lady of the message seems to have read with special insight the "signs of the times," the signs of our time.

John Paul II also spoke of Fatima during this homily in these significant terms: "The appeal of the Lady of the message of Fatima is so deeply rooted in the Gospel and the whole of Tradition that the Church feels that the message imposes a commitment on her."

The pope decided to renew the consecration in March 1984, with letters being sent to all the world's bishops in good time, including the Orthodox, asking them to join him in this action. On 25 March 1984, the feast of the Annunciation, Pope John Paul II duly renewed the act of consecration in St Peter's Basilica in Rome, before the statue of Our Lady from the site of the apparitions at Fatima, which was specially brought from the shrine for the occasion. Although the text used did not mention Russia, the pope did specifically recall the acts of consecration made by Pope Pius XII in 1942 and 1952, the latter being essentially concerned with Russia. It also appears that John Paul II paused during the ceremony, and, according to the then bishop of Leiria-Fatima, Alberto Cosme do Amaral, quietly included Russia in the consecration. This action is understandable, given the delicate political situation, and, it has been argued, with the understanding that God was leaving the pope, as head of the Church on earth, to decide the precise form the act should take.

Certainly, Russia was in the pope's mind in the following reference: "In a special way we entrust and consecrate to you those individuals and nations which particularly need to be thus entrusted and consecrated." Although not all the world's bishops joined in the act of consecration, it appears that a "moral totality" did, thus satisfying the request of the Blessed Virgin. Following this consecration, Sr Lucia was again visited by the Apostolic Nuncio; this time, she told him that the consecration of Russia had indeed been accomplished, and that God had accepted it. Thus, after nearly seventy years, the act of collegial consecration was finally accomplished.[1]

Apparently the following day, 26 March, Pope John Paul II posed a question about the consecration, and was told by Fr Luis Kondor, the vice-postulator for the causes of Jacinta and Francisco, that he had spoken to Sr Lucia before coming to Rome, and that she had said that the Holy Father would do all that was within his power, an answer which satisfied the pope. As Fr Andrew Apostoli notes: "The Pope was happy with this reply. After all, if the Pope did all he could and it was not enough, then the consecration could never be made by him or any other pope."

Sr Lucia later confirmed in writing that the consecration had been properly done, in the way that Our Lady wanted, saying that when people asked her, she said: "'Yes.' From that time, it is made!" And there are several further instances of her stating that the consecration had been carried out correctly.[2]

THE COLLAPSE OF COMMUNISM

It's hard not to see a connection between the consecration made in 1984 and the rise to power of Mikhail Gorbachev in Russia, in March 1985, when he became General Secretary of the Communist Party. Realizing the dangerous situation of the Soviet Union, he began a program of reform based on restructuring and openness. This led to greater democratization in Russia, a more tolerant attitude to religious believers and fruitful arms reductions talks with the United States. It also led, ultimately, to the collapse of Communism in Russia and Eastern Europe.

This, however, was for the future; and, from 1988, Gorbachev was able to introduce major political changes, including a democratic Russian parliament. At the same time, he began to ease restrictions on religion, on the pragmatic basis that the country needed the energies of believers if it was to rebuild itself. This was also probably an acknowledgment of the fact that Communism had been unable to crush Christianity, despite exercising total control over it for more than seventy years. Meanwhile, popular unrest in Eastern Europe, in protest of Communist rule, led to the end of the Warsaw Pact, in 1989, as Gorbachev made it clear that Russia was not going to intervene to repress emerging democratic movements in countries such as Poland. In December 1989, President Gorbachev met the pope at the Vatican, surely an unbelievable scenario just a few years previously.[3]

FURTHER FATIMA DEVELOPMENTS

Fatima had received further papal support when, earlier in the year, on 13 May 1989, Pope John Paul II had declared Jacinta and Francisco "venerable," the first stage in the canonization process. In May 1991, a decade after the assassination attempt, the pope returned to Fatima to give thanks to the Blessed Virgin for the marvelous fruits of the 1984 consecration and for saving his life. But he warned that although Marxism was losing its influence, there was a danger of its being replaced by another form of atheism equally hostile to Christian morality, a reference to Western materialism. Later in the same year, in August 1991, an attempted coup against President Gorbachev failed, and the Soviet Union as a belligerent world power began to collapse. Given Russia's military might, this dissolution was far more peaceful than had been feared.

These massive changes in Russia and Eastern Europe support the view that the consecration of 1984 was carried out largely in accordance with Our Lady's wishes. The Blessed Virgin promised the conversion of Russia if her wishes were complied with, but she did not say that this would happen overnight. Seventy years of Communist misrule could not be put right in a few years. The conversion of the Roman Empire took centuries to fully accomplish, although the decisive blow was struck by the Emperor Constantine early in the fourth century at the battle of the Milvian Bridge—but only after three hundred years of persecution for the early Church.

If it took that long to convert the Roman Empire—despite the tremendous graces poured out as a result of Christ's crucifixion and resurrection, to say nothing of all the sufferings of the early martyrs—then there is surely a need to be cautious about demanding quick results with regard to Russia's conversion.

THE CONVERSION OF RUSSIA

Comparisons have been made between what happened in Mexico after Guadalupe in 1531, when there were mass conversions to Catholicism within a few decades, and the lack of a like process in Russia in recent years. But this is to lose sight of the fact that the apparitions, and the miraculous *Tilma* which resulted from them, were common knowledge in the country. In addition, the evangelization of Mexico was greatly helped by the presence of Franciscan missionaries who were able to minister to the people. Regarding Fatima, too, the apparitions, and in particular the miracle of the sun, were common knowledge in Portugal, and it was essentially a matter of reinvigorating the Catholic sentiments of the people, who had been adversely affected by vicious governmental persecution.

But in the case of Russia, the situation is completely different.

Not only was there no great public miracle in Russia either in 1917 or 1984, but in addition the Catholic population of Russia is tiny, and equally crucially, there are very few priests or missionaries available for evangelization.

There is no case in history of a large country being converted without either some sort of miraculous intervention in the country itself, or intense missionary activity—with the latter preferably accompanied by miracles. Neither of these conditions was or is present in Russia, and so its conversion looks like being a long drawn-out process, one which will require either a much larger Catholic presence in the country, or the renewal/conversion of the Russian Orthodox Church.

And it has to be remembered that Communism did a huge amount of damage to religion, both in terms of the number of churches destroyed and, more crucially, regarding the terrible persecutions which believers had to endure, as well as the pervasive atheistic indoctrination to which they were subject for nearly three quarters of a century. It is clearly impossible that the destructive legacy of such a regime could be undone in a short space of time, especially given that the damage was inflicted over two or three generations.

There is still much to be done, but it is difficult to argue that there have not been huge changes in Russia in recent years. Russian society is by no means tranquil, there is a great deal of corruption and an increasingly authoritarian government, but at least the vicious persecutions of the past are over, and there are some signs of hope for a religious renewal. In particular, there has been a noticeable thaw in relations between the Catholic and Russian Orthodox Churches in recent years, during the pontificates of Popes Benedict XVI and Francis. Clearly, though, the conversion of Russia does seem some way off, which only underlines the need for the greater promotion of, and participation in, the Five First Saturdays devotion on the part of Catholics generally.[4]

FATIMA AND MEDJUGORJE CONTRASTED

It is clear, then, that the contrast between Fatima and Medjugorje could hardly be greater. As we have seen, the course of the Fatima apparitions from May to October 1917 is radically different from the early events at Medjugorje. Portugal was completely transformed as its people lived out the message of Fatima, while by contrast, following the alleged visions at Medjugorje, there was no lasting spiritual revival amongst the people living in the surrounding areas. Indeed, it could be said that those followers of Medjugorje who became embroiled in the cause of Croatian nationalism were a strong contributory factor in the violence which erupted during the 1990s.

In particular, elements from the July 1917 Fatima secret have been shown to have come true over the course of time, in contrast to the supposed "secrets" of Medjugorje, while the Fatima miracle of the sun, in October 1917, dwarfs any other claimed "miracles" at Medjugorje.

The later apparitions to Sr Lucia, which developed the important link between the consecration of Russia and the Five First Saturdays devotion, likewise indicate how crucial this devotion is, and why it is necessary that it should become much better known throughout the Church. Unfortunately, one of the reasons this is not happening is the popularity of Medjugorje, which has little practical emphasis on this important devotion.

The consecrations of Portugal to Mary's Immaculate Heart by the Portuguese bishops during the 1930s were instrumental in keeping the country out of both the Spanish Civil War and World War II, whereas Medjugorje was unable to prevent Yugoslavia, during the early 90s, from becoming the scene of the bitterest fighting in Europe for decades.

Finally, the profound power and impact of Fatima is shown by the fact that the consecration of the world to Mary's Immaculate Heart made by Pius XII in 1942 was able to shorten the Second World War, while Pope John Paul II's collegial consecration in 1984 led to the virtually peaceful collapse of Communism in Russia and Eastern Europe.

What can Medjugorje possibly offer in comparison with this unique association of Fatima with the papacy, which has been of such profound significance for the world?

SOME QUESTIONS FOR MEDJUGORJE SUPPORTERS

Thus, supporters of Medjugorje have to ask themselves some crucial questions.

Why, for example, having warned about the "errors of Russia" at Fatima, did the "Gospa" at Medjugorje not warn about the threat presented by Communism to the salvation of the local people? Or why, if Mary really was appearing at Medjugorje, did it take the pope's consecration to Our Lady of Fatima in 1984 to bring an end to the Communist persecution of the Church in Eastern Europe? If

Medjugorje was the continuation and fulfillment of Fatima—"the last apparition on earth"—why didn't the "Gospa" perform a great public miracle there, like the miracle of the sun at Fatima?

But if there was no great miracle at Medjugorje, the results of the pope's act of consecration to the Immaculate Heart of Mary in 1984, that is, the virtually peaceful collapse of Communism in the Soviet Union and Eastern Europe, are quite plain. There has been a great burgeoning of vocations in the countries of Central and Eastern Europe, where there are many thousands of seminarians studying for ordination. Tragically, in the West, where there has been minimal compliance with the requests of the Blessed Virgin at Fatima, congregations are falling and seminaries are being closed because vocations are drying up.

So how can we explain the ongoing crisis of faith in the Church in the West, if Mary did in truth begin to appear at Medjugorje as recently as 1981, and Medjugorje is supposed to have far surpassed Fatima in its efficacy and power? Millions of people have visited Medjugorje and a vast amount of information about it has been circulated throughout the Church, but where are the concrete results of all this activity which stand comparison with those effected in Portugal after 1917, and in Eastern Europe after Pope John Paul II's consecration in 1984?

In sum, why is Medjugorje still a subject of ongoing doubt, dispute and disagreement in the Church, whereas, as detailed above, Fatima brought about a marvelous and harmonious spiritual renewal of the Church throughout Portugal, and today Our Lady's message is welcomed in many dioceses throughout the world where it contributes to the authentic spiritual renewal of many Catholics? These are some of the questions which any convinced supporter of Medjugorje needs to answer, but meanwhile it is clear that the spiritual effects of Medjugorje have been minimal in comparison with the great blessings bestowed on the Church through the message of Fatima.

MORE RECENT FATIMA DEVELOPMENTS

In 1999, it was announced that Pope John Paul would beatify Francisco and Jacinta in Fatima on 13 May 2000. On the evening of 12 May, a crowd of 650,000 greeted the Holy Father as he arrived at the Cova da Iria on his third pilgrimage to the shrine as pope. The next morning, he returned to the Cova for the Beatification Mass, stopping off at the Basilica to meet privately with 93-year-old Sr Lucia. During the Mass, the Holy Father read out the text of beatification, which allowed for the celebration of a local feast for the two children on 20 February each year, the anniversary of Jacinta's death in 1920. And as we will see, both Popes Benedict and Francis have continued the close association of the modern papacy with Fatima, with the latter canonizing the two seers in May 2017 at the Portuguese shrine during the centenary year of the apparitions.

Towards the end of the Mass, Cardinal Sodano, the then Vatican Secretary of State, unexpectedly announced, at the pope's behest, the imminent publication of the third part of the secret of Fatima along with an official commentary. He revealed, too, that part of the text dealt with the Holy Father, and described it as a "prophetic vision similar to those found in Sacred Scripture," which had to be interpreted in symbolic terms. He further described the contents as being concerned with the persecutions suffered by the Church and successive popes during the twentieth century, and particularly that "the bishop clothed in white," whom the children witnessed being shot, was Pope John Paul II. A little over a month later, the full text of the third part of the secret, originally set down by Sr Lucia in the 1940s, was released by the Holy See, along with a commentary by Cardinal Joseph Ratzinger.

The importance of Fatima in the life of the Church was further confirmed by the act of the Polish pope, on 8 October 2000, of entrusting the third millennium to Mary. The statue of Our Lady of Fatima at the Capelinha was again specially brought to Rome for the occasion, a move of particular symbolic importance in the Jubilee Year. As in the case of the 1984 collegial consecration, all the bishops of the world were encouraged to join in this new act of entrustment. Thus these developments, the beatification — and later canonization — of Francisco and Jacinta, the revelation of the third part of the secret, and the dedication of the third millennium to Our Lady, indicate the crucial importance of the message of Fatima in the life of the Church.

It is clear that this message was not confined to one period of time, but rather has continued to develop over the course of the twentieth century; indeed, it is not complete yet, and further developments can be expected. In short, the implications of the message of Fatima still have to be taken up by the Church as a whole in the twenty-first century.[5]

POPE BENEDICT IN FATIMA

This was apparent in the remarks of Pope Benedict XVI, during his journey, in May 2010, to Fatima, for the tenth anniversary celebrations of the beatification of Jacinta and Francisco Marto. Even on the flight to Lisbon, on 11 May 2010, the pope was at pains to emphasize the crucial importance of Fatima for the Church: "I want to say how happy I am to be going to Fatima, to pray before Our Lady of Fatima. For us, Fatima ... has *a message for the entire world* and touches history here and now, and sheds light on this history."

And in relation to the third part of the secret of Fatima, he went on to say: "Beyond [the] great vision of the suffering of the Pope, which we can in the first place refer to Pope John Paul II, an indication is given of realities involving *the future of the Church*, which are gradually taking shape and becoming evident."[6]

As part of his homily during Mass at Fatima, on 13 May, the 93rd anniversary of the first apparition of Our Lady, he said: "I have come to Fatima, because today the pilgrim Church, willed by her Son as the instrument of evangelization and the sacrament of salvation, *converges upon this place*." Further on he said: "We would be mistaken to think that Fatima's prophetic mission is complete," before concluding, "May the seven years which separate us from the centenary of the apparitions hasten the fulfillment of the prophecy of the triumph of the Immaculate Heart of Mary, to the glory of the Most Holy Trinity."[7]

Note that Pope Benedict spoke of Fatima being a "message for the entire world," one involving "the future of the Church" — contrast this fulsome support with the hesitant and perplexed attitude of the Church towards Medjugorje over so many years.

In November 2010, a book-length interview with Pope Benedict, conducted by the journalist Peter Seewald, was published. In this, the pope dealt with questions from Seewald, some on quite controversial issues. The book included a chapter entitled "Mary and the Message of Fatima," and in this the pope set out his thoughts not only on Fatima but also on the importance of Marian devotion for the Church generally. For instance, in speaking of Our Lady, he remarks: "Throughout history, God has never ceased to use her as the light through which he leads us to himself," using Guadalupe in Mexico, and his recent experiences during his pilgrimage to Fatima earlier in the year, to illustrate this point.[8]

MEDJUGORJE A CONTINUATION OF FATIMA?

Despite this lack of official ecclesial enthusiasm for Medjugorje, some of its supporters have claimed that it is a continuation of Fatima.[9] But if this is the case why has there been virtually no mention of Mary's Immaculate Heart in the messages? This was the devotion which God wished to establish in the world, as Our Lady told Lucia at Fatima on 13 July 1917. The reality is that there can only be one continuation of Fatima, and that is voluntary compliance with Our Lady's requests, according to the teaching, acts and example of Popes John Paul II, Benedict XVI and now Francis — until the world experiences the triumph of her Immaculate Heart, which she promised would finally come.

It is certainly true that the Medjugorje messages do give a cursory mention to some of the more important themes from Fatima, including the necessity of saying the rosary. But essentials like this are buried in the sheer profusion of questionable, banal and endlessly repetitive messages. Thus, it is quite incorrect to regard Medjugorje as having any sort of genuine link with Fatima.

In illustration of this, a Dutch woman, Mrs. Hildegard Alles, concerned about reports that Sr Lucia was receiving messages from Our Lady about what she was allegedly doing in Medjugorje, wrote to the Bishop of Fatima, in 1998, requesting a clarification. This letter was passed on to Dr Luciano Cristino, the director of SESDI [Department of Studies and Publications] at the Fatima Sanctuary, who replied saying that such an allegation was "completely false."

This point, that Sr Lucia was not receiving any heavenly revelations, whether regarding Medjugorje or otherwise, was further emphasized in December 2001. It was then revealed, in connection with the release of the third part of the Fatima secret, that Sr Lucia had met then Archbishop Bertone, the secretary of the Congregation for the Doctrine of the Faith, and amongst other things had said. "If I had received new revelations, I would have told no one, but I would have communicated them directly to the Holy Father."[10]

However, it does seem that sometime after the collegial consecration of 1984, Sr Lucia *did* receive a direct revelation from heaven confirming that the consecration had been carried out correctly. In an interview, the archbishop, now a cardinal, spoke of an "apparition in which the Virgin showed Sr Lucia that she accepted and was pleased with John Paul II's consecration of the world and Russia to her Immaculate Heart." Indeed, in the 2001 meeting referred to above, Sr Lucia herself stated: "I have already said that the consecration that Our Lady desired was accomplished in 1984, and was accepted in heaven."

The cardinal also reaffirmed the point—questioned by some—that the complete text of the third part of the secret of Fatima had been revealed in 2000, saying: "I completely deny that the full secret has not been revealed.... I brought the text to Sr. Lucia... and [she] exclaimed, 'This is my text, these are my pages, this is my envelope and this is my writing. There is nothing else.'"[11] And this was also the position of Cardinal Ratzinger in his theological commentary, where he quite categorically states that for the first time the third part of the secret is "being published in its entirety."[12]

The following Medjugorje message, which explicitly mentions Fatima, is dated 25 August 1991: "Dear Children... I want you to make sacrifices for nine days so that, with your help, all that I mean to carry out through the secrets which I started giving at Fatima may be achieved.... Thank you for your response to my call!"[13]

This message, of itself, is a strong indication that Medjugorje is false. We just don't find any explicit reference to the other apparitions in the approved, genuine, historical Marian apparitions.

THE FIVE FIRST SATURDAYS DEVOTION

It is important to note that as early as the July 1917 apparition at Fatima, the Blessed Virgin was jointly linking the consecration of Russia to Mary's Immaculate Heart and the Five First Saturdays devotion of reparation, as being amongst the means by which manifold evils would be undone and peace brought to the world. Having mentioned all the problems facing the Church in the world, she explicitly said: "To prevent this, I shall come to ask for the consecration of Russia to my Immaculate Heart, and the Communion of Reparation on the First Saturdays."

We have looked at the incident in which the Blessed Virgin appeared to Sr Lucia in December 1925, and spoke to her about the Five First Saturdays devotion, which involved her promise to:

> assist at the hour of death, with all the graces necessary for salvation, all those who, on the first Saturday of five consecutive months, go to confession and receive Holy Communion, recite five decades of the Rosary and keep me company for

a quarter of an hour while meditating on the mysteries of the Rosary, with the intention of making reparation to me.

There is also the letter Sr Lucia wrote to her confessor in 1930, in which she said:

> If I am not mistaken, Our Dear Lord God promises to end the persecution of Russia, if the Holy Father condescends to make, and likewise ordains the Bishops of the Catholic World to make, a solemn and public act of reparation and consecration of Russia to the Most Holy Hearts of Jesus and Mary. In response to the ending of this persecution, His Holiness is to promise to approve of and recommend the practice of the already mentioned devotion of reparation.[14]

It is extremely important to note the explicit link between the consecration of Russia and the Five First Saturdays devotion, but it does not seem as though many in the Church are really aware of this. The active persecution of Christians in Russia is over now, although no one is pretending that life there is easy, or that there are not human rights abuses — but as a state-sponsored activity, such persecution has ceased.

It seems, then, that the full conversion of Russia promised by Our Lady may well not happen until this First Saturdays devotion of reparation is widely known and practiced. Pope St John Paul II gave us an example by fulfilling Our Lady's requests to a quite unprecedented extent, and now it would appear that a response is required from the whole Church.

If the Five First Saturdays devotion was properly implemented throughout the Church, with full backing from the pope and all the bishops, it would have a profound impact. Not only would it be a great encouragement to frequent reception of the sacraments, the primary sources of grace, but it would also give Catholics an assurance of eternal salvation through its promise of the grace of final perseverance. Great graces that are being held in store for the Church by God would undoubtedly be released *if* large numbers of Catholics really took this devotion to heart. Would it be too much to believe that, just as the collegial consecration led to the downfall of Communism in Russia, so also the widespread implementation of the First Saturdays devotion could lead to both the conversion of Russia, *and* a great revival for the Church in the West?

Whereas the Five First Saturdays devotion is particularly intended to call for a response from priests and laity, the collegial consecration was specifically directed to the pope and the bishops in union with him. Both aspects together, then, invite the whole people of God to play their respective parts in fulfilling the requests of Our Lady of Fatima.

Thus, the Five First Saturdays devotion of reparation is one of the "missing links" in the message of Fatima, and its adoption would appear to be far more important than has hitherto been realized. In fact, what is needed is nothing less than a worldwide movement to promote this devotion, along the lines of the Divine Mercy movement. But instead of this happening, the energies of large numbers of well-meaning Catholics have been diverted into promoting Medjugorje, which has thus become a serious stumbling block to a genuine renewal of the whole Church.

During the June 1917 apparition, Lucia was told by Our Lady that unlike Jacinta and Francisco, who would shortly be going to heaven, she would have to remain behind for "some time to come." The reason for this was that Jesus wanted to establish devotion to Mary's Immaculate Heart throughout the world. The Blessed Mother then continued: "I promise salvation to whoever embraces it; these souls will be dear to God, like flowers put by me to adorn his throne."

This promise of salvation is for everyone without exception, and as indicated above the Five First Saturdays devotion forms an integral part of the Fatima message, one which the Church, principally in the persons of her priests and laity, now needs to enthusiastically accept and promote. If this is done, then we can expect a new Marian era and a wonderful rebirth for the Church, all of which will eventually lead to the long-awaited triumph of Mary's Immaculate Heart.

25
Medjugorje Developments from 2011

THE WORK OF THE COMMISSION

As detailed in Chapter 22, "The Vatican and Medjugorje," an official international commission to investigate Medjugorje was authorized by Pope Benedict XVI in March 2010, under the auspices of the Congregation for the Doctrine of the Faith, and led by Cardinal Camillo Ruini. The work of the Commission continued until it issued a report in early 2014, and this was then passed on to the CDF for evaluation.

Various reports were in circulation in 2011 to the effect that the Medjugorje visionaries were to be interviewed by the International Commission, and in May 2011, the Croatian newspaper *Vecernji list*, quoting unnamed sources, published an article which claimed that they would testify before the International Commission investigating Medjugorje the following month. According to the paper, the Commission had previously interviewed Bishop Ratko Peric of Mostar-Duvno, and the Provincial of the Herzegovina Franciscans, Fr Ivan Sesar, although it was not known if the visionaries would undergo any new scientific tests.[1]

The following month, on 14 June, the Swiss-based International Catholic Press Agency provided information about a short interview in which Cardinal Ruini was asked if an official evaluation of Medjugorje could be expected soon, given the proximity of the thirtieth anniversary of the beginning of the alleged events later in the month. He replied that the International Commission was "still far from being able to publish an official judgment" concerning the alleged Marian apparitions at Medjugorje, and he also emphasized the duty of the Commission to keep its work confidential.[2]

Later that month, the Italian writer Vittorio Messori, who famously interviewed the then Cardinal Ratzinger in the 1980s — with the resultant text published as *The Ratzinger Report* (*Rapporto sulla fede*) — wrote an article for the Italian newspaper *Corriere della Sera*, in which he spoke of the "dilemma of Medjugorje." According to Messori there were two possibilities: that the International Commission could rule — against the position of the local Ordinary — that the visions are authentic, with the result being a "catastrophe" for the pastoral authority of the bishop of Mostar-Duvno; or alternatively, the Commission could rule that the alleged visions are not authentic, but rather due to deceit, misunderstanding or a deliberate hoax, resulting in a pastoral catastrophe for millions of sincere but misled believers in the visions.[3]

But as Medjugorje commentator Louis Bélanger points out, the essentially negative verdicts of preceding Medjugorje Commissions, which have been detailed in this book, that is, verdicts of *non constat de supernaturalitate* ("the supernaturality has not been proven"), argue against Messori's contentions. Bélanger quotes from the dissertation by canon lawyer Fr Andrew Kingham, "The Norms for Judging Alleged Apparitions and Private Revelations," as follows:

> The verdict of "non constat de supernaturalitate" can be manipulated by supporters of alleged apparitions, especially in protracted occurrences, to suggest that the diocesan bishop is unable to give an affirmative judgment until the phenomena cease or when a prophecy is fulfilled. *Therefore, in order to give greater clarity, the meaning of "non constat de supernaturalitate" should be understood to mean a negative decision.* That is, the phenomenon is not supernatural because no evidence has been found to prove the case. Given the facts of the case brought before the commission of investigation, if it is impossible to give an affirmative judgment, then the case should be closed with a verdict of "non constat de supernaturalitate."[4]

And as Bélanger further points out, if Messori is right regarding his first contention, and a positive verdict is returned, then not only will the pastoral authority of the local bishops have been adversely affected, but also that of all those involved in the various commissions, including experts, priests, bishops, archbishops, cardinals, the Congregation for the Doctrine of the Faith and even Pope Benedict XVI himself. That would mean that all those individuals, over a period of many years, had failed to recognize an authentic apparition of the Blessed Virgin, which is surely, as Bélanger says, "highly improbable," if not a "practical impossibility."

Consequently, Messori's dilemma disappears, and what remains is the necessity for the Church to proclaim the truth about Medjugorje, even if this does involve acknowledging that many millions of sincere believers have indeed been misled over the alleged visions, and are actually the victims of a falsehood.[5]

In November 2011, Cardinal Schönborn again hosted one of the Medjugorje visionaries, Ivan Dragicevic, in his cathedral in Vienna, as part of a televised event. Dragicevic claimed that the Virgin Mary appeared at 6:40 pm, just before Mass, and blessed all those present, and also that those connected via the internet, and their religious items, had also been blessed during the vision. This event took place despite the fact that the Bishops of Bosnia-Herzegovina and Croatia do not permit any of the Medjugorje visionaries to have alleged visions on Church property.[6]

MEDJUGORJE DEVELOPMENTS IN 2012

Early in January 2012, Bishop Ratko Peric defended his predecessor, Bishop Pavao Zanic, against a renewed charge of collaborating with the Communist authorities in ex-Yugoslavia. This accusation was made by four pro-Medjugorje journalists in a book published in Croatian in 2011, entitled: *The Mystery of Medjugorje*. As we have seen in chapter 12, "Medjugorje and the Theologians," this was a charge previously made by Fr Ljudevit Rupcic, and also in the film *Gospa*; the latter in particular was refuted by the Mostar Chancery office in 1995. But as Bishop Peric pointed out on this occasion, Bishop Zanic's position on Medjugorje was consistently opposed to that of the Communists and thus such a charge was groundless.[7]

On 14 February, the Italian News Agency, ASCA, reported that the archbishop of Sarajevo, Cardinal Vinko Puljic, a member of the International Commission, had stated that the members wanted to finish their work by the end of the year, and that then the concluding report could be presented by Cardinal Ruini to Pope Benedict XVI, so he could render judgment on the case.[8]

In early December 2012, the French magazine *La Vie* ran a story claiming that the International Commission was expected to present its report to Pope Benedict by the end of the month. But a few days later, the US-based *National Catholic Register* stated that Fr Federico Lombardi, the official Vatican spokesman, had said, after speaking to Cardinal Ruini, that such speculation was "not true" and that the work of the Commission would take longer, and that it first had to give its report to the Congregation for the Doctrine of the Faith, before it could be passed on to the pope.[9]

MEDJUGORJE DEVELOPMENTS IN 2013

Cardinal Ruini gave an interview in mid-January 2013, in which he stated that the Commission still had work to do on its Medjugorje report, but that "there won't be a public declaration, because it's not the commission's duty to say anything to the public." He went on to say, "The role of the commission is to give a reasonable explanation to the Congregation for the Doctrine of the Faith, which will not be published officially."

However, in a rather sad reflection on the state of things, the cardinal also said that it was likely that the Commission's report would be "leaked." He finished by saying: "The motivation for the commission is to form an opinion and pass it along to the Congregation for the Doctrine of the Faith. They will then evaluate it and decide whether to get the Pope involved."[10]

It was also reported that later in the year, in August, there would be a pilgrimage to the Holy Land involving Medjugorje visionary Vicka Ivankovic-Mijatovic, who was scheduled to have alleged apparitions in Bethlehem, among other places.[11]

According to published reports, there were at least seventeen appearances by various Medjugorje visionaries in Italy during 2011–2012, activities which could be seen as an attempt to influence the Commission through the Italian media.

It is also perhaps worth noting that Medjugorje visionary Marija Pavlovic-Lunetti is reported to have said: "The act of forming the Commission was a positive act. The Church is often not interested in the sensations. It has its own position and is not in a hurry. It took decades until the official recognition of the shrine in Lourdes or Fatima. So it is with Medjugorje. I am convinced that the Vatican recognizes the authenticity of the apparitions, but only when they stop and when we visionaries have died."[12]

This quote is questionable, particularly regarding the fact that Pavlovic-Lunetti is mistaken in saying that it required "decades" for official recognition of Lourdes and Fatima. In fact, while it took thirteen years for Fatima to be approved, in 1930, Lourdes was approved only four years after the apparitions to St Bernadette. In other words, both were approved while at least some of their respective visionaries were still alive.

The announcement from Pope Benedict XVI, on 11 February 2013, the Feast of Our Lady of Lourdes, that he would be abdicating as pontiff came as a shock to the whole Catholic world. But it became apparent in due course that the work of the Commission would continue under his successor, Pope Francis.

PUBLICATION OF *MEDJUGORJE: THE FIRST DAYS*

In July 2013, Fr James Mulligan published another book on Medjugorje, entitled *Medjugorje: The First Days*, which consists largely of transcripts of the original tapes of the visionaries. In this he was following in the footsteps of Fr Ivo Sivric and Daria Klanac, who, as we have seen, both published their own transcripts of those conversations. In his foreword, Fr Mulligan acknowledges the work of Fr Sivric, describing his translation as "basically sound"; but he claims that Fr Sivric was hampered by a lack of understanding of some of the modern and colloquial expressions of the young visionaries. There is probably some justification for this view, but as he noted, this doesn't affect the essential validity of Fr Sivric's transcriptions.

Fr Mulligan also claimed to have had access to a larger amount of material for his transcriptions, but makes no mention of Daria Klanac's previous work, although she is credited as being one of the translators of this new work. He asserts that the transcriptions he provides point "very strongly to the authenticity of Medjugorje,"[13] but as we will see, this is very far from being the case.

If we look at how these new transcripts affect some of the points made in this book previously, then we can see that they actually strengthen them, and certainly don't contradict the arguments already made. As in the case of the differences between the Sivric and Klanac transcriptions, the differences between Fr Mulligan's transcriptions and previous ones are mainly cosmetic, although there are some instances where there are definite discrepancies, and some of these will be looked at in more detail further on.

Certainly, the new transcripts do nothing to diminish the fact, as demonstrated already in chapter 6, "Three More Days of Visions," that there were only supposed to be another three appearances of the "Gospa" to the visionaries after Tuesday, 30 June 1981, and that they were due to finish on Friday, 3 July. The text in Fr Mulligan's book states this quite explicitly, as this part of the conversation between Fr Zovko and Mirjana, who was with the other visionaries (apart from Ivan), on the evening of 30 June, makes clear:

Fr Zovko: "Please describe to me what you were talking about with the Gospa."

Mirjana: "I asked how many days will she stay with us. She said, 'Three days.'"

Fr Zovko: "More?"

Mirjana: "Three days more. That means until Friday."[14]

Likewise, in the section in chapter 6 headed "The Visionaries as Reliable Witnesses," we saw how Vicka was in fact an unreliable witness, in that in the interview she had with Fr Bubalo in 1983, she claimed that the visionaries had been "kidnapped" by the two social workers and tricked into going with them. But, as noted, this was not the case, and the visionaries had actually agreed to go with the young women.

This point, too, comes out quite clearly in the new transcripts. During the same 30 June interview, the question of this outing came up, and Fr Zovko asked about it, saying, "Who was the first who thought of going to that place?" to which the visionaries replied in unison: "We all did." Later on in the interview, Fr Zovko came back to this point asking: "Who told you to go to that other hill and try there?" to which the visionaries responded: "We did, we decided ourselves."[15]

However, there *is* a clear discrepancy between the Sivric and Mulligan versions regarding another part of the interview, when Fr Zovko was discussing with some of the visionaries the question of how many people could be expected to turn up for the next apparition. First we have the text from the Fr Sivric version.

Mirjana: "I think that a great number of people will not come. *After all, it is going to last just a few more days in the church.* Some of these who are on the hillside came to have fun or to see the people. When the Gospa comes to the church, there won't be disorder in the church anymore."[16]

Note that this dialogue reiterates the point that the apparitions are only going to last "just a few more days." Now compare this with the same dialogue in the Fr Mulligan version:

Mirjana: "I think that a large number of people will not come. *Only the true Christians will follow us to the church.* And the people up on the hill may have come to mock us, and they will go. Or perhaps they've come to see if it really is Our Lady? Here, in the church, those who do not believe will not follow."[17]

There is obviously quite a discrepancy between Fr Sivric's transcription of Mirjana's words as, "After all, it is going to last just a few more days in the church," and Fr Mulligan's: "Only the true Christians will follow us to the church."

There are many possible reasons for this, but rather than speculate, we can look at another discrepancy, this time from the interview with Jakov done on the evening of 28 June 1981. Here is Fr Sivric's version.

> Jakov: "All of a sudden, she appears in front of us. We look up and see the Gospa coming. There she is! There she is! And Grgo is taking pictures."
> Fr Zovko: "What is he taking?"
> Jakov: "He is taking pictures of some sort of mist."[18]

And this is Fr Mulligan's version of the same dialogue:

> Jakov: "She suddenly appears before us like this. When we look up when the Lady comes we shout, 'Here she is, here she is,' and Grgo records it."
> Fr Zovko: "What does he record?"
> Jakov: "Grgo has a tape-recorder and records."[19]

Obviously there is a discrepancy here regarding whether Grgo was taking photographs or using a tape-recorder, and these examples underline the need for an official Church-approved transcription of the tapes in the major world languages. Then the most important sections could be made available via the internet, thus greatly assisting the faithful in making up their own minds about Medjugorje.

In sum, *Medjugorje: The First Days*, does not radically alter the situation regarding the validity of the tape transcripts, nor does it invalidate the work of Fr Sivric. It may possibly provide some clarifications of marginal points, but it does nothing to obviate the major points made in this book, such as the fact that the visions were supposed to end on Friday, 3 July 1981, or that Vicka is an unreliable witness.

POPE FRANCIS AND MEDJUGORJE

Turning now to Pope Francis, the Church was certainly left in no doubt about how he viewed Fatima when, on the morning of 13 October 2013, in St Peter's Square, before a congregation of more than 100,000, he entrusted the world to the Blessed Virgin in the presence of the statue of Our Lady of Fatima from the Capelinha at Fatima.

This ceremony was part of the "Marian Day" weekend which was part of the Year of Faith celebrations, and which coincided with the 96th anniversary of the last apparition at Fatima, on 13 October 1917.[20]

Prior to that, Pope Francis had ensured that his pontificate was consecrated to Our Lady of Fatima on his behalf, on 13 May 2013, by the Cardinal of Lisbon, again, a strong signal of his support for Fatima, and a sign of the way that he intended to maintain the close links between the Papacy and Fatima established by his predecessors, and particularly Pope St John Paul II.[21]

Meanwhile, earlier that month, the Italian news site *Corrispondenza Romana* had published an item claiming that in September, at the *Domus Sanctae Marthae* in the Vatican, where the pope resides, Pope Francis, when speaking on the theme, "there is no Christian without Jesus," had criticized "revelationist" believers and had apparently been skeptical about the alleged apparitions at Medjugorje.

But when the pope's address was published on the Vatican news site and in *L'Osservatore Romano,* the alleged references to Medjugorje had seemingly been removed, and the pope was reported as saying only, "There is another group of Christians without Christ: those who look for rarities and curiosities that come from private revelations." He then went on to warn about people seeking "the spectacle of a revelation, to experience something new," when they should be focusing on the Gospel.[22]

However, a further report in the middle of the following month, November, seemed to lend credence to the earlier story about Pope Francis being skeptical about Medjugorje. It was reported that during Mass on the morning of 14 November, the pope preached a homily in which he warned that curiosities "distance us from the Gospel, from the Holy Spirit, from peace and wisdom, from the glory of God, from the beauty of God." He went on to say we should reject the attitude of those who say, "I know a visionary, who receives letters from Our Lady…[but] She is not a postmaster, sending messages every day."[23]

While these remarks were not directed specifically to the activities of the Medjugorje visionaries, they certainly seemed to reveal a marked skepticism about claims of alleged visions, especially those said to be occurring every day, as in the case of Medjugorje.

Meanwhile, in early November 2013, with regard to Medjugorje, the Congregation for the Doctrine of the Faith issued a directive to bishops. This information was released via a letter addressed to the General Secretary of the United States Conference of Catholic Bishops, Msgr Ronny Jenkins, which came from Archbishop Carlo Maria Viganò, the US Apostolic Nuncio.

In this letter, dated 21 October 2013, the Nuncio stated that he was writing at the request of the Prefect of the CDF, Archbishop (later Cardinal) Gerhard Müller, who was advising the US Bishops about the activities of Medjugorje visionary Ivan Dragicevic, who was scheduled to appear at various parishes around the country, to the effect that, "Clerics and the faithful are not permitted to participate in meetings, conferences or public celebrations during which the credibility of such 'apparitions' would be taken for granted." Thus in order to avoid "scandal and confusion," the archbishop asked that the bishops be informed about this "as soon as possible."

The fact that both clerics *and* faithful were included in this prohibition came as a shock to many Medjugorje supporters, who had believed that until a final decision was reached such participation in Medjugorje events was allowed. And as a result of this letter, scheduled public appearances by Medjugorje visionary Ivan Dragicevic, due in late October in the US, were actually canceled.[24]

MEDJUGORJE DEVELOPMENTS IN 2014

On 18 January 2014, Vatican Radio announced that Fr Federico Lombardi had confirmed that the Medjugorje International Commission had just had its last meeting the previous day, and that it had completed its work, and would be submitting the outcome of its studies to the Congregation for the Doctrine of the Faith.[25]

As might be expected, this announcement generated speculation as to the verdict of the Commission, particularly in an article published at VaticanInsider.com, which is part of the Italian *La Stampa* news service, and which was dated 19 January 2014. Under the headline, "Verdict on Medjugorje nears as Commission claims apparitions are 'no hoax,'" journalists Giacomo Galeazzi and Andrea Tornielli stated, "The verdict could be positive albeit partial but no concrete decision has yet been reached."

They go on to say, "Vatican Insider has learnt that the Commission has focused mainly on the first phase of apparitions. There is apparently no proof of any tricks, hoaxes or abuse of popular credulity. However, it is proving difficult for the Church to form a definitive verdict on the supernatural nature of a phenomenon that is ongoing."[26]

The difficulty with this statement is that word "apparently," which clearly indicates we are dealing with speculation, and also raises the possibility that someone on the Commission had broken their agreement not to speak about its secret deliberations. Even if that is not the case, and it is just a question of an unnamed person's theological opinion, it is still a question of unproven speculation.²⁷

On 23 January 2014, it was reported that Pope Francis had met with Cardinal Camillo Ruini, the Commission chairman, that day, and although Fr Federico Lombardi, the Vatican spokesman, didn't disclose the reason for the meeting, it is thought that the cardinal discussed the Commission's findings with the pope.²⁸

MEDJUGORJE DEVELOPMENTS IN 2015

In March 2015, it was reported that Ivan Dragicevic had been banned from speaking at an event in St Charles, Missouri, scheduled for 18 March, following the circulation of a memo to the priests and deacons of his archdiocese by Archbishop Robert Carlson, in which he said, "I have received a request from the Congregation for the Doctrine of the Faith to remind everyone that they are not to participate in events that promote the so-called visionaries of Medjugorje and in particular Mr. Ivan Dragicevic."²⁹

However, following this, as reported on the pro-Medjugorje website *Medjugorje Today*, on 17 March, Dragicevic went ahead and had an alleged vision in a private home in the city, in the presence of about 75 people, despite the fact that Archbishop Carlson had also said, "No other such events should be scheduled." This would certainly appear to include visionary activities which equate with having a public event at a private residence. Rather paradoxically, Dragicevic then claimed that he had "always been obedient to the authority of the Church," and would continue to be so.³⁰

The reality is that Ivan's stance contradicts the CDF ruling detailed previously, which stated, "Clerics and the faithful are not permitted to participate in *meetings*, conferences or public celebrations during which the credibility of such 'apparitions' would be taken for granted."³¹

Medjugorje author and supporter Wayne Weible then claimed that this CDF statement had in fact misquoted the Zadar declaration of 1991, since the CDF ruling, as delivered in a letter from Archbishop Carlo Maria Viganò, the US Apostolic Nuncio, quoted the Zadar text as follows, "On the basis of the research that has been done, it is not possible to state that there were apparitions or supernatural revelations," whereas Weible claimed it should read: "On the basis of the investigations, so far it cannot be affirmed that one is dealing with supernatural apparitions and revelations."

However, a number of versions of this text are in circulation on the internet and in books, and it can be argued that the difference between the two above texts is not really crucial, and that the CDF version is a legitimate paraphrase. And in any event, as detailed above, the Zadar declaration is in essence negative.[32]

Around this time, on 20 March, it was reported that there had been no mention of Medjugorje during the *ad limina* visit to Rome of the Bishops of Bosnia-Herzegovina, which lasted from 10–17 March. Rather, Pope Francis had focused his remarks on the practical difficulties facing the Church in the region.[33]

On 12 May, it was reported that the local bishop of Padua, in Italy, had banned visionary Ivan Dragicevic from appearing in his diocese on 22 May, in compliance with Vatican directives, and also that a proposed visit by Vicka to Brazil, from 24–26 May, had likewise been canceled.[34]

On 16 May, at a Confirmation ceremony in Medjugorje, the local Ordinary, Bishop Ratko Peric, reaffirmed his opposition to acceptance of the claims by the visionaries regarding messages and alleged visions.[35]

26
The Ruini Commission Report

MORE ON POPE FRANCIS AND MEDJUGORJE

On 22 May 2015, it was reported by Andrea Gagliarducci that Pope Francis would not be visiting Medjugorje during his one-day visit to Bosnia-Herzegovina on 6 June. Gagliarducci quoted a source in the CDF who said that "the Vatican's caution around the supposed apparitions" is due to their exceptional nature, and that "it was never the case in history that the Virgin Mary appeared so continuously and so constantly over the years," and that "the tradition of Marian apparitions shows that they are limited to a given period in the life of any visionary."[1]

On the return flight from his 6 June visit to Sarajevo, Pope Francis said that an announcement about Medjugorje would soon be made, following a recent CDF meeting: "We're at this point of making decisions... and then they will be announced." The pope also said that the Cardinal Ruini Commission had done "good work."[2]

A few days later, on 9 June, Vatican Radio reported on the homily the pope had given at Mass the previous day. In this, he had criticized those Christians "who forget they have been anointed and given the guarantee of the Spirit, so they are always searching for some 'novelty' in their Christian identity. They say 'Where are the visionaries who can tell us exactly what message Our Lady will be sending at 4 o'clock this afternoon?'"[3]

Fr Salvatore Perrella, one of the members of the Medjugorje Commission, seemingly supported the position that the pope was in fact referring to Medjugorje, in an article which appeared in the Italian newspaper *Avvenire*. In fact, he stated that Pope Francis is, by his words, actually preparing people for a decision regarding Medjugorje.

After describing the positive and negative criteria by which the Commission had analyzed the case of Medjugorje, Fr Perrella discussed the possible conclusions which the Commission could come to including regarding it as definitely supernatural, *constat de supernaturalitate* ("the supernatural character is established"), or as definitely not supernatural, *non constat de supernaturalitate* ("the supernatural character is not established"), in line with the provisions of *Normae Congregationis*.[4]

As noted elsewhere, although the traditional third possibility, *constat de non supernaturalitate* ("the non-supernatural character is established"), is not mentioned in *Normae Congregationis*, Fr Perrella did apparently allude to this in his article when he referred to a "third possibility" being available to theologians.

In any event, on 12 June, the Italian "ACI Stampa" internet service reported on remarks made by Cardinal Ruini, who stated that so far what was in circulation about Medjugorje was only rumors, that the plenary session of the Congregation for the Doctrine of the Faith has not yet taken place, and that no one on the Commission could say anything definite because its findings are "sub secreto pontificio," that is, to be kept in strictest confidence.[5]

On 12 June, too, the *National Catholic Register* carried a report by Edward Pentin, in which speculation that a decision regarding Medjugorje was imminent was played down, following comments from Vatican spokesman, Fr Federico Lombardi, who said that it was "hard to say" when a ruling would come, but that it was not likely to happen before the Vatican summer break.[6]

Meanwhile, on 9 June, in an article on the *National Catholic Register* website by Simcha Fisher, entitled "Does It Matter If Medjugorje Is Real or Not?," the author quite clearly stated her disbelief in Medjugorje, citing a number of cogent reasons for this, including the negative position of the original bishop, Pavao Zanic, allegations of sexual misconduct, plus the latest statements and actions of Pope Francis. She points to disobedience as being one of its major fruits, and in particular, the fact that some of its adherents say that it doesn't matter whether it's true or not, because the "fruits" are good.[7]

On 22 June, the *Te Deum laudamus!* blog carried a post entitled "Pope Francis revealed blunt thoughts on Medjugorje in an interview in a Brazilian book." In this it was revealed that the pope had apparently made some "rather blunt comments" about Medjugorje and the visionaries while in Rio de Janeiro for World Youth Day, and that these remarks have now been published in a book by Fr Alexander Awi Mello, entitled *Ela é minha mãe: Encontros de papa Francis com Mary*, which can be rendered in English as, *She's My Mother: Encounters of Pope Francis with Mary* (although the book had not been translated into English at the time of the post).

In this, the pope reportedly expressed disapproval of Medjugorje, criticizing the idea that Our Lady would appear at a particular time according to the agenda set by the visionaries. But he also apparently conceded that miracles are possible there.[8]

However, another report on this topic claimed, "The Holy Father voiced his suspicion that some people who claim visions have psychological problems, and others are deliberately deceiving the public."[9]

POPE FRANCIS'S STATEMENTS ON MEDJUGORJE

A few days later, on 24 June 2015, the "anniversary date" of the first alleged Medjugorje vision, pro-Medjugorje Italian journalist Vittorio Messori issued a warning[10] that a negative judgment of the visions could engender "something like a schism." He argued that Medjugorje had greatly boosted the post-Vatican II Church, and that the faith of many people had been rekindled after visiting it. In the words of the report on the CatholicCulture.org site, "Messori suggested that Pope Francis would be prudent to take no official position regarding the authenticity of the apparitions, but simply to take note of the spiritual fruits."[11]

As if to illustrate the febrile atmosphere that surrounds Medjugorje, claims were made by Italian journalists that the Congregation for the Doctrine of the Faith, at a *feria quarta* meeting on June 24, had reached a negative decision about Medjugorje as a place of supernatural activity, but judged that it could be regarded as a "place of prayer."[12]

However on 26 June, the *National Catholic Register* site reported that, according to the Vatican, "Contrary to reports in Italian media, no decision has been made regarding certain doctrinal and disciplinary aspects of alleged Marian apparitions at Medjugorje." Edward Pentin said that Fr Ciro Benedettini of the Vatican Press Office had told him, "Officials of the Congregation for the Doctrine of the Faith (CDF) had not yet met to review the findings of a three-year commission that investigated the Medjugorje phenomenon."[13]

Then in August, the pro-Medjugorje site *Medjugorje Today* ran a story saying, "The boom of Italian pilgrims in Medjugorje has ceased as a result of Pope Francis' words on visionaries who claim to have daily apparitions," with one pilgrimage organizer estimating that the number of pilgrims had halved since 2013, with the economic crisis being given as a major factor in this.[14]

This downturn was also discussed in a story by Elisabetta Povoledo in the *New York Times*, dated 26 August. She noted, "Already, since the pope announced in June that a decision was imminent, the numbers of Italians — once the bulk of the pilgrims here — have fallen by half." She also interviewed Sante Frigo, an Italian married to a pilgrim guide in Medjugorje, who said, "From the point of view of the pilgrimage supply chain, it's been a catastrophe."[15]

In her September 2015 report, Sr Emmanuel Maillard, a well-known Medjugorje enthusiast, lamented the various restrictions that were being put in place on the alleged visionaries in the town:

> Marija no longer opens the Magnificat Center for her daily apparition. Ivan and Jakov still go to the Rotunda in the afternoon with Father Marinko to pray with the pilgrims, but without giving the messages. The Information Center no longer releases the message received on the 2nd of the month by Mirjana as it did previously. This Summer Ivan did not invite the pilgrims to participate in the apparition at night on the mountain with his prayer group, etc.

She went on to say, "These restrictions are probably local and prudent measures before Pope Francis' announcement on Medjugorje."[16]

In December, *National Geographic* magazine published a lengthy article by Maureen Orth entitled "How the Virgin Mary Became the World's Most Powerful Woman."[17]

This article began with a brief account of Medjugorje, and went on to make a number of references to it, although it did also deal with genuine shrines such as Guadalupe and Lourdes. The information about Medjugorje was mostly focused on alleged cures associated with it, but what was really significant was the fact that there was absolutely no mention of Fatima anywhere in the article. So the place where the greatest miracle of the twentieth century took place, and where the authentic Marian message from Our Lady was given to mankind, one which has been publicly supported by all the popes since Pius XII, was ignored, and instead Medjugorje was highlighted. Surely, this is indicative of a crisis in the Church, and one which needs to be speedily resolved?

MEDJUGORJE DEVELOPMENTS IN 2016

According to AsiaNews.it, Pope Francis returned to a previous theme in his remarks during Mass at the Casa Santa Marta on 18 April 2016. He warned that Jesus is the door to eternal life and that people should not trust "those who indicate another route, such as fortune tellers and alleged visionaries."[18]

In a column written for the British paper *The Catholic Herald*, dated 29 April 2016, a London priest who goes under the penname of Pastor Iuventus indicated his thoughts about Medjugorje under the headline "Fear and Discomfort in Medjugorje." In this he expressed his concerns, in part, as follows:

> Official ecclesiastical judgment has never credited the apparitions there with supernatural quality. Neither the visionaries' state during their apparitions nor the thousands of miracles claimed have been subjected to rigorous, objective or conclusive scientific testing. What I found at Medjugorje was a cult of the alleged visionaries which left me feeling more uncomfortable and fearful than I have ever felt in any place of pilgrimage.

Then, on 3 July, *Croatia News* announced that it was expected that Pope Francis would soon appoint a special Vatican administrator for Medjugorje, which would assume the status of a shrine, with the parish still being under the control of the Franciscans of the Herzegovina province. According to the report, this would have possibly meant the end of the long-running dispute between the Franciscans and the local bishops of Mostar.[19]

But the following day, Fr Federico Lombardi, the Vatican spokesman, said in Rome that such reports were "premature," and that this was just one possible idea under consideration, and that no decision had actually been made.[20]

MIRJANA'S BOOK, *MY HEART WILL TRIUMPH*

A book by Medjugorje visionary Mirjana Soldo was published in August 2016, with the title *My Heart Will Triumph*, and this recounts her life story and involvement with Medjugorje.

The first thing to note about it is that the title is a rather strange one, given that the triumph of Our Lady's Immaculate Heart is a theme that is much more associated with Fatima. Similarly, the cover has a picture of a blue-veiled Gospa figure rather than the gray veil usually associated with Medjugorje. The question must be asked: is this an attempt to make it seem more like approved Marian apparitions?

As regards the contents, there are aspects of these which tend to back up the previous points made about Mirjana and the early days of the visions. For example, she confirms the fact that the visions were supposed to end quickly, saying, "Something kept telling me that she'd appear for just a few more days, and I related this to the other visionaries."

However, she then qualifies this by saying, "At some point, we began believing it was true."

It's as if, though, she didn't really believe this, and in fact, after speaking about the emotional pressure she was under, carries on to say, "But deep down, I desperately wanted the apparitions to continue. How would I go back to living a normal life after experiencing Heaven?"[21]

Perhaps here we have a revelation of one of the driving forces behind the continued claims of visions, that is, the desire on the part of Mirjana, and possibly some of the other visionaries, that they *should* continue.

But as we have seen above, according to St John of the Cross, the desire to see something supernatural is very dangerous since it gives the devil the possibility of fulfilling such a desire in his own way.

Another puzzling aspect of the book is the fact that although Mirjana mentions speaking to Fr Zovko on the evening of 28 June 1981, and even recounts some of their conversation, what they say does not match anything in either Fr Sivric's or Daria Klanac's transcriptions of the taping done on that evening.[22]

On the question of Mirjana's mental and emotional states, which have been discussed above, the book is quite revealing. This is what she says about some of her early experiences:

> Although I could not see it at the time, life in Sarajevo was difficult for my parents. Dad worked during the day and spent most of the nights studying and taking classes to be able to work in a radiology ward. Mom worked as a cook at a large company. She left our apartment every day at 5 am and came home exhausted every afternoon. They were unable to pay someone to babysit me in the years before I could be enrolled in school. So, by the time I turned five, I stayed at home alone, which was stressful for Mom and Dad.[23]

Surely, being left repeatedly on her own virtually all day, at such a young age, must have had a profound effect on her emotions and personality. It cannot be said that this type of information is reassuring as to Mirjana's general emotional state and thus her suitability to act as a genuine seer.

CARDINAL MÜLLER INTERVIEW AND POPE FRANCIS'S MEDJUGORJE REMARKS

On 27 September, Medjugorje visionary Ivan Dragicevic once more visited St Stephen's Cathedral in Vienna, and claimed that the Gospa appeared to him. Afterwards, Dragicevic "shared" aspects of his encounter with those present, including the alleged message he had received.[24]

On 11 November, the Croatian newspaper *Slobodna Dalmacija* published an interview with Cardinal Gerhard Müller, the Prefect of the Congregation for the Doctrine of the Faith, which touched briefly on the topic of Medjugorje.

When asked if the alleged visions there were of supernatural character, and of the ultimate fate of Medjugorje, he replied that it was necessary to wait for a decision from the highest authority in the Church. He went on to say that a mature Catholic veneration of the Blessed Virgin did not depend on phenomena such as apparitions or messages, but rather on traditional Church teaching on her person and role.[25]

In Rome, on 25 November, Pope Francis addressed 140 Superiors General of male religious orders and congregations during their 88th General Assembly, and he also took questions. When asked why he had chosen Marian themes for the next three World Youth Days leading up to the Youth Days in Panama, he said that he had done this in response to what people in Latin America had asked for, that is, a "strong Marian presence."

But he went on to say that he wanted to focus on "the real Madonna! Not the Madonna at the head of a post office that every day sends a different letter, saying: 'My children, do this and then the next day do that.' No, not that Madonna. The real Madonna is the [one] who generates Jesus in our hearts, a Mother. This fashion for a superstar Madonna, who seeks the limelight, is not Catholic."[26]

This would appear to be a repetition of his remarks in November 2013, and June 2015, as reported above, which were widely regarded as being critical of Medjugorje.

MEDJUGORJE DEVELOPMENTS IN 2017

In early February 2017, it was announced by the Vatican that Pope Francis was appointing Polish Archbishop Henryk Hoser of Warszawa-Praga as a special envoy to Medjugorje. The announcement said that his mission "has the aim of acquiring a deeper knowledge of the pastoral situation there and above all, of the needs of the faithful who go there in pilgrimage, and on the basis of this, to suggest possible pastoral initiatives for the future."

The announcement went on to say that the archbishop's mission would have an "exclusively pastoral character" and that it was a role that was expected to finish by the summer, and further that he would be in contact with Bishop Peric, the local Franciscans and the local faithful.

It was stressed that his role was not that of an apostolic visitation — these are classed by the Vatican as exceptional initiatives of the Holy See which involve "sending a Visitor or Visitors to evaluate an ecclesiastical institute such as a seminary, diocese, or religious institute. Apostolic Visitations are intended to assist the institute in question to improve the way in which it carries out its function in the life of the Church."

Nor would the envoy be looking at the merits of the alleged visions, which, since they are "questions of doctrine," come under the responsibility of the CDF.[27]

Meanwhile, on the Diocese of Mostar-Duvno website, in a statement issued on 9 February and headlined "The True Madonna and the 'Post Office Manager,'" Bishop Ratko Peric commented on the remarks made by the pope the previous November, about the "Real Madonna," and not "the Madonna at the head of a post office that every day sends a different letter," saying this was "the way the Pope distinguishes the true from the false Madonna."

The bishop then went on to outline numerous aspects of the alleged visions which gave cause for concern, as detailed previously in this book.[28]

It was also reported that Archbishop Hoser had taken part in a telephone interview with Vatican Radio on Monday 25 February, in which he spoke of the high numbers of pilgrims still coming to Medjugorje, and how this represented a challenge for the Church. He also spoke of Medjugorje in these terms: "On the one hand are the phenomena and are the messages of the Mother of God genuine? This was the subject of the investigation by the special commission led by Cardinal Ruini. The second aspect is that which has been entrusted to me: it is about organizing pastoral care, in agreement and harmony with the ecclesiastical hierarchy on the ground."[29]

The Ruini Commission Report

The exact significance of this development is hard to quantify. On the one hand the reported remarks of the pope before Christmas indicate a continuing skepticism about the activities of alleged visionaries, and particularly, it is argued, of those involved in Medjugorje. But on the other hand, this new pastoral mission, which will look at "possible pastoral initiatives for the future," seems to indicate a sympathetic approach to Medjugorje.

But it is also possible that this initiative may ultimately mean that the Vatican will be more directly involved in determining what happens there. Some may argue, of course, that it is not appropriate to think in terms of pastoral solutions to the problem of Medjugorje until the more basic question of authenticity has been determined.

POPE FRANCIS AND "TOURISM IN MEDJUGORJE"

A report published on 21 February, on the *Total Croatia News* website, headlined "Pope Francis Endangers Tourism in Medjugorje," was quite revealing, and not just because of the use of the word "tourism" in the headline.

According to one owner of a travel agency, Gianni Mauro, "Every year more than 200,000 pilgrims from Italy used to come to Medjugorje, but by the summer of 2016 that number had decreased to only about 50 people per ferry coming from Italy."

He thought the reason for this decline was twofold: first, the economic crisis affecting Italy at the time, and second, the negative remarks about Medjugorje attributed to Pope Francis.

Another travel agency owner, Rea Karnincic, confirmed that, "the number of pilgrims had been rapidly falling for two years." She expressed the hope that Pope Francis would provide an official position on Medjugorje so as to end the uncertainty. Apparently, though, pilgrim numbers from Poland are growing — and this may be significant given the appointment of Archbishop Hoser.

Regarding pilgrim numbers in general to Medjugorje, the article stated that there were no official figures, only estimates based on the number of Holy Communions received. As regards pilgrim accommodation, "It is estimated that there are around 20,000 beds in various accommodation facilities, but there are no firm data." The article concludes by saying that this is not to be wondered at, since "70 percent of [such] buildings have been constructed illegally."[30]

On 27 February, Bishop Ratko Peric, the local Ordinary, commented in a public statement on the Diocese of Mostar-Duvno website under the heading "The First Seven Days of the 'Apparitions' in Medjugorje." He said that from the early 1980s, "the position of this chancery throughout all this time has been clear and resolute: this is not an authentic apparition of the Blessed Virgin Mary."

In this statement, the bishop goes on to speak of the evidence provided by the transcriptions of the cassettes made during the first days of the alleged visions—highlighting a number of the dubious aspects of these claimed apparitions which have been dealt with in this book—before concluding that there have been no supernatural apparitions or revelations in Medjugorje.[31]

And on 3 March, the Italian website *Lettera43* published an interview with Cardinal Müller of the CDF, in which he spoke of "exaggeration" regarding phenomena such as Medjugorje.[32]

POPE FRANCIS AND THE RUINI COMMISSION

Then on 13 May, on his journey back to Rome from Fatima, where he had just canonized Jacinta and Francisco Marto, Pope Francis held an in-flight press conference. During this, among other things, he discussed Medjugorje. He was asked what he thought about "shrines" like Medjugorje, and the religious fervor surrounding them.

The pope responded by saying that presumed apparitions, such as Medjugorje, aren't part of the public, ordinary Magisterium of the Church. Then he remarked that he was aware of problems concerning it, but that investigations were continuing and he hoped that the truth about it would come out. He then mentioned the Ruini Commission and described the report it produced as "very, very good," while also saying that the Congregation for the Doctrine of the Faith, under Cardinal Müller, had expressed some "doubts" about the phenomenon and sent all the documentation, including evidence opposed to the position of the Ruini Commission, to the members of the *Feria Quarta* CDF monthly meeting. The pope indicated that he would have preferred it if the CDF had sent those observations to him directly.

He then went on to say that the Ruini report indicated that the "first apparitions" must continue to be studied. But speaking of alleged current apparitions, Pope Francis said the report had its doubts, which he would personally express more strongly, in line with his previous criticism of the idea of the Madonna as the head of a telegraphic office who sends out daily messages.

So the pope distinguished between the early apparitions and the later ones, which are apparently not to be regarded as supernatural — and then spoke about the pastoral aspects of Medjugorje which he had sent Archbishop Hoser to investigate.³³

RUINI COMMISSION REPORT DETAILS LEAKED

Writing a few days later, Italian journalist Andrea Tornielli apparently revealed the way the Ruini Commission members had voted regarding Medjugorje, despite the fact that its deliberations were supposed to be kept secret. This indicates that a member, or possibly more than one member, of the Commission has broken their commitment to secrecy. In any event, Tornielli claimed that there had been "thirteen votes in favor of recognizing the supernatural nature of the first seven appearances in Medjugorje," with one vote against and one suspended.

He also said that the Commission met seventeen times and examined all the documents on the case held in the Vatican, at the parish of Medjugorje, and in the secret service archives of the former Yugoslavia. The members also apparently interviewed all the alleged seers and other witnesses, and visited Medjugorje itself in April 2012.

So, according to Tornielli, the majority of the Commission voted in favor of recognizing the first seven visions, those which took place between 24 June and 30 June 1981. But regarding all the other claimed visions, which are described as the "second phase of the apparitions," there was apparently more mixed voting as regards the spiritual fruits of Medjugorje — depending on whether or not the behavior of the visionaries was taken into account. In coming to these conclusions, the Commission apparently took note of the following: the long-running conflict between the Bishops of Mostar and the Franciscans; the pre-announced nature of the apparitions; the repetitive nature of the messages; that the visions continued despite the fact that they were supposed to end; and also concerns about the problems caused by the "apocalyptic flavor" of some of the alleged secrets emanating from the visionaries.

But as regards looking at Medjugorje from a positive perspective, the Commission apparently argued the six visionaries were "psychically normal," and that "nothing of what they had seen was influenced by either the Franciscans of the parish or any other subjects." They were commended for resisting the attempts to threaten them made by the police, and the Commission also "rejected the hypothesis of a demonic origin of the apparitions."

It also called for an end to the ban on official diocesan and parish pilgrimages to Medjugorje, and the majority of the Commission "voted in favor of the constitution of 'an authority dependent on the Holy See' in Medjugorje as well as the transformation of the parish into a pontifical sanctuary." This is said to be a pastoral decision which "would not imply the recognition of the supernatural nature of the apparitions."[34]

THE IMPLICATIONS OF THE RUINI COMMISSION REPORT

The tone of Tornielli's account gives the impression that Medjugorje has been approved, but in fact a majority positive vote was given to only seven out of the alleged tens of thousands of visions said to have taken place since 1981. Regarding these visions — the "second phase of the apparitions" — apparently two members of the Commission voted against them being supernatural, and twelve offered no opinion about them, which means they received no votes in favor of them having a supernatural origin.[35]

The belief of the Commission members that the visionaries were "psychically normal," and that "nothing of what they had seen was influenced by either the Franciscans of the parish or any other subjects," seems rather surprising in the light of the publicly available negative evidence about these matters, which has been extensively detailed earlier in this book.

On 18 May, one of the commission members, Fr Salvatore Perrella, was interviewed by *Avvenire*. He said that the "commission did not make a definitive pronouncement," but rather decided to distinguish between what happened at the beginning and what has happened since then. He is reported as saying, "The Commission has cut the case into two segments. The first part concerns the seven initial apparitions — let's call it the founding core — which seemed credible. The other part, that is, the sequel to the apparitions that would continue, has left the Commission perplexed."

Fr Perrella also noted that the facts about Medjugorje are so complex "that the pontiff is free to conduct a further investigation."[36]

This suggests that the views of the Commission members are far from definitive, a position which finds support in the pope's remarks during the in-flight press conference that the initial apparitions must continue to be studied.[37] Thus, if the transcripts of the original tapes were not studied in any detail by the Ruini Commission, this leaves open the possibility for such a study in the future.

What are we to make, then, of the Commission's findings? The first thing to note is that the Ruini Commission is a purely advisory body whose role is to offer its findings to the Congregation for the Doctrine of the Faith, which then makes recommendations regarding Medjugorje.

Apart from that, neither Andrea Tornielli nor Fr Perrella mention the transcripts of the original tape-recordings of the visionaries, which constitute the primary evidence about the whole phenomenon. Did the Commission study the transcripts, which now exist in at least three differing but largely complementary printed versions? And on what basis did the Commission rule out diabolical involvement at Medjugorje? If Medjugorje is to be properly understood, we need to know exactly what the sources consulted by the Commission members were that led to them voting for a supernatural origin for the initial visions.

And in fact, as we will see, the actual contents of the Ruini Report were revealed in February 2020, and it certainly appears to be the case from a study of this text that the Commission did not carry out an in-depth study of these transcripts.

NUMEROUS MEDJUGORJE ANOMALIES

We are left with the fact that there are a number of very strange events recorded as happening during the first seven apparitions, as is clear from the transcripts. For example, the evidence they provide presents us with a "Gospa" who was reportedly holding a baby which she then hid from the visionaries — surely a very strange thing for the real Blessed Virgin to do. And there are also the incidents where "she" laughed with them, or when her hands were trembling, or when Vicka touched the Gospa and her fingers bounced off "her" as though they were made of steel. As Vicka herself said, "We kept touching her and kissing her, and she kept laughing." And likewise, the assertion that the Vision told the visionaries that she would remain with them as long as they wanted, is very strange.

In addition, the clear evidence presented in this book shows that there was simply no message of any significance given to the visionaries during the first week or so of the visions, and this was publicly acknowledged by Fr Zovko. And in fact, the Vision apparently said nothing unless questioned by the visionaries — surely a very odd procedure, one which prompted Fr Zovko to say, "So, there is no message."

And there is also a further stumbling block to belief in the supernatural nature of these early visions; the fact that Ivanka and Mirjana, actually went initially to Podbrdo, where the early visions took place, to smoke and listen to rock music.

The biggest problem, though, as we have seen, with the messages emanating from the early visions, is the clear evidence that they were supposed to end on 3 July, three days after the vision on Tuesday, 30 June.

Tornielli's reporting about the views of the Ruini Commission leaves us with an unsettling anomaly. If the Commission members believe that the Blessed Virgin appeared to the visionaries on the seven occasions, starting in June 1981, and not afterwards, that implies that the visionaries first received a tremendous privilege from Heaven. They saw the Mother of God, who has been assumed into glory. Such an experience must have a tremendous impact on the beholder — it implies a transformative experience. And then, we are asked to believe that after seven such experiences, the same seers proceeded immediately, the very next day, to start giving out false reports of more alleged visions, perhaps on their own initiative, perhaps in concert with others, perhaps for patriotic or other reasons — but for all that, false reports which now amount to tens of thousands of extra visions.

The implication of the Ruini Report is that Our Lady appeared to the visionaries in the full knowledge that once she had stopped appearing to them they would fabricate further visions. And as she could foretell the future with regard to, for example, Russia, as at Fatima in July 1917, then she would surely have been aware of what the Medjugorje visionaries would do.

This seems to be the fatal objection to the idea that the first visions were supernatural. How would the Church regard Lourdes or Fatima if either St Bernadette or the seers had gone on to falsify visions after the original and genuine ones were over?

It might be objected at this point that the case of the La Salette seers, Mélanie and Maximin, shows that genuine Marian visionaries can go on to produce fabrications. But what happened with them is very different from what has happened at Medjugorje. Regarding Mélanie, in later life she published a book falsely claiming that it contained the full text of the secret given to them by Our Lady when she appeared to them in 1846. This secret has never been officially revealed. This wasn't a case, then, of her claiming new apparitions but of expanding on the message received at the single vision they experienced. So the case of La Salette is not relevant in this respect to Medjugorje. It is the sheer scale of the extra visions claimed at Medjugorje which is the real problem.

And this problem becomes even more serious if we consider all the other negative aspects about Medjugorje which have unfolded over the years, including the clear disobedience of some of the Franciscans involved with the visionaries: Fr Tomislav Vlasic in particular, but also Fr Zovko, who was disciplined on a number of occasions.

Given all that, the reader must decide if it is credible to say that the Blessed Virgin really would have appeared to the visionaries during the first week or so, knowing all that would happen in the following decades.

27
The Vatican and Medjugorje

FURTHER MEDJUGORJE DEVELOPMENTS IN 2017

Regarding the economic activities of the visionaries, a program about them, *PiazzaPulita*, was aired on Italian television (LA7) on 30 March 2017. Marco Corvaglia highlights this program on his site, and also has information about Marija there. In 2010 she founded an association with the aim of collecting funds for the construction of a "Spirituality Center" to be named "Magnificat" on land owned by her in Bijakovici. But it turns out that this building, which has 54 rooms, a conference room and a chapel, and which was opened in 2012, is now used as a four-star hotel. According to the TV program, in order to be present at one of Marija's apparitions you have to book a room — and payment is in cash.[1]

In mid-2017, the old charge that Bishop Zanic had been a Communist collaborator, which was looked at in chapter 12, "Medjugorje and the Theologians," was renewed in a film entitled *From Fatima to Medjugorje*.[2] This lurid production claimed that both Bishop Zanic and his successor, Bishop Peric, were collaborators with the Communist secret police — but, as had happened previously, the Mostar Chancery energetically rejected these allegations as calumny. The Mostar diocese Vicar General, Fr Zeljko Majic, energetically rebutted the claims, characterizing them as calumny, in a lengthy response which was posted on the diocesan website.[3]

In this, he stated, "Everything said in the film about the supposed 'cooperation' of our shepherds Pavao and Ratko with the anti-God and anti-Church secret security, is a blasphemous calumny and has no foundation, nor any involvement with the persons being slandered: it serves only as defamation not just of the individuals but of the Church herself!"

ARCHBISHOP HOSER ON MEDJUGORJE

Then in August 2017, an interview with Archbishop Hoser conducted by the Polish Catholic Information Agency (KAI) appeared on a Polish Catholic news site Deon.pl. The archbishop was quoted as saying, "Everything indicates that the apparitions will be recognized, perhaps even this year...." When asked what he regarded as being the most important phenomenon in Medjugorje, apart from the alleged revelations, he pointed to the number of pilgrims going to confession, and what he described as "real conversions." He also had words of praise for the work of Fr Slavko Barbaric.

The archbishop claimed that there are no doctrinal errors in the content of the messages—but also said that he had not studied the content of the revelations because that was not his role. When asked if it was possible for the Holy See to recognize the truth of the revelations if the local bishop considered them to be false, he replied in the affirmative, and also stated that his assessment of the pastoral aspects of Medjugorje was positive.[4]

The archbishop's interview was criticized at the Croatian online portal, *Vjera I Djela* ("Faith and Works"), on the grounds of a lack of impartiality and objectivity in focusing on the fruits of the alleged apparitions at the expense of ignoring their doctrinal aspects. Amongst other things, he was also accused of prejudging any decision of the Holy See.[5]

MIRJANA AND DEMONIC ACTIVITY?

On 18 September 2017, an article appeared on the Spirit Daily website entitled, "Demonic Howls Erupt During Apparition." The basis of this story came from the newsletter of Sr Emmanuel Maillard. The account speaks of how on 2 September, as Mirjana Soldo was "receiving her monthly apparition" in the presence of a large crowd, "a rather common phenomenon occurred once again. But on this day, it was on a scale I had never seen before." The report goes on to say, "People in large numbers began to howl blasphemies and yell like animals as soon as the Blessed Mother appeared."

The report from Sr Maillard continues, saying, "This went on for some time, and then everything gradually calmed down. When people who are tormented by demons are in the presence of Our Lady these demons sometimes manifest their anger in this way." A video accompanied this story, and on it, one can hear in the background a very disturbing cacophony of howls and screams which continues for some time, and which certainly has the feeling of the demonic about it.[6]

An alternative explanation, though, is that this was not a genuine Marian apparition. In this interpretation, there was no authentic apparition, but a *simulation* of one by Soldo which became an occasion for demonic activities to become manifest. This interpretation is supported by the fact that, according to Sr Maillard, this is a "rather common phenomenon." Whatever may be said about this, it is surely not a good sign as to the authenticity of Soldo's claims of further and continual visions.

CARDINAL PAROLIN AND ARCHBISHOP HOSER ON MEDJUGORJE

On 1 November, the Italian daily newspaper *La Stampa* published a report on the visit of the Vatican Secretary of State, Cardinal Parolin, to Croatia, under the headline "Medjugorje, Parolin, 'The Holy See wants to regulate the phenomenon.'"

The cardinal answered questions from journalists, and spoke of the Ruini Commission, whose task had been to clarify the phenomenon of the apparitions, while also emphasizing the need for pastoral care for pilgrims to Medjugorje.[7]

A report then appeared on the *Aleteia* website, on 7 December 2017, under the headline "Official pilgrimages to Medjugorje are being authorized, confirms Pope Francis' envoy." In this article, Archbishop Hoser was quoted as saying, "The devotion of Medjugorje is allowed. It's not prohibited, and need not be done in secret.... Today, dioceses and other institutions can organize official pilgrimages. It's no longer a problem." The archbishop went on to say, "This is a phenomenon. And what confirms the authenticity of the place is the large amount of charitable institutions that exist around the sanctuary. And another aspect as well: the great effort that is being made at the level of Christian formation."[8]

It might be remarked that the authenticity of an alleged place of apparitions in the eyes of the Church requires more than the presence of charitable institutions or formation centers.

An interview with Archbishop Hoser appeared shortly after the *Aleteia* article, on 10 December, in *Il Giornale,* under the headline "Medjugorje, pilgrimages yes. But not for the apparitions." In this interview, amongst other things, the archbishop, on his own initiative, distinguished between worship and apparitions at Medjugorje, saying that if a bishop wanted to organize a prayer pilgrimage to Medjugorje, that was no problem, but that organizing pilgrimages to go there for the apparitions was not authorized, because "the problem of the visionaries has not yet been solved."[9]

ARCHBISHOP HOSER AS SPECIAL ENVOY TO MEDJUGORJE

At the end of May 2018, Archbishop Hoser's mandate as special envoy to Medjugorje was extended indefinitely by Pope Francis. As Apostolic Visitator, he has a particular responsibility both for the pastoral needs of pilgrims and for the local Medjugorje parish community. The Vatican communiqué announcing this news laid stress on the "exclusively pastoral" nature of the archbishop's task, and described this as being to "ensure a stable and continuous accompaniment of the parish community of Medjugorje and of the faithful who go there on pilgrimage, whose needs require particular attention."[10]

The then director of the Vatican Press Office, Greg Burke, stressed the "pastoral, not doctrinal nature" of Hoser's mission and said that this announcement "does not enter into the doctrinal questions" regarding the truthfulness of the Marian apparitions of Medjugorje. Burke also said that the appointment did not represent the conclusion of Medjugorje, but should rather be seen as the "next step."[11]

Just exactly what this "next step" was leading towards with respect to a judgment on Medjugorje was not made clear.

On Sunday 22 July, Archbishop Hoser took up his mandate as Apostolic Visitator in Medjugorje, beginning with a Mass in St James's Church. During his homily he pointed to the positive aspects of Marian devotion locally, including Holy Mass, adoration, confessions, the rosary and the way of the cross, but he made no comment concerning the legitimacy of the alleged visions.[12]

Just prior to this event, Bishop Peric had, apparently, in a conversation in which the Apostolic Nuncio also took part, informed Archbishop Hoser that he continued to believe that the alleged apparitions at Medjugorje were "not credible," and this position included those in the "first seven or ten days of 1981."[13]

FR MANFRED HAUKE ON MEDJUGORJE

In the 1 August edition of the German newspaper, *Die Tagespost*, Fr Manfred Hauke was interviewed about Archbishop Hoser's pastoral role. He commented that it wasn't reassuring to separate the truth of the messages from pastoral matters. He went on to say that the question of authenticity must first be asked and only then can the pastoral answer be given, including any concerns for those who come as pilgrims. When asked why this was so, he spoke of the many problems in accepting the Medjugorje apparitions and messages as genuine, as detailed previously in this book. He also warned that it was necessary for all the relevant facts about Medjugorje to be brought to light to prevent the Church from being further compromised by this matter.[14]

Fr Hauke also set out his views in some detail in a lengthy interview with Dr Eva Doppelbauer for *Gloria TV* on 27 August, in which he discussed and explained many aspects of the whole Medjugorje question. In particular, he made the point that the Ruini Commission had apparently overlooked the transcripts of the original tapes in its deliberations, and said, "Failing to basically evaluate a historical source of this rank is scandalous from a scholarly point of view."[15]

In addition, beyond these interviews, Fr Hauke also produced a more academic work on the early days of the alleged apparitions in a number of languages, including French. In this brief work, Fr Hauke looks at the work of the Ruini Commission as regards events during the first ten days at Medjugorje, and concludes that the Commission did not make an in-depth study of the tapes.[16]

EXPANSION PLANS FOR MEDJUGORJE

On 20 September, an article appeared on the *Crux* news site authored by Jonathan Luxmoore. In this he reported that Archbishop Hoser had, with regard to Medjugorje, "outlined plans for expansion, including more Masses in different languages and facilities for young pilgrims who flock to the site of the alleged Marian apparitions."

Luxmoore went on to quote the archbishop as saying, "Medjugorje represents Europe's spiritual lungs, a place where millions discover God and the beauties of the Church," and "We now have to re-create its infrastructure, firstly by securing its liturgical space. We also need to expand its areas for retreats and provide new places for celebrating the Eucharist, especially for pilgrims." The archbishop also said that many visitors come from Western Europe, "where the church has atrophied" but now is "suddenly experiencing God's grace."[17]

Early the next month, on 6 October, Archbishop Hoser expanded on his remarks, as further reported by *Crux* in an article headlined "Papal envoy compares Medjugorje to Fatima and Lourdes." The Polish prelate was quoted as saying, "I believe that the message of peace, which is central here in Medjugorje, is intended for the whole world," before going on to put the message allegedly being delivered there on a par with those given at Lourdes and Fatima. He also described Medjugorje as "the confessional of the world," claiming that it attracted "two and a half million pilgrims a year."

But despite this fulsome praise, the archbishop said that the position of the Church regarding Medjugorje continued to be one of "wait and see." He finished by saying, "Pope Francis has taken the biggest step by sending his representative here. Pope Francis wants to develop pastoral activities in Medjugorje and thus confirms the value of this place."[18]

The reader will recall that regarding the alleged Medjugorje secrets, in the early 80s Mirjana said that she would give a "miraculous" sheet of paper with details of them to Fr Petar Ljubicic ten days before the first secret became a reality. In his book, Fr Sivric includes a translation of a letter by Fr Ljubicic dated 4 September 1985, in which he gives details about this.

But as time went on, Mirjana changed her story, and in 2015 she claimed that the situation now was that Our Lady would show her the priest who would be asked to reveal the secrets. And by 2018, Mirjana was claiming, and this was recorded on video on 26 October of that year, that actually she had never chosen Fr Ljubicic for this task in the first place.[19]

POPE FRANCIS AND CHIARA AMIRANTE OF NEW HORIZONS

On 2 November, the *Aleteia* site posted an article based on a conversation about Medjugorje between Chiara Amirante, the foundress of the *Nuovi Orizzonti* ("New Horizons") community, and Pope Francis. Amirante claimed that she had been authorized to make the contents of this interview public. She said that Pope Francis told her positive things about Medjugorje. While discussing this topic with the pope, Amirante stated, contrary to the generally accepted figure of tens of thousands of alleged visions, that there had only actually been 682, and that this had given rise to some perplexity and perhaps confused the pope.

At this point, Pope Francis, according to Amirante, apparently said that he was in fact the one who had "saved" Medjugorje from those in the Church who were opposed to it. He also said his heart was with Medjugorje, and that he has sent Archbishop Hoser because he believed that the fruits are many and undeniable. According to Amirante he said that his previously expressed personal opinion, that Our Lady is not a postmaster of the post office sending out messages every day, had been held because of "erroneous information that the Madonna was giving appointments at all hours, every day." Amirante further stated that the pope said that he was "taking steps with my delegate Hoser... to protect everything that is beautiful at Medjugorje," and that there would soon be a new statement about his position.[20]

MEDJUGORJE MLADIFEST YOUTH FESTIVAL

On 13 May 2019, the *Vatican News* site carried an article with the headline "Pope authorizes pilgrimages to Medjugorje," in which an announcement made by the Apostolic Visitator, Archbishop Hoser, and the Apostolic Nuncio of Bosnia-Herzegovina, Archbishop Luigi Pezzuto, was publicized. This announcement was essentially a repetition of information previously made public, regarding papal authorization for pilgrimages by dioceses and parishes to Medjugorje, with the proviso that this was not to be interpreted as authentication of the alleged apparitions.[21]

In her May 2019 online report, Sr Emmanuel Maillard announced that because of a request by "the authorities"—presumably by the Holy See—"as is the case for all websites associated with Medjugorje, we will no longer be able to publish the link to Mirjana's [monthly] apparition."[22] This was apparently to avoid the impression that any sort of formal authentication of the alleged visions had been given by the Church.

On 30 July, the British Catholic weekly *The Tablet* ran a story entitled "Vatican dignitaries head to Medjugorje amid reports of imminent recognition." The reporter, Jonathan Luxmoore, related that according to a report on *Vatican Radio*, a Vatican delegation was, for the first time, due to visit Medjugorje. This was for the Mladifest youth festival there in early August, which would be opened by Cardinal Angelo De Donatis, the papal vicar of the Rome diocese. This event was then due to be closed by Archbishop Rino Fisichella and Archbishop José Carballo, president of the Pontifical Council for Promoting the New Evangelization and secretary of the Vatican's Congregation Institutes of Consecrated Life and Societies of Apostolic Life respectively.

However, as Luxmoore pointed out, the *Vatican Radio* report "added that its presence did not mean 'tacit recognition' of alleged Marian apparitions at the site, which are currently undergoing separate examination and evaluation by the Catholic Church." Luxmoore also noted, "The Vatican's nuncio to Bosnia-Herzegovina, Archbishop Luigi Pezzuto, who will also form part of the official delegation, told *Avvenire* that the Virgin Mary was at the center of life at Medjugorje, 'regardless of any supernatural facts.'"[23]

Luxmoore reported on the festival for the *Crux* news site on 7 August. Apparently, 60,000 young people from 97 countries were present there on 5 August, along with fourteen archbishops and bishops and approximately 700 priests when Archbishop Rino Fisichella spoke to them. According to *Radio Medjugorje*, parts of the festival had been watched by more than 2.8 million people around the world.[24]

On 18 March 2020, the *Catholic News Agency* carried a story about Mirjana, that she had said that the Gospa would no longer be appearing to her on the second of every month, which she claimed had been happening since the 1980s.[25]

And on 11 July 2020, the pope accepted the resignation of Bishop Ratko Peric, who retired from the diocese of Mostar-Duvno at the age of 76. His successor is Bishop Petar Palic, who was formerly the bishop of the diocese of Hvar in Croatia.[26]

A further development, though not a surprising one, was the report of the excommunication of ex-Fr Tomislav Vlasic, the former spiritual director of the visionaries, which was carried on various Catholic news sites. As we have seen, Vlasic was laicized in 2009, and this further announcement came from the diocese of Brescia due to the fact that he had continued to attempt to carry on a ministry with various groups and individuals, and continued to call himself a priest and religious, which also continued to "cause serious scandal among the faithful, committing acts gravely detrimental to ecclesial communion and to obedience to church authorities."

According to a statement published on 23 October by the Brescia diocesan press office, "The Congregation for the Doctrine of the Faith formally communicated to the bishop of Brescia that on July 15, 2020, the congregation issued a declarative decree regarding Mr. Tomislav Vlasic. The decree declared that Mr. Vlasic incurred the penalty of excommunication."[27]

28
The Contents of the Ruini Commission Report are Revealed

LEAKED COPIES OF RUINI REPORT PUBLISHED

Meanwhile, the most important Medjugorje development in 2020 came on 7 February, when David Murgia, an Italian religious journalist and Medjugorje supporter, claimed on his blog, *Il Segno di Giona* ("The Sign of Jonah"), that he was in possession of an authentic copy of the Ruini Commission Report, and was now reproducing excerpts from this online.[1] This report was translated by Richard Chonak, and appeared on his *Catholic Light* blog, after he had removed some of Murgia's comments from the translation.[2]

Regarding the alleged Medjugorje visions, Murgia quotes the Ruini Report as saying, "From the point of view of its [i.e., Medjugorje's] possible supernatural origin, this can then be recognized, in a sufficient and reasonable way, in the first seven alleged apparitions, which are attested to have taken place from June 24 to July 3, 1981."

The document is further quoted as saying, "The hypothesis of a demonic origin from the beginnings of the phenomenon appears gratuitous and unfounded... by the positive fruits derived from the phenomenon itself," and, "On the basis of these data, the International Commission considers that it can affirm with reasonable certainty that the first seven apparitions prove to be intrinsically credible."

The members of the commission also apparently voted to agree that the beginning of the phenomenon was "not attributable to human dynamics alone, but having a supernatural origin," and they also excluded "individual or mass manipulation."

REPORT HIGHLIGHTS PROBLEMS WITH VISIONARIES

But according to the leaked Report, not all the claims of the visionaries were accepted as authentic, since "the International Commission has had to consider the repetitive banality of some of the communications which the witnesses declare they received from the Gospa, and likewise the lack of... transcendence, which is proper to supernatural character." And the text also declared that the secrets allegedly revealed to the visionaries, and similar texts, "cannot enjoy any ecclesiastical approval." The commission also advised that for any ongoing events "the linguistic formulation of the alleged messages of the Madonna . . . should take place in the presence of the priest entrusted with the spiritual accompaniment of the alleged seer."

Richard Chonak comments on this point:

> This is astounding advice, urging authorities to have the alleged messages from Heaven processed through a doctrinal inspection before they are ever spoken or written. It would become impossible to separate the mystical phenomenon itself from the human activity of its overseers, and so judging the authenticity of new messages on the grounds of their compatibility with sound doctrine would become practically impossible. An intervention like this did actually happen in the past: at the time in the 1980s messages were recorded in the parish's "Chronicle of the apparitions" maintained by then-friar Tomislav Vlasic, eventually laicized in 2009 after his own doctrine and behavior were investigated by the CDF. Some questionable points of doctrine were recorded in the Chronicle as messages from the Madonna with no apparent objection from him.[3]

The Commission also acknowledged that the visionaries "now effectively have a relation, ambiguous in certain aspects, with money (and with what in general can be called a preoccupation with their own 'wellbeing')." But the text goes on to claim that this is not due to "immorality" but to a lack of spiritual support and "solid discernment," while noting a mixture of innocence and calculation in their characters. It also acknowledges that their behavior has seen manifestations of "certain ambivalences and ambiguities."

One particular visionary, whose name was withheld by Murgia (as "Redacted" below), was accused of lying "multiple times" and of lacking credibility in the way this person spoke of his or her alleged "experiences with the Gospa."

The text goes on to say that,

> The alleged seers have appeared substantially credible in their witness of the first seven apparitions, and also through the succeeding alleged apparitions, it does not seem possible to deny their subjective good faith, independent of judgment on the reality of the event. This positive evaluation, however,

does not extend to [Redacted], on whose credibility serious and demonstrated reservations have emerged. Also, as regards moral conduct and in particular the question of the *quaestus lucri* [gain, profit], the position of [Redacted] is more compromised than that of the other alleged seers.

Furthermore, the text states, "Church authority must keep watch over the economic activities of the alleged seers connected with the Medjugorje phenomenon, especially in the case of [Redacted]."

On the personal qualities of the visionaries, the leaked Report has this to say:

> Attention and pastoral care must be addressed to them above all, toward the development and deepening of their spiritual life and their sense of belonging to the Church. They do not in fact appear mature either in their faith or in their ecclesiality, and at certain times not even in their psychological consistency. The fact that none of them have been really followed by a spiritual director in their personal journey can at least explain these lacks in part.

Richard Chonak makes this general comment at this point on his blog: "I find it puzzling that the commission found the first seven alleged apparitions were able to arouse faith and a sense of belonging to the Church so well that the commission considered it a sign of the events' supernatural origin; and yet the ensuing... years have not brought the seers to mature faith or self-understanding as members of the Church."

The report goes on to say that the Commission "recognizes that the alleged seers, in their public statements, do not intend to take the place of the Church, and they do keep her doctrine in mind, in a sufficiently balanced way. However, there are strong tendencies to draw attention to themselves and their current alleged visions, rather than on the Christocentric and ecclesial substance of Marian spirituality."[4]

The above considerations, then, were the important points from the excerpts of the Ruini Commission report which Murgia claimed to have access to.

RUINI REPORT PUBLISHED AS TWO SEPARATE EBOOKS

The alleged text of the Ruini Report was then published in full, in Italian, as an eBook, both by Murgia and by another Italian writer, Saverio Gaeta, who, as we have seen, is a Medjugorje supporter and who likewise claimed to have a copy of the report. Then the Murgia text was translated into English and is now available online.[5]

The initial question to ask about this text concerns its legitimacy — is this actually the authentic Ruini Report? The answer would seem to be yes, since the Murgia and Gaeta versions are the same, apart from the fact that Gaeta did not withhold any details of names and Murgia added some extra material relating to the chronology of the events of the first eleven days at Medjugorje, and also included the testimony of Darinka Sumanovic-Glamuzina, a doctor who witnessed the sixth alleged apparition.

In addition, Murgia is employed by *TV2000*, a television station owned by the Italian Episcopal Conference, and apparently on receipt of the text of the Ruini Report was able to confirm with members of the Ruini Commission that the document was genuine.[6] Likewise, Gaeta is a well-known author, and his version of the report was published by the reputable Pauline Books organization. If these publications were not reliable, then undoubtedly there would have been an intervention by the Church — but this did not happen. Therefore, we can conclude that the authors have published the genuine text of the Ruini Commission Report.

A detailed analysis of the Report, however, raises serious questions about its soundness, especially regarding the assertion that the first seven alleged apparitions had a supernatural origin, while ruling out a possible demonic origin for them as something "gratuitous and unfounded." And it is surely deeply worrying as regards the whole Medjugorje phenomenon that the Commission could find that one of the seers was accused of repeatedly lying and of lacking credibility.

GENERAL ANALYSIS OF THE RUINI REPORT

To come back to the Report itself, as mentioned above, the Murgia text was translated into English and is now available online as a PDF.[7] An examination of the full document is rather illuminating.

The remit of the Commission is described as being to "present a detailed Report with the relative *votum* [votes] on the supernaturality or otherwise of the phenomenon, suggesting also the most opportune pastoral solutions to apply in this regard."

The members of the Commission, which is described as an "International Commission of Inquiry on Medjugorje" are then listed, beginning with Cardinal Ruini, as detailed earlier in this book.[8]

The Contents of the Ruini Commission Report are Revealed

The first thing to note about this Commission is the use of the word "international." Is that word really justified given the actual makeup of the Commission? The fact is that of its members over a third are from the countries which made up ex-Yugoslavia, and the majority of the others are either from Italy or ex-Communist Eastern European countries.

So far from being genuinely international, the Commission largely came from ex-Yugoslavia, Italy and a few other countries. There were no representatives from the wider Catholic world, and no laymen or lay women. In fact, almost the entire Commission could be described as "male and clerical" — the single exception being a religious sister — and this is despite the fact that the vast majority of pilgrims to Medjugorje have been and still are lay people — and surely some sort of grasp of the lay mentality on this issue is essential if a true understanding of Medjugorje is to be possible, to say nothing of the expertise that suitably qualified lay people would also have brought to the Commission.

This is not to criticize the actual members of the Commission, but rather to point out that its fundamental structure was flawed. In order to be truly "international" and more representative of the Church as a whole, the Commission should have been drawn from a much wider geographical area — in fact, the whole world, given the worldwide impact of Medjugorje — and likewise there should have been an appropriate number of lay persons involved.

While it is true that it was important to have a Commission which included membership of those with authority in the Church — cardinals, bishops and so on — and also those familiar with the culture of the Balkans, the danger of such an exclusive and rather narrow approach is that the deliberations of the Commission would be too insular and constrained — which unfortunately seems to have been the case.

In any event, at best, the Commission could be described as a "regional" Commission, but it is stretching things to describe it as being truly "international."

REPORT POSITS "TWO PHASES" TO THE VISIONS

Coming now to the actual content of the Report, the first part, the "1.1 Initial profile of the phenomenon," looks at the origins of Medjugorje, and seeks to come to a tentative explanation as to what happened there during the early days. As the text indicates, the initial visions, leaving aside their actual cause for the moment, were quite distinctive.

It is very difficult if not impossible to attribute them to the influence of the local Franciscans — they seem rather to be much more of a reflection of objective events. This is a point with which the impartial observer of the whole Medjugorje phenomenon could not argue. In that sense it would seem that the Commission was right to identify the initial alleged visions as the most important.

However, another statement in this section is more questionable: "There are the testimonies that there was pressure on the Bishop, who, probably for this and certainly for the subsequent affirmations of some alleged visionaries on the pronouncements of the Gospa regarding the Herzegovina Question, changed his opinion on the authenticity of the phenomenon."[9]

As we have seen in chapter 12, the charge that Bishop Zanic changed his mind about the alleged visions due to Communist pressure was categorically denied by the Vicar General of the diocese of Mostar in 1995.[10]

Moving on to the next part of the document, "1.2 The reasons for identifying two phases," the text lays out the reasons for such a division between the earliest visions and later ones, and argues that the first five visions, those which took place on Mount Podbrdo, represent those visions which respond best to a situation free from improper elements of influence. The Commission also decided to include two other alleged visions, these being the one which took place at Cerno, a village not far from Medjugorje, and the other a vision at the rectory in Medjugorje. This choice was justified in the case of Cerno because of the alleged "martyrdom dimension" (*la dimensione martiriale*) connected with the events there.[11]

THE INFLUENCE OF FATIMA AND KIBEHO ON THE REPORT

This is a reference to the alleged abduction of the visionaries on 30 June 1981, an incident which was discussed in some detail at the beginning of Chapter 6, "Three More Days of Visions." The idea the Report seems to be putting forward here is that the visionaries were in some way "martyrs" for the way that they resisted a Communist plot to abduct them. But as we have seen, this was not the case, and in fact the visionaries agreed to go with the two young ladies who accompanied them on that occasion.

The Contents of the Ruini Commission Report are Revealed

It's possible here that the Commission allowed itself to be unduly influenced by things that have happened in previous genuine apparitions. And indeed in the "Introductory Considerations" at the beginning of the report, as part of the criteria to be followed, the way that the "Mariophanies" at La Salette, Lourdes, Fatima and Kibeho in Rwanda were regarded by the local bishop as regards authenticity is highlighted as guidance for the ensuing treatment of Medjugorje.[12]

Regarding Fatima and the "martyrdom" incident at Cerno, as noted previously, the connection which comes immediately to mind is the incident on 13 August 1917, when the three seers were kidnapped by the local mayor and ultimately threatened with being boiled in oil. The children fully believed that this is what would happen to them but were so determined not to reveal the secret they had been given by the Blessed Virgin that they were prepared to undergo martyrdom. But no meaningful comparison can be drawn with this incident and what happened at Cerno, and the use of the word "martyrdom" for the latter is unnecessary.

What happened at Kibeho may likewise have influenced the Commission with regard to the rationale behind splitting the Medjugorje visions into two phases, since we find a somewhat similar division regarding Kibeho.

Here, on 29 June 2001, Bishop Augustin Misago of Gikongoro issued a declaration on the alleged apparitions at Kibeho. These began in November 1981, when six young women and a boy claimed to have seen the Blessed Virgin — although only the visions of three of the young women have received episcopal approval. What complicates matters is that in 1988, the then bishop approved public devotion relating to Kibeho, having deliberately put aside questions regarding the actual authenticity of the alleged apparitions. In addition, there was also the question of deciding which visionaries were to be believed given that a "large number of people" were also claiming visions — and so a decision on this was also left for the future.

The fact that the visions of the three female visionaries whose experiences were seen as authentic lasted for periods ranging from six months to eight years was probably also a factor influencing the Commission, given the large number of claimed visions at Medjugorje, even if it has only decided in favor of the first seven alleged visions.[13]

But in both cases, this pattern does not follow the one found in past approved apparitions of Our Lady, where the number of appearances has usually been quite small, in addition to which they have been completed within a relatively short time period—indeed as short as one apparition in the cases of La Salette and Knock, for example.

Also, the fact that with Kibeho we have a situation where the bishop in 1988 decided to approve a local devotion even though the question of authenticity had not been decided may also have influenced the Ruini Commission in coming to its position on Medjugorje.

In any event, the Report highlights several reasons for this division of the visions into two phases, including the fact that the later visions were "scheduled" at a determined time.

THE REPORT ON THE FIRST SEVEN VISIONS

In the next section of the Report, "1.3 Reasons to affirm the supernatural origin of the beginning of the phenomenon," the Commission then sets out to evaluate the initial seven visions according to the criteria set out in *Normae Congregationis*, the CDF guidelines on apparition discernment—these were originally issued in 1978, and then officially made public in 2012.[14] As the reader will recall, we have already examined some of these criteria in chapter 18 of this book, "Clarifying the Case of Medjugorje."

At this point, though, as Marco Corvaglia points out,[15] we can note that there are some problems with identifying what actually constitute the first seven apparitions which the Commission decided were genuine. Between 24 and 29 June, that is, up to the evening before the Cerno vision, there are actually *six* claimed visions, not five. In addition, the other vision which took place at the rectory in Medjugorje happened not the evening after Cerno, that is, 1 July, but the following evening, Thursday, 2 July, which was actually the ninth day of the apparitions starting from 24 June. The day in between, 1 July, saw a claimed vision in a police van, as we will see further on.

In adding the six apparitions at Podbrdo to the ones at Cerno and the rectory, we have a total of eight visions, and not seven as identified by the Commission. So the choice of only seven of these would appear to have been an arbitrary decision, especially since the Report does specifically state that they are assessing the period from "from 24 June to 3 July 1981"[16] which is actually a period of ten days.

Marco Corvaglia relates that Saverio Gaeta gets around this discrepancy by arguing that the Commission started counting the days only from 25 June, and that the first day, 24 June, should be considered only as a "premise," since two of the witnesses of that day's vision, Ivan Ivankovic and Milka Pavlovic, the 13-year-old sister of Marija, were not summoned to the Vatican by the Commission to render their testimony.[17]

But regarding the discrepancy noted above, that is, that the period from 24 June to 3 July is ten and not seven days, Marco Corvaglia reports that Gaeta attributes this "evident inconsistency" to a flaw in the composition of the Commission. In other words, there was an absence of an expert on the history of what actually took place in Medjugorje, which is clearly a serious defect for a body charged with coming to a judgement about the alleged visions.[18]

THE VISION AS "QUEEN OF PEACE" AND HER MESSAGES

The Report gives as a reason for affirming the supernatural origin of the first seven alleged visions that they agree in a way which is consistent, unaltered, essential and simple regarding two points, that is, that the Gospa appeared to the visionaries as the "Queen of Peace," and that she allegedly made requests to them and through her messages, to believers.

Let's examine the first of these claims, that the Gospa appeared to the visionaries as the "Queen of Peace" during the first seven visions, that is, in effect this was the specific title that the Vision wanted to be known by.

When Vicka was questioned about the title "Queen of Peace" by Fr Bubalo during an interview, he asked her, "It is commonly known, Vicka, that you, the Seers, have called the Virgin the Queen of Peace. How did the idea occur to you to do so?"

In reply, Vicka said, "Why we didn't give her that title, rather, she, herself, gave it."[19]

Interestingly, if we look at the transcripts of the tapes over the period up to 30 June 1981, there is no apparent mention of the term "Queen of Peace," or any request from the "Gospa" that she be given that title. When the word peace does appear, it is in a number of the "farewells" given to the visionaries which usually comprise a form of words such as, "Go in God's peace."

The same is true of the first section of Vicka's diary, which covers the period up to 6 September 1981.[20] Instead, the only real title, or self-description, given by the "Gospa" on the transcripts is that of "Blessed Virgin Mary," which occurs a number of times.[21]

Moreover, it is in Vicka's diary that the first substantial mention of the theme of peace, apart from the word being used as part of a farewell, is found. In the entry for 25 August — that is, two months after the visions began — Vicka describes how she, Mirjana, Jakov and Ivanka allegedly saw the cross on Krizevac change into the Gospa, and then as she started to disappear, the cross reappeared, and across the sky "'MIR' [PEACE] was written in golden letters."[22]

In his interview with her, Fr Bubalo pressed Vicka regarding the title of "Queen of Peace," asking her *when* and *where* that title was given. But instead of answering the question in a straightforward way, she said: "Well you know that she, from the start, often spoke of peace."

Vicka then went on to mention an alleged incident when the "Gospa" appeared to Marija holding a cross and said, "Peace, peace and only peace," before speaking of the necessity of peace being established between God and mankind. But in her answer, Vicka makes no mention of the origin of the term "Queen of Peace."

Fr Bubalo continued to press her: "But did the Virgin announce peace in any other fashion?"

To this, Vicka repeated her previous assertions, saying, "Oh, so many times! So often in her apparitions she would leave the words 'Peace — peace to men!' inscribed. And the like."

Fr Bubalo was not satisfied with this rather cryptic response and wanted to know if there had been a more general call to peace, and this gave Vicka a chance to talk about the incident where the word "peace" was seen in golden letters at Krizevac, and to claim that many other people had also seen them.

Fr Bubalo, though, was not to be diverted, and he came back to his original point: "But it continues to be unclear to me as to how you came to call her the Queen of Peace."

Vicka's response was aggressive and also somewhat unclear. "Lord, I told you Father, she herself applied the name, and you again ... now."

She continued with an account of how a friar, known to both of them but not identified, came and asked them to inquire of the Gospa regarding any special name she might have for herself, before saying, "We asked her some two or three days running, and she told us 'I am the Queen of Peace.' We wrote that down and gave it to the Friars in the Parish House. And she didn't say it only then. At that time she said it formally. Now, is it clear to you?"[23]

The Contents of the Ruini Commission Report are Revealed

The most obvious question to ask about this response is, if this is the case, why didn't Vicka just give Fr Bubalo this information in an unequivocal way?

QUEEN OF PEACE OR BLESSED VIRGIN MARY?

The transcripts of the tapes, however, have no reference to this announcement in the first days of the visions, or to the friars receiving it in written form, even though the visionaries are on record as actually asking the Gospa her name. This detail occurs on one of the transcripts found in Fr Mulligan's book—though not those of Fr Sivric or Daria Klanac—dated 28 June, in which Fr Zovko interviewed Vicka. She describes the chaotic conditions on Podbrdo as the visionaries were jostled by the onlookers who wanted to know the name of the Vision. Vicka said that Mirjana then asked the "Gospa" her name and was told, "I am the Blessed Virgin Mary."[24]

This testimony is backed up by the transcript of Fr Zovko's interview with Mirjana, also on 28 June, in which, in response to a question about what they had asked her, she said, "We asked her what was her name. She told us: 'The Blessed Virgin Mary.'" Mirjana repeated this testimony in a further interview with Fr Zovko that evening.[25]

And this is also the case with the interview between Vicka and Fr Tomislav Vlasic, which took place on 3 March 1982, that is just over eight months after the visions began. In this, Vicka states quite clearly that when they asked the Vision its name, they were told, "I am the Blessed Virgin Mary."[26]

So the visionaries did ask the Gospa her name on the evening of 27th June, and the answer she gave was "the Blessed Virgin Mary," and *not* the "Queen of Peace." And so it is very difficult, indeed impossible, to reconcile what was said here with Vicka's later testimony, and likewise, to understand why she didn't speak of this title with Fr Vlasic when he interviewed her.

But when Fr Vlasic produced a personal testimony, dated 22 April 1983, he stated therein that, "When the children asked her if she would be known by various names, she introduced herself as 'Queen of Peace.'" And this is also what Ivanka said in an interview she gave to Fr Svetozar Kraljevic, which took place on 27 February 1983. In this, when asked the Madonna's name, she replied, "The Queen of Peace," and further explained that she thought this was because she "means to reconcile the world."[27]

This is clearly, then, the story that was in circulation just under two years after the alleged visions began, but which is not present in the earliest testimonies.

One explanation for this strange situation may be that, as previously noted, Bishop Zanic's predecessor, Bishop Cule, had, in 1977, set up a shrine dedicated to the Blessed Virgin as "Queen of Peace" at Hrasno, which is about 25 miles away from Medjugorje. It may be then that the insistence on this title for the Gospa was a deliberate move to counter the influence of Hrasno, or perhaps to link Medjugorje with the earlier devotion in the public mind, thus facilitating its acceptance more generally.

Having said all that, though, as we will see, there was an incident involving Dr Darinka Sumanovic-Glamuzina, who was a witness to one of the early visions on Podbrdo, where the term "Queen of Peace" was apparently used — but only once.

But even allowing for this, generally speaking this was not a title that the Gospa attributed to herself in any sort of consistent way, and thus the assertion in the Ruini Commission Report is questionable.

29
The Medjugorje Messages as Suspect

THE CONTENT OF THE MEDJUGORJE MESSAGES

The Report then goes on to say that regarding the content of the requests made to the visionaries, and the message given through them to believers, their testimonies agree in a constant and unaltered manner on the following four points: the fervent return to faith, true conversion, assiduous prayer and fasting, and the continuous invocation of peace.

However, as detailed in chapter 3 of this book, "The Medjugorje Tapes and the Visionaries," based on the evidence from the transcripts of the taped interviews with the visionaries, the actual content of the visions is suspect. And so it is necessary to look again at the earliest visions in order to bring out the fact that there is really no consistent message to be found there, contrary to the above assertions in the Report.

This is quite clear regarding the visions which took place on the first and second days, 24 and 25 June 1981, when there was no message as such during either of them apart from the "Gospa" apparently saying "Go in God's peace."[1] One curious anomaly coming from this period, though, is that, according to Ivan, the color of the Gospa's dress was *blue* rather than gray as was reported by the other visionaries.[2]

On the third day, Friday, 26 June, Ivanka asked the Vision why she had come, and was told: "Because there were a lot of faithful, that we must be together." Then after personal questions about their deceased relatives from her and Mirjana, they asked the "Gospa" if she was going to come again, and received the reply, "Tomorrow at the same place."

According to Jakov, on this occasion, too, the "Gospa" may also have also said that the people were being gathered at Podbrdo so that "all of us might be at peace," and that, "we should be at peace, that all of us should reconcile."[3]

There is an "invocation of peace" here, but whether these remarks constitute a "continuous invocation of peace" as the Report claims, is another matter. And such an invocation also requires an explanation of the means by which this peace is to be brought about. At Fatima, on a number of occasions, Our Lady told the children to pray the rosary to obtain peace for the world and the end of the war. But there was no such exhortation at Medjugorje, and in fact according to the Fr Sivric transcripts, the "Gospa" said nothing at all about the rosary — which is all the more strange considering that at Fatima, the Blessed Virgin called herself "the Lady of the Rosary," and Medjugorje is alleged to be a continuation of Fatima.

Regarding the vision on the fourth day, Saturday, 27 June, during his interview with Marija, Fr Cuvalo asked her if the "Gospa" had told them anything, to which she replied, "She didn't."[4]

And when Fr Zovko interviewed Mirjana that Saturday afternoon, she said that she asked the "Gospa" to leave a sign so that the people would believe. Fr Zovko, worried by the fact that so little was being related by the Vision, said, "She had to give you some message. Mirjana, please ask her this evening to tell us what she wants us to do, all of us."

Similar concerns, though with somewhat different wording, are expressed in the version of the transcripts in the book *Medjugorje: The First Days*, by Fr James Mulligan. He quotes Fr Zovko as saying, "Ok, why did she appear if she has no message to give?" to which Mirjana responded, "I don't know." Daria Klanac has a comparable transcription in her *Aux Sources de Medjugorje*.[5]

In the interview with Mirjana on the morning of the same day, she remarked to Fr Zovko that the Vision had called them her "angels," and, as we have seen, had also claimed to be the Blessed Virgin Mary. In response to a query of hers about drugs and epilepsy, the "Gospa" had said, "My children, there has always been so much injustice in the world."[6]

Mirjana also said that they were continually asking for a sign, but without any positive response, and that on asking if "she" had any message for the Franciscans, they were told that they should firmly believe. Regarding the people in general, the message was, "Blessed are those who did not see but believe!" and "Let them believe as if they see me!"[7]

THERE IS NO MESSAGE

On the fifth day, Sunday, 28 June, Mirjana was interviewed by Fr Zovko in the evening, following the vision of that day. At one point in the interview, he said to her, "What did she tell you?" She responded that they had asked the "Gospa" to appear to the people who had gathered, and then asked "her" why she didn't appear in the church. Apparently there was no answer to this question—but Mirjana remarked that, "She keeps turning around, she looks out over the people, she smiles [and says]: "Blessed are those who don't see and believe! Believe firmly as if you see me!""[8]

A little further on, Mirjana said, "She doesn't answer our questions, only when we ask her to leave us some sign, she only smiles and disappears as soon as we ask her that. When we asked her the first time, she disappeared. When we asked her the second time, she said: 'Go in God's peace!' and again she disappeared."[9]

Also, Mirjana reported that in answer to their question, "Why are these people gathering here?"—a question that they put to the "Gospa" repeatedly—she "continually answers that question by constantly saying that we should not lose our faith and that we should be together all the time. All the time the same thing. Then she keeps telling us: 'My angels.'"[10]

Mirjana also asked a question about the Franciscans, and the response was, "Let them believe as firmly as if they see me!" Then, after some further rather inconclusive questioning, Fr Zovko said: "Why didn't she give you a message when you asked for it? What are people expected to do? Why doesn't she appear in the church?" Mirjana made no response to these questions.[11]

Fr Zovko then questioned her further before saying, "She should leave some message to you, communicate something to you. Otherwise this is just clowning. She comes, you see her, she keeps quiet, you keep quiet and that doesn't look convincing? Do you know that, Mirjana?"

She replied that she knew that and that it would not be convincing for her either, but a little further on insisted that they believed that what they had seen was the Gospa, and that she had said, "I am the Blessed Virgin Mary."[12]

However, at the end of the interview, Fr Zovko put this question, "The Gospa never spoke first until you asked her some questions?" to which Mirjana responded, "No. We always asked her something." Then Fr Zovko said, "Thus there is no message."[13]

Fr Zovko also interviewed Ivanka that evening, Sunday, 28 June, and, pondering the apparent lack of any coherent message, said to her, "She didn't tell you: 'I appear to you because of that and that. I require from you that and that. Do this and do that.' She doesn't tell you to pray nor that you go to see somebody. She doesn't tell you to fast nor to tell the people this and that."[14]

Fr Zovko expressed himself in a similar way during an interview with Ivan that same evening: "Listen! Those who have seen the Gospa always say that she tells them to fast, pray, believe more strongly, and you did not feel anything like this. Is that so?"[15]

Both Ivanka and Ivan responded in a rather incoherent way, but apart from this testimony, as we have already seen in chapter 4, "True and False Visions of Light," there is evidence from a tape-recording made of the visionaries while they were allegedly seeing the Gospa on Mount Podbrdo, and which Fr Bubalo played for Vicka. From that live recording, as far as receiving a message goes, we have the following points, gleaned from what Vicka said out loud as the purported words of the Gospa: firstly, that priests should be "firm of faith" and then those who did not see her but believed were blessed—a point repeated later on. Then after that the Gospa said she would come again to the same place, and that she wanted people to both sing and pray. But to the question as to what she wished of the people gathered there, there was no response. And likewise, there was no response to the request for a sign.[16]

On the sixth day, Monday, 29 June, as noted previously, Fr Zovko read out a declaration on the visions after Mass in which he said that having "listened again to the cassettes, I must insist that there is no public revelation here. If anything is being revealed, it is of a private nature, for the children's benefit alone. Whether this will change I do not know. So far, Our Lady has said nothing that is meant for anyone else."[17]

FR ZOVKO AND IVANKA... AND FR VLASIC

On the morning of Tuesday, 30 June, the seventh day, Fr Zovko interviewed Ivanka. There is rather a curious beginning to this interview in the Fr Mulligan and Daria Klanac versions which is absent in Fr Sivric's book.

Fr Mulligan's transcript begins with Fr Zovko saying, "Do you want me to record or not? It's not important. You know why." To this Ivanka responds, "You can record." Daria Klanac has very similar wording except that she has the last sentence from Fr Zovko as a question, i.e., "Do you know why?" Fr Zovko then goes on to say, "It's not important. It's not important at all."[18]

Obviously, it matters whether the sentence above is rendered as "You know why," or "Do you know why?" that is, either as a statement or a question. And in context, rendering it as a statement seems to be more logical, since, if, as Klanac claims, it was a question, then we would have expected Ivanka to answer that question in some way, whereas she just says, "You can record."

It is from this point on that Fr Sivric's transcription begins, with the following continuation of the above sentence as it is found in the Fr Mulligan and Daria Klanac transcriptions: "Iva, tell me, what is your real name," which Fr Mulligan renders as: "Tell me this, Iva. What do they call you?"[19]

It may be a coincidence, but it is certainly strange that these first exchanges were removed from the tape that Fr Sivric listened to, given that it involved abruptly removing the first part of Fr Zovko's further exchange with Ivanka midway through what he was saying.

It's as if something was being revealed which, for some reason, someone listening to the original tape didn't want to be made public, namely, that for some reason Fr Zovko considered that from that point on, it would be unnecessary to make any more recordings based on some prior reason he had given to the visionaries, which is alluded to in the statement, "You know why." And in fact, that was the last day that recordings were made.

Previous to this, as already noted, Fr Tomislav Vlasic had come to Medjugorje, on 29 June, and spoken to at least some of the visionaries. He gives details of this in a testimony he provided, and in which he makes the following remark regarding the unorganized way the people were praying on Podbrdo, such that he "felt a need to bring the people to the church, to pray in the church, and to try and help them to understand what had happened."[20]

It would be surprising if Fr Vlasic had not conferred about this with his fellow Franciscan, Fr Zovko, and so this probably further explains the latter's insistence that future visions should take place in the church.

And apart from that, the reader will recall that it was pointed out previously that at a Charismatic conference held in Rome in May 1981, Fr Vlasic was made aware of the "prophecy" of Sr Briege McKenna that he would be "in a twin-towered church sitting in a chair and surrounded by a great crowd," which clearly pointed to St James's parish church in Medjugorje. Given that, it's not surprising that Fr Vlasic was anxious to meet the visionaries and also to ensure that future visions should take place in the church. And this is quite apart from the fact, as also previously noted, that on 29 June 1981, Fr Zovko had been told by the Communist authorities that it was now a requirement that the crowds gathering at Podbrdo should be moved into the church.

FR ZOVKO'S FRUSTRATION AT VISIONARIES' RESPONSES

In any event, Fr Zovko's frustration at the way things were turning out is apparent in this remark to Ivanka a little way into the interview: "You didn't change. It means you remained the same in spite of the fact that you claimed you had seen the Gospa. Why didn't this influence you? You aren't afraid, you don't undertake anything, and she doesn't tell you anything. So far she never, first, told you anything."[21] The priest then went on to make another point, not waiting for Ivanka to respond, a further sign of his dissatisfaction.

As previously noted, they also discussed the questions that had been put to the "Gospa" during the previous evening's vision. The first of these, put by Ivanka, concerned their ability to endure, to which the "Gospa" apparently replied: "You will . . . my dear," before saying, "Go in God's peace!" The second concerned how long she was going to remain with them, to which the reply was as long as they wished, as long as they wanted.[22]

Fr Zovko also asked her if the "Gospa" taught her any prayer, to which Ivanka replied, "Nothing at all." To this Fr Zovko said, "Why? Until now, she taught those she talked with. She taught those in Fatima how to pray the rosary, and she said to pray for fellow sinners." To this, Ivanka replied, "She didn't. Whatever we ask her she answers. Otherwise, she doesn't talk."[23]

Vicka was also interviewed that morning, and as already noted, she related that she had asked the "Gospa" what she wanted to happen at Podbrdo, but that from "her" reaction, it was apparent that she didn't know what to say, to which Fr Zovko responded: "What kind of Gospa is it who doesn't know? Then she is smaller than a child."[24]

This was the evening when the visionaries claimed a vision at Cerno, a village about 3 or 4 miles away from Medjugorje, and the occasion of the non-existent "abduction" incident. After this, all the visionaries apart from Ivan were interviewed by Fr Zovko, along with the two young women who had taken them to Cerno.

As we have seen, during this interview Fr Zovko asked Mirjana if she had said anything to the "Gospa," to which she responded that she had—that she had asked her "how many days she is going to remain with us. Exactly how many days she will remain with us. She said: 'Three days'... which means until Friday."[25]

VISIONS IN A POLICE VAN AND AT THE CHURCH

On Wednesday, 1 July, the eighth day, according to Vicka's account in Fr Bubalo's book, *A Thousand Encounters with the Blessed Virgin Mary in Medjugorje,* that day's vision took place in a car, or rather a van, after she, Marija and Ivanka had been picked up by the secret police. However, Vicka was unable to say whether the vehicle was in motion or stationary, as she claimed they could only see the Gospa, and nothing else. Apparently the Vision told them not to be afraid.[26]

According to Vicka's account, too, as given in Fr Bubalo's book, it seems that the first vision to take place at the church at Medjugorje happened the next day, Thursday, 2 July, before Mass. This event was taped and Fr Bubalo played part of the tape for Vicka during one of their interviews. This excerpt begins with Fr Zovko saying, "Now the children who have had their apparition with the Virgin, and at the conclusion of this mass, [sic] wish to pray for you and yours at home." Then a little further on, Jakov is recorded as saying, "Today, I asked the Virgin to leave some sort of sign... and she shook her head like this [affirmatively] and then disappeared.... At the end of her visit she said to us: Goodbye, my dear angels."[27]

The implications of this recording are that the visionaries had their alleged vision for that day before Mass, presumably on church premises, since Fr Zovko spoke of an apparition in the singular, and Jakov used the word "today."

NO COHERENT MESSAGES GIVEN TO THE VISIONARIES

Given all of the above, then, what are we to make of the Ruini Report's assertion that the Gospa allegedly made requests to the visionaries, and that these can be seen as giving rise to a series of messages meant for believers?

The evidence from the transcripts does not show any systematic giving of requests to the visionaries, in comparison with what happened at (for example) Lourdes and Fatima. Regarding those apparitions, and particularly in the case of Fatima, there was a clear, consistent and coherent message given to the seers, one which can easily be identified.

But with Medjugorje things are very different—here there was no clear teaching given by the Gospa, in the sense of her imparting information to the visionaries in a systematic way; rather, as we have seen, for the most part, the visionaries initiated any conversation. And to describe the responses which were given by the Vision as a "message" is inflating a few scattered remarks far beyond their real significance, especially given the fact that it was the visionaries who were questioning the Gospa, rather than the latter imparting a message as such.

Taking the four points made in the Ruini Report as regards an alleged message individually, then, firstly, as regards the "fervent return to faith," on the transcripts this only exists as a few exhortations to having a firmer faith, and to a greater belief in the supernatural, or at most, according to Mirjana, the repetition of the idea that they "should not lose their faith."

As regards the second, "true conversion," it is difficult to discern anything in the transcripts corresponding to this.

As regards the third point, a concern with "assiduous prayer and fasting," these themes are conspicuous by their absence on the tapes—a fact which prompted Fr Zovko to ask why the Gospa hadn't taught the visionaries any prayers, nor told them to fast.

And with the fourth point, "the continuous invocation of peace," all we have are a few remarks that people should be at peace and be reconciled, and the farewell words "Go in God's peace."

Thus the reality is that, contrary to the assertions made in the Report, there was actually no substantial message given by the "Gospa," and this comes across very strongly on the tapes—and it should be remembered that the transcripts of these are almost the only reliable evidence we have as to what actually happened during the early days at Medjugorje.

It may be, though, that in formulating these points, the Commission was influenced by the above-mentioned interview between Vicka and Fr Vlasic, on 3 March 1982, in which, when asked by the priest about what messages the Gospa gave them, she replied, "Her main message is that she calls the world to peace, conversion, prayer and penance."[28]

The lack of a meaningful message was a point that Fr Zovko frequently returned to, complaining that there was no message being given, and so what were the people expected to do, to the point that he described what was happening as "clowning." He also complained about the fact that the Gospa never spoke to them unless the visionaries put a question first—thus he concluded that there was therefore no message.

But there was one definite point on which a message was given, on Tuesday, 30 June, when the visionaries were told that the Gospa would only remain with them for a further three days, that is, until the following Friday. That is a message which comes across quite clearly on the tapes, but it is one which many Medjugorje supporters have never heard, or if they have heard of it, have chosen to ignore it.

THE REPORT AND DEMONIC INFLUENCES

The Commission Report then makes the following declaration about a possible demonic origin for the events at Medjugorje: "(b) The hypothesis of a demonic origin from the beginnings of the phenomenon appears gratuitous and unfounded, being in contrast with what was observed on the initial profile of the phenomenon (see point 1.1), as well as with the positive fruits derived from the phenomenon itself (see point 2 'Subsequent history of the phenomenon')."[29]

Here the Commission is indicating, in point 1.1, the apparently healthy and normal state of the visionaries at the time, plus the fact that it did not seem that the local Franciscans were responsible for influencing them, and also that they stood up to Communist pressure, as all being signs of the genuineness of their initial experiences. These points are seemingly valid as far as they go, but they do not exclude the hypothesis of a demonic origin for the visions.

Regarding point 2, the "Subsequent history of the phenomenon," the fact that there have been "good fruits" arising from visits to Medjugorje is likewise of no absolute significance as to excluding the demonic—how Medjugorje arose and how it developed are two separate considerations, and it is quite possible for it to have had a demonic origin and for subsequent good fruits to also be present, as has been demonstrated earlier in this book.[30]

And in fact, Fr Zovko was clearly concerned that the visions might indeed be demonic. When he interviewed Mirjana on 28 June, he asked her what she thought was the "greatest reason" for accepting that what they were seeing was indeed the Gospa. In reply she said, "We believe that's the Gospa. She said: 'I am the Blessed Virgin Mary.'"

To this Fr Zovko said, "Of course, she said that. Aren't you perhaps afraid that satan [sic] can pretend and say: 'I am the Blessed Virgin Mary.'" He further pointed out that there have in fact been instances of this happening.[31]

He came back to this point in his interview with Ivanka that same evening, saying, "If you didn't pray anything special, didn't thank God, that disturbs me terribly, look, since it sometimes happens that the devil says, pretends and says, 'I'm Jesus' or 'I'm the Gospa' or 'I'm this or that saint,' in order to deceive people. We read of all these things in the lives of the saints. What do you think of that?"

In reply, Ivanka said that she thought that the devil would have run away from the prayer on the hillside on the third evening, and also this was the occasion when Vicka sprinkled holy water on the "Gospa," but that this did not drive the Vision away.

However, in response, Fr Zovko astutely pointed out that this incident showed that at this stage, the visionaries themselves had some doubts about whether what they were seeing was actually the Gospa or not.[32]

HOLY WATER NOT INFALLIBLE REGARDING THE DEMONIC

And in any case, as we have seen, this was not actually holy water, but a mixture of blessed salt and ordinary water, which is not at all the same thing. Moreover, even genuine holy water is not necessarily an infallible remedy against diabolic influence. This is clear from an incident in the life of St John Bosco. At one point, his sleep was being disturbed by noises coming from the attic above his bedroom, noises like the sound of heavy stones being flung down onto the wooden floor. He thought it might be rats or other animals, but scraps of food he left in the attic overnight were untouched the next morning. Then he cleared out all the old junk that was in the attic so there was nothing to make a sound, and yet the noise continued.

He spoke about these disturbances to his spiritual director, Fr—later Saint—Joseph Cafasso, who advised him to sprinkle the attic with holy water. He did this but the "terrible racket" went on. He even set up a ladder to the trap door to the attic, so as to speedily find out what was making the noise. But on hearing it one night, and rushing up the ladder, he could see nothing, and so accepted he was definitely dealing with a diabolical infestation. To combat this, he finally hung a small picture of the Blessed Virgin on the wall of the attic and from that point on, the sound was never heard again.[33]

Thus holy water is not a cure-all as regards demonic influence, and so the fact that Vicka used a mixture of blessed salt and plain water does not mean that what the visionaries saw really was the Blessed Virgin — it could still have been a demonic imposture.

In sum, if the visionaries had doubts that what they were seeing was really Our Lady, and if Fr Zovko could seriously propose that perhaps what they were seeing was of demonic origin, then surely it was incorrect for the Commission to rule out this possibility — and without apparently looking at the evidence in any depth. And this is quite apart from all the points made previously in this book which clearly do point strongly to a diabolic origin for the visions.

30

More Problems Highlighted by the Report

THE COMMISSION REPORT VS THE ZADAR DECLARATION

The Commission Report also makes this statement regarding the earliest visions:

> (c) In the case of the first seven alleged apparitions, the International Commission found that the testimonies agree, also here, in a manner constant, unaltered, essential, simple and modest on the following elements: [1] the subject, the Gospa, manifests and maintains an indissoluble bond with the Christ of God and her person and gestures are not understandable outside of this bond; [2] the requests/messages of the subject, the Gospa, have a theological structural dimension, both in their cognitive-intellectual dimension, and in their practical-operative dimension; [3] the manifestation of the Gospa revives in the alleged visionaries the sense of their belonging to the Church.[1]

This statement presents some difficulties, in the sense that regarding point 1, where exactly is the evidence in the actions and words of the so-called Gospa during these early events for such a bond with Christ? There are a very few scattered references to "Jesus" or "Christ" in the transcripts, but these can by no stretch of the imagination be described as an "indissoluble bond."

And likewise with the second point, if this is saying that the theology underlying the "messages" of the Gospa is consistent with the traditions of the Church and has solid practical and intellectual aspects, then, again, where is the evidence for this is in the very brief utterances or actions of the Gospa during the earliest visions?

In any event, on the basis of this reasoning and the information given above, which it could be argued is flawed, the Report goes on to say:

> (d) On the basis of these data, the International Commission considers that it can affirm with reasonable certainty that the first seven apparitions prove to be intrinsically credible,

as they were capable of fostering in those who saw them an awakening of faith, a conversion in their way of life, and a renewed sense of belonging to the Church.[2]

But as Marco Corvaglia points out,[3] and as we have seen, if these initial apparitions were genuine, how was it that the Yugoslav Episcopal Conference was able to issue its Zadar declaration, in April 1991, which stated, "On the basis of investigation up till now, it cannot be established that one is dealing with supernatural apparitions and revelations"? There is clearly a major contradiction here.

And it must be emphasized that even if the three points made above are true, they do not constitute any sort of proof as regards authenticity — the only way that can be determined is by actually examining the details of the earliest visions. And this information is only reliably found in the tape transcripts. Therefore it must be concluded with regret that on this crucial point the Commission adopted a flawed approach and its findings do not stand up to scrutiny.

PROBLEMATIC ELEMENTS

Now we move on to the next part of the Report, entitled "2. Subsequent History of the Phenomenon." Under the subheading "2.3 Aspects related mainly to the behavior of the alleged visionaries," point (c), we find this statement:

> The main problem of the messages does not concern essentially the original events of the first seven apparitions, but what followed (especially starting from their problematic "transcriptions," "entrustments," "applications" to ecclesiastical situations and people).

The first part of this statement is very much open to question, since it is precisely the original events which need to be investigated with the most care. But likewise, this is an acknowledgment on the part of the Commission that there are definite problems regarding what happened after the first seven visions, and the text goes on to describe some of these, including the "repetitive banality" of some of the alleged messages from the Gospa, and the status of matters such as the "great sign" and the ten "secrets."

Regarding the latter, the Commission, "considered itself unable to order the alleged visionaries to reveal the content of the 'secrets,'" perhaps in part because "the alleged visionaries describe them as hidden realities which, by order of the Gospa, cannot be revealed until the opportune moment, which will be shown to them exclusively by the Madonna."[4]

The statement is quite revealing, and shows that the Commission really adopted an incorrect approach in dealing with the visionaries on this point. It could certainly be argued that having been given an explicit mandate by the Church, the Commission had every right to inquire into all aspects of the Medjugorje phenomenon. But instead of doing this, it rather displayed an attitude almost amounting to subservience to the visionaries, in treating their explanations as somehow above suspicion and not to be questioned because they emanated from the "Gospa."

The next statement in the report is equally questionable:

> (d) In any case, the form with which these realities are attested seems to *recall and consolidate a role* and *physiognomy* of the witnesses of apparitions/Mariophanies that has gradually imposed itself in the Christian religious collective imagination over time and above all starting from the Mariophanic events from Fatima onwards.[5]

What this seems to be saying is that the overall Medjugorje phenomenon — in terms of the visions and the visionaries in themselves, and the messages they passed on — is in some sense a continuation of the way in which genuine Marian apparitions in the Church have developed since the time of Fatima.

But given all the material which has been discussed in this book, and particularly the comparisons drawn between Fatima and Medjugorje — to the detriment of the latter — it does not seem credible to say that Medjugorje is in any significant way a continuation of those Marian apparitions which have been approved by the Church in the twentieth century, such as Fatima, Banneux and Beauraing.

In the case of those approved apparitions, we are dealing with a relatively brief duration of weeks or months, and the imparting of a coherent message, along with (in some cases) clearly miraculous signs; whereas the Medjugorje phenomenon, which has now been going on for four decades, provides no evidence of having a genuine message to impart, nor does it have anything definitely miraculous about it, while it has also been a cause of deep divisiveness in the Church.

MONEY AND LIES

The next section of the Report is entitled: "2.4 Present credibility of the alleged visionaries." In point (a) this deals with allegations of impropriety regarding monetary gain amongst them, and also discusses whether any of them is subject to "significant and altering psychological pathologies," that is, to any type of mental imbalance.

The Report acknowledges that there are problems regarding the first point, but excuses the visionaries on the grounds that they often lacked a "solid discernment and a coherent orientation," and also because of a lack of suitable spiritual guides. Because of this, the Report contends that the relative "impenetrability" of the visionaries has probably been heightened, so that they are at times "innocent" and at other times "calculated."

But this excusing of the visionaries of blame for having "a relation, ambiguous in certain aspects, with money (and with what in general can be called a preoccupation with their own 'wellbeing'),"[6] is surely something that can't just be explained away as a result of a lack of direction and discernment. The visionaries are now adults and have been for many years, with a responsibility, like every Christian, to live up to the moral law—and if, as some of them claim, they have been seeing the Blessed Virgin on a regular basis for four decades now, that responsibility is even more pressing and indeed overwhelming—they ought to have been living saintly lives long ago.

If, in comparison with Medjugorje, a handful of apparitions of Our Lady set Bernadette Soubirous and Jacinta and Francisco Marto on the road to sainthood, then surely more, much more, is to be expected of the Medjugorje visionaries if there is any truth in their claims.

As regards the "impenetrability" of the visionaries, what the Report seems to be saying here, in a roundabout way, is that they have not been as cooperative as they should have been, that they have at times deliberately put up a calculated barrier in their dealings with the Commission members.

The Report concludes this point (a), by saying:

> This negative dynamic reaches its apex in the case of Ivan Dragicevic, whose continuing meetings and conferences on the Medjugorje phenomenon seem to constitute his only work and support. He has also lied multiple times and is also less credible in the way he speaks of experiences with the Gospa.[7]

Surely the realization and acceptance of the fact that Ivan has lied "multiple times" should have set alarm bells ringing for the Commission members? Here is a person who has claimed to be seeing the Blessed Virgin for decades, and yet they find him guilty of lying and of a lack of credibility!

The Report goes on to admit, "(b) The International Commission notes, in any case, that the *events subsequent to the first seven apparitions* constitute a *real problem*, which makes very difficult an evaluation in conformity to that which can be recognized in the *original sign*."[8]

THREE MORE DAYS ... AND SUBJECTIVISM

The next section of the Report begins as follows:

> From the original documents made available to the International Commission, it appears that the then adolescents had declared that the phenomenon would *end*. But as we know, *this has not happened*. Where does the impulse towards this very long successive continuity really come from? The question is reasonable, all the more if we consider that the places, conditions, times and relative predictability of the alleged appearances *in progress* have substantially changed: they now occur with predictable and often even organized rhythms.[9]

Here is an acknowledgment that the visions were in fact supposed to end on Friday, 3 July 1981, which makes the subsequent thousands of alleged visions more than suspect. The Report seeks to explain this inconsistency as follows:

> In the course of the various hearings, moreover, the International Commission perceived in many *ways the great difference of narrative* that exists between the original events and the current events. The alleged visionaries, in fact, appeared without emotions and took on an almost professional air in mentioning the phenomenon *in progress*; when, on the other hand, in the transcripts of the 1981 interviews, the freshness and ingenuity of the children who try to report the lived experience during the first apparitions emerge — with indisputable evidence. These connotations, by contrast, give great credibility to the accounts of that time; but, at the same time, they show a noticeably changed attitude, not only on an emotional level, and in relation to a certain "addiction" to repetition, but, according to what appears, even in the public and spectacular

forms of the present alleged visions or apparitions, among other things for the "ease" of their management.[10]

This section of the Report is interesting for a number of reasons, not least for the way in which it implies that the visionaries' accounts of the original visions were based on real events. This is also the position of this book — except that the evidence points to them as having a diabolic rather than supernatural origin. It is also important because it highlights the fact that the later alleged visions and messages are far more likely to have been fabricated by the visionaries and thus have none of the emotional attachment they felt for the original visions.

And equally, this part of the Report is of interest because it mentions the fact that the Commission members were aware of the transcripts of the original 1981 interviews and their contents. But the problem is that despite this, the methodology of the Commission appears to have been unsound, because instead of looking in depth at the *content* of the original visions, the focus is more on the subjective element, that is, the transcripts being more animated, in terms of the "the freshness and ingenuity" of the visionaries as opposed to the way they spoke of their later alleged experiences. Just because they spoke of the original visions in a more emotional way, though, doesn't mean that those experiences were actually supernatural.

Section 2.4 of the Report concludes as follows:

> Considering that such difference in narrative (and credibility) cannot be ascribed to reasons of psychological disorder or even outright immorality — if not perhaps in the case of Ivan Dragicevic — the problem of the witnesses' present credibility remains. The Commission has therefore hypothesized diverse interpretations of this fact, interpreting it as a "degradation" or as a "rarefaction" of the original phenomenon.[11]

PASTORAL RECOMMENDATIONS

The second half of the Ruini Report is entitled "Suggestions for the Practical Management of the Phenomenon." It argues that the approach hitherto taken towards Medjugorje should be modified, such that:

> The supranational diffusion of the veneration of the "Madonna of Medjugorje" and in particular of the pilgrimages to Medjugorje, with the abundant fruits of grace that resulted from it,

recommends in turn that a positive pastoral attitude should be assumed, aimed at favoring and promoting the fruits of goodness and at the same time to contrast, and, if necessary, to repress the ambiguous, dangerous or even frankly negative aspects that are also present in the phenomenon, as was noted in the first part of this Report.[12]

Here again, there is an assumption that because of some alleged good fruits associated with pilgrimages to Medjugorje, a "positive pastoral attitude" should be assumed towards it, rather than a focus on whether or not its origins are genuinely supernatural—and this is despite the fact that here the Report explicitly acknowledges the presence of "dangerous" and "frankly negative aspects."

The text then goes on to speak about the need to promote suitable pastoral initiatives, so as to encourage a healthy Marian spirituality, "characterized by the renewal of faith, by a spirit of penance and a sense of belonging, faithfulness and obedience to the Church, in accordance with the meaning of the initial apparitions and the widespread attitude among the pilgrims who go to Medjugorje."[13]

But as we have seen, as regards the "meaning of the initial apparitions," the reality is that they effectively have no meaning, since they contain no coherent message.

The following section of the Report is entitled "2. Forms in which the Authority of the Church in Medjugorje should be exercised," with a subheading of "2.1 Reasons why this problem arises." Here, the document argues that adequate pastoral care in Medjugorje is impossible because of the attitude of Bishop Peric, and envisages either a change in his attitude or his "transfer to another position," or alternatively, the establishment of a "new ecclesiastical district" to include the parish of Medjugorje.

The Report then goes on to argue that if the ban on "official" pilgrimages is lifted, the parish church at Medjugorje could be regarded as a "shrine" or "sanctuary" by the Holy See, in accordance with Canon Law, even if "the erection of a sanctuary does not in itself imply any recognition or even reference to apparitions of supernatural origin." And it further states, "Usually, in pontifical sanctuaries, direct dependence on the Holy See is ensured through the appointment of a pontifical Delegate, different from the rector of the sanctuary."

On this point, though, the Report concludes that such a step may be too radical, given that it would lead to the assumption amongst the media and believers that "the Church approves the Medjugorje phenomenon in its entirety." Instead it comments, "Such an erection... requires great prudence and could, if anything, take place at a later time, while for now it could be suitable to establish in Medjugorje only an ecclesiastical authority depending directly on the Holy See."[14]

THE VISIONARIES AS AN EMBARRASSMENT

The Report then looks at how the visionaries should be dealt with in a section headed "3. Attitudes to be taken towards the alleged Visionaries," under the subheading "3.1 Objectives to be achieved."

The first paragraph of this section is as follows:

> As is clear from the first part of this Report, the alleged visionaries have appeared substantially credible in their witness of the first seven apparitions, and also through the succeeding alleged apparitions, it does not seem possible to deny their subjective good faith, independent of judgment on the reality of the event. This positive evaluation, however, does not extend to Ivan Dragicevic, on whose credibility serious and demonstrated reservations have emerged. Also, as regards moral conduct and in particular the question of the *quaestus lucri*, the position of Ivan Dragicevic is more compromised than that of the other alleged visionaries.[15]

It is difficult to understand the comment here regarding the visionaries that "it does not seem possible to deny their subjective good faith," regarding the alleged visions beyond the initial ones. How can there be talk of "good faith" if the Commission has rejected these later claims?

Also, concerning the remark about Ivan's position being compromised, this does not completely absolve the other visionaries, since it says he is "more compromised" than they, and thus that they too are also compromised to some extent by a preoccupation with worldly matters, in a way which is unworthy of genuine seers.

The Report then goes on to say regarding the visionaries:

> In the judgment of the International Commission... attention and pastoral care must, above all, be addressed to them, toward the development and deepening of their spiritual life and their sense of belonging to the Church. They do not in fact appear mature either in their faith or in their ecclesiality, and at certain times not even in their psychological consistency.[16]

More Problems Highlighted by the Report

This is really an astonishing admission — that after decades of alleged visions, daily visions in some cases — the visionaries as a whole have not developed a deep spiritual life nor a sense of belonging to the Church, and that, in fact, their faith, and at times their psychological consistency, show signs of immaturity.

The Report tries to mitigate these points by saying that the above problems can be explained, at least in part, by a lack of suitable spiritual direction for the visionaries. But surely their primary "spiritual director" for decades now, at least for some of the visionaries, has been the Blessed Virgin, and so if their claims are genuine then the problem should not arise.

The Report then goes on to say that regarding the visionaries, there are "strong tendencies to draw attention to themselves and their current alleged visions, rather than on the Christocentric and ecclesial substance of Marian spirituality."

Again, would genuine seers, after decades of personal direct instruction at the hands of Our Lady, continue to be attention-seekers and act in a way which even the average Christian would not stoop to?

The Report then proposes a solution to this problem of the less-than-perfect visionaries:

> If, as is desired by this International Commission, the Church will take a more positive attitude towards the Medjugorje phenomenon, committing herself to promoting the fruits of grace, it appears necessary that the centrality of the place of grace of Medjugorje emerge more clearly than the personal events and present experiences of the alleged visionaries, for which the Church cannot and must not be held responsible.[17]

In other words, the activities of the visionaries — the supposed recipients of heavenly favors far beyond anything any Catholic would even dream of — are an embarrassment, and they should be sidelined in favor of promoting Medjugorje itself, to the extent that the Church should not be responsible for their activities in any way.

MORE BAD FRUITS

The Report continues with recommendations that the alleged visionaries should have their own spiritual guides, that they should do a yearly spiritual retreat, and study the *Catechism*, and also that they should not broadcast their alleged visions in a public manner, nor accept invitations to conferences or other events. On the one hand, these points reveal the mediocre spiritual level of the visionaries, while they also highlight their desire for publicity, factors which after decades of alleged visions of the Blessed Mother are very difficult to explain or understand.

Ivan comes in for particular criticism in the following statement, but the implication of the words used is that at least some of the other visionaries are not blameless: "Church authority must keep watch over the economic activities of the alleged visionaries connected with the Medjugorje phenomenon, especially in the case of Ivan Dragicevic."[18]

Surely if the visionaries were genuine recipients of heavenly messages, it would be totally unnecessary to suggest that such a provision be made?

After commenting that oversight is needed regarding the canonical situation of various new religious communities, and that there is a need to "screen their activities, even from an economic and financial point of view," the text goes on to say, "This will protect the pilgrims from the various risks of sectarian drift, the formation of 'parallel churches,' [and] economic abuse."

In other words, some, at least, of the new communities in Medjugorje are suspect, and pilgrims need to be protected from their influence or the danger of being exploited by them. This is surely a sorry commentary on the general state of religious life in Medjugorje.

And that things are not well in the wider world beyond Medjugorje is apparent from this further statement from the Report:

> In many nations and ecclesiastical districts, there are numerous groups of Marian prayer and devotion which are inspired by the Medjugorje phenomenon and its spirituality. However, they are often not sufficiently followed and accompanied spiritually. Autonomous initiatives organized outside of any pastoral control and sometimes giving rise to dangerous deviations, find ample space.[19]

Again, surely this reflects badly on the whole Medjugorje phenomenon, that movements, groups and so on growing out of it can cause such problems — surely this is a bad fruit?

DR SUMANOVIC-GLAMUZINA'S TESTIMONY

At the end of the Report we find the testimony of Dr Darinka Sumanovic-Glamuzina, who was interviewed by the Commission when they visited Medjugorje as part of their investigations. And it is significant, too, that near the beginning of the Report her position was highlighted as follows:

> The signed witness exists from Dr. Darinka Sumanovic-Glamuzina, collected during the site visit to Medjugorje from the International Commission, which recounts the happening in an extrinsic and neutral perspective. She was present at the place during the very first days of the history of the phenomenon and remained convinced—although she was very skeptical in the beginning—of the authenticity of the alleged apparitions.[20]

What is surprising about the doctor's testimony is how subjective it is, and equally surprising is the fact that the Commission considered it so important that it was the only such evidence included in the Report.

Dr Sumanovic-Glamuzina, who was a non-practicing Catholic at the time, testified that she met the visionaries before one of the early apparitions, actually on the fifth day according to the testimony of Ivanka made on 30 June. The doctor went up Podbrdo with them, and had "an experience of the Madonna that changed her," so much so that "after the event...she felt full of energy."

The impression she made on the Commission is worth noting: "It struck us that this person, after so many years, in recounting that event, was very excited, turning red in the face, with tears in the eyes." In other words, the emphasis is on the emotional aspects of the testimony, which the Report goes on to contrast with the matter-of-fact way one of the visionaries had spoken to them the day before.[21]

Dr Sumanovic-Glamuzina relates that she had been sent to observe the visionaries from a psychological point of view, since she thought they might be being manipulated or subject to some form of "collective hypnosis." But she also states that "everything happening was outside of what I, as a doctor, knew as hypnosis or manipulation." She then goes on to relate that she apparently even believed at one point that what she was seeing was some sort of alien manifestation, since she says that, "At a certain moment, I even thought it was an object of the universe, something that belongs to another reality."

But just then, the visionaries began to pray the rosary in a way that she "had never experienced before" and then they announced that the Gospa had arrived, saying, "Here She is." At this stage then, the doctor wanted to investigate the phenomenon and possibly expose it from a medical and scientific point of view.[22]

However, it is obvious from what happened next that her apparently objective approach had been compromised by the emotional impact of what was happening, since she testifies that she asked Vicka if she could put some questions to the Vision, although she still claimed to be doubtful at this point. Then, after Vicka said, "Madonna, can this woman ask You questions?" the doctor describes her response: "This was a new shock to me because she had contacted something and asked permission so that I could have contact. This immediately put me in a position to think that someone is actually there. Someone is there."[23]

So in a moment, Dr Sumanovic-Glamuzina went from being doubtful to thinking that there really was something there — not on the basis of any subjective evidence, though, but purely, it would seem, based on what Vicka had said.

THE DOCTOR CHANGES HER MIND

The doctor then asked Vicka to inquire as to who the Vision actually was, and Vicka, after listening for an answer, said, "The Madonna says that she is the Queen of Peace."

As we have seen from the information above, the use of this term is the exception, and on those occasions when the visionaries asked the Vision "her" name, they were told, "The Blessed Virgin Mary." There is certainly no mention of the term "Queen of Peace" in the transcripts where they deal with the doctor and the "unbelieving Judases" incident, as we saw in chapter 5, "The Visions Continue." Moreover, Vicka does not mention this in her interview with Fr Bubalo — which is surprising given her later insistence that this was the self-description of the Gospa.

In any event, Dr Sumanovic-Glamuzina's testimony at this point is very revealing: "I hope you understand this situation: a continuous contact between Vicka, Our Lady and me is taking place."[24]

From this, we can infer that the doctor believed that the Gospa was actually appearing to the visionaries. She had been drawn in so as to think that what she was experiencing was genuinely supernatural. Sumanovic-Glamuzina goes on to describe her thoughts, including why such a title as "Queen of Peace" was necessary — since they were at peace — and also why the Gospa would appear in such a primitive

More Problems Highlighted by the Report

place. This prompted her to put a further question, which in turn brought a response via Vicka about the faith of the people locally.

The doctor then asked if she could touch the Vision and Vicka responded that she could. Although claiming to still be in a state of doubt, Sumanovic-Glamuzina knelt down and put her hand at the place where Vicka told her that Our Lady was. We can read Vicka's own account of this incident in Fr Bubalo's book, where in one of his interviews with her she told him that the doctor had "approached and touched the Virgin." This prompted Fr Bubalo to say, "How did she know where to touch, since she could not see the Virgin?" Vicka told him that she directed the doctor, who touched the Gospa on her left shoulder.[25]

There is a potential anomaly here, though; the doctor kneels down but is also able to touch the Gospa's shoulder. It is just possible to do that, depending on how tall each person is, but if the Gospa was on a cloud and floating above the ground, her shoulders would probably have been at least seven feet off the ground, which would make touching them effectively impossible.

Be that as it may, Dr Sumanovic-Glamuzina then tells us that she was aware she was "entering into something very dangerous" such that she was "on an edge" to the extent that at that moment she felt "destroyed," and "collapsed." She also says that the situation seemed to her "to be ... on a very subtle border between the desire of the children that I touch this 'someone' and my unbelief." Perhaps, though, she also wanted to touch the Vision herself, but was unwilling to admit this.[26]

FROM SKEPTICISM TO BELIEF

Here, we can pause and reflect. Firstly, this testimony is, despite its strongly emotional aspects, again evidence that indicates that the visionaries were actually seeing and hearing "something" beyond the natural, and that that "something" could also affect others in the vicinity. What it does *not* prove is that this "something" was genuinely supernatural, that is, from God — rather it seems to point to something evil, especially given the doctor's words that she felt she was entering into "something very dangerous." Could this feeling have been a divine warning to her to not go any further, not to make any attempt to touch the Vision?

Whether that is the case or not, the doctor's further testimony is also very revealing:

In the following seconds, I try, like a robot, to touch something and an incredible thing happens: something that words cannot describe, something inexplicable. I feel that this "something" or "someone" is gone. I don't see anything, but I feel it's gone. I feel that it is no longer here. Behind me I hear Vicka's words: "The Madonna has gone away." After a second, I then heard these words from Vicka. I back off with so much shame. I was so ashamed inside. I felt a great humility inside of me in front of the miracle that was in front of me.[27]

This testimony further points to the doctor experiencing something beyond the natural, to the extent that she is now talking about a "miracle." And we also have the testimony of Ivanka, as recorded by Fr Zovko on 30 June, that when Dr Sumanovic-Glamuzina touched the "Gospa" the Vision departed, and that the doctor had told them that she had seen the cloud when this happened. Vicka also told Fr Bubalo that later on, when the doctor was at her house, she declared, "When she touched her [the Vision] she felt some sort of tingling through her hand."[28]

So the whole thing could be described as a conversion experience from scientific skepticism to a form of belief—but again, it must be pointed out that this doesn't imply a genuinely supernatural experience, rather something beyond the natural, which, given all we know about what happened at Medjugorje, is more likely to have been demonic than divine.

Dr Sumanovic-Glamuzina then describes how she felt: "Inside me, I felt a kind of energy, not like the one that made Saint Paul fall from the horse, but something similar. I am a doctor and I have a very clear perception. All my cells were different. I was aware of having experienced a physical metamorphosis. The external appearance has remained the same, but the internal aspect had completely changed."

Again, the subjective nature of what the doctor experienced, and the fact that she believed it was supernatural, comes out in her subsequent testimony, as she relates that then, as they were going back down, she asked Mirjana what "Our Lady" had told her, which is the point at which she was told about the "unbelieving Judases" remark. The result of all this is the doctor's statement that she "went up the hill being a certain type of person and went down like another person."[29]

This is all very well, but none of the above proves anything supernatural happened to her, and ultimately it is all subjective. And yet the Commission chose to give prominence to this account, and effectively posit it as being an important reason for their believing that the initial visions were supernatural, as is clear from this statement from the Report: "The data and considerations proposed in dealing with the initial profile of the phenomenon (point 1.1) constitute, as has already been mentioned, reasons for affirming the supernatural origin of its beginnings."[30]

VOTES OF THE COMMISSION

Various votes were taken on aspects of the issues dealt with by the Commission, and these are recorded in the body of the Report. These included votes on the supernaturality of the beginning of the phenomenon; on the effects of the phenomenon regardless of the behavior of the alleged visionaries; on the supernaturality of aspects of the subsequent history of the phenomenon related to the behavior of the alleged visionaries; on present bans on pilgrimages to Medjugorje; and on the forms in which ecclesiastical authority should be exercised in Medjugorje.

The results of these votes saw a majority of the Commission in favor of regarding the first seven visions as supernatural; a majority seeing "positive" or "mixed, mainly positive" results regarding the effects of the phenomenon regardless of the behavior of the alleged visionaries; a majority "not yet decided" (*nondum decernendum*) regarding the subsequent history of the phenomenon as related to the visionaries; a majority in favor of lifting the bans on pilgrimages to Medjugorje; a majority in favor of ecclesiastical authority there being dependent on the Holy See; and likewise a majority in favor of the erection of a pontifical sanctuary in Medjugorje.[31]

The overall position of the Commission is summed up at the end of the Report as follows:

> Both the supernatural origin of the beginnings of the phenomenon, and the abundance of the fruits of grace, as well as the unwanted effect of the current prohibitions, which ended up facilitating initiatives not conforming to the thought and discipline of the Church, suggests [it would be appropriate] to modify the line hitherto carried out by the ecclesiastical authority and to assume a more positive pastoral attitude, aimed at favoring and promoting the fruits of grace, while

at the same time contrasting ambiguous, dangerous or negative aspects.[32]

According to Saverio Gaeta, it seems that after the Commission delivered its verdict to the Congregation for the Doctrine of the Faith, the latter body, after examining it, regarded it in a negative light as being partial and biased towards Medjugorje. This point was noted previously with reference to the "doubts" expressed by the CDF about the phenomenon.

Gaeta wrote of a "harsh attack by the Congregation against the Report of the International Commission," and says that the Congregation came to the following verdict: "The results achieved by the International Commission should not be taken into account; and plausibly, a decree of rejection of the apparitions of Medjugorje had to be reached."

But Gaeta also states that subsequently, Pope Francis had the Commission Report examined by other theologians who, on the contrary, supported the Commission's investigative methodology.[33]

VERDICT ON THE REPORT

It would seem, then, that the Commission Report is a vindication of Medjugorje, but as Kevin Symonds points out, this may turn out ultimately to be a pyrrhic victory because the whole Medjugorje phenomenon has been going on for forty years now, with, as he says, "'messages' upon endless messages." This has given its supporters a definite view of what the place stands for. But if only the first seven "apparitions" are accepted, then "nearly forty years of history gets thrown right out the window."

Symonds argues that this will force Medjugorje supporters to "re-evaluate the meaning and message of Medjugorje." He states further, "It will be a tremendous blow to the Medjugorje phenomenon, as it is presently understood."[34]

How then can we assess the Commission's report in an overall sense? Certainly, it seems fair to say that its makeup should have been far more "international" than it actually was, and also that it should have contained a greater number of qualified theologians and also some qualified lay people. Indeed, the Commission which was set up by the Yugoslav Episcopal Conference to study Medjugorje, which met between April 1987 and September 1990, and which issued the Zadar declaration in 1991, was actually larger than the Ruini Commission.

More Problems Highlighted by the Report

The latter may also have been unduly influenced by the events at Kibeho in focusing on the alleged good fruits associated with Medjugorje, and likewise it seems to have been too inclined to downplay the importance of the lack of spirituality of the visionaries, and to make excuses for them. At the same time, while acknowledging that Ivan is guilty of lying, there is an unwillingness in the Report to investigate the distinct possibility that the visionaries as a whole may well be lying about their later alleged experiences.

The fact is that it does not go into sufficient detail as to why it came to the particular decisions that were reached, and in general, the Commission members seem to have looked at Medjugorje with an undue focus on the good fruits.

In a general sense, it could be said that the Report replicated the mistakes made by the some of the unofficial medical and scientific investigations into Medjugorje, that is, a lack of rigor in its investigations, as well as displaying an exaggerated deference to the visionaries in treating them as respected religious figures rather than possible fraudsters.

Also, in the same way that members of, for example, Dr Henri Joyeux's team in the main did not really have the expertise to deal with alleged visionaries, so also with the Commission: it lacked experts with detailed knowledge of what actually happened at Medjugorje.

Moreover — and this is a remark which also applies to many clerics who are Medjugorje supporters — the report shows signs of an excessive focus on the numbers going to confession, as this statement from it describing the situation in Medjugorje shows:

> Special importance is given to sacramental confessions, which occur in huge numbers in Medjugorje. Therefore, the confessionals must be increased, guaranteeing the external conditions for the respect of the secret, and a precise discipline of the confessors must be ensured, checking their identity and suitability.[35]

While acknowledging the crucial importance of this sacrament for the spiritual life, it cannot become the touchstone by which the truth of the events at Medjugorje are judged. And so the numbers going to confession there should not be allowed to overshadow all other considerations as to authenticity.

Similarly, we have the fact that, as we have seen, the Zadar declaration was in essence negative. This was the point made by Fr Andrew Kingham, which is worth quoting again:

The meaning of "non constat de supernaturalitate" should be understood to mean a negative decision. That is, the phenomenon is not supernatural because no evidence has been found to prove the case. Given the facts of the case brought before the commission of investigation, if it is impossible to give an affirmative judgment, then the case should be closed with a verdict of "non constat de supernaturalitate."

Finally, Saverio Gaeta's remark about the composition of the Commission, that it lacked an expert on the history of the events at Medjugorje, is, surely, given the essential nature of such a person for body like the Commission, a fatal flaw which effectively nullifies its judgments.

These criticisms are made with reluctance—but the truth about Medjugorje demands that it be examined in an objective and complete manner.

31
Some Conclusions

WE HAVE LOOKED, THEN, AT THE HISTORICAL background to Medjugorje, and seen how the long-running dispute between, on the one hand, the Franciscans of Herzegovina, and on the other hand, the local bishops and the Vatican, is one of the keys to understanding why Medjugorje has become such a problem for the Church. In addition, we have seen how the link between the Charismatic Movement and the visions has facilitated their acceptance by many Catholics, despite the fact that there has been no Church approval for Medjugorje. Similarly, we have analyzed the crucial role that Fr René Laurentin played in the promotion of the visions, as well as the effect of the numerous books supportive of Medjugorje. This combination of factors, and more, has assured Medjugorje its present high profile, despite the serious problems involved in accepting it as genuine.

We have also seen that both the contents of the visions themselves and the activities of the visionaries have been far from satisfactory. The early accounts about Medjugorje were mostly based on late interviews, whereas the primary source material, the transcripts of the very revealing tapes made during the first week or so of the visions, has been largely ignored. These transcripts indicate that whatever the visionaries saw during this period, it was *not* the Blessed Mother. Moreover, they also reveal that there was no real message from the "Gospa," and that the visions were supposed to end very quickly.

It has also been demonstrated that the arguments often put forward in support of the visions are without serious foundation, and that the wordy and repetitive messages bear almost no relation to what the Blessed Virgin has previously said during her approved apparitions. Similarly, the evidence for miraculous healings and other allegedly supernatural events at Medjugorje has been assessed and found wanting. The activities of some of the Franciscans involved in Medjugorje have been sadly disedifying, while the horrific violence which took place in the vicinity of Medjugorje in the early 90s — when pilgrims were mostly absent — surely could not have taken place if Our Lady had truly been appearing there.

While acknowledging that there have been some good fruits arising from Medjugorje, it has been shown that these cannot be used as the sole criterion for assessing the truth of the visions. Likewise, the fact that Medjugorje has been accepted by so many Catholics is not of itself an argument in favor of authenticity. We are still living through the upheavals which have been affecting the Church since the 60s, and it is against this confused and troubled background that the popularity of Medjugorje must be judged.

Mary Craig tells us that on 30 June 1981, a week after the visions began, Fr Zovko made the following admission to Frs Tomislav Pervan and Ivan Dugandzic, saying that it would be "awful" if, in the future, "newspaper headlines proclaim that twenty, thirty, maybe even fifty thousand people have been the victims of a hoax on our bleak and barren hillside."[1]

The reality is that, forty years later, Fr Zovko's warning has apparently been borne out — except that he greatly underestimated the numbers involved.

THE CHURCH IN CRISIS

This, then, is the situation which confronts the Church and the papacy, forty years after the beginning of the visions in 1981. As we have seen, there has been no official Church approval of Medjugorje on a doctrinal level; rather it has been regarded as an ongoing problem.

The Church in the West has still not recovered from the aftermath of the cultural revolution which, in the wake of Vatican II, threatened to overwhelm it. Catechesis has largely collapsed, and the result has been large numbers of ill-formed Catholics, who have turned out to be easy prey for those involved in promoting suspect visions. Similarly, the loss of a sense of the sacred which followed the changes in the liturgy has left many Catholics looking for spiritual solace elsewhere. In addition, influential theologians have played a large part in giving questionable visions like Medjugorje a degree of respectability and mass appeal. These are probably the main reasons why Medjugorje has had such an impact on the Church, and they indicate the difficulties faced by the Holy See in formulating a policy to deal with it.

POPE JOHN PAUL II'S POSITION

Indeed, Pope John Paul II found himself in a situation very like that outlined by Christ in the parable of the wheat and the weeds (Matt 13:24–30).

> The kingdom of heaven may be compared to a man who sowed good seed in his field; but while men were sleeping, his enemy came and sowed weeds among the wheat, and went away. So when the plants came up and bore grain, then the weeds appeared also. And the servants of the householder came and said to him, "Sir, did you not sow good seed in your field? How then has it weeds?" He said to them, "An enemy has done this." The servants said to him, "Then do you want us to go and gather them?" But he said, "No; lest in gathering the weeds you root up the wheat along with them. Let both grow together until the harvest; and at harvest time I will tell the reapers, Gather the weeds first and bind them in bundles to be burned, but gather the wheat into my barn."

Pope John Paul II was the householder who — regardless of his own private position — had to deal with the Medjugorje "weeds" which were sown in the field of the Church. The point of the parable is that in the beginning, when both the weeds and the wheat sprout, they are very difficult to distinguish. In the same way, at the beginning, many of the signs associated with Medjugorje seemed good. Thus it had to be given time to develop. But, having been given that time, it is now quite clear that the weeds are largely just that, weeds. They have grown up and are threatening to overwhelm the good seed, that is, the message of Fatima, as well as other aspects of the Church's life and mission.

Unfortunately, Medjugorje is proving to be a long-lasting plant, and it doesn't look as though it will wither away by itself; rather some sort of negative declaration coming from the highest levels of the Church will be necessary. At the same time, the good seed must be protected and promoted, that is, the message of Fatima must be proclaimed much more strongly throughout the Church. While sites of alleged visions such as Medjugorje continue to attract large crowds, rank-and-file Catholics are neglecting Fatima, despite the fact that it has attracted unprecedented approval from the Church.

THE TRUTH OF FATIMA: THE PROBLEMS WITH MEDJUGORJE

As we have seen above, the truth and power of the Fatima message have become quite clear over the years. But despite all this, and the lack of any official backing for Medjugorje on the doctrinal level, the latter has mysteriously maintained a very high level of support among Catholics.

If Medjugorje was nothing more than a series of false visions, then the Church is resilient enough to cope with that. There have been false visions and false visionaries throughout Church history, but sooner or later they become manifest and remedial action is taken. It is true that for forty years now, millions of people have been misled into believing in Medjugorje in good faith, but in a pastoral sense, over time, that damage can be undone.

But Medjugorje is much more than a passing difficulty which can be shrugged off with little in the way of ill effects. The truth is that it has played a very damaging role in diverting Catholics from Fatima. The reader might ask: is Fatima really that crucial? And the answer most certainly is "Yes," it is that vital. It represents an unprecedented intervention on the part of the Blessed Virgin in order to bring back to Christ a world which is increasingly denying and rejecting the Gospel of eternal salvation, precisely as she warned us at Fatima. Its effects are still being worked out over a century after the original apparitions, and its message will be of great importance for many decades to come.

During the July 1917 apparition, Our Lady, as part of the secret, told the children, "In the end, my Immaculate Heart will triumph ... and a period of peace will be granted to the world." This is an extremely complex subject,[2] but suffice it to say that the most realistic interpretation of these words involves seeing in them a prophecy of a great worldwide triumph for the Church, and a time of global peace. We only have to look around us to see how many conflicts are raging, conflicts which often have deep historical roots and which do not seem, humanly speaking, to be capable of resolution. The threat of further violence is ever present, and it is difficult to see how there can be genuine peace in the world unless there is a major change in the present way of thinking. Just as the growth of Christendom in the Middle Ages was an imperfect example of the way that a society based on Catholicism could be lived out, so also we need to look forward to a new Christendom, a new "Civilization of Love," a worldwide civilization based on the teaching of the Church, as Pope John Paul II proclaimed during his pontificate.

TRIUMPH OF THE IMMACULATE HEART OF MARY

If the triumph of Mary's Immaculate Heart is nothing more than a patching up of the present system so that it can creak along, then it will be a very poor triumph. We are talking here of a radical transformation of the world — otherwise the use of the word "triumph" is completely inappropriate. And it should be obvious, too, that such a triumph is not going to happen overnight. The deep-seated problems presently convulsing the world are not, it would seem, going to be solved in a decade or two.

This idea, that the triumph of Mary's Immaculate Heart is going to be of worldwide importance, is clearly present in the writings of some well-known Marian saints.

St Louis de Montfort, author of the famous *True Devotion to Mary*, wrote, in the early eighteenth century, of the "great saints of the latter times," who by their word and example "shall draw the *whole world* to true devotion to Mary." He also described how they would, "imbued with the spirit of Mary... work great wonders in the world, so as to destroy sin and to establish the Kingdom of Jesus Christ, her Son, upon the ruins of the kingdom of this corrupt world."[3]

This prophecy, incidentally, only emphasizes the point made above about the conversion of Russia, that is, that this will not happen until there are sufficient apostolic workers on the ground to bring it about, perhaps even to the extent of their working miracles to this end — Russia will certainly not be converted in a religious vacuum. St Louis indeed said that the *whole world* would be drawn to Mary, but also that this would not happen without a great deal of heroic evangelizing work.

Before her death in 1876, St Catherine Labouré, the seer of the Rue du Bac in Paris, made the following fascinating prediction, one which certainly seems to equate with Our Lady's words at Fatima: "Oh, how wonderful it will be to hear, 'Mary is Queen of the Universe....' It will be a time of peace, joy and good fortune that will last long; she will be carried as a banner and she will make a tour of the world."[4]

Similarly, one of St John Bosco's most famous prophetic dreams apparently casts light on the triumph of Mary's Immaculate Heart. This famous nineteenth-century educator, the founder of the Salesian Order, quite often told his pupils the details of his mysterious dreams, one of which apparently concerned the future of the papacy and the Church. He saw the Catholic Church as a great ship, with a future pope as its captain in the midst of storms, being increasingly attacked by irreligious forces, as other boats, representing persecutions of all sorts, seemed about to destroy it. But at the last moment, the pope managed to steer his ship towards two great columns, one representing the Eucharist and the other the Blessed Virgin, and a great period of peace then descended on the Church and the world. This prophecy ties in very well with the message of Fatima, that, following persecutions and the recognition of Mary's importance and her association with the Eucharist, the world will be given a period of peace.[5]

More recently, St Maximilian Kolbe, the great martyr of Auschwitz, summed up the situation succinctly when he said that mankind "will find true happiness only when Mary Immaculate reigns over the *whole world*."[6]

And this point only underlines the importance of Fatima, since as Archbishop Fulton Sheen noted in his book *The World's First Love*, which was published as long ago as 1952, Our Lady's choice of Fatima, a place in Portugal with such a striking Muslim name, is surely of great significance. Fatima was the name of Muhammad's favorite daughter, and the town received its name following the Muslim occupation of Portugal. Muslims make up one-fifth of the population of the world, and so clearly there is not going to be global peace without a major Muslim involvement. And since there is a definite and quite significant place given to Mary in the Qur'an, the message of Fatima is of crucial importance in the evangelization of the Muslim world.

The fact, too, that the Angel of Peace, when he appeared to the Fatima children, asked them to pray in a particular way is surely noteworthy; he knelt down, and bowed his head until his forehead touched the ground, using the type of prayer posture favored by many Muslims. In addition, angels appear many times in the Qur'an and belief in angels is very important in Islam.

Archbishop Sheen asks "why the Blessed Mother... should have revealed herself in the insignificant little village of Fatima, so that to all future generations she would be known as 'Our Lady of Fatima.'" He answers this question by saying:

> Since nothing ever happens out of heaven except with a finesse of all details, I believe that the Blessed Virgin chose to be known as "Our Lady of Fatima" as a pledge and a sign of hope to the Moslem people, and as an assurance that they, who show her so much respect, will one day accept her Divine Son, too.[7]

And indeed, Pope John Paul II himself said in *Crossing the Threshold of Hope*: "Christ will conquer through [Mary], because he wants the Church's victories now and in the future to be linked to her."[8]

Some Conclusions

FATIMA IS THE ANSWER

Thus, genuine Marian devotion, as contained in the message of Fatima, in reality provides a blueprint for the whole Church for the foreseeable future, and particularly, as we have seen, in regard to the promotion of the Five First Saturdays devotion. For that reason alone it is of enormous importance.

But if we also consider what has just been said about the significance of Fatima regarding the evangelization of the Muslim world, in addition to the previous points made about how the Fatima message is intimately related to the conversion of Russia, and thus presumably to the future unity between the Catholic and Orthodox Churches, then the absolutely vital role of Fatima, and Marian devotion generally, in the Church in the future becomes even more apparent.

Many Anglicans, too, have a great devotion to Our Lady, and indeed, the Ordinariate for those Anglicans in England and Wales wishing to enter into full communion with the Church is officially entitled "The Personal Ordinariate of Our Lady of Walsingham." And the Ordinariate is growing in a number of English-speaking countries around the world.

And obviously, too, Fatima can appeal to atheists and non-believers just as much today as it did at the time of the miracle of the sun.

Moreover, Fatima should also have an appeal for Jewish people, since Sr Lucia reported seeing a star near the bottom of Our Lady's tunic at Fatima, and this has been linked with the Old Testament story of Queen Esther, whose name means "star." She intervened to save the Jewish people on the thirteenth of the month, just as Mary appeared at Fatima on the thirteenth day of each month between May and October 1917.[9] And this is obviously quite apart from the fact that the Blessed Virgin was Jewish, and so has a special love and concern for the Jewish people.

In addition, a previous work of this author, *Marian Apparitions, the Bible, and the Modern World*, sought to show that there is a typological connection between the major approved Marian apparitions and various incidents in the Bible which have traditionally been seen as types or foreshadowings of Mary. Thus the message of the approved apparitions, and particularly Fatima, ought likewise to appeal to those people who take the Bible seriously, including Orthodox Jews and evangelical Protestants.

Thus, Medjugorje, by hindering the message of Fatima, is doing far more damage than is apparent at first sight. Not only is it obstructing the propagation of the Fatima message amongst Catholics worldwide, and amongst non-believers generally, but it is also indirectly blighting future efforts at evangelization and the promotion of Christian unity.

All of this is not to say, though, that Fatima, of itself, is a panacea for all the problems in the Church—rather its message is meant to be seen as part of a complete renewal of Catholicism, one involving evangelization, catechesis, liturgy, and so on. But factors in this renewal, such as the importance of the Five First Saturdays devotion, have certainly been seriously underrated.

For the good of the Church, then, it is necessary that a genuine and properly regulated Marian piety and practice once more become part of normal Catholic life. This is precisely what the Second Vatican Council intended by means of the teaching about Our Lady in chapter eight of *Lumen Gentium*, which clearly indicates the importance of her place in the Church. And the unprecedented Marian teachings of Pope John Paul II likewise indicate that the Church should be much more focused on the role of Mary, a role which has also been emphasized by Pope Benedict XVI and Pope Francis.

Thus the genuine enthusiasm and any real achievements attached to Medjugorje, where these exist, need to be integrated into mainstream Marian Catholicism. This means that the apparently genuine conversions and spiritual good points coming from Medjugorje—for example, the large numbers involved in receiving the sacraments—somehow need to be harnessed to the ordinary Marian "channels" which exist in the Church, particularly those involving Fatima.

If this kind of integration does not happen, though, the Medjugorje movement will continue to divert the faithful away from Fatima, and thus further the risk of their estrangement from the true life of the Church. There are signs to indicate this is already happening, particularly in terms of disobedience to lawful Episcopal authority. Either the "good fruits" of Medjugorje are properly appropriated, or there is a danger that they will evaporate in an excess of enthusiasm, or worse, lead to the formation of schismatic or even heretical groups. It has certainly been the case in the past that groups which have started out with the best of intentions have deviated from normality and ended up in opposition to the Church, so this is not a far-fetched scenario, as we have seen regarding Montanism.

Some Conclusions

Regrettably, what seems to be happening with regard to Medjugorje nowadays is the development of a sect-like or cult-like mentality among a number of its supporters. This obviously does *not* include ordinary believers who have perhaps been once or twice to Medjugorje but who do not have any particularly strong attraction towards it. Rather it involves a small but very vocal and influential minority, who have become fervent promoters of Medjugorje — writing books, organizing pilgrimages, or being in some way or other financially involved in it — as well as people who become fanatically attached to Medjugorje and will accept no criticism of it, no matter how well-founded.

There are probably hundreds of websites around the world, in many languages, devoted to Medjugorje, certainly numerous companies offering pilgrimages, and hundreds of books and other Medjugorje items available through various websites. In addition, in Medjugorje itself a whole industry has grown up to service the needs of pilgrims, and properties are available for sale in the town. So there are large vested interests dependent on Medjugorje in one way or another.

PROBLEMS AND DANGERS

What many adherents of Medjugorje don't seem to realize is that they are out on a limb in their espousal of the visions and the visionaries. Instead of following the safe and sure path of the Fatima message, a message which has received an abundance of support from the Church, including encouragement from all the popes since Pius XII, and further confirmation via the collegial consecration in 1984, as well as the beatification and canonization of Jacinta and Francisco, some people are choosing to follow the strange byway of belief in Medjugorje.

It is like having to get home late at night, and facing a choice between two footpaths. One is well-lit and safe, but quite long, while there is a short-cut across dangerous ground, without any streetlights, and in an area known for its high crime rate. Admittedly, the short cut means less work and may even be somewhat "exciting," but in real life would any sensible person risk going off the normal path and on to a strange and possibly dangerous one? It would be foolish to take such a risk just to save a few minutes, but how much more foolish regarding spiritual matters which may have eternal implications?

There have been suggestions, as in the Ruini Report, that even if Medjugorje is not recognized as supernatural, it should still be regarded as a "shrine" of some sort, which pilgrims could still visit.

But as Fr Manfred Hauke points out, in an interview conducted before the announcement of the International Commission on Medjugorje, this is a questionable approach. He further commented:

> If a new investigative commission reaches a recognition that certain characteristics indissolubly connected with the phenomenon of the apparitions speak against their authenticity, then the love of truth demands that this be made known with all clarity and that Catholic Christians be warned expressly against "pilgrimages."

He also warned that if the Church does not effectively deal with the problem of Medjugorje, then "anti-Catholic groups will do the job and with pleasure."[10] In other words, they, and the media, will do their own investigations of the various problems and scandals surrounding Medjugorje and give the Church more unwelcome publicity, as happened with the sex-abuse crisis.

And Fr Hauke also pointed to the danger concerning the apparent patience extended to the enthusiasm regarding Medjugorje by the Church, which could mean it becoming "a boomerang that attacks the Church from [within], if the groups previously connected with the Bosnian 'place of pilgrimage,' [becoming] finally disillusioned, should turn against the Faith and the Church."

This is the danger of a breakaway, cult-like "Medjugorje Church" being formed, which was referred to above, but this could also be applied to individual believers turning their backs on the Church, to form a large group of disillusioned ex-believers.

FORTY YEARS OF VISIONS OR RELIGIOUS FRAUD?

If you are a Medjugorje supporter, and you have stayed with the book this far, you may be feeling rather upset that you have not previously been informed about the questionable activities that have been described above, and which have gone on for so long and caused so many problems for the Church. It is painful to have to face the fact that someone or something has led us astray. We feel cheated. It is easy, once a person realizes that Medjugorje is not genuine, particularly if they have invested a lot of spiritual capital in the visions, to become somewhat bitter and resentful. But if anyone feels that way, they should rather turn towards Our Lady as she has revealed herself at Fatima. There, contrary to the situation regarding Medjugorje, they can have complete moral certainty that the message of Fatima

Some Conclusions

is good, truthful, and life-giving, and also in total harmony with the Church and the Gospel.

As Mary herself told us in June 1917, her Immaculate Heart will be our refuge on our journey, and the secure and trustworthy way to lead us to God. If we truly live the message of Fatima, she will save us from being deceived. Given this, our task is to do all we can to help bring about the triumph of Mary's Immaculate Heart, by complying unreservedly with her requests, following the sublime example of Francisco, Jacinta and Lucia.

Thus, all those genuinely devoted to the Blessed Virgin should examine their position, and look at the Church's approach to both Fatima and Medjugorje. It has given the fullest possible support to the former, whereas it has given no official doctrinal support to the latter. To continue to support Medjugorje means to continue on a misguided quest for "signs and wonders," to continue on a doubtful path that will probably end in disappointment and quite possibly disaster.

This book has sought to give readers a real understanding of Medjugorje, and while we can definitely affirm that Fatima is of heavenly origin, sadly, the only rational conclusion about Medjugorje is that, so far from being a case of "forty years of visions," all the indications are that it has instead turned out to be an enormous religious fraud.

THE FUTURE OF MEDJUGORJE?

In the end, what can be expected regarding Medjugorje in the future? Given all the evidence discussed in this book, it would appear that, despite the Ruini Report's position on the first seven alleged visions, there is, in the long term, very little chance that a favorable judgment regarding Medjugorje will be given by the Church.

The whole phenomenon could have been dealt with authoritatively at an early stage, but it was allowed to grow and has now entangled itself in the life of the Church. Thus it may be necessary to let it run its course, until the visionaries are dead, or they admit it is a deceit, or perhaps until some truly adverse circumstances occur, for example, a great scandal unfolding at some point in the future — although it should be said Medjugorje has already survived enough scandals to sink the proverbial battleship.

It could well be many years before a definite judgement can be rendered, when all the present actors in this on-going tragedy have finally left the stage. It will probably be the case, then, that at some point in the future a truly International Commission with the mandate of getting to the truth about Medjugorje will be established. Apart from anything else, this is necessary in order for the Church to be the bearer of truth to the world, following in the footsteps of Christ, the Way, the *Truth* and the Life.

An ideal ruling from the critical point of view would be a clear negative judgment, *constat de non supernaturalitate*, accompanied by a ban on pilgrimages and on any form of promotion of Medjugorje. It might be necessary to add a warning of censure in case of disobedience.[11]

In any event, such a Commission will need to have an explicit focus on the alleged visions, and particularly on the transcripts of the original tapes rather than on the "fruits" of Medjugorje. In the meantime, an agreed-upon, Vatican-approved version of these tapes could be produced, translated into the major world languages, and put on the internet for all to see, along with any other relevant documentation.

The truth is that Medjugorje is a spiritual malaise which is damaging the Church; and at the same time Catholics must be strongly encouraged to support Fatima, Lourdes and other approved apparitions, while being actively discouraged from supporting Medjugorje.

For now, the genuine Fatima message will continue to suffer as good Catholics are led astray by Medjugorje, with grievous adverse consequences for both the Church and the world.

ENDNOTES

NOTE FOR THE INTRODUCTION
1. See Saverio Gaeta, *Medjugorje: 1. La vera storia* (San Paolo Edizioni, 2020), p. 141, https://www.vu.nl/en/Images/20131112_Rapport_Commissie_Baud_Engelse_versie_definitief_tcm270-365093.pdf, and https://hrcak.srce.hr/file/165671 (11_Jolic_Bax.pdf); the Italian version of *Medjugorje Revisited* is: *Comprendere Medjugorje: Visioni celesti o inganno religioso?* (Eupress FTL–Edizioni Cantagalli s.r.l, Lugano/Siena, 2017).

NOTES FOR CHAPTER 1
1. Ivo Sivric, OFM, *The Hidden Side of Medjugorje, Volume 1*, ed. L Bélanger, trans. S. Rini (Psilog Inc., Saint-François-du-Lac, 1989), p. 195, n. 214.
2. John R. Lampe, *Yugoslavia as History: Twice There Was a Country*, 2nd edition (Cambridge University Press, Cambridge, 2000), pp. 19–20; cf. Marko Attila Hoare, *The History of Bosnia: From the Middle Ages to the Present Day* (Saqi Books, London, 2007), pp. 41–42, 58, and Michael A. Sells, *The Bridge Betrayed: Religion and Genocide in Bosnia* (University of California Press, Berkeley/Los Angeles, 1998), p. 33.
3. Sivric, *The Hidden Side of Medjugorje, Vol. I*, p. 117; Lampe, *Yugoslavia as History*, pp. 23, 67; cf. Hoare, *The History of Bosnia*, p. 78. An archdiocese was created at Sarajevo in 1881, and the first archbishop was Josef Stadler, who did much to expand the school system, while also building a cathedral and numerous churches.
4. Marcus Tanner, *Croatia: A Nation Forged in War* (Yale University Press, New Haven, 1997), pp. 150–52, 155; Mary Craig, *Spark from Heaven: The Mystery of the Madonna of Medjugorje* (Spire, London, 1991), p. 46, n. 8; Lampe, *Yugoslavia as History*, pp. 208–213; Leslie Benson, *Yugoslavia: A Concise History* (Palgrave Macmillan, Basingstoke, 2004), pp. 52–53, 63, 77–78; cf. Sells, *The Bridge Betrayed*, pp. 60–62, 99; Vjekoslav Perica, *Balkan Idols: Religion and Nationalism in Yugoslav States* (Oxford University Press, New York, 2002), p. 118; E. Michael Jones, *The Medjugorje Deception: Queen of Peace, Ethnic Cleansing, Ruined Lives* (Fidelity Press, South Bend, 1998), pp. 2, 68.
5. This criticism did not necessarily apply to every individual Franciscan or parish, but is a general observation about the overall situation within the Order in Bosnia-Hercegovina.
6. Jones, *The Medjugorje Deception*, pp. 25–26, 54–55, 74; Sivric, *The Hidden Side of Medjugorje, Volume 1*, pp. 115–18.
7. Jones, *The Medjugorje Deception*, pp. 60–62; Daria Klanac, *Medjugorje, Réponses aux objections* (Le Sarment, 2001), pp. 26–27.

NOTES FOR CHAPTER 2
1. Jones, *The Medjugorje Deception*, pp. 43–46; Sivric, *The Hidden Side of Medjugorje, Volume 1*, p. 105; cf. Klanac, *Medjugorje, Réponses aux objections*, p. 46.

2. Jones, *The Medjugorje Deception*, pp. 43–47; Craig, *Spark from Heaven*, p. 56; cf. *Visions on Demand: The Medjugorje Conspiracy*, 60 min., Network 5 International, 1997, video, available on YouTube at: https://www.youtube.com/watch?v=koWigNN1fS8; Gaeta, *Medjugorje: 1. La vera storia*, p. 26; https://medjugorje.org/svetletter.htm.

3. René Laurentin, *Medjugorje Testament: Hostility Abounds, Grace Superabounds* (Ave Maria Press, Toronto, 1999), pp. 93, 214.

4. Jones, *The Medjugorje Deception*, pp. 50–52.

5. Ibid., pp. 53–54.

6. Denis Nolan, *Medjugorje: A Time for Truth and a Time for Action* (Queenship Publishing, Santa Barbara, 1993), pp. 24, 181.

7. Perica, *Balkan Idols*, p. 109.

8. Dates of birth from: Michael Davies, *Medjugorje After Fifteen Years: The Message and the Meaning* (The Remnant Press, St Paul, 1998), pp. 5–6. Other sources give variations on these dates.

9. Sivric, *The Hidden Side of Medjugorje, Volume 1*, pp. 32, 35, 36.

10. Agnes Horvath and Arpad Szakolczai, *The Dissolution of Communist Power: The Case of Hungary* (Routledge, 1992), pp. xiii, 1, 216–17, 220.

11. Katherine Verdery, *What Was Socialism, and What Comes Next?* (Princeton University Press, Princeton, 1996), pp. 21–27.

12. L. Rooney and R. Faricy, *Mary Queen of Peace. Is the Mother of God Appearing in Medjugorje?* (Fowler Wright, Leominster, 1984), pp. 28–29. The correct spelling is "Tardif."

13. Sivric, *The Hidden Side of Medjugorje, Volume 1*, pp. 105–106, n. 183; cf. *Visions on Demand* video.

14. Wayne Weible, *The Final Harvest: Medjugorje at the End of the Century* (Paraclete Press, Brewster, 1999), p. 4. Emphasis added.

15. Rudo Franken, *A Journey to Medjugorje: Objections to the Apparitions* (Roggel en Neer, 1999), p. 49; René Laurentin and Ljudevit Rupcic, trans. F. Martin, *Is the Virgin Mary Appearing at Medjugorje?* (The Word Among Us Press, Gaithersburg, 1988), pp. 20–21.

16. Laurentin and Rupcic, *Virgin Mary Appearing at Medjugorje?* pp. 97–98.

17. Morton T. Kelsey, *Tongue Speaking: The History and Meaning of Charismatic Experience* (Crossroad, New York, 1981), pp. 55–58, 60–65.

18. Ibid., pp. xii–xiii; Walter Hollenweger, *The Pentecostals* (SCM Press Ltd., London, 1972), pp. 8–9.

19. René Laurentin, *Catholic Pentecostalism* (Darton, Longman and Todd, London, 1977), pp. 12–13.

20. Ibid., pp. 107–10.

21. Kelsey, *Tongue Speaking*, pp. xiii–xvi, 208.

22. Ibid., pp. 223–25, 231.

23. Laurentin, *Catholic Pentecostalism*, p. 9; Laurentin & Rupcic, *Virgin Mary Appearing at Medjugorje?* p. 3.

24. Laurentin and Rupcic, *Virgin Mary Appearing at Medjugorje?* p. 21.

25. Ronald Knox, *Enthusiasm, A Chapter in the History of Religion* (Collins, London, 1987), pp. 26–27, 29–30, 33–35, 38; Hans Lietzmann, *A History of*

the Early Church, Vol. I (James Clarke & Co., Cambridge, 1993), pp. 462–65; Christine Trevett, *Montanism: Gender, Authority and the New Prophecy* (Cambridge University Press, 2002), pp. 2, 13, 78–79; "Montanists," in *The Catholic Encyclopedia*, at: www.newadvent.org/cathen/10521a.htm.

26. Knox, *Enthusiasm*, pp. 33, 37, 38; Lietzmann, *A History of the Early Church, Vol. I* (James Clarke & Co., Cambridge, 1993), pp. 465–67; Trevett, *Montanism: Gender, Authority and the New Prophecy*, pp. 31, 101.

27. Trevett, *Montanism*, pp. 3, 158, 167–69, 185, 210, 221.

28. Ibid., pp. 186, 210–12, 214–15.

29. Laurentin, *Catholic Pentecostalism*, pp. 136–37; Gaeta, *Medjugorje: 1. La vera storia*, p. 28.

30. Knox, *Enthusiasm*, pp. 37–38, 48–49; Lietzmann, *A History of the Early Church, Vol. I*, pp. 465–468.

31. Knox, *Enthusiasm*, p. 30.

32. Trevett, *Montanism*, pp. 39–40.

33. Knox, *Enthusiasm*, p. 25.

34. Ibid., pp. 31–33.

35. Knox, *Enthusiasm*, p. 34; Trevett, *Montanism*, pp. 1–2, 227.

36. Knox, *Enthusiasm*, pp. 38–39; Lietzmann, *A History of the Early Church, Vol. I*, pp. 462–63.

NOTES FOR CHAPTER 3

1. Jones, *The Medjugorje Deception*, pp. 83–84; Daria Klanac, *Aux Sources de Medjugorje* (Éditions Sciences et Culture, Montréal, 1998), p. 178; Sivric, *The Hidden Side of Medjugorje, Vol. I*, p. 102. However, it is true that both the children of La Salette, and to a lesser extent St Bernadette, also had less than ideal family backgrounds, so this factor is not necessarily decisive even though it does have to be taken into account.

2. Svetozar Kraljevic, OFM, *The Apparitions of Our Lady at Medjugorje*, ed. M. Scanlan (Franciscan Herald Press, Chicago, 1984), p. 152. Emphasis added.

3. Craig, *Spark from Heaven*, p. 119.

4. Jones, *The Medjugorje Deception*, pp. 84–86, 350–51, 353.

5. Sister Lucia, *Fatima in Lucia's Own Words II*, ed., Louis Kondor (Secretariado dos Pastorinhos, Fatima, 1999).

6. Although Sr Lucia's father did drink, she categorically states that he was not a drunkard, as some exaggerated accounts of Fatima have made out, and particularly that he never disturbed the "peace and tranquility of the family environment." Thus in no sense was her family "dysfunctional." Sister Lucia, *Fatima in Lucia's Own Words II*, p. 143.

7. Klanac, *Aux Sources de Medjugorje*, p. 12.

8. Donal Anthony Foley, *Marian Apparitions, the Bible, and the Modern World* (Gracewing, Leominster, 2002), pp. 138, 159.

9. Ibid., pp. 245, 250, 281, 290, 292.

10. Augustin Poulain, *Revelations and Visions* (Alba House, New York, 1998), p. 79. The italic emphases in the original text have been removed.

11. Craig, *Spark from Heaven*, pp. 57–59, 75; Michael O'Carroll, *Medjugorje: Facts, Documents, Theology* (Veritas, Dublin, 1986), p. 34.

12. Sivric, *The Hidden Side of Medjugorje, Vol. I*, pp. 55–56, 59, 87.

13. Klanac, *Aux Sources de Medjugorje*, pp. 11–12.

14. An example which shows how similar they are can be seen at: http://theotokos.org.uk/wp-content/uploads/2020/07/sivric-klanac-french-comparison.pdf; cf. this translation of some of the Klanac text from French to English: http://theotokos.org.uk/wp-content/uploads/2020/07/klanac-french-english.pdf.

15. Klanac, *Aux Sources de Medjugorje*, p. 68.

16. Cf. Ivo Sivric, *La face cachée de Medjugorje, tome I* (Éditions Psilog, Saint-François-du-Lac, 1988), pp. 303–309; and Klanac, *Aux Sources de Medjugorje*, pp. 127–31.

17. Cf. Klanac, *Aux Sources de Medjugorje*, pp. 69–81, and Sivric, *La face cachée de Medjugorje*, pp. 247–51.

18. Cf. Klanac, *Aux Sources de Medjugorje*, pp. 97–100, and Sivric, *La face cachée de Medjugorje*, pp. 267–68.

19. Klanac, *Aux Sources de Medjugorje*, pp. 93–95.

20. Ibid., p. 83.

21. Klanac, *Aux Sources de Medjugorje*, pp. 168, 176, 178–79, 181, 183.

22. Ljudevit Rupcic and Viktor Nuic, *Once Again the Truth about Medjugorje* (K. Kresmir, Zagreb, 2002), pp. 61–62, 79.

23. en.louisbelanger.com; See: "Are our primary sources authentic?" and "Are our transcriptions reliable?"

24. Sivric, *The Hidden Side of Medjugorje, Vol. I*, p. 26; en.louisbelanger.com/the-hidden-side-of-medjugorje. It seems that Fr Sivric's hearing was less acute that that of Daria Klanac, so in the absence of agreed official transcripts of the tapes, both versions need to be used, where possible.

25. Jones, *The Medjugorje Deception*, pp. 73–75; Laurentin and Rupcic, *Virgin Mary Appearing at Medjugorje?* p. 38; Craig, *Spark from Heaven*, pp. 20–21.

26. Another witness on this first day was 13-year-old Milka Pavlovic, Marija's sister. See Sivric, *The Hidden Side of Medjugorje, Vol. I*, p. 36.

27. Sivric, *The Hidden Side of Medjugorje, Vol. I*, pp. 220–21; en.louisbelanger.com: "Medjupedia: A pause—The construction of the 'Lady of Medjugorje,' 30 September 2010."

28. Albert Farges, *Mystical Phenomena*, trans. S. P. Jacques (Burns, Oates & Washbourne Ltd., London, 1926), pp. 330–31. This book received an approbation from Pope Benedict XV; Sivric, *The Hidden Side of Medjugorje, Vol. I*, p. 224; cf. James Mulligan, *Medjugorje: The First Days* (Boanerges Press, Bijakovici, 2013), p. 95.

29. Manfred Hauke, "The prophetic role of Mary in apparitions," in *Introduction to Mariology* (Catholic University of America Press, Washington, D. C., 2021), chap. 9, p. 6. Originally published as *Introduzione alla Mariologia* (EuPress FTL, Lugano, Switzerland, 2008), pp. 303–329; available at: http://catholiclight.stblogs.org/index.php/2010/12/.

Notes for Chapter 4

30. Sivric, *The Hidden Side of Medjugorje, Vol. I*, pp. 243–44, 286. See also: Marco Corvaglia, "Nota documentaria sui messaggi dei primi anni" in *La verità su Medjugorje: Il grande inganno* (Lindau, Turin, 2018), pp. 11–13.

31. Sivric, *The Hidden Side of Medjugorje, Vol. I*, pp. 205–206; cf. Mulligan, *Medjugorje: The First Days*, p. 64.

32. René Laurentin and René Lejeune, *Messages and Teachings of Mary at Medjugorje: Chronological Corpus of the Messages* (The Riehle Foundation, Milford, 1988), pp. ix, 20.

33. Laurentin, *Medjugorje Testament*, p. 81.

34. Weible, *The Final Harvest*, p. 11.

35. F. Sanchez-Ventura y Pascual, *The Apparitions of Garabandal*, trans. A de Bertodano (San Miguel Publishing Co., Detroit, 1976), pp. 32–34.

36. Sivric, *The Hidden Side of Medjugorje, Vol. I*, p. 271; cf. Klanac, *Aux Sources de Medjugorje*, p. 96 and Mulligan, *Medjugorje: The First Days*, p. 124.

37. Craig, *Spark from Heaven*, pp. 58, 60; Sivric, *The Hidden Side of Medjugorje, Vol. I*, p. 264; cf. Klanac, *Aux Sources de Medjugorje*, p. 88. See also similar comments by Ivanka in Sivric, *The Hidden Side of Medjugorje, Vol. I*, p. 305.

38. Sivric, *The Hidden Side of Medjugorje, Vol. I*, p. 60.

39. Sivric, *The Hidden Side of Medjugorje, Vol. I*, p. 254; cf. Klanac, *Aux Sources de Medjugorje*, p. 70.

40. Sivric, *The Hidden Side of Medjugorje, Vol. I*, pp. 260, 263; cf. Klanac, *Aux Sources de Medjugorje*, pp. 83–84, and Mulligan, *Medjugorje: The First Days*, p. 74.

41. Farges, *Mystical Phenomena*, pp. 336–37. Emphasis added.

42. Sivric, *The Hidden Side of Medjugorje, Vol. I*, p. 214; cf. Mulligan, *Medjugorje: The First Days*, p. 70.

43. Sivric, *The Hidden Side of Medjugorje, Vol. I*, pp. 209–210; cf. Mulligan, *Medjugorje: The First Days*, p. 66.

44. Sivric, *The Hidden Side of Medjugorje, Vol. I*, pp. 206–7, 213, 224, 228, 244.

45. Ibid., pp. 208, 301, 320; Kraljevic, *The Apparitions of Our Lady at Medjugorje*, p. 154; cf. Mulligan, *Medjugorje: The First Days*, p. 66.

NOTES FOR CHAPTER 4

1. Sivric, *The Hidden Side of Medjugorje, Vol. I*, p. 211. The square brackets with italicized wording are present in the original texts given by Fr Sivric; cf. Mulligan, *Medjugorje: The First Days*, p. 68.

2. Sivric, *The Hidden Side of Medjugorje, Vol. I*, pp. 59, 211–13, 255–56; cf. Klanac, *Aux Sources de Medjugorje*, pp. 70–71, and Cf. Mulligan, *Medjugorje: The First Days*, pp. 49–50, 68–69.

3. Janko Bubalo, *A Thousand Encounters with the Blessed Virgin Mary in Medjugorje* (Friends of Medjugorje, Chicago, 1996), p. 17.

4. Sivric, *The Hidden Side of Medjugorje, Vol. I*, pp. 216, 225–28; cf. Mulligan, *Medjugorje: The First Days*, pp. 96–97.

5. Sivric, *The Hidden Side of Medjugorje, Vol. I*, pp. 231–34; cf. Mulligan, *Medjugorje: The First Days*, pp. 79–81.

6. Sivric, *The Hidden Side of Medjugorje, Vol. I*, pp. 237, 238; cf. Mulligan, *Medjugorje: The First Days*, pp. 84–85.
7. Sivric, *The Hidden Side of Medjugorje, Vol. I*, pp. 239–40; cf. Mulligan, *Medjugorje: The First Days*, pp. 85–86.
8. Sivric, *The Hidden Side of Medjugorje, Vol. I*, p. 263; cf. Klanac, *Aux Sources de Medjugorje*, pp. 86–87, and Mulligan, *Medjugorje: The First Days*, pp. 76–77.
9. Sivric, *The Hidden Side of Medjugorje, Vol. I*, pp. 263–64; cf. Klanac, *Aux Sources de Medjugorje*, p. 87, and Mulligan, *Medjugorje: The First Days*, p. 77.
10. Sivric, *The Hidden Side of Medjugorje, Vol. I*, pp. 278, 284; Mulligan, *Medjugorje: The First Days*, pp. 150, 171–72.
11. Sivric, *The Hidden Side of Medjugorje, Vol. I*, pp. 281–82; cf. Klanac, *Aux Sources de Medjugorje*, pp. 117–18, and Mulligan, *Medjugorje: The First Days*, p. 148.
12. Sivric, *The Hidden Side of Medjugorje, Vol. I*, pp. 284, 286; cf. Klanac, *Aux Sources de Medjugorje*, p. 121, and Mulligan, *Medjugorje: The First Days*, pp. 149–50.
13. Bubalo, *Thousand Encounters*, pp. 29–30.
14. Giorgio Gagliardi and Marco Margnelli, *Le apparizioni della Madonna* (Riza Scienze, Milan, 1987), pp. 29–31, cited in: Corvaglia, *La verità su Medjugorje*, pp. 216–20.
15. Sivric, *The Hidden Side of Medjugorje, Vol. I*, pp. 287–88, 294–95, 312; cf. Klanac, *Aux Sources de Medjugorje*, pp. 102, 122, 130–31, and Mulligan, *Medjugorje: The First Days*, pp. 145, 152–53, 157.
16. Sivric, *The Hidden Side of Medjugorje, Vol. I*, p. 57.
17. Klanac, *Aux Sources de Medjugorje*, pp. 123, 125–26; cf. Sivric, *The Hidden Side of Medjugorje, Vol. I*, pp. 288–89, 291–92, and Mulligan, *Medjugorje: The First Days*, pp. 153, 155.
18. Sivric, *The Hidden Side of Medjugorje, Vol. I*, p. 304. Cf Mulligan, *Medjugorje: The First Days*, p. 165.
19. Sivric, *The Hidden Side of Medjugorje, Vol. I*, p. 342; Klanac, *Aux Sources de Medjugorje*, p. 155, and Mulligan, *Medjugorje: The First Days*, p. 215.
20. Craig, *Spark from Heaven*, pp. 65, 68, 72–73; cf. Sivric, *The Hidden Side of Medjugorje, Vol. I*, p. 376, and Mulligan, *Medjugorje: The First Days*, p. 246.
21. Laurentin and Lejeune, *Messages and Teachings*, p. 60.
22. Cited by Frances Parkinson Keyes, "Bernadette and the Beautiful Lady," in J. Delaney, ed., *A Woman Clothed with the Sun* (Doubleday, New York, 1961), p. 122.
23. René Laurentin, *The Life of Catherine Labouré*, trans., P. Inwood (Collins, London, 1983), pp. 73–76.
24. Jean Jaouen, *A Grace Called La Salette*, trans. N. Théroux (La Salette Publications, Attleboro, 1991), pp. 40–42, 49–50; John Beevers, *The Sun Her Mantle* (Browne and Nolan Ltd., Dublin, 1954), pp. 26–28.
25. John de Marchi, I. M. C., *Fatima from the Beginning*, trans. I. M. Kingsbury (Missões Consolata, Fatima, 1983), pp. 50–51.

Notes for Chapter 5

26. Kondor, *Fatima in Lucia's Own Words*, pp. 60–62; cf. the similar accounts in the *Fourth Memoir* of this volume, pp. 150–53. Some secondary accounts of this incident may give the impression that the Angel only gradually assumed his final appearance before the children, and thus that this would invalidate the argument given above. But clearly, Sr Lucia's memoirs are the primary source for the history of the Fatima apparitions, and thus her account here is not comparable with what happened at Medjugorje.

27. Farges, *Mystical Phenomena*, pp. 358–59.

28. Léon Cristiani, *Evidence of Satan in the Modern World* (TAN, Rockford, 1974), pp. 58–60. Emphasis added.

29. Courtenay Bartholomew, *A Scientist Researches Mary Mother of All Nations* (Queenship Publishing Company, Goleta, 1999), p. 175.

30. Raoul Auclair, *The Lady of All Peoples*, trans. E. Massecar (L'Armée de Marie, Inc., Québec, 1978), pp. 113, 119, 121, 127, 131. Emphasis added. For information on the problems with accepting the Amsterdam visions see: http://theotokos.org.uk/controverted-apparitions-at-amsterdam. Both the original Ordinary, Bishop Huibers and Pope John XXIII strongly disapproved of the alleged events at Amsterdam, and a notification by the Sacred Congregation for the Doctrine of the Faith appeared in *L'Osservatore Romano*, on 27 June 1974 to that effect. However, a more recent bishop, Msgr Punt, on 31 May 2002, issued a statement on these alleged apparitions in which he apparently regards them as having a "supernatural origin" but makes no mention of the previous condemnations. In sum, the status of the Amsterdam visions is questionable, and indeed some of the "messages" are simply grotesque. For examples of this see: http://theotokos.org.uk/problems-with-the-amsterdam-visions-and-ida-peerdeman/.

31. Marlene Maloney, "Necedah Revisited: Anatomy of a Phony Apparition," in *Fidelity Magazine*, Feb. 1989, p. 22; Kevin Orlin Johnson, *Apparitions: Mystic Phenomena and What They Mean* (Pangaeus Press, Dallas, 1995), p. 333.

32. Mark Garvey, *Searching for Mary* (Plume, New York, 1998), p. 42.

NOTES FOR CHAPTER 5

1. Sivric, *The Hidden Side of Medjugorje, Vol. I*, pp. 127–31, 297. Emphasis added; cf. Klanac, *Aux Sources de Medjugorje*, p. 104.

2. Rooney & Faricy, *Mary Queen of Peace*, pp. 73–74; Craig, *Spark from Heaven*, p. 108; Sivric, *The Hidden Side of Medjugorje, Vol. I*, pp. 128–29. Fr Sivric also states his belief that Bishop Zanic was not firm enough at the beginning regarding Medjugorje, after which his reaction was somewhat excessive, in that he "became too emotionally involved in his position against Medjugorje and the Franciscans," whereas he should have "remained calmer," p. 131.

3. Lucy Rooney and Robert Faricy, *Medjugorje Journal: Mary Speaks to the World* (McCrimmons, Great Wakering, 1987), pp. 93–96. The 1978 CDF document on apparition discernment is available online at: http://www.vatican.va/roman_curia/congregations/ Cfaith/documents/rc_con_Cfaith_doc_19780225_norme-apparizioni_en.html.

4. Joachim Bouflet, *Medjugorje, ou la fabrication du surnaturel* (Éditions Salvator, Paris, 1998), pp. 204–205, 223–24.

5. Ljudevit Rupcic, *The Truth about Medjugorje* (Ljubuski-Humac, 1990), p. 13.
6. Laurentin, *Medjugorje Testament*, p. 87.
7. Rupcic and Nuic, *Once Again the Truth about Medjugorje*, pp. 229-32.
8. Klanac, *Aux Sources de Medjugorje*, pp. 133, 135; cf. Sivric, *The Hidden Side of Medjugorje*, Vol. I, pp. 316-19, and Mulligan, *Medjugorje: The First Days*, pp. 194-96.
9. Klanac, *Aux Sources de Medjugorje*, p. 135; cf. Sivric, *The Hidden Side of Medjugorje*, Vol. I, p. 319, and Mulligan, *Medjugorje: The First Days*, p. 196. Fr Mulligan's version has "doubting Judases"; Bubalo, *Thousand Encounters*, p. 37.
10. Laurentin and Lejeune, *Messages and Teachings*, p. 36; cf. Jones, *The Medjugorje Deception*, pp. 78-79, 152.
11. Cf. Gagliardi and Margnelli, *Le apparizioni della Madonna*, pp. 29-31.
12. Sivric, *The Hidden Side of Medjugorje*, Vol. I, p. 321; cf. Klanac, *Aux Sources de Medjugorje*, p. 137, and Mulligan, *Medjugorje: The First Days*, pp. 197-98.
13. Sivric, *The Hidden Side of Medjugorje*, Vol. I, pp. 323-24; cf. Klanac, *Aux Sources de Medjugorje*, pp. 139-40, and Mulligan, *Medjugorje: The First Days*, p. 199.
14. Sivric, *The Hidden Side of Medjugorje*, Vol. I, pp. 324-25; cf. Klanac, *Aux Sources de Medjugorje*, pp. 140-41, and Mulligan, *Medjugorje: The First Days*, pp. 200-1.
15. Sivric, *The Hidden Side of Medjugorje*, Vol. I, pp. 326-28; cf. Klanac, *Aux Sources de Medjugorje*, p. 141, and Mulligan, *Medjugorje: The First Days*, pp. 201-2.
16. Klanac, *Aux Sources de Medjugorje*, p. 147; cf. Sivric, *The Hidden Side of Medjugorje*, Vol. I, pp. 329-31, and Mulligan, *Medjugorje: The First Days*, pp. 205-7.
17. Sivric, *The Hidden Side of Medjugorje*, Vol. I, pp. 332-33; cf. Klanac, *Aux Sources de Medjugorje*, pp. 148-49, and Mulligan, *Medjugorje: The First Days*, pp. 207-8.
18. Sivric, *The Hidden Side of Medjugorje*, Vol. I, pp. 336-39; cf. Mulligan, *Medjugorje: The First Days*, pp. 211-13.
19. Klanac, *Aux Sources de Medjugorje*, pp. 155-56, 158; cf. Sivric, *The Hidden Side of Medjugorje*, Vol. I, pp. 341-44, and Mulligan, *Medjugorje: The First Days*, pp. 214-17.
20. Kraljevic, *The Apparitions of Our Lady at Medjugorje*, p. 115.
21. Sivric, *The Hidden Side of Medjugorje*, Vol. I, pp. 105-6.

NOTES FOR CHAPTER 6

1. Sivric, *The Hidden Side of Medjugorje*, Vol. I, pp. 347, 349, 365; Klanac, *Aux Sources de Medjugorje*, pp. 160, 162, 178, and Mulligan, *Medjugorje: The First Days*, pp. 220-21, 239.
2. Sivric, *The Hidden Side of Medjugorje*, Vol. I, pp. 358, 364-65; Klanac, *Aux Sources de Medjugorje*, pp. 170, 176-77, and Mulligan, *Medjugorje: The First Days*, pp. 231, 237-38.
3. Sivric, *The Hidden Side of Medjugorje*, Vol. I, pp. 366, 369; Klanac, *Aux Sources de Medjugorje*, pp. 179, 182, and Mulligan, *Medjugorje: The First Days*, pp. 239, 241.

Notes for Chapter 6

4. Sivric, *The Hidden Side of Medjugorje*, Vol. I, pp. 357–58; Klanac, *Aux Sources de Medjugorje*, p. 170, and Mulligan, *Medjugorje: The First Days*, pp. 230–31.

5. Sivric, *The Hidden Side of Medjugorje*, Vol. I, pp. 350, 352; Klanac, *Aux Sources de Medjugorje*, p. 163, 165, and Mulligan, *Medjugorje: The First Days*, pp. 223, 225.

6. Sivric, *The Hidden Side of Medjugorje*, Vol. I, pp. 63–64, 345–46, parentheses in original text; cf. Klanac, *Aux Sources de Medjugorje*, pp. 159–60, and Mulligan, *Medjugorje: The First Days*, pp. 219–20.

7. Sivric, *The Hidden Side of Medjugorje*, Vol. I, pp. 347, 373–74; cf. Mulligan, *Medjugorje: The First Days*, pp. 244. Bubalo, *Thousand Encounters*, p. 58.

8. Klanac, *Aux Sources de Medjugorje*, pp. 160, 170; cf. Sivric, *The Hidden Side of Medjugorje*, Vol. I, pp. 347–59, 371, and Mulligan, *Medjugorje: The First Days*, p. 220.

9. Sivric, *The Hidden Side of Medjugorje*, Vol. I, pp. 360–61, 364, 371; Craig, *Spark from Heaven*, p. 74; cf. Klanac, *Aux Sources de Medjugorje*, 174, 184, and Mulligan, *Medjugorje: The First Days*, pp. 235, 242.

10. Bubalo, *Thousand Encounters*, pp. 41–42.

11. Sivric, *The Hidden Side of Medjugorje*, Vol. I, pp. 347, 366; cf. Klanac, *Aux Sources de Medjugorje*, p. 179, and Mulligan, *Medjugorje: The First Days*, p. 239.

12. Rupcic and Nuic, *Once Again the Truth about Medjugorje*, pp. 79–80. Some of the footnotes on these two pages are incorrectly numbered.

13. Ibid., pp. 80–81.

14. Ibid., p. 82.

15. Rupcic and Nuic, *Once Again the Truth about Medjugorje*, pp. 85–87; Klanac, *Aux Sources de Medjugorje*, p. 36.

16. Laurentin, *Medjugorje Testament*, p. 228. It should be noted, though, that there cannot be any errors in the Bible, only in our interpretations of it.

17. Klanac, *Aux Sources de Medjugorje*, p. 37.

18. Ibid., p. 184; the original French text is: P. JOZO: Soit! Ceci m'intéresse. Encore trois fois. Donc, quand finissent-elles ces visions? MICA: Ils ont dit: "Tout de suite." Plus tard, ils ont dit: "Ça finit vendredi." P. JOZO: Mais où est-ce que cela va finir vendredi? JAKOV: A l'église. MIRJANA: Si Gospa ne nous le dit pas, peut-être que pour le dernier jour, elle désire que ce soit sur la colline!

19. Ljudevit Rupcic, *The Great Falsification: The Hidden Face of Medjugorje by Ivo Sivric*, p. 3, cited in Nolan, *Medjugorje: A Time for Truth*, p. 200.

20. Sivric, *The Hidden Side of Medjugorje*, Vol. I, p. 37.

21. Sivric, *The Hidden Side of Medjugorje*, Vol. I, pp. 64, 360. Daria Klanac attributes this statement to Mirjana (*Aux Sources de Medjugorje*, p. 172), but the point is it seems that this young lady was also related to at least one of the visionaries.

22. Nolan, *Medjugorje: A Time for Truth*, p. 200.

23. O'Carroll, *Medjugorje: Facts, Documents, Theology*, pp. 103–35.

24. Rupcic, *The Great Falsification*, p. 4, cited in Nolan, *Medjugorje: A Time for Truth*, pp. 201–2.

25. "Le père Jozo Zovko interroge Jakov Colo au matin du 27 juin 1981"; link at: www.comprendre-medjugorje.info/fr/sources.html. The recording of the 27 June interview with Mirjana is also at this page, plus transcriptions of a number of the tapes in Croatian and French.

26. Rupcic, *The Great Falsification*, p. 4, cited in Nolan, *Medjugorje: A Time for Truth*, p. 202.

27. Ibid., p. 202.

28. Ibid., p. 202.

29. Bubalo, *Thousand Encounters*, pp. 37, 41; Sivric, *The Hidden Side of Medjugorje, Vol. I*, pp. 359–60; cf. Klanac, *Aux Sources de Medjugorje*, 171–72, and Mulligan, *Medjugorje: The First Days*, p. 232.

30. Nolan, *Medjugorje: A Time for Truth*, p. 200; Daniel Klimek claims that the visionaries were "lured" and kept "against their will" by the women, but as the tape transcripts show, this is incorrect; cf. ministryvalues.com/index.php?option=com_content&task=view &id=1366&Itemid=125. Note: The Ministry Values site is no longer in operation, but it can be accessed via: https://web.archive.org/web/20160312112100/ministryvalues.com/index.php?option=com_content&task=view&id=1366&Itemid=125. It appears though that not all of Klimek's points are now at the original site, but they are being included here since historically that was the case.

31. Bubalo, *Thousand Encounters*, p. 125; Sivric, *The Hidden Side of Medjugorje, Vol. I*, pp. 222, 224, 228, Cf. Mulligan, *Medjugorje: The First Days*, pp. 94–95, 98; Marco Corvaglia gives further examples in his, *Medjugorje: è tutto falso* (Anteprima, Turin, 2007), p. 29. For some unknown reason, Daria Klanac failed to publish her own version of this tape.

32. Rupcic, *The Great Falsification*, p. 4, cited in Nolan, *Medjugorje: A Time for Truth*, p. 201.

33. Klanac, *Aux Sources de Medjugorje*, p. 126; cf. Sivric, *The Hidden Side of Medjugorje, Vol. I*, pp. 60, 292, and Mulligan, *Medjugorje: The First Days*, p. 155.

34. Klanac, *Aux Sources de Medjugorje*, pp. 136–37; cf. Sivric, *The Hidden Side of Medjugorje, Vol. I*, p. 320, and Mulligan, *Medjugorje: The First Days*, p. 197.

35. Sivric, *The Hidden Side of Medjugorje, Vol. I*, pp. 62, 378; cf. Klanac, *Aux Sources de Medjugorje*, p. 190, and Mulligan, *Medjugorje: The First Days*, p. 247.

36. Craig, *Spark from Heaven*, p. 71.

37. Kraljevic, *The Apparitions of Our Lady at Medjugorje*, pp. 41–42.

38. Jones, *The Medjugorje Deception*, pp. 88–89.

39. Sivric, *The Hidden Side of Medjugorje, Vol. I*, pp. 67–68.

40. Rupcic and Nuic, *Once Again the Truth about Medjugorje*, p. 84.

41. Rupcic, cited in O'Carroll, *Medjugorje: Facts, Documents, Theology*, p. 110. Emphasis added.

42. Kraljevic, *The Apparitions of Our Lady at Medjugorje*, pp. 191–92; Laurentin and Rupcic, *Virgin Mary Appearing at Medjugorje?* pp. 1, 3.

43. Sivric, *The Hidden Side of Medjugorje, Vol. I*, pp. 68, 176–77, 257, 260; cf. Klanac, *Aux Sources de Medjugorje*, pp. 74–75, 82–83, and Mulligan, *Medjugorje: The First Days*, p. 73; Kraljevic, *The Apparitions of Our Lady at Medjugorje*, p. 39.

44. Sivric, *The Hidden Side of Medjugorje*, Vol. I, p. 206; cf. Mulligan, *Medjugorje: The First Days*, p. 64.

45. The situation is somewhat complicated because, according to Fr Laurentin, there were actually only eighteen rather than nineteen apparitions in total at Lourdes. But we are concerned here with popular perceptions, and it is the number of apparitions which the villagers, the visionaries and Fr Zovko respectively, *believed* had taken place which really matters. See René Laurentin, *Bernadette of Lourdes* (Darton, Longman, & Todd, London, 1998), pp. 31–90; René Laurentin, *Lourdes: récit authentique des apparitions* (P. Lethielleux, Paris, 1987), p. 250.

46. Laurentin & Lejeune, *Messages and Teachings*, p. 153.

47. en.louisbelanger.com/2010/10/20/medjugorje-the-grand-concealment-2-three-more-days-duplicity-rene-laurentin/.

48. Sivric, *The Hidden Side of Medjugorje*, Vol. I, p. 177; Laurentin, *Bernadette of Lourdes*, p. 40.

49. Sivric, *The Hidden Side of Medjugorje*, Vol. I, pp. 178, 324–25.

50. Sivric, *The Hidden Side of Medjugorje*, Vol. I, pp. 178–83. On a connected point, Fr Sivric believed that from the point when the visionaries moved their visions into the church, in January 1982, they were inaudible, whereas before this they spoke loudly. However he may have been mistaken in this, and so not all his theories as to what was happening there have necessarily turned out to be correct. We have to distinguish, then, between what is on the tapes and was transcribed by Fr Sivric, and any theories of his own as to the cause of the Medjugorje visions, where there is room for error; cf. Sivric, *The Hidden Side of Medjugorje*, Vol. I, pp. 178–79.

NOTES FOR CHAPTER 7

1. Craig, *Spark from Heaven*, pp. 20–21; cf. Sullivan, *The Miracle Detective*, pp. 71–72.

2. https://web.archive.org/web/20041223120520/www.stichtingvaak.nl/main_bestanden/Ave2Juni01.PDF. Mark Waterinckx, "Hrasno Het Echte Heiligdom Van De Kraljica Mira," p. 15.

3. Sivric, *The Hidden Side of Medjugorje*, Vol. I, pp. 208–10; cf. Mulligan, *Medjugorje: The First Days*, pp. 66–67.

4. Sanchez-Ventura y Pascual, *The Apparitions of Garabandal*, pp. 46–49; Joseph Pelletier, *Our Lady Comes to Garabandal* (Assumption Publications, Worcester, 1971), pp. 35–36.

5. Sanchez-Ventura y Pascual, *The Apparitions of Garabandal*, pp. 67–72; Pelletier, *Our Lady Comes to Garabandal*, p. 67.

6. Sivric, *The Hidden Side of Medjugorje*, Vol. I, pp. 212–13, 244, 261; cf. Mulligan, *Medjugorje: The First Days*, pp. 69–70, 75.

7. Kraljevic, *The Apparitions of Our Lady at Medjugorje*, p. 12.

8. Sivric, *The Hidden Side of Medjugorje*, Vol. I, pp. 211–12; cf. Mulligan, *Medjugorje: The First Days*, pp. 68–69.

9. en.louisbelanger.com/.

10. Sivric, *The Hidden Side of Medjugorje, Vol. I*, pp. 238, 263; cf. Mulligan, *Medjugorje: The First Days*, p. 85.

11. Sivric, *The Hidden Side of Medjugorje, Vol. I*, pp. 286, 294–95; cf. Mulligan, *Medjugorje: The First Days*, pp. 151, 157; Craig, *Spark from Heaven*, p. 65.

12. See the relevant chapters in Foley, *Marian Apparitions*, for more details on this point. The actual, and generally very brief, words said by Mary during a number of her approved apparitions can also be accessed via the links at: http://theotokos.org.uk/major-approved-apparitions/.

13. Robert M. Maloy, "The Virgin of the Poor," in *A Woman Clothed with the Sun* (Doubleday, New York, 1961), pp. 247–62; L. Wuillaume, *Banneux: A Message for Our Time* (Banneux Shrine, 1995), pp. 3–34.

14. Kondor, *Fatima in Lucia's Own Words*, pp. 158–60.

15. Klanac, *Aux Sources de Medjugorje*, p. 160; Sivric, *The Hidden Side of Medjugorje, Vol. I*, pp. 63–64, 345–47, and Mulligan, *Medjugorje: The First Days*, pp. 219–20.

16. Craig, *Spark from Heaven*, p. 70.

17. Sivric, *The Hidden Side of Medjugorje, Vol. I*, pp. 70–71, 245.

18. Ibid., p. 73.

19. Sivric, *The Hidden Side of Medjugorje, Vol. I*, p. 74; Bubalo, *Thousand Encounters*, p. 157.

20. Laurentin and Lejeune, *Messages and Teachings*, pp. 159–62; Bubalo, *Thousand Encounters*, p. 158. The word "spontaneously" is used in the Bubalo text, but it is clear from the context that what is actually meant is "instantaneously."

21. Rupcic and Nuic, *Once Again the Truth about Medjugorje*, pp. 89–92; Sivric, *The Hidden Side of Medjugorje, Vol. I*, p. 248.

22. Kondor, *Fatima in Lucia's Own Words*, p. 161.

23. Sanchez-Ventura y Pascual, *The Apparitions of Garabandal*, pp. 134–35, 138.

24. Cf. Pelletier, *Our Lady Comes to Garabandal*, pp. 114–15.

25. Laurentin and Rupcic, *Virgin Mary Appearing at Medjugorje?* p. 70.

26. Jones, *The Medjugorje Deception*, pp. 91–93; Sivric, *The Hidden Side of Medjugorje, Vol. I*, pp. 33, 74.

27. Perica, *Balkan Idols*, pp. 111–12; Jones, *The Medjugorje Deception*, pp. 95, 107; Sivric, *The Hidden Side of Medjugorje, Vol. I*, pp. 58–59.

28. Jones, *The Medjugorje Deception*, p. 70.

NOTES FOR CHAPTER 8

1. Jones, *The Medjugorje Deception*, p. 94; *Corpus Chronologique des Messages* (Paris: OEIL, 1988); Sivric, *The Hidden Side of Medjugorje, Vol. I*, pp. 10–12, 95, 250; Bubalo, *Thousand Encounters*, pp. 90–92; cf. Corvaglia, *La verità su Medjugorje*, pp. 123–25; G. Sercambi, *Le Croniche, Vol. II* (Giusti, Rome, 1892), pp. 291–93. The book by the Italian researcher Marco Corvaglia is a comprehensive critical study of Medjugorje.

2. René Laurentin, *Eight Years* (The Riehle Foundation, Milford, 1989), p. 38, cited in Nolan, *Medjugorje: A Time for Truth*, p. 328.

3. Sivric, *The Hidden Side of Medjugorje, Vol. I*, pp. 92–95.

Notes for Chapter 8

4. Paolo Apolito, *Apparitions of the Madonna at Oliveto Citra: Local Visions and Cosmic Drama*, trans. W. Christian (Pennsylvania State University Press, Pennsylvania, 1998), pp. 63–64.
5. Poulain, *Revelations and Visions*, p. 84.
6. O'Carroll, *Medjugorje: Facts, Documents, Theology*, pp. 159, 165.
7. Ibid., p. 168.
8. Bishop Ratko Peric, "The deviations of Medjugorje," 25 January 2010, at: catholiclight.stblogs.org/archives/2010/03/the-deviations-of-medjugorje.html. It is also possible that St Joseph is in heaven, body and soul.
9. Bishop Ratko Peric, "The deviations of Medjugorje," 25 January 2010, at: catholiclight.stblogs.org/archives/2010/03/the-deviations-of-medjugorje.html; Laurentin and Lejeune, *Messages and Teachings*, pp. 344–49.
10. catholiclight.stblogs.org/archives/2009/10/context-of-the.html; Vicka Ivankovic, *The Third Diary*, handwritten manuscript, copy in the diocesan curia at Mostar.
11. Laurentin & Lejeune, *Messages and Teachings*, p. 189. Emphasis added.
12. Ludwig Ott, *Fundamentals of Catholic Dogma* (TAN Books and Publishers, Rockford, 1974), pp. 489–90.
13. Laurentin and Lejeune, *Messages and Teachings*, p. 191. Emphasis added.
14. Cf. Ott, *Fundamentals of Catholic Dogma*, pp. 212–15.
15. Louis de Montfort, *The Secret of Mary* (TAN Books and Publishers, Rockford, 1998), p. 11.
16. See: www.medjugorje.org/olmpage.htm for a list of these messages.
17. *Cover Up: The Hidden Agenda*, 1 hour 20 min., Network 5 International, 1998, video; Weible, *The Final Harvest*, p. 24.
18. Jordan Aumann, *Spiritual Theology* (Sheed and Ward, London, 1995), p. 430.
19. Bouflet, *Medjugorje, ou la fabrication du surnaturel*, p. 136.
20. René Laurentin and Henri Joyeux, *Scientific and Medical Studies on the Apparitions of Medjugorje* (Veritas Publications, Dublin, 1987), pp. 77–78, 84; Sivric, *The Hidden Side of Medjugorje, Vol. I*, p. 297; cf. Klanac, *Aux Sources de Medjugorje*, p. 104, and Mulligan, *Medjugorje: The First Days*, p. 159.
21. http://www.miraclehunter.com/marian_apparitions/approved_apparitions/laus/; Fr Augustin Poulain argued: "If the revelations or visions are very numerous, this circumstance, *taken alone*, does not constitute an unfavorable sign." But in this he was thinking of such revelations to saints, rather than the way the modern approved Marian apparitions have occurred, and so there has been a development since the time when his book was originally published, at the beginning of the twentieth century. Poulain, *Revelations and Visions*, p. 84.
22. Cf. the information at: https://championshrine.org/; although Adele was older than is usual for the seers of approved apparitions, this is understandable given her mission. She was told by Our Lady: "Gather the children in this wild country and teach them what they should know for salvation." This obviously involved her traveling around, an activity unsuitable for a child; and later she became a sister and founded a religious community.
23. Bubalo, *Thousand Encounters*, pp. 186–87.

24. Cf. www.frankrega.com/somethingmissing.htm; there is a concordance at: https://www.medjugorje.ws/en/messages/concordance.
25. Laurentin and Rupcic, *Virgin Mary Appearing at Medjugorje?* p. 143.
26. Jones, *The Medjugorje Deception*, p. 65.
27. Bouflet, *Medjugorje, ou la fabrication du surnaturel*, pp. 201–2.
28. "The Gospa and Instigation to Insubordination" at: en.marcocorvaglia.com/la-gospa-e-l-istigazione; cf. Canons 201, 601. See also: https://medjugorje-documents.blogspot.com/2010/11/1975-decree-romanis-pontificibus.html.
29. en.marcocorvaglia.com/la-gospa-e-l-istigazione.
30. Laurentin and Lejeune, *Messages and Teachings*, p. 329. Other versions of this message, which are substantially the same, are given here too; cf. en.marcocorvaglia.com/la-gospa-e-l-istigazione and Sivric, *The Hidden Side of Medjugorje, Vol. I*, p. 120.
31. en.marcocorvaglia.com/la-gospa-e-l-istigazione; cf. Pavao Zanic, *The Truth about Medjugorje*, March 1990, para. 7.
32. en.marcocorvaglia.com/la-gospa-e-l-istigazione; cf. Pavao Zanic, *The Truth about Medjugorje*, March 1990, para. 12. The last answer regarding the pope appears as the following in the original transcription: *Nek Pope govori, kako ja kazem onak jest.*
33. en.marcocorvaglia.com/la-gospa-e-l-istigazione.
34. en.marcocorvaglia.com/la-gospa-e-l-istigazione; cf. R. Laurentin, *Dernières Nouvelles de Medjugorje*, n. 13 (OEIL, 1994), p. 49.
35. en.marcocorvaglia.com/la-gospa-e-l-istigazione.
36. medjugorjedocuments.blogspot.com/2008/04/fr-rene-laurentin-disinformations-by.html; this decree was published in the official bulletin, *Vrhbosna*, 2/1996, p. 142.
37. Bouflet, *Medjugorje, ou la fabrication du surnaturel*, p. 136; also, Sivric, *The Hidden Side of Medjugorje*, Vol. I, p. 131; see also: catholiclight.stblogs.org/archives/2009/10/medjugorje-cont.html; Interview with Fr Manfred Hauke by Regina Eineg, "Don't let the devotees fall into the void," in *Die Tagespost*, 2 February 2010, pp. 6–7.
38. *Cover Up: The Hidden Agenda*, 1 hour 20 min., Network 5 International, 1998, video.
39. catholiclight.stblogs.org/archives/2009/10/context-of-the.html; Slavko Barbaric (handwritten), *Chronicle of the Apparitions*, vol. III, p. 247; cf. Corvaglia, *La verità su Medjugorje*, p. 140; Laurentin and Lejeune, *Messages and Teachings*, p. 253.
40. *Vrhbosna*, official Newsletter of the Diocese of the Metropolis of Sarajevo, n.1/2000, p. 65.
41. E. Michael Jones, *Medjugorje: The Untold Story* (Fidelity Press, South Bend, 1993), pp. 64–65; cf. Perica, *Balkan Idols*, p. 111. The controversy involving Frs Ivica Vego and Ivan Prusina and Bishop Zanic is fully explained at: en.marcocorvaglia.com/la-gospa-e-l-istigazione and also at this site: medjugorjedocuments.blogspot.com/2008/04/fr-rene-laurentin-disinformations-by.html.
42. Karl Rahner, SJ, *Visions and Prophecies* (Burns & Oates, London, 1963), pp. 31–39, n. 37, 51, n. 47.
43. Ibid., pp. 130–31.

NOTES FOR CHAPTER 9

1. Franken, *A Journey to Medjugorje*, pp. 28–30.
2. Davies, *Medjugorje After Fifteen Years*, pp. 62–63.
3. Weible, *The Final Harvest*, p. 116.
4. Sivric, *The Hidden Side of Medjugorje, Vol. I*, pp. 136–37.
5. O'Carroll, *Medjugorje: Facts, Documents, Theology*, 142–45.
6. Davies, *Medjugorje After Fifteen Years*, pp. 24–25.
7. Jones, *The Medjugorje Deception*, pp. 105–7; Sivric, *The Hidden Side of Medjugorje, Vol. I*, p. 102.
8. Jones, *The Medjugorje Deception*, pp. 107–8; cf. Sivric, *The Hidden Side of Medjugorje, Vol. I*, p. 129; Laurentin and Rupcic, *Virgin Mary Appearing at Medjugorje?* pp. 142–44.

NOTES FOR CHAPTER 10

1. Foley, *Marian Apparitions*, pp. 224–26.
2. Ibid., pp. 231–33.
3. Ibid., pp. 234–38.
4. Ibid., pp. 238–43.
5. Ibid., pp. 243–50.
6. Ibid., pp. 250–51.
7. Ibid., pp. 251, 270–72.
8. Ibid., pp. 251–52.
9. Ibid., pp. 304–5.
10. Ibid., pp. 305–7.
11. Ibid., pp. 312–15.
12. Michel de la Sainte Trinité, *Fatima Revealed... and Discarded*, tr. T. Tindal-Robertson (Augustine Publishing, Devon, 1988), chapters 2–5, quotations from pp. 11, 45, 48; Francis Johnston, *Fatima: The Great Sign* (Augustine Publishing, Devon, 1980), pp. 23, 38, 85.
13. Foley, *Marian Apparitions*, pp. 347, 360.

NOTES FOR CHAPTER 11

1. Jones, *The Medjugorje Deception*, pp. 53–54; Klanac, *Aux Sources de Medjugorje*, p. 9.
2. O'Carroll, *Medjugorje: Facts, Documents, Theology*, pp. 50–51.
3. Cf. https://web.archive.org/web/20160312112100/ministryvalues.com/index.php?option=com_content&task=view&id=1366&itemid=125.
4. Sullivan, *The Miracle Detective*, pp. 83–107, quote p. 107, emphasis added, 210.
5. Ibid., pp. 22, 119, 122, 125, 137, 160, 210, passim.
6. Paolo Apolito, *The Internet and the Madonna: Religious Visionary Experience on the Web*, trans. A. Shugaar (The University of Chicago Press, Chicago, 2005), pp. 36–37.
7. Laurentin and Rupcic, *Virgin Mary Appearing at Medjugorje?* p. 77.
8. Mark Miravalle, *The Message of Medjugorje: The Marian Message to the Modern World* (University Press of America, Lanham, 1986), pp. xv–xvi.

9. Nolan, *Medjugorje: A Time for Truth*, pp. xi–xiv.
10. Ibid., p. 123.
11. Ibid., p. 123.
12. Ibid., pp. 221, 223. We can see some examples of this in Nolan's citing of Professor Janet Smith as supportive of Medjugorje; he quotes an article by her which was written in April 1989, many years previously. That was during the period when a huge amount of propaganda about Medjugorje was in circulation, and when there was very little critical material available. Smith was largely repeating the positive information about Medjugorje which was then available, and following a visit there had obviously been favorably impressed. She mentions solar "miracles" and rosaries changing color as evidence, and also the large numbers of people who have gone there. Some of the things that she pointed to have subsequently turned out to be false, and in general her position on Medjugorje as a whole has been overtaken by events, including claims concerning the poverty of the visionaries; the "bloody handkerchief" incident; the reliability of Fr Laurentin; and the reputations of Fr Zovko and Fr Vlasic; cf. pp. 224–35.
13. O'Carroll, *Medjugorje: Facts, Documents, Theology*, pp. 50, 53. Emphasis added in both cases.
14. Laurentin and Rupcic, *Virgin Mary Appearing at Medjugorje?* p. 7.
15. Laurentin and Lejeune, *Messages and Teachings*, pp. 14–15.
16. Bernard Billet, et al., *Vraies et Fausses Apparitions dans L'Église* (P. Lethielleux, Paris, 1971), pp. 8–19; Yves Chiron, *Enquête sur les Apparitions de la Vierge* (Éditions J'ai Lu, Paris, 1995), p. 462.
17. Apolito, *The Internet and the Madonna*, p. 23.
18. Laurentin and Rupcic, *Virgin Mary Appearing at Medjugorje?* pp. 3, 106.
19. Poulain, *Revelations and Visions*, pp. 70–73.
20. Rooney and Faricy, *Medjugorje Journal*, p. 92.
21. Bouflet, *Faussaires de Dieu* (Presses de la Renaissance, Paris, 2000), p. 89; *Acta Apostolicae Sedis*, 1951, 561; Bouflet, *Medjugorje, ou la fabrication du surnaturel*, pp. 208–9.
22. Laurentin and Rupcic, *Virgin Mary Appearing at Medjugorje?* pp. 83, 106.
23. Ibid., p. 83.
24. Ibid., p. 105.
25. Ibid., p. 130.
26. William Most, *Mary in Our Life* (Mercier Press, Cork, 1955), p. 219.
27. Laurentin and Rupcic, *Virgin Mary Appearing at Medjugorje?* p. 120.
28. Kraljevic, *The Apparitions of Our Lady at Medjugorje*, p. 124.
29. Laurentin and Rupcic, *Virgin Mary Appearing at Medjugorje?* pp. 136–37.

NOTES FOR CHAPTER 12

1. Laurentin and Rupcic, *Virgin Mary Appearing at Medjugorje?* pp. 135–36, 145; O'Carroll, *Medjugorje: Facts, Documents, Theology*, pp. 54–56, 201; Rooney and Faricy, *Mary Queen of Peace*, p. 12.
2. See: Anne Barbeau Gardiner, "The Dubious Adrienne von Speyr," in *New Oxford Review*, September 2002, at: https://web.archive.org/web/20151208084256/http://www.newoxfordreview.org/article.jsp?did=0902-gardiner.

Notes for Chapter 13

3. Ratko Peric, *Ogledalo Pravde [Mirror of Justice]* (Mostar, 2001), p. 55, as cited in "Medjugorje: Secrets, Messages, Vocations, Prayers, Confessions, Commissions," a talk given at Maynooth, Co. Dublin, on February 17, 2004.

4. This information comes from a personal communication to the author from Fr Peter Joseph, who was reliably informed about this at the time.

5. Laurentin and Rupcic, *Virgin Mary Appearing at Medjugorje?* p. 113.

6. Ibid., p. 2.

7. Sivric, *The Hidden Side of Medjugorje, Vol. I*, pp. 53, 141.

8. te-deum.blogspot.com/2010/10/st-francis-of-assisi-and-bishop-of.html.

9. Cf. Information at: en.marcocorvaglia.com/il-vescovo-si-oppone (www.marcocorvaglia.com/risposte-a-saverio-gaeta-parte-3).

10. Laurentin and Lejeune, *Messages and Teachings*, p. 11. Emphasis added.

11. O'Carroll, *Medjugorje: Facts, Documents, Theology*, p. 195.

12. In some respects, it is one of the counterparts of the "parallel magisterium of theologians," which the Congregation for the Doctrine of the Faith Instruction, *Donum Veritatis*, "On the Ecclesial Vocation of the Theologian," deals with in regard to dissenting theologians; cf. also information found at this site: www.vatican.va/roman_curia/congregations/Cfaith/documents/rc_con_Cfaith_doc_19900524_theologian-vocation_en.html.

13. O'Carroll, *Medjugorje: Facts, Documents, Theology*, pp. 191–95; Laurentin and Lejeune, *Messages and Teachings*, p. 15.

14. Rupcic, *The Truth about Medjugorje*, pp. 69–75.

15. Ratko Peric, *Criteria for Discerning Apparitions: Regarding the Events of Medjugorje* (Mostar, 1995), p. 17.

16. See Michael Davies, "A Letter From Monsignor Zanic to Father Tomislav Pervan, 25 March 1985" in *Medjugorje after Twenty-One Years, 1981–2002: The Definitive History*, p. 35.

NOTES FOR CHAPTER 13

1. Sivric, *The Hidden Side of Medjugorje, Vol. I*, pp. 91, 270–71, 315; cf. Mulligan, *Medjugorje: The First Days*, p. 193; Laurentin and Rupcic, *Virgin Mary Appearing at Medjugorje?* pp. 27, 125, 134; Laurent Volken, *Visions, Revelations, and the Church*, trans. E. Gallaher (P. J. Kenedy & Sons, New York, 1963) p. 161; Craig, *Spark from Heaven*, p. 174; Laurentin and Joyeux, *Scientific and Medical*, p. 12.

2. Laurentin and Joyeux, *Scientific and Medical*, pp. 46–49, 53–55.

3. It might also be said that some of Joyeux's ideas are not exactly mainstream: in 2002, he was criticized in a newspaper article for his espousal of some fringe ideas, namely instinct therapy and crudivorism, that is, practices concerned with the supposed benefits of the eating of raw food. It is claimed that such a diet can cure all sorts of illnesses, but there is no hard scientific data to support such a notion. Cf: https://en.marcocorvaglia.com/scienziati-di-medjugorje.

4. Laurentin et al., *Medjugorje Today* (Franciscan University Press, Steubenville, 1990), p. 53; the 1985 interview in *Paris Match* mentioned below in the text has the word "polygraphy" in brackets in a statement about the experiments carried out, but gives no details; cf. as cited in Nolan, *Medjugorje: A Time for Truth*, p. 136.

5. Laurentin and Joyeux, *Scientific and Medical*, pp. 13, 20–27, 47.
6. Ibid., p. 25.
7. Ibid., p. 24.
8. Cited in Nolan, *Medjugorje: A Time for Truth*, p. 141.
9. See: Laurentin and Joyeux, *Scientific and Medical*, pp. 13, 23–24, 26–27, 33; cf. Corvaglia, *La verità su Medjugorje*, pp. 314–15.
10. Laurentin and Joyeux, *Scientific and Medical*, pp. 13, 23; the work of Dr Frigerio and Dr Cigada is cited in: Corvaglia, *La verità su Medjugorje*, pp. 313, 320, 332–33.
11. Cited in Nolan, *Medjugorje: A Time for Truth*, p. 141. For background information about aspects of Dr Margnelli's attitude and experience see: https://en.marcocorvaglia.com/scienziati-di-medjugorje.
12. Laurentin and Joyeux, *Scientific and Medical*, pp. 20, 23–24. Emphasis added.
13. Francesco D'Alpa, *La Scienza e Medjugorje, Vol. I: Il Caso Joyeux* (Laiko.it, 2010), pp. 17–18, passim. This e-book is available as a PDF from: en.marcocorvaglia.com/risorse-utili-medjugorje.
14. Laurentin and Joyeux, *Scientific and Medical*, pp. 6–7. The general line of argument against supernaturality for this section is adapted from: https://web.archive.org/web/20170401082231/skeptiCfiles.org/think/lucifer1.htm. The use of this material was criticized by Daniel Klimek, but this website is atheistic rather than satanic. Thus, the use of the material can be justified on the grounds that the author was using his reasoning powers to validly assess the alleged visions, and has actually made some valuable critical points not available elsewhere. In sum, we should be looking to what is being said, rather than in an overly critical way at who might have said it; cf. https://web.archive.org/web/20160312112100/ministryvalues.com/index.php?option=com_content&task=view&id=1366&Itemid=125.
15. Laurentin and Joyeux, *Scientific and Medical*, p. 7. Another observer, Dr Lucia Capello (pp. 14–15), claimed that some of the visions she observed ended with "perfect simultaneity" but it is difficult to reconcile this with Fr Laurentin's testimony, and more generally with the available video footage.
16. *All I Need Is a Miracle* (Bounty Hill Media Productions, 1991), video.
17. *Marian Apparitions of the 20th Century* (Marian Communications Ltd., Lima, Pennsylvania, 1991), video.
18. See "A Literature Review on Reaction Time," by Robert J. Kosinski, at: https://fon.hum.uva.nl/rob/Courses/InformationInSpeech/CDROM/Literature/LOTwinterschool2006/biae.clemson.edu/bpc/bp/Lab/110/reaction.htm.
19. Laurentin and Joyeux, *Scientific and Medical*, p. 7.
20. Laurentin and Joyeux, *Scientific and Medical*, pp. 26, 28, 70–71, 75–76.
21. *Visions on Demand* video.
22. Translated *Il Tempo* interview cited in Nolan, *Medjugorje: A Time for Truth*, p. 144.
23. Laurentin and Joyeux, *Scientific and Medical*, pp. 29, 36, 52; emphasis added.

24. Sharkey and Debergh, *Our Lady of Beauraing* (Abbey Press, Indiana, 1973), pp. 132–36.
25. Laurentin and Joyeux, *Scientific and Medical*, p. 9.
26. Laurentin, *Bernadette of Lourdes*, p. 34.
27. Laurentin and Joyeux, *Scientific and Medical*, p. 114.
28. Laurentin and Rupcic, *Virgin Mary Appearing at Medjugorje?* p. 128; O'Carroll, *Medjugorje: Facts, Documents, Theology*, p. 66.
29. *All I Need Is a Miracle* video, plus information personally received from Louis Bélanger.
30. Cf. Corvaglia, *La verità su Medjugorje*, pp. 328–29; https://web.archive.org/web/20081121100405/http://nuke.associa zionereginadellapace.org/.
31. See: www.medjugorje.org/science3.htm.
32. *Medjugorje Messenger* interview, cited in Nolan, *Medjugorje: A Time for Truth*, pp. 139–40.
33. Corvaglia, *La verità su Medjugorje*, p. 284.
34. Klanac, *Medjugorje, Réponses aux objections*, pp. 150–51.
35. Corvaglia, *La verità su Medjugorje*, p. 305.
36. Corvaglia, *La verità su Medjugorje*, pp. 341–42; Laurentin, *Medjugorje Testament*, p. 59.
37. https://en.marcocorvaglia.com/sulle-estasi-sincronizzate-mentivan; cf. Andreas Resch & Giorgio Gagliardi, *I Veggenti di Medjugorje. Ricerca Psicofisiologica* [The seers of Medjugorje. Psychophysiological inquiry] (Resch Verlag, Innsbruck, Austria, 2000), pp. 19, 45, 47, 96.
38. Corvaglia, *La verità su Medjugorje*, pp. 332–33; www.youtube.com/watch?v=BL93mg7Q_70; Resch and Gagliardi, *I Veggenti di Medjugorje*, p. 163.
39. Cf. en.marcocorvaglia.com/ricevo-dal-dr-giorgio-gagliardi.
40. Laurentin, *Medjugorje Testament*, pp. 220–24; see also the information at: antipolygraph.org/.
41. en.marcocorvaglia.com/la-scienza-non-prova-nulla-parte-1.
42. Corvaglia, *La verità su Medjugorje*, pp. 337–43.
43. Laurentin and Joyeux, *Scientific and Medical*, pp. 19, 21, 23, 50; cf. Corvaglia, *La verità su Medjugorje*, pp. 337–43, for further examples of this type of thing.
44. Corvaglia, *La verità su Medjugorje*, p. 338.
45. Corvaglia, *La verità su Medjugorje*, p. 340; René Laurentin, *Latest News of Medjugorje No 6* (The Rihele Foundation, Milford, 1987), pp. 6, 7.
46. René Laurentin, *Dernières Nouvelles de Medjugorje* n. 8 (OEIL, Paris, 1989), p. 26, cited in Corvaglia, *La verità su Medjugorje*, p. 340.
47. René Laurentin, *Dernières Nouvelles de Medjugorje* n. 9 (OEIL, Paris, 1990), pp. 19, 28, cited in Corvaglia, *La verità su Medjugorje*, p. 341.
48. René Laurentin, *Dernières Nouvelles de Medjugorje* n. 11 (OEIL, Paris, 1992), p. 56, cited in Corvaglia, *La verità su Medjugorje*, p. 341.
49. René Laurentin, *Dernières Nouvelles de Medjugorje* n. 15 (OEIL, Paris, 1996), p. 38, cited in Corvaglia, *La verità su Medjugorje*, p. 341.
50. Cf. Resch & Gagliardi, *I Veggenti di Medjugorje*, p. 18, cited in Corvaglia, *La verità su Medjugorje*, p. 341.

51. Corvaglia, *La verità su Medjugorje*, p. 342. For an update with information about the rather strange views/positions adopted by Dr Joyeux and some of his associates, see: https://en.marcocorvaglia.com/scienziati-di-medjugorje and https://en.marcocorvaglia.com/ scienziati-schierati-parte-2.

52. Resch and Gagliardi, *I Veggenti di Medjugorje*, pp. 171, 205, 207, cited in Corvaglia, *La verità su Medjugorje*, p. 342.

53. Corvaglia, *La verità su Medjugorje*, p. 343; Resch and Gagliardi, *I Veggenti di Medjugorje*, p. 207.

NOTES FOR CHAPTER 14

1. Jones, *Medjugorje: The Untold Story*, pp. 1–3.
2. Sivric, *The Hidden Side of Medjugorje, Vol. I*, pp. 78–79, 82–84. Mark Waterinckx's evidence was communicated personally to the author.
3. Craig, *Spark from Heaven*, pp. 255–56.
4. Sharkey and Debergh, *Our Lady of Beauraing*, p. 74.
5. John of the Cross, "Ascent of Mount Carmel," in *Complete Works, Vol. I*, pp. 106–8; John of the Cross, "Ascent of Mount Carmel," in *Collected Works*, p. 230.
6. Teresa of Avila, *Interior Castle*, Sixth Mansion, ch. IX, 13, 15, cited in Poulain, *Revelations and Visions*, p. 125. Emphasis added to first quote.
7. Nolan, *Medjugorje: A Time for Truth*, p. 182.
8. Maloney, "Necedah Revisited," in *Fidelity Magazine*, Feb 1989, p. 18.
9. Ibid., pp. 18, 21, 23.
10. Sivric, *The Hidden Side of Medjugorje, Vol. I*, pp. 79–81.
11. C. Malanga and R. Pinotti, *I fenomeni B.V.M.: Le manifestazioni mariane in una nuova luce* (Montadori, Milan, 1990), cited in Apolito, *Apparitions of the Madonna at Oliveto Citra*, pp. 95–96. There are examples of this type of thing available at: www.youtube.com/watch?v=YPRxNalkWIM and www.youtube.com/watch?v=afosoQ-uWBo. The commentaries by those involved make it clear that they are looking through the viewfinders of their video cameras, whereas other people nearby are not seeing anything or reacting at all.
12. Michael J. Mazza, *The Catholic Church and Medjugorje*, p. 10.
13. Laurentin and Lejeune, *Messages and Teachings*, p. 69.
14. en.marcocorvaglia.com/miracoli-del-sole-e-altro-parte-1; the report by August Meessen can be accessed via: www.meessen.net/AMeessen/MirSun.pdf.
15. en.marcocorvaglia.com/miracoli-del-sole-e-altro-parte-1; https://web.archive.org/web/20140517035729/; www.youtube.com/watch?v=ZroaQw7XPcg; "The Visionaries from Medjugorje tried by Science," 2004, FilmGruppMünchen; Marco Corvaglia has a webpage showing the way alleged miracles of the sun at Medjugorje can be reproduced; cf. en.marcocorvaglia.com/miracoli-del-sole-e-altro-parte-2.
16. Jones, *Medjugorje: The Untold Story*, pp. 25–26.
17. en.marcocorvaglia.com/miracoli-del-sole-e-altro-parte-1; see also information in *British Journal of Ophthalmology*, "Solar retinopathy following religious rituals," 1988, 72, 931–34, available at: www.ncbi.nlm.nih.gov/pmc/articles/PMC1041624/; Ralph R. Nix and David J. Apple, "Solar Retinopathy from Sungazing in Medjugorje," published in the *Journal of the Louisiana State Medical Society*, August 1987,

volume 139, 8, pp. 36–40; Randy V. Field, et al., "Medjugorje Maculopathy," *New England Journal of Medicine*, Volume 318, 18, May 1988, p. 1207.

18. Sivric, *The Hidden Side of Medjugorje, Vol. I*, pp. 155–56, 199 n. 311; cf. Vittorio Guerrera, *Medjugorje: A Closer Look* (Maryheart Crusaders, Meriden, 1995), p. 66; cf. Laurentin and Joyeux, *Scientific and Medical*, pp. 98–99. Fr Laurentin points out that Dr Mangiapan's negative statement was preceded by references to some nine cases, "which would merit a more careful enquiry." There is no indication, though, that subsequent enquiries have given grounds for believing that these alleged cures, or any others, have been genuinely supernatural.

19. Guerrera, *Medjugorje: A Closer Look*, pp. 65–66; Cf. Jones, *Medjugorje: The Untold Story*, p. 22.

20. Rupcic cited in O'Carroll, *Medjugorje: Facts, Documents, Theology*, p. 125.

21. Sullivan, *The Miracle Detective*, p. 217.

22. *All I Need Is a Miracle* video.

NOTES FOR CHAPTER 15

1. Jones, *The Medjugorje Deception*, p. 54.
2. Ibid., p. 65.
3. Joseph Ratzinger with Vittorio Messori, *The Ratzinger Report: An Exclusive Interview on the State of the Church* (Fowler Wright Books, Leominster, 1985), pp. 111–12.
4. O'Carroll, *Medjugorje: Facts, Documents, Theology*, pp. 149–54.
5. Ratzinger, *The Ratzinger Report*, pp. 111–12.
6. Jones, *The Medjugorje Deception*, p. 66.
7. Ibid., pp. 113–14; Perica, *Balkan Idols*, p. 113.
8. https://www.marcocorvaglia.com/risposte-a-saverio-gaeta-parte-3.
9. Sivric, *The Hidden Side of Medjugorje, Vol. I*, p. 135.
10. Peric, *Criteria for Discerning Apparitions*, pp. 9–10. From *La Civiltà Cattolica*, 19 October 1985.
11. Jones, *The Medjugorje Deception*, pp. 124–25; Sivric, *The Hidden Side of Medjugorje, Vol. I*, pp. 53, 187, n. 42; cf. medjugorjedocuments.blogspot.com/2009/09/what-did-archbishop-bertone-really-say.html.
12. Sivric, *The Hidden Side of Medjugorje, Vol. I*, p. 141.
13. Jones, *The Medjugorje Deception*, pp. 125–27; *The Hidden Side of Medjugorje, Vol. I*, p. 129.
14. Cf. Sivric, *The Hidden Side of Medjugorje, Vol. I*, pp. 142–43.
15. Guerrera, *Medjugorje: A Closer Look* (Prot. No. 909/88/5), p. 64.
16. www.medjugorje.org/framorth1.htm.
17. Sivric, *The Hidden Side of Medjugorje, Vol. I*, pp. 15–16, 37. See *Dernières Nouvelles* (No. 7), 1988.

NOTES FOR CHAPTER 16

1. Bubalo, *Thousand Encounters*, p. 17. For other examples of Vicka's irreverent way of answering Fr Bubalo see pp. 10, 15, 17–18, 28, 31, 39, 42, 64, 78, 93, 152, 177.

2. Bubalo, *Thousand Encounters*, pp. 215–16. Emphasis added. Fr Vlasic quote from: Lucy Rooney and Robert Faricy, *Medjugorje Unfolds: Mary Speaks to the World* (Fowler Wright Books Ltd., Leominster, 1985), p. 55; *All I Need Is a Miracle* video.

3. Bubalo, *Thousand Encounters*, pp. 216–17.

4. Kondor, *Fatima in Lucia's Own Words*, pp. 105–106.

5. Cf. en.marcocorvaglia.com/una-prova-pratica; Bubalo, *Thousand Encounters*, pp. 47, 166, 167.

6. Guerrera, *Medjugorje: A Closer Look*, pp. 40–41; Jones, *The Medjugorje Deception*, pp. 117–18; *All I Need Is a Miracle* video; cf. www.youtube.com/watch?v=xXVERLoaOwA and en.marcocorvaglia.com/una-prova-pratica; www.youtube.com/watch?v=EDmW2mDfrIo.

7. en.marcocorvaglia.com/una-prova-pratical. Emphasis added. Marco Corvaglia provides a translation of Vicka's words, as recorded on the video; see also information in Klanac, *Medjugorje, Réponses aux objections*, pp. 77–78; www.youtube.com/watch?v=7FjFrEy113w.

8. René Laurentin, *Dernières Nouvelles de Medjugorje*, n.3 (OEIL, 1985), p. 32.

9. Laurentin, *Bernadette of Lourdes*, pp. 84–85.

10. Ibid., p. 75.

11. Jones, *The Medjugorje Deception*, pp. 101–2; Sivric, *The Hidden Side of Medjugorje, Vol. I*, pp. 53, 74–77.

12. O'Carroll, *Medjugorje: Facts, Documents, Theology*, p. 206.

13. Sullivan, *The Miracle Detective*, p. 158; Laurentin, *Medjugorje Testament*, pp. 81–83.

14. Weible, *The Final Harvest*, pp. 98, 164.

15. catholiclight.stblogs.org/archives/2009/10/context-of-the.html.

16. Jones, *Medjugorje: The Untold Story*, pp. 89–91; Guerrera, *Medjugorje: A Closer Look*, pp. 68–70; Laurentin and Lejeune, *Messages and Teachings*, p. 166; cf. *Visions on Demand* video.

17. Davies, *Medjugorje After Fifteen Years*, pp. 32–33. Frs Rupcic and Nuic, in their *Once Again the Truth about Medjugorje*, p. 32, claim that Marija was not speaking about her own messages, but those allegedly received by Agnes Heupel, but it is not clear what they base this idea on.

18. Weible, *The Final Harvest*, p. 166.

19. Sivric, *The Hidden Side of Medjugorje, Vol. I*, pp. 100–1.

20. Kraljevic, *The Apparitions of Our Lady at Medjugorje*, p. 133.

21. Ibid., p. 136; Aumann, *Spiritual Theology*, p. 412.

22. en.louisbelanger.com/2011/02/28/medjugorje-%E2%80%9Creality-tele-visions%E2%80%9D-and-the-cruel-absence-of-pastoral-care/.

23. Sivric, *The Hidden Side of Medjugorje, Vol. I*, pp. 96–100; Bouflet, *Medjugorje, ou la fabrication du surnaturel*, p. 178; Craig, *Spark from Heaven*, pp. 240, 299; cf. Bubalo, *Thousand Encounters*, pp. 283–87.

24. Aumann, *Spiritual Theology*, p. 430.

25. Donald DeMarco "The Goodness of Guilt," *National Catholic Register* (January 21–27, 2001), located on the internet at: https://www.catholiceducation.org/en/culture/catholic-contributions/the-goodness-of-guilt.html.

26. For critical evidence, see particularly Jones, *The Medjugorje Deception*, pp. 46–50, 75, 77, 84, 96, 114; cf. also *Visions on Demand* video. For the opposite point of view see: Nolan, *Medjugorje: A Time for Truth*, pp. 183, 245–48, 320–27, and Klanac, *Medjugorje, Réponses aux objections*, pp. 49–53; cf. en.marcocorvaglia.com/lodato-dalla-gospa-e-scomunicato.

27. Jones, *The Medjugorje Deception*, pp. 147, 164–65, 370; Laurentin and Lejeune, *Messages and Teachings*, p. 168. Laurentin, *Dernières Nouvelles de Medjugorje*, Nr. 15, June 1996, p. 34. Mark Waterinckx gives explicit testimony about the allegations concerning Fr Zovko on the *Cover Up* video, with this being based on his own firsthand experiences as a former close friend of Fr Zovko over many years. Furthermore, these details have been personally confirmed to the author by Mark Waterinckx. The details of the suspensions of Fr Zovko are contained in the Mostar Chancery documents numbers 622/89 and 423/94; cf. also *Cover Up* video. Details of the third suspension can be found at: https://www.marcocorvaglia.com/padre-jozo-decreto-di-sospensione; the decree was published in *Vrhbosna*, 3/2004, pp. 293–98 (843/2004).

28. Letter from Bishop Peric to Fr Rudo Franken, 7 February 2000, cited in Michael Davies, *Medjugorje after Twenty-One Years, 1981–2002: The Definitive History*, pp. 148–49.

NOTES FOR CHAPTER 17

1. Lampe, *Yugoslavia as History*, pp. 353–54, 360–64; Jones, *The Medjugorje Deception*, 167–74; Benson, *Yugoslavia: A Concise History*, 157.

2. Davies, *Medjugorje after Twenty-One Years, 1981–2002*, p. 86.

3. Jones, *The Medjugorje Deception*, pp. 184–86. According to Jones, the details of the Zadar declaration had been leaked to reporters from the CNS in "late 1990." So it was obviously finalized by that date, and thus Cardinal Ratzinger would have been aware of the decision of the Yugoslav bishops before it was officially issued, in April 1991.

4. From the Introduction in Janice T. Connell, *The Visions of the Children* (St Martin's Press, New York, 1992), p. xv.

5. *30 DAYS* (March 1991), p. 55.

6. Lampe, *Yugoslavia as History*, pp. 365, 369–71; Jones, *The Medjugorje Deception*, pp. 188–89, 191; Jones, *Medjugorje: The Untold Story*, p. 124.

7. Jones, *The Medjugorje Deception*, pp. 189–92, 194; Benson, *Yugoslavia: A Concise History*, p. 162; Sells, *The Bridge Betrayed*, pp. 72, 95.

8. Lampe, *Yugoslavia as History*, pp. 372–73; *The Medjugorje Deception*, pp. 233, 235–38.

9. Sullivan, *The Miracle Detective*, p. 191; cf. "Ministry Values site, Klimek article."

10. www.medjugorje.eu/messages/; Slavko Barbaric, *Mother, Lead us to Peace!* (Grude, Herceg–Bosna, Grafotisak, 1994), p. xii, cited in Claverie, *Les guerres de la Vierge* (Gallimard, 2003), p. 238.

11. Jones, *The Medjugorje Deception*, pp. 246–47, 267; cf. Lampe, *Yugoslavia as History*, 376–77.

12. Sullivan, *The Miracle Detective*, pp. 268–71; Mart Bax, *Medjugorje: Religion, Politics, and Violence* (VU Uitgeverij, Amsterdam, 1995), p. 113.

13. Ed Vulliamy, *Seasons in Hell: Understanding Bosnia's War* (Simon & Schuster, London, 1994), pp. 60–61, 259–60.

14. Michael Sells, "Crosses of Blood: Sacred Space, Religion, and Violence in Bosnia-Hercegovina," in *Sociology of Religion 2003*, 64:3, p. 320; https://academic.oup.com/socrel/article-abstract/64/3/309/1662482.

15. Sells, *The Bridge Betrayed*, pp. 102–5; cf. Laura Silber and Allan Little, *The Death of Yugoslavia* (Penguin Books/BBC Books, London, 1996), pp. 299–300. Other accounts say that the monks at Zitomislic were buried alive, see Craig, *Spark from Heaven*, p. 46.

16. Vulliamy, *Seasons in Hell*, pp. 320–30.

17. Sells, *The Bridge Betrayed*, pp. 105–6; Perica, *Balkan Idols*, p. 172.

18. en.marcocorvaglia.com/scandali-d-erzegovina; cf. https://web.archive.org/web/20180829174415/, http://24sata.info/vijesti/intervju/204762-vencel-culjak-medjugorju-se-ne-pise-dobro.html and Tobias Greiff, *Violent Places: Everyday Politics and Public Lives in Post-Dayton Bosnia and Herzegovina* (Nomos Verlagsgesellschaft, 2018), p. 123.

19. https://www.theguardian.com/world/2001/apr/06/2.

20. en.louisbelanger.com/ "Medjupedia: A pause—The construction of the 'Lady of Medjugorje,' 30 September 2010"; see also the Christmas 2000 bulletin at: www.medjugorje.hr/files/html/enpb2000.html.

21. Sells, *The Bridge Betrayed*, p. 107; Perica, *Balkan Idols*, pp. 114, 118–22, 172–73.

22. Sells, *The Bridge Betrayed*, p. 113; Perica, *Balkan Idols*, pp. 114, 118–22.

23. Some people might argue that the case of Mélanie and Maximin, to whom Our Lady appeared at La Salette in the nineteenth century, and whose later lives were far from exemplary, shows that what happens in the aftermath of an apparition is not necessarily of significance. But clearly, the scale and nature of the "problems" in the Medjugorje area during the war is of a completely different order to what happened regarding the La Salette children later on, and moreover, there was only one apparition at La Salette in contrast to the claims of tens of thousands at Medjugorje.

NOTES FOR CHAPTER 18

1. Jones, *The Medjugorje Deception*, pp. 200–201; for further information on Cardinal Ratzinger's letter, see the information on the EWTN website at: https://web.archive.org/web/20190705235205/; http://www.ewtn.com/expert/answers/poem_of_the_man.htm; and for information about the *L'Osservatore Romano* report of its condemnation, see: Corvaglia, *La verità su Medjugorje*, p. 136.

2. Elliot Miller and Kenneth R. Samples, *The Cult of the Virgin: Catholic Mariology and the Apparitions of Mary* (Baker Book House, Grand Rapids, 1994), pp. 150, 177.

3. Jones, *The Medjugorje Deception*, p. 240.

4. Ibid., p. 295.

5. Jones, *The Medjugorje Deception*, pp. xvii, xix, 297, 304, 309–10; cf. *Visions on Demand* video.
6. Laurentin, *Medjugorje Testament*, p. 96.
7. See Davies, *Medjugorje after Fifteen Years*, p. 78.
8. Réginald-Omez, *Psychical Phenomena*, Faith and Fact Books, 36 (Burns & Oates, London, 1959), pp. 84–85.
9. Louis de Montfort, *True Devotion to the Blessed Virgin*, nn. 90–91.
10. See Donal Anthony Foley, "Marian Apparitions — Some Lessons from History," in *Homiletic and Pastoral Review*, June 2001, also at: http://theotokos.org.uk/article-marian-apparitions-and-history/.
11. Aumann, *Spiritual Theology*, pp. 420–21.
12. Ibid., pp. 402–3.
13. Ibid., pp. 403, 412.
14. Johnson, *Apparitions: Mystic Phenomena and What They Mean*, pp. 286–88; Michael Walsh, *The Apparition at Knock* (St Jarlath's College, Tuam, 1959), p. 10.
15. Manfred Hauke, *Introduction to Mariology*, Chapter 9, "The prophetic role of Mary in apparitions," p. 2.
16. *De Servorum Dei*, III, 53, xxii, II.
17. Most, *Mary in Our Life*, p. 217.
18. Joseph de Sainte-Marie, OCD, *Reflections on the Act of Consecration at Fatima of Pope John Paul II on 13th May 1982*, trans., W. Lawson (Augustine Publishing Company, Devon, 1983), pp. 23–24; see also Ranwez, "The Value of the Episcopal Declarations concerning the events at Beauraing," in *Marian Library Studies*, 96, pp. 3–4.
19. Hauke, *Introduction to Mariology*, Chapter 9, "The prophetic role of Mary in apparitions," p. 2.
20. Augustin Poulain, *The Graces of Interior Prayer* (Kegan Paul, London, 1912), pp. 349–50.
21. Walsh, *The Apparition at Knock*, 13–14; Louis Lochet, *Apparitions of Our Lady: Their Place in the Life of the Church* (Herder, Freiburg, 1960), 34–35.
22. Hauke, *Introduction to Mariology*, Chapter 9, "The prophetic role of Mary in apparitions," p. 19. Since this book was published, Jacinta and Francisco Marto have been canonized.
23. The full title is: *Normae S. Congregationis pro doctrina fidei de modo procedendi in diudicandis praesumptis apparitionibus ac revelationibus*. http://www.vatican.va/roman_curia/congregations/Cfaith/documents/rc_con_Cfaith_doc_19780225_norme-apparizioni_en.html.
24. Interestingly, the traditional third possibility, *constat de non supernaturalitate* ("the non-supernatural character is established"), is not mentioned in *Normae Congregationis*. It is difficult to say how significant this is, since it is unlikely that the Congregation would apply a "hermeneutic of discontinuity" in regard to the previous teaching and practice of the Church in this area.
25. Davies, *Medjugorje After Fifteen Years*, pp. 85–88.
26. Jones, *The Medjugorje Deception*, p. 362.

27. Jones, *The Medjugorje Deception*, p. 368; cf. the letter, at: www.catholic-culture.org/culture/library/view.Cfm?id=317& repos=1&subrepos=0&searchid=726078.

28. Cf. medjugorjedocuments.blogspot.com/2009/09/what-did-archbishop-bertone-really-say.html; www.catholicculture.org/culture/ library/view.Cfm?id=317&repos=1&subrepos=0&searchid=726078.

29. Davies, *Medjugorje After Fifteen Years*, pp. 89–91.

30. Cf. medjugorjedocuments.blogspot.com/2008/04/fr-rene-laurentin-dis-informations-by.html.

31. Davies, *Medjugorje After Fifteen Years*, pp. 97–99, 159–63; Laurentin, *Medjugorje Testament*, p. 99.

32. Davies, *Medjugorje after Twenty-One Years*, pp. 111–12 (Prot. No. 32343/97 & Prot. No. 32344/97).

33. An unofficial translation of this letter can be found at: https://www.ewtn.com/catholicism/library/letter-to-bishop-gilbert-aubry-2048; cf. Kevin Orlin Johnson, *Twenty Questions About Medjugorje: What Rome Really Said* (Pangaeus Press, Dallas, 1999), pp. 6–8.

34. Cf. https://www.ewtn.com/catholicism/library/letter-to-bishop-gilbert-aubry-2048; medjugorjedocuments.blogspot.com/2009/09/what-did-archbishop-bertone-really-say.html.

35. Johnson, *Twenty Questions About Medjugorje*, pp. 8–12.

36. medjugorjedocuments.blogspot.com/2009/05/february-20-1999-decree-romanis.html.

37. medjugorjedocuments.blogspot.com/2009/05/february-20-1999-decree-romanis.html (capitalization of some of the words in the quote has been altered).

NOTES FOR CHAPTER 19

1. Sivric, *The Hidden Side of Medjugorje*, Vol. I, pp. 71–72, 156.
2. Rooney & Faricy, *Mary Queen of Peace*, pp. 32, 75.
3. Maloney, "Necedah Revisited" in *Fidelity Magazine*, February, 1989, pp. 21, 22–23.
4. O'Carroll, *Medjugorje: Facts, Documents, Theology*, pp. x, 13.
5. Laurentin and Lejeune, *Messages and Teachings*, p. 27.
6. Sivric, *The Hidden Side of Medjugorje*, Vol. I, pp. 156–57, 158. The information about quarrelling came via a personal communication to the author from Mark Waterinckx.
7. Rooney and Faricy, *Medjugorje Journal*, pp. 101, 107.
8. Craig, *Spark from Heaven*, p. 164.
9. Weible, *The Final Harvest*, pp. 155–56.
10. Moira Noonan, *Ransomed from Darkness* (North Bay Books, El Sobrante, 2005), pp. 55–96.
11. David Baldwin, *Medjugorje* (CTS, London, 2002), p. 75; Gina Hutchings, *Youth 2000* (CTS, London, 2001), pp. 4, 8–10, 70.
12. Emmanuel Maillard quote from: James Mulligan, *Medjugorje: What's Happening?* (Dusty Sandals Press, London, 2008), p. 211; cf. te-deum.blogspot.com/2009/04/letter-from-bishop-peric-medjugorje-to.html; te-deum.blogspot.

com/2009/04/letter-from-bishop-peric-medjugorje-to_03.html; Davies, *Medjugorje After Fifteen Years*, pp. 89–91.

13. Craig, *Spark from Heaven*, pp. 178–79.

14. Johnson, *Twenty Questions About Medjugorje*, pp. 13–14; Davies, *Medjugorje After Fifteen Years*, pp. 67–69.

15. Cf. Jones, *The Medjugorje Deception*, p. 53.

16. Ibid., p. 53.

17. *The Troubadour*, 8 December 1983, p. 1; 14 November 1986; 6 February 1987; 27 March 1987, p. 3; 2 February 1989; 27 September 1990; 20 February 1992, p. 3; 18 February 2000.

18. Weible, *The Final Harvest*, p. 125.

19. Cf. Apolito, *The Internet and the Madonna*, pp. 3, 4.

20. Nolan, *Medjugorje: A Time for Truth*, p. 161.

21. O'Carroll, *Medjugorje: Facts, Documents, Theology*, pp. 145–46.

22. Sanchez-Ventura y Pascual, *The Apparitions of Garabandal*, pp. 88, 92.

23. Johnson, *Twenty Questions About Medjugorje*, pp. 14–16; cf. Apolito, *The Internet and the Madonna*, pp. 30, 44–45, 46–47.

24. Volken, *Visions, Revelations, and the Church*, p. 166.

25. Chiron, *Enquête sur les Apparitions de la Vierge*, pp. 462–64.

26. René Laurentin, *The Apparitions of the Blessed Virgin Mary Today* (Veritas Publications, Dublin 1991), pp. 141–46.

27. Jones, *The Medjugorje Deception*, p. xiv. The information about Fr Sivric was passed on to the author by Mary Broome, who knew him personally when he lived in St Louis, Missouri.

NOTES FOR CHAPTER 20

1. Nolan, *Medjugorje: A Time for Truth*, pp. 181–82; cf. https://web.archive.org/web/20160312112100/ministryvalues.com/index.php?option=com_content&task=view&id=1366&Itemid=125. The accusation that Nolan's conclusions following this statement have been ignored—as made at the above link—is not true, since the points he makes there are dealt with elsewhere in this book.

2. Weible, *The Final Harvest*, pp. 155–56.

3. See: https://web.archive.org/web/20160312112100/ministryvalues.com/index.php?option=com_content&task=view&id=1366&Itemid=125.

4. See Mark Garvey, *Searching for Mary*, for this type of thing in the US.

5. Bouflet, *Medjugorje, ou la fabrication du surnaturel*, pp. 185–88.

6. Jones, *The Medjugorje Deception*, pp. xviii, 352, 359.

7. *The Sunday Times*, 29 December 2002, "Village grows rich on Virgin visions," by Tom Walker, Medjugorje, Bosnia.

8. https://www.medjugorje.org/pilgrimages/medjugorje-pilgrimages.htm.

9. Johnson, *Twenty Questions About Medjugorje*, pp. 3–4.

10. Ibid., pp. 4–6.

11. Nolan, *Medjugorje: A Time for Truth*, pp. 109–22.

12. Johnson, *Twenty Questions About Medjugorje*, p. 19; Donovan, "Bayside Unveiled," in *Fidelity Magazine*, March 1988, pp. 34–35; Davies, *Medjugorje after Twenty-One Years, 1981–2002*, p. 86.

13. John of the Cross, "Ascent of Mount Carmel," in *Collected Works*, p. 226.
14. Noonan, *Ransomed from Darkness*, pp. 51–53.
15. Kraljevic, *The Apparitions of Our Lady at Medjugorje*, pp. 125–26.
16. Although such incidents were not unknown in the lives of saints such as Padre Pio, such persons are clearly in a different category to the Medjugorje visionaries.
17. Kondor, *Fatima in Lucia's Own Words*, pp. 137–38.
18. Kraljevic, *The Apparitions of Our Lady at Medjugorje*, pp. 156–57.
19. Laurentin and Lejeune, *Messages and Teachings*, pp. 38, 157.

NOTES FOR CHAPTER 21

1. *Homiletic and Pastoral Review Magazine* (letter to the editor), pp. 5–6, July 2002.
2. Davies, *Medjugorje after Twenty-One Years, 1981–2002*, p. 151.
3. Ibid., pp. 152–53.
4. Ibid., pp. 138–42.
5. Ibid., pp. 142–43.
6. Ibid., pp. 138, 143–46.
7. *L'Osservatore Romano*, Vatican, October 17, 2001. See also CWNews.com, Vatican, October 10, 2001, ref. 16570, https://www.catholicculture.org/news/features/index.Cfm?recnum=16570. The ungrammatical nature of the latter part of this text is present in the original.
8. *The Catholic Weekly* (Australia), 14 July 2002.
9. https://www.irishexaminer.com/news/arid-20145694.html.
10. *The Catholic Herald*, 29 November, 2002.
11. Baldwin, *Medjugorje*, pp. 43–44; https://www.catholicnewsagency.com/news/medjugorje-visionary-says-monthly-apparitions-have-come-to-an-end-63003. There seem to be differing accounts from various sources as to the exact status of each visionary as regards receiving visions at present.
12. "The Visionaries from Medjugorje tried by Science," 2004, FilmGrupp-München, c. 1 hour 8 minutes.
13. Joseph Deery, *Our Lady of Lourdes* (Brown & Nolan, Dublin, 1958), p. 25.
14. "Medjugorje: Secrets, Messages, Vocations, Prayers, Confessions, Commissions," a talk given at Maynooth, Co. Dublin, on February 17, 2004.
15. http://theotokos.org.uk/wp-content/uploads/2020/07/bishop-piacenza.pdf.
16. Roy Abraham Varghese, *God-Sent: A History of the Accredited Apparitions of Mary* (The Crossroad Publishing Company, New York, 2000), p. 171.
17. For details see: catholiclight.stblogs.org/archives/2008/02/korean-bishop-e.html.
18. Varghese, *God-Sent*, p. 190.
19. Ibid., pp. 184–85, 188.
20. Ibid., p. 189.
21. Mark Miravalle, *Introduction to Medjugorje* (Queenship Publishing, Goleta, 2004), pp. 5–6.

22. Denis Nolan, *Medjugorje and the Church* (Queenship Publishing, Goleta, 2007), p. ix; for information about Bishop Hnilica, see Jones, *Medjugorje: The Untold Story*, pp. 133–49.
23. Nolan, *Medjugorje and the Church*, p. 23.
24. Ibid., p. 153.
25. Ibid., p. 155.
26. Ibid., pp. 160, 171.
27. Ibid., pp. 178–79.
28. Mark Miravalle and Wayne Weible, *Are the Medjugorje Apparitions Authentic?* (New Hope Press, Hiawassee, 2008), p. 21. See also the section above in Chapter 11, "The Visionaries Compared with the Saints."
29. Miravalle and Weible, *Are the Medjugorje Apparitions Authentic?* p. 20.
30. Ibid., pp. 21–22.
31. Ibid., p. 26.
32. Ibid.
33. Ibid., p. 27.
34. Ibid., p. 40.
35. Mulligan, *Medjugorje: What's Happening?* p. 12.
36. Ibid., p. 14.
37. Ibid., pp. 42, 48. Emphasis added to this and subsequent quote, p. 42.
38. Ibid., pp. 53–54.
39. Ibid., pp. 58–59.
40. Ibid., pp. 107–8.
41. Ibid., pp. 108, 133–40.
42. Ibid., pp. 170–77.
43. The pictures of Fr Vlasic on pp. 31 and 72 in the first edition are missing in the revised edition; see pages 170 and 175 respectively in the first and revised editions for the name removal.

NOTES FOR CHAPTER 22

1. From the interview with Msgr. Ratko Peric, bishop of Mostar-Duvno, released to the *Crkva na Kamenu* ("The Church on the Rock"), monthly pastoral bulletin of the Dioceses of Mostar-Duvno and Trebinje-Mrkan, nr. 4/2006, pp. 22–24, after his Ad Limina visit from 23–28 February 2006.
2. chiesa.espresso.repubblica.it/articolo/37078?eng=y; www.nationalcatholicreporter.org/word/word072205.htm.
3. See: https://www.catholicregister.org/item/8367-army-of-mary-excommunicated.
4. https://web.archive.org/web/20110827141212/www.zenit.org/article-16018?l=english.
5. See information at: te-deum.blogspot.com/2006/07/homily-of-bishop-ratko-peric-of.html.
6. www.cafarus.ch/cet.medjugorje.html.
7. See: medjugorjedocuments.blogspot.com/2010/09/2005-article-about-cardinal-bertone-on.html and www.corriere.it/Primo_Piano/Cronache/2005/02_Febbraio/24/medjugorje.shtml.

8. Cardinal Tarcisio Bertone with Giuseppe de Carli, *The Last Secret of Fatima* (Doubleday, New York, 2008), pp. 95–96.

9. Bertone, *The Last Secret of Fatima*, pp. 107–8.

10. See Catholic News Service report, "Papal preacher won't lecture in Medjugorje after bishop nixes plan," 20 June 2007.

11. www.medjugorje.ws/en/articles/competence-puljic/.

12. See Catholic Herald report, "Vatican will reject Medjugorje, says bishop," 6 June 2008. From private correspondence I have received from a reliable academic source concerning information passed on to him by a cleric who knew Bishop Gemma, who was the bishop of the Isernia-Venafro diocese in Italy from 1990 to 2006, it appears that he discouraged people in his diocese from visiting Medjugorje during his tenure as bishop. He suffered the first of a series of strokes in 1997 which apparently affected his behavior and judgement, and this is a factor which has to be taken into account in judging his position on Medjugorje. However, it could also be argued that his experience as an exorcist means he could well have perceived something diabolical about the alleged apparitions, despite his poor state of physical health.

13. Letter from CDF: prot. 144/1985-27164.

14. www.medjugorje.org/laurentinstatement.htm.

15. Teresa of Avila, *The Interior Castle*, tr. Benedictines of Stanbrook (Benzinger Brothers, New York, 1912), p. 119.

16. See translation at: catholiclight.stblogs.org/archives/2008/10/petrus-intervie.html.

17. Laurentin and Rupcic, *Virgin Mary Appearing at Medjugorje?* p. 138. Emphasis added.

18. For a copy of the original text and an English translation see: catholiclight.stblogs.org/archives/2009/07/medjugorje-bomb.html.

19. Bubalo, *Thousand Encounters*, p. 58; see also information at: Corvaglia, *La verità su Medjugorje*, pp. 76–77.

20. Laurentin and Lejeune, *Messages and Teachings*, pp. 165–66, 182, 201. Emphasis added.

21. See: https://web.archive.org/web/20100408165324/www.catholicnews.com/data/stories/cns/0904306.htm; also see English translation of the documents described at: catholiclight.stblogs.org/archives/2009/09/new-directives.html.

22. See: blogs.reuters.com/faithworld/2009/10/07/vatican-ruling-on-disputed-medjugorje-shrine-expected-soon/.

23. See: www.catholicnewsagency.com/news/17714/cardinal-schonborns-visit-to-medjugorje-not-a-statement-spokesman-says.

24. Cf. information in comments made by Diane M. Korzeniewski at: https://catholicherald.co.uk/medjugorje-is-generating-what-the-devil-loves-most-disobedience; papal comment on Maciel in: Pope Benedict XVI with Peter Seewald, *Light of the World: The Pope, the Church, and the Signs of the Times* (CTS/Ignatius Press, 2010), p. 39.

25. See: www.catholicnewsagency.com/news/bosnian_cardinal_denies_claims_of_vatican_commission_for_medjugorje/.

26. Corvaglia, *La verità su Medjugorje*, p. 145; Bishop Peric's remarks were reported in *Crkva na Kamenu*, 5/2007, 33–35.
27. See: te-deum.blogspot.com/2010/09/another-slap-from-vienna-as-cardinal.html.
28. Cf. comments from Diane M. Korzeniewski at te-deum.blogspot.com/2011/02/medjugorje-controversy.html.
29. See the 12 January 2010 *Petrus* internet report as translated at: catholiclight.stblogs.org/archives/2010/01/from-petrus-car.html.
30. See: www.catholicnewsagency.com/news/vatican_commission_to_reportedly_investigate_medjugorje_apparitions/.
31. See: www.catholicnewsagency.com/news/holy_see_confirms_formation_of_medjugorje_commission/.
32. See: www.catholicnewsagency.com/news/possibility_of_new_diocese_for_medjugorje_floated/ and www.ncregister.com/blog/new_medjugorje_diocese/.
33. See: www.catholicnewsagency.com/news/vatican_announces_members_of_medjugorje_commission/.
34. www.marcocorvaglia.com/madonnina-di-civitavecchia-parte-1.
35. medjugorjedocuments.blogspot.com/2010/04/archbishop-derrico-papal-nuncio-to-bih.html.
36. https://www.catholicnews.com/services/englishnews/2011/is-seeing-believing-how-the-church-faces-claims-of-marian-apparitions-cns-1100252.Cfm.

NOTES FOR CHAPTER 23

1. www.medjugorje.ws/en/articles/caritas-of-birmingham/.
2. www.medjugorje.ws/en/articles/caritas-of-birmingham-not-roman-catholic-organization/.
3. www.medjugorje.ws/en/articles/a-friend-of-medjugorje-terry-colafrancesco-cult-leader-caritas-of-birmingham/.
4. www.caritasofbirmingham.com/; https://www.medjugorje.com/medjugorje-messages/latest-25-message.html.
5. www.caritasofbirmingham.com/tabernacle.html.
6. www.terrycolafrancesco.com/; "Spreading the word of Caritas: Headquarters grows as visionary returns to Alabama," at: blog.al.com/spotnews/2011/03/spreading_the_word_of_caritas.html.
7. www.caritasofbirmingham.com/other-outreaches.html.
8. www.caritasofbirmingham.com/pilgrimages.html; pilgrimage.medjugorje.com/.
9. www.caritasofbirmingham.com/caritas-prayer-gatherings.html; the web page has not been updated in some time, so it is unclear if these events are still going on.
10. blog.al.com/spotnews/2011/03/spreading_the_word_of_caritas.html.
11. blog.al.com/spotnews/2011/03/spreading_the_word_of_caritas.html; see also: en.marcocorvaglia.com/a-proposito-di-marija for more details of allegations against Caritas.
12. https://www.medjugorje.ws/en/articles/caritas-of-birmingham/.

13. https://www.catholicnews.com/services/englishnews/2011/pilgrims-flock-to-medjugorje-while-vatican-studies-alleged-apparitions.Cfm.

NOTES FOR CHAPTER 24

1. Foley, *Marian Apparitions*, pp. 350–51. For a discussion on the validity of the collegial consecration, see pages 352–56; see also, Andrew Apostoli, *Fatima for Today: The Urgent Marian Message of Hope* (Ignatius Press, San Francisco, 2010), pp. 189–96.
2. Apostoli, *Fatima for Today*, pp. 189–99; quote p. 196.
3. Foley, *Marian Apparitions*, pp. 360–61.
4. Foley, *Marian Apparitions*, pp. 361–62; Apostoli, *Fatima for Today*, p. 258; cf. "Fatima, Church Unity, and the Conversion of Russia: A Catholic Russia?" by James Likoudis, originally published in the Catholic magazine *Immaculate Heart Messenger*, issue of January-March 2000.
5. Foley, *Marian Apparitions, the Bible, and the Modern World*, pp. 362–66.
6. www.vatican.va/holy_father/benedict_xvi/speeches/2010/may/documents/hf_ben-xvi_spe_20100511_portogallo-interview_en.html. Emphasis added.
7. "Homily, Mass in Fatima 13 May 2010;" https://www.ewtn.com/catholicism/library/homily-mass-in-fatima-13-may-2010-6854.
8. Pope Benedict/Seewald, *Light of the World*, pp. 163–64.
9. For example, see: Nolan, *Medjugorje: A Time for Truth*, passim.
10. SESDI, 1J5.1/11.209, 1998 11 10, 5938; CWNews.com, Vatican, 20 December 2001.
11. *Inside the Vatican*, December 2004, p. 39; CWNews.com, Vatican, 20 December 2001; cf. Apostoli, *Fatima for Today*, pp. 263–68.
12. www.vatican.va/roman_curia/congregations/Cfaith/documents/rc_con_Cfaith_doc_20000626_message-fatima_en.html; cf. Pope Benedict/Seewald, *Light of the World*, p. 165.
13. *Medjugorje: All Our Lady's Messages* (Edizioni Martini, n.d.), p. 88; also available at: www.medjugorje.org/olmpage.htm.
14. Antonio Martins and Robert Fox, *Documents on Fatima & the Memoirs of Sr Lucia* (Fatima Family Apostolate, Alexandria, 1992), p. 246.

NOTES FOR CHAPTER 25

1. See http://www.vecernji.hr/hrvatska/papina-komisija-pozvala-vidioce-iz-medjugorja-na-novo-ispitivanje-292309 via Google translation, and http://www.miraclehunter.com/news/ (scroll down to "Interview with Member of Medjugorje Commission").
2. http://en.louisbelanger.com/tag/medjugorje-commission/ — third item.
3. http://en.louisbelanger.com/2011/06/27/%E2%80%9Cfor-the-holy-see-medjugorje-is-a-tormenting-dilemma%E2%80%9Dvittorio-messori-%E2%80%93-part-1/; http://www.corriere.it/cronache/11_giugno_22/dialoghi-madomma-dilemma-medjugorje_fe39ac3c-9c8d-11e0-ad47-baea6e4ae360.shtml.
4. http://en.louisbelanger.com/2011/08/15/for-the-holy-see-medjugorje-is-a-tormenting-dilemma-vittorio-messori-right-wrong-there-is-no-dilemma-part-2/; Kingham, pp. 213–14. Emphasis added.

Notes for Chapter 25

5. http://en.louisbelanger.com/2011/08/15/for-the-holy-see-medjugorje-is-a-tormenting-dilemma-vittorio-messori-right-wrong-there-is-no-dilemma-part-2/. Although it could also be said that if the Holy See were to review a case of alleged visions, and contradict the local Ordinary, then that would be a strengthening and not a weakening of the Faith. But that would assume that overwhelming new evidence was available which would warrant such a stance, which does not appear to be the case with Medjugorje.

6. http://www.catholicculture.org/news/headlines/index.Cfm?storyid=12407; cf. comments from Diane M. Korzeniewski at http://te-deum.blogspot.co.uk/2011/11/medjugorje-and-situational-collegiality.html?spref=fb.

7. http://catholiclight.stblogs.org/index.php/2012/01/bp-peric-defend/; see also: http://te-deum.blogspot.co.uk/2012/02/medjugorje-commission-to-end-its-work.html (scroll down).

8. http://te-deum.blogspot.co.uk/2012/02/medjugorje-commission-to-end-its-work.html; http://en.louisbelanger.com/2012/02/16/medjugorje-commission-our-work-is-continuing-but-we-need-to-finish-it-this-year-cardinal-vinko-puljic-2012-02-14/; http://catholiclight.stblogs.org/index.php/2012/02/cardinal-puljic/.

9. http://www.ncregister.com/blog/edward-pentin/vatican-medjugorje-commission-findings-not-imminent.

10. http://te-deum.blogspot.co.uk/2013/01/cardinal-ruini-speaks-about-medjugorje.html.

11. http://te-deum.blogspot.co.uk/2013/01/cardinal-ruini-speaks-about-medjugorje.html. Scroll down to "Visions on demand travel to Holy Land. What?"

12. http://catholiclane.com/sabotaging-medjugorje-commission/.

13. Mulligan, *Medjugorje: The First Days*, pp. 1, 3.

14. Mulligan, *Medjugorje: The First Days*, p. 219.

15. Mulligan, *Medjugorje: The First Days*, pp. 223, 232.

16. Sivric, *The Hidden Side of Medjugorje, Vol. I*, p. 352.

17. Mulligan, *Medjugorje: The First Days*, p. 226.

18. Sivric, *The Hidden Side of Medjugorje, Vol. I*, p. 277.

19. Mulligan, *Medjugorje: The First Days*, p. 171.

20. https://www.catholicnewsagency.com/news/pope-entrusts-world-to-immaculate-heart-of-mary.

21. http://www.zenit.org/en/articles/francis-pontificate-consecrated-to-our-lady-of-fatima.

22. http://www.corrispondenzaromana.it/notizie-brevi/papa-francesco-contro-medjugorie/; http://catholiclight.stblogs.org/index.php/2013/10/is-pope-francis-against-medjugorje/.

23. https://www.catholicculture.org/news/headlines/index.Cfm?storyid=19676.

24. http://rorate-caeli.blogspot.com/2013/11/cdf-prefect-on-medjugorje.html; cf. http://wdtprs.com/blog/2013/11/cdf-directs-clerics-faithful-not-to-attend-conferences-favorable-to-medjugorje/.

25. http://www.ncregister.com/blog/edward-pentin/vatican-commission-completes-medjugorje-investigation; cf. http://www.ansa.it/web/notizie/rubriche/politica/2014/01/18/Commissione-chiude-lavori-Medjugorje_9920072.html.

26. https://www.lastampa.it/vatican-insider/en/2014/01/19/news/verdict-on-medjugorje-nears-as-commission-claims-apparitions-are-no-hoax-1.35936797.

27. http://te-deum.blogspot.co.uk/2014/01/vatican-insider-report-on-medjugorje.html; http://www.ncregister.com/blog/jimmy-akin/does-vatican-insider-have-the-inside-scoop-on-medjugorje-11-things-to-know.

28. http://www.ncregister.com/blog/edward-pentin/pope-meets-head-of-medjugorje-commission. See also: http://catholiclight.stblogs.org/index.php/2014/01/verdict-watch-for-medjugorje/ for a commentary on these events.

29. http://www.stltoday.com/lifestyles/faith-and-values/archdiocese-of-st-louis-cancels-st-charles-speech-by-man/article_218Cf267-d7ac-5e2b-93a5-03ca9a06d648.html. Note: this web page is not available in areas subject to GDPR practices.

30. http://te-deum.blogspot.co.uk/2015/03/ivan-dragicevic-thumbs-nose-at-cdf.html; https://www.catholicculture.org/news/headlines/index.Cfm?storyid=24329.

31. Cf. https://www.facebook.com/groups/256661721134929/permalink/608584042609360/; http://wdtprs.com/blog/2013/11/cdf-directs-clerics-faithful-not-to-attend-conferences-favorable-to-medjugorje/.

32. http://www.catholicstand.com/wayne-weible-papal-nuncio-response/. See this article by Kevin Symonds for a more detailed discussion of Weible's arguments, and also: https://www.facebook.com/groups/256661721134929/permalink/610872872380477/. The original Weible article has since disappeared from this location: http://www.medjugorjetoday.tv/14259/arrangement-ban-is-based-on-misquotation/ but the Kevin Symonds reply has sufficient details to make the exchange understandable.

33. http://en.radiovaticana.va/news/2015/03/16/pope_francis_receives_bishops_of_bosnia_and_herzegovina/1129673.

34. http://te-deum.blogspot.co.uk/2015/05/medjugorje-fallout-more-cancellations.html; https://www.catholic.org/news/international/europe/story.php?id=60435.

35. http://catholiclight.stblogs.org/index.php/2015/05/bishop-ratko-peric-at-medjugorje-unity-is-more-important-than-charisms/.

NOTES FOR CHAPTER 26

1. http://www.catholicnewsagency.com/news/pope-francis-bosnian-visit-to-steer-clear-of-medjugorje-40577/.

2. http://www.catholicnewsagency.com/news/pope-francis-on-medjugorje-its-almost-decision-time-19185/.

3. http://en.radiovaticana.va/news/2015/06/09/pope_francis_dont_weaken_or_water_down_christian_identity/1150231; http://www.catholicnewsagency.com/news/days-after-medjuorge-comment-pope-downplays-predictable-visions-20781/.

4. http://www.avvenire.it/Chiesa/Pagine/Ecco-i-criteri-per-valutare-il-fenomeno-Medjugorje.aspx.

5. http://www.acistampa.com/story/ruini-su-medjugorje-finora-solo-indiscrezioni-0781.

6. https://www.ncregister.com/daily-news/vatican-spokesman-medjugorje-decision-will-take-months.

Notes for Chapter 26

7. http://www.ncregister.com/blog/simcha-fisher/does-it-matter-if-medjugorje-is-real-or-not.

8. http://te-deum.blogspot.co.uk/2015/06/pope-francis-revealed-blunt-thoughts-on.html.

9. https://www.catholicculture.org/news/headlines/index.Cfm?storyid=25343.

10. http://www.ilgiornale.it/news/cronache/messori-avverte-papa-francesco-se-dir-no-medjugorie-si-risch-1144480.html.

11. https://www.catholicculture.org/news/headlines/index.Cfm?storyid=25343.

12. https://www.catholicculture.org/news/headlines/index.Cfm?storyid=25356; http://www.ilgiornale.it/news/politica/medjugorje-papa-isola-veggenti-1144889.html.

13. http://www.ncregister.com/daily-news/vatican-remains-mum-on-medjugorje-no-decision-has-been-made; http://www.lastampa.it/2015/06/26/vaticaninsider/eng/the-vatican/medjugorje-no-decision-yet-xOzm5ygStuoGAd8JwWqZUJ/pagina.html.

14. https://www.facebook.com/groups/256661721134929/permalink/681308628670234/.

15. http://www.nytimes.com/2015/08/27/world/europe/catholic-church-virgin-mary-apparitions-medjugorje.html?_r=0.

16. https://sremmanuel.org/newsletter/september-2015-report-4/.

17. https://www.nationalgeographic.com/magazine/2015/12/virgin-mary-worlds-most-powerful-woman/.

18. http://www.asianews.it/news-en/Pope%3A-follow-Jesus-on-the-path-of-life-and-do-not-trust-fortune-tellers-and-alleged-visionaries-37254.html.

19. http://www.total-croatia-news.com/item/12828-vatican-to-take-over-administration-of-medugorje. But given the fact that the conflict over parishes long preceded the alleged apparitions and St James Parish is not one of the disputed parishes, this claim is rather puzzling.

20. www.ncregister.com/blog/fr-lombardi-reports-of-vatican-administrator-for-medjugorje-premature.

21. Mirjana Soldo, *My Heart Will Triumph* (CatholicShop Publishing, Cocoa, 2016), p. 53.

22. Soldo, *My Heart Will Triumph*, pp. 54–55.

23. Soldo, *My Heart Will Triumph*, p. 20.

24. "Ivan's encounter with Our Lady in Vienna on September 27, 2016," http://marytv.tv/?p=640.

25. http://slobodnadalmacija.hr/novosti/hrvatska/clanak/id/449169/kardinal-gerhard-ludwig-muller-drugi-covjek-vatikana-molim-se-stepincu-njegov-grob-treba-biti-jedno-od-glavnih-odredista-meunarodnih-hodocasca.

26. http://www.corriere.it/english/17_febbraio_09/pope-francis-there-is-corruption-the-vatican-but-m-at-peace-5f115a68-eeaa-11e6-b691-ec49635e90c8.shtml.

27. http://www.ncregister.com/blog/edward-pentin/pope-francis-appoints-polish-archbishop-to-be-special-envoy-to-medjugorje; http://en.radiovaticana.va/

news/2017/02/11/pope_appoints_special_envoy_to_medjugorje/1291940; http://www.vatican.va/resources/resources_glossary-terms_en.html.

28. http://www.md-tm.ba/clanci/true-madonna-and-post-office-manager.

29. http://crownofstars.blogspot.co.uk/2017/02/high-number-of-medjugorje-pilgrims.html.

30. https://www.total-croatia-news.com/lifestyle/16782-pope-francis-endangers-tourism-in-medugorje.

31. http://md-tm.ba/clanci/first-seven-days-apparitions-medjugorje; cf. https://www.total-croatia-news.com/lifestyle/17006-local-bishop-there-were-no-apparitions-of-virgin-mary-in-medugorje.

32. https://kevinsymonds.com/2017/03/; http://www.lettera43.it/it/articoli/cronaca/2017/03/03/medjugorje-il-cardinale-scettico-troppe-esagerazioni/208966/.

33. http://www.catholicnewsagency.com/amp/news/full-text-of-may-13-in-flight-interview-with-pope-francis-12886/; https://kevinsymonds.com/2017/05/14/pope-francis-medjugorje/; http://www.lastampa.it/2017/05/13/vaticaninsider/eng/the-vatican/medjugorje-doubts-and-openings-of-the-pope-drhXLmmf3xzVtBohNoHpoM/pagina.html; it appears that Tornielli was mistaken in believing that the Ruini report went to the *Feria Quarta*. The literal words of Pope Francis seem to indicate that he intervened before the *Feria Quarta* meeting; cf. the link to Kevin Symonds' site above; http://w2.vatican.va/content/francesco/en/speeches/2017/may/documents/papa-francesco_20170513_voloritorno-fatima.html.

34. http://www.lastampa.it/2017/05/16/vaticaninsider/eng/the-vatican/medjugorje-the-findings-of-the-ruini-report-hvBaZ3ssAeDicj dmEcS3UN/pagina.html; http://www.catholicnews.com/services/englishnews/2017/prudence-pastoral-concern-guided-medjugorje-commission-member-says.Cfm.

35. https://www.churchmilitant.com/news/article/dispelling-the-spin-on-medjugorje.

36. https://www.avvenire.it/chiesa/pagine/medjugorje-papa-madonna-postina; http://www.catholicnews.com/services/englishnews/20 17/prudence-pastoral-concern-guided-medjugorje-commission-member-says.Cfm; https://aleteia.org/2017/05/22/a-member-of-the-medjugorje-commission-explains-the-popes-skepticism/.

37. http://www.catholicnewsagency.com/amp/news/full-text-of-may-13-in-flight-interview-with-pope-francis-12886/.

NOTES FOR CHAPTER 27

1. en.marcocorvaglia.com/i-veggenti-e-il-denaro-parte-1, and en.marcocorvaglia.com/i-veggenti-e-il-denaro-parte-2. Also, various stories related to the activities of the visionaries have continued to surface, including one concerning Mirjana, who, with her husband, is the owner of a luxury four-star beachfront villa which they rent to tourists. She was accused of illegally constructing a cement patio encroaching on the local public beach, but when contacted by a reporter, she claimed to know nothing about it. Also, Ivan paid more than $8,000 in property taxes for his US home, which is valued at over $700,000, in 2018. And regarding pilgrim accommodation generally in Medjugorje, as Marco Corvaglia points out, there have been numerous infringements of the law regarding the non-issuance of receipts, tax evasion and the employment of

Notes for Chapter 27

persons working illegally. https://www.redfin.com/MA/Peabody/5-Emily-Ln-01960/home/11349781#property-history.

2. This video appears to be no longer available on YouTube. A copy, however, has been preserved by Kevin J. Symonds, author of *Refractions of Light: 201 Answers on Apparitions, Visions and the Catholic Church* (En Route Books and Media, St. Louis, Missouri, 2017).

3. http://www.md-tm.ba/clanci/calumnies-film. See also, https://www.md-tm.ba/clanci/sedlars-calumnies, and https://www.md-tm.ba/clanci/generals-stubborn-calumnies. The Mostar-Duvno website also, on 23 June, published a lengthy article entitled "On the Medjugorje Zealots or How the 'Gospa' Contradicts the Madonna" (https://www.cnak.ba/osvrti/the-medjugorje-zealots-or-how-the-gospa-contradicts-the-madonna/). This drew a response from Fr Karlo Lovrić, parish vicar in Medjugorje, "The fictional Lady is an excellent pastor" (https://www.vjeraidjela.com/izmisljena-gospa-odlican-pastorizator/), which in turn prompted a further response from Kevin Symonds, "A Response to Fr. Karlo Lovrić on Medjugorje" (https://www.cnak.ba/osvrti/a-response-to-fr-karlo-lovric-medjugorje/).

4. https://deon.pl/kosciol/wszystko-wskazuje-na-to-ze-objawienia-beda-uznane-abp-hoser-odpowiada-na-zarzuty-dot-medjugorie,448292.

5. https://www.vjeraidjela.com/medjugorje-fanaticism-and-the-papal-envoy-archbishop-hoser/. See also: https://kevinsymonds.com/2017/08/18/hoser-on-medjugorje/.

6. https://spiritdaily.org/blog/spiritual-warfare/demonic-howls-erupt-during-apparition. The video can also be seen at: https://www.youtube.com/watch?v=fjcyyjJUOgg. Another example of this can be seen at: https://www.youtube.com/watch?v=NpQqS7WnK18&.

7. https://www.lastampa.it/vatican-insider/en/2017/11/01/news/medjugorje-parolin-the-holy-see-wants-to-regulate-the-phenomenon-1.34377637.

8. https://aleteia.org/2017/12/07/official-pilgrimages-to-medjugorje-are-being-authorized-confirms-pope-francis-envoy/.

9. https://www.ilgiornale.it/news/politica/medjugorje-pellegrinaggi-s-non-apparizioni-1472328.html; cf. https://catholicherald.co.uk/papal-envoy-backtracks-on-medjugorje-remarks/. This article on the Mostar-Duvno website points out some of the inconsistencies between the two interviews given by Archbishop Hoser: https://www.cnak.ba/osvrti/instructions-for-medjugorje-pilgrims/ and there is further criticism here: https://www.cnak.ba/osvrti/by-what-authority-is-archbishop-hoser-proclaiming-medjugorje-a-shrine/.

10. https://kevinsymonds.com/2018/05/31/hoser-av-medjugorje/; cf. https://www.catholicnewsagency.com/news/pope-francis-names-apostolic-visitor-for-pastoral-care-in-medjugorje-42036; http://press.vatican.va/content/salastampa/it/bollettino/pubblico/2018/05/31/0399/00875.html.

11. https://www.lastampa.it/vatican-insider/en/2018/05/31/news/medjugorje-the-pope-appoints-hoser-as-permanent-visitor-1.34021267.

12. https://www.catholicnewsagency.com/news/apostolic-visitor-to-medjugorje-begins-pastoral-mandate-20137; cf. https://www.vaticannews.va/en/church/news/2018-07/archbishop-hoser-envoy-medjugorje-st-james-apparition-mary.html.

13. https://www.total-croatia-news.com/lifestyle/29987-bishop-medjugorje-apparitions-are-not-credible; cf. https://www.katholisch.de/artikel/18388-ortsbischof-zweifelt-an-erscheinungen-in-medjugorje and also https://www.vjeraidjela.com/from-the-athanasius-of-mostar-to-henryk-of-medjugorje/.

14. http://catholiclight.stblogs.org/index.php/2018/08/the-courage-to-reveal/; cf. https://www.die-tagespost.de/kirche-aktuell/Mut-zur-Aufdeckung;art312,190845 and https://www.die-tagespost.de/kirche-aktuell/Medjugorje-Hauke-kritisiert-Vatikan-fuer-Umgang-mit-Erscheinungen;art312,190873.

15. http://catholiclight.stblogs.org/index.php/2018/08/medjugorje-first-ten-days/; cf. https://gloria.tv/post/Nrhajf2qbFiu1aMNSUVzWeA1V.

16. *Les premières apparitions de la Gospa à Medjugorje et leur évaluation. Bref status* (Le Mans, France), 2020, 28 pp, http://d.auzenet.free.fr/e_books/sp7_medjugorje.pdf; Italian version: *Le prime "apparizioni" della "Gospa" a Medjugorje e la loro valutazione. Breve status quaestionis* (Rivista teologica di Lugano, 2018), 433-62; German Version: *Die ersten "Erscheinungen" der "Gospa" in Medjugorje und ihr Ursprung. Kurzer status quaestionis.* (Forum Katholische Theologie, 2018), 262-89; Spanish Version: *Las primeras "apariciones" de la "Gospa" en Medjugorje y su evaluación* (Corrispondenza romana, 2019), 28 pp, https://es.corrispondenzaromana.it/las-primeras-apariciones-de-la-gospa-en-medjugorje-y-su-evaluacion/.

17. https://cruxnow.com/church-in-europe/2018/09/popes-delegate-outlines-plans-for-expansion-at-medjugorje-shrine/.

18. https://cruxnow.com/church-in-europe/2018/10/papal-envoy-compares-medjugorje-to-fatima-and-lourdes/.

19. https://en.marcocorvaglia.com/ho-scelto-padre-petar-anzi-no; Sivric, *The Hidden Side of Medjugorje, Vol. I*, p. 102.

20. https://it.aleteia.org/2018/11/02/chiara-amirante-papa-francesco-mi-ha-detto-ho-salvato-io-madonna-medjugorje/; cf. https://gloria.tv/post/g78NWX-rMZxmS4pjB2xH12xQYe — this page also has a video clip of Amirante speaking about this matter to a group.

21. https://www.vaticannews.va/en/pope/news/2019-05/pope-authorizes-pilgrimages-to-medjugorje.html; cf. https://cruxnow.com/church-in-europe/2019/05/pope-okays-pilgrimage-to-medjugorje-says-apparitions-need-study/ and also a commentary on this news from Andrea Tornielli: https://www.vaticannews.va/en/pope/news/2019-05/medjugorje-the-marian-faith-and-the-decision-of-the-pastor.html and this critical commentary at: https://www.vjeraidjela.com/what-does-the-holy-sees-statement-that-pilgrimages-to-medjugorje-are-authorized-really-mean/.

22. https://sremmanuel.org/newsletter/may-2019-report/.

23. https://www.thetablet.co.uk/news/11928/vatican-dignitaries-head-to-medjugorje-amid-reports-of-imminent-recognition; cf. https://www.avvenire.it/chiesa/pagine/hoser-medjugorje-faro-spirituale.

24. https://cruxnow.com/church-in-europe/2019/08/vatican-confirms-medjugorje-approval-by-joining-youth-festival/.

25. "Medjugorje 'visionary' says monthly apparitions have come to an end," at https://www.catholicnewsagency.com/news/medjugorje-visionary-says-monthly-apparitions-have-come-to-an-end-63003.

26. http://press.vatican.va/content/salastampa/en/bollettino/pubblico/2020/07/11/200711c.html.

27. https://www.catholicnewsagency.com/news/tomislav-vlasic-former-spiritual-director-of-medjugorje-visionaries-excommunicated-80554; https://www.ncronline.org/news/world/former-spiritual-adviser-medjugorje-visionaries-excommunicated; cf. catholiclight.stblogs.org/archives/2009/07/medjugorje-bomb.html307. There were some claims made by Medjugorje supporters that Vlasic was not in fact the spiritual director of the visionaries in the early 80s, but these claims are not valid: en.marcocorvaglia.com/lodato-dalla-gospa-e-scomunicato, and https://kevinsymonds.com/2020/11/05/reply-nolan-medjugorje/.

NOTES FOR CHAPTER 28

1. https://ilsegnodigiona.com/2020/02/07/rapporto-su-medjugorje-la-relazione-top-secret-della-commissione-pontificia-esclusa-origine-demoniaca-nessuna-manipolazione-vere-le-prime-sette-apparizioni-banali-i-messaggi-della-go/.

2. http://catholiclight.stblogs.org/index.php/2020/02/a-leak-from-the-medj-study-commission/.

3. Cf. http://catholiclight.stblogs.org/index.php/2008/09/the-father-of-t/ and http://catholiclight.stblogs.org/index.php/2010/03/the-deviations-of-medjugorje/.

4. http://catholiclight.stblogs.org/index.php/2020/02/a-leak-from-the-medj-study-commission/.

5. https://kevinsymondsdotcom.files.wordpress.com/2020/02/murgia-ruini-dossier-enpolished_1.2.pdf (Alternative text at: https://www.academia.edu/42068907/Final_Relatio_International_Commision_of_inquiry_on_Medjugorje); cf. the Murgia book: https://www.amazon.it/rapporto-medjugorje-documento-commissione-pontificia-ebook/dp/B084YHD2JM and the Gaeta book: https://www.amazon.it/Dossier-Medjugorje-Relazione-Commissione-apparizioni-ebook/dp/B0851NKYVM. Gaeta's website is at: https://saveriogaeta.it/.

6. In his book, *Rapporto su Medjugorje: Il Documento Segreto della Commissione Pontificia* ("Report on Medjugorje: The Secret Document of the Pontifical Commission"), p. 11, Murgia says: "Il sono un giornalista. E faccio questo mestiere da quasi vent'anni. E Mai mi sarie sognato di pubbblicare un documento del genere senze fare mille verifiche. Cosa che ho fatto anche con qualcuno dei componenti della stessa Commissione Pontificia." That is, as a journalist of long standing, he would not have published a document like this without proper verification, and without checking with members of the Commission.

7. https://kevinsymondsdotcom.files.wordpress.com/2020/02/murgia-ruini-dossier-enpolished_1.2.pdf.

8. Ibid., p. 1.

9. Ibid., p. 3.

10. See also, en.marcocorvaglia.com/medjugorje-e-la-chiesa-parte-2 and https://en.marcocorvaglia.com/il-vescovo-si-oppone (https://www.marcocorvaglia.com/risposte-a-saverio-gaeta-parte-3).

11. https://kevinsymondsdotcom.files.wordpress.com/2020/02/murgia-ruini-dossier-enpolished_1.2.pdf, pp. 5–6.

12. Ibid., p. 3.

13. https://www.ewtn.com/catholicism/library/judgement-on-the-apparitions-of-kibeho-5709 and http://miraclehunter.com/marian_apparitions/approved_apparitions/kibeho_rwanda/.

14. *Acta Apostolicae Sedis* 104 (2012), 497–504. The text is available online on the Vatican's website: http://www.vatican.va/roman_curia/congregations/Cfaith/documents/rc_con_Cfaith_doc_19780225_norme-apparizioni_en.html.

15. https://en.marcocorvaglia.com/medjugorje-e-la-chiesa.

16. https://kevinsymondsdotcom.files.wordpress.com/2020/02/murgia-ruini-dossier-enpolished_1.2.pdf p. 7; cf. http://catholiclight.stblogs.org/index.php/2018/08/medjugorje-first-ten-days/.

17. https://en.marcocorvaglia.com/medjugorje-e-la-chiesa; Saverio Gaeta, *Dossier Medjugorje* (San Paolo Edizioni, 2020), pp. 66–67.

18. Ibid., p. 65.

19. Bubalo, *Thousand Encounters*, p. 117.

20. For example, as in Sivric, *The Hidden Side of Medjugorje*, Vol. I, pp. 224, 242, 243–51, 253, 254, 276, 278, 283, 295, 317, 361; cf. Mulligan, *Medjugorje: The First Days*, pp. 87, 94, 149, 157, 169, 171, and Klanac, *Aux Sources de Medjugorje*, p. 69.

21. Sivric, *The Hidden Side of Medjugorje*, Vol. I, pp. 268, 288, 303; cf. Mulligan, *Medjugorje: The First Days*, pp. 120, 130, 153, 164, and Klanac *Aux Sources de Medjugorje*, pp. 91, 123.

22. Sivric, *The Hidden Side of Medjugorje*, Vol. I, p. 247.

23. Bubalo, *Thousand Encounters*, pp. 117–18.

24. Mulligan, *Medjugorje: The First Days*, p. 130.

25. Sivric, *The Hidden Side of Medjugorje*, Vol. I, p. 268, 288; cf. Mulligan, *Medjugorje: The First Days*, p. 121, 153, and Klanac, *Aux Sources de Medjugorje*, p. 91, 123.

26. Kraljevic, *The Apparitions of Our Lady at Medjugorje*, p. 17. There seems to be some confusion here on Vicka's part in referring to this as happening on the third day, that is 26 June, as the other visionaries refer to the fourth day.

27. Ibid., pp. 117, 146.

NOTES FOR CHAPTER 29

1. Sivric, *The Hidden Side of Medjugorje*, Vol. I, pp. 224, 253, 254; cf. Mulligan, *Medjugorje: The First Days*, p. 94, and Klanac, *Aux Sources de Medjugorje*, p. 69.

2. Sivric, *The Hidden Side of Medjugorje*, Vol. I, p. 223; cf. Mulligan, *Medjugorje: The First Days*, p. 94.

3. Sivric, *The Hidden Side of Medjugorje*, Vol. I, pp. 211–12, 253. See also pages 225 and 226 for similar statements from Ivan; cf. Mulligan, *Medjugorje: The First Days*, pp. 68–69 and Klanac, *Aux Sources de Medjugorje*, p. 69.

4. Sivric, *The Hidden Side of Medjugorje, Vol. I*, p. 238; cf. Mulligan, *Medjugorje: The First Days*, p. 79. Fr Mulligan places this interview on 27 June, whereas Fr Sivric dates it to 28 June—this is probably just a typo on the part of Fr Sivric.

5. Sivric, *The Hidden Side of Medjugorje, Vol. I*, p. 263; cf. Mulligan, *Medjugorje: The First Days*, p. 77, and Klanac, *Aux Sources de Medjugorje*, p. 87. There is a somewhat unusual difference in the ordering of sentences between, on the one hand the Sivric transcription, and on the other hand those of Mulligan and Klanac regarding this section of the tape—normally they are quite similar.

6. Sivric, *The Hidden Side of Medjugorje, Vol. I*, pp. 267–68; cf. Mulligan, *Medjugorje: The First Days*, pp. 120–21, and Klanac *Aux Sources de Medjugorje*, p. 91.

7. Sivric, *The Hidden Side of Medjugorje, Vol. I*, pp. 268–69; Jakov also reported similar remarks, p. 273; cf. Mulligan, *Medjugorje: The First Days*, pp. 120–21, and Klanac, *Aux Sources de Medjugorje*, p. 92.

8. Sivric, *The Hidden Side of Medjugorje, Vol. I*, pp. 282–83, parentheses in original text; cf. Mulligan, *Medjugorje: The First Days*, p. 149, and Klanac *Aux Sources de Medjugorje*, p. 118. Fr Mulligan's text has similar wording for this quote, although there is a difference for the latter part, i.e., "They strongly believe as if they saw me."

9. Sivric, *The Hidden Side of Medjugorje, Vol. I*, pp. 283; cf. Mulligan, *Medjugorje: The First Days*, p. 149, and Klanac, *Aux Sources de Medjugorje*, p. 118. In this case, for the first part of the quote, Fr Mulligan's text contradicts that of Fr Sivric, i.e., "She answered some questions." The same is true of Daria Klanac, who has, "Elle répond à nos questions." Overall, though, this is not a highly significant difference.

10. Sivric, *The Hidden Side of Medjugorje, Vol. I*, pp. 284; cf. Mulligan, *Medjugorje: The First Days*, p. 150, and Klanac, *Aux Sources de Medjugorje*, p. 119.

11. Sivric, *The Hidden Side of Medjugorje, Vol. I*, pp. 285–86; cf. Mulligan, *Medjugorje: The First Days*, p. 151, and Klanac, *Aux Sources de Medjugorje*, p. 119. Fr Mulligan's wording is similar, except that with reference to the Gospa appearing in church, he has, "Why doesn't she announce it in church?"

12. Sivric, *The Hidden Side of Medjugorje, Vol. I*, p. 288; cf. Mulligan, *Medjugorje: The First Days*, pp. 152–53, and Klanac, *Aux Sources de Medjugorje*, pp. 122–23, and Kraljevic, *The Apparitions of Our Lady at Medjugorje*, p. 24.

13. Sivric, *The Hidden Side of Medjugorje, Vol. I*, p. 292; cf. Mulligan, *Medjugorje: The First Days*, p. 155, and Klanac, *Aux Sources de Medjugorje*, p. 126.

14. Sivric, *The Hidden Side of Medjugorje, Vol. I*, p. 297; cf. Mulligan, *Medjugorje: The First Days*, p. 159, and Klanac, *Aux Sources de Medjugorje*, p. 104.

15. Sivric, *The Hidden Side of Medjugorje, Vol. I*, p. 312; cf. Mulligan, *Medjugorje: The First Days*, p. 145, and Klanac, *Aux Sources de Medjugorje*, p. 131.

16. Bubalo, *Thousand Encounters*, pp. 29–30.

17. Craig, *Spark from Heaven*, pp. 65, 68.

18. Mulligan, *Medjugorje: The First Days*, p. 193; cf. Klanac, *Aux Sources de Medjugorje*, p. 132, and Sivric, *The Hidden Side of Medjugorje, Vol. I*, p. 315. Klanac's text reads: "P. JOZO: Désires-tu que j'enregistre ou pas? Ça n'a pas d'importance! Tu sais pourquoi? IVANKA: Vous pouvez enregistrer. P. JOZO: Ce n'est pas important. Cela n'a aucune importance."

19. Sivric, *The Hidden Side of Medjugorje, Vol. I*, p. 315; cf. Mulligan, *Medjugorje: The First Days*, p. 193, and Klanac, *Aux Sources de Medjugorje*, p. 132. Klanac's transcription is: "Dis-moi, Iva, quel est ton vrai nom?"
20. Kraljevic, *The Apparitions of Our Lady at Medjugorje*, p. 115.
21. Sivric, *The Hidden Side of Medjugorje, Vol. I*, pp. 317; cf. Mulligan, *Medjugorje: The First Days*, p. 195, and Klanac, *Aux Sources de Medjugorje*, p. 134.
22. Sivric, *The Hidden Side of Medjugorje, Vol. I*, pp. 318–19; cf. Mulligan, *Medjugorje: The First Days*, p. 196, and Klanac, *Aux Sources de Medjugorje*, p. 135.
23. Sivric, *The Hidden Side of Medjugorje, Vol. I*, p. 320; cf. Mulligan, *Medjugorje: The First Days*, p. 197, and Klanac, *Aux Sources de Medjugorje*, p. 136.
24. Sivric, *The Hidden Side of Medjugorje, Vol. I*, p. 342; cf. Mulligan, *Medjugorje: The First Days*, p. 197, and Klanac, *Aux Sources de Medjugorje*, p. 155.
25. Sivric, *The Hidden Side of Medjugorje, Vol. I*, p. 346; cf. Mulligan, *Medjugorje: The First Days*, p. 219, and Klanac, *Aux Sources de Medjugorje*, p. 159.
26. Bubalo, *Thousand Encounters*, pp. 47–48.
27. Bubalo, *Thousand Encounters*, pp. 70–71. [affirmatively] in brackets is in original text.
28. Kraljevic, *The Apparitions of Our Lady at Medjugorje*, p. 17.
29. https://kevinsymondsdotcom.files.wordpress.com/2020/02/murgia-ruini-dossier-enpolished_1.2.pdf, p. 9.
30. Ibid., p. 10.
31. Sivric, *The Hidden Side of Medjugorje, Vol. I*, pp. 288–89; cf. Mulligan, *Medjugorje: The First Days*, p. 153, and Klanac, *Aux Sources de Medjugorje*, p. 123.
32. Sivric, *The Hidden Side of Medjugorje, Vol. I*, p. 303; cf. Mulligan, *Medjugorje: The First Days*, p. 164, and Klanac, *Aux Sources de Medjugorje*, p. 109.
33. *The Biographical Memoirs of St. John Bosco, Vol. III* (The Salesian Society, 1966), p. 23. PDF available from: https://www.sdb.org/en/Don_Bosco_Resources/Biographical_Material.

NOTES FOR CHAPTER 30

1. https://kevinsymondsdotcom.files.wordpress.com/2020/02/murgia-ruini-dossier-enpolished_1.2.pdf, p. 9. The numbers in square brackets indicate bullet points in the original text.
2. Ibid., p. 9.
3. https://en.marcocorvaglia.com/medjugorje-e-la-chiesa.
4. https://kevinsymondsdotcom.files.wordpress.com/2020/02/murgia-ruini-dossier-enpolished_1.2.pdf, p. 12.
5. Ibid., p. 12, italics as in original text.
6. Ibid., p. 13.
7. Ibid.
8. Ibid., p. 14, italics as in original text.
9. Ibid.
10. Ibid.
11. Ibid.
12. Ibid., p. 15.
13. Ibid.

Notes for Chapter 31

14. Ibid., pp. 16–17.
15. Ibid., p. 18.
16. Ibid., pp. 18–19.
17. Ibid., p. 19.
18. Ibid.
19. Ibid., p. 21.
20. Ibid., p. 4.
21. Ibid., pp. 24–25; Sivric, *The Hidden Side of Medjugorje, Vol. I*, p. 319; cf. Mulligan, *Medjugorje: The First Days*, p. 196, and Klanac, *Aux Sources de Medjugorje*, p. 136.
22. Ibid., p. 25; cf. https://en.marcocorvaglia.com/medjugorje-e-la-chiesa-parte-2.
23. Ibid., p. 25. This encounter between Vicka and the Doctor is problematic because the visionaries were supposed to be in ecstasy during their visions of the Gospa. In that case, how could Vicka talk to Sumanovic-Glamuzina?
24. Ibid., pp. 25–26.
25. https://kevinsymondsdotcom.files.wordpress.com/2020/02/murgia-ruini-dossier-enpolished_1.2.pdf, pp. 12, 26; Bubalo, *Thousand Encounters*, p. 36.
26. https://kevinsymondsdotcom.files.wordpress.com/2020/02/murgia-ruini-dossier-enpolished_1.2.pdf, pp. 12, 26.
27. Ibid., p. 26. It should also be noted that there is a possible discrepancy between the doctor's testimony here and the testimony she provided in 2008, in which she says of this incident: "I attempt to feel something with my hand, but . . . nothing." http://www.comprendre-medjugorje.info/en/comprehending_medjugorje/supplement-ii-the-testimony-of-dr-glamuzina.html. This was also the conclusion of René Laurentin, as published in 1987, in *6 années d'apparitions, juin 1987* (Dernières Nouvelles, 6), Paris 1987, pp. 20–21: "Le docteur . . . demanda . . . de toucher l'apparition (. . .). Mais elle ne se souvient pas d'avoir éprouvé aucune sensation, come on le lui fait dire."
28. Sivric, *The Hidden Side of Medjugorje, Vol. I*, p. 319; cf. Mulligan, *Medjugorje: The First Days*, p. 196, and Klanac, *Aux Sources de Medjugorje*, p. 136; Bubalo, *Thousand Encounters*, p. 36.
29. Ibid., p. 27.
30. Ibid., p. 7.
31. Ibid., pp. 9, 11, 14, 16, 18, 22, 23.
32. Ibid., p. 23.
33. Saverio Gaeta, *Dossier Medjugorje*, pp. 11–12, as quoted at: https://www.marcocorvaglia.com/medjugorje/medjugorje-e-la-chiesa.html.
34. "Medjugorje: New Excerpts" at https://kevinsymonds.com/2020/02/18/medjugorje-new-excerpts/.
35. https://kevinsymondsdotcom.files.wordpress.com/2020/02/murgia-ruini-dossier-enpolished_1.2.pdf, pp. 12, 20.

NOTES FOR CHAPTER 31

1. Craig, *Spark from Heaven*, p. 71.
2. See Johnston, *Fatima: The Great Sign*, for more details on this subject.

3. Louis de Montfort, *True Devotion to Mary* (TAN Books and Publishers, Rockford, 1985), 27, emphasis added; De Montfort, *The Secret of Mary*, 45.

4. Joseph Dirvin, CM, *Saint Catherine Labouré of the Miraculous Medal* (TAN Books and Publishers, Rockford, 1984), p. 208.

5. See E. M. Brown, ed., *Dreams, Visions and Prophecies of Don Bosco* (Don Bosco Publications, New Rochelle, 1986), pp. 105–8.

6. Maximilian Kolbe, *The Crusade of Mary Immaculate* (Crusade of Mary Immaculate Press, Manchester, 2000), p. 66. Emphasis added.

7. Fulton Sheen, *The World's First Love* (McGraw-Hill Book Company, Inc., New York, 1952), pp. 205–7, also at: www.archive.org/details/worldsfirstlove013240mbp; cf. Apostoli, *Fatima for Today*, pp. 12, 23.

8. John Paul II, *Crossing the Threshold of Hope* (Jonathan Cape, 1994), p. 221.

9. Cf. Thomas McGlynn, *Vision of Fatima* (Skeffington and Son, London, 1951), p. 53; and Francis Johnston, *Fatima: The Great Sign*, p. 9.

10. Interview with Fr Manfred Hauke by Regina Eineg, "Don't let the devotees fall into the void," in *Die Tagespost*, 2 February 2010, pp. 6–7.

11. If the pope should wish to rule out any appeal against such a decision, he could add his approval of the directives *in forma specifica*. If an ecclesiastical document from a Vatican dicastery is given *in forma specifica*, this means that it has special papal approval, has the canonical force of a formal papal act, and that normally no further appeal to the pope regarding it is possible. See *Consecrated Phrases: A Latin Theological Dictionary* (Liturgical Press, Collegeville, 1998, p. 62).

BIBLIOGRAPHY

Apolito, Paolo. *Apparitions of the Madonna at Oliveto Citra: Local Visions and Cosmic Drama*. Translated by W. Christian. University Park, PA: Pennsylvania State University Press, 1998.

———. *The Internet and the Madonna: Religious Visionary Experience on the Web*. Translated by A. Shugaar. Chicago: The University of Chicago Press, 2005.

Apostoli, Andrew. *Fatima for Today: The Urgent Marian Message of Hope*. San Francisco: Ignatius Press, 2010.

Aumann, Jordan, OP. *Spiritual Theology*. London: Sheed and Ward, 1995.

Bax, Mart. *Medjugorje: Religion, Politics, and Violence in Rural Bosnia*. Amsterdam: VU Uitgeverij, 1995.

Beevers, John. *The Sun Her Mantle*. Dublin: Browne and Nolan, 1954.

Benedict XVI with Peter Seewald. *Light of the World: The Pope, the Church, and the Signs of the Times*. San Francisco: CTS/Ignatius Press, 2010.

Benson, Leslie. *Yugoslavia: A Concise History*. Basingstoke, Hampshire: Palgrave Macmillan, 2004.

Bertone, Tarcisio, with Giuseppe de Carli. *The Last Secret of Fatima*. New York: Doubleday, 2008.

Billet, Bernard, Joaquin-Maria Alonso, Boris Bobrinskoy, Marc Oraison, and René Laurentin. *Vraies et Fausses Apparitions dans L'Eglise*. Paris: P. Lethielleux, 1971.

Bouflet, Joachim. *Medjugorje, ou la fabrication du surnaturel*. Paris: Éditions Salvator, 1999.

———. *Faussaires de Dieu*. Paris: Presses de la Renaissance, 2000.

Bouflet, Joachim and Philippe Boutry. *Un signe dans le ciel: Les apparitions de la Vierge*. Paris: Grasset, 1997.

Brown, E. M., ed. *Dreams, Visions and Prophecies of Don Bosco*. New Rochelle: Don Bosco Publications, 1986.

Chiron, Yves. *Enquête sur les Apparitions de la Vierge*. Paris: Éditions J'ai Lu, 1995.

Corvaglia, Marco. *Medjugorje. È tutto falso*. Turin: Anteprima Edizioni, 2007.

Craig, Mary. *Spark from Heaven: The Mystery of the Madonna of Medjugorje*. London: Spire, 1991.

D'Alpa, Francesco. *La Scienza e Medjugorje, Vol. I: Il Caso Joyeux*. N.p.: Laiko.it, 2010.

Davies, Michael. *Medjugorje After Fifteen Years: The Message and the Meaning*. St. Paul: The Remnant Press, 1998.

_____. *Medjugorje after Twenty-One Years, 1981–2002: The Definitive History* (available as an internet download from: https://tinyurl.com/medjugorje-davies).
Deery, Joseph. *Our Lady of Lourdes*. Dublin: Brown & Nolan, 1958.
Delaney, John. *A Woman Clothed with the Sun*. New York: Doubleday, 1961.
De Marchi, John, I.M.C. *Fatima from the Beginning*. Translated by I.M. Kingsbury. Fatima: Missões Consolata, 1983.
De Montfort, Louis. *True Devotion to Mary*. Rockford, IL: TAN Books and Publishers, 1985.
_____. *The Secret of Mary*. Rockford, IL: TAN Books and Publishers, 1998.
Dirvin, Joseph, C.M. *Saint Catherine Labouré of the Miraculous Medal*. Rockford, IL: TAN Books and Publishers, 1984.
Farges, Albert. *Mystical Phenomena*. Translated by S.P. Jacques. London: Burns, Oates & Washbourne, 1926.
Foley, Donal Anthony. *Marian Apparitions, the Bible, and the Modern World*. Leominster, MA: Gracewing, 2002.
_____. *Comprendere Medjugorje. Visioni celesti o inganno religioso?* Lugano–Siena: Eupress FTL-Edizioni Cantagalli, 2017.
Franken, Rudo. *A Journey to Medjugorje: Objections to the Apparitions*. Roggel en Neer: Rudo Franken, 1999.
Gaeta, Saverio. *Medjugorje: 1. La vera storia*. Cinisello Balsamo, Italy: San Paolo Edizioni, 2020.
Garvey, Mark. *Searching for Mary*. New York: Plume, 1998.
Guerrera, Vittorio. *Medjugorje: A Closer Look*. Meriden, CT: Maryheart Crusaders, 1995.
Hauke, Manfred. "The prophetic role of Mary in apparitions," in *Introduction to Mariology*. Washington, D.C: Catholic University of America Press, 2021. Originally published as *Introduzione alla Mariologia* (Lugano: EUPress FTL, 2008).
Hoare, Marko Attila. *The History of Bosnia: From the Middle Ages to the Present Day*. London: Saqi Books, 2007.
Horvath, Agnes and Arpad Szakolczai. *The Dissolution of Communist Power: The Case of Hungary*. London: Routledge, 1992.
Jaouen, Jean. *A Grace Called La Salette*. Translated by N. Théroux. Attleboro, MA: La Salette Publications, 1991.
John of the Cross. *The Complete Works of Saint John of the Cross*. 3 vols. Translated by E. Allison Peers. London: Burns & Oates, 1943.
_____. *The Collected Works of Saint John of the Cross*. Translated by Kieran Kavanagh and Otilio Rodriguez. Washington: ICS Publications, 1991.
Johnston, Francis. *Fatima: The Great Sign*. Chulmleigh, Devon: Augustine Publishing, 1980.

Johnson, Kevin Orlin. *Twenty Questions About Medjugorje: What Rome Really Said.* Dallas: Pangaeus Press, 1999.

_____. *Apparitions: Mystic Phenomena and What They Mean.* Dallas: Pangaeus Press, 1995.

Jones, E. Michael. *Medjugorje: The Untold Story.* South Bend, IN: Fidelity Press, 1993.

_____. *The Medjugorje Deception: Queen of Peace, Ethnic Cleansing, Ruined Lives.* South Bend, IN: Fidelity Press, 1998.

Klanac, Daria. *Aux Sources de Medjugorje.* Montréal: Éditions Sciences et Culture, 1998.

_____. *Medjugorje, Réponses aux objections.* N.p.: Le Sarment, 2001.

Kolbe, Maximilian. *The Crusade of Mary Immaculate.* Urmston, Manchester: Crusade of Mary Immaculate Press, 2000.

Knox, Ronald. *Enthusiasm, A Chapter in the History of Religion.* London: Collins, 1987.

Kondor, Louis, ed. *Fatima in Lucia's Own Words I.* Fatima: Postulation Centre, 1976.

_____. *Fatima in Lucia's Own Words II.* Fatima: Postulation Centre, 1999.

Kraljevic, Svetozar, OFM. *The Apparitions of Our Lady at Medjugorje.* Edited by M. Scanlan. Chicago: Franciscan Herald Press, 1984.

Lampe, John R. *Yugoslavia as History: Twice There Was a Country.* 2nd ed. Cambridge: Cambridge University Press, 2000.

Laurentin, René. *Catholic Pentecostalism.* London: Darton, Longman and Todd, 1977.

_____. *The Life of Catherine Labouré.* Translated by P. Inwood. London: Collins, 1983.

_____. *The Apparitions of the Blessed Virgin Mary Today.* Dublin: Veritas Publications, 1991.

_____. *Bernadette of Lourdes.* Translated by J. Drury. London: Darton, Longman & Todd, 1998.

_____. *Medjugorje Testament: Hostility Abounds, Grace Superabounds.* Toronto: Ave Maria Press, 1999.

Laurentin, René and René Lejeune. *Messages and Teachings of Mary at Medjugorje: Chronological Corpus of the Messages.* Milford, OH: The Riehle Foundation, 1988.

Laurentin, René and Ljudevit Rupcic. *Is the Virgin Mary Appearing at Medjugorje?* Translated by F. Martin. Gaithersburg, MD: The Word Among Us Press, 1988.

Lietzmann, Hans. *A History of the Early Church.* Vol. 1. Cambridge: James Clarke, 1993.

Lochet, Louis. *Apparitions of Our Lady: Their Place in the Life of the Church.* Freiburg, Germany: Herder, 1960.

Martins, Antonio and Robert Fox. *Documents on Fatima & the Memoirs of Sr Lucia*. Alexandria, SD: Fatima Family Apostolate, 1992.
McGlynn, Thomas. *Vision of Fatima*. London: Skeffington and Son, 1951.
Miller, Elliot and Kenneth R. Samples. *The Cult of the Virgin: Catholic Mariology and the Apparitions of Mary*. Grand Rapids, MI: Baker Book House, 1994.
Miravalle, Mark. *The Message of Medjugorje: The Marian Message to the Modern World*. Lanham, MD: University Press of America, 1986.
_____. *Introduction to Medjugorje*. Goleta, CA: Queenship Publishing, 2004.
Miravalle, Mark and Wayne Weible. *Are the Medjugorje Apparitions Authentic?* Hiawassee, GA: New Hope Press, 2008.
Most, William. *Mary in Our Life*. Cork, Ireland: The Mercier Press, 1955.
Mulligan, James. *Medjugorje: What's Happening?* London: Dusty Sandals Press, 2008.
Nolan, Denis. *Medjugorje: A Time for Truth and a Time for Action*. Goleta, CA: Queenship Publishing, 1993.
_____. *Medjugorje and the Church*. Goleta, CA: Queenship Publishing, 2007.
Noonan, Moira. *Ransomed from Darkness*. El Sobrante, CA: North Bay Books, 2005.
O'Carroll, Michael, CSSp. *Medjugorje: Facts, Documents, Theology*. Dublin: Veritas, 1986.
Ott, Ludwig. *Fundamentals of Catholic Dogma*. Rockford, IL: TAN Books and Publishers, 1974.
Pelletier, Joseph. *Our Lady Comes to Garabandal*. Worcester, MA: Assumption Publications, 1971.
Peric, Ratko. "Criteria for Discerning Apparitions: Regarding the Events of Medjugorje," in *Prijestolje Mudrosti* [The Throne of Wisdom]. Mostar: Crkva na Kamenu, 1995.
Perica, Vjekoslav. *Balkan Idols: Religion and Nationalism in Yugoslav States*. New York: Oxford University Press, 2002.
Poulain, Augustin. *The Graces of Interior Prayer*. London: Kegan Paul, 1912.
_____. *Revelations and Visions*. New York: Alba House, 1998.
Rahner, Karl. *Visions and Prophecies*. London: Burns & Oates, 1963.
Ratzinger, Joseph with Vittorio Messori. *The Ratzinger Report: An Exclusive Interview on the State of the Church*. Leominster, MA: Fowler Wright Books, 1985.
Rooney, Lucy and Robert Faricy. *Mary Queen of Peace: Is the Mother of God Appearing in Medjugorje?* Leominster, MA: Fowler Wright, 1984.
_____. *Medjugorje Journal: Mary Speaks to the World*. Great Wakering, Essex: McCrimmons, 1987.
Rupcic, Ljudevit. *The Truth about Medjugorje*. N.p.: Ljubuski-Humac, 1990.

Rupcic, Ljudevit and Viktor Nuic. *Once Again the Truth about Medjugorje.* Zagreb: K. Kresmir, 2002.
Sanchez-Ventura y Pascual, F. *The Apparitions of Garabandal.* Translated by A. de Bertodano. Detroit: San Miguel Publishing, 1976.
Sells, Michael. *The Bridge Betrayed: Religion and Genocide in Bosnia.* Berkeley and Los Angeles: University of California Press, 1998.
Sharkey, D. and J. Debergh. *Our Lady of Beauraing.* St. Meinrad, IN: Abbey Press, 1973.
Sheen, Fulton. *The World's First Love.* New York: McGraw-Hill Book Company, 1952.
Silber, Laura and Allan Little. *The Death of Yugoslavia.* London: Penguin/BBC Books, 1996.
Sivric, Ivo, OFM. *The Hidden Side of Medjugorje.* Vol. 1. Edited by L. Bélanger. Translated by S. Rini. Saint-François-du-Lac, Quebec: Éditions Psilog, 1989.
_____. *La face cachée de Medjugorje, tome I.* Saint-François-du-Lac, Quebec: Éditions Psilog, 1988.
Sullivan, Randall. *The Miracle Detective: An Investigation of Holy Visions.* London: Little Brown, 2004.
Tanqueray, Adolphe. *The Spiritual Life.* Tournai, Belgium: Desclée, 1950.
Tindal-Robertson, Timothy. *Message of Fatima.* London: Catholic Truth Society, 1998.
Trevett, Christine. *Montanism: Gender, Authority and the New Prophecy.* Cambridge: Cambridge University Press, 2002.
Varghese, Roy Abraham. *God-Sent: A History of the Accredited Apparitions of Mary.* New York: The Crossroad Publishing Company, 2000.
Verdery, Katherine. *What Was Socialism, and What Comes Next?* Princeton: Princeton University Press, 1996.
Volken, Laurent. *Visions, Revelations, and the Church.* Translated by E. Gallaher. New York: P.J. Kenedy & Sons, 1963.
Vulliamy, Ed. *Seasons in Hell: Understanding Bosnia's War.* London: Simon & Schuster, 1994.
Walsh, Michael. *The Apparition at Knock.* Tuam, Galway: St Jarlath's College, 1959.
Weible, Wayne. *The Final Harvest: Medjugorje at the End of the Century.* Brewster, MA: Paraclete Press, 1999.
Wuillaume, L. *Banneux: A Message for Our Time.* Banneux: Banneux Shrine, 1995.

MEDJUGORJE/FATIMA RESOURCES

RECOMMENDED MEDJUGORJE RESOURCES
Marco Corvaglia has a critical site on Medjugorje, entitled: "The Medjugorje Illusion" at: https://en.marcocorvaglia.com/
Kevin Symonds has information on Medjugorje here: https://kevinsymonds.com/
Richard Chonak has Medjugorje-related material on his blog at: http://catholiclight.stblogs.org/
Information also at: http://en.louisbelanger.com/
The Diocese of Mostar site is at: https://www.md-tm.ba/
Theotokos Books Information at: http://theotokos.org.uk/information-about-medjugorje/

RECOMMENDED FATIMA RESOURCES
Official Fatima Sanctuary website: https://www.fatima.pt/en
World Apostolate of Fatima, International Secretariat: http://www.world-fatima.com/en/
Theotokos Books Fatima information at: http://theotokos.org.uk/fatima-apparitions/

INDEX

A

"abduction of visionaries," 382
addiction, to spiritual experiences,
    271–72
"All I Need Is a Miracle," video, 189
alleged supernatural signs at
    Medjugorje, 179–80
Alles, Hildegard, 336
Amaral, Bishop, of Leiria-Fatima, 328
Amirante, Chiara,
    and Pope Francis, 374
Amorth, Fr Gabriele, 196
Amsterdam visions, 47–48
Andjelkovic, Fr Petar OFM, 221
Angel of Portugal, 121
apocalypticism,
    and Charismatic Movement, 7
    and Medjugorje, 268
apocryphal writings, 229–30
apparitions, Marian, *see* Marian
    apparitions
Aubry, Bishop Gilbert,
    query about Medjugorje to CDF,
    243
Aumann, Fr Jordan, 103
    on characteristics of genuine seers,
    210
    on discernment, 231
    on genuine divine revelations, 210
    on signs of diabolical spirit, 209,
    232
    on signs of divine spirit, 231–32
    on spirit of docility/humility, 232
Awi Mello, Fr Alexander, 354

B

bad fruits,
    and Medjugorje, 247–50
Banneux, 88, 104

Barbaric, Fr Slavko,
    allegedly in Heaven, 282
    as controlling visions, 111
    death of, Dec 2000, 282
    as deprived of faculty to hear
        confessions, 112
    and prophecy of war, 218
    as spiritual director of visionaries,
        95
    as vetting Gospa messages, 207
    as visiting war crimes suspects,
        222
Basile, Diane, 188
Bax, Mart,
    criticism of by Robert Jolic, xxv
    and Saverio Gaeta criticisms, xxv
Beauraing, 9, 25, 44, 140, 104, 167, 181
Bélanger, Louis,
    as critical of Vittorio Messori, 342
    on duplicating states of
        consciousness, 168
    on inducing visions, 112
    on Medjugorje tapes, 30
Benedict XIV, Pope,
    on private revelations, 233
Benedict XVI, Pope,
    on Fatima, 2006, 300–17
    interview with Peter Seewald, 335
    visit to Fatima, 2010, 335
    see also Ratzinger, Cardinal
        Joseph
Bernadette Soubirous, St,
    ecstasies of, 203–4
    as rejecting money, 204
Bertone, Archbishop Tarcisio,
    and Bishop Aubry inquiry,
        243–44
    on Medjugorje pilgrimages, 244
    as Medjugorje skeptic, 301–2
    meeting with Sr Lucia, 336
    upholds Zadar declaration, 243

Bible,
    as critical of excessive talk, 102
Bilic-Brajcic, Venka, 188
Billet, Bernard, 141
bishop, local
    as responsible for discerning apparitions, 235, 238
bishops,
    collegiality of, importance of, 312–13
Bishops' Conference, Yugoslav, 195, 213, 216
    and Zadar declaration, 274
bishops, local,
    as responsible for discerning apparitions, 235
"bloody handkerchief" incident, 97
Bosnia-Herzegovina, 2, 213, 216–17
Bouflet, Joachim,
    on journeys of visionaries, 269
    on Vicka as hysteric, 209
Bovone, Archbishop Alberto,
    letter to Bishops of Italy, 194
Brincard, Henri, Bishop of Puy-en-Velay,
    on Medjugorje, 282–84
Brise, Adele, 105
British Journal of Ophthalmology, 187
Bubalo, Fr Janko, 24, 39, 41, 106, 199, 209
    as aware of original tapes, 26
    and bloody handkerchief incident, 97
    interviews of with Vicka, 199, 385–87
    on three more days of visions, 65
    and Vicka's recollections, 73, 199–200
Burresi, Fr Luigi, (Br Gino), decree against, 299

C

candle flame, and St Bernadette, 204

Canon Law,
    Franciscans in breach of, 242
    and private revelations, 227
Cantalamessa, Fr Raniero, 303
Capljina,
    church entrance bricked up, 242
    and violence against Muslims, 220
Caporello, Msgr Egidio, 194
Caritas of Birmingham, 321–26
Catechism of the Catholic Church,
    on authentic charisms, 8
    on dishonesty, 279
    on private revelations, 233
Catholic Church, crisis in, 420
    crisis of faith in, 273–74
    and discernment of Medjugorje, 191, 193
    necessity for renewal of, 426
    position of on visions, 233–35
    on private revelations, 233
Cenacolo community, 252
Cerno 61, 118, 296
Charismatic Renewal/Movement, 5–8
Chiron, Yves,
    on alleged modern visions, 141, 263
    interviewed Bishop Peric, 240
Chonak, Richard, 377–78
Church, Catholic, *see* Catholic Church
Churchill, Winston, 127
Cigada, Dr Mario, 161, 172
Citluk, 44, 157
civil war, in Yugoslavia,
    and Medjugorje, 218–19
Civitavecchia statue, 317
Colafrancesco, Terry, 322–25
collegial consecration, 328, 336
    and Communism, 330, 332
    by John Paul II in 1984, 327–29
Colo, Jakov,
    ceased daily visions in 1998, 286
    family background of, 23
    outburst about police, 65

Index

Commission, International, on Medjugorje, *see* Ruini Commission
Communism, 10–11
  fall of, 217–18, 329
Communist regime, Yugoslav,
  and concerns about visions, 44
  as opposed to Medjugorje, 95
  as supportive of Medjugorje, 193
concentration camps, 220–21
Confession, Sacrament of,
  at Medjugorje, 247
Congregation for the Doctrine of the Faith,
  attitude towards Medjugorje, 310
  and judgment of alleged revelations, 227, 239
  as negative towards Ruini Report, 416
  reported position on Medjugorje, 355
  as supportive of Medjugorje bishops, 310
  2013 directive to Bishops, 348–49
constat de non supernaturalitate, 215, 241
constat de supernaturalitate, 237
Corvaglia, Marco,
  on subjective nature of scientific tests, 169
Craig, Mary,
  description of visionaries, 23
  on Fr Zovko's declaration, 44
  and Medjugorje dancing sun, 180
  on Vicka in "hysterical stupor," 209–10
criminality in Medjugorje during civil war, 219
crisis of faith in Church, and Medjugorje, 273–74
Croatia,
  declared independence, 1991, 216
  effect on of Medjugorje, 194
  Mirjana prophecy about, 217

Croatian nationalism, 30, 222–23
  and Medjugorje, 220
Cule, Petar, Bishop of Mostar, 3
  and Hrasno Shrine, 388
cures, alleged, at Medjugorje,
  as not proven/unsatisfactory, 188–89

D

D'Alpa, Dr Francesco, 163
death threats,
  and Medjugorje authors, 264
D'Errico, Archbishop, 317
diabolical activity, possible, at Medjugorje, 275–77
  on true and false Marian devotion, 228–29, 231
desire for miracles, *see* miracles, desire for
diabolical visions, 145
discernment, 108, 140, 162, 170, 177
disobedience, 261–62
dos Santos, Sr Lucia,
  further apparitions to, 336
  no messages from Mary re Medjugorje, 336
doubting Thomases incident, 55,
Dragicevic, Ivan, 8, 39, 42, 61, 64, 86, 113, 179, 269, 420
  accused of lying, 404–5
  details of "sign," 204–5
  disobedience of, 205, 350
  public appearances of canceled, 349–51
  threatening letter of, 113
  wrote down "sign," 205
Dragicevic, Mirjana,
  cessation of monthly visions, 376
  changed story about secrets, 374
  emotional stability/state of 208–9, 358
  on Medjugorje as last apparitions, 208–9

"My Heart Will Triumph book,"
  357–58
  and possible demonic activity, 370
  "prophecy" about Croatia, 217–18
  as recipient of ten secrets, 374
  on three more days, 57, 63

E

ecstasies, alleged, of visionaries,
  158–62, 169, 172, 175
ecstasies, genuine,
  and St Bernadette, 203
EEG tests on visionaries, 162–63
entrustment of third millennium
  to Mary, 334
ethnic cleansing, 216
exorcism of visionaries suggested, 90
eye damage, due to sun-gazing, 187

F

faith, as opposed to signs, 259
false prophets, 261–62, 265, 268–69
Farges, Msgr, 32, 36, 47
Faricy, Fr Robert, 21, 52, 144, 149,
  249, 478
  on Zadar declaration, 214
fasting, as not request of Gospa, 103
Fatima,
  as answer to Medjugorje, 425–26
  contrasted with Medjugorje,
    331–32, 421–22
  importance of, 231
  in Ruini Report, 383
First Saturdays devotion,
  and consecration of Russia,
    337–38
  implementation of required, 338
  and revival of Church, 338
  promotion of necessary, 339
Francis, Pope,
  and Chiara Amirante, 374
  and Fatima, 347–48

as critical of Medjugorje, 354, 359,
  362
on Medjugorje, 362
not visiting Medjugorje, 353
impact on pilgrimages, 355, 361
as critical of some revelations/
  visionaries, 348, 353, 356
on Ruini Commission, 353, 362
Franciscans, Herzegovinian,
  disobedience of to Bishops,
    241–42
  disobedience of to Rome, 278
  and Hercegovacka banka, 221–22
  and Zagreb church, 221
Franciscan Univ. of Steubenville
  and Medjugorje, 253–54
Franic, Archbishop Frane, 117
  and Ivan's "sign," 205
  consulted Gospa, 258
French-Italian scientific theological
  commission, 169–70
Frigerio, Dr Luigi, 161, 168, 174
  and "Queen of Peace Society,"
    168
  and Vicka larynx test, 166

G

Gaeta, Saverio, xxv, 5, 18
  and leaked Ruini Report, 379–80
Gagliardi, Dr Giorgio,
  and 1998 Italian tests, 171–72
Gagliarducci, Andrea, 353
Garabandal, 34, 84–85, 93–94,
  258–59
Gemma, Bishop Andrea,
  on Medjugorje as diabolical, 303
Giguère, Marie-Paule, 300–4
good fruits, and Medjugorje,
  247–48, 250, 260–61
  Christ's teaching on, 260–61
  as motive for visionaries, 117
Gorbachev, Mikhail,
  met Pope in 1989, 329

Gospa,
- self-description as "Blessed Virgin Mary," 387
- as supportive of Fr Vlasic, 309

guilt, effects of, 211–24

H

Hague International Criminal Court, 222
hallucination, 38, 43, 47, 124, 158–59
Hauke, Fr Manfred,
- on holiness of seers, 236
- interviews of, 372–73
- on need for truth about Medjugorje, 428
- on private revelations, 233–34

HDZ, Croatian political party, 213
heaven,
- according to Vicka, 199

hell,
- according to Vicka, 200
- and Fatima seers, 200–1

Heupel, Agnes, 95, 207
"Hidden Side of Medjugorje" book, 197
Hill, John, 253
holy water, 398–99
HOS, right-wing Croat forces, 219
Hoser, Archbishop Henryk,
- appointed as special envoy, 359–60, 372
- expansion plans for Medjugorje, 373
- interviewed on Medjugorje, 360, 369, 371
- at Medjugorje, 372
- on Medjugorje messages, 370
- pastoral nature of mission, 372
- on pilgrimages to Medjugorje, 371

Hrasno shrine, 83, 241, 388
HVO, Bosnian Croat army, 219
hysteria, 212
- alleged in case of Vicka, 209

I

Immaculate Heart of Mary,
- triumph of, 339, 422–24

inaudible voices of visionaries, alleged, 166
Index of Forbidden Books,
- and alleged visionary messages, 227
- and *Poem of the Man-God*, 225

Italian medical tests 1998, 171–72
Ivan Dragicevic, *see* Dragicevic, Ivan
Ivanka Ivankovic, *see* Ivankovic, Ivanka
Ivankovic, Ivan, original visionary, 31
Ivankovic, Ivanka,
- and unusual Fr Zovko interview, 392

Ivankovic, Marinko, 23, 37, 54, 56, 58, 277
Ivankovic, Mica, 61–66
Ivankovic, Vicka,
- allegedly had brain tumor, 210
- as avoiding tests, 171
- and bloody handkerchief incident, 97
- credibility of, 199
- and dropping of baby Jesus, 201–203
- experiences of heaven, 199
- in Ireland, 2011, 285
- and journey to hell, 200
- physical and psychological state of, 209–10
- and *Poem of the Man-God*, 225
- public appearances of canceled, 351
- seen by psychiatrists, 209–10
- vision of in police van, 395

J

Jakov Colo, *see* Colo, Jakov
Jesus Christ,
- and parable of wheat and weeds, 420
- teaching on "good fruits," 260

John of the Cross, St, 182, 265
   on desire for revelations, 182, 257
   on diabolical deceptions, 274–75
John Paul II, Pope,
   and beatification of Fatima seers, 333–34
   and Medjugorje, 4, 195–96, 420–21
   on suspect visionary spirituality, 226
   and third part of Fatima secret, 334
Jones, E. Michael,
   and assault on Bishop Peric, 226
   received death threat, 264
Joyeux, Dr Henri,
   and medical tests on visionaries, 159
   on medical tests as not decisive, 168

K

Kibeho, alleged apparitions at, 263
   in Ruini Report, 383–84
Klanac, Daria, 25–29, 68, 345
Kraljevic, Fr Svetozar, 23–24, 58, 75, 78, 134, 137, 151, 208, 253
Kuharic, Cardinal, 170, 195, 221, 242

L

Laghi, Archbishop Pio, 196
La Salette,
   compared with Medjugorje, 366–67
Laurentin, Fr René,
   as backpedaling on Medjugorje, 306–8
   on Ivan's sign, 206
   on medical tests, 159, 171
   response to Bishop Gemma, 306
   letter, threatening, from Ivan, 113

Levada, Cardinal William, 299
lie detector tests, 159, 173
light phenomena, and Vision, 35, 37, 45–46
Ljubicic, Fr Petar,
   and Mirjana secrets, 118, 374
Lorenz, Konrad,
   and "imprinting" of Medjugorje, 255–66
Lourdes, 45, 47, 56, 78–81, 87, 91, 119, 130, 133, 140, 142, 188, 203, 233, 235, 268
Luburic, Don Ante,
   on Fr Laurentin "disinformations," 110, 242
   on Franciscan disobedience, 241–42
Lucia, Sr, of Fatima, see dos Santos, Sr Lucia

M

Maciel Degollado, Fr Marcial, 311
Maillard, Sr Emmanuel, 356, 370, 375
Mangiapan, Dr,
   and alleged miracles/cures at Medjugorje, 188
Margnelli, Dr Marco, 161
Marian apparitions,
   average number small, 105
   discernment and authenticity of, 234–35
   and false revelations, 230–31
   qualities of, 46, 87, 104
   as special case of private revelation, 234
Marija Pavlovic, see Pavlovic, Marija
Martin, Jean-Louis,
   and Baby Jesus incident, 201–2
Marto, Francisco,
   beatified, 329
   and diabolical vision, 277
Marto, Jacinta, beatified, 329

Index

Mary, Blessed Virgin,
  alleged birthday of, 111
  alleged threatening message of, 113
  characteristics of approved apparitions of, 35, 38
  impersonated by devil, 32
  messages always serious/brief, 87–88
  worldwide reports of visions of, 263
McKenna, Sr Briege,
  and vision of Fr Vlasic, 12
media, Catholic, and Medjugorje, 272
medical tests on visionaries, 159–60, 168–69, 171–73, 175–77, 188, 209–10
Medjugorje,
  and alleged signs, 179, 267
  anomalies concerning, 365–66
  books about, 287–98
  cult-like aspects of, 427
  dangers of believing in, 427
  and Fatima, 331–32, 337
  final judgment on likely in future, 429–30
  general conclusions about, 419–20
  impact on Church, 256
  and lack of message from Gospa, 390–92
  messages, *see* messages, Medjugorje
  and modern media, 257
  not continuation of Fatima, 336, 356
  as opposed to Fatima, 428–29
  pilgrim numbers to, 361
  pilgrimages to, 240–41, 371
  and possible evil atmosphere, 275
  priestly criticism of, 357
  as promoted by Catholic media, 272–73
  questions concerning, 332–33
  reasons for popularity, 270–71
  spirituality of supporters, 272
  violence in, 219–34
  visionaries, *see* visionaries, Medjugorje
  Visionary entity, *see* Gospa
  visions at, *see* visions, Medjugorje
Meessen, Prof Auguste, 186
messages, Medjugorje,
  as lacking in coherence, 395–97
messages, visionary,
  as subject to Canon Law, 227
  submission of to diocesan bishop, 227
Messori, Vittorio, 191, 341
  "schism," warning of, 355
Milosevic, Slobodan, 213, 216
miracles, desire for, 259–60
Miravalle, Mark,
  books of, on Medjugorje, 292–94
Mirjana Dragicevic, *see* Dragicevic, Mirjana
Mladifest youth festival, 375–76
money,
  and visionaries, 204
Most, Fr William,
  on diabolical visions, 145
  on types of private revelations, 234
Murgia, David,
  and leaked Ruini Report, 377–80
Müller, Cardinal Gerhard,
  as critical of promotion of Medjugorje, 349, 362
  interview with re Medjugorje, 359
Mulligan, Fr James,
  books by on Medjugorje, 295–98, 345–56

N

National Geographic magazine, 356
Necedah, 183–84, 248
neo-Nazis, 219

Nolan, Denis,
    books by, problems with, 138–40,
        289–93
    admits Medjugorje problems, 267
    on secular media and Medjugorje,
        273
non constat de supernaturalitate,
    170, 215, 237, 241, 317, 342, 353
    Fr Andrew Kingham on, 342
    as not supportive of Medjugorje,
        215
Noonan, Moira,
    on New Age experiences, 250
    on New Age incident, 275–76
Normae Congregationis, CDF
    document, 170, 195, 236–40,
    292, 316, 353–54, 384
Novak, Srecko Franjo, 242–43

O

O'Carroll, Fr Michael, 152–54
    on Medjugorje spirituality,
        248–49
Ottaviani, Cardinal,
    warning about false visions, 228
Our Lady, *see* Mary, Blessed Virgin

P

Papacy,
    and private revelations, 235–36
Parolin, Cardinal Pietro, 371
Pavlovic, Fr Tadija,
    as scandalized by visionaries, 77
    on last day of visions, 76
Pavlovic, Marija,
    on formation of Ruini
        Commission, 344
    and Fr Vlasic's religious
        community, 95, 207–8
    and joke about Christ, 281
    messages of, and retraction, 207

and *Poem of the Man-God*, 225
and "Spirituality Center," 369
Pell, Cardinal George,
    and visionary Vicka, 285
Pentin, Edward, 354–55
Peric, Ratko, Bishop of Mostar
    assaulted by mob, 226
    as critical of Medjugorje, 360–62
    on disorders at Medjugorje, 226,
        240
    Maynooth address, Feb 2004, 287
    on Medjugorje, 240, 282
    as not part of International
        Commission, 316
    pastoral visitation of Medjugorje,
        309
Perica, Vjekoslav, 222–23
and Pope Benedict XVI, 299
    preached at Medjugorje, 2006,
        301
    stated visions not supernatural,
        241
Perko, Archbishop Franc,
    on Zadar declaration, 214–15
Perrella, Fr Salvatore, 318
    on *non constat de*
        supernaturalitate, 353
    on Pope Francis and Medjugorje,
        353
    on Ruini Commission
        conclusions, 353, 364
Pervan, Fr Tomislav,
    and Croatian independence,
        222–23
    and exorcism of visionaries, 90
    as Medjugorje parish priest, Mar,
        1985, 115
    as supporting nationalist
        propaganda, 221
Pezzuto, Archbishop Luigi, 375
Pius XII, Pope, 126–27, 130
Podbrdo, 8, 31, 37, 43–44, 51, 57,
    62–63, 79, 81, 90–91, 95, 179
polygraphy, *see* lie detector tests

Poulain, Fr Augustin,
  on credibility of revelations, 26, 99, 143, 234
psychiatrists, group of, examine Vicka, 209–10
Puljic, Cardinal Vinko,
  on Medjugorje, 285, 303, 310–12, 343
Puljic, Fr Zelimir,
  and interview with Ivan, 205

Q

"Queen of Peace," Vision as,
  according to Vicka, 385–87
  Gospa as Queen of Peace?, 387
  and Hrasno shrine, 388
  term not in tape transcripts, 387–88

R

Ratzinger, Cardinal Joseph, 53, 144, 191–93, 195, 214, 225, 283, 343
reaction time of visionaries, 164–65, 168–70
Rencurel, Benoîte, 104, 318
Resch, Fr Andreas,
  and 1998 Italian tests, 171, 176–77
Revelation, public and private, 233–34
revelations, alleged, 263–64
Romanis Pontificibus, 29, 108, 244–45, 278
rosaries changing color, 184
Rue du Bac, 45, 102, 423
Ruini, Cardinal Camillo, 317
  and International Commission, 23–24, 314, 344, 354
Ruini Commission, 314, 341
  as advisory body, 365
  as aware of tape transcripts, 406
  flawed structure of, 381, 385
  implications of, 364
  leaked version of Report genuine, 380
  members of, 315–16
  problems with stance of, 366
  rejected demonic hypothesis, 397
  Report details leaked, 363–64, 377–79
  to take time to reach decision, 341
  and tape transcripts of visionaries, 365
  as truly international?, 381
Ruini Commission Report,
  CDF negative towards, 416
  on contents of messages, 389–90
  on deficiencies of visionaries, 409–10
  on first seven visions, 384–85
  on first seven visions as credible, 401–2
  general analysis/assessment of, 380, 416–18
  on general credibility of visionaries, 408
  on impropriety regarding money, 404
  influence of Fatima and Kibeho on, 382–84
  on Ivan lying multiple times, 405
  on Medjugorje as Holy See "shrine," 407–8
  overall conclusions of Report, 415
  pastoral recommendations of, 406–7
  posits two phases to visions, 381–82, 405
  on problems with subsequent visions, 402–3
  rejected demonic hypothesis, 397
  support of Pope Francis, 416
  testimony of Dr Sumanovic-Glamuzina, 410–15
  on "three more days" of visions, 405
  Vision as "Queen of Peace," 385

on visions re approved apparitions, 403
votes of the Commission members, 415
Ryden, Vassula, 227

S

Santini, Prof. Maurizio,
and alogmeter test, 168–69
Saraiva Martins, Cardinal José, 313
Satan, as promoting Medjugorje, 306–7
Schalueck, Fr Herman, 211
schism, danger of, and Medjugorje, 321
Schönborn, Cardinal Christoph, 310, 312
hosted Medjugorje event, 343
scientific tests, on visionaries, *see* medical tests on visionaries
secrets, of Medjugorje visionaries, 13, 107, 118, 167–68, 254, 286–87, 374, 377, 402
secular media
as supportive of Medjugorje, 273
self-censorship, under communism, 10
Sells, Michael, historian,
on resurgence of Croatian nationalism, 220, 222
sensitivity-training programs, 5
Seper, Cardinal Franjo, 52, 107–8
sexual allegations and Medjugorje, 135, 211, 304
Sgreva, Fr Gianni, 257–58
sign, at Medjugorje,
and Ivan, 204–5
Sivric, Fr Ivo,
and anti-Medjugorje book, 196–97
and Croatian folk culture, 97
expertise of on Medjugorje, 197
explanation for alleged signs, 180
on last day of visions, 76

on local prophecies, 98
on Medjugorje local culture, 98
on Medjugorje quarrels, 75
and mental stability of Mirjana, 208
objective view of Medjugorje, 249
on solar miracles at Medjugorje, 184
and tapes of visionaries, 27
tape transcription difficulties of, 27–28
and translation of texts, 27
smoking,
and Mirjana, 34
of visionaries at Podbrdo, 33
solar miracles, alleged,
at Medjugorje, 184
and video films, 185
witnessed by Mary Craig, 180
Sr Lucia, of Fatima, *see* dos Santos, Lucia
Staehlin, Carlos,
visionary experiment of, 113
Stopar, Dr Ludvik, 157
hypnotized Marija, 167
Sullivan, Randal,
on alleged Medjugorje cures, 188–89
on violence in Medjugorje, 219
on Ivan's sign, 206
Sumanovic-Glamuzina, Doctor,
testimony of re Medjugorje, 410–15
sun-gazing, at Medjugorje, 186
dangers of, 187
and Prof Meessen experiments, 186
Surmanci,
and mass killing of Serbs, 28, 121, 219, 223, 295
Symonds, Kevin,
on Ruini Report, 416
Szakolczai, Arpad,
on effects of communism, 10

T

tapes of visionaries,
  differences between transcripts, 345–47
  and later accounts of visionaries, 346
television,
  influence of on visionaries, 10
  and Medjugorje messages, 145
  and Medjugorje visionaries, 9
Teresa of Avila, St,
  on desire for revelations, 182
  on diabolical wiles, 307
Thavis, John, 214
The Poem of the Man-God,
  as placed on index, 225
The Sunday Times,
  report on Medjugorje visionaries, 269
third part of Fatima secret, 334
"three more days of visions," 57, 63, 65–66, 68, 346
Tornielli, Andrea, 349, 366
  and creation of new diocese, 314–15
  on International Commission verdict, 349–50
  and leaking of Ruini Report details, 363–64
transcripts of tapes of visionaries, *see* tapes of visionaries
Tudjman, Franjo, 213, 216, 220–21, 242

U

"unbelieving Judases" incident, 55, 120
Ustasha, 2, 94, 220, 295

V

Valtorta, Maria, 225
Van Hoof, Mary Ann,
  blessed religious objects, 184
  career as visionary, 248
  and Necedah false visions, 48
Varghese, Roy Abraham, 287–89
Vasilj-Gluvic, Ljubica, 29, 61, 64
Vatican,
  and administrator for Medjugorje, 357
Vicka Ivankovic, *see* Ivankovic, Vicka
Viganò, Archbishop Carlo Maria, 349
violence,
  in Medjugorje, 219
  in vicinity of Medjugorje, 218
visionaries,
  activities of, 262
  and alleged miracles, 184
  growth in reports of, 260
  and position of Church, 141
visionaries, Medjugorje,
  claims of daily visions, 286
  as emotionally vulnerable, 23
  as justifying activities because of "good fruits," 117
  lifestyle of, 269–70
  and money, 204
  as promoters of Medjugorje, 344
  promoting pilgrimages, 270, 344
  as uncooperative, 174–77
  as victims of Medjugorje, 81
visions, alleged,
  as appearing from cloud, 47
  attitude of Bishops towards, 235
  at Beauraing, 181
  as condemned, 144
  danger of illusion/deception, 233
  diabolical, 32, 145, 275, 277
  fabrication of, 274
  as gradually appearing, 35, 47
  at Lourdes, 47
  and malformed laity, 420
  at Necedah, 183, 248
  position of Church on, 233
  prior to Medjugorje, influence of, 94
  as result of intense desire, 182
  since 1930s, 140–41

Vlasic, Fr Tomislav,
  and CDF charges, 304–5
  excommunication of, 376
  laicized by Pope Benedict XVI, 308–9
  wanted visions in church, 393–94
Volken, Fr Laurent,
  on disobedience, 261
  on psychological testing, 157
von Balthasar, Fr Hans Urs, 149
vows, religious,
  and chastity, 211
Vulliamy, Ed,
  on criminality in Medjugorje during civil war, 219
VU University Amsterdam, xxv

W

Waterinckx, Mark,
  on alleged signs, 180
  on quarreling in Medjugorje, 249
Waters, Patricia,
  on Fr Barbaric, 111
  on nature of Medjugorje visions, 102
Weible, Wayne,
  conversion experience of, 294
  on impact of Medjugorje, 256
  on Medjugorje commercialism, 117, 249
  on unhealthy desire for messages, 267
  and visionaries smoking, 34

Willesee, Terry, 189
wristwatch sign, 33

Y

Youth 2000, 251
Yugoslavia,
  civil war in, 213, 216
  communist government of and Medjugorje, 193–94

Z

Zadar declaration,
  as accepted by CDF, 243
  details of, 213–14
  as essentially negative, 417–18
  interpretations of, 215
  as pro-Medjugorje?, 214–16
  re the Ruini Commission, 402, 416
  and Wayne Weible, 350–51
Zanic, Pavao, Bishop of Mostar,
  accused of collaborating with communists, 343, 369
  Episcopal palace of destroyed, 226
  not relieved of Medjugorje dossier, 239, 283
Zovko, Fr Jozo,
  as disciplined three times, 211–12
  disobedience of, 312
  as frustrated with visionaries, 394
  no permission for Washington Mass, 286
  sexual allegations against, 211

ABOUT THE AUTHOR

DONAL ANTHONY FOLEY lives in England, has degrees in Humanities and Theology, and previously worked as a part-time teacher. After a walking pilgrimage to Fatima in the early 1980s, he became interested in the topic of Marian apparitions, particularly how to distinguish between true and false ones. This led to the publication of his *Marian Apparitions, the Bible and the Modern World*, and the creation of the www.theotokos.org.uk site. He has also been involved in self-publishing and the promotion of Fatima. More recently he has written some Catholic-themed young adult books, the *Glaston Chronicles*.

www.ingramcontent.com/pod-product-compliance
Lightning Source LLC
Chambersburg PA
CBHW030212170426
43201CB00006B/58